Delinquency and Juvenile Justice

Recent Titles in
Bibliographies and Indexes in Sociology

Latin America, 1983–1987: A Social Science Bibliography
Robert L. Delorme, compiler

Social Support Networks: A Bibliography, 1983–1987
David E. Biegel, Kathleen J. Farkas, Neil Abell, Jacqueline Goodin, and Bruce Friedman, compilers

Diffusion of Innovations: A Select Bibliography
Klaus Musmann and William H. Kennedy, compilers

Native American Youth and Alcohol: An Annotated Bibliography
Michael L. Lobb and Thomas D. Watts

The Homosexual and Society: An Annotated Bibliography
Robert B. Marks Ridinger, compiler

Pro-Choice/Pro-Life; An Annotated, Selected Bibliography (1972–1989)
Richard Fitzsimmons and Joan P. Diana, compilers

Sikhs in North America: An Annotated Bibliography
Darshan Singh Tatla

Adoption Literature for Children and Young Adults: An Annotated Bibliography
Susan G. Miles

Homelessness in America, 1893–1992: An Annotated Bibliography
Rod Van Whitlock, Bernard Lubin, and Jean R. Sailors, compilers

The Multilevel Design: A Guide with an Annotated Bibliography, 1980–1993
Harry J.M. Hüttner and Pieter van den Eeden

Pro-Choice/Pro-Life Issues in the 1990s: An Annotated, Selected Bibliography
Richard Fitzsimmons and Joan P. Diana

Work-Family Research: An Annotated Bibliography
Teri Ann Lilly, Marcie Pitt-Catsouphes, and Bradley K. Googins, compilers

Delinquency and Juvenile Justice

An International Bibliography

Compiled by Clayton A. Hartjen and S. Priyadarsini

Bibliographies and Indexes in Sociology, Number 26

PRAEGER

Westport, Connecticut
London

Library of Congress Cataloging-in-Publication Data

Hartjen, Clayton A., 1943–
Delinquency and juvenile justice : an international bibliography / compiled by Clayton A. Hartjen and S. Priyadarsini.
p. cm.—(Bibliographies and indexes in sociology, ISSN 0742–6895 ; no. 26)
Includes index.
ISBN 0–313–32098–5 (alk. paper)
1. Juvenile delinquency—Bibliography. 2. Juvenile justice, Administration of—Bibliography. I. Priyadarsini, S., 1943– II. Title. III. Series.
Z5703.4.J88H376 2004
[HV9069]
016.36436—dc22 2003062434

British Library Cataloguing in Publication Data is available.

Library of Congress Catalog Card Number: 2003062434
ISBN: 0–313–32098–5
ISSN: 0742–6895

First published in 2004

Praeger Publishers, 88 Post Road West, Westport, CT 06881
An imprint of Greenwood Publishing Group, Inc.
www.praeger.com

Printed in the United States of America

The paper used in this book complies with the Permanent Paper Standard issued by the National Information Standards Organization (Z39.48–1984).

10 9 8 7 6 5 4 3 2 1

This work is dedicated to the memory of our parents:
Alfred C. Hartjen, Ruth J. Hartjen, M. P. Sarangapani, and M. S. Rukmini

CONTENTS

PREFACE

A large number and variety of sources were used to compile this bibliography, including our personal collection and others' libraries, and materials supplied to us by criminologists in various parts of the world. Primarily, however, the publications referenced in this volume were located from the shelves of the criminal justice collection at Rutgers University in Newark. We are indebted to Phyllis Schultz, the information specialist who is largely responsible for that collection, for her assistance in locating relevant materials for this volume. Her knowledge, assistance, and patience with our persistent pestering are gratefully appreciated and this volume could not have been compiled without her help. We are also indebted to our friend, Professor Doris Guilloton for her assistance in translating numerous publications referenced in this volume. Her contributions to copy editing and locating our mistakes are also appreciated. Numerous other individuals helped us enthusiastically in many ways to make this arduous task easier. We are greatly indebted to them all.

We apologize in advance to those who would be upset that their publication(s) have not been included, either due to lack of availability, accessibility, linguistic barriers, or simple decision-making on our part to reference specific publications. While we sought to be as comprehensive and exhaustive in compiling these references as we possibly could, undoubtedly we have not included everything that has been written on the topic of youth and their misbehavior. Rather than a census, this volume then should be considered a survey of the international literature on youth crime and society's response to it.

INTRODUCTION

In compiling this bibliography, we sought to bring together as much of the literature regarding delinquency and the operation of juvenile judicial and correctional agencies around the world as we could locate and abstract. The bulk of the research and writing in criminology remains highly, if not intentionally, ethnocentric and culturally bound. The field does exhibit a growing awareness, not only of the international dimensions of the phenomena we study, but also of the potential insights we might gain from research in political/judicial systems and societies outside the boundaries of our own societies. Our purpose in this volume, therefore, has been to provide a ready source for locating publications on diverse topics regarding youth crime and justice from as many countries as possible. Although this is probably the most international and comprehensive bibliography on the subject yet compiled, undoubtedly not every publication on the subject matter has been included. Since our concern here is to bring together the widely dispersed references on the delinquency of, and abuse and neglect of, minors in specific countries around the world, as well as laws regarding and the operation of various agencies that deal with young people accused of or victimized by crimes, unless specifically identified with a particular country or multiple countries, publications on delinquent behavior in general (such as theories of crime/delinquency *per se*), commentary or opinions on the behavior of youths as such, and the like, are excluded.

The references included were gathered and annotated over a period of several years by both compilers. The publications included roughly cover a quarter-century of criminological research and writings (from 1975 through 2001) and draw upon materials published as books, anthologies, chapters in anthologies, articles in scholarly journals, government reports, and documents of various kinds. The bulk of the literature referenced represents publications of scholarly research and literature in academic journals or government reports, although commentary, country-identifiable theoretical arguments, and legislation are also included throughout. Dissertations, mass-media publications, and documents such as legislative hearings, are largely excluded. On the occasions where they are included, the publications were of some particular relevance or provide one of the very few sources of information of any kind for a particular country. We have tried to organize multiple publications of specific authors from the most recent to the earliest of the author's works. And, unless specified at the end of the citation, the language of the publication is English.

The references are limited to publications on youth-crime or delinquency, and juvenile justice. To be chosen for inclusion, a publication had to be clearly identified as involving one or the other realm, and the ages of subjects studied or the scope of some agency's authority had to clearly indicate that it concerned persons below age 21, which we set as the upper limit for our definition of being "delinquent." Some publications using the term "delinquent" or similar terminology were excluded when, upon reading, it was found that they either did not concern juveniles or the focus of discussion was unclear. In this regard, it was the intent of our literature search to locate materials dealing either with the behavior of, or reaction to, juveniles in diverse parts of the world. While we cannot claim to be either exhaustive or comprehensive in including relevant publications, it is our hope that persons interested in exploring this literature find this bibliography a useful tool in their pursuit.

Titles were translated into English and the original language title is included in parentheses. The titles of journals, however, are left in the original language for ease of location by users of the bibliography. In trying to avoid awkward verbatim translations of publication titles, we may have been less precise than the author(s) originally intended. But by translating titles as close to common criminological usages as possible, we hope we have made them more comprehensible, relevant, and useful to the English-speaking audience. However much we wanted to include other works that we were aware of, in some cases obtaining them was physically impossible. Any and all such omissions and errors in translation, are solely our responsibility.

Two broad categories, "Behavior" and "Justice", corresponding to the two dominant concerns of the discipline -- the study of criminal/delinquent behavior and the study of the administration and effects of criminal/juvenile justice -- were employed in sorting references into groupings. These categories offer users a rough guide for locating references of particular relevance to their respective interests. For each reference listed, a brief annotation is provided. Each annotation is offered as a short synopsis of the publication's content and focus. They are not meant to be fully descriptive of the publication and should only be used as guides for locating publications of particular interest to users. It is expected that once located, users will seek and explore the publication in pursuit of their special interests.

Of course, not all references clearly fit into one or the other category, and some publications encompass each since the author(s) deal with both behaviors and the consequent judicial processes. Clearly some readers may not agree with our decision to locate a particular reference under the heading "Behavior" versus "Justice." Our guiding principle in making categorization choices was the "primary focus" of the publication. Thus, for example, an article concerning the deterrent impact of some correctional program could have been listed either as “behavior” or “justice” depending on whether the primary focus of the author(s) was on the operation of the correctional program or on explaining the etiology, continuation, or rate of delinquent behavior. In some cases the choice was quite arbitrary, although we attempted to be consistent in making these decisions.

Within each broad topic category, this bibliography lists references by individual country for ease of locating relevant literature for specific localities. As users will soon realize, for many countries the number of references we could locate and abstract is quite sparse. Although extreme differences in the literature referenced by country could, to some extent, reflect limitations in our search abilities and language skills, it also clearly reflects the lack of research and information on delinquency and juvenile justice for much of the world. Some countries, such as the United States and various Western European nations, produce an immense volume of literature in this area while regarding other countries, indeed entire regions of the World, nothing is known. To the extent that the disparities in literature referenced in this volume for various countries or regions are reflective of the entire discipline, it is clear that criminology has a long way to go before it can truly be called a global undertaking. What gaps in our knowledge and theory are occasioned by these gaps in research and literature can only be speculated on. At minimum, much remains to be learnt, particularly in non-industrialized, developing regions of the world.

Locating a reference within a particular country was not always straightforward. With glasnost, perestroika and the break up of the Soviet Union, and other changes in country names and borders in recent decades, it was not always clear what country a particular reference concerned. It became necessary, thus, to often use broad "country" categories rather than specific nation-state names to group references. In this regard, references from the Soviet Union, for example, are listed under the title "Russian Federation" in this volume, unless a specific country is identifiable as the locus of the research or commentary. Similarly, references for England, Wales, Scotland and Northern Ireland are listed as "United Kingdom" because much of this literature involved research in two or more of these localities, or did not clearly indicate the location of the study. Similarly, for other countries, such as the United States and its territories, a single "country" category is employed. Rather than using official country names, generic names more familiar to most potential users are employed for ease of reference (e.g., China versus the People’s Republic of China, and Germany versus the Federal Republic of Germany, where unification has made distinguishing the two German states a mute issue).

Since many references involved research or commentary on two or more localities, a "Multi-National" section is included at the end of each topic grouping. References in these sections include comparative research, multinational anthologies on a single topic, or international inquiries. Including these references as separate listings saved numerous duplicate listings as well as highlighting the cross-national scope of delinquency research which, even if limited, provides another dimension to an international bibliography not readily available elsewhere. Persons interested in specific countries should consult the Subject Index to locate references for individual countries included in these sections.

Given the diversity of topics covered by the literature referenced, it was decided that individual references would be organized by author, rather than by some specific topic such as offence rates, treatment outcome, gender, or whatever. We hope the index will be of value to users in locating specific references on particular topics. While the organization of the selection of references by authors' names offers a quick way of locating publications by specific authors within the topic and country headings, an Author Index is also provided to help find all referenced publications by individual authors. The Subject Index would likewise help locate references on specific topics cutting across the author/country organization of the bibliography.

It is our hope that this bibliography will not only be of value to individuals who are looking for literature on delinquency and juvenile justice around the world, but will also serve as a map of the extent and nature of criminological inquiry regarding the phenomena. Covering approximately a quarter-century of research and commentary (from 1975 through 2001), this bibliography provides an encapsulated view of the state of our knowledge and the scope of criminological inquiry. Equally important, it reveals the wide gaps that exist in both. In this regard, this bibliography provides criminologists direction as to where we might seek to inquire further, and what needs to be investigated in the future.

BEHAVIOR

The references contained in this section include publications primarily concerned with delinquent behavior and youth crime as reflected in the research and commentary produced for various countries. Included are publications on the etiology of delinquency, its epidemiology, character, and distribution. Also included are various forms of youthful misconduct, such as gang delinquency, violence, bullying, and sexual misconduct. Publications regarding the victimization of young people at home, school, and elsewhere, by peers and adults, are also listed. References to status offenders, at-risk and homeless youths, and the like, are also included.

Argentina

0001 Defense For Children International *Trafficking And Sale Of Children In Argentina*. Argentina Secretariat for Human Development and Family Welfare, Ministry of Health and Social Welfare, Republic of Argentina: Buenos Aires, Argentina, 1989. This report on the trafficking and sale of Argentinean children for domestic and foreign adoption identifies societal factors conducive to child-selling, and recommendations are presented for ameliorating the trafficking. 60p.

Australia

0002 Alder, Christine & Hunter, Nicole Australia, pp 1-13 in Hoffman, Allan M. & Summers, Randal W. (eds.) *Teen Violence: A Global View*. Westport, Connecticut: Greenwood, 2001. This chapter briefly describes the trends in Australian juvenile violence, the contributing factors, and the system-wide responsesthrough "family conferencing".

0003 Baker, Joanne *Juveniles In Crime-Part 1: Participation Rates And Risk Factors*. Sydney, Australia: New South Wales Bureau of Crime Statistics and Research, 1998. Findings of a large-scale self-reported delinquency study of secondary school male and female students in New South Wales in 1996 show that gender, drug-use, perceived school performance, ethnicity, aboriginality, level of supervision are risk factors and delinquency peaks at 14-16 years of age.

0004 Bessant, Judith & Watts, Rob Masculinity And Violence: An Ethnographic Exploration Of The Bodgies, 1948-1958, pp 189-220 in Hazlehurst, Kayleen & Hazlehurst, Cameron (eds.) *Gangs And Youth Subcultures: International Explorations*. New Brunswick, New Jersey: Transaction, 1998. This chapter offers a critique of youth-gang theory and an extensive analysis of the Bodgies of the 1950s Australia.

0005 Bessant, Judith & Watts, Rob Young People And Violence, pp 105-122 in Chappell, Duncan & Eggers, Sandra (eds.) *Australian Violence*. Canberra, Australia: Australian Institute of Criminology, 1995. Interviews with youths in suburban Melbourne lead to the conclusion that issues of personal integrity, righteous anger, codes of toughness, loyalty and turf-protection are motives to their violence.

0006 Bessant, Judith & Hil, Richard (eds.) *Youth, Crime & The Media*. Hobart, Australia: National Clearinghouse For Youth Studies, 1997. This anthology addresses the various dimensions of Australian media's portrayal of young peopleas a threat and objects of fear. 234p.

0007 Bessant, Judith The American 'Juvenile Underclass' And The Cultural Colonization Of Young Australians Under Conditions Of Modernity, *Journal Of Gang Research* 2:15-33, 1994. This article provides a theoretical perspective on the impact of North-American "youth cultures" and lifestyles on young Australians.

0008 Borowski, Allan & Murray, James M. (eds.) *Juvenile Delinquency In Australia*. North Ryde, New South Wales, Australia: Methuen, 1985. This anthology covers a wide spectrum of topics such as the causes of delinquency, the Aboriginal juvenile offender, the mentally retarded juvenile offender, the Children's Courts, diversionprograms, and juvenile probation. 438p.

0009 Borowski, Allan Programmes For Violent Juvenile Offenders: What Works? *Australian And New Zealand Journal Of Criminology* 19:155-162, 1986. This article offers a review of effective American programs for violent youths that the author feels may apply to Australia.

0010 Braithwaite, John & Braithwaite, Valerie An Exploratory Study Of Delinquency And The Nature Of Schooling, *Australian And New Zealand Journal Of Criminology* 14:25-32, 1978. This article reports that there is no support for the hypothesis that a less competitive school system will eliminate many of the structural strains that create juvenile delinquency.

0011 Braithwaite, John *Inequality, Crime, And Public Policy.* Boston, Massachu-setts: Routledge, 1979. Along with discussion of Australia and the United States, the author discusses the theory and research evidence on the interaction among class, slums, and crime including discussion of wealth, power, and public policy, chapters 4-9 focus on juvenile delinquency. 332p.

0012 Broadhurst, Roderic & Ferrante, Anna Trends In Juvenile Crime And Justice, pp 79-95 in Harding, Richard (eds.) *Repeat Juvenile Offenders: The Failure Of Selective Incapacitation In Western Australia.* Nedlands, Australia: Crime Research Centre, University of Western Australia, 1995. Diverse data-sources on the characteristics of juvenile offenders, their offenses, convictions and penalties, detention, and recidivism are analyzed and reported.

0013 Carcach, Carlos & Keverett, Simon *Recidivism Among Juvenile Offenders: An Analysis Of Times To Reappearance In Court.* Griffith, Australia: Australian Institute of Criminology, 1999. When adjudicated juveniles were followed up over five years, the authors found that there was about a 18 months' lapse between consecutive court appearances and offending. 25p.

0014 Carroll, Annemaree; Hattie, John; Durkin, Kevin & Houghton, Stephen Goal-Setting And Reputation Enhancement: Behavioural Choices Among Delinquent, At-Risk And Not At-Risk Adolescents, *Legal And Criminological Psychology* 6:165-184, 2001. This research investigates the relationships among goal setting, reputation enhancement and delinquent behavior in adolescents.

0015 Collins, Mark F. & Wilson, Richard M. Automobile Theft: Estimating The Size Of The Criminal Population, *Journal Of Quantitative Criminology* 6:395-409, 1990. Compares different offender estimation methods for car theft that have reliable incidence figures to assess the relative merit of each technique using arrest records of adults and juveniles charged with the offense.

0016 Dagger, Dianne & Mukherjee, Satyanshu *National Trends For Persons In Juvenile Corrective Institutions And Adult Prisons 1981 To 1992.* Canberra, Australia: Australian Institute of Criminology, 1994. Data on persons in juvenile corrective institutions shows that the rate of incarceration in such and, the rate of persons under 20 years old in juvenile institutions and adult prisons all declined between 1982 and 1992. 25p.

0017 Dunstan, John A. P. & Roberts, Scott F. Ecology, Delinquency And Socioeconomic Status, *British Journal Of Criminology* 20:329-343, 1980. An examination of the complex relationship of socioeconomic status to delinquency using a variety of dimensions for measuring socioeconomic status suggests a very strong link between poverty and officially recorded delinquency but not socioecomic status as such.

0018 Durkin, Kevin & Houghton, Stephen Children's And Adolescents' Stereotypes Of Tattooed People As Delinquent, *Legal And Criminological Psychology* 5:153-164, 2000. This study found that by the age of 6 children develop negative criminal stereotypes implying that adolescents who chose to get tattoo are aware of such stigma.

0019 Easteal, Patricia Weiser *Vietnamese Refugees: Crime Rates Of Minors And Youths In New South Wales.* Canberra, Australia: Australian Institute of Criminology, 1989. Examination of the crime rate for Vietnamese refugees, aged 10 to 24, in New South Wales, Australia demonstrates lack of empirical evidence for the media portrayal of rampant youth violence in the Vietnamese community. 46p.

0020 Francis, Ronald D. *Migrant Crime In Australia.* St. Lucia, Australia: University of Queensland, 1981. Official data and research findings of all immigrants including juveniles are evaluated in terms of the immigrants' relationship to Australian criminal justice system. 217p.

0021 Freeman, Karen *Young People And Crime.* Sydney, Australia: Bureau of Crime Statistics and Research, 1996. Reports on trends in juvenile crime and justice in New South Wales, Australia including information on criminal prosecution of juveniles, sources of information about juvenile crime, current statistics on offenses committed by juveniles as well as offender characteristics, and patterns of juvenile offending. 8p.

0022 Geason, Susan & Wilson, Paul R. *Preventing Graffiti And Vandalism.* Canberra, Australia: Australian Institute of Criminology, 1990. Describes various criminological theories of vandalism, and suggests planning, management, architectural and design strategies for minimizing vandalism and graffiti. 83p. Appendix.

0023 Goldstein, Mandy & Heaven, Patrick C. L. Perceptions Of The Family, Delinquency, And Emotional Adjustment Among Youth, *Personality And Individual Differences* 29:1169-1178, 2000. This study explored the relationships between perceived family processes and adolescent emotional and behavioral adjustment among a sample of youth in Australia.

0024 Grichting, Wolfgang L. The Subjective Probability Of Being Labelled Criminal In Juvenile Corrections, *Australian And New Zealand Journal Of Criminology* 12:162-174, 1979. When asked to estimate how the correctional staff might view certain illegality, institutionalized male and female youths in Australia indicate their fear of being labeled irrespective of their being first-offenders, recidivists, status-offenders, or more serious law violators.

0025 Gullone, Eleonora & Moore, Susan Adolescent Risk-Taking And The Five Factor Model Of Personality, *Journal Of Adolescence* 23:393-407, 2000. A study of risk-taking among Melbourne boys and girls, concludes that together with age, sex and personality traits predicts rebellious risk behavior rather than thrill seeking deviance.

0026 Harding, Richard Youth, Crime And Justice, pp 91-110 in Seventh United Nations Congress On The Prevention Of Crime And Treatment Of Offenders. *Australian Discussion Papers*. Canberra, Australia: Australian Institute of Criminology, 1985. This chapter offers a brief discussion of the nature and extent of youth crime in Australia, speculation on causes, and some discussion of responses to the problem.

0027 Harris, Tracey E. & Lennings, Chris J. Suicide And Adolescence, *International Journal Of Offender Therapy And Comparative Criminology* 37:263-270, 1993. Explores the role of family background, substance abuse, depression and hopelessness in predicting past suicidal behavior among adolescent offenders.

0028 Heaven, P. C. L.; Caputi, P.; Trivellion-Scott, D. & Swinton, T. Personality And Group Influences On Self-Reported Delinquent Behaviour, *Personality And Individual Differences* 28:1143-1158, 2000. This article reports the results of two data sets in which the links among the Eysenckian personality factors, identification with delinquent peers, and self-reported delinquency among high school students are examined.

0029 Heaven, Patrick C. L. Family Of Origin, Personality, And Self-Reported Delinquency, *Journal Of Adolescence* 17:445-459, 1994. Findings among a sample of female and male Catholic high-school students in New South Wales confirm the effects of family process and individual personality on youth violence and participation in vandalism/theft.

0030 Heaven, Patrick C. L. Personality And Self-Reported Delinquency: Analysis Of The "Big Five" Personality Dimensions, *Personality And Individual Differences* 20:47-54, 1996. The results of two studies into the "Big Five" personality factors associated with interpersonal violence and vandalism/theft are reported in this paper.

0031 Heaven, Patrick C. L. Personality And Self-Reported Delinquency: A Longitudinal Analysis, *Journal Of Child Psychology And Psychiatry* 37:747-751, 1996. This study assessed the personality factors associated with self-reported delinquency.

0032 Heaven, Patrick C. L. & Virgen, Michael Personality, Perceptions Of Family And Peer Influences, And Males' Self-Reported Delinquency, *Personality And Individual Differences* 30:321-331, 2001. This research sought to assess the joint influences of personality factors, family control, and delinquent companionship on males' self-reported delinquency.

0033 Henderson, Monica; Henderson, Peter & Kiernan, Carol Missing Persons: Incidence, Issues And Impacts, *Trends And Issues Australian Institute Of Criminology* 144:1-6, 2000. This article provides some data on the age and gender of missing persons demonstrating that 11-17 year olds make up the largest missing person category.

0034 Hil, Richard A Gloomy Vista? 'Globalization,' Juvenile Crime And Social Order---An Australian Perspective, *Crime, Law And Social Change* 33:369-384, 2000. This article discusses the link between globalization and youth crime, and the tendency for youth problem to be equated to the crime problem.

0035 Ireland, Steve Juvenile Alcohol Consumption A Cause For Concern, pp 187-207 in Vernon, Julia (eds.) *Alcohol And Crime*. Canberra, Australia: Australian Institute of Criminology, 1990. Describes the development of a multi-disciplinary 1982 self-reported research program on drinking and driving of male and female students from 10th grade.

0036 Kraus, J. Causes Of Juvenile Delinquency As Perceived By Juveniles, *International Journal Of Offender Therapy And Comparative Criminology*, 21:79-86, 1977. Australian adolescents' opinions on what causes delinquency among their peers.

0037 Kraus, J. & Bowmaker, B. How Delinquent Are The Delinquents—A Study Of Self-Reported Offences, *Australian And New Zealand Journal Of Criminology* 15:163-169, 1982. This self-report study on the "true" extent of delinquency among committed male offenders concludes that half of them "got away with" at least six out of every ten serious offenses, and 70 percent "got away with" at least four out of ten offenses.

0038 Kraus, J. Foster Children Grown Up: Parameters Of Care And Adult Delinquency, *Children And Youth Services Review* 3:99-114, 1981. This follow-up study of a male and female birth cohort who were discharged from wardship on their 18th birthday found that the number of foster care placements for both gender groups, and court appearances and earlier first conviction for males, and later first convictions of females were related positively to convictions but not to imprisonments.

0039 Kraus, J. Juvenile Unemployment And Delinquency, *Australian And New Zealand Journal Of Criminology* 12:37-42, 1979. A longitudinal analysis of the association between unemployment and delinquency rates of working-age male juveniles and others in New South Wales found no relationship between the two variables although adjudicated juveniles have higher unemployment rates.

0040 Kraus, J. Delinquency And Socioeconomic Status As Factors In Illiteracy Of Male Juveniles, *Australian And New Zealand Journal Of Criminology* 10:195-203, 1977. The author's analysis reveals that low socioeconomic status and illiteracy have greater association with delinquency rate of the area of residence.

0041 Kraus, J. The Deterrent Effect Of Fines And Probation On Male Juvenile Offenders, *Australian And New Zealand Journal Of Criminology* 7:231-240, 1975. Recidivism research among male youths fined and sentenced to probation found that those who engaged in larceny tended to commit more serious offenses and do so more frequently after fines.

0042 Kraus, J. Trends In Juvenile Delinquency, pp 155-162 in Chappell, Duncan & Wilson, Paul (eds.) *The Australian Criminal Justice System. 2nd Ed.* Chatswood, Australia: Butterworths, 1977. Summarizes earlier findings on trends in Australian juvenile delinquency and juvenile court policy and practices.

0043 Kraus, J. Trends In Violent Crime And Public Concern, *Australian Journal of Forensic Sciences* 11:192-208, 1979. Although mostly on adult crime, this article includes a table of persons under 18 who were convicted for willful damage to school property and other such adolescent acts besides homicide, assault, rape, and robbery from 1968-1976.

0044 Legislative Assembly Of Queensland Parliamentary Travelsafe Committee *Brisbane's Citytrain Network - Part Two: Passenger Security*. Queensland, Australia, 1998.This is a report by 12-18 year olds on the incidents of assault in the city public transportation system. 132p.

0045 Lennings, Christopher & Pritchard, Monica Prevalence Of Drug use Prior To Detention Among Residents Of Youth Detention Centres In Queensland, *Drug and Alcohol Review* 18:145-152, 1999. This article describes the prior drug-use behavior and demographics of 118 young people in detention.

0046 Levy, Kenneth St. C. The Contribution Of Self-Concept In The Etiology Of Adolescent Delinquency, *Adolescence* 32:671-686, 1997. This study of 230 adolescents from high schools and correctional institutions in Australia who are non-delinquent, non-institutionalized delinquent, or institutionalized delinquent confirms the importance of the relationship between self-concept and delinquency.

0047 Lovegrove, S. A. Personality And Short-Term Re-Offence Behavior Among Young Australian Male Probationers, *Australian And New Zealand Journal Of Criminology* 11:13-18, 1978. In an extension of an earlier study concludes that the young, male offenders (probationers) cannot be identified very effectively by using socialization, alienation and delinquency proneness scales.

0048 Mason, Gail & Wilson, Paul Sport, Recreation And Juvenile Crime: An Assessment Of The Impact Of Sport And Recreation Upon Aboriginal And Non-Aboriginal Youth Offenders. Canberra, Australia: Australian Institute of Criminology, 1988. It is argued that sports and recreational programs are only one aspect in improving the social, economic and political opportunities for youth. 183p.

0049 McKissack, Ian & Simcock, Robert Delinquency, Hostility And The Effects Of Institutional Training, *Australian And New Zealand Journal Of Criminology* 8:231-234, 1975. In this study of two matched groups of adolescents, it was found that delinquent behavior is an integral part of the hostility of institutionalized hard-core delinquents compared to recent first offender inmates.

0050 Moore, David *The Lads In Action: Social Process In An Urban Youth Subculture*. Hants, United Kingdom: Ashgate, 1994. This ethnography describes the social processes that create and maintain the distinctive urban life-style activities of males belonging to the skinhead subculture in Perth, Western Australia. 161p.

0051 Mukherjee, Satyanshu K.; Jacobsen, Evelyn & Walker, John R. *Sourcebook Of Australian Criminal & Social Statistics: 1900-1980*. Canberra, Australia: Australian Institute of Criminology, 1981. Besides a wide variety of criminal justice and crime data for all of Australia, this volume includes information pertaining to the age and gender of arrested offenders, police force statistics, courts, and prisons statistics. 333p.

0052 Mukherjee, Satyanshu K.; Scandia, Anita; Dagger, Dianne & Matthews, Wendy *Sourecbook Of Australian Criminal And social Statistics*. Canberra, Australia: Australian Institute of Criminology, 1989. Section 5 on juvenile statistics for all of Australia and each of its states provides data on gender, age, residence, types of offenses and sanctions. 661p.

0053 Mukherjee, Satyanshu K.;Walker, John R.; Psaila, Trish; Scandia, Anita; & Dagger, Dianne *The Size Of The Crime Problem In Australia*. Phillip, Australia: Australian Institute of Criminology, 1987. Analyses of official and crime victim survey data suggest that juveniles are over-represented in arrests for breaking and entering, stealing, and vehicle theft in all of Australia, and its various states and territories and includes Canadian crime rates as well. 111p.

0054 New South Wales Australia Ombudsman *Policing Public Safety: Report Under 5.6 Of The Crime Legislation Amendment (Police And Public Safety) Act 1998*. New South Wales, Australia, 1998. Chapters 7 & 8 include a discussion of parents who allow children to carry knives to schools, as well as some age and gender data on people who were issued "directions" and penalties, revealing a disproportionate rate for indigenous youth. 380p.

0055 Ogden, E. J .D. & De L Horne, D. J. An Australian Residential Youth Training Centre: Population Study, *Australian And New Zealand Journal Of Criminology* 9:49-54, 1996. This research studied boys in Turana Youth Centre, Victoria and found that most of their offenses related to theft.

0056 Ogilvie, Emma Masculine Obsessions: An Examination Of Criminology, Criminality And Gender, *Australian And New Zealand Journal Of Criminology* 29:205-226, 1996. Using data from a large-scale sibling study and in-depth interviews with serious offenders, this study concludes that combining both methods with self-report studies and official statistics provides a better understanding of the process by which juveniles become delinquent.

0057 Peiser, Nadine C. & Heaven, Patrick C. L. Family Influences On Self-reported Delinquency Among High School Students, *Journal Of Adolescence* 19:557-568, 1996. A self-reported study of boys and girls on the interactions among self esteem, perceived family relationships, parental discipline style and delinquency concludes that among boys, parents' punitive discipline style and high delinquency while among girls, intuitive disciplinary style and low levels of deliquency were correlated.

0058 Perrone, Santina & White, Rob Young people And Gangs, *Trends and Issues in Crime and Criminal Justice* 167:1-6, 2000. This study concludes that the Australian concern for gang activity is the result of media myth and that the bands of Australian youths cannot be defined as gangs in the American sense.

0059 Polk, Kenneth & White, Rob Economic Adversity And Criminal Behavior: Rethinking Youth Unemployment And Crime, *The Australian And New Zealand Journal Of Criminology* 32:284-302, 1999. This paper argues that changes in the economies and the consumption behavior around the shopping mall have an impact on adolescent behavior and enforcement statistics.

0060 Polk, Kenneth Youth Violence: Myth And Reality, pp 51-70 in Chappell, Duncan & Eggers, Sandra (eds.) *Australian Violence: Contemporary Perspectives II*. Canberra, Australia: Australian Institute of Criminology, 1995. Percentages of juveniles involved in various crimes in Australia and its states and their victimization data demonstrate, that contrary to media and other portrayals, most violence involves adults.

0061 Poynting, Scott; Noble, Greg & Tabar, Paul Middle Eastern Appearances: "Ethnic Groups," Moral Panic And Media Framing, *Australian And New Zealand Journal Of Criminology* 34:67-90, 2001. This research found that the media played a strong role in the portrayals of ethnic youth and crime in a suburb of Sydney during 1998-2000.

0062 Putnins, Aldis L. Victim Awareness Programs For Delinquent Youths: Effects On Moral Reasoning, *Adolescence* 32:709-714, 1997. Attendance at the Victim Awareness Program significantly increased scores on measures of socio-moral reasoning and maturity among incarcerated delinquents in a treatment group.

0063 Queensland Criminal Justice Commission *Children, Crime And Justice In Queensland*. Brisbane, Australia: Research Paper Series, Vol. 2, Number 2, 1995. Provides statistics on the juvenile justice system in Queensland since the enactment of the Juvenile Justice Act 1992 and the Children's Court Act 1992. 19p.

0064 Read, Hilary & Alder, Christine Job Retention: Employment Problems Of Youth From Youth Training Centers, *Australian And New Zealand Journal Of Criminology* 21:67-80, 1988. Interviews with a group of adolescent youths released into employment by a Youth Training Center reveal the following six factors as the most important in job retention: type of job, support; emotional and personality problems, effects of institutionalization, stigma, and peers.

0065 Richards, Ian & Sullivan, Ann Psychotherapy For Delinquents, *Journal Of Adolescence* 19: 63-73, 1996. The authors review delinquency and psychotherapy literature and describe their treatment program for 45 Australian boys and 2 girls that is based on attachment theory.

0066 Rigby, Ken & Cox, Ian The Contribution Of Bullying At School And Low Self-Esteem To Acts Of Delinquency Among Australian Teenagers, *Personality And Individual Differences* 21:609-612, 1996. Using a survey of school children ages 13-17, this study presents factors associated with delinquent behavior and reports that girls reported less delinquent behavior than boys.

0067 Roberts, Gwenneth Young People And Violence: A Focus On Schools, pp 105-122 in Chappell, Duncan & Eggers, Sandra (eds.) *Australian Violence: Contemporary Perspectives II*. Canberra, Australia: Australian Institute of Criminology, 1995. Interviews with Melbourne youths indicate that for them issues of personal integrity, anger, codes of toughness, loyalty and protection of territory are motivating issues for violence.

0068 Russell, Kate Inmates With Alcohol And Other Drug Problems: What About The Next Generation? *Current Issues In Criminal Justice* 7:237-245, 1995. The author addresses the issue of the intergenerationality of criminality.

0069 Salmelainen, Pia *The Correlates Of Offending Frequency: A Study Of Juvenile Theft Offenders In Detention*. Sydney, Australia: New South Wales Bureau of Crime Statistics and Research, 1995. This study suggests that the factors related to lifestyle are most important in offending frequency, although different factors seemed more or less important, depending on offense type. 81p.

0070 Sanson-Fisher, R. Aborigines In Crime Statistics: An Interaction Between Poverty And Detectors, *Australian And New Zealand Journal Of Criminology* 11:71-80, 1978. This paper examines the overrepresentation of the Aborigines in official crime statistics in the context of a complex interaction of factors such as the juveniles' opportunity to conform, survival skills, motivation, and cultural differences.

0071 Sanson-Fisher, R. & Woollacott, H. & Mulligan, B. Knowledge Of The Law: The Disadvantaged Delinquent? *Australian And New Zealand Journal Of Criminology* 13:204-214, 1980. This study concludes that the non-offenders were significantly less delinquent and scored better on the questions relating to their knowledge of their rights than the institutionalized group although both groups showed a disturbingly limited knowledge of many laws.

0072 Sarantakos, Sotirios Cohabitation, Marriage And Delinquency: The Significance Of Family Environment, *Australian And New Zealand Journal Of Criminology* 30:187-199, 1997. Drawing on data from 233 children with cohabiting parents and 279 with married parents, it was found that there were proportionally more offenders from families of cohabiting than of married couples.

0073 Sheehan, Mary & Nucifora, J. The Young, Delinquency, Drink And Driving, pp 95-105 in Vernon, Julia (eds.) *Alcohol And Crime*. Canberra, Australia: Australian Institute of Criminology, 1990. Discusses Australian juveniles involvement with alcohol and related problem behaviors including sources of alcohol, relationship with known drinkers, frequency of use etc.

0074 Slee, Roger Pathologies Of School Violence: A Reconsideration, pp 16-23 in Bessant, Judith; Carrington, Kerry & Cook, Sandy (eds.) *Culture Of Crime And Violence: The Australian Experience*. Bundoora, Australia: La Trobe University Press, 1995. This chapter considers violence in schools as not a major issue and suggests that schools have the potential to shape a "more peaceful future."

0075 Stevenson, Richard J.; Forsythe, Lubica M. V. & Weatherburn, Don The Stolen Goods Market In New South Wales, Australia: An Analysis Of Disposal Avenues And Tactics, *British Journal Of Criminology* 41:101-118, 2001. This study concludes that most youths steal "on commission,"and juveniles were stealing to support their cannabis habit while adults were involved with heroin.

0076 Trimboli, Lily & Coumarelos, Christine *Cannabis And Crime*. Sydney, Australia: New South Wales Bureau of Crime Statistics and Research, 1998. Reviews the Australian literature and household and school research during the 1990s that reveals widespread use of cannabis. 16p.

0077 Vinson, T. & Homel, R. Crime And Disadvantage, *British Journal Of Criminology* 15:21-31, 1975. Nine socio-medical indices used in this study to identify "high-risk" areas in minor New Castle, Australia suburbs prone to high rates of juvenile delinquency show that neighborhoods with high delinquency rate also exhibit other forms of economic and social disadvantages.

0078 Walker, Linley Chivalrous Masculinity Among Juvenile Offenders In Western Sydney: A New Perspective On Young Working Class Men And Crime, *Current Issues In Criminal Justice* 9:279-293, 1998. This article provides a criminal ethnography on one case study regarding social and cultural variables in Australia and their relationship to crime.

0079 Warner, Catherine A Study Of The Self-Reported Crime Of A Group Of Male And Female High School Students, *Australian And New Zealand Journal Of Criminology* 15:255-272, 1982. A survey of male and female youths from an urban high school of mixed socioeconomic strata concludes that there is substantial hidden delinquency, and that boys admit to more infractions than girls.

0080 Warren, Ian & Aumair, Megan Media Depictions And Public Discourses On 'Gangs' In Melbourne, 1989-1991, pp 221-244 in Hazlehurst, Kayleen & Hazlehurst, Cameron (eds.) *Gangs And Youth Subcultures: International Explorations*. New Brunswick, New Jersey: Transaction, 1998. This chapter describes how media depictions of youth gangs in Australia help generated a "moral panic" about gang violence.

0081 Weatherburn, Don & Lind, Bronwyn *Social And Economic Stress, Child Neglect And Juvenile Delinquency*. Sydney, Australia: New South Wales Bureau of Crime Statistics and Research, 1997. This report includes discussions of economic stress and the parenting process, the role of social stresses and supports in child maltreatment, neglect and abuse, as well juvenile participation in crime, and predictors of juvenile participation in property and violent crime. 55p.

0082 Weatherburn, Don; Lind, Bronwyn & Ku, Simon 'Hotbeds Of Crime?' Crime And Public Housing In Urban Society, *Crime & Delinquency* 45:256-271, 1999. This study concludes that a concentration of public housing in an area causes the breakdown of social control mechanism and thereby, increasing neighborhood crime problem.

0083 Weir, Karen & Ford, Dennis Modification Of The Behaviors Of Delinquent Youth In A Token Economy: Lentara Project, *Australian And New Zealand Journal Of Criminology* 10:153-164, 1977. A small study of "token economy" in a community based treatment facility suggests that such behavior modification may help reinforce positive behavior among delinquent and pre-delinquent boys.

0084 White, Rob (ed.) *Australian Youth Subcultures: On The Margins And In The Main Stream*. Hobart, Tasmania: Australian Clearinghouse for Youth Studies, 1999. The articles in this anthology are organized under six topics on social, economic, and behavioral aspects of youth culture. 221p.

0085 White, Rob Making Ends Meet: Young People, Work And The Criminal Economy, *Australian And New Zealand Journal Of Criminology* 22:136-150, 1989. This article explores the relationship between juvenile delinquency and the participation of young people in the formal and the informal sectors of the Australian economy.

0086 White, Rob *No Space Of Their Own: Young People And Social Control In Australia*. New York, New York: Cambridge, 1990. A critique of the relationship between the young and increasing adult social control measures in Australia that the author feels is delegating the former to a permanent under class status. 237p.

0087 White, Rob The Business Of Youth Crime Prevention, pp 164-184 in O'Malley, Pat & Sutton, Adam (eds.) *Crime Prevention In Australia: Issues In Policy And Research*. Leichhardt, Australia: Federation Press, 1997. This chapter reviews the Midland Gate Streetwork crime prevention program for Australian youth and discusses the socioeconomic trends that contribute to their alienation, marginalization and criminalization.

0088 Williams, Paul Alcohol-Related Social Disorder And Rural Youth: Part 1-Victims, *Trends And Issues In Crime And Criminal Justice* 140:1-6, 1999. The author uses three successive waves of national drug use surveys in Australia, and concludes that alcohol consumption has been increasing among youths, particularly among the rural youths.

0089 Wilson, Paul & Arnold, Josid *Street Kids: Australia's Alienated Young*. Victoria, Australia: Collins Dove, 1986. Based on personal interviews of alienated youths it was found that they were involved in sundry delinquency, alcohoism, drug abuse, prostitution, suicide attempts or serious crimes. 121p.

0090 Wilson, Paul & Lincoln, Robyn Young People, Economic Crisis, Social Control And Crime, *Current Issues In Criminal Justice* 4:110-116, 1992. This article addresses why young people in Australia, and in other countries, are more criminally involved as a result of their being unemployed

Austria

0091 Grafl, Christian Juvenile Delinquency In Austria In The Eighties, pp 29-32 in Junger-Tas, Josine; Boendermaker, Leonieke & Van Der Laan, Peter H. (eds.) *The Future Of The Juvenile Justice System (L'Avenir Du Système Pénal Des Mineurs)*. Leuven, Belgium: Acco, 1991. This chapter presents empirical studies on delinquency that is known to the police, female juvenile delinquency, and information on juveniles convicted by the courts in Austria.

Barbados

0092 Ramoutar, Karen M. Social Class And Crime In A Caribbean Community *Inter-national Journal Of The Sociology Of Law* 23:273-293, 1995. In this exploration of social class and criminal behavior in Barbados it was found that no differences except for drug offenses existed between rich and poor communities in the amount of criminal and delinquent activity taking place.

Belgium

0093 Born, M.; Chevalier, V. & Humblet, I. Resilience, Desistance And Delinquent Career Of Adolescent Offenders, *Journal Of Adolescence* 20:679-694, 1997. This study identifies factors that predict persistent and increased/decreased delinquency between early childhood and adolescence.

0094 Born, Michel & Gavray, Claire Self-Reported Delinquency In Liége, Belgium, pp 131-155 in Junger-Tas, Josine; Terlouw, Gert-Jan & Klein, Malcolm W. (eds.) *Delinquent Behavior Among Young People In The Western World: First Results Of The International Self-Report Delinquency Study*. Amsterdam/New York: Kugler, 1994. Chapter reports the findings form a self-reported delinquen- ncy survey carried out in the city of Liége, Belgium.

0095 Gavray, C. Deviant Path Between Adolescence And Adulthood (Trajectoire Déviante À La Lisière Entre Adolescence Et Âge Adulte), *Déviance Et Société* 21:273-288, 1997. This longitudinal study of self-reported criminality among a representative sample of youths of Liege found that criminal behavior was not necessarily abandoned upon becoming an adult, school discontinuation or obtaining a job. French.

0096 Hermans, Philip The Expression Of Guilt By Moroccan Adolescents: Ethnocentric Interpretations By Western Teachers And Social Workers, *International Journal Of Educational Research* 31:303-316, 1999. In this study of the Belgian teachers' attitudes to their Moroccan students questions their views of these students' illegal conduct.

0097 Junger-Tas, Josine Hidden Delinquency And Judicial Selection In Belgium, pp 70-94 in Friday, Paul C. & Stewart, V. Lorne (eds.) *Youth Crime And Juvenile Justice: International Perspectives*. New York: Praeger, 1977. Interviews of youths living in one city in Belgium reveals that two-thirds of the sample reported having engaged in some delinquent acts of which most were against property.

0098 Mauwissen, Eric & Delaet-van Gasse, Joëlle Some Aspects Of The Fates Of Young Delinquents In Belgium During The 19th Century (Quelques Aspects Du Sort Réservé Aux Jeunes Délinquants En Belgique Au XIXè Siècle), pp 625-654 in Hess, Albert G. & Clement, Priscilla F. (eds.) *History Of Juvenile Delinquency: A Collection Of Essays On Crime Committed By Young Offenders, In History And In Selected Countries, Vol.2.* Aalen, Germany: Scientia Verlag, 1993. This chapter provides an extensive discussion of the law, system of justice and extent and nature of delinquency in Belgium during the 19th century. French with English summary.

0099 Van Welzenis, Ingrid The Self-Concept Of Societally Vulnerable And Delinquent Boys Within The Context Of School And Leisure Activities, *Journal Of Adolescence* 20:695-705, 1997. This study examines whether delinquent and non-delinquent boys in a medium-sized Belgian city have different self-concepts.

0100 Vettenburg, Nicole Preventing Juvenile Delinquency By Making The Curriculum More Attractive (La Prevention De La Délinquance Juvénile Par L'offre Scolaire Attractive), pp 181-191 in Junger-Tas, Josine, Boendermaker, Leonieke & Van Der Laan, Peter H. (eds.) *The Future Of Juvenile Justice System (L'Avenir Du Système Pénal Des Mineurs).* Leuven, The Netherlands: Acco, 1991. A study in Flemish Belgium on school performance, family life, delinquent behavior, contact with the police and judiciary concludes that the school, particularly the interaction with the teachers, has great impact on the delinquent behavior. French.

0101 Vettenburg, Nicole & Walgrave, Lode School Experiences, Delinquency And Social Vulnerabilities (Expériences Scolaires, Délinquance Et Vulnérabilité Sociétale), *Revue Internationale De Criminologie Et De Police Technique* 44:174-189, 1991. This study on the relationship among school performance, delinquency and social maladjustment focused on school students and dropouts in two phases in Flanders, Belgium. French with English summary.

Brazil

0102 Barker, Gary & Loewenstein, Irene Where The Boys Are: Attitudes Related To Masculinity, Fatherhood, And Violence Toward Women Among Low-Income Adolescent And Young Adult Males In Rio De Janeiro, Brazil, *Youth And Society* 29:166-196, 1997. This study of male and female youths on gender roles and violence found that these 14-30 year old males feel violence toward women acceptable.

0103 Carlo, Gustavo; Koller, Silvia & Eisenberg, Nancy Prosocial Moral Reasoning In Institutionalized Delinquent, Orphaned, And Non-institutionalized Brazilian Adolescents, *Journal Of Adolescent Research* 13:363-376, 1998. This study comparing prosocial moral reasoning of institutionalized Brazilian delinquents and non-institutionalized adolescents reports that the former prefer lower levels of prosocial moral reasoning and not internalized types of pro-social moral reasoning.

0104 Huggins, Martha K. & Mesquita, Myriam P. Scapegoating Outsiders: The Murders Of Street Youth In Modern Brazil, *Policing And Society* 5:265-280, 1995. The authors analyze life and death by murders of homeless youths in contemporary Brazil.

0105 Inciardi, James A. & Surratt, Hilary L. Children In The Streets Of Brazil: Drug Use, Crime, Violence, And HIV Risks, *Substance Use & Misuse* 33:1461-1480, 1998. The lifestyle and illegal substance-use by street urchins in Brazil are described.

0106 Penglase, Ben *Final Justice: Police And Death Squad Homicides Of Adolescents In Brazil.* New York, New York: Human Rights Watch/Americas, 1994. This report on the murder of children in four states in Brazil found a pattern of killings by on-duty police officers during the course of their official duties and unofficial death squads of off-duty officers. 140p.

0107 Salvador, Celia Sociocultural Roots of Violence: Street Children In Brazil, pp 163-170 in Chiland, Colette & Young, J. Gerald (eds.) *Children And Violence.* Northvale, New Jersey: Jason Aronson, 1993. This brief chapter describes the state of street children and some of the Brazilian efforts to deal with them.

Cameroon

0108 Ade, Catherine M. Juvenile Delinquency As Reflected By Offenders Of The Borstal Institute Of Cameroon, *International Journal Of Comparative And Applied Criminal* Justice 19:257-268, 1995. This study presents profiles of 67 juvenile offenders institutionalized in the Buea Reformtory School of the Republic of Cameroon.

0109 Matchinda, Brigitte The Impact Of Home Background On The Decision Of Children To Run Away: The Case Of Yaounde City Street Children In Cameroon, *Child Abuse And Neglect* 23:245-255, 1999. This study describes the backgrounds of street children and their home backgrounds in sub-Saharan Cameroon.

Canada

0110 Adlaf, Edward M. Recent Studies Of Cocaine Use And Abuse In Canada, *Canadian Journal Of Criminology* 34:1-13,1992. The author reviews the various data on cocaine and other illegal substance use and convictions for related offenses in the various Canadian provinces among street youths 15 years and older.

0111 Adlaf, Edward M.; Smart, Reginald G. & Walsh, Gordon W. Is The Association Between Drug Use And Delinquency Weakening? *Addiction* 89:1675-1681,1994. This study of the association between drug use and delinquency among Ontario juveniles found that drug use and drug selling declined significantly while reported non-drug-related delinquency increased.

0112 Ambert, Anne Marie & Gagnon, Louise D. What Is The Experience Of Parents Of Young Lawbreakers? (Que Sait-On De L'Expérience Existentielle Des Parents Des Jeunes Contrevenants?) *Criminologie* 28:2:131-142, 1995. This article on the negative effects and experiences of 116 Montreal parents whose children were delinquents analyzes the statistics on stress, fatigue, health and general happiness. French.

0113 Amorso, Donald M. & Ware, Edward E. Youth's Perception of Police As A Function Of Attitudes Towards Parents, Teachers And Self, *Canadian Journal Of Criminology* 25:191-200,1983. In this study of young students in Ontario, it was found that attitudes towards teachers but not towards self or parents, were the best predictors of attitudes toward the police.

0114 Anderson, Laurence E. & Walsh, James A. Prediction Of Adult Criminal Status From Juvenile Psychological Assessment, *Criminal Justice And Behavior* 25:226-239,1998. This follow-up study of juvenile offenders in an assessment center in Canada uses discriminate-function analysis to arrive at the best variables which distinguish between those who as adults have a serious criminal record and those without.

0115 Andre, Glenn; Kendall, Kathleen & Pease, Ken Health And Offense Histories Of Young Offenders In Saskatoon, Canada, *Criminal Behaviour And Mental Health* 4:163-180, 1994. The relationship between health and juvenile criminality in Saskatchewan reveals little association between any specific disease and juvenile offending.

0116 Andrews, Don A. Recidivism Is Predictable And Can Be Influenced: Using Risk Assessment To Reduce Recidivism, *Forum On Corrections Research* 1:11-17, 1989. This article is a critique of the principles of risk and need and how juvenile offenders can be managed efficiently and humanely while their recidivism is lowered.

0117 Avakame, Edem F. Modeling The Patriarchal Factor In Juvenile Delinquency: Is There Room For Peers, Church, And Television? *Criminal Justice And Behavior* 24:477-494, 1997. This study of parental relations and controls on offspring's delinquency and taste for risk did not find any support for the role of patriarchal gender-role attitudes suggesting the importance of factors beyond the nuclear family and its socialization methods.

0118 Avakame, Edem Frank *Gender, Family-Class Structure, And Juvenile Delinquency: A Partial Replication And Extension Of Power-Control Theory*. Edmonton, Canada: University of Alberta Centre for Criminological Research, 1993. In this research of extra-familial socializing agents on gender subjectivities, risk tolerance, and proclivity for delinquency, the evidence highlights the impor tance of direct parental controls in delinquency prevention. 40p.

0119 Badgley, Robin Symposium Report: Report Of The Committee On Sexual Offenses Against Children And Youths In Canada, *Canadian Criminology Forum* 7:145-156, 1985. This report of the proceedings of a conference under the auspices of the Center for Criminology and the Institute of Child Study at the University of Toronto in 1985 is on the findings of the Badgley Committee Report on Sexual Offenses Against Children and Youth.

0120 Baron, Stephen W. & Hartnagel, Timothy F. Attributions, Affect, And Crime: Street Youths' Reactions To Unemployment, *Criminology* 35:409-434, 1997. This study found that familial and school factors had minimal influence on current criminal behavior while more relevant were the immediate factors such as homelessness, drug or alcohol use, and criminal peers who were engaged in illegal activities.

0121 Baron, Stephen W. Canadian Male Street Skinheads: Street Gang Or Street Terrorists?, *Canadian Review Of Sociology And Anthropology* 34:125-154, 1997. This ethnographic study of 14 Edmonton male skinheads living on the streets describes their violent behavior and political consciousness.

0122 Baron, Stephen W. & Hartnagel, Timothy F. Street Youth And Criminal Violence, *Journal Of Research In Crime And Delinqeuncy* 35:166-192, 1998. This self-report study in Edmonton found that longer exposure to the street subculture and criminal peers lead to concern for honor, protection and retribution, and these youths had a history of physical abuse at home and were at greater the risk for violence on the street.

0123 Baron, Stephen W. & Kennedy, Leslie W. Deterrence And Homeless Male Street Youths, *Canadian Journal Of Criminology* 40:27-60, 1998. This study of the threat of formal punishment on the criminal behavior of homeless male Canadian street youths concludes that while many street youths feared legal sanctions, more serious offenders them did not.

0124 Baron, Stephen W. & Tindall, David B. Network Structure And Delinquent Attitudes Within A Juvenile Gang, *Social Networks* 15:255-273, 1993. The authors examine juvenile delinquency, social bonds and group structures from a social network approach.

0125 Bartek, Sophie E. ; Krebs, Dennis L. & Taylor, Michael C. Coping, Defending, And The Relations Between Moral Judgment And Moral Behavior In Prostitutes And Other Female Juvenile Delinquents, *Journal Of Abnormal Psychology* 102:66-73,1993. Among female delinquents and same-age non-delinquents, it was found that compared to non-delinquents, the delinquents had lower scores on moral maturity and coping but higher scores on defensiveness.

0126 Beare, Margaret E. ; Clarke, Curtis & Gordon, Robert *Youth At Risk: Literacy, Substance Abuse, And Criminality.* Ottawa, Canada: Canadian Association of Chiefs of Police, 1996. The authors focus on the relationships among street youths, youth illiteracy and its causes, drug abuse, delinquency and crime, the role of the police, characteristics of successful programs, issues and resources related to increasing literacy and drug awareness within each Canadian province. 252p.

0127 Biron, Louise & LeBlanc, Marc Family Components And Home-Based Delinquency, *British Journal Of Criminology* 17:157-168, 1977. The results of this self-report questionnaire study of students in eight public high schools of Montreal indicate that the structural aspects of family living may have been over-valued in previous research at the expense of the more influential, but more difficult to measure, psycho-sociological factors.

0128 Biron, Louise L. & Ladouceur, Carol The Boy Next Door: Local Teen-Age Burglars In Montreal, *Security Journal* 2:200-204, 1991. This Montreal self-report study using the rational choice perspective, explores decision-making from the point of view of the teenage burglars.

0129 Biron, Louise; Gagnon, Rosette & LeBlanc, Marc *Girls' Delinquency (La Délinquance Des Filles)*, Montreal, Canada: University of Montreal, 1980. This is a review of research and theories of female delinquency in the context of women's movement and children's rights. 208p. French.

0130 Bonta, J.; Lipinski, S. & Marin, M. Aboriginal Recidivists, *Forum On Corrections Research* 5:9-10, 1993. This study of 282 Canadian male Aboriginal offenders describes the age at first offense, conviction, and recidivism.

0131 Brannigan, Augustine & Caputo, Tullio *Studying Runaways And Street Youth In Canada: Conceptual And Research Design Issues*. Ottawa, Canada: Solicitor General Canada, 1993. This is a pilot study on the process of becoming a runaway in Calgary, the factors related to leaving the street, and the responses and effectiveness of services designed for runaways and street youth. 217p.

0132 Brannigan, Augustine & Fleischman, John Juvenile Prostitution And Mental Health: Policing Delinquency Or Treating Pathology? *Canadian Journal Of Law And Society*, 4:77-98,1989. This article addresses juvenile prostitution in Canada, its extent and if such behavior is the result of prior abuse.

0133 Brannigan, Augustine Self Control, Social Control And Evolutionary Psychology: Towards An Integrated Perspective on Crime, *Canadian Journal Of Criminology* 39:403-431, 1997. This is a review of the various developments in control theory of delinquency and crime and a defense of a developmental-evolutionary perspective.

0134 Brendgen, Mara; Vitaro, Frank & Bukowski, William M. Affiliation With Del-inquent Friends: Contributions Of Parents, Self-Esteem, Delinquent Behavior, And Rejection By Peers, *Journal Of Early Adolescence* 18:244-265, 1998. This examines if a perceived lack of closeness with parents is related to associating with delinquent friends and mediated by a lack of self-esteem.

0135 Brendgen, Mara; Vitaro, Frank & Bukowski, William M. Stability And Variability Of Adolescents' Affiliation With Delinquent Friends: Predictors And Consequences, *Social Development* 9:205-225, 2000. This study of delinquent behavior over a two-year period found that attitude toward delinquent behavior was the main predictor of stability versus change in affiliation with delinquent or non-delinquent friends.

0136 Cabrera, Natasha J. Violence By And Against Children In Canada, pp 126-152 in Ross, Jeffrey Ian (ed.) *Violence In Canada*. Don Mills, Canada: Oxford, 1995. This article summarizes various Canadian research findings on physical and sexual violence by and against children, responses to such violence by the criminal justice system and treatments.

0137 Canada Correctional Research And Development *A Profile of Homicide Offenders In Canada: A Research Brief.* Ottawa, Canada: Correctional Services of Canada, 1995. This publication provides a brief summary of gang-related homicide. 11p.

0138 Canada National Clearinghouse On Family Violence *The Invisible Boy: Revisioning The Victimization Of Male Children And Teens.* Ottawa, Canada: Canada Health, 1996. This report highlights the issues of male child victimization in Canada including physical and sexual or psychological maltreatment and neglect, corporal punishment, suicide, and community- and school-based violence. 68p.

0139 Canada National Crime Prevention Council *The Dollars And Sense Of Comprehensive Crime Prevention Strategy For Canada.* Ottawa, Canada: National Crime Prevention Council, 1997. This report recommends multifaceted social development programs such as early education, home visits, social skills groups, limiting access to guns and alcohol, reduction in poverty, and treatment for children. 14p.

0140 Canada Solicitor General Information Systems And Statistics Division *Statistics Handbook 1977.* Ottawa, Canada, 1978. This is a statistical compilation of juvenile and adult Canadian crimes and criminal justice system with data on police, court, juvenile justice, and corrections, details on drug offenses and convictions, and penitentiary statistics. 143p.

0141 Canada Statistics *A Graphical Overview Of Crime And The Administration Of Criminal Justice In Canada.* Ottawa, Canada: Canadian Centre for Justice Statistics, 1996. This report includes juvenile and adult crimes and criminal justice system and corrections in general. 215p.

0142 Canadian Association Of The Chiefs Of Police *Organized Crime Committee Report.* Ottawa, Canada: Canadian Association of the Chiefs of Police, 1993. A review of organized crime, this report includes a section on youth gangs, with highlights of each province's youth gangs of the 1990s. 100p.

0143 Caplan, Paula J. ; Awad, George A.; Wilks, Corinne & White, Georgina Sex Differences In A Delinquent Clinic Population, *British Journal Of Criminology* 20:311-328, 1980. This is a large-scale study of 7-16 year old boys and girls referred to Toronto family court clinic for assessment.

0144 Caputo, T. ; Weiler, R. & Kelly, K. *Phase II Of The Runaways And Street Youth Project: The Saskatoon Case Study. Final Report.* Ottawa, Canada: Policing Division, Solicitor General Canada, 1994. This study of the community response to street youths in Saskatoon, its cost and effectiveness, concludes that the majority of youths using social services were runaways and street youth who were predominantly Aboriginal, with long-term and multifaceted problems. 111p.

0145 Carrington, Peter J. Trends In Youth Crime In Canada 1977-1996, *Canadian Journal Of Criminology* 41:1-32, 1999. Using uniform crime report data, this study traces trends in Canadian youth crime from 1977 to 1996 and concludes that the level of police-reported youth crime in Canada has changed little since the 1980s.

0146 Carrington, Peter J. Has Violent Youth Crime Decreased? *Canadian Journal Of Criminology* 37:61-73, 1995. The author critiques claims of increases in youth crime in Canada during the 1990s.

0147 Carrington, Peter J. & Moyer, Sharon Trends In Youth Crime And Police Response, Pre- And Post-YOA, *Canadian Journal Of Criminology* 36:1-28, 1994. This study of the impact of Canada's Young Offenders Act (1984) on official youth crime and the police response to it found no evidence of support for the popular belief that the YOA had resulted in more, and more serious, youth crime in Canada.

0148 Clark, Barry M. & O'Reilly-Fleming, Thomas Out Of The Carceral Straightjacket: Under Twelves And The Law, *Canadian Journal Of Criminology* 36:305-327, 1994. Focusing on under-12-year olds, the authors surveyed 27 police forces that showed that although offending is common, serious violent offenses are rare in this age group.

0149 Connell, Anne & Farrington, David P. Bullying Among Incarcerated Young Offenders: Developing An Interview Schedule And Some Preliminary Results, *Journal Of Adolescence* 19:75-93, 1996. This questionnaire study reports on measuring bullying and victimization using a sample of incarcerate young offenders.

0150 Cormier, Bruno M. & Markus, Baila A Longitudinal Study Of Adolescent Murderers, *Bulletin Of The American Academy Of Psychiatry And The Law* 8:240-260, 1980. This paper on longitudinal patterns of the evolution of adolescent murderers concludes that their seeming indifference, lack of guilt and feelings toward the act they committed are only defenses that could be dealt with a knowledge of the psychodynamics of the adolescents.

0151 Corrado, Raymond R.; Cohen, Irwin M. & Odgers, Candice Canada, pp 15-32 in Hoffman, Allan M. & Summers, Randal W. (eds.) *Teen Violence: A Global View*. Westport, Connecticut: Greenwood, 2001. This chapter describes the nature and extent of teen violence in Canada and the responses of Canadian autorities to it.

0152 Csapo, Marg & Vanasse, Cécile Aggression And Delinquency In Adolescence: Similar Or Different Behaviors? (Agression Et Délinquance Chez L'Adolescent: Conduites Analogues Ou Différentes?), *Criminologie* 16:67-76,1983. Based on a survey of youths on attachment to parents, punishment and delinquent friends it was found that social integration is important in avoiding illegal behavior. French.

0153 Cusson, Maurice *Why Delinquency?* Toronto, Canada: University of Toronto, 1983. The author focuses on strategic analysis of delinquent behavior and its significance to the delinquent within the context of social structure and opportunity. 193p.

0154 Doob, Anthony N. & Sprott, Jane B. Is The 'Quality' Of Youth Violence Becoming More Serious? *Canadian Journal Of Criminology* 40:185-194, 1998. Using official Canadian juvenile crime and justice statistics to examine the assertion that youth violence is becoming more violent in Canada, this analysis found no empirical evidence for such an assertion.

0155 Dozois, Jean Adolescent And Sexual Aggressor: Results Of A Study (Adolescent Et Agresseur Sexuel: Bilan D'Une Recherche), *Criminologie* 27:71-85, 1994. Interviews with a small sample of juvenile sex offenders in the Montreal area were the basis for this study on adolescent sexual aggression. French with English-summary.

0156 Farrington, David Critical Examination Of The Environmental And Familial Effects On Delinquency (Examen Critique Des Influences Environmentales Et Familiales De La Délinquance), *Criminologie* 27:23-48, 1994. Summarizes and discusses various theories of delinquency such as high impulsivity, low intelligence, family and neighborhood factors. French with English summary.

0157 Fisher, Joan *Missing Children Research Project Volume 1: Findings Of The Study. A Focus On Runaways.* Alberta, Canada: Ministry Secretariat, Solicitor General Canada, 1989. This study investigated the extent and nature of missing children cases in Canada. 56p. Appendix.

0158 Fleming, Zachery; Brantingham, Patricia & Brantingham, Paul Exploring Auto Thefts In British Columbia, pp 47-90 in Clarke, Ronald V. (ed.) *Crime Prevention Studies, Vol. 3*. Monsey, New York: Criminal Justice press, 1994. This research on car theft concludes that most such thefts were committed not by profit-motivated, organized adult entrepreneurs but by thrill-seeking young offenders.

0159 Forth, Adelle & Tobin, Fred Psychopathy And Young Offenders: Rates Of Childhood Maltreatment, *Forum On Corrections Research* 7:20-22, 1995. Combining self-report survey, files and interviews of 95 male incarcerated youths tend to report being victims of abuse, neglect etc.

0160 Fréchette, Marcel & LeBlanc, Marc *Hidden Adolescent Delinquency (La Délinquance Cachée À L'Adolescence)*. Montreal: Université de Montréal. Groupe de Recherche sur L'Inadaptation Juvenile, 1979. Hidden delinquency among adolescents in Montreal, Canada was examined in this study comparing self-reported delinquent behaviors of public school students and wards of the juvenile court. 239p. French.

0161 Gabor, Thomas Trends In Youth Crime: Some Evidence Pointing To Increases In The Severity And Volume Of Violence On The Part Of Young People, *Canadian Journal Of Criminology* 41:385-392, 1999. This is a critique of the limitations of Canadian official police and court data on youthful crime.

0162 Gal, Marlo & Hoge, Robert D. A Profile Of The Adolescent Sex Offender, *Forum On Corrections Research* 11:7-11, 1999. The authors provide a profile of the juvenile sex offender.

0163 Gomme, Ian M. Predictors Of Status And Criminal Offences Among Male And Female Adolescents In An Ontario Community, *Canadian Journal Of Criminology* 27:147-159, 1985. This 1978 study of male and female students was an attempt to test the difference in the male/female delinquency that found delinquent peer association was a better predictor for males than females.

0164 Gordon, Robert M. Criminal Business Organizations, Street Gangs And 'Wanna-be' Groups: A Vancouver Perspective, *Canadian Journal Of Criminology* 42:39-60, 2000. Based on the 1995 Greater Vancouver Gang Study, the author discusses the causes and behavior of street gangs.

0165 Gordon, Robert M. Street Gangs And Criminal Business Organisations: A Canadian Perspective, pp 165-187 in Hazlehurst, Kayleen & Hazlehurst, Cameron (eds.) *Gangs And Youth Subcultures: International Explorations*. New Brunswick, New Jersey: Transaction, 1998. This chapter describes the Vancouver street gang "Los Diablos" which had juvenile members and its involvement in criminal and other activity vis-à-vis the "Lotus" criminal organization.

0166 Grady, Bill O.; Bright, Robert & Cohen, Eric Sub-Employment And Street Youths: An Analysis Of The Impact Of Squeegee Cleaning On Homeless Youths, *Security Journal* 11:315-323, 1998. This study suggests that squeegee work was related to a reduction in criminal activity among homeless youths in Toronto.

0167 Gretton, Heather M.; McBride, Michelle; Hare, Robert D.; O'Shaughnessy, Roy & Kumka, Gary Psychopathy And Recidivism In Adolescent Sex Offenders, *Criminal Justice And Behavior* 28:427-449, 2001. This study uses available information on 220 adolescent males in an outpatient sex offender treatment program to study their total, violent, and non-violent reoffense rates.

0168 Griffiths, Curt Taylor The Use Of Community Service Orders And Restitution In The Canadian North: The Prospects And Problems Of 'Localized' Corrections, pp 145-153 in Galaway, Burt & Hudson, Joe (eds.) *Criminal Justice, Restitution, and Reconciliation*. Monsey, New York: Criminal Justice Press, 1990. The author reviews the use of community service for juveniles and adults as an alternative sentence in Canadian Northwest territories, issues and problems in its use, and its failures.

0169 Groulx, France Consumption Of Psychotropic Drugs, Delinquency And Placement in Rehabilitation Centers (Consommation Des Psychotropes, Activités Délictuellles Et Placement Des Adolescents En Centre De Réadaptation). Montreal, Canada: Centre International de Criminologie Comparée, University of Montreal, 1992. This study examines the use of psychotropic drugs from the perspective of 20 adolescent offend-ers in Canadian treatment centers. French. 116p.

0170 Haapasalo, Jaana & Tremblay, Richard E. Physically Aggressive Boys From Age 6 To 12: Family Background, Parenting Behavior, And Prediction Of Delinquency *Journal of Consulting And Clinical Psychology* 62:1044-1052, 1994. This 10-year longitudinal study of boys in Montreal Schools found that high levels of fighting were correlated with high self-reported delinquency.

0171 Hagan, John & Kay, Fiona Gender And Delinquency In White-Collar Families: A Power-Control Perspective, *Crime and Delinquency* 36:391-407, 1990. In this study of power/control perspective, the authors examine juveniles' violations of patents and copyrights laws in copying of audio and video tapes, and of computer software.

0172 Hagan, John & McCarthy, Bill *Mean Streets: Youth Crime And Homelessness*. Cambridge, United Kingdom: Cambridge University Press, 1997. This is a study of street youths in Toronto and Vancouver, Canada that includes their family and social histories, living conditions and criminal experiences. 299p.

0173 Hagan, John; Gillis, A. R. & Simpson, John The Class Structure Of Gender And Delinquency: Toward A Power-Control Theory Of Common

Delinquent Behavior, *American Journal Of Sociology* 90:1151-1178, 1985. This is a 1979 survey of a neo-Marxian class-based, power-control theory of gender and delinquency among 458 students from seven secondary schools in the Tronto area and their parents.

0174 Hartnagel, Timothy F. Labor Market Problems In The Transition From School To Work And Illegal Drug Use: A Panel Study Of Canadian Youth, pp 61-90 in Blau, Zena Smith & Hagan, John (eds.) *Current Perspectives On Aging And The Life Cycle: Delinquency And Disrepute In The Life Course, Vol. 4*. Greenwich, Connecticut: JAI Press, 1995. This chapter reports findings from a four-year panel study examining the impact of labor market difficulties on illegal drug use in a sample of recent Canadian high school and university graduates in three cities.

0175 Hartnagel, Timothy F. & Tanner, Julian Class, Schooling And Delinquency: A Further Examination, *Canadian Journal Of Criminology* 24:155-172, 1982. In their research on 733 junior and high school students in Edmonton, the authors found support for school status theory rather than class background model of adolescent delinquency.

0176 Hatch, Alison & Griffiths, Curt T. Youth Crime In Canada: Observations For Cross-Cultural Analysis, *International Journal Of Comparative And Applied Criminal Justice*, 16:165-183, 1992. The authors provide a description of rates and patterns of youth crime in Canada.

0177 Hendrick, Dianne & LaChance, Marc A Profile Of The Young Offender, *Forum On Corrections Research* 3:17-21, 1991. Youth court survey data from around Canada except Ontario and Northwest Provinces were analyzed regarding age, disposition, and length of sentences.

0178 Hodgson, James F. *Games Pimps Play: Pimps, Players And Wives-In-Law. A Qualitative Analysis Of Street Prostitution*. Toronto, Canada: Canadian Scholars' Press, 1997. This is an ethnographic study of the interactions between adolecent- female street prostitutes and pimps. 149p.

0179 Hoge, Robert D.; Andrews, D. A. & Leschied, Alan W. An Investigation Of Risk And Protective Factors In A Sample Of Youthful Offenders, *Journal Of Child Psychology And Psychiatry* 37: 419-424, 1996. This study of potential risk and protective factors in relation to criminal activity and adjustment in the Montreal area found that risk variables were correlated with increased re-offending and low overall adjustment, while the presence of protective factors were associated with more positive outcomes.

0180 Hornick, Joseph P.; Bolitho, Floyd H. & LeClaire, Denise *Young Offenders And The Sexual Abuse Of Children*. Ottawa, Canada: Department of Justice Canada, 1994. This study describes the characteristics of victims and provides data on the accused and case outcomes based on data collected in research on child sexual assault in Canada that found that most of the victims were female. 123p. Appendix.

0181 Hundleby, John D. Personality And The Prediction Of Delinquency And Drug Use, *British Journal Of Criminology* 26:129-146, 1986. When school boys and adolescents entering training schools were followed up three years later, it was found that drug use and alienation were related to various indices, but predicting recidivism not successful.

0182 Jacob, Martine; McKibben, André & Proulx, Jean Descriptive And Comparative Study Of A Population Of Adolescent Sexual Aggressors (Étude Descriptive Et Comparative D'Une Population D'Adolescents Agresseurs Sexuels), *Criminologie* 26:133-163, 1993. Two groups of sexually aggressive - against children and against adults - adolescents in a medium security psychiatric facility are compared. French with English summary.

0183 Jamieson, Wanda & LaPrairie, Carol *Native Criminal Justice Research Issues And Data Sources*. Ottawa, Canada: Ministry of the Solicitor General, 1987. This is a review of the research and literature as well as sources on topics involving juvenile offenders, natives and criminal justice. 84p.

0184 Janus, Mark David Physical Abuse In Canadian Runaway Adolescents, *Child Abuse And Neglect* 19:433-447, 1995. Eighty-six percent of the male and female juveniles reported at least one physically abusive experience in this study on the nature and extent of physical abuse among Canadian runaways.

0185 Jung, Sandy; Rawana, Edward P. & Lod, Byron Risk Classification For Young Offenders, *Forum On Corrections Research* 9:23-25, 1997. The authors developed and tested an instrument for identifying youths at-risk in an Ontario mental health facility for boys and girls and conclude the measure was able to delineate between recidivists and non-recidivists.

0186 Keane, Carl; Gillis, A. R. & Hagan, John Deterrence And Amplification Of Juvenile Delinquency By Police Contact: The Importance Of Gender And Risk-Orientation, *British Journal Of Criminology* 29:336-352, 1989. In this study of the relationship between deterrence and deviance among a sample of males and females, it was found that the deviance of boys is amplified by police contacts while that of girls is deterred.

0187 Kendall, Kathleen; Andre, Glenn & Pease, Ken Health Histories Of Juvenile Offenders And A Matched Control Group In Saskatchewan, Canada, *Criminal Behaviour And Mental Health* 2:269-286, 1992. The health histories of 1,647 young offenders and a matched cohort of non-offenders when examined failed to reveal any relationship between delinquency and general health.

0188 Kennedy, Leslie W. & Baron, Stephen W. Routine Activities And A Subculture Of Violence: A Study Of Violence On The Street, *Journal Of Research In Crime And Delinqeuncy* 30:88-112, 1993. This case study of street violence concludes that the routine activities approach is inadequate in explaining how interactions escalate to violence, and should include a component to be integrated in to the subcultural approach.

0189 Kennedy, Leslie W. & Sacco, Vincent F. (eds.) *Crime Counts: A Criminal Event Analysis*. Toroto, Canada: Nelson, 1996. Of the 17 articles in this anthology, juvenile crime and justice is interspersed through out while chapter 14 specifically deals with juvenile crime. 321p.

0190 Kerr, Margaret; Tremblay, Richard E. & Pagani, Linda Boys' Behavioral Inhibition And The Risk Of Later Delinquency, *Archives Of General Psychiatry* 54:809-816, 1997. This is a research on the protective effect of behavioral inhibitions in the development of delinquency among both disruptive and non-disruptive boys.

0191 Kijewski, Kristina The Effect Of The Decision To Charge Upon Subsequent Behavior, *Canadian Journal Of Criminology* 25:201-208, 1983. Official records of 142 juveniles were used to test the labeling perspective and it was concluded that subsequent illegality was irrespective of being warned or charged.

0192 Kinsman, Gary & Brock, Deborah Patriarchal Relations Ignored: A Critique Of The Badgley Report On Sexual Offences Against Children And Youth, *Canadian Criminology Forum* 8:15-29, 1986. In this essay the authors critique the Badgley Report on the prevalence of sexual offenses against minors that recommends Canadian legislation to protect youth and children.

0193 LaForest, Suzette & Paradis, Richard Adolescents And Sexual Delinquency (Adolescents Et Délinquance Sexuelle), *Criminologie* 23:95-116, 1990. This Quebec study is on adolescent sex offenders under group therapy. French with English summary.

0194 Lagier, Pierre-Marie & Dickner, Sonia The Likelihood Of Adult Criminality Among Juvenile Delinquents: Temporary Insignificant Juvenile Delinquency (De La Délinquance Juvénile À La Probable Absence De Criminalité Adult: Le Délinquant Temporaire Insignificant [DIT]), *Canadian Journal Of Criminology* 28:243-262, 1986. This research was an attempt to delineate the criminal personality from the insignificant, temporary juvenile illegality of youth who do not have adult criminal records. French with English summary.

0195 Lagier, Pierre-Marie On Juvenile Delinquency And The Eventual Absence Of Adult Criminality: The Temporarily Serious Delinquent (De La Délinquance Juvénile À L'Eventuelle Absence De Criminalité Adulte: Le Délinquant Temporaire Grave [DTG]), *Canadian Journal Of Criminology* 26:13-28, 1984. The author uses the concept of differential criminal personality to explain disappearance of adult criminality among his sample of former serious delinquents. French with English abstract.

0196 Lagier, Pierre-Marie Juvenile Delinquency And True Criminality: The Persistent Serious Delinquent (DPG) (De La Délinquance Juvénile À La Vraie Criminalité: Le Délinquant Persistant Grave [DPG]), *Canadian Journal Of Criminology* 24:141-153, 1982. In this study of 30 wards of the Montreal juvenile court the author focuses on the self-reported delinquency and personality characteristics of these juveniles and claims that that it is not the degree but the kind of illegality that delineates the delinquent from the non-delinquent youths. French with English summary.

0197 LaGrange, Teresa C. & Silverman, Robert A. Low Self-Control And Opportunity: Testing The General Theory Of Crime As An Explanation For Gender Differences In Delinquency, *Criminology* 37:41-72, 1999. When the general theory of crime was tested for its ability to explain gender differences in the delinquency of secondary school students in Canada, there was partial support for it.

0198 Lanctôt, Nadine & LeBlanc, Marc Girl Members Of Marginal Gangs: A Decreasing Antisocial Potential In Gang Dynamics? (Les Adolescentes Membres Des Bandes Marginales: Un Potentiel Antisocial Atténué Par La Dynamique De La Bande?), *Criminologie* 30:111-130, 1997. The personal and social characteristics of female gang members are described in this study of 150 girls convicted in juvenile courts during 1992-93. French with English summary.

0199 Lanctôt, Nadine & LeBlanc, Marc The Participation Of Boys In A Marginal Gang: A Phenomemon Of Selection And Opportunities (La Participation Des Garçons À Une Bande Marginale: Un Phénomène De Sélection Et D'Opportunitiés), *Canadian Journal Of Criminology*

38:375-400, 1996. In this 1992-93 study of 505 boys, the authors found that the most dysfunctional boys are selected for gang membership irrespective of the gang's structure. French with English summary.

0200 Landau, Barbara The Adolescent Female Offender, *Canadian Journal Of Criminology* 17:146-153, 1975. This article describes the distinct demographics of the female juvenile offender, the various laws that relate to their behaviors, and the court processes.

0201 Langevin, R.; Paitich, D.; Orchard, B.; Handy, L.; & Russon, A. Childhood And Family Background Of Killers Seen For Psychiatric Assessment: A Controlled Study, *Bulletin Of The American Academy Of Psychiatry And The Law* 11:331-342, 1983. Using diverse sources of data on violent killers, nonviolent offenders and a normal control group the authors conclude that inadequate and violent parenting cannot predict antisocial behavior.

0202 Langley, Michael An Alternative Approach To Delinquency Analysis And Management, *Canadian Journal Of Criminology* 18:204-224, 1976. Prevailing conceptions, definitions, and models of delinquency are reviewed by the author.

0203 LeBlanc, Marc & Lapointe, Cindy Sexual Aggression Among Boys: A Comparison Of Aggressors And Other Adolescents In Difficulty (Agression Sexuelle Chez Les Garçons: Comparaison Des Agresseurs, Des Aggresses Et Des Agresseurs Avec Les Autres Adolecents En Difficulte), *Canadian Journal Of Criminology* 41:479-511, 1999. This study of Montreal official delinquents concludes that the sexual aggressors had greater social and psychological problems although they resembled their victims more. French with English summary.

0204 LeBlanc, Marc & Kaspy, Nathalie Trajectories Of Delinquency And Problem Behavior: Comparison Of Social And Personal Control Characteristics Of Adjudicated Boys, *Journal Of Quantitative Criminology* 14:181-214, 1998. This study of boys in Montreal investigated the differences between delinquents with synchronous trajectories and those with non-synchronous trajectories and concludes that personal control variables, rather than social control variables, were more effective in discriminating between trajectories.

0205 LeBlanc, Marc Socialization Or Propensity? Does Integrative Control Theory Apply To Adjudicated Boys? *Studies On Crime & Crime Prevention* 6:200-223, 1997. In this self-report study testing learning, propensity and control theories, the author found support for the various dimensions of social control theory.

0206 LeBlanc, Marc & Girard, Stephane The Generality Of Deviance: Replication Over Two Decades With A Canadian Sample Of Adjudicated Boys, *Canadian Journal Of Criminology* 39:171-183, 1997. This study of the presence of "general deviance" among French-speaking adjudicated boys in Canada addresses the stability of general deviance across cultures and over time studies showing increasing aggression.

0207 LeBlanc, Marc Changing Patterns In The Perpetration Of Offenses Over Time: Trajectories From Early Adolescence To The Early 30's, *Studies On Crime And Crime Prevention* 5:151-165, 1996. On factor analysis, the author found two of the three categories of modus operandi of adolescent delinquency persist into the late twenties and early thirties.

0208 LeBlanc, Marc Family, School, Delinquency And Criminality, The Predictive Power Of An Elaborated Social Control Theory For Males, *Criminal Behaviour And Mental Health* 4:101-117, 1994. Based on a large-scale Montreal study to predict late-adolescent delinquency and adult criminality, this research reports that only three of eighteen variables to predict adult criminality were highly significant.

0209 LeBlanc, Marc; McDuff, Pierre & Tremblay, Richard E. The Emergence Of Behavior Disorders And The Consequences For The Course Of Latency (L'Émergence Des Troubles De Comportement Et Ses Conséquences Au Cours De La Latence), *Canadian Journal Of Criminology* 36:103-136, 1994. This study of behavior disorders among children in Montreal shows that frequent sanctions by school authorities and insufficient investment in school activities, followed by vagrancy frequenting arcades and associating with deviant peers are the antecedents to such problem behavior. French with English summary.

0210 LeBlanc, Marc An Analysis Of Social Change And Adolescent Delinquency As Revealed In The Writings Of Denis Szabo (Changement Social Et Délinquances Des Adolescents, Une Analyse À La Lumière Des Écrits De Denis Szabo), *Criminologie* 26:13-28, 1993. The author discusses how delinquency of the "affluent society" of 1960s-70s and the "scarcity" epoch of 1980s-90s in spite of structural and modal personality changes, the nature and level of self-reported delinquency in adolescence has not changed from Szabos' revelatory writings on youthful misconduct.

0211 LeBlanc, Marc Late Adolescence Deceleration Of Criminal Activity And Development Of Self- And Social-Control, *Studies On Crime & Crime Prevention* 2:51-68, 1993. Comparing Montreal male court wards over 2-year period, the author concludes that there is a reduction in self-reported criminality while social and self-control increase.

0212 LeBlanc, Marc; Valliéres, Évelyne & McDuff, Pierre The Prediction Of Males' Adolescent And Adult Offending From School Experience, *Canadian Journal Of Criminology* 35:4459-478, 1993. This longitudinal study of the relationship among school performance and experience, graduation and criminality found that self-reported criminality as well as adult official record are predicted by the former.

0213 LeBlanc, Marc; Cote, Gilles & Loeber, Rolf Temporal Paths In Delinquency: Stability, Regression, And Progression Analyzed With Panel Data From An Adolescent And A Delinquent Male Sample, *Canadian Journal Of Criminology* 33:23-44, 1991. Research in Montreal on juveniles' progression from less to more serious forms of delinquency and specialization in delinquent activities found that over time delinquency remained stable or progress, with a lesser tendency to de-escalate.

0214 LeBlanc, Marc & Fréchette, Marcel *Male Criminal Activity From Childhood Through Youth: Multilevel And Developmental Perspectives*. New York & Berlin: Springer-Verlag, 1989. This authors examined delinquency patterns in samples of male adolescents and convicted youths from Montreal and found progression of criminal activity that resembled an occupation that became more and more serious and sophisticated over time. 228p.

0215 LeBlanc, Marc & Fréchette, Marcel The Delinquent Personality Syndrome (Le Syndrome De Personnalité Déliquante, *Revue Internationale De Criminologie Et De Police Technique* 40:133-146, 1987. The authors argue that with increasing delinquent personality, there is greater separation of the delinquent from his social milieu.

0216 LeBlanc, Marc The Criminal Career: Definition And Prediction (La Carrière Criminelle: Définition Et Prédiction), *Criminologie* 19:79-99, 1986. This paper advocating the concept of a criminal career in dealing with youthful misconduct, Montreal court wards and other adolescents were studied for their criminal activities – frequency, variety, gravity, and duration. French with English summary.

0217 LeBlanc, Marc For An Integrative Approach To Delinquent Behavior (Pour Une Approche Intégrative De La Conduite Délinquante Des Adolescents), *Criminologie* 19:73-95, 1986. Reviewing various theoretical approaches, the author emphasizes a multi-disciplinary integrative approach for understanding and dealing with youthful misbehavior. French with English summary.

0218 LeBlanc, Marc Adolescent Delinquency: Hidden And Known Delinquency (La Délinquance À L'Adolescence: De La Délinquance Cachées Et De La Délinquance Apparente), *Annals De Vaucresson*

14:19-50, 1976-1977. This study of hidden and known delinquency found that while most respondents engaged in hidden delinquency, known delinquency constituted only a fraction of the acts committed.

0219 Ledingham, Jane E.; Ledingham, C. Anne & Richardson, John E. *The Effects Of Media Violence On Children*. Ottawa, Canada: National Clearinghouse on Family Violence, Health and Welfare Canada, 1993. This summary of the existing research on the effects of media violence on children argues that although exposure to television violence has an important and consistent relationship to aggression, the positive effects of television viewing on may be more significant than the negative effects. 17p.

0220 Linden, Rick & Currie, Raymond Religiosity And Drug Use: A Test Of Social Control Theory, *Canadian Journal Of Criminology And Corrections* 19:346-355, 1977. The social control and drug use examined in this research indicates a weak-to-moderate relationship between church attendance of 15-24 year olds and their attitudes and respect for conventional authority.

0221 Lo, Lucia Exploring Teenage Shoplifting Behavior: A Choice And Constraint Approach, *Environment And Behavior* 26:613-639, 1994. This field study of teenagers found that those who shoplifted did it for fun and excitement and may have done so under some peer pressure, and shoplifted small objects during moderate circulation in large stores far away from home.

0222 Loeber, Rolf Risk Factors And The Development Of Disruptive And Antisocial Behavior In Children, *Forum On Corrections Research* 3:22-28, 1991. This psychological study of the manifestations of various problem behaviors found that the strongest predictors of delinquency for boys are aggression, drug use and stealing.

0223 Loeber, Rolf & Stouthamer-Loeber, Magda The Predicition Of Delinquency (La Prédiction De La Délinquance), *Criminologie* 19:33-48, 1986. The authors carried out a meta-analysis of diverse longitiudinal male and female delinquency studies of behavioral problems, family conditions etc. French with English summary.

0224 Lowman, John & Fraser, Laura *Violence Against Persons Who Prostitute: The Experience Of Prostitution*. Ottawa, Canada: Canadian Department of Justice, 1996. Albeit on prostitutes in general, this volume includes minors who engage in sex trade as well. 230p.

0225 Lowman, J.; Jackson, M. A.; Palys, T. S. & Gavigan, S. *Regulating Sex: An Anthology On The Findings And Recommendations Of The Badgley*

And Fraser Reports. Burnaby, British Columbia: Simon Fraser University School of Criminology, 1986. The 12 articles in this volume deal with the Badgley and Fraser commission reports on diverse issues of sexual abuse of children including juvenile prostitution. 223p.

0226 MacDougall, Jyl *Violence In The Schools: Program And Policies For Prevention*. Toronto: Canadian Education Association, 1993. This report on the problem of violence in schools provides practical examples of policies and programs of Canada in reducing violent attitudes and incidents. 76p.

0227 Markwart, Alan & Corrado, Raymond R. A Response To Carrington, *Canadian Journal Of Criminology* 37:74-87, 1995. This is the authors' defense against criticism of their claims of increasing youth crime in Canada during the 1990s.

0228 Marron, Kevin *Apprenticed In Crime: Young Offenders, The Law, And Crime In Canada*. Toronto: Seal Books, 1992. This journalistic description of trends in Canadian youth crime and the response of the justice system raises also the issues of treatment of children as adults when they commit heinous crimes, as well as punishment versus treatment. 335p.

0229 Mathews, Frederick *Familiar Strangers: A Study Of Adolescent Prostitution. Rev. Ed.* Ontario, Canada: Central Toronto Youth Services, 1989. Juvenile prostitutes formed the basis of this study of social effects model in that they are actors and interpreters of the values, attitudes and beliefs that prevail in the larger society. 54p.

0230 Mathews, Frederick *Youth Gangs On Youth Gangs*. Ottawa, Canada: Solicitor General Canada, Police Policy and Research Division, 1993. This report on policy recommendations, examines the problem of youth gangs in Toronto and southern Ontario as well as responses and changes in delivery of services to victims, gang members, and at-risk and non-offending youth. 111p.

0231 Matthews, Peter C. Neglect And Violence Toward Children, *Canadian Journal Of Family Law* 3:369-376, 1980. This article discusses issues on clinical observations and legal responses to violence toward and neglect of children in Canada.

0232 McCarthy, Bill & Hagan, John Homelessness: A Criminogenic Situation? *British Journal Of Criminology* 31:393-410, 1991. This study of 390 Toronto adolescent homeless youths found support for Don Gibbons' position that the motivations for particular crimes may exist, not in the actor's psychological or social history, but in various criminogenic situations in which the individual is located.

0233 McCarthy, Bill & Hagan, John Mean Streets: The Theoretical Significance Of Situational Delinquency Among Homeless Youths, *American Journal Of Sociology* 98:597-627, 1992. This study of situational delinquency among homeless Toronto youths testing an integration of strain and control theories found consistent evidence of the effects of adverse situational conditions on criminality.

0234 McCarthy, Bill *On The Streets: Youth In Vancouver.* Vancouver, Canada: Research, Evaluation and Statistics Branch, British Columbia Ministry of Social Services, 1995. This research on the street youths in Vancouver has a description of the respondents' demographic characteristics, home and street experiences as well as the factors that increase their criminality. 52p.

0235 McCarthy, Bill The Attitudes And Actions Of Others: Tutelage And Sutherland's Theory Of Differential Association, *British Journal Of Criminology* 36:135-147, 1996. This 1987-88 study of 390 homeless youths up to age 19 found that when past criminal behavior is controlled for, tutelage is an important element in drug selling, theft and prostitution.

0236 McCarthy, Bill; Hagan, John & Cohen, Lawrence E. Uncertainty, Cooperation And Crime: Understanding The Decision To Co-Offend, *Social Forces* 77:155-184, 1998. This study of factors that influence the decision to engage in co-offending found that the adversity of street life was important in the context for criminal cooperation, particularly collaboration.

0237 McCarthy, John D. & Hoge, Dean R. The Dynamics Of Self-Esteem And Delinquency, *American Journal Of Sociology* 90:396-410, 1984. In their sample of Catholic and public school boys and girls, the authors found a negligible effect of self-esteem on self-reported delinquency and an opposite effect across age, ;types of family, race, and mother's education.

0238 McGinnis, Janice Dickin Bogeymen And The Law: Crime Comics And Pornography, *Ottawa Law Review* 20:3-23, 1988. The author argues against censorship of violent and pornographic crime comics in that their role in incidence of youthful and other violence isn't well established and advocates the repeal of such law in Canada.

0239 Meloff, William & Silverman, Robert A. Canadian Kids Who Kill, *Canadian Journal Of Criminology* 34:15-34, 1992. The authors describe the cases of Canadian youths charged with homicide between 1961 and 1983 with a variety of information on offense behavior and comparisons with New York City offenders.

0240 Motiuk, Laurence L. *An Examination Of Sex Offender Case Histories In Federal Corrections.* Ottawa, Canada: Canada Correctional Service, 1993. Case files of 785 sex offenders were analyzed for their family history of abuse/neglect, institutionalizaion, and prior arrest records for violence and sexual offenses. 70p.

0241 Murphy, Brian C. & Shinyei, Martha J. Cons And Straights: Comparative Free Behavior Rates Of 25 Delinquents And 25 Non-delinquents Matched For Age And Legal Occupation In British Columbia, Canada, *Canadian Journal Of Criminology And Corrections* 18:343-361, 1976. This study comparing relative involvement in different kinds of legal and illegal behaviors among official delinquents and non-delinquents in British Columbia found that the two groups were not significantly different from one another in some illegal behaviors.

0242 O'Bireck, Gary M. (ed.) *Not A Kid Anymore: Canadian Youth, Crime, And Subcultures.* Scarborough, Canada: Nelson Canada, 1996. The articles in this anthology are organized in terms of theoretical, methodological, empirical and substantive issues in Canadian juvenile delinquency. 402p.

0243 Offord, D. R.; Poushinsky, Mary F. & Sullivan, Kathryn School Performance, IQ And Delinquency, *British Journal Of Criminology* 18:110-127, 1978. This study of Ottawa juvenile court cases under probation and aftercare found very little difference between delinquents with and without school performance problems.

0244 Ouimet, Marc Aggregation Bias In Ecological Research: How Social Disorganization And Criminal Opportunities Shape Spatial Distribution Of Delinquents In Montreal, *Canadian Journal Of Criminology* 42:135-156, 2000. The author found that while social disorganization variables predict rates of offenders and juvenile crimes in Montreal census tracts, opportunity theory variables seems to be strong predictors at neighborhood level.

0245 Paetsch, Joanne J. & Bertrand, Lorne D. Victimization And Delinquency Among Canadian Youth, *Adolescence* 34:351-367, 1999. This study examining the extent of victimization and delinquency among 962 students in a large Canadian city found victimization to be high and over one-half reported committing at least one delinquentact during the past year.

0246 Pagani, Linda; Tremblay, Richard E.; Vitaro, Frank & Parent, Sophie Does Preschool Help Prevent Delinquency In Boys With A History Of Perinatal Complications? *Criminology* 36:245-267, 1998. Using a quasi-experimental design, this study examined a sample of boys from the most disadvantaged areas of Montreal to see if preschool intervention program moderates the effects of perinatal complications.

0247 Parizeau, Alice *Parenting And Delinquent Youth.* Lexington, Massachusetts: Lexington Books, 1980. This Quebec research of both inmate parents and youths in a detention center demonstrates that while their parents failed to provide social and family stability, ambition, a sociocultural model of behavior, and positive life goals, the unfairness of the onus placed on juveniles held responsible to the court for their actions 179p.

0248 Pronovost, Louison & LeBlanc, Marc Transition Status And Delinquency (Transition Statutaire Et Délinquance) *Canadian Journal Of Criminology* 22:288-297, 1980. The authors conclude that among their sample of 12-18 year olds, being employed among school dropouts in later adolescence reduced delinquency.

0249 Regoeczi, Wendy C. Adolescent Victimization And Offending: Assessing The Extent Of The Link, *Canadian Journal Of Criminology* 42:493-505, 2000. Data from cases of 12-17 year old homicide victims between 1985-1995 found that while the victims had no prior record or illegal behavior, the offenders did.

0250 Reitsma-Street, M. & Offord, D. R. Girl Delinquents And Their Sisters: A Challenge For Practice, *Canadian Social Work Review* 8:11-27, 1991. This article reports that delinquent and non-delinquent sisters lacked the ability to meet their material needs and feel closer to, nurtured by, and doing more things with, more females than males.

0251 Roberts, Julian Sexual Assault Is A Crime Of Violence, *Canadian Journal Of Criminology* 37:88-93, 1995. The author argues that increases in youthful assault, if categorized as violent crime, would reveal increasing crime in Canada during the 1990s.

0252 Rondeau, Roger Violence Until Death? Reflections On Two Homicide Cases (Violents Jusqu'au Meurtre? Réflexions Sur Deux Cas D'Homicide) *Criminologie* 23:75-93, 1990. The author narrates the case history of two youths accused of murder in Quebec. French with English summary.

0253 Ross, R. R.; McKay, H. B.; Palmer, W. R. & Kenny, C. J. Self-Mutilation In Adolescent Female Offenders, *Canadian Journal Of*

Criminology 20:375-392, 1978. This paper discusses a long-term study of one form of self-mutilation (carving or cutting of the body) frequent among female juveniles in training schools.

0254 Ryan, Colleen; Mathews, Fred & Banner, Jorhdin *Student Perceptions Of Violence: Summary Of Preliminary Findings*. Toronto, Canada: Central Toronto Youth Services, 1993. This survey of students' perceptions of school violence, victimization and violent offenses of fellow students was conducted in two middle schools in Ontario. 124p.

0255 Samuelson, Leslie; Hartnagel, Timothy F. & Krahn, Harvey Crime And Social Control Among High School Dropouts, *Journal Of Crime And Justice* 18:129-165, 1995. This study concludes that besides weak social controls, free time, boredom, and interaction with deviant peers provided additional opportunities and inducements for criminal behavior.

0256 Schissel, Bernard & Fedec, Kari The Selling Of Innocence: The Gestalt Of Danger In The Lives Of Youth Prostitutes, *Canadian Journal Of Criminology* 41:33-56, 1999. This study of violence involving juvenile prostitutes found that they ran a high risk of being assaulted by a predator, or self-injury indirectly through high-risk behavior.

0257 Schissel, Bernard *Blaming Children: Youth Crime, Moral Panic And The Politics Of Hate*. Halifax, Canada: Fernwood, 1997. The author explores the moral panic against youth and juvenile crime in Canada from 1961 to 1994 and argues that it was a product of the media and its ties to information/political systems. 133p.

0258 Shields, Ian W. & Jordan, Shelley A. Young Sex Offenders: A Comparison With A Control Group Of Non-Sex Offenders, *Forum On Corrections Research* 7:17-19, 1995. This psychological study of regional detention center inmates who were juveniles when they committed the offense found the sex offenders, more often than non-sex offenders, report being victims of sexual aggression.

0259 Silverman, Robert A. Trends In Canadian Youth Homicide: Some Unanticipated Consequences Of A Change In The Law, *Canadian Journal Of Criminology* 32:651-656, 1990. It was found that rates of homicide perpetrated by Canadian youth have not varied much over the past 13 years.

0260 Silverman, Robert A. & Kennedy, Leslie *Deadly Deeds: Murders In Canada*. Scarborough, Canada: Nelson, 1993. There are sections on "Canadian Youth Offenders" in chapter 8 and "special offender groups" in chapter 6 of this book. 270p.

0261 Simourd, D. J.; Hoge, R. D. & Andrews, D. A. & Leschied, A. W. An Empirically-Based Typology Of Male Young Offenders, *Canadian Journal Of Criminology* 36:447-461, 1994. The authors' report on their attempt to develop a typology of youthful offenders from the properties of the Youth Level Of Service Inventory.

0262 Sinclair, Roberta Lynn & Dell, Colleen Anne Recent Trends In Youth Crime, *Forum On Corrections Research* 11:39-42, 1999. As suggested by the title, the authors trace recent youth crime trends in Canada.

0263 Skilling, Tracy A.; Quinsey, Vernon L. & Craig, Wendy M. Evidence Of A Taxon Underlying Serious Antisocial Behavior In Boys, *Criminal Justice And Behavior* 28:450-470, 2001. Taxometric analyses yielded evidence of an underlying taxon, and two other tests of consistency strengthened the conclusion that a taxon underlies serious antisocial behavior in children.

0264 Smith, Ronald B.; Bertrand, Lorne D. & Arnold, Bruce L. *A Study Of The Level And Nature Of Youth Crime And Violence In Calgary.* Ottawa, Canada: Solicitor General Canada, 1995. This report based on student and community surveys, police files, and interviews with serious habitual offenders examines the nature and scope of youth crime and violence in Calgary, Canada. 133p. Appendix.

0265 Sprott, Jane B. & Doob, Anthony Bad, Sad, And Rejected: The Lives Of Aggressive Children, *Canadian Journal Of Criminology* 42:123-133, 2000. In this report on a large-scale longitudinal study of aggression among young children, authors argue against criminalizing 10-11 year olds.

0266 Strange, Carolyn *Toronto's Girl Problem: The Perils And Pleasures Of The City, 1880-1930.* Toronto, Canada: University of Toronto, 1995. This book is on the history of the relationship between industrialization, urbanization, modernization, social control and behavior of young girls. 299p.

0267 Sullivan, Terry The Politics Of Juvenile Prostitution, pp 177-191 in Lowman, J.; Jackson, M. A.; Palys, T. S. & Gavigan, S. *Regulating Sex: An Anthology On The Findings And Recommendations Of The Badgley And Fraser Reports.* Burnaby, British Columbia: Simon Fraser University-School of Criminology, 1986. This article deals with the juvenile law and prostitution, the economics of juvenile prostitutions, and professional regulation of the family.

0268 Tanner, Julian *Teenage Troubles: Youth And Deviance In Canada.* Toronto, Canada: Nelson, 1996. This book analyzes theory and research related to youthful deviance in Canadian society. 262p.

0269 Tremblay, Pierre; Clermont, Yvan & Cusson, Maurice Jockeys And Joyriders: Changing Patterns In Car Theft Opportunity Structures, *British Journal Of Criminology* 34:307-321, 1994. This study of Statistics Canada's data on Quebec car theft patterns from 1963-1988 tested the two models—joyriders and jockeys—of auto theft.

0270 Tremblay, R. E.; Zhon, R. M.; Gagnon, C.; Vitaro, H. & Boileau, H. Violent Boys: Development And Prevention, *Forum On Corrections Research* 3:29-35, 1991. The authors report on a 1984 longitudinal study of 916 francophone underprivileged Montreal boys and delinquency.

0271 Tremblay, Richard E.; Desmarais-Gervais, Lise; LeBlanc, Marc & Schwartzmann, Alexandre Predicting Juvenile Court Contacts Of Young People: Using The Evaluation Of Behavior Of Primary School Pairs (La Prédiction Des Contacts Avec Le Tribunal De La Jeunesse: Utilisation De L'Évaluation Du Comportement Par Les Pairs Au Début De L'École Primaire), *Criminologie* 19:49-77, 1986. This study of 493 girls and 499 boys found that girls who were aggressive-withdrawn were more likely to have a court record 7-8 years later. French with English summary.

0272 Turmel, André Childhood And Normalcy Classification, Numerical Regularities, And Tabulations, *International Journal Of Education Research* 27:661-672, 1998. This article discusses the changing status of childhood at the turn of the 19th century in Canada.

0273 Vasey, Paul *Kids In The Jail: Why Do Our Young Offenders Do The Things They Do*. Windsor, Canada: Black Moss Press, 1995. This volume presents a journalistic profile of juvenile offenders in a Canadian maximum-security jail for young offenders. 271p.

0274 Vaz, Edmund W. & Lodhi, Abdul Q. *Crime And Delinquency In Canada*. Scarborough, Ontario: Prentice-Hall, 1979. This anthology has 5 articles on "theory and research on juvenile delinquency" and 7 articles on "crime as a market transaction" focusing on various trends in crime and juvenile delinquency in Canada. 390p.

0275 Vingilis, Evelyn; Ogborne, Alan; Kejewski, Kristina & Salutin, Lorne A Study Of A Sample Of Young People Charged With Underage Drinking, *Canadian Journal Of Criminology* 22:457-463, 1980. This is a study of the socioeconomic, family, and substance abuse factors in a sample of male and female 16-18 year olds charged by the Toronto court for underage drinking.

0276 Vingilis, Evelyn; Mann, Robert; Adlaf, Edward M. & Kejewski, Kristina Young Drinking Offenders: Relationships Among Demographic, Behavioural And Attitudinal Variables At Conviction And Status Seventeen Months Later, *Canadian Journal Of Criminology* 27:317-325, 1985. This Toronto study of youths charged with minor consumption or possession of alcohol found that while family and peer variables correlated with drinking behavior, legal sanctions have very little effect on subsequent drinking.

0277 Vitaro, F. & Tremblay, Richard E. Delinquency Prevention: The Role Of Mediating Factors In Pairs (Prévention De La Délinquance: Le Rôle Médiateur Des Pairs), *Criminologie* 31:49-66, 1998. The researchers tested to see if friends' characteristics had a mediating effect on early disruptive behavior of 8-9 year olds and later delinquency when they were 13-14 years of age. French with English summary.

0278 Wade, Terrance J. & Brannigan, Augustine The Genesis Of Adolescent Risk-Taking: Pathways Through Family, School, And Peers, *Canadian Journal Of Sociology* 23:1-19, 1998. This study testing social control theory of Sampson and Laub found that the effects of family attachment on risk-taking is moderated by both school and peer involvement.

0279 Walker, Sandra Gail *Weapons Use In Canadian Schools.* Ottawa, Canada: Solicitor General Canada, 1994. Using multiple research methods, this study examined the type and extent of weapons used by youths in Canadian schools, the reasons for such use, and the systems' responses. 32p.

0280 Webber, Marlene *Street Kids: The Tragedy Of Canada's Runaways.* Toronto, Canada: University of Toronto Press, 1991. This is a study of the reasons given by Canadian youths for running away from home, the nature of homelessness, and possible intervention strategies. 261p.

0281 Welsh, Lesley A.; Archambault, Francis X. & Janus, Mark David *Running For Their Lives: Physical And Sexual Abuse Of Runaway Adolescents.* New York, New York: Garland, 1995. The problems of adolescent runaways are analyzed and the interrelationships among their self-esteem, the incidence and nature of physical and sexual abuse experienced at home and on the street are examined . 107p.

0282 West, W. Gordon Educational Reforms And Delinquency, *Crime Et/And Justice* 6:41-52, 1978. This essay on the effect of recent educational reforms on youthful illegality in Canada by weakening the schools' control over young people concludes that the recent reforms are not adequate to alter the established relationship between school and delinquency.

0283 West, W. Gordon *Young Offenders And The State: A Canadian Perspective On Delinquency.* Toronto, Canada: Butterworths, 1984. This book approaches juvenile delinquency from the conflict perspective of the social and legal status of children and youth in Canada while integrating research from around the world. 269p.

0284 Wilgosh, Lorraine & Paitich, Daniel An Examination Of Sex Differences In A Clinical Sample Of Juvenile Offenders, *Canadian Journal Of Criminology* 20:75-78, 1978. This research exploring male/female delinquency in Canada found no clear differences between the two gender groups in age, intelligence, and achievement, delinquency and recidivism, but there were striking variations in the nature of the offenses committed and family interaction patterns.

0285 Wilgosh, Lorraine & Paitich, Daniel Characteristics Of Juvenile Offenders, Grouped According To Psychiatric Description And Their Parents, *Canadian Journal Of Criminology* 18:267-271, 1976. This study of Toronto delinquent boys and girls concludes that those with greater psychiatric problems come from families with greater family interaction problems.

0286 Wine, Shelley *A Motherhood Issue: The Impact Of Criminal Justice System Involvement On Women And Their Children.* Ottawa, Canada: Ministry of Solicitor General, 1992. This user report has a small section that discusses intergenerational crime involving the children of women in custody. 136p.

0287 Wong, Siu Kwong Acculturation, Peer Relations, And Delinquent Behavior Of Chinese-Canadian Youth, *Adolescence* 34:107-119, 1999. This research on the links among acculturation, peer relations and delinquency among Chinese-Canadian youths in Winnipeg found that adherence to Chinese culture was related to lower delinquency while the opposite was true for North American acculturation.

0288 Wong, Siu Kwong Delinquency Of Chinese-Canadian Youth: A Test Of Opportunity, Control, And Intergeneration Conflict Theories, *Youth And Society* 29:112-133, 1997. This study of the relationship between acculturation and concludes that there was not enough support for opportunity and control theories, but found evidence of intergenerational conflict theory.

0289 Worling, James R. Sexual Abuse Histories Of Adolescent Male Sex Offenders: Differences On The Basis Of The Age And Gender Of Their Victims, *Journal Of Abnormal Psychology* 104:610-613, 1995. This study hypothesized that more adolescent offenders who assault male children would report a history of sexual abuse compared to those who offend against female children, peers or adults, and found support for the hypothesis.

China

0290 Curran, Daniel J. & Cook, Sandra Growing Fears, Rising Crime: Juveniles And China's Justice System, *Crime & Delinquency* 39:296-315, 1993. This article examines fear of crime and distrust of the justice system among youths in China, as well as Chinese scholars' theories to explain the rising delinquent behavior.

0291 Daosheng, Shao *Preliminary Study Of China's Juvenile Delinquency.* Beijing, China: Foreign Language Press, 1992. This volume attemps to explain the apparent rise in juvenile delinquency in China to the disruptive forces of the cultural revolution resulting in changes in values regarding money, and the family. 174p.

0292 Epstein, Irving (ed.) Juvenile Delinquency In China, *Chinese Education A Journal Of Translation* 19:1-107, 1986. This is a special issue of translated articles of various authors from China on the social causes of juvenile delinquency, the family factors shaping juvenile crimes and mistakes, work-study schools, the psychological causes and psychoanalysis of juvenile delinquency, new trends in the development of juvenile delinquent gangs, identifying hoodlum cliques, and the struggle against criminal youth groups.

0293 Fu, Hualing Juvenile Delinquency In Post-Mao China, *International Journal Of Comparative And Applied Criminal Justice* 16:263-272, 1992. Article provides estimates of the forms and extent of delinquency in China.

0294 Sheu, Chuen Jim Juvenile Delinquency In The Republic Of China: A Chinese Empirical Study Of Social Control Theory, *International Journal Of Comparative And Applied Criminal Justice* 12:59-71, 1988. Based on self-report data, this study examined the increase in delinquency in the Republic of China and argues that social control theory is the most appropriate theory to explain the origin of, as well as the increase in, delinquency.

0295 Wong, Dennis S. W. Changes In Juvenile Justice In China, *Youth And Society* 32:492-509, 2001. This article discusses juvenile and youth crime trends during the past 40 years in China.

0296 Wong, Dennis S. W. Delinquency Control And Juvenile Justice In China, *Australian And New Zealand Journal Of Criminology* 32:27-41,

1999. This review of recent developments in juvenile justice in the People's Republic of China suggests that the improvement in the economy has been associated with a genuine rise in delinquency.

0297 Xiang, Guo Delinquency And Its Prevention In China, *International Journal Of Comparative And Applied Criminal Justice* 43:61-70, 1999. This is a brief description of current trends in juvenile delinquency in China.

0298 Xiaoming Li, Xiaoyi Fang & Stanton, Bonita Cigarette Smoking Among School Boys In Beijing, China, *Journal Of Adolescence* 22:621-625, 1999. On the basis of data collected in 1997 from 23 middle school youths in Beijing, the author reports 15% of the students with a higher rate for males admit to smoking and that smoking is to be related to "problem" behavior.

0299 Zhang, Lening & Messner, Steven F. Family Deviance And Delinquency In China, *Criminology* 33:359-388, 1995. Research conducted from surveys of family deviance and delinquency in Tianjin, China finds that family deviance is positively correlated with official delinquency status and exhibits indirect effects via family controls and moral commitments.

0300 Zhang, Lening; Messner, Steven F. & Lu, Zhou Gang Crime And Its Punishment In China, *Journal Of Criminal Justice* 25:289-302, 1997. This study describes selected characteristics of youth gangs, gang crime, and official punishment in contemporary China, and compares them to those commonly reported in the United States.

Colombia

0301 Klevens, Joanne; Restrepo, Ofelia; Roca, Juanita & Martinez, Adriana Comparison Of Offenders With Early-And Late-Starting Antisocial Behavior In Colombia, *International Journal Of Offender Therapy And Comparative Criminology* 44:194-203, 2000. This research is on childhood versus adolescent onset of delinquency, ages at onset, and type of-offense, characteristics of family of origin, and personal history.

0302 Rubio, Mauricio *Social Capital, Education And Delinquency In Colombia (Capital Social, Educación Y Delincuencia Juvenil En Colombia).* Santa Fé de Bogotá, Colombia: Centro de Estudios Sobre Desarrollo Economico Universidad, 1996. The author argues that juvenile delinquency in Colombia is related to problems of the educational system and to "capital social perverso" (perverted social capital), an elaboration of Coleman's concept of social capital. 68p. Spanish.

Cuba

0303 Salas, Luis P. Juvenile Delinquency In Postrevolutionary Cuba: Characteristics And Cuban Explanations, *Cuban Studies/Estudies Cubanos* 9:43-61, 1979. The author argues that juvenile delinquency in Cuba takes many of the same forms found in other societies, both socialist and capitalist.

Denmark

0304 Guttridge, Patricia; Gabrielli, William F. Jr.; Mednick, Sarnoff A. & Van Dusen, Katherine Teilmann Criminal Violence In A Birth Cohort, pp 211-224 in Van Dusen, Katherine Teilmann & Mednick, Sarnoff A. (eds.) *Prospective Studies In Crime And Delinquency*. Boston, Massachusetts: Kluwer-Nijhoff, 1983. This chapter presents an analysis of a sample of a Copenhagen male cohort whose police records were analyzed for the age at first arrest, type of offenses committed, and the number of offenses.

0305 Kandel, Elizabeth & Mednick, Sarnoff A. Perinatal Complications Predict Violent Offending, *Criminology* 29:519-529, 1991. This study, based on a cohort sample of 216 people born in Copenhagen between 1959-1960 concludes that birth trauma and violent offending in later life were significantly associated.

0306 Kramp, Peter; Israelson, Lise; Mortensen, Karen Vibeke & Aarkrog, Tove Serious Juvenile Offenders: Demographic Variables, Diagnostic Problems And Therapeutic Possibilities, *International Journal Of Law And Psychiatry* 10:63-73, 1987. In a sample of juveniles referred by courts for treatment at a Copenhagen psychiatric clinic, a majority had exhibited severe emotional and behavioral problems since early childhood.

0307 Mednick, Brigitte R.; Baker, Robert L. & Carothers, Linn E. Patterns Of Family Instability And Crime: The Association Of Timing Of The Family's Disruption With Subsequent Adolescent And Young Adult Criminality, *Journal Of Youth And Adolescence* 19:201-220, 1990. Using maternal interviews and official records of male youths, this follow-up study suggests selected correlates of family disruption in adolescence may contribute to young-adulthood criminal behavior.

0308 Moffitt, Terrie E.; Mednick, Sarnoff A. & Gabrielli, William F. Jr. Predicting Careers Of Criminal Violence: Descriptive Data And Predispositional Factors, pp 12-34 in Brizer, David A. & Crowner, Martha L. (eds.) *Current Approaches To The Prediction Of Violence*. Washington,

D.C.: American Psychiatric Press, 1989. This study found that there is specialization in violent crimes among juveniles, and that such violence can be traced to their early aggressive tendencies as well as heritability and perinatal health.

0309 Nielson, Beth Grothe Young Offender Ideologies And The Danish Discourse, pp 56-65 in Booth, Tim (ed.) *Juvenile Justice In New The Europe* Sheffield, United Kingdom: Sheffield University, 1991. This chapter discusses the issues related to the process of "crime problem" being equated with the "youth problem" in Denmark.

0310 Tehrani, J. A.; Brennan, P. A. & Hodgins, S. Mental Illness And Criminal Violence, *Social Psychiatry And Psychiatric Epidemiology* 33:s81-s84, 1998. From the record of 9125 birth records, this study concludes that there is an increased risk of children of mentally ill parents toward criminal violence.

Egypt

0311 Feucht, Erika Juvenile Misbehavior In Ancient Egypt, pp 61-70 in Hess, Albert G. & Clement, Priscilla F. (eds.) *History Of Juvenile Delinquency: A Collection Of Essays On Crime Committed By Young Offenders, In History And In Selected Countries, Vol. I.* Aalen, Germany: Scientia Verlag, 1990. This chapter offers a brief description of attitudes toward children and their misbehavior in Ancient Egypt.

0312 Souryal, Sam S. Juvenile Delinquency In The Cross-Cultural Context: The Egyptian Experience, *International Journal Of Comparative And Applied Criminal Justice* 16:329-352, 1992. This article describes the forms and extent of delinquency in Egypt providing tables of data on trends and forms of offense behavior.

Ethiopia

0313 Lalor, Kevin Street Children: A Comparative Perspective, *Child Abuse And Neglect* 23:759-770, 1999. This study describes findings from research on the victimization and widespread abuse of "street children" in Ethiopia, and draws comparisons to the experiences of homeless Latin-American youths.

0314 Terefe, Dereje & Mengistu, Derese Violence In Ethiopian Schools: A Study Of Some Schools In Addis Ababa, pp 34-56 in Ohsako, Toshio (ed.) *Violence At School: Global Issues And Interventions*. Paris, France: United Nations Educational, Scientific and Cultural Organization, 1997.

This chapter describes some aspects of violence in Ethiopian schools and outlines the policies and procedures designed to deal with it.

Finland

0315 Aromaa, Kauko Self-Reported Delinquency In Helsinki, Finland, 1992, pp14-41 in Junger-Tas, Josine; Terlouw, Gert-Jan & Klein, Malcolm W. (eds.) *Delinquent Behavior Among Young People In The Western World: First Results Of The International Self-Report Delinquency Study*. Amsterdam/New York: Kugler, 1994. This chapter reports the findings from a self-reported delinquency survey carried out in Helsinki.

0316 Hamalainen, M. & Pulkkinnen, L. Problem Behavior As A Precursor Of Male Criminality, *Development And Psychopathology* 8:443-455, 1996. In this investigation, it was found that the risk for different types of offenses was highest for boys who exhibited escalating conduct problems and academic failure during the school years.

0317 Hamalainen, Minna & Pulkkinnen, Lea Aggressive And Non-prosocial Behaviour As Precursors Of Criminality, *Studies On Crime And Crime Prevention* 4:6-21, 1995. Based on a sample of 8-14 year olds, this study of the precursors of criminality reports that convicted males had more aggressive and lower prosocial behavior than those who had not been arrested.

0318 Huesmann, L. Rowell; Lagerspetz, Kristi & Eron, Leonard D. Intervening Variables In The T.V. Violence-Aggression Relation: Evidence From Two Cities, *Developmental Psychology* 20:746-775, 1984. American and Finnish children were interviewed and tested as part of a longitudinal investigation of the impact of TV violence on behavior. 314p.

0319 Kivivuori, Janne Delinquent Behavior, Psychosomatic Symptoms And The Idea Of Healthy Delinquency, *Journal Of Scandinavian Studies In Criminology And Crime Prevention* 1:121-139, 2000. This study examined the association between self-reported delinquent behavior and psychosomatic symptoms among a nationally representative sample of 15-16 year old Finnish adolescents.

0320 Kivivuori, Janne Delinquent Phases: The Case Of Temporally Intensified Shoplifting Behavior, *British Journal Of Criminology* 38:663-680, 1998. This research investigating features of shoplifting by Finnish adolescents also explores if and how such behavioral phases are related to sex, age, other offense behavior and social control variables.

0321 Kivivuori, Janne *The Criminal And Delinquent Behavior Of Young People 1995: Results And Experience From The First year Of The Ongoing Study of Youth Criminality (Nuorten Rikollinen Ja Kielletty Toiminta 1995: Nuorisorikollisuuden Seurantahankkeen Ensimmaisen Vuoden Tuloksia Ja Kokemuksia).* Helsinki, Finland: Oikeuspoliittinen Tutkimuslaitos, 1995. This questionnaire research on juvenile delinquency in Finland reports that delinquency is widely prevalent among school children. 60p. Appendix. Finnish.

0322 Kivivuori, Janne *Understand And Punish: The Culture Of Juvenile Transgressions In The Context Of A Welfare State.* Helsinki, Finland: National Research Institute of Legal Policy, 1994. This study describing the meanings attached to delinquency and criminal transgressions by youths in Helsinki, discusses the relationship between modern understanding professions and the cultural formation of juvenile transgressions. 277p.

0323 Koivisto, Hanna & Haapasalo, Jaana Childhood Maltreatment And Adulthood Psychopathy In Light Of File-Based Assessments Among Mental State Examinees, *Studies On Crime And Crime Prevention* 5:91-104, 1996. This study examines the child abuse and neglect experiences of a sample of 52 offenders in Finland who were rated using the file-based Psychopathy Check List.

0324 Peltoniemi, Teuvo Child Abuse And Physical Punishment Of Children In Finland, *Child Abuse And Neglect* 7:33-36, 1983. A study of attitudes toward child abuse and physical punishment of children based on poll data on family violence in Finland and Sweden is reported in this article.

0325 Peltoniemi, Teuvo *The Detection Of Family Violence (Perhevakivallan Ilmitulo).* Helsinki, Finland: Research Institute of Legal Policy, 1982. Data on 173 cases of family violence handled by the police in Turku, Finland when analyzed indicate that three percent of the young children, and one percent of the teen-aged children report such violence while ten percent of the women and ten percent of the men experience family violence. 89p.

0326 Rantakallio, P.; Myhrman A. & Koiranen, M. Juvenile Offenders, With Special Reference To Sex Differences, *Social Psychiatry & Psychiatric Epidemiology* 30:113-120, 1995. This article on juvenile offenders from Northern Finland, reports their social and demographic characteristics, frequency and forms of offense by gender.

0327 Rasanen, P.; Hirvenoja, R. & Hakko, H. A Portrait Of The Juvenile Arsonist, *Forensic Science International* 73:41-47, 1995. This study on whether juvenile arsonists differ from violent juvenile criminals in regard to suicide and mental problems, found that suicide was more common among the arsonists than the violent offenders.

0328 Sariola, Heikki & Uutela, Antti The Prevalence And Context Of Family Violence Against Children In Finland, *Child Abuse And Neglect* 16:823-832, 1992. The researchers investigated the prevalence and context of violence against children in Finland.

0329 Virkkunen, Matti Parental Deprivation And Recidivism In Juvenile Delinquents, *British Journal Of Criminology* 16:378-384, 1976. The significance of parental deprivation in the recidivism of young offenders was studied among 16-20 year-old juvenile offenders sentenced to prison in Finland.

France

0330 Addad, M. & Benezech, M. Schizophrenia And Delinquency: A Medico-Social Study Of 116 Psychotics Of Whom 63 Are Delinquents Confined In Special Hospitals, pp 69-101 in Shoham, S. Giora & Grahame, Anthony (eds.) *Israel Studies In Criminology, Vol. 5.* Ramat Gan, Israel: Turtledove Publishing, 1979. This study compares the relationship between psychoses and type of offenses among non-delinquent schizophrenics and schizophrenic offenders in five psychiatric hospitals in France.

0331 Alarie, Sophie & Brochu, Serge Listening To "Heavy Metal" And Deviancy: A Complex Link (Audition De Musique "Heavy Metal" Et Déviance: Un Lien Complexe), *Revue Internationale De Criminologie Et De Police Technique* 49:300-311, 1996. This essay concludes that the impact of musical styles on problem behaviors is still uncertain. French.

0332 Body-Gendrot, Sophie Urban Violence In France: The Quest For New Policies, pp 33-44 in Bruinsma, G. J. N. & Van Der Vijver, C. D. (eds.) *Public Safety In Europe.* Enschede, The Netherlands: International Police Institute Twente, 1999. This is a discussion of the causes of youth violence and vandalism in public transportation as an expression of immigrant ethnic experience in urban France.

0333 Bosanquet, Nick & Magee, Jayne Adolescents And Smoking: Evidence From France And Spain, *Journal Of Adolescence* 22:601-605, 1999. Although not on delinquency *per se*, this paper reports that almost a third of 12-18 year old French male and female youths smoke in spite of the age-restrictions on tobacco use.

0334 Bourgeois, Frédérique & Dieppedale, Dominique *The Police And The Social Test (La Police À L'Épreuve Du Social)*. Paris, France: Institut Des Hautes Etudes De La Sécurité Intérieur, 1993. Part 2 contains delinquency data on two districts of, France after the 1983 riots. French. 147p.

0335 Brion, F. & Tulkens, F. Cultural Conflict And Delinquency: Questioning The Evidence (Conflit De Culture Et Délinquance: Interroger L'Évidence), *Déviance Et Société* 22:235-262, 1998. This paper espouses the view that labeling certain behaviors of immigrants and their children reflects the "state-based establishment" line instead of asking what it is that makes us think their behavior to be deviant. French with English summary.

0336 Carra, C. & Sicot, F. Disorder And Violence At School (Perturbations Et Violence À L'École), *Déviance Et Société* 20:85-97, 1996. Article summarizes research and theories on violence and school disturbances. French.

0337 Esterle, Maryse Etiology Of Delinquent Conduct In A Study Of A Gang (Contribution À L'Étiologie De La Conduite Délinquante À Travers L'Étude D'Une Bande), *Revue International De Criminologie Et De Police Technique* 43:203-221, 1990. This article provides a case study of some gang members in a community outside of Paris. French.

0338 Esterle-Hedibel, M. Joy-Riding And Vandalism Of Cars: Motivations For Theft And Destruction Of Cars By Youth Gangs In Public Areas (Virées, Incendies Et Vols De Voitures: Motivations Aux Vols Et Aux Dégradations De Voitures Dans Les Bandes De Jeunes De Milieu Populaire), *Déviance Et Société* 20:119-139, 1996. In this participant observation study of Arab youth gangs in French suburbs, it was found that the "borrowed" car has symbolic and practical value such as group cohesion, enhanced prestige among peers, and thumbing noses at the larger society, although the status symbols and aspirations of the mainstream are imitated. French with English summary.

0339 Favard, Anne-Marie Childhood In Danger: Findings And Ideas (L'Enfance En Danger: Des Faits Et Des Idées), *Revue Internationale De Criminologie Et De Police Technique* 64:80-93, 1991. This paper presents an anyalysis of children in danger due to violence, abuse, neglect in urban and rual settings of France. French.

0340 Fiacre, Patricia Juvenile Repeat Offenders: Followup Of The Judicial Trajectories Of A Population (Les Jeunes Délinquants Réitérants: Suivi De Trajectoires Judiciaires D'Une Population). Paris, France: Ministère D'Intérieur. Institut des Hautes Études de la Sécurité Intérieure, 1996. Using official records, the author tracked the progress into adulthood of twenty two juvenile delinquents in France. French. 109p.

0341 Fornes, Paul; Druihe, Laurent & Lecomte, Dominique Childhood Homicide In Paris, 1990-1993: A Report Of 81 Cases, *Journal Of Forensic Sciences* 40:201-204, 1994. This article investigated the incidence and character of homicides involving child victims in Paris and it suburbs from 1990 to 1993 with epidemiological and autopsy data for victims from a few days after birth up to age 14.

0342 Fornes, Paul; Druihe, Laurent & Lecomte, Dominique Homicide Among Youth And Young Adults 15 Through 29 Years Of Age. A Report Of 138 Cases From Paris And Its Suburbs, 1991-1993, *Journal Of Forensic Sciences* 41:837-840, 1996. Based on autopsy and police records of homicides of 15-29 year olds over a 3-year period in Paris and its suburbs, this analysis concludes that the rate of homicides was relatively constant at 2.4 homicides per 100,000 and the victims were mainly over age 20.

0343 Fuchs, Rachel Ginnis Crimes Against Children In Nineteenth Century France: Child Abuse, *Law And Human Behavior* 6:237-260, 1982. This study describes the origins of child abuse as a widespread social problem in 19th Century France.

0344 Khosrokhavar, T. Violence And Its Avatars In Vulnerable Neighborhoods (La Violence Et Ses Avatars Dans Les Quartiers Sensibles), *Déviance Et Société* 24:425-440, 2000. The author argues that the nature of youth violence is a product of gender, ethnicity, and subcultures of the neighborhood and the segregation, stigmatization and exclusion by French society. French with English summary.

0345 LaCombe, P. & Moulin, C. Delinquent Minors Amidst Repression, Media, Enforcement, Education And Responsibility (Les Mineurs Délinquants, Entre Répression, Médiatisation, Sanction, Éducation Et Reponsabilisation), *Déviance Et Société* 24:167-186, 2000. This article reports research concerning delinquent careers of youths using life history techniques. French with English summary.

0346 Lagrée, J.-Ch. Adolescents And Marginality: The Case A Of A New Housing Development (Adolescence Et Marginalité: Le Cas D'Une Ville Nouvelle), *Déviance Et Societé* 4:349-369, 1980. This analysis discusses the various factors that make lower class youth of a new housing colony marginal while excluding their participation in the larger socioeconomic structure. French.

0347 Lagrée, Jean-Charles & Fai, Paula Lew Girls In Street Gangs In The Suburbs Of Paris, pp 80-95 in Cain, Maureen (ed.) *Growing Up Good:*

Policing The Behavior Of Girls in Europe. Newbury Park, California: Sage, 1989. Describes the marginality of a sample of 38 youths gang members of different gender, race, age and social class groups who were interviewed during 1984.

0348 Leca, Marie-Hélène Cognitive Reasoning And Juvenile Delinquency (Carences Cognitives Et Délinquance Juvénile), *Revue Internationale De Criminologie Et De Police Technique* 69:288-299, 1996. This article reports a study of 51 subjects whose cognitive reasoning ability and delinquency involvement were the focus of inquiry.

0349 Monteil, Catherine & Musitelli, François *Vandalism (Les Destructions Et Dégradations).* Paris, France: Institut des Hautes Etudes de la Sécurité Intérieure, 1995. From an analysis of police statistics on the extent of reported vandalism in France during 1980-1993, it is concluded that the increase in vandalism of private property, especially vehicles, began in 1989 with most involving a higher proportion of youths. 56p. French.

0350 Peretti-Watel, P. Theories Of Deviance And Delinquency: Self-Reports In A School Environment (Théories De La Déviance Et Délinquance: Auto-Reportée En Milieu Scolaire), *Déviance Et Societé* 25:235-256, 2001. Based on self-report data from French school children, this study concludes thate there are three deviant profiles: casual predation, casual acts of violence, and a combination of the two. French.

0351 Portelli, Serge Family Crime And Violations Of The Law (Crimes Et Délits De Famille L'État Du Droit) *Les Cahiers De La Sécurité Intérieur* 28:75-100, 1997. Discusses the issue of family violence involving children and the loss of paternal power under the new family law, and recommends that criminal law be resorted to in cases of family violence. French with English summary.

0352 Selosse, Jacques (ed.) *Working With The Families Of At-Risk Youths (Le Travail Avec Les Familles De Jeunes Marginaux).* Vaucresson, France: Centre De Formation Et De Recherche De L'Éducation Surveillée, 1979. This anthology has sections devoted to socio-historical, cultural diversity and Arab immigrants, family therapy, social work, correctional education, and socio-judicial perspectives of family and adolescents, and child protection hearings. French and English. 601p.

0353 Tournier, Pierre The Detention Of Minors: Followup Observations Of An Incoming Cohort (La Détention Des Mineurs: Observation Suivie D'Une Cohorte D'Entrants). Paris, France: Ministère de la Justice), 1991. This volume has many tables on a cohort of delinquent youths whose dossiers were analyzed for the length of sentence and the post release delinquent behavior exhibited by the youths. 109p. French.

0354 Van Zanten, A. Neighborhood Or School? Deviance And Sociability Of Adolescents In A Junior Highschool In A Suburb (Le Quartier Ou L'École? Déviance Et Sociabilité Adolescente Dans Un Collège De Banlieue), *Déviance Et Société* 24:377-401, 2000. This article argues that adolescents from disadvantaged neighborhoods are already oriented to either school culture or street culture and the processes of school propels some toward deviant behavior depending upon the strength of their friendship networks, class room sociability and inter-ethnic relationships. French with English summary.

Germany

0355 Albrecht, H.-J. & Kury, H. (eds.) *Research On Crime And Criminal Justice At The Max Planck Institute: Summaries, Kriminologische Forschungsberichte, Vol. 83*. Freiburg, Germany: Max Planck Institute for Foreign and International Criminal Law, 1998. This anthology includes English language summaries of studies conducted at the Max Planck Institute for Foreign and International Criminal Law, and juvenile delinquency is among the diverse topics covered by the volume. 104p.

0356 Boehnke, Klaus; Hagan, John & Merkens, Hans Right-Wing Extremism Among German Adolescents: Risk Factors And Protective Factors, *Applied Psychology* 1:109-126, 1998. The study provides empirical evidence on risks for and protective factors against juvenile delinquency and right-wing extremism among German youth from East and West Berlin.

0357 Boers, Klaus; Class, Michael & Kur, Peter Self-Reported Delinquency In Germany After The Reunification, pp 343-353 in Junger-Tas, Josine; Terlouw, Gert-Jan & Klein, Malcolm W. (eds.) *Delinquent Behavior Among Young People In The Western World: First Results Of The International Self-Report Delinquency Study*. Amsterdam/New York: Kugler, 1994. This chapter reports the findings of a self-reported delinquency survey carried out in Germany.

0358 Buchholz, Erich Reasons For The Low Rate Of Delinquency In The German Democratic Republic, *Eurocriminology* 1:61-75, 1987. The author reports that juvenile delinquency declined in East Germany by one third, while crime in West Germany and much of Europe was increasing.

0359 Buchholz, Erich The German Democratic Republic, pp 61-90 in Stewart, V. Lorne (ed.) *Justice And Troubled Children Around The World, Vol. 4*. New York, New York: New York University Press, 1982. This discussion addresses the reasons why elinquency may exist in a socialist state where the conditions for such behavior are assumed to not exist.

0360 Bytheway, Bill The Statistical Association Between Social Class And Self-Reported Delinquency, *International Journal Of Criminology And Penology* 3:243-251, 1975. The author reviews the literature and concludes that there is a real, albeit statistically small, negative association between social class and delinquency.

0361 Diedrich, Ingo; Meyer, Anja & Roessner, Dieter Contesting The Limits Of Society: A Critique of Control Theory And The Disorganization Approach (Der Kampf Um Den Limes Der Gesellschaft: Eine Kritik Der Kontrolltheorie Und De Desintegration), *Kriminologisches Journal* 31:82-106, 1999. Based on a study of youth violene in Halle/Saale, Germany, the findings of this study raise questions regarding control theory and disintegration approach.

0362 Dobash, Russell P.; Dobash, Emerson; Ballintyne, Scott; Schumann, Karl; Kaulitzki, Reiner & Garth, Hans-Werner Ignorance And Suspicion: Young People And Criminal Justice In Scotland And Germany, *British Journal Of Criminology* 30:306-320, 1990. This study of young people's contacts with and perceptions of criminal justice in the two countries reports that contacts with authorities were described in negative terms by the youths and had negative impact on subsequent behavior in both places.

0363 Douglas, Marie C. Ausländer Raus! Nazi Raus! An Observation Of German Skins And Jugendgangen, *International Journal Of Comparative And Applied Criminal Justice* 16:129-134, 1992. This article on the "Skins" (skinheads) and youth gangs of the newly united Germany dating back to 1984 found that the typical member of the movement is an unemployed and uneducated male aged 14 to 21 state welfare recipient living at home.

0364 Dussich, Von John *New Perspectives In Control Theory: Social Coping Of Youth Under Supervision.* Köln, West Germany: Carl Heymans Verlag KG, 1985. Testing Friday's social coping model on young male offenders who had recently undergone probation or parole supervision in Hanover lend considerable support to the "Spaceround" Integration model and the Social Coping model. 306p.

0365 Egon, Stephan Personality And Attitude Measurement In Two Studies Of Self-Reported Delinquency And Victimization, *International Journal Of Criminology And Penology* 5:275-287, 1977. The author presents a critique of victimization surveys and discusses the results of a self-reported delinquency survey carried out in Stuttgart, Germany.

0366 Engel, Uwe & Hurrelmann, Klaus Delinquent Behavior In Adolescence: Potential And Constraints Of Preventive Strategies In School Settings, pp 167-184 in Albrecht, Peter Alexis & Backes, Otto (eds.) *Crime Prevention And Intervention: Legal And Ethical Problems*. Berlin: Walter de Gruyter, 1989. Results of a self-report survey confirm that delinquent behavior is associated with anticipation of unfavorable chances for mobility, feelings of injustice regarding basic status allocation, and achievement-related status dynamics.

0367 Enzmann, Dirk; Pfeiffer, Christian & Wetzels, Peter Youth Violence In Germany: A Study Of Victimisation And Delinquency In Four Major Cities, pp 93-262 in Bruinsma, G. J. N. & Van Der Vijver, C. D. (eds.) *Public Safety In Europe*. Enschede, The Netherlands: Febodruk, 1999. This chapter provides data and graphs on juvenile violence in Leipzig, Hamburg, Hanover, and Stuttgart.

0368 Freiburg, Arnold Juvenile Delinquency In The German Democratic Republic (Zur Jugendkriminalit In Der DDR), *Kölner Zeitschrift Für Soziologie Und Sozialpsychologie* 27:489-537, 1975. Based on official records, this report suggests that since the end of World War II, both adult crime and juvenile delinquency rates were substantially lower in the German Democratic Republic than in the Federal Republic.

0369 Hagan, John; Hefler, Gerd & Classen, Gabriele Subterranean Sources Of Subcultural Delinquency Beyond The American Dream, *Criminology* 36:309-341, 1998. Based on a study of German youths, this article examines whether subcultural forms of earlier crime and delinquency represent rejections or distorted reflections of the core values of market-oriented societies and offers evidence suggesting such a subterranean causal link to core values of market society and argues that the strands of this web can lead to subcultural delinquency.

0370 Hagan, John; Merkens, Hans & Boehnke, Klaus Delinquency And Disdain: Social Capital And The Control Of Right-Wing Extremism Among East And West Berlin Youth, *American Journal Of Sociology* 100:1028-1052, 1995. This study analyzes links between subterranean traditions of right-wing extremism and school delinquency suggesting that weakened informal social controls and anomic aspirations lead to delinquent drift, and extremist and delinquent involvements.

0371 Hess, Ulrike *A Sociological Analysis Of Xenophobic Violence In Germany (Fremdenfeindliche Gewalt In Deutschland—Eine Soziologische Analyse)*. Munich, Germany: Profil Verlag, 1996. This analysis attempts to explain xenophobic, including juvenile, violence in Germany since 1989 within the framework of Norbert Elias' sociology of figuration. 330p.

0372 Hummel, Peter; Thömke, Volker; Oldenbürger, Hartman A. & Specht, Friedrich Male Adolescent Sex Offenders Against Children: Similarities And Differences Between Those Offenders With And Those Without A History Of Sexual Abuse, *Journal Of Adolescence* 23:305-317, 2000. This study compares a defined sample of male adolescents with regard to their personal development, family characteristics and the types of offenses they committed.

0373 Hurrelmann, Klaus & Engel, Uwe Delinquency As A Symptom Of Adolescents' Orientation Toward Status And Success, *Journal Of Youth And Adolescence* 21:119-138, 1992. Based on survey data of students in Germany, this study supports the idea that an adolescent's failure in being accepted by the peer group and failure in establishing an undisputed social position in such a group, must be seen as a risk factor for deviance.

0374 Jäger, Joachim Crime Control And Its Rationale (Kriminalitatskontrolle Und Vernunft), *Schriftenreihe Der Polizei Führungsakademie* 1:58-65, 1986. This report contends that crimes committed by minors and young adults decreased in West Germany in the mid-1980s and suggests the reasons and the policy implications. German with English summary.

0375 Jehle, Jörg-Martin *Pre-Trial Custody Of Juveniles And Young Adults Preceding And Following Reunification (Entwicklung Der Untersuchungshaft Bei Jugendlichen Und Heranwachsenden Vor Und Nach Der Wiedervereinigung)*. Bonn, Germany: Forum Verlag Godesberg, 1995. This study investigated arrest rates of juveniles and young adults in Germany and changes in the imposition of pretrial custody by juvenile criminal courts during the reunification period. 160p.

0376 Johnson, Eric A. & McHale, Vincent E. Socioeconomic Aspects Of The Delinquency Rate In Imperial Germany, 1882 – 1914, *Journal Of Social History* 13:384-402, 1980. This study assessed cross-temporal and cross-sectional variations in juvenile delinquency in Germany during 1882 –1914 and concludes that the relationship between delinquency rates and urban industrial development in nineteenth century Germany was largely indirect, and fluctuated over time.

0377 Kaiser, Günther & Jehle, Jörg-Martin (eds.) Criminological Victimology: New Perspectives And Findings, Vol. 2 (Kriminologische Opferforschung: Neue Perspektiven Und Erkenntnisse, Teilband II). Heidelberg, Germany: Kriminalistik Verlag, 1995. This anthology includes papers on the results of a victimization survey of sexually abused children. 246p.

0378 Kaiser, Günther Juvenile Delinquency In The Federal Republic Of Germany, *International Journal Of Comparative And Applied Criminal Justice* 16:185-204, 1992. This article details the nature and extent of juvenile delinquency in contemporary Germany.

0379 Karstedt-Henke, Susanne & Crasmöller, Bernhard Risks Of Being Detected, Chances Of Getting Away, pp 33-62 in Junger-Tas, Josine; Boendermaker, Leonieke & Van Der Laan, Peter H. (eds.) *The Future Of The Juvenile Justice System (L'Avenir Du Système Pénal Des Mineurs).* Leuven, Belgium: Acco, 1991. This chapter describes research on juvenile offenders and their offenses within their social network of friends, parents, and school.

0380 Kersten, Joachim German Youth Subcultures: History, Typology And Gender-Orientations, pp 67-94 in Hazlehurst, Kayleen & Hazlehurst, Cameron (eds.) *Gangs And Youth Subcultures: International Explorations.* New Brunswick, New Jersey: Transaction, 1998. This paper offers an extensive discussion of the history, contemporary organization, behavior and possible explanations of youth groups in Germany.

0381 Klein, Michael Are East German Juveniles More Delinquent Than Those In West Germany? (Verhalten Sich Jugendliche In Ostdeutschland Haeufiger Delinquent Als Jugendliche In Westdeutschland?), *Monatsschrift Für Kriminologie Und Strafrechtsreform* 80:148-164, 1997. From the official police crime statistics, the author assess differences and the differences attributable to differences in police strategy in the rates of delinquency in East and West Germany.

0382 Kraus, Ludwig & Rolinski, Klaus Officially Recorded Recidivism Among Delinquents After Their Social Behavioral Training (Rückfall Nach Sozialem Training Auf Der Grundlage Offiziell Registrierter Delinquenz), *Monatsschrift Für Kriminologie Und Strafrechtsreform* 75:32-46, 1992. This study examines the criminal behavior of German juveniles who participated in courses designed for learning social behavioral skills.

0383 Krober, Hans-Ludwig; Scheurer, Heinz; Richter, Paul & Saß, Henning Causes Of Recidivism Among Violent Criminal Offenders: The Heidelberg Delinquency Project (Ursachen Der Rückfälligkeit Von Gewaltstraftätern: Ergebnisse Des Heidelberg Delinquenzprojekts), *Monatsschrift Für Kriminologie Und Strafrechtsreform* 76:227-241, 1993. The Heidelberg Delinquency Study explores social, psychological and biological factors that may be important in the development and persistence of violence crimes.

0384 Kube, Edwin Collective Violence Among Young People: A Serious Challenge To Government And Society, *Eurocriminology* 7:39-51, 1994.

This review examines the incidence and prevention of collective violence, particularly crimes committed by youth gangs and crimes against foreign nationals, by young people in Germany.

0385 Loll, Bernd Uwe *Predicting The Criminality Of German And Alien Resident Youth. (Prognose Der Jugendkriminalität Von Deutschen Und Ausländern)*. Wiesbaden, Germany: Bundeskriminalamt, 1990. This study tested the accuracy of crime prediction models on German youths whose parents are native and foreign born, predicting a rise in the crime index for Hamburg and Germany as a whole and. 217p.

0386 Maggs, Jennifer L. & Hurrelmann, Klaus Do Substance Use And Delinquency Have Differential Associations With Adolescents' Peer Relations? *International Journal Of Behavior Development* 22:367-388, 1998. This study tested the idea that adolescent substance use, but not delinquency, would be associated with positive peer relations and found increased frequency and intensity of peer relations with substance use, but not consistently with delinquency.

0387 Nohl-Arnd, Michael Immigrant Youth: Empirical Research On Turkish Gangs And Cliques (Jugend In Der Migration: Tuerkische Banden Und Cliquen In Empirischer Analyse), *Interkulturelle Erziehung In Praxis Und Theorie, Vol. 19*. Baltmannsweiler, Germany: Schneider Verlag Hohengehren, 1996. This author focuses on socialization of male Turkish youths in Germany some of whom developed subcultural orientations and position outside the maintream, and the author argues that for some of these groups ethnic discrimination becomes an escalating factor in the use of violence. 175p.

0388 Obergfell-Fuchs, Joachim & Fuchs, Ina Fine-Tuning A Model For The Diversion Of Youths: A Comparative Study Of Jena And Freiburg 1991/92 and 1993 (Einstellungsmuster Von Jugendlichen. Eine Vergleichende Untersuchung In Jena Und Freiburg 1991/92 Und 1993), pp 215-254 in Kaiser, Günther & Kury, Helmut (eds.) *Criminological Research In The 1990s (Kriminologische Forschung In Den 90er Jahren)*. Freiburg, Germany: Max Planck Institute For Foreign and International Penal Law, 1993. The impact of German unification on the illegal behavior of juveniles in East and West Germany is compared. German.

0389 Oberwittler, D.; Blank, T.; Köllisch, T. & Naplava, T. *Working Report 1/2001: Social Life Conditions And Juvenile Delinquency - Results Of The 1999 MPI-School Investigation In Freiburg And Köln (Arbeitsberichte 1/2001: Soziale Lebenslagen Und Delinquenz Von Jugendlichen - Ergebnisse Der MIP-Schulbefragung 1999 In Freiburg Und Köln)*. Freiburg im Breisgau, Germany: Max Planck Institute for Foreign and

International Penal Law, 2001. This research from Cologne concludes that above all else, peers and time spent with peers, affect delinquency particularly among immigrants. German.

0390 Pfeiffer, Christian & Wetzels, Peter The Structure And Development Of Juvenile Violence In Germany: A Proposition Paper Based On Current Research Findings. Hanover: Kriminologisches Forschungsinstitut Niedersachsen, 1999. Based on research on juvenile violence, it is argued that crime-policy focusing solely on intensified repression is neither far-sighted nor likely to bring positive results.

0391 Plate, Monika Trends In Juvenile Delinquency In The Federal Republic Of Germany, pp 63-68 in Junger-Tas, Josine; Boendermaker, Leonieke & Van Der Laan, Peter H. (eds.) *The Future Of The Juvenile Justice System (L'Avenir Du Système Pénal Des Mineurs)*. Leuven, Belgium: Acco, 1991. Analysis of empirical data on delinquency in Germany are presented.

0392 Schumann, Karl F. The Deviant Apprentice: The Impact Of The German Dual System Of Vocational Training On Juvenile Delinquency, pp 91-104 in Blau, Zena Smith & Hagan, John (eds.) *Current Perspectives On Aging And The Life Cycle: Delinquency And Disrepute In The Life Course, Vol. 4.* Greenwich, Connecticut: JAI Press, 1995. This chapter describes the dual educational system in Germany where in compar son to other countries, vocational training may retard delinquency.

0393 Sutterer, Peter & Karger, Thomas Self-Reported Juvenile Delinquency In Mannheim, Germany, pp 156-185 in Junger-Tas, Josine; Terlouw, Gert-Jan & Klein, Malcolm W. (eds.) *Delinquent Behavior Among Young People In The Western World: First Results Of The International Self-Report Delinquency Study*. Amsterdam/New York: Kugler, 1994. This chapter reports findings from a self-reported delinquency survey carried out in Mannheim, Germany.

0394 Traulsen, M. Youthful Criminality In Comparative Perspective: Offense Behavior Of Young People In Sachsen (Jugendkriminalität Im Vergleich: Die Kriminalität Junger Menschen In Sachsen), *Kriminalistik* 49:47-50, 1995. Data on selected offenses obtained from official records to compare rates of offending by young people in the former East German state of Saxony and the West German states of Baden-Württemberg and North Rhine Westphalia show that the percentage of all suspects who were under age 21 in 1992 was considerably higher in the former East German state than in the two West German states. German.

0395 Villmow, Bernard & Johnson, Elmer H. Self-Reported Delinquency: Age And Class Statuses: And The Control Network Of A Small City In

West Germany, *International Journal Of Comparative And Applied Criminal Justice* 6:53-59, 1982. This study presents findings of a self-report survey of delinquencies of 14 - 25 year olds in Baden-Wurttemberg, West Germany.

0396 Villmow, Bernard & Johnson, Elmer H. Self-Reported Delinquency In A Small City In West Germany: Delinquents, Victims, And Offender/Victims, *International Journal Of Comparative And Applied Criminal Justice* 5:144-152, 1981. Self-reports were used to address several issues on youthful crime in a small-city setting.

0397 Volker, Grundies Delinquency Among Ethnic German Immigrant Youths (Kriminalitätsbelastung Junger Aussiedler), *Monatsschrift Für Kriminologie Und Strafrechtsreform* 83:290-305, 2000. Using police statistics, this study investigated criminality among "Aussiedler" (Eastern European) youth who migrated to Germany. German.

0398 Waite, Robert G. Political Change, Economic Crisis And Juvenile Delinquency In Germany, 1870 To 1945, pp 347-383 in Hess, Albert G. & Clement, Priscilla F. (eds.) *History Of Juvenile Delinquency: A Collection Of Essays On Crime Committed By Young Offenders, In History And In Selected Countries Volume I.* Aalen, Germany: Scientia Verlag, 1990. This chapter discusses the impact of changes in political, social, and economic systems in Germany on the delinquent behavior of young people.

0399 Williams, Christopher R.; Arrigo, Bruce A. & Klaus, Stephanie Germany, pp 47-57 in Hoffman, Allan M. & Summers, Randal W. (eds.) *Teen Violence: A Global View.* Westport, Connecticut: Greenwood, 2001. This chapter offers an overview of teen violence and a brief discussion of anti-violence programs in Germany.

Ghana

0400 Weinberg, Kirson S. Shaw-Mckay Theories Of Delinquency In Cross-Cultural Context, pp 167-185 in Short, James F. (ed.) *Delinquency, Crime, And Society.* Chicago, Illinois: University of Chicago Press, 1976. This chapter compares factors related to delinquency in Accra, Ghana.

Greece

0401 Hatzichristou, Chryse & Papadatos,Yiannis Juvenile Delinquents' Perceptions Of Childhood Parental Rearing Patterns, *Child Abuse And Neglect* 17:487-494, 1993. This study examines a sample of the delinquents in all Greek institutions and prisons on their perceptions of childhood abuse and neglect in their parents' child rearing.

0402 Spinellis, Calliope D.; Apospori, Eleni; Kranidioti, Maria; Symiyianni, Yiota & Angelopoulou, Nina Key-Findings Of A Preliminary Self-Report Delinquency Study In Athens, Greece, pp 288-318 in Junger-Tas, Josine; Terlouw, Gert-Jan & Klein, Malcolm W. (eds.) *Delinquent Behavior Among Young People In The Western World: First Results Of The International Self-Report Delinquency Study*. Amsterdam/New York: Kugler, 1994. This chapter reports the findings from a self-reported delinquency survey carried out in the city of Athens, Greece.

0403 Van Looy, Herman Youth Violence In Ancient Athens: 5th And 4th Century B.C., pp 71-126 in Hess, Albert G. & Clement, Priscilla F. (eds.) *History Of Juvenile Delinquency: A Collection Of Essays On Crime Committed By Young Offenders, In History And In Selected Countries, Vol. I.* Aalen, Germany: Scientia Verlag, 1990. Based on information regarding the "leisured" classes of ancient Greece, this chapter offers an extensive discussion of youth violence, including gang behavior, in Athens during the 4th and 5th centuries B.C.

0404 Vidali, Sophie Youth Deviance And Social Exclusion In Greece, pp 339-349 in Ruggiero, Vincenzo; South, Nigel & Taylor, Ian (eds.) *The New European Criminology: Crime And Social Order In Europe.* New York, New York: Routledge, 1998. Using secondary sources, this chapter discusses the politicization, evolution of youth subcultures, and marginalization and their impact on criminalization of youth in Athens.

Guyana

0405 Dodd, David J. & Parris, Michael An Urban Plantation: Aspects Of Crime And Delinquency In Georgetown, Guyana, *International Journal Of Criminology And Penology* 5:31-61, 1977. In this study of the incidence of delinquent behavior and its determinants in Georgetown, the authors suggest that crimes tend to be committed largely by Afro-Guyanese teenagers and young adult males, most of whom live in poor urban neighborhoods.

Hong Kong

0406 Cheung, Yuet W. Family, School, Peer, And Media Predictors Of Adolescent Deviant Behavior In Hong Kong, *Journal Of Youth And Adolescence* 26:569-596, 1997. This study attempts to assess the importance of family, peer group, and school and media variables in the delinquent behavior of Hong Kong secondary-school children.

0407 Cheung, Yuet Wah & Ng, Agnes M. C. Social Factors In Adolescent Deviant Behavior In Hong Kong: An Integrated Theoretical Approach, *International Journal Of Comparative And Applied Criminal Justice* 12:27-45, 1988. Using variables from major theories, this study sought to identify the social correlates of deviant behavior among Hong Kong school children.

0408 Gaylord, Mark S. Hong Kong, pp 160-174 in Shoemaker, Donald J. (ed.) *International Handbook On Juvenile Justice*. Westport, Connecticut: Greenwood, 1996. This chapter offers an extensive discussion of the juvenile justice system of Hong Kong.

0409 Japan Ministry Of Justice Research And Training Institute Hong Kong, pp 3-7 in *Asia Crime Report No. 1*. Tokyo, Japan: United Nations Asia and Far East Institute, 1993. Chapter provides some official data on rates of juvenile delinquency in Hong Kong.

0410 Kwan, Tsung Pui The Correction Of Young Offenders In Hong Kong, pp 43-50 in Hideo, Utsuro (ed.) *Materials Produced During The 78th International Seminar On Contemporary Achievements And Future Perspectives In Policies For Corrections*. Tokyo, Japan: UNAFEI, 1988. The institutions for dealing with juvenile offenders in Hong Kong are described and offers data on characteristics of young offenders and processing.

0411 Lee, Francis W. L.; Lo, T. Wing & Wong, Dennis S. W. Intervention In The Decision Making Of Youth Gangs, *Groupwork* 9:292-302, 1996. This study sought to identify the structural and subcultural factors that influence decision making by Hong Kong gang youths.

0412 Leung, Kwok & Lau, Sing Effects Of Self-Concept And Perceived Disapproval Of Delinquent Behavior In School Children, *Journal Of Youth And Adolescence* 18:345-359, 1989. Based on data from students in Hong Kong schools, this study sought to reveal the intricate relationships between self-concept and delinquent behavior.

0413 Vagg, Jon Delinquency And Shame: Data From Hong Kong, *British Journal Of Criminology* 38:247-264, 1998. Based on published self-report and offender studies, this study examines Braithwaite's theory of "reintegrative shaming" in pre-1997 Hong Kong and suggests some modification of the idea.

0414 Wong, Connie S. Y.; Tang, Catherine S. K. & Schwarzer, Ralf Psychological Correlates Of Substance Use: Comparing High School

Students With Incarcerated Offenders In Hong Kong, *Journal Of Drug Education* 27:147-172, 1997. The prevalence of drug use among Hong Kong youth from self-reproted behavior was the focus of this research.

0415 Wong, Ngai-Ying & Lau, S. Effects Of Self-monitoring And Perceived Approval Of Delinquent Behavior Among Hong Kong Adolescents, *Journal Of Youth And Adolescence* 22:191-200, 1993. The mediating effects of self-monitoring on behavior and perceptions of approval from relevant others was the subject of this research.

0416 Yip, Tak Chu Juvenile Delinquency And Drug Abuse Problems In Hong Kong, pp 118-126 in United Nations Asia And Far East Institute (ed.) *Resource Material Series No 21.* Tokyo, Japan: UNAFEI, 1982. This document presents trends in delinquency, reasons for an upsurge in these rates, some information on juvenile justice administration and treatment of drug abusing youths.

Hungary

0417 Vigh, Jozsef Problems Of Crime Causation In Hungary, *Eurocriminology* 3:147-157, 1990. In this review of post World War II crime trends and judicial policy in Poland, it was found that during the 1980s, the number and proportion of crimes committed by children and juveniles increased sharply.

0418 Walter, Michael & Fischer, Wolfgang Juvenile Delinquency Structures And Forms Of Dealing With It In Budapest And Hamburg, *International Journal Of Offender Therapy And Comparative Criminology* 33:1-20, 1989. In this study comparing delinquency in Budapest, Hungary and Hamburg, West Germany a striking correspondence between the rates was found.

Iceland

0419 Bernburg, Jon Gunnar & Thorlindsson, Thorolfur Adolescent Violence, Social Control, And The Subculture Of Delinquency: Factors Related To Violent Behavior And Nonviolent Delinquency, *Youth And Society* 30:445-460, 1999. This study attempts to determine if violence is part of a general subculture of delinquency and investigates the relationship of variables adapted from social control theories to violent and nonviolent delinquency.

0420 Sigurdsson, Jon F. & Gudjonsson, Gisli H. The Psychological Characteristics Of 'False Confessors.' A Study Among Icelandic Prison Inmates And Juvenile Offenders, *Personality And Individual Differences*

20:321-329, 1996. Data obtained from psychological tests were used in comparing the psychological characteristics of 62 prison inmates who claimed to have made a "false confession" during a police interview with those of other inmates.

0421 Sigurdsson, Jon F. & Gudjonsson, Gisli H. The Psychological Characteristics Of Juvenile Alcohol And Drug Users, *Journal Of Adolescence* 19:41-46, 1996. In a study investigating whether personality tests could differentiate between alcohol and drug users among juvenile offenders, it was found that the scores of drug users and others differed.

0422 Skinner, William F. Delinquency, Crime, And Development: A Case Study Of Iceland, *Journal Of Research In Crime And Delinquency* 23:268-294, 1986. This research presents data on the occurrence of 17 types of delinquency among a sample of young adolescents residing in Reykjavik.

India

0423 Channabasavanna, S. M.; Mohan, Isaac K. & Bhaskar, M. S. Juvenile Delinquency: A Social-Demographic Study, *Indian Journal Of Criminology And Criminalistics* 1:47-49, 1981. This article offers a brief discussion of the social-demographic characteristics of delinquency in an Indian city.

0424 Hartjen, Clayton A. & Kethineni, Sesharajani Delinquency In Comparative Perspective: India, *International Journal Of Comparative And Applied Criminal Justice* 16:317-328, 1992. Article describes rates and forms of delinquency in India.

0425 Hartjen, Clayton A. Delinquency, Development, And Social Integration In India, *Social Problems* 29:464-473, 1982. Several socioeconomic features of Indian society ensure that young people are integrated into the dominant social system and deter the development of an adolescent subculture separate from adult society.

0426 Japan Ministry Of Justice Research And Training Institute India, pp 8-13 in United Nations Asia And Far East Institute (ed.) *Asia Crime Report No. 1*. Tokyo, Japan: UNAFEI, 1993. Official rates of juvenile delinquency in India are the subject of this chapter.

0427 Priyadarsini, S. Crime News In Newspapers: A Case Study In Tamil Nadu, India, *Deviant Behavior* 5:313-326, 1984. The attitudes and perceptions of the public regarding youthful misconduct as reflected in newspaper coverage is the focus of this research.

0428 Priyadarsini, S. Public Perceptions Of Drinking By Juveniles In India, *Journal Of Studies On Alcohol*, 42:7:594-603, 1981. Attitudes of the public toward illegal juvenile alcohol use in a 'dry' state in India is explored in this article based on survey data.

0429 Sandhu, Harjit S. Low Rates Of Delinquency And Crime In India. *Indian Journal Of Criminology* 15:9-16, 1987. The author argues that the Indian family serves as insulation against delinquency by virtue of its support, responsibility, and desire to maintain a good reputation in the community.

0430 Sarkar, Chandana *Juvenile Delinquency In India: An Etiological Analysis*. Delhi, India: Daya Publishing House, 1987. Based on interviews and official statistics, this book describes a study of the etiology of delinquency in India claiming that industrialization and urbanization is behind the rising offense rate.

0431 Sharma, D. D. *Young Delinquents In India*. Jaipur, India: Printwell, 1996. This is a volume bsed on interviews and observations condcted in three reformatories in the state of Rajasthan. 209p.

0432 Wani, Abdul Latif Juvenile Delinquency In India, *Social Defence* 20:5-17, 1984. This review of official rates of juvenile delinquency suggests that it is not as serious a problem as faced by other countries.

Indonesia

0433 Hadisuprapto, Paulus Attachment And Delinquency In Javanese Society pp 61-70 in Strang, Heather & Vernon, Julia (eds.) *International Trends In Crime: East Meets West*. Canberra, Australia: Australian Institute of Criminology, 1992. This chapter reports the results of a self-report delinquency study in Java designed to test notions of attachment and delinquency.

Iran

0434 Nakhshab, Sirous *Juvenile Delinquency In Tehran, Iran: An Examination Of Sutherland's Theory Of Differential Association*. Ann Arbor, Michigan: University Microfilms International, 1979. In this research the delinquent acts of juveniles in Tehran were used to test Sutherland's theory of differential association. 153p.

Iraq

0435 Al-Jumaily, Fathia H. *Rural Migration And Juvenile Delinquency In Iraq: A Case Study Of Medenat Al-Thowrah In Baghdad.* Ann Arbor, Michigan: University Microfilms International, 1984. This is a study of juvenile delinquency among the urban immigrants and non-immigrants in Iraq. 129p.

0436 Chambers, Carl D. & Inciardi, James A. Deviant Behavior In The Middle East: A Study Of Delinquency In Iraq, *Criminology* 9:291-315, 1971. This study of deviant behavior among juveniles in Iraq provided a baseline of information on the incidence and types of delinquency, characteristics of delinquents, alternative handling of detected offenders, and rehabilitative efforts for those adjudicated.

Ireland

0437 Harvey, Brian & Menton, Mary Ireland's Young Homeless, *Children And Youth Services Review* 11:31-43, 1989. Historical context of homeless children, the origins of National Child Care Service, and data on age of hostel residents are some of the topics included in this article.

0438 Shorts, Ivor D. Delinquency By Association? Outcome Of Joint Participation By At-Risk And Convicted Youths In A Community-Based Program, *British Journal Of Criminology* 26:156-163, 1986. Testing differential association ideas, this study found that there is no relationship between contact in the program by at-risk minors with convicted offenders and more serious future criminality.

Israel

0439 Addad, Moshe & Leslau, Avraham Immoral Judgement, Extraversion, Neuroticism, And Criminal Behavior, *International Journal Of Offender Therapy And Comparative Criminology* 34:1-13, 1990. This article reports on a study focusing on the moral development and delinquency of Israeli adults and juveniles.

0440 Barnea, Zipora; Teichman, Meir & Rahav, Giora Substance Use And Abuse Among Deviant And Non-Deviant Adolescents In Israel, *Journal Of Drug Education* 23:223-236, 1993. This study investigated if young people's use of psychoactive substances is strongly associated with social deviance.

0441 Cohen, Ben-Zion & Zeira, Ruth Social Control, Delinquency, And Victimization Among Kibbutz Adolescents, *International Journal Of*

Offender Therapy And Comparative Criminology 43:503-513, 1999. The results of a multivariate analysis of youths' behavior in a kibbutz are consistent with social control theory.

0442 Cromer, Gerald Drama As Catharsis And Catalyst: Two Ways Of Preventing Delinquency, *International Journal Of Offender Therapy And Comparative Criminology* 22:91-96, 1978. This paper asserts that drama groups in deprived areas in Israel have proved valuable in involving young people in creative work in which they express their despair and feelings of alienation and force the community to understand their grievances.

0443 Geiger, Brenda & Fischer, Michael *Family, Justice, And Delinquency*. Westport, Connecticut: Greenwood Press, 1995. This study examined self-reported delinquency among communally-reared children on an Israeli kibbutz and children raised in the traditional nuclear family. 143p.

0444 Hassin, Yael Jewish And Arab Juvenile Delinquency In Israel: The Problem And Its Remedies, *International Journal Of Comparative And Applied Criminal Justice* 11:213-230, 1987. This paper presents a review of juvenile delinquency in Israel, focusing on legislation, theoretical models, and the agencies for juvenile justice.

0445 Hassin, Yael Juvenile Delinquency In Israel 1948-1977: Patterns And Trends, pp 25-50 in Spitzer, Steven (ed.) *Research In Law, Deviance And Social Control, Vol. 5*. Greenwich, Connecticut: JAI Press, 1983. Based on official data, this study investigated the main trends and patterns of juvenile delinquency in Israel from its inception in 1948 until 1977.

0446 Hassin, Yael Illicit Driving (Joy Riding) By Minors In Israel, *Crime And Social Deviance* 10:57-73, 1982. This study examined illicit driving in Israel and developed a typology of youths who were convicted of illicit driving.

0447 Iram, Yaacov School Violence In Israel, pp 72-84 in Ohsako, Toshio (ed.) *Violence At School: Global Issues And Interventions*. Paris, France: United Nations Educational, Scientific and Cultural Organization, 1997. This chapter describes some aspects of violence in schools in Israel.

0448 Nachson, Israel & Rotenberg, Mordechai Perception Of Violence By Institutionalized Offenders, *Journal Of Criminal Law And Criminology* 68:454-457, 1977. This study examined the effect on perception of personal experiences with violence and reports that juvenile delinquents gave more violent responses than did the control subjects.

0449 Rahav, Giora Israel, pp 68-71 in Hoffman, Allan M. & Summers, Randal W. (eds.) *Teen Violence: A Global View*. Westport, Connecticut: Greenwood, 2001. This chapter in a multi-country anthology describes violence by teens in Israel and official responses to it.

0450 Rahav, Giora Birth Order And Delinquency, *British Journal Of Criminology* 20:385-395, 1980. This study found that the relationship between birth-order and delinquency in Israel is mixed.

0451 Rahav, Giora Delinquency And Certain Structural Characteristics Of The Family, pp 20-36 in Shoham, S. Giora (ed.) *Israel Studies In Criminology Volume VII*. Dobbs Ferry, New York: Sheridan House, 1984. The behavioral and other characteristics of young offenders in Israel is the focus of this descriptive study.

0452 Rahav, Giora Family Relations And Delinquency In Israel, *Criminology* 14:259-270, 1976. The connection between intrafamily relationships and delinquency among different social strata in Israel was studied in this sample of boys who were arrested in the Tel Aviv metropolitan area.

0453 Rahav, Giora Family Size And Delinquency, *Sociology And Social Research* 66:42-51, 1981. Estimates of official delinquency rates for Israel show that they rise rapidly as the number of children in the family increases.

0454 Sagi, Abraham & Eisikovits, Zvi Juvenile Delinquency And Moral Development, *Criminal Justice And Behavior* 8:79-93, 1981. A morality test administered to a sample of youths in Israel found that in most measures of moral development, nondelinquents scored better than delinquents.

0455 Sherer, Moshe Peer Group Norms Among Jewish And Arab Juveniles In Israel, *Criminal Justice And Behavior* 18:267-286, 1991. This study of Jewish and Arab youths in Israel found that the Arab street corner youths express more negative norms compared to Arab or Israli school or Israeli street corner youths.

0456 Shichor, David & Amir, Menachem Some Ethnic Aspects Of Official Delinquency In Israel, *California Sociologist* 2:69-83, 1979. An analysis of official data on juvenile delinquency in Israel found that juveniles of Asian-African descent were more delinquent than were juveniles of European or American descent.

0457 Shichor, David & Kirschenbaum, Alan Juvenile Delinquency And New Towns: The Case Of Israel, pp 95-108 in Friday, Paul C. & Stewart, V. Lorne (eds.) *Youth Crime And Juvenile Justice: International Perspec-*

tives. New York, Praeger, 1977. This study sought to explore the extent and depth of juvenile delinquency in Israeli development (new) towns and to investigated the connections between this phenomenon and various socioeconomic indicators.

0458 Shoham, Efrat Family Characteristics Of Delinquent Youth In Time Of War, *International Journal Of Offender Therapy And Comparative Criminology* 38:247-258, 1994. This research sought to find if rising delinquency during war time in Israel is associated with family variables.

0459 Shoham, S. Giora Drug And Alcohol Involvement Among Israeli Youth, pp 54-87 in Shoham, S. Giora (ed.) *Israel Studies In Criminology Volume VII*. Dobbs Ferry, New York: Sheridan House, 1984. The author found a connection between peer/family relationships and drug involvement among Israeli 9th-12th graders.

0460 Shoham, S. Giora; Segal, Esther & Rahav, Giora Secularization, Deviance And Delinquency Among Israeli Arab Villagers, pp 72-85 in Shoham, S. Giora (ed.) *Israel Studies In Criminology, Vol. 3*. Jerusalem, Israel: Jerusalem Academic Press, 1976. The authors examine cultural conflict theory among a sample of 17-25 year old Arab males.

0461 Somer, Eli & Braunstein, Anat Are Children Exposed To Interparental Violence Being Psychologically Maltreated? *Aggression And Violent Behavior* 4:449-456, 1999. This paper reviews research on childhood witnessing of interparental violence.

0462 Weller, Leonard & Tiel, Armon Self-Concept And Perception Of Parents, Teachers And Friends Of First-Time and Recidivist Delinquents, pp 86-96 in Shoham, S. Giora (ed.) *Israel Studies In Criminology, Vol. 3*. Jerusalem, Israel: Jerusalem Academic Press, 1976. Youths were interviewed to examine how self-concept and attitudes might relate to behavior.

Italy

0463 Baldry, Anna C. & Farrington, David P. Types Of Bullying Among Italian School Children, *Journal Of Adolescence* 22:423-426, 1999. This study describes the types and frequencies of bullying experienced by boys and girls in a middle school in Rome.

0464 Baldry, Anna Constanza Italy, pp 73-85 in Hoffman, Allan M. & Summers, Randal W. (eds.) *Teen Violence: A Global View*. Westport, Connecticut: Greenwood Press, 2001. This chapter describes Italy's low delinquency rate and lack of public perception of teen violence.

0465 Gatti, Uberto & Verde, Alfredo Moving Away From The Penal System: An Italian Approach To The Problem Of Juvenile Delinquency (S'Éloigner Du Système Penal: Une Approache Du Probléme De La Délinquance Juvénile En Italie), *Revue Internationale De Criminologie Et De Police Technique* 41:49-65, 1988. This study traces the increase in juvenile delinquency in Genoa, Italy to the breakdown of social control in employment, family, school and peer control. French, with English summary.

0466 Charmet, Gustavo Pietropolli New Forms Of Juvenile Delinquency: Psychological Aspects, pp 73-78 in United Nations Crime Prevention And Criminal Justice Program International Scientific And Professional Advisory Council (ed.) *Juveniles And Delinquency: In The Italian And European Context.* Milan, Italy, 1995 This chapter analyses the psychological aspects of some of the new forms of juvenile delinquency that have been observed in the metropolitan Milan.

0467 De Leo, Gaetano New Forms Of Juvenile Delinquency: Criminological Aspects, pp 79-86 in United Nations Crime Prevention And Criminal Justice Program International Scientific And Professional Advisory Council (ed.) *Juveniles And Delinquency: In The Italian And European Context.* Milan, Italy, 1995. This chapter briefly describes four new forms of delinquency that are becoming recognizable in Italy.

0468 Eyben, Emiel Youthful (Mis)behavior In Roman Antiquity, pp 127-230 in Hess, Albert G & Clement, Priscilla F. (eds.) *History Of Juvenile Delinquency: A Collection Of Essays On Crime Committed By Young Offenders, In History And In Selected Countries, Vol. I.* Aalen, Germany: Scientia Verlag, 1990. This chapter offers an extensive description of youth in Ancient Rome, focusing on lifestyles, status, and hings that may have influenced misconduct on their part.

0469 Gatti, Uberto; Fossa, Giovanni; Lusetti, Eleonara; Marugo, Maria Ida; Russo, Gaetana & Traverso, Giovanni Battista Self-Reported Delinquency In Three Italian Cities, pp 267-287 in Junger-Tas, Josine; Terlouw, Gert-Jan & Klein, Malcolm W. (eds.) *Delinquent Behavior Among Young People In The Western World: First Results Of The International Self-Report Delinquency Study.* Amsterdam/New York: Kugler, 1994. The authors present findings from a self-reported delinquency survey carried out in Genoa, Messina and Siena, Italy.

0470 Sorcioni, Maurizio The Drift Of Juvenile Deviance: An Analysis Of The Italian Situation, pp 9-30 in United Nations Crime Prevention And Criminal Justice Program International Scientific And Professional Advisory Council (ed.) *Juveniles And Delinquency: In The Italian And Euro-*

pean Context. Milan, Italy, 1995. This chapter describes the structure of juvenile "deviance" in Italy based on available data and some innovations in juvenile justice proceedings.

0471 Stefanizzi, Sonia Reflections On Juvenile Delinquency In The Urban Area Of Milan, pp 31-32 in United Nations Crime Prevention And Criminal Justice Program International Scientific And Professional Advisory Council (ed.) *Juveniles And Delinquency: In The Italian And European Context.* Milan, Italy, 1995. This brief chapter describes some observations on studies designed to assess marginality and urban space on the genesis of delinquency in Milan.

Ivory Coast

0472 Brillon, Yves Acculturation, Deviance And Criminality In Black Africa (Acculuration, Déviance Et Criminalité En Afrique Noire), *Revue Internationale De Criminologie Et De Police Technique* 60:385-393, 1987. This article deals with the role of ancestral tradition in the life of African youth and the urban realities that propel them into delinquency.

0473 Hérault, Georges Youth, Street Culture And Urban Violence In Africa: Factors, Parameters And Strategies For Change (Jeunes, Culture De La Rue Et Violence Urbaine En Afrique: Invariants, Paramètres Et Stratégies Du Changement), pp 1-8 in Hérault, Georges & Adesanmi, Pius (eds.) *Youth, Street Culture And Urban Violence In Africa: Proceedings Of The International Symposium In Abidjan 5-7 May, 1997 (Jeunes, Culture De La Rue Et Violence Urbaine En Afrique: Actes Du Symposium International D'Abidjan 5-7 Mai 1997).* Ibadan, Nigeria: French Institute for Research in Africa, 1997. Based on a 1994 study in the Ivory Coast, the author addreses the causes and the spiral of violence among youth as well as various strategies to combat it. 415p. French.

0474 Koudou, Opadou Family Life: Their Characteristics And Their Effects On The Development Of Socially Maladjusted Children In The Ivory Coast (Les Évènement De Vie Familiale: Leurs Caracteristiques Et Effets Sur Le Développement Des Comportements Inadaptés Sociaux Chez L'Enfant De 8 À 14 Ans En Côte D'Ivoire) *Revue Internationale De Criminologie Et De Police Technique* 49:94-104, 1996. This article addresses the role of family factors in the Ivory Coast and delinquency. French with English summary.

0475 Koudou, Opadou "Secondary" Family Dissociation In The Ivory Coast And Delinquent Behavior Of Adolescents (Familles Dissociées "Secondaieres" En Côte D'Ivoire Et Compartement Délinquant Des Adolescents), *Revue Internationale De Criminologie Et De Police Technique* 67:179-186, 1994. In this article the author explores the role of family dissociation in juvenile delinquency in the Ivory Coast.

0476 Ouizan-Bi, Hughes The Street Children Of Abidjan: Research And Local Reality (Les Enfants De La Rue À Abidjan De La Recherche-Action À L'action De Terrain), pp 281-284 in Hérault, Georges & Adesanmi, Pius (eds.) *Youth, Street Culture And Urban Violence In Africa: Proceedings Of The International Symposium In Abidjan 5-7 May, 1997 (Jeunes, Culture De La Rue Et Violence Urbaine En Afrique: Actes Du Symposium International D'Abidjan 5-7 Mai 1997)*. Ibadan, Nigeria: French Institute for Research in Africa, 1997. This chapter summarizes the ages, gender, level of education, family and economic situation of the street children in Abidjan. French.

0477 Poitou, Danièle Traditional Practices And Processes Of Marginalization Of African Youth (Pratiques Traditionelles Et Processus De Marginalisation De La Jeunesse Africaine), *Revue Internationale De Criminologie Et De Police Technique*:60:394-407, 1987. This articles deals with the role and structure of the family, education and social habits in the life of youth who are marginalized in Africa.

0478 Sissoko, Alain Abidjan: A Relatively Well-Managed Case? (Abidjan: Une Situation Relativement Bien Maîtrisée?), pp 247-284 in Hérault, Georges & Adesanmi, Pius (eds.) *Youth, Street Culture And Urban Violence In Africa: Proceedings Of The International Symposium In Abidjan 5-7 May, 1997 (Jeunes, Culture De La Rue Et Violence Urbaine En Afrique: Actes Du Symposium International D'Abidjan 5-7 Mai 1997).* Ibadan, Nigeria: French Institute for Research in Africa, 1997. This chapter concerns street children in Abidjan, their survival activities and criminal subculture. French with English summary.

Jamaica

0479 Allen, Frederick Jamaica, pp 87-96 in Hoffman, Allan M. & Summers, Randal W. (eds.) *Teen Violence: A Global View*. Westport, Connecticut: Greenwood, 2001. Discusses the rising teen violence in Jamaica due to poverty, single parent households, and other socioeconomic factors.

0480 Mahabir, Cynthia Crime In The Caribbean: Robbers, Hustlers and Warriors, *International Journal Of The Sociology Of Law* 16:315-338, 1988. Article describes how urban gangs developed in post-war Jamaica and Trinidad.

Japan

0481 Becker, Carl B. Report From Japan: Causes And Controls Of Crime In Japan, *Journal of Criminal Justice* 16:425-435, 1988. Recent upward trends in juvenile crime in Japan are discussed with a description of the informal social control mechanism of "ijime" (ridicule) among school children.

0482 Cook, Schura Euller Social And Cultural Factors Significant For Low Crime Rates In Japan, pp 181-192 in Hideo, Utsuro (ed.) *Material Produced During The 78th International Seminar On Contemporary Achievements And Future Perspective In Policies For Corrections*. Tokyo, Japan: UNAFEI, 1988. This article describes the various historical, social and cultural aspects of Japanese society that seem to inhibit delinquency and crime.

0483 Crystal, David S. Concepts Of Deviance In Children And Adolescents: The Case Of Japan, *Deviant Behavior* 15:2421-266, 1994. The author reviews the theoretical, clinical and research findings in light of current Japanese concern with bullying, school problems and violence against parents.

0484 Fenwick, Charles R. Culture, Philosophy And Crime: The Japanese Experience, *International Journal Of Comparative And Applied Criminal Justice* 9:67-81, 1985. The author tries to account for the varied Japanse trends in crime within the context of the cultural traditions Japan.

0485 Fenwick, Charles R. The Juvenile Delinquency Problem In Japan: Application Of A Role Relationship Model, *International Journal Of Comparative And Applied Criminal Justice* 7:119-128, 1983. The author argues that recent increases in youth crime in Japan can be explained by the role relationship model that increasing attachment to peers due to breakdown of informal social control and relationships enhances the probability of delinquency.

0486 Goldstein, Susan & Ibaraki, Toshio Japan: Aggression And Aggression Control In Japanese Society, pp 313-324 in Goldstein, Arnold & Segall, Marshall H. (eds.) *Aggression in Global Perspective*. New York, New York: Pergamon, 1983. This chapter has a section on intra-school violence and a table of intra-family violence offenders by gender and age.

0487 Harada, Yutaka & Yonezato, S. Stability And Change In The Longitudinal Patterns Of Delinquency: A Comparison Of Two Birth Cohorts, *Reports Of The National Research Institute Of Police Science* 38:83-92, 1997. This study of offending among Japanese juveniles analyzes the offense histories of two birth cohorts up to age 19 found a sharp decline in offending in the later teenage years. Japanese with English summary.

0488 Harada, Yutaka Adjustment To School, Life Course Transitions, And Changes In Delinquent Behavior In Japan, pp 35-60 in Blau, Zena Smith & Hagan, John (ed.) *Current Perspective On Aging And The Life Cycle: Delinquency And Disrepute In The Life Course, Vol. 4*. Greenwich, Connecticut: JAI Press, 1995. The author examines the relationship between educational sorting and the variation between early peak and sharp decline in adolescent crime.

0489 Harada, Yutaka An Event History Analysis On The Effect Of School Maladjustment, *Reports Of The National Research Institute Of Police Science* 32:38-52, 1991. The arrest records of about 10,000 males and females from a 1970 birth-cohort reveals that those who have problems with school tend to become recidivists and often this subsequent delinquency declines once the juveniles have graduated from junior high school. Japanese with English summary.

0490 Harada, Yutaka; Suzuki, Shingo; Inokuchi, Yumiko & Suzuki, Mamoru A Study On The Prevalence And Backgrounds Of Self-reported Deviant Behavior Among Junior And Senior high school Students, *Reports Of The National Research Institute Of Police Science* 36:65-81, 1995. Reports on the 1995 incidence and prevalence of delinquent behavior of male and female junior and senior high school students. Japanese with English summary.

0491 Hoshino, Kanehiro Community Programs For Preventing Delinquency And Internalization Of The Bond To Conventional Society, *Reports Of The National Research Institute Of Police Science* 30:149-163, 1989. This study found support for several aspects of social bond theory among 2408 juveniles studied. Japanese with English summary.

0492 Inokuchi, Yumiko The Relationships Between The Counseling Skills Applied To Guardians And Changes In The Problematic Behavior Of Children, *Reports Of The National Research Institute Of Police Science* 35:1-12, 1994. The different outcomes of counselors' attitudes toward juvenile delinquents who were receiving counseling for delinquency prevention are discussed in this research paper. Japanese with English summary.

0493 Inoue, Yutaka; Matsuhasi, Akihide & Kiyonaga, Kenji The Relations Between Frequency Of Subsequent Delinquency And Misconduct Committed By Juveniles Under 14 Years Of Age, *Reports Of The National Research Institute Of Police Science* 30:49-56, 1989. The authors feel misconduct continues among male delinquents born in 1972 and arrested at 14 in Aichi and Thiba refectures. Japanese with English summary.

0494 Ito, Fujie An Analysis Of The Background Of Sexual Misconducts, *Reports Of The National Research Institute Of Police Science* 28:63-71, 1987. The author found that among 623 sexually delinquent girls compared with 1431 non-delinquent girls from junior and senior high school, there are a weak attachment to mother, parental conflict, fewer female friends at school and more males friends on street, greater dependency on males, a lack of moral sense, undervaluing of women's generosity and sincerity. Japanese with English summary.

0495 Ito, Fujie Relationship Between The Extent Of Deviance In Life Style And The Types Of Sexual Misconducts, *Reports Of The National Research Institute Of Police Science* 28:52-62, 1987. The author found that girls subject to police guidance due to sexual misconduct varied from serious to mild deviance. Japanese with English summary.

0496 Japan Ministry Of Justice *Summary Of The White Paper On Crime 1998*. Ministry of Justice: Tokyo, Japan: Research and Training Institute,1998. The English-language summary of the Ministry of Justice's annual White Paper on Crime for 1998 presents official data highlights juvenile delinquency and trends in crime as well as criminal justice system activities. 35p.

0497 Japan Ministry Of Justice *Summary Of The White Paper On Crime: 1979*. Tokyo, Japan: Research and Training Institute, 1980. Several articles deal with typology of delinquent behavior among the residents in a training school, characteristics and outcomes of the juveniles admitted to classification homes and the differential treatment of juvenile delinquents. 66p.

0498 Japan Ministry Of Justice *Summary Of The White Paper On Crime 1978*. Tokyo, Japan: Research and Training Institute, 1979. Violent crimes committed by youthful extremists are discussed and chapter IV has a flow chart of the Japanese juvenile justice system and a discussion of juvenile delinquency in Japan. 66p.

0499 Japan Ministry Of Justice *Bulletin Of The Criminological Research Department, 1977*. Tokyo, Japan: Research and Training Institute, 1978. This report presents the findings of a multi-year study of juvenile delinquents in custody. 31p.

0500 Japan Ministry Of Justice *Summary Of The White Paper On Crime 1977*. Tokyo, Japan: Research and Training Institute, 1978. This report includes, under the topic on special crimes and criminals in section III, data on juveniles' involvement in crime. 55p.

0501 Japan Ministry Of Justice *Summary Of The White Paper On Crime: 1976*. Tokyo, Japan: Research and Training Institute, 1977. Part III deals with juvenile crime trends, statistics on penal code and other special law offenders and their age groups, data on their offenses, school and employment status, disposition and treatment. 53p.

0502 Japan Ministry Of Justice *Bulletin Of The Criminological Research Department 1976*. Tokyo, Japan: Research and Training Institute, 1977. This report has several short pieces by multiple authors who deal with various factors that contribute to juvenile delinquency. 36p.

0503 Japan Ministry Of Justice *Summary Of The White Paper On Crime: 1975*. Tokyo, Japan: Research and Training Institute , 1976. This official data on crime in general has some details on juvenile offenders and their offenses. 47p.

0504 Japan Ministry Of Justice *Bulletin Of The Criminological Research Department 1975*. Tokyo, Japan: Research and Training Institute, 1976. This document has a number of papers on delinquency and the impact of juvenile corrections. 58p.

0505 Japan Ministry Of Justice Research And Training Institute Japan, pp 14-24 in United Nations Asia And Far East Institute (ed.) *Asia Crime Report No. 1*. Tokyo, Japan:UNAFEI, 1993. Chapter provides some official data on juvenile delinquency rates in Japan.

0506 Kersten, Joachim Street Youths, Bosozoku, And Yakuza: Subculture Formation And Societal Reactions In Japan, *Crime & Delinquency* 39:277-295, 1993. Criticizing the Western notions of Japanese "shame culture" or policing as the cause of low rates of Japanese crime, this article describes the importance, size, and the characteristics of youth subcultures in contemporary Japan.

0507 Kiyonaga, Kenji An Examination Of The Causation Of Subsequent Delinquency By Path Analysis, *Reports Of The National Research Institute Of Police Science* 25:33-42, 1984. This study found that those who had delinquent tendency before 13 had subsequent delinquency involving bodily injury while those who were at high school-level when arrested tend to be involved in property-type offenses. Japanese with English summary.

0508 Kiyonaga, Kenji Effects Of Delinquent Career Before Fourteen Years Old On Subsequent Delinquency, *Report Of The National Research Insti-*

tute Of Police Science 24:26-32, 1983. The author studied the arrest records for recidivism of 520 male delinquents born in 1963 in Aichin prefecture. Japanese with English summary.

0509 Kiyonaga, Kenji The Delinquent Career By Types Of Frequency Of Misbehaviors, *Reports Of The National Research Institute Of Police Science* 23:1-8, 1982. Reports on a 1979-1981 two-year follow-up study of delinquent boys and girls for their re-arrest behavior, family and hous hold characteristics, and academic performance. Japanese with English summary.

0510 Kiyonaga, Kenji; Hoshino, Kanehiro; Uchiyama, Ayako & Ito, Fujie The Relationship Between The Permissiveness To And Experience Of Deviant Behaviors, *Reports Of The National Research Institute Of Police Science* 29:62-81, 1988. The researchers conclude that there is no significant difference between delinquent and non-delinquent male and female school students' attitudes toward serious violations of law, certain infringement of mores and folkways or minor violations of family and school norms. Japanese with English summary.

0511 Kiyonaga, Kenji; Mugishima, Fumio & Takahashi, Yoshiaki Situations Of The Delinquency And The Attitudes Toward Bullying, *Reports Of The National Research Institute Of Police Science* 26:38-55, 1999. The author describes his study and findings from a sample of 304 male and 91 female juveniles arrested for bullying related violence in 1985. English summary.

0512 Kobayashi, Juichi & Suzuki, Mamoru An Empirical Examination Of The Effects Of Community Activities For Preventing Delinquency - Neighborhood-Level Analysis, *Reports Of The National Research Institute Of Police Science* 41:28-38, 2001. This study concludes that neighborhoods with high level of psychological bonds between generations due to older residents' participation in the community activities correlate with lower levels of delinquency. Japanese with English summary.

0513 Kobayashi, Juichi An Analysis Of The Perceptual Difference Between Juvenile Delinquents And Their Parents, *Report Of The National Research Institute Of Police Science* 31:34-48, 1990. This research found that while parents deny their responsibility for their children's delinquency, their delinquent progeny attribute their misconduct to family and parents. Japanese with English summary.

0514 Kobayashi, Juichi Characteristics Of Organized Crime In Japan And Their Policy Implications, *Asian Journal Of Crime Prevention And Criminal Justice* 8:135-176, 1990. While describing organized crime, the author briefly discusses the status of juvenile delinquent gangs with some tables of data on the socioeconomic backgrounds of the organized gang members.

0515 Kobayashi, Juichi Parents' Attribution Of Responsibility For Delinquency Of Their Own And Others, *Report Of The National Research Institute Of Police Science* 31:20-33, 1990. Parents' of delinquent children are less eager to change their attitudes toward their offspring and attribute their children's delinquency to school, teachers and friends as well as attributing personality, school problems and bad social conditions as the cause of delinquency in general. Japanese with English summary.

0516 Kobayashi, Juichi Juveniles' Attribution Of Responsibility For Delinquency Of Their Own And Others, *Report Of The National Research Institute Of Police Science* 30:51-67, 1989. Non-delinquent and recorded delinquent boys' self-report study concludes that more of those who were delinquent evade responsibility for their behavior and seem unwilling to change their behavior by blaming family, friends or school. Japanese with English summary.

0517 Kobayashi, Juichi; Nishimura, Haruo; Takahashi, Yoshiaki; Tozaki, Yoshifumi & Suzuki, Shingo Relations Of School Life And Peers At The Time Of Arrest To Subsequent Delinquency, *Reports Of The National Research Institute Of Police Science* 29:15-26, 1988. The authors found those male and female juveniles who committed more new offenses/recidivists regardless of gender feel more alienated from teachers, schoolmates, school work and club activities and had more friends outside school who were prone to delinquency. Japanese with English summary.

0518 Kobayashi, Juichi A Study On The Junior High school Students' Attitudes Toward Violence: The Structure Of factors Eliciting Violence, *Report Of The National Research Institute Of Police Science* 28:15-26, 1987. More than 1000 male and female students' attitudes toward violence in regard to verbal abuse and intimidation, ignoring or treating someone as an outsider, forcing someone to behave against will, breaking someone's property intentionally, pulling hair, kicking or hitting, injuring with a weapon and so on. Japanese with English summary.

0519 Kumagai, Fumie Filial Violence In Japan, *Victimology* 8:173-194, 1983. This large scale study of 15 and 16-year old abusive and battering adolescents found that mothers were often the victims of these youths with poor peer-relation and lack of social experience.

0520 Ladbrook, Denis A. Why are Crime Rates Higher In Urban Than In Rural Areas? - Evidence From Japan, *The Australian And New Zealand*

Journal Of Criminology 21:81-103, 1988. This article explains rural-urban crime rate difference in terms of social structural variables such as density, migration, and has a good discussion of the demographics of youth in population and crime.

0521 Matsushita, Teruo Youthful Extremism In Japan, pp 97-104 in United Nations Asia And Far East Institute (ed.) *Resource Material Series No. 13.* Tokyo, Japan:UNAFEI, 1977. The author discusses, although not juveniles directly, the recent youthful extremism among Japanese radicals.

0522 Miyazawa, Koichi & Cook, Schura Euller Juvenile Delinquency And Juvenile Justice In Japan, *International Annals Of Criminology* 28:55-65, 1990. This review explores reasons for the relatively low Japanese juvenile delinquency rates compared to other industrialized nations.

0523 Morita, Shoichi; Yokokoshi, Aiko; Muroi, Seiicho & Okudaira, Hiromi A Study On The Educational Activities In Juvenile Training Schools, pp 17-19 in *Bulletin Of The Criminological Research Department*, Ministry of Justice: Tokyo, Japan, 1982. This report is based on the illegal behavior of 3652 boys and girls in the training institutions.

0524 Moriyama, Tadashi The Response To Delinquency By Formal Agencies In Japan: Could It Change Reality, pp 269-278 in Hackler, Jim (ed.) *Official Responses to Problem Juveniles: Some International Reflections.* Euskadi, Spain: The Oñati International Institute for the Sociology of Law, 1991. Discusses delinquency in Japan and feels that the Japanese response reaffirms the belief that much juvenile behavior is temporary and shaming has greater effect than harsh response from the juvenile justice system.

0525 Motoaki, Hiroshi; Souma, Ichiro & Kimura, Hiroshi Behavioral Characteristics Of Juvenile Deviators In Japan: A Study Of The Current Status Of Deviant Behavior Among Japanese High School Boys And Girls, *Japanese Psychological Research* 32:181-191, 1990. This study attempts to predict the delinquent behavior of juveniles by detecting early proclivity for maladjusted deviant behavior.

0526 Mugishima, Fumio; Kiyonaga, Kenji & Takahashi, Yoshiaki On The Occurrence Of The Delinquency And The Attributes Of The Subjects, *Reports Of The National Research Institute Of Police Science* 28:28-37, 1999. This research on male and female delinquents who were arrested found that those youths with poor school performance and those in junior high school tended to engage in delinquency. Japanese with English summary.

0527 Mugishima, Fumio; Kiyonaga, Kenji & Takahashi, Yoshiaki An Investigation Of The Delinquency Related To Bullying: 1. On The Occurrence Of The Delinquency And The Attributes Of The Subjects, *Reports Of The National Research Institute Of Police Science* 26:28-37, 1985. This study investigates the actual conditions of bullying by surveying the records of all delinquents arrested of related offenses related during June-July, 1985. Japanese with English summary.

0528 Nishimura, Haruo; Suzuki, Shingo; Kobayashi, Juichi & Takahashi, Yoshiaki A Study On Subsequent Delinquency During Three Years Among Junior And Senior High School Students Arrested By The Police, *Reports Of The National Research Institute Of Police Science* 30:28-48, 1989. Research on several thousand male and female 12-16 year old students lead the authors to conclude that the earlier the youths' involvement, more numerous are their subsequent illegality and they engage in same kind of deviance. Japanese with English summary.

0529 Nishimura, Haruo; Suzuki, Shingo & Takahashi, Yoshiaki Weakening Of Social Bonds Or Flourishing Of Deviant Motivations? An Empirical Test Of The Control Theory, *Reports Of The National Research Institute Of Police Science* 25:1-12, 1984. This self-report study of Tokyo high school students reports on delinquent and academic behavior, perceptions of parental attitudes, and self-concept. Japanese with English summary.

0530 Nishimura, Haruo A Comparative Analysis On Perception Of Juvenile Delinquency By Social Categories *Reports Of The National Research Institute Of Police Science* 24:1-15, 1983. Attitudes of adults', teachers, family court officers and corrections officers, probation workers and police officers perceptions of delinquency. Japanese with English summary.

0531 Nishimura, Haruo; Suzuki, Shingo & Takahashi, Yoshiaki An Analysis Of The Conditions Conducive To Juvenile Delinquent Involvement Among High School Students: On Their Deterioration On Inner Control, *Reports Of The National Research Institute Of Police Science* 23:27-50, 1982. Both males and female students' self-reported penal code violations and "misbehaviors" concludes that as delinquency involvement increases, so does out of school involvement. Japanese with English summary.

0532 O'Donoghue, Joseph Violence In Schools, pp 101-108 in Adler, Lenore Loeb & Denmark, Florence L. (eds.) *Violence And The Prevention Of Violence*. Westport, Connecticut: Praeger, 1995. The volume has a summary of Japanese school violence research along with school violence in the United States.

0533 Richeson, Scott *Juvenile Deviance In Japan: Result Of Culture, Institute, Or Community?* Chicago, Illinois: Office of International Criminal Justice, University of Illinois at Chicago, 1997. This review of various explanations for Japan's comparatively low rate of juvenile and young adult criminality argues that the following three factors are important: community policing, institutional and a unique culturally constructed reaction to crime. 60p.

0534 Saisho, Atsuro; Sato, Tsuneko; Yokokoshi, Aiko; Watanabe, Yoshiaki & Sawata, Naoko A Study On The Contents Of Juvenile Delinquency (Second Report) Current Situation Of Juvenile Delinquency By Crime Types, pp 15-16 in *Bulletin Of The Criminological Research Department*, Ministry of Justice: Tokyo, Japan, 1982. This is a very brief description of types of illegality committed by the inmates of juvenile training schools. Saito, Toyoji. Juvenile Delinquency In Japan In The 1980s, *Eurocriminology* 5-6:91-122, 1993. Using official data from diverse sources, this study describes juvenile delinquency trends in Japan in the 1980s.

0535 Sato, Ikuya *Kamikaze Biker: Parody And Anomy In Affluent Japan.* Chicago, Illinois: University of Chicago Press, 1991. This study of the behavior of Japanese "bosozoku"-- hot-rodders and motorcycle gangs -- concludes their youthful behaviors are a form of play and thrill seeking. 277p.

0536 Schneider, Hans Joachim Crime And Its Control In Japan And The Federal Republic Of Germany, *Indian Journal Of Criminology* 17:31-41, 1989. The author compares some crime data from Japan and Germany and discusses the possible causes, includeing an absence of youth subculture, for Japan's low incidence.

0537 Shelley, Louise I. *Crime And Modernization: The Impact Of Industrialization And Urbanization On Crime.* Carbondale, Illinois: Southern Illinois University, 1981. There is a discussion of youthful offenders that includes a brief discussion of Japan. 186p.

0538 Suzuki, Mamoru; Suzuki, Shingo & Harada, Yutaka An Analysis Of The Relationship Between The Level Of Self-Reported Deviant Behavior And Socio-Psychological Factors Size, *Reports Of The National Research Institute Of Police Science* 37:28-39, 1996. This is a 1994-95 self-report study of 950 male and 902 female junior high school and high-school students' 19 deviant behaviors. Japanese with English summary.

0539 Suzuki, Shingo; Inokuchi, Yumiko; Takahawa, Kazumi; Kobayashi, Juichi; Okeda, Seijun & Takahashi, Yoshiaki A Study Of Juvenile Co-Offending: An Analysis Of Offending Process By Offense Type And

Group Size, *Reports Of The National Research Institute Of Police Science* 35:13-29, 1994. The offending patterns of co-offending juveniles are studies in this research of 1659 juveniles of whom 640 had arrest records. Japanese with English summary.

0540 Suzuki, Shingo & Takahawa, Kazumi A Study On The Relationship Between Changes Of Juveniles' Difficulties Faced In Puberty And Self-Reported Delinquency, *Reports Of The National Research Institute Of Police Science* 34:34-44, 1993. This study of junior high school students reports that there is a relationship between perceived difficulties in puberty and delinquent behavior particularly among the older youths. Japanese with English summary.

0541 Suzuki, Shingo & Takahawa, Kazumi Relationship Between Parental Control And Self-Reported Delinquency, *Reports Of The National Research Institute Of Police Science* 33:74-84, 1992. The male and female students surveyed indicate that those youths who were more involved in delinquency also report parents who are concerned with their children's habits. Japanese with English summary.

0542 Suzuki, Shingo An Analysis On Relation Of Coping Resources And Psychological Stress To Delinquency Involvement, *Reports Of The National Research Institute Of Police Science* 30:13-27, 1989. The author found that among male and female students self-control was negatively correlated with both psychological stress and delinquency involvement. Japanese with English summary.

0543 Suzuki, Shingo An Analysis Of Experience Of Stressful Life Events And Developmental And Psychological Changes As Stress Factors, *Reports Of The National Research Institute Of Police Science* 29:27-43, 1988. Self-reported delinquency involvement of 1285 boys and girls in junior high school reveals the importance of stress factors in delinquency. Japanese with English summary.

0544 Suzuki, Shingo Recent Trends In Self-Reported Delinquency Of Junior High School Students Involvement, *Reports Of The National Research Institute Of Police Science* 28:23-27, 1987. It was found that stressful life events, daily disturbance and developmental psychological changes were related to psychological stresses and delinquency involvement among junior high school students. Japanese with English summary.

0545 Suzuki, Shingo; Nishimura, Haruo & Takahashi, Yoshiaki An Analysis Of Conditions Conducive To Delinquency Involvement Among High School And Junior High School Students: On Their Weakened Bonds To Family And School, *Reports Of The National Research Institute Of Police Science 23*:51-69, 1982. This study found that delinquent boys and girls were more maladjusted and discontented with their family and school and had more friends outside school. Japanese with English summary.

0546 Suzuki, Shingo; Nishimura, Haruo & Takahashi, Yoshiaki Patterns Of Self Concept Conducive To Deviant Behavior Among Junior And Senior High School Students, *Reports Of The National Research Institute Of Police Science* 25:42-59, 1984. A survey of several thousand boys and girls from junior and senior high schools focuses on the importance of self-concept in deviant behavior. Japanese with English summary.

0547 Takahashi, Yoshiaki & Shishido, Choichi A Study Of Delinquent Deterrence Through Perceptions, *Reports Of The National Research Institute Of Police Science* 32:14-23, 1991. This 1990 survey of boys and girls in junior and high school tries to measure their perceptions the pain of sanctions and their deterrence. Japanese with English summary.

0548 Takahashi, Yoshiaki; Suzuki, Shingo; Shishido, Choichi; Kobayashi, Juichi & Hoshino, Kanehiro Relationships Between Identity With family And Delinquency, *Reports Of The National Research Institute Of Police Science* 31:1-13, 1990. This research of school boys and girls tries to establish the interaction between the strength of school and family identity and past delinquency and current misbehavior. Japanese with English summary.

0549 Takakuwa, Kazumi; Inokuchi, Yumiko; Hoshino, Kanehiro & Okeda, Seijun Changes In The Lifestyle Of juveniles, *Reports Of The National Research Institute Of Police Science* 34:36-52, 1993. This document reports research into the effects of shorter school-week among delinquent and non-delinquent junior and senior high school students. Japanese with English summary.

0550 Takakuwa, Kazumi; Takahashi, Yoshiaki & Suzuki, Shingo A Follow-up Study On Delinquent Careers Of Glue-Sniffers, *Reports Of The National Research Institute Of Police Science* 33:14-19, 1992. This research based on data from male and female high school students studied the relationship between family, school and family problems and glue-sniffing re-arrest for glue-sniffers delinquency. Japanese with English summary.

0551 Takakuwa, Kazumi; Tamura, Masayuki & Kurusu, Hiromichi Characteristics Of Juveniles Homicide Cases: The Differences By Offenders' Age Groups, *Reports Of The National Research Institute Of Police Science* 35:13-23, 1994. Police records of 14-19 year olds in involved in homicide cases were examined for the patterns and context of their offenses behavior. Japanese with English summary.

0552 Tamura, Masayuki & Mugishima, Fumio An Estimation Of Dark Figures Of Shoplifting Through A Victimization Survey Of Shops, *Reports Of The National Research Institute Of Police Science* 32:1-13, 1991. This is a study of shoplifting in shops selling products that appeal to young people near schools and other areas of youths' assembly. Japanese with English summary.

0553 Tamura, Masayuki A Pattern Analysis Of Delinquent Gangs: On The Traits Of Members' Personality, *Reports Of The National Research Institute Of Police Science* 25:34-41, 1984. The personality traits of boys and girls and different types of delinquency involvement were investigated. Japanese with English summary.

0554 Tamura, Masayuki The Contact With Harmful Environment And Delinquent Behavior, *Reports Of The National Research Institute Of Police Science* 34:61-70, 1993. Male and female junior and senior high-school students were surveyed for the impact of harmful environmental factors such as bars and pubs, pinball parlor, horse race betting, porno movies, soft porno videos and telephone clubs on their delinquent conduct. Japanese with English summary.

0555 Tanioka, Ichiro & Glaser, Daniel School Uniforms, Routine Activities, And The Social Control Of Delinquency In Japan, *Youth And Society* 23:50-75, 1991. This test found support for the hypotheses that frequency of delinquency varies directly with motivated individuals but varies inversely with the guardians' ability to detect and control, as well as with the strength of social bonds between offenders so inclined and their intimate handlers.

0556 Tokoi, Zen Japanese Rehabilitation Services And Community Involvement, pp 85-93 in United Nnations Asia And Far East Institute (ed.) *Resource Material Series No. 14 Parts 1 & 2*. Tokyo, Japan, 1978. The author examines the effects of social change on juvenile crime. 155p.

0557 Uchiyama, Ayako & Amano, Sachiko Parent-Child Relations And Daily Life Of Delinquents: Psychological Interaction Between Parents And Child, *Reports Of The National Research Institute Of Police Science* 34:19-33, 1993. This is a study of perceptual gap between parents and their delinquent progeny compared with non-delinquent school students and their parents. Japanese with English summary.

0558 Uchiyama, Ayako; Okeda, Seijun; Hoshino, Kanehiro; Harada, Yutaka & Mugishima, Fumio Juveniles' Perception Of Boryokudan Represented In The Mass Media, *Reports Of The National Research Institute Of Po-*

lice Science 33:15-25, 1992. A survey of male and female delinquent and non-delinquent youths reveals that their major source of positive images on organized gangs is the mass media and this is particularly more so among delinquents. Japanese with English summary.

0559 Uchiyama, Ayako & Amano, Sachiko Parent-Child Relations And Daily Life Of Delinquents: Habit Formation In Daily Life, *Reports Of The National Research Institute Of Police Science* 32:19-35, 1991. This survey of parents and delinquent and non-delinquent young people tries to establish the relationship between parents' consistency, training and the offsprings' rating of their parent and delinquency. Japanese with English summary.

0560 Uchiyama, Ayako A Study On The Environmental Influence Upon Juvenile Delinquency In Amusement Quarters: Behavior Change After Resorting To Amusement Quarters, *Reports Of The National Research Institute Of Police Science* 26:56-69, 1985. This report is on juvenile delinquents and victims of sex related offenses who after visiting amusement places in Japan exhibit changes in behavior (particularly more frequently among girls) and those who had delinquent careers. Japanese with English summary.

0561 Uchiyama, Ayako A Study On The Daily Life Of Juveniles Committing A Shoplifting, *Reports Of The National Research Institute Of Police Science* 23:70-84, 1982. This study tests the relationship between good daily habits and delinquent and non-delinquent patterns of behavior among youths accused of shoplifting and non-delinquent youths. Japanese with English summary.

0562 Vaughn, Michael S. & Huang, Frank F. Y. Delinquency In The Land Of The Rising Sun: And Analysis Of Juvenile Property Crime In Japan During The Shoma Era, *International Journal of Comparative And Applied Criminal Justice* 16:273-300, 1992. Article describes delinquency in Japan from 1936-1988.

0563 Vaughn, Michael S. Are Japanese Police Practices Increasing Teenaged Arrest Rates? Long-Term Juvenile Delinquency Trends In Nippon From 1936 To 1987, *Police Studies* 13:33-44, 1990. This study of arrest rates for Japanese youth crime during the war, immediate postwar years and modernization eras concludes that total juvenile arrests in Japan have increased at a faster pace than felonious offenses.

0564 Wagatsuma, Hiroshi *Heritage Of Endurance: Family Patterns And Delinquency Formation In Urban Japan*. Berkeley, California: University of California, 1984. A psycho-cultural study of lower class families in Tokyo, this research found evidence of parental attitudes' bearing on juveniles engaging in deviant behavior. 500p.

0565 Watanabe, Kazumi; Tamura, Masayuki & Kurusu, Hiromichi Characteristics Of Juvenile Homicide Cases: Two Differences By Offender-Victim Relationships, *Reports Of The National Institute Of Political Science* 36:29-36, 1995. Most juvenile homicide cases involve unrelated/non-familial other juveniles with prior delinquency and parental behavioral problems. Japanese with English summary.

0566 Yajima, Masami Pre-Delinquent Student Subcultures In Japan: A Comparative Analysis Of Junior High School Students And Adults *International Journal Of Comparative And Applied Criminal Justice* 12:159-175, 1988. This article is based on a survey of more than 1000 boys' and girls' and adults' attitude to vignettes of deviant behavior such as shoplifting, joyriding motorcycles, and disobedience.

0567 Yonekawa, Shigenobu & Hoshino, Kanehiro The Juvenile Delinquents' Ways Of Spending Their Holidays And Their Wishes For Participation In Community Activities, *Reports Of The National Research Institute Of Police Science* 34:1-18, 1993. A large-scale study of delinquent and non-delinquent males and females reveals that the delinquent youths tend not to participate in community activities. Japanese with English summary.

0568 Yonezato, Seiji An Analysis Of The Effect Of Academic Achievement On Delinquent Involvement, *Reports Of The National Research Institute Of Police Science* 33:42-50, 1992. This is a research on the interaction between academic failure and delinquency among male adolescents. Japanese with English summary.

Jordan

0569 Daher, Abatah Dabaan *Levels Of Depression And Anxiety Among Male Juvenile Delinquents And Non-Delinquents In Jordan.* Indiana, Pennsylvania: Department of Criminology, Indiana University of Pennsylvania, 1992. This study sought to determine the level of depression and anxiety among male juvenile delinquents and non-delinquents in Jordan. 135p.

0570 Hussinat, Mohammad M. *Leisure And Crime.* New Delhi, India: Rawat Publications, 1997. The focus of this research is the correlation between leisure and crime among youth in Jordan. 236p.

0571 Irfaifeh, Ayed Awad *Causes Of Juvenile Delinquency In Jordan.* Ann Arbor, Michigan: University Microfilms International, 1990. Using self-reports from 147 male students, this research tests social bonding as a way of preventing delinquency in Jordanian society. 221p.

0572 Obeidat, Zougan Bullying And Violence In The Jordanian School, pp 20-33 in Ohsako, Toshio (ed.) *Violence At School: Global Issues And Interventions.* Paris, France: United Nations Educational Scientific and Cultural Organization, 1997. This chapter offers extensive information on violence in schools and some measures, actual and proposed, to deal with it.

0573 Rbeihat, Sabri A. *Explaining Male Delinquency In Jordan.* Los Angeles, California: Department of Sociology, University of Southern California, 1988. The author addresses the usefulness of official statistics on juvenile delinquency in Jordan and the applicability of various theories in explaining delinquency. 137p.

Kenya

0574 Rodriguez-Torrès, Deyssi Nairobi: Direct From Nairobi's Street Gangs (Nairobi: Les Gangs De La Rue En Direct), pp 9-87 in Hérault, Georges & Adesanmi, Pius (eds.) *Youth, Street Culture And Urban Violence In Africa: Proceedings Of The International Symposium In Abidjan 5-7 May, 1997 (Jeunes, Culture De La Rue Et Violence Urbaine En Afrique: Actes Du Symposium International D'Abidjan 5-7 Mai 1997).* Ibadan, Nigeria: French Institute for Research in Africa, 1997. This study analyses social signs and modes of social and physical survival of street children in Nairobi as well as their involvement in delinquency and violence. French with English Summary.

Kuwait

0575 Murty, K. S.; Al-Lanqawi, Abdullah M. & Roebuck, Julian B. Self-Reported Juvenile Delinquency In Kuwait, *International Journal Of Comparative And Applied Criminal Justice* 14:49-63, 1990. This study explored offense behavior using self-reported delinquency data from 483 male students in Kuwait.

Latvia

0576 Kinis, Uldis Child Criminality In Latvia, pp 176-177 in Cavadino, Paul (ed.) *Children Who Kill.* Winchester, United Kingdom: Waterside, 1996. This brief discussion offers some data on serious violent crime by juveniles and a short discussion of official reaction.

Malaysia

0577 Edwards, Arthur Youth And Crime In Malaysia, *The Asia Journal Of Crime Prevention And Criminal Justice* 8:85-91, 1990. This article provides an overview of youth involvement in crime in Malaysia, secret society activities, runaway and neglected children, and various topics on juvenile justice.

Mexico

0578 Juarez, Francisco; Medina-Mora, Elena; Berenzon, Shoshana; Villatoro, Jorge A.; Carreno, Silvia; Lopez, Elsa K.; Galvan, Jorge & Rojas, Estela Antisocial Behavior: Its Relation To Selected Sociodemographic Variables And Alcohol And Drug Use Among Mexican Students, *Substance Use And Misuse* 33:1437-1459, 1998. This study focuses on self-reported alcohol, other drug use and antisocial behavior of Mexican school children.

Netherlands

0579 Baerveldt, Chris Schools And The Prevention Of Petty Crime: Search For A Missing Link, *Journal Of Quantitative Criminology* 8:79-94, 1992. This study considers the influence of schools, and their staff members, on the delinquent behavior of Dutch pupils.

0580 Beke, B. M. W. A. & Kleiman, W. M. *Youth And Violence: An Analysis Of The 'Hard Core' (Jongeren En Geweldscriminaliteit: Een Nadere Analyze Van De 'Harde Kern')*, Hague, The Netherlands: Ministry of Justice, 1992. This study examines the crime patterns and social background of "hard-core" delinquents. 63p. Dutch with English summary.

0581 Blom, Maria & Van Den Berg, Ton A Typology Of The Life And Work Styles of Heroin Prostitutes, pp 55-69 in Cain, Maureen (ed.) *Growing Up Good: Policing the Behavior of Girls in Europe*. Newbury Park, California: Sage, 1989. Discusses how among Amsterdam's heroin addicted Dutch prostitutes including runaway minors, life and work-style have evolved from a male to a feminized career model.

0582 Boendermaker, L. Graduates Of Residential Judicial Treatment For Juveniles: A One-Year Follow-Up *(Eind Goed Al Goed?De Leefsituatie Van Jongeren Een Jaar Na Vertrek Uit Een Justitiële Behandelintichtin).* Hague, The Netherlands: Ministry of Justice, 1998. A follow-up study of Dutch juveniles under judicial treatment concludes that two-thirds of the juveniles stayed out of trouble while one-third continued to be delinquent. 135p. Dutch with English summary.

0583 Bol, M. W.; Terlouw, G. J. & Blees, L. W. *Young And Violent: Violent Crime Among Juveniles In The Netherlands - Trends And Causes*. Hague, The Netherlands: Ministry of Justice, 1998. This is a comprehensive review of the literature on juvenile violence in the Netherlands since 1985, and also describes the interviews with Dutch violent young offenders. 173p.

0584 Bruinsma, Gerben, J. N. Differential Association Theory Reconsidered: An Extension And Its Empirical Test, *Journal Of Quantitative Criminology* 8:29-49, 1992. This study tests a version of differential association theory, drawing on self-report data of male and female Dutch youths.

0585 Buikhuisen, Wouter & Mednick, Sarnoff A. (eds.) *Explaining Criminal Behavior: Interdisciplinary Approaches*. Leiden, The Netherlands: E. J. Brill, 1988. Section I of this anthology deals with theories of delinquency and Section II "precursors" of delinquency and crime. 260p.

0586 De Haan, Willem J. M. Violence In Troubled Neighborhoods, pp 75-91 in Bruinsma, G. J. N. & Van Der Vijver, C. D. (eds.) *Public Safety In Europe*. Enschede, The Netherlands: Febodruk, 1999. Although focusing on violence in general, this article has a small section on juvenile violence and "public disorder" incidents involving minority youths in the Netherlands.

0587 De Waard, Jaap *The Dutch Criminal Justice System: English Written Information*. Hague, The Netherlands: Crime prevention Directorate, Ministry of Justice, 1990. This annotated bibliography of the various English-language sources for information on crime and criminal justice system in the Netherlands has numerous references on delinquency. 86p.

0588 Eijken, A. W. M. *The Size Of The Crime Problem In The Netherlands: Criminality, Victimization And Prevention In The Period 1980-1990. (Criminaliteitsbeeld Van Nederland: Criminaliteit, Onveiligheid En Preventie In De Period 1980-1990)*. Gravenhage, The Netherlands: Netherlands Ministry of Justice, 1991. Reports on the Dutch crime statistics from the 1970's to 1990's and includes data on juveniles that demonstrates how they are most often the victims of crimes. 70p.

0589 Eijken, A. W. M. An Overview Of Crime In The Netherlands: Types, Extent, Prevention, Punishment And Victim Support In The period 1980-1993. (Criminsliteitsbeeld Van Nederland: Aard, Omvang, Preventie, Bestraffing En Zorg Vgoor Slachtoffers Van Criminaliteit In De Periode 1980-1993). Hague, The Netherlands: Ministry of Justice, 1994. Overall extent, distribution, loss, victims' and offenders' profiles are covered in this document. 126p. Dutch with English summary.

0590 Hakkert, Alfred; Smulders, Antoon & Eijken, Ton *Youth Groups (Groepscriminaliteit)*. Hague, The Netherlands: Ministry of Justice, 1998. A review of the literature on criminal youth groups in the Netherlands, and discusses the group processes and crimes such as vandalism, drugs, intimidation, arson, and riots. 131p. Dutch with English summary.

0591 Hakkert, Alfred Group Delinquency In The Netherlands: Some Findings From An Exploratory Study, *International Review Of Law, Computers & Technology* 12:453-474, 1998. This paper presents a number of findings from a Dutch self-report study.

0592 Janssen, Jacques & Dechesne, Mark The Psychological Importance Of Youth Culture, *Youth & Society*, 31:152-167, 1999. Based on 53 Dutch 16-19 year old students, this report uses vignettes to study the applicability of terror management theory in students' responses to the story and the youthful protagonists.

0593 Junger, M. Delinquency And Ethnicity: An Investigation Of Social Factors Relating To Delinquency Among Moroccan, Turkish, Surinamese And Dutch Boys. Deventer, The Netherlands: Kluwer, 1990. This study examines the causes of higher involvement in juvenile crime among ethnic minorities in Holland. 175p.

0594 Junger, Marianne; Stroebe, Wolfgang & Van Der Laan, André M. Delinquency, Health Behaviour And Health, *British Journal Of Health Psychology* 6:103-120, 2001. The authors investigated Dutch 13-24 year olds to examine any relationship between self-reported alcohol, drug and tobacco use and delinquent behavior and somatic, chronic and general health conditions of a sample of 3, 677.

0595 Junger, Marianne & Marshall, Ineke Haen The Interethnic Generalizability Of Social Control Theory: An Empirical Test, *Journal Of Research In Crime And Delinquency* 34:79-112, 1997. Social control theory is used to model the self-reported delinquent behavior of Surinamese, Moroccan, Turkish, and Dutch boys.

0596 Junger, Marianne & Wiegersma, Auke The Relations Between Accidents, Deviance And Leisure Time, *Criminal Behavior And Mental Health* 5:144-173, 1995. This study examines the relationship between mild deviance and involvement in accidents; and concludes that the correlates of problem behavior and involvement in accidents are similar.

0597 Junger, Marianne & Polder, Wim Religiosity, Religious Climate, And Delinquency Among Ethnic Groups In The Netherlands, *British Journal*

Of Criminology 33:416-435, 1993. Reports on a study of the effect of religiosity on delinquent behavior among boys of various ethnic groups in the Netherlands.

0598 Junger, Marianne & Polder, Wim Some Explanations Of Crime Among Four Ethnic Groups In The Netherlands, *Journal Of Quantitative Criminology* 8:51-78, 1992. This study examines the higher degree of criminal involvement and arrest rates among ethnic minority boys as compared to indigenous boys in the Netherlands, and speculates the possible causes of this involvement.

0599 Junger, Marianne Ethnic Minorities And Causes Of Crime, pp 129-154 in Junger-Tas, Josine; Boendermaker, Leonieke & Van Der Laan, Peter H. (eds.) *The Future Of The Juvenile Justice System (L'Avenir Du Système Pénal Des Mineurs)*. Leuven, Belgium: Acco, 1991. This essay attempts to answer the question of whether ethnic minority juveniles in the Netherlands are more frequently engaged in criminal activities or not.

0600 Junger, Marianne Discrepancies Between Police And Self-Report Data For Dutch Racial Minorities, *British Journal Of Criminology* 29:273-284, 1989. This study assesses the validity of self-reported delinquency data among minority groups in the Netherlands.

0601 Junger, Marianne Social Control Theory Versus Differential Associaiton – A Test On Panel Data, pp 77-103 in Junger-Tas, Josine & Block, Richard L. (eds.) *Juvenile Delinquency In The Netherlands, 1988*. Amstelveen, The Netherlands: Kugler, 1988. This study tests modes derived from social control and differential association theories. Support was found for both theories.

0602 Junger-Tas, Josine & Van Kesteren, John *Bullying And Delinquency In A Dutch School Population*. Hague, The Netherlands: Kugler, 1999. This study of bullying among Dutch elementary and secondary school students 9-16 years old, Japanese, Norwegian, Engliush and Washington state found that about one-fifth of primary and secondary school Dutch pupils reported being frequently bullied, and about the same proportion admitted to bullying behavior. 106 p. Appendix.

0603 Junger-Tas, Josine Changes In The Family And Their Impact On Delinquency, *European Journal On Criminal Policy And Research* 1:22-51, 1993. Article provides a summary of the various research, and attributes the causal factors as socioeconomic and cultural forces of contemporary life.

0604 Junger-Tas, Josine Juvenile Delinquency In The Netherlands: Trends And Perspectives, *International Journal Of Comparative And Applied Criminal Justice* 16:207-229, 1992. Article describes the extent and nature of delinquency in the Netherlands.

0605 Junger-Tas, Josine An Empirical Test Of Social Control Theory, *Journal Of Quantitative Criminology* 8:9-28, 1992. In a test of social control theory using self-report and official data on juveniles in the Netherlands there appeared to be a strong and inverse relation between changes in social integration, or the bond with society, and the frequency of offending.

0606 Junger-Tas, Josine Self-Reported Delinquency Research In Holland With A Perspective On International Comparison, pp 17-42 in Klein, Malcolm W. (ed.) *Cross-National Research In Self-Reported Crime And Delinquency*. Dordrecht, The Netherlands: Kluwer, 1989. This paper discusses the way in which the self-report method is used in Dutch criminological research and examines the issue of constructing a common instrument for comparative study.

0607 Junger-Tas, Josine Patterns In Delinquent Behavior, pp 13-37 in Junger-Tas, Josine & Block, Richard L. (eds.) *Juvenile Delinquency In The Netherlands, 1988*. Amstelveen, The Netherlands: Kugler, 1988. In this study testing social control theory, the authors used official statistics and self-report data to differentiate between conforming and more or less delinquent juveniles in the Netherlands.

0608 Junger-Tas, Josine & Junger, Marianne *Juvenile Delinquency II: The Impact Of Judicial Intervention*. Hague, The Netherlands: Ministry of Justice, 1985. This study examines the effects of judicial intervention and changes in social integration on later behavior of delinquent youths in the Netherlands. 61p.

0609 Junger-Tas, Josine *Young Immigrants In The Netherlands And Their Contacts With The Police*. Hague: The Netherlands Ministry of Justice, 1985. Uses demographic and arrest data to highlight the disproportionate numbers of the ethnic minority juveniles whom the welfare services and the juvenile justice system serve. 21p.

0610 Junger-Tas, Josine *Recent Trends In Juvenile Delinquency And Reactions Of The Juvenile Justice System*. Hague, Netherlands: Research and Documentation Center, Ministry of Justice, 1984. Discusses the widespread nature of delinquency in the Netherlands and the increasing emphasis on the rights of juveniles as well as diversification of the penal measures. 51p.

0611 Kruissink, M. & Essers, A. A. M. *Trends In Juvenile Delinquency: 1980-1999 (Ontwikkeling Van De Jeugd-Criminaliteit: Period 1980-1999)*. Hague, The Netherlands: Ministry of Justice, 2001. This document provides a wealth of official and self-report data on delinquency rates in the Netherlands. 49p. Dutch with English Summary.

0612 Landsheer, J. A.; Hart, H. T. & Kox, W. Delinquent Values And Victim Damage: Exploring The Limits Of Neutralization Theory, *British Journal Of Criminology* 34:44-53, 1994. Using "Neutralization" theory, the authors tested the hypothesis that techniques of neutralization are dependent on the possibility of ignoring the damage caused by delinquent acts.

0613 Landsheer, Johannes A. Age And Adolescent Delinquency: The Changing Relationship Among Age, Delinquent Attitudes And Delinquent Activity, *Criminal Justice And Behavior* 26:373-388, 1999. Article reports the findings of a study of attitudes of Dutch 12 to 24 year olds toward illegal behavior.

0614 Lenssen, V. Simone A. M.; Doreleijers, Theo A. H.; Van Dijk, Mirjam E. & Hartman, Catherina A. Girls In Detention: What Are Their Characteristics? A Project To Explore And Document The Character Of This Target Group And The Significant Ways In Which It Differs From One Consisting Of Boys, *Journal Of Adolescence* 23:287-303, 2000. This article from behavioral and psychiatric perspective, discusses the differences between male and female juvenile delinquency.

0615 Leuw, Ed *Delinquency And Ethnic Minorities: A Criminological Analysis (Criminaliteit En Etnische Minderheden: Een Criminologische Analyses)*. Hague, The Netherlands: Wetenschappelijk Onderzoek en Documentatiecentrum, 1997. This review summarizes empirical data on and interpretations of crimes of ethnic minorities—juvenile and adult—in the Netherlands. 61p. Appendix. Dutch with English summary.

0616 Moser, Françoise & Doreleijers, Theo A. H. An Explorative Study Of Juvenile Delinquents With Attention-Deficit/Hyperactivity Disorder, *European Journal On Criminal Policy And Research* 5:67-81, 1997. A study of official delinquents in the Hague concluded that delinquents with Attention Deficit/Hyperactivity Disorder (ADHD) were younger and exhibited problem behaviors compared to offenders who did not have ADHD.

0617 Netherlands Central Bureau Of Statistics *Justice And Prisons*. Hague, The Netherlands. Reprinted from "Statistical Yearbook of the Netherlands", pp. 361-388, 1979. Provides various official statistics including data on juvenile offenders from 1965 to 1978.

0618 Sagel-Grande, Irene Juvenile Delinquency And Age, pp 69-78 in Junger-Tas, Josine; Boendermaker, Leonieke & Van Der Laan, Peter H. (eds.) *The Future Of The Juvenile Justice System (L'Avenir Du Système Pénal Des Mineurs)*. Leuven, Belgium: Acco, 1991. This study based on Dutch data provides a brief discussion of the relative involvement in delinquency and age of youths.

0619 Scholte, Evert M. Factors Predicting Continued Violence Into Young Adulthood, *Journal of Adolescence* 22:3-20, 1999. This empirical study highlights crime- producing factors of adolescent offending that predict continued violence into young adulthood.

0620 Scholte, Evert M. Social Control Theory, Educational Intervention, And The Prevention Of Delinquency, pp 167-180 in Junger-Tas, Josine; Boendermaker, Leonieke & Van Der Laan, Peter H. (eds.) *The Future Of The Juvenile Justice System (L'Avenir Du Système Pénal Des Mineurs)*. Leuven, Belgium: Acco, 1991. This essay reports research based on social control theory on educational intervention as a form of social control to prevent delinquency.

0621 Stanger, Catherine; Achenbach, Thomas M. & Verhulst, Frank C. Accelerated Longitudinal Comparisons Of Aggressive Versus Delinquent Syndromes, *Development And Psychopathology* 9:43-58, 1997. A longitudinal study examines similarities and differences between the developmental trajectories of aggressive versus delinquent syndromes in childhood and adolescence.

0622 Steinmetz, Carl H. D. Aggression In A Youth Club – An Observation Study In A Town In The West Of Holland, pp 105-144 in Junger-Tas, Josine & Block, Richard L. (eds.) *Juvenile Delinquency In The Netherlands, 1988*. Amstelveen, The Netherlands: Kugler, 1988. This study of the involvement in acts of aggression found that experiences as victim and witness alone could result in a spiral of violence, supporting a social learning theory explanation of institutional violence.

0623 Tavecchio, L. W. C.; Stams, G. J. J. M. & Brugman, D. Moral Judgement And Delinquency In Homeless Youths, *Journal Of Moral Education* 28:63-79, 1999. This study behavior based on samples of homeless and institutionalized youths investigated the impact of an individual's life condition and the relationship between moral judgment and delinquent conduct.

0624 Terlouw, Gert-Jan & Bruinsma, Gerben J. N. Self-Reported Delinquency In The Netherlands, pp 102-130 in Junger-Tas, Josine; Terlouw,

Gert-Jan & Klein, Malcolm W. (eds.) *Delinquent Behavior Among Young People In The Western World: First Results Of The International Self-Report Delinquency Study.* Amsterdam/New York: Kugler, 1994. Chapter reports the findings from a self-reported delinquency survey carried out in the Netherlands.

0625 Terlouw, Gert-Jan The International Juvenile Self-Report Delinquency Survey: Some Problems In International Data Collection And Results Of The Dutch Pilot Study, pp 104-128 in Farrington, David P. & Walklate, Sandra (eds.) *Offenders And Victims: Theory And Policy* London, United Kingdom: Kings College Institute for the Study and Treatment of Delinquency, 1992. Discusses some of the issues and problems in the construction of a questionnaire for a comparative self-report study and its Dutch pilot study.

0626 Van Der Heiden-Attema, N. & Bol, M. W. Difficult Youth: Risk And Protective Factors For The Development Of Delinquent Behaviour In High-Risk Juveniles *(Moeilijke Jeugd: Risico—En Protectieve Factoren En De Ontwikkeling Van Delinquent Gedrag In Een Groep Risicojongeren)*. Hague, The Netherlands: Ministry of Justice, 2000. Reports on the bio-psycho-social risk variables among 106 delinquent and 112 non-delinquent youths in Leiden, the Netherlands. 120p. Dutch.

0627 Van Der Laan, Peter H. *Surinamese, Turkish And Moroccan Youngsters In Dutch Residential Care.* Hague, The Netherlands: Coordinating Committee on Research into Child Care and Protection, 1985. This study examines behavior problems leading to placement of juveniles from ethnic minorities in Dutch child-care and child-protection institutions and homes. 40p.

0628 Van Der Ploeg, J. D. Homelessness: A Multidimensional Problem, *Children And Youth Services Review* 11:45-60, 1989. This study of homeless juveniles in Amsterdam found that homelessness is a multidimensional dilemma that merits an integrated policy of youth care.

New Zealand

0629 Bartusch, Dawn R. Jeglum; Lynam, Donald R.; Moffitt, Terrie E. & Silva, Phil A. Is Age Important? Testing A General Versus A Developmental Theory Of Antisocial Behavior, *Criminology* 35:13-48, 1997. In this study testing competing hypotheses derived from "general theory" and "developmental theory" found support for developmental theory.

0630 Begg, Dorothy J.; Langley, John D. & Moffitt, Terrie Sport And Delinquency: An Examination Of The Deterrence Hypothesis In A Longitudinal Study. *British Journal Of Sports Medicine* 30:335-341, 1996. Whether participation in sports in mid-adolescence would deter delinquent behavior in late adolescence was the subject of this research.

0631 Bimler, David & Kirkland, John School Truants And Truancy Motivation Sorted Out With Multidimensional Scaling, *Journal Of Adolescent Research* 16:75-102, 2001. Multivariate techniques were applied to the problem of school truancy.

0632 Caspi, Avshalom; Lynam, Donald & Moffitt, Terrie E. Unraveling Girls' Delinquency: Biological, Dispositional, And Contextual Contributions To Adolescent Misbehavior, *Developmental Psychology* 29:19-30, 1993. In this study of the relationship between biological maturation and delinquency among girls, it was found that the impact of menstral timing on delinquency was moderated by the sex composition of schools.

0633 Entner Wright, Bradley R.; Caspi, Avshalom & Moffitt, Terrie E. Reconsidering The Relationship Between SES And Delinquency: Causation But Not Correlation, *Criminology* 37:175-194, 1999. This study proposes socioeconomic status has both a negative and positive indirect effect on delinquency that, in tandem, results in little overall correlation between the two.

0634 Fergusson, David M.; Horwood, L. John & Nagin, Daniel S. Offending Trajectories In A New Zealand Birth Cohort, *Criminology* 38:525-551, 2000. This paper develops a latent class modeling method to examine variation in offending trajectories to test the predictions of the trajectory theories.

0635 Fergusson, David M.; Horwood, L. John & Lloyd, Michael A Latent Class Model Of Child Offending, *Criminal Behaviour And Mental Health* 1:90-106, 1991. In this paper the authors propose a latent class model to estimate the magnitude and direction of errors of measurement in reports of youthful offending.

0636 Fergusson, D. M.; Lynskey, M. T. & Horwood, L. J. The Effects Of Unemployment On Juvenile Offending, *Criminal Behavior And Mental Health* 7:49-68, 1997. This study examining the associations between duration of unemployment and measures of youthful offending found that young people who were jobless for six months or longer had higher mean levels of offending as well as offense rates for specific types of crime.

0637 Fergusson, D. M.; Lynskey, M. T. & Horwood, L. J. Truancy In Adolescence, *New Zealand Journal Of Educational Studies* 30:25-37, 1995. This paper examines the development of truancy in a Christ

Church birth cohort of school children.

0638 Fergusson, D. M.; Horwood, L. J. & Lynskey, M. T. Ethnicity, Social Background And Young Offending: A 14-Year Longitudinal Study, *Australian And New Zealand Journal Of Criminology* 26:155-170, 1993. The authors analyzed the relationship between ethnicity and rates of violent, property and other offenses.

0639 Fergusson, D. M.; Fifield, J. K. & Slater, S. W. *Social Background, School Performance, Adjustment And Juvenile Offending: A Path Analytic Model.* Joint Committee on Young Offenders New Zealand, Research Report No. 5, 1976. This study reports that the impact of social background variables on offending is mainly direct. 21p.

0640 Fergusson, D. M.; Donnell, Anne & Slater, S. W. *The Effects Of Race And Socio-Economic Status On Juvenile Offending Statistics.* Wellington, New Zealand: Shearer Joint Committee on Young Offenders, 1975. This study examined the extent to which differences in offending statistics vary systematically by race and socio-economic status. 31p.

0641 Hampton, Ross E. *Sentencing In A Children's Court And Labeling Theory.* Wellington, New Zealand: Department of Justice, 1975. This study of the juvenile adjudication process in New Zealand tests the hypothesis that youths who receive more severe sentences are more likely to re-offend. 84p.

0642 Henry, Bill; Moffitt, Terrie E. & Robins, Lee Early Family Predictors Of Child And Adolescent Antisocial Behaviour: Who Are The Mothers Of Delinquents? *Criminal Behaviour And Mental Health* 3:97-118, 1993. This study tests the usefulness of maternal and familial characteristics in identifying children at-risk.

0643 Moffitt, Terrie E.; Caspi, Avshalom & Dickson, Nigel Childhood-Onset Versus Adolescent-Onset Antisocial Conduct Problems In Males: Natural History From Ages 3 To 18 Years, *Development And Psychopathology* 8:399-424, 1996. The distinction between childhood-onset and adolescent-onset of delinquency was investigated in this article.

0644 Moffitt, Terrie E.; Caspi, Avshalom; Silva, Phil A. & Stouthamer-Loeber, Magda Individual Differences In Personality And Intelligence Are Linked To Crime: Cross-Context Evidence From Nations, Neighborhoods, Genders, Races, And Age-Cohorts, pp 1-34 in Blau, Zena Smith & Hagan, John (eds.) *Current Perspectives On Aging And The Life Cycle: Delinquency And Disrepute In The Life Course, Vol. 4.* Greenwich, Connecticut: JAI Press, 1995. The findings from a comparative study of

tive study of intelligence and delinquency among youth in New Zealand and the United States.

0645 Moffitt, Terrie E.; Lynam, Donald R. & Silva, Phil A. Neuropsychological Tests Predicting Persistent Male Delinquency, *Criminology* 32:277-300, 1994. The relationship between extent of neuropsychological deficit and self-reported delinquency is the subject of this research.

0646 Moffitt, Terrie E.; Silva, Phil A.; Lynam, Donald R. & Henry, Bill Self-Reported Delinquency At Age 18: New Zealand's Dunedin Multi-Disciplinary Health And Development Study, pp 354-369 in Junger-Tas, Josine; Terlouw, Gert-Jan & Klein, Malcolm W. (eds.) *Delinquent Behavior Among Young People In The Western World: First Results Of The International Self-Report Delinquency Study*. Amsterdam/New York: Kugler, 1994. Chapter reports the results of a self-reported delinquency survey carried out in New Zealand.

0647 Moffitt, Terrie E. Juvenile Delinquency And Attention Deficit Disorder: Boys' Developmental Trajectories From Age 3 To Age 15, *Child Development* 61:893-910, 1990. Using longitudinal data, this study analyzed the delinquent behavior of a birth cohort of New Zealand boys.

0648 Moffitt, Terrie E. & Henry, Bill Neuropsychological Assessment Of Executive Functions In Self-Reported Delinquents, *Development And Psychopathology* 1:105-118, 1989. Using self-reprot data, this study assessed five tests of executive functions on a cohort of boys and girls.

0649 Moffitt, Terrie E. Accommodating Self-Report Methods To A Low-Delinquency Culture: A Longitudinal Study From New Zealand, pp 43-66 in Klein, Malcolm W. (ed.) *Cross-National Research In Self-Reported Crime And Delinquency*. Dordrecht, The Netherlands: Kluwer, 1989. This study investigated individual variation in anti-social behavior among a group of youths who were likely to report little serious delinquency.

0650 Moffitt, Terrie E. & Silva, Phil A. Neuropsychological Deficit And Self-Reported Delinquency In An Unselected Birth Cohort, *Journal Of The American Academy Of Child And Adolescent Psychiatry* 27:233-240, 1988. This study examines the prevalence of neuropsychological deficit and self-reported delinquency in a birth cohort of Dunedin's 13 year olds.

0651 Moffitt, Terrie E. & Silva, Phil A. Self-Reported Delinquency: Results From An Instrument For New Zealand, *Australian And New Zealand Journal Of Criminology* 21:227-240, 1988. The authors present the results of a self-reported delinquency survey in Dunedin, New Zealand.

0652 O'Connell, B. M. *The Home Situations Of Juvenile Offenders*. Wellington, New Zealand: New Zealand Social Welfare Department, 1975. This study provides information on the home situation of children in the New Zealand Children's Court who appeared either for an offense or on complaints of misbehavior. 21p.

0653 Winter, Pahmi 'Pulling The Teams Out Of The Dark Room': The Politicisation Of The Mongrel Mob, pp 245-266 in Hazlehurst, Kayleen & Hazlehurst, Cameron (eds.) *Gangs And Youth Subcultures: International Explorations*. New Brunswick, New Jersey: Transaction, 1998. This chapter offers a case study of how a youth gang called the Mongrel Mob became a political issue in New Zealand and their policy impact.

0654 Woodward, Lianne J. & Fergusson, David M. Childhood And Adolescent Predictors Of Physical Assault: A Prospective Longitudinal Study, *Criminology* 38:233-261, 2000. Longitudinal data on more than 1,000 New Zealand children were used to examine contextual, lifestyle, and childhood risk factors associated with young people's exposure to physical assault in late adolescence.

Nigeria

0655 Adisa, Jinmi Lagos: Street Culture And Families In The Street, pp 89-145 in Hérault, Georges & Adesanmi, Pius (eds.) *Youth, Street Culture And Urban Violence In Africa: Proceedings Of The International Symposium In Abidjan 5-7 May, 1997 (Jeunes, Culture De La Rue Et Violence Urbaine En Afrique: Actes Du Symposium International D'Abidjan 5-7 Mai 1997)*. Ibadan, Nigeria: French Institute for Research in Africa, 1997. This chapter reports findings from an interview study of Lagos street culture and its relationship to criminality among urban youth. English with French summary.

0656 Albert, Olawale Kano: Religious Fundamentalism And Violence, pp 285-328 in Hérault, Georges & Adesanmi, Pius (eds.) *Youth, Street Culture And Urban Violence In Africa: Proceedings Of The International Symposium In Abidjan 5-7 May, 1997 (Jeunes, Culture De La Rue Et Violence Urbaine En Afrique: Actes Du Symposium International D'Abidjan 5-7 Mai 1997)*. Ibadan, Nigeria: French Institute for Research in Africa, 1997. This is based on an extensive Kano study on the relationships between youth violence and religious fundamentalism. English with French summary.

0657 Denga, Daniel I. Juvenile Delinquency Among Polygynous Families In Nigeria, *Journal Of Social Psychology* 114:3-7, 1981. The author focused on the relationship between polygynous/monogamous family life and juvenile delinquency in Nigerian familes with delinquent offspring.

0658 Ebbe, Obi N. I. Juvenile Delinquency In Nigeria: The Problem Of Application Of Western Theories, *International Journal Of Comparative And Applied Criminal Justice* 16:353-370, 1992. Rates and patterns of delinquency in Nigeria aer presented along with tables of official data to assess the extent to which Western theories can explain juvenile delinquency in Nigeria.

0659 Ebbe, Obi N. I. Crime And Delinquency In Metropolitan Lagos: A Study Of 'Crime And Delinquency Area' Theory, *Social Forces* 67:751-765, 1989. The applicability of "delinquency area" theory to Lagos was tested by this research.

0660 Ebbe, Obi N. I. Ecological Distribution Of Juvenile Delinquency In Metropolitan Lagos, *International Journal Of Comparative And Applied Criminal Justice* 8:187-197, 1984. This paper presents the ecology of delinquency in the metropolitan city of Lagos, Nigeria to show where delinquency occurs and among whom.

0661 Odekunle, Femi Patterns Of Delinquency And Formalized Control Policy In Nigeria, pp 114-124 in Brusten, M.; Graham, J.; Herriger, N. & Malinowski, P. (eds.) *Youth Crime, Social Control And Prevention: Theoretical Perspectives And Policy Implications—Studies From Nine Different Countries*. Pfaffenweiler: Centauras-Verlagsgesellschaft, 1986. This chapter provides data on youth crime in Nigeria and some description and evaluation of formal control procedures.

0662 Ogunlesi, A. O. Nigerian Juvenile Offenders: A Case-Controlled Study, *Forensic Science International* 44:187-192, 1990. Using a sample of Nigerian male juveniles under custody, this study sought to identify risk factors in delinquent behavior.

0663 Ojile, Emmanuel Juvenile Delinquency In The Northern States Of Nigeria, *The Journal Of Social Psychology* 133:405-406, 1993. This study confirms the existence of delinquency in northern Nigeria and argues that it exists for the same reasons dedlinquency is found in other societies.

0664 Ononye, Frank & Morakinyo, Olufemi Drug Abuse, Psychopathology, And Juvenile Delinquency In South-Western Nigeria, *Journal Of Stiftung Forensic Psychiatry* 5:527-537, 1994. The possible interactions among drug abuse, psychopathology, and delinquency among a sample of Nigerian youths under custody is the focus of this research.

Norway

0665 Aromaa, Kauko Finland, Sweden And Norway: Increasing Concern With A Relatively Stable Situaiton (Finnland, Schweden Und Norwegen: Zunehmende Besorgnis Bei Relativ Stabiler Lage), pp 59-64 in Friedrich Ebert Stiftung (ed.) *Child and Juvenile Delinquency In Germany (Kinder- Und Jugendkriminalität In Deutschland*). Friedrich Ebert Stiftung: Berlin, Germany, 1996. This brief chapter provides an assessment of juvenile delinquency in Norway, Finland and Sweden. German.

0666 Bendixen, Mons & Olweus, Dan Measurement Of Antisocial Behavior In Early Adolescence And Adolescence: Psychometric Properties And Substantive Findings *Criminal Behavior And Mental Health* 9:323-354, 1999. Reports the findings of a self-report survey of 2,430 Bergen boys and girls aged 10-16.

0667 Farrington, David P. Understanding And Preventing Bullying, pp 381-458 in Tonry, Michael (ed.) *Crime And Justice: A Review Of Research Volume 17*. Chicago, Illinois: University of Chicago Press, 1993. Has summary of the current literature on bullying and victimization of children in institutions including the schools in Scandinavia, and provides a description of the Norwegian national campaign against bullying.

0668 Hydle, Ida Juvenile Delinquency: A Norwegian Perspective, pp 35-41 in United Nations Crime Prevention And Criminal Justice Program International Scientific And Professional Advisory Council (ed.) *Juveniles And Delinquency*. Milan, Italy, 1995. Has summaries of various Norwegian delinquency research and a good table of rates and demographics for 14-24 year olds charged with crime.

0669 Joutsen, Matti Treatment, Punishment, Control: Juvenile Delinquency In Scandinavia, pp 599-623 in Hess, Albert G. & Clement, Priscilla F. (eds.) *History Of Juvenile Delinquency II: A Collection Of Essays On Crimes Committed By Young Offenders*. Aalen, Germany: Scientia Verlag, 1993. The authors provide a survey of juvenile delinquency in Scandinavia, including Norway.

0670 Kjelsberg, E. & Dahl, A. A. A Long-term Follow-Up Study Of Adolescent Psychiatric In-Patients. Part II. Predictors Of Delinquency, *Acta Psychiatrica Scandinavica* 99:237-242, 1999. Using the National register of criminal psychiatric inpatients were followed-up for their involvement in delinquency, and 77% of the disruptive, ward-rule violating, psychoactive substance using males with personality disorder tended to have criminal records in the follow up.

0671 Kjelsberg, E. & Dahl, A. A. High Delinquency, Disability And Mortality - A Register Study Of Former Adolescent Psychiatric Inpatients, *Acta Psychiatrica Scandinavica* 98:34-40, 1998. This report of a follow-up study of former male and female inpatients in psychiatry concludes that delinquency, disability and mortality were, compared to the general population, pronounced among this group.

0672 Skogen, Ketil & Wichström, Lars Social Class And Delinquency (Kriminalitet Og Klasse*), Nordisk Tidsskrift For Kriminalvidenskab* 82:32-59, 1995. Results of a self-reported delinquency survey of a random national sample of almost 12,00 Norwegian 13-20 year old youths are the subject of this analysis. Norwegian.

0673 Olweus, Dan Bullying: What We Know And What We Can Do (Mobbning: Vad Vet Vi Och Vad Kan Vi Göra), pp 67-80 in Sweden National Council For Crime Prevention (ed.) *Crime Prevention Work In Schools*. Stockholm, Sweden: Sweden National Council For Crime prevention, 1989. Recounts the experiences of Norway-wide measures to combat victimization among school children. Swedish.

0674 Pedersen, Willy Crime And Punishment In Norwegian Mid-adolescents: A Normal Population Study, *Journal Of Scandinavian Studies In Criminology And Crime Prevention* 1:87-104, 2000. Comparing a national representative sample of adolescents' self-reported crimes with official police records, this research concludes that 3.7% of the boys and 1.9% of the girls had received some penal sanction during the preceding year and their participation in crime was higher than that of the national Norwegian sample.

0675 Pedersen, Willy & Wichström, Lars Patterns Of Delinquency In Norwegian Adolescents, *British Journal Of Criminology* 35:543-562, 1995. Reports on age and gender-based disparity in a large-scale self-report survey of delinquency among Norwegian males and females.

0676 Pedersen, Willy Parental Relations, Mental Health, And Delinquency In Adolescents, *Adolescence* 29:975-990, 1994. The data from a longitudinal survey of 573 Norwegian youths are examined for the relationship between parental bonding and delinquency.

0677 Rossow, Ingeborg; Pape, Hilde & Wichström, Lars Young,Wet & Wild? Associations Between Alcohol Intoxication And Violent Behavior In Adolescence, *Addiction* 94:1017-1031, 1999. Of the surveyed Norwegian school students, boys report more violent and criminal behavior at a younger age and with increasing frequency, and increasing incidents of intoxication when in the "wet" environment of their peers and family.

0678 Storvoll, Elizabet E. & Hovland, Arild The Ullersmo Project: "Scared Straight" (Ullersmoprosjekter:"Scared Straight"), *Nordisk Tidsskrift For Kriminalvidenskab* 85:122-135, 1998. This evaluation of the Ullersmo Project modeled after the "scared straight" program to prevent delinquency found that the project was a failure due to various factors including follow-up preparations. Norwegian.

Papua New Guinea

0679 Dinnen, Sinclair Urban Raskolism And Criminal Groups In Papua New Guinea, pp 267-306 in Hazlehurst, Kayleen & Hazlehurst, Cameron (eds.) *Gangs And Youth Subcultures: International Explorations*. New Brunswick, New Jersey: Transaction, 1998. This chapter describes criminal gangs in Papua New Guinea focusing on raskolism as an example.

0680 Sundeen, Richard A. Juvenile Arrests In Papua New Guinea, pp 124-141 in Jensen, Gary F. (ed.) *Sociology Of Delinquency*. Beverly Hills, California: Sage, 1981. The author presents numerous tables and summaries of arrests, charges, offense and age of juveniles for law violations in this Pacific island nation.

Philippines

0681 Maxwell, Sheila Royo A Focus On Familial Strain: Antisocial Behavior And Delinquency In Filipino Society, *Sociological Inquiry* 71:265-292, 2001. This study tests ideas based on Agnew's general strain theory among a sample of grade-school students in urban and rural schools in the Philippines.

0682 Shoemaker, Donald J. Male And Female Delinquency In The Philippines: A Comparative Analysis, *Youth And Society* 25:299-329, 1994. Using the results of a self-report survey, this study compared the delinquency of male and female students in the Philippines.

0683 Shoemaker, Donald J. Delinquency In The Philippines: A Description, *Philippine Sociological Review* 40:83-103, 1992. This research based on a self-report survey among high school, college, and school dropout Filipinos found that several attitudinal factors and delinquent behavior are closely associated.

Poland

0684 Batawia, Stanislaw Problems Of Social Maladjustment And Crime In Poland (Zagadnienia Nieprzystosowania Spotecznego I Przestepczosci W

Polsce). Wroclaw, Poland: Polska Akademia Nauk, 1978. This report provides official data on juveniles appearing before courts in Poland. Polish. 493p.

0685 Feshbach, Seymour & Fraczek, Adam (eds.) *Aggression And Behavior Change: Biological And Social Processes*. New York: Praeger, 1979. This anthology on psychological factors and issues in aggression includes a review of studies on various intervention programs for children with aggression and other behavioral problems, and delinquent subcultures. 299p.

0686 Jarosz, Maria Disintegration Of The Family In The Etiology Of Deviant Behavior, *Deviant Behavior* 2:1-13, 1980. This is a psychological study of juvenile delinquency and dysfunctions in familes with child support payment problems.

0687 Jasinski, Jerzy (ed.) *Problems Of Social Maladjustment And Crime In Poland*. Wroclaw, Poland: Polish Academy of Sciences, Department of Criminology, 1989. This anthology contains chapters on drug dependence, social maladjustment, and the effect of peer groups on juvenile delinquency. 294p. Appendix.

0688 Jasinski, Jerzy Crime: Manifestations, Patterns And Trends Of Crime "Traditional" Versue "New" Crime; Juvenile Crime; Fear Of Crime. *European Journal Of Crime, Criminal Law And Criminal Justice* 7:374-386, 1999. Although generally about crime and crime trends in Soviet block countries, this article has some information and data on juvenile illegal behavior as well.

0689 Kocur, Jozef & Aleksandrowicz, Jerzy Psychiatric And Psycho-Social Conditions Of The Crime Of Group Rape, *Eurocriminology* 11:151-161, 1997. Gang rape involving Polish juvenile offenders is the focus of this research.

0690 Wójcik, Dobrochna Juvenile Delinquency And Victims Of Crime, pp 73-76 in Jasinski, Jerzy & Siemaszko, Andrzej (eds.) *Crime Control In Poland*. Warsaw, Poland: Institute of Justice, Police Ministry of Justice, 1995. This paper discusses juvenile delinquency and crime victims in Poland.

Portugal

0691 Gersaõ, Eliana & Lisboa, Manuel The Self-Reported Delinquency Study In Portugal, pp 212-237 in Junger-Tas, Josine; Terlouw, Gert-Jan & Klein, Malcolm W. (eds.) *Delinquent Behavior Among Young People In The Western World: First Results Of The International Self-Report De-*

linquency Study. Amsterdam/New York: Kugler, 1994. Chapter reports the findings from a self-reported delinquency survey carried out in Portugal.

Russian Federation

0692 Andreev, Vladimir What's Happening To The Children? *Russian Social Science Review* 40: 41-53, 1999. The author offers some observations on Russia's young people, and examines the influence of the West on their behavior and attitudes, and offers some reasons as to why some youngsters are running away from home.

0693 Antonian, Iu M. The Sociopsychological Consequences Of Urbanization And Their Influence On Crime, *Soviet Law And Government* 15:51-65, 1976. This article on urbanization and crime discusses the impact of nuclear family and lack of community on juvenile crime/deviance.

0694 Beermann, R. Delinquency In The Estonian SSR, *Review Of Socialist Law* 7:99-112, 1981. This article provides information on delinquency rates during the 1960s with some tables on gender and other variables along with a brief description of delinquency laws.

0695 Bocharova, Oksana & Lerner, Anton Characteristics Of The Way Of Life Of Adolescents, *Russian Social Science Review* 42:15-26, 2001. This article discusses a study examining the generational attitudes, including attitudes toward the law and values of upper-grade students in Russia.

0696 Borodin, Stanislav V. The Soviet Union, pp 125-141 in Stewart, V. Lorne (ed.) *Justice And Troubled Children Around The World, Vol. I.* New York, New York: New York University Press, 1980. This chapter describes the "holistic"(home, school, and community) Soviet approach to child development and their relationship to delinquency among Soviet youth.

0697 Butler, W. E. Crime In The Soviet Union: Early Glimpses Of The True Story, *British Journal Of Criminology* 32:144-159, 1992. Provides some official 1990 crime data with some statistics on juveniles.

0698 Creuziger, Clementine G. K. Russia's Unwanted Children: A Cultural Anthropological Study Of Marginalized Children In Moscow And St. Petersburg, *Childhood A Global Journal Of Child Research* 4:343-358, 1997. This study describes the plight of various groups of marginalized children (orphans and children with some family ties in special boarding homes, and street children) in Russia.

0699 Dashkov, Gennady V. Quantitative And Qualitative Changes In Crime In The USSR, *British Journal Of Criminology* 32:160-166, 1992. Reports on the changes during 1987-1990 with a small section on juvenile crimes.

0700 Dobson, Richard B. Youth Problems In The Soviet Union pp 227-251 in Jones, Anthony; Connor, Walter D. & Powell, David E. (eds.) *Soviet Social Problems*. Boulder, Colorado: Westview Press, 1991. There is a discussion of the nature and sources of youth problems such as gangs, youth subcultures, drugs and crimes within the socioeconomic contexts of urbanization, leisure time, and spread of Western pop culture.

0701 Dolgova, Azalia The Characteristics Of Circumstances Linked With Juvenile Delinquency, pp 81-89 in USSR Academy Of Sciences (ed.) *Social Sciences Today*. Moscow, Russia: International Social Defence Society, 1981. Discusses the interaction among juvenile delinquency and socioeconomic characteristics such as family, informal groups, industrial development, urbanization, educational establishments etc.

0702 Finckenauer, James O. Legal Socialization Theory: A Precursor To Comparative Research In The Soviet Union, pp 71-85 in Laufer, William S. & Adler, Freda (eds.) *Advances in Criminological Theory, Vol. 2*. New Brunswick, New Jersey: Transaction, 1990. This summary of various studies on behavior, attitudes and values toward law in general in both the Soviet Union and the United States includes a small section on juvenile delinquency.

0703 Finckenauer, James O. Two Worlds Of Deviance: Russia And The United States, pp 193-206 in White, Susan O. (ed.) *Handbook Of Youth And Justice*. New York, New York: Kluwer/Plenum, 2001. A sample of Moscow school youth's perceptions of their peers' impact on deviance and some statistics on the nature and trends in delinquency as well as the unique Russian experience and responses are presented along with a comparative overview of the two countries' juvenile justice approaches.

0704 Finckenauer, James O.; Weidner, Robert R. & Terrill, William C. Delinquency Among A Sample Of Russian Youth: A Test Of Power-Control Theory, *International Criminal Justice Review* 8:15-32, 1998. In a 1992-survey of Moscow juveniles to test the family and structural variables of control theory and peer influence, this study found that the latter was a better predictor of delinquent behavior.

0705 Finckenauer, James O. *Russian Youth: Law, Deviance And The Pursuit Of Freedom*. New Brunswick, New Jersey: Transaction, 1995. This cross-cultural study of Russian and American youths focuses on their legal socialization and how shifting legal contexts in post-Soviet Union

Russia may have influenced the illegal behavior of Russian youth. 237P.

0706 Finckenauer, James O. & Kelly, Linda Juvenile Delinquency And Youth Subcultures In The Former Soviet Union, *International Journal Of Comparative And Applied Criminal Justice* 16:247-261, 1992. Article describes the extent of and changes in delinquency in Russia after the dissolution of the former Soviet Union.

0707 Finckenauer, James O. Corrections In The Soviet Union, *Prison Journal*, 68:41-50, 1988. Soviet youth is one of the subjects in this article on issues and problems of Soviet corrections such as purposes and forms of punishment, and labor as a correctional measure.

0708 Finckenauer, James O. Juvenile Delinquency In The USSR: Social Structural Explanations, *International Journal Of Comparative And Applied Criminal Justice* 12:73-80, 1988. The author examines delinquency and certain theories of delinquency in the context of Soviet social structural variables.

0709 Iagodin, G. A. Only A Free School Will Educate A Free Person, *The Soviet Review* Nov.-Dec:76-88, 1991. The author's view on the relationships among Soviet law, media and the teaching profession on the socialization and morality of children are discussed in this article.

0710 Juviler, Peter & Forschner, Brian E. Juvenile Delinquency In The Soviet Union, *Prison Journal* 58:18-30, 1978. This paper offers estimates of delinquency rates and the official Soviet responses to young offenders prior to the breakup of the Soviet Union.

0711 Karpukhin, O. I. The Young People Of Russia: Characteristics Of Their Socialization And Self-Determination, *Russian Social Science Review* 42:4-14, 2001. This article discusses a study that focused on the socialization and self-determination of Russian youth, and their possible implications for delinquency.

0712 Markowitz, Fran Not Nationalists: Russian Teenagers' Soulful A-Politics, *Europe-Asia Studies* 51:1183-1198, 1999. This school-based ethnography of 16 year-old youths in Russian cities documents aspects of the teenage subculture and political orientation of modern Russian youth.

0713 McClellan, Dorothy Spektorov Soviet Youth: A View From The Inside, *Crime And Social Justice* 29:1-25, 1987. This article based on interviews with Soviet scholars and graduate students in criminology and related fields as well as published literature describes issues of youth crime in the USSR.

0714 Mikhailovskaya, Inga B. Crime In Post-Totalitarian Russia, *Cahiers De Defense Sociale,* pp 35-50, 1996. This author provides some official crime statistics by age of offenders in the various former republics of the USSR from 1976-1992.

0715 Mikhailovskaya, Inga B. Criminality In Post-Totalitarian Russia, *Revue Internationale De Criminologie Et De Police Technique* 48:277-293, 1994. This volume has some statistics on recorded crimes and demographics such as gender of those between 14-17 who were accused of crimes, sentences etc. in the Soviet Union and the member republics. French with English summary.

0716 Mukhina, V. S. Psychological Help For Children Being Brought Up In Boarding-Type Institutions, *The Soviet Review* 32:70-83, 1991. The need for stress-management for the residents in institutions for orphans, children deprived of parental care and children of certain northern nationalities is the focus of this discussion.

0717 Pankratov, V. V. Study Of The Problem Of Juvenile Delinquency And Crime Of Young Adults, pp 43-45 in USSR All Union Institute Of Problems Of Strengthening Of Legality (ed.) *Scientific Information On Problems Of Crime Combating Research Findings Of 1989.* Moscow, USSR: All Union Institute of Problems of Strengthening of Legality, 1990. This is a report on crime and juvenile delinquency prevention aswell as their control in the Soviet Union.

0718 Rawlinson, Paddy Criminal Heirs - Organised Crime And Russia's Youth, pp 95-115 in Hazlehurst, Kayleen & Hazlehurst, Cameron (eds.) *Gangs And Youth Subcultures: International Explorations.* New Brunswick, New Jersey: Transaction, 1998. Article has a brief history of crime in the Soviet Union, and the relationship among youth, party, and antisocial groups.

0719 Rawlinson, Patricia Russian Organized Crime - Moving Beyond Ideology, pp 242-263 in Ruggiero, Vincenzo; South, Nigel & Taylor, Ian. *The New European Criminology: Crime And Social Order In Europe.* London, United Kingdom: Routledge, 1998. Provides the backdrop for viewing juvenile crime in the post-perestroika/glasnost era.

0720 Riordan, Jim (ed.) *Soviet Youth Culture.* Bloomington, Indiana: Indiana University, 1989. Six articles in this anthology cover a variety of topics on juveniles and youth in the Soviet Union. 148p.

0721 Ruchkin, V. V.; Eisenmann, M. & Cloninger, C. R. Behavior Emotional Problems In Male Juvenile Delinquents And Controls In Russia: The Role Of Personality Traits, *Acta Psychiatrica Scandinavica* 98:231-236,

1998. Self-report study of male institutionalized youths in northern Russia and matched school-boys found statistically significant differences in personality traits and problem behavior scores of the delinquents and non-delinquents.

0722 Ruchkin, V. V.; Eisenmann, M. & Hägglöf, B. Parental Rearing And Problem Behaviors In Male Delinquent Adolescents Versus Controls In Northern Russia, *Social Psychiatry And Psychiatric Epidemiology* 33:477-482, 1998. This study found that the institutionalized delinquents had higher problem-behavior scores and were treated more severely by parents although lack of parental emotional warmth in both the institutionalized youth and control group seemed to cause problem behavior.

0723 Ruchkin, Vladislav V., Eisenmann, Martin & Hägglöf, Bruno Coping Styles In Delinquent Adolescents And Controls: The Role Of Personality And Parental Rearing, *Journal Of Youth And Adolescence* 28:05-717, 1999. This study concludes that novelty seeking, harm-avoidance, and self-directedness as well as parental discipline and emotional warmth varied between the delinquent and non-delinquent youths.

0724 Rybinskii, E. M. The Position Of Children In Russia, *Russian Social Science Review* 37: 78-95, 1996. This article provides an analysis of the impact of the post-Soviet transition period in Russia on its children and young population.

0725 Serio, Joseph (ed.) *USSR Crime Statistics And Summaries: 1989 And 1990*. Chicago, Illinois: University of Illinois, 1992. This publication has data, tables, pie charts and graphs on Russian illegality with the age distribution of juveniles accused, percentages of juveniles committing crimes in each republic, as well as the different types of crimes they committed during 1988 and 1989. 114p.

0726 Shestakov, Dmitry A. & Shestakova, Natalia D. Comparative Juvenile Justice: An Overview Of Russia, pp 205-232 in Winterdyk, John (ed.) *Juvenile Justice System: International Perspective*. Toronto, Canada: Canadian Scholars' Press, 1997. Topics covered vary from the turbulent evolution of Russian law, a flow chart of the juvenile justice system, official data on juvenile crimes to the processes from initial contact and preliminary hearing to trial.

0727 Stolee, Margaret K. Homeless Children In The USSR, 1917-1957, *Soviet Studies* 60:64-83, 1988. Historic review of literature and eyewitness accounts of the homeless young and their involvement in crime preceding, during and after the Russian revolution.

0728 Sturova, M. P. The System Of Education And Youth Crime, *Russian Social Science Review* 42:36-49, 2001. This article discusses the relationship between quality of education and youth crime in Russia, and includes a discussion of the common problems of upbringing seen in schools and reviews the programs aimed at adolescents.

0729 Tatidinova, T. G. Young People And Organized Crime, *Russian Social Science Review* 42:50-63, 2001. This article describes results of a study to determine the extent to which the *obshchak* organized crime influences school youngsters in Russia as well as criminal ideology.

0730 Thornton, William E. & Voigt, Lydia Russia, pp 98-117 in Hoffman, Allan M. & Summers, Randal W. (eds.) *Teen Violence: A Global View.* Westport, Connecticut: Greenwood Press, 2001. This Chapter offers an over view of teen violence in Russia along with statistical data on juvenile crime over the decade.

0731 United Nations Interregional Crime And Justice Research Institute & Russian Federation Ministry Of The Interior Research Institute *Crime and Crime Prevention In Moscow.* Rome, Italy: United Nations, 1994. Chapter 4 has characteristics (gender, age, recidivists, and minors) of those charged with crime in Moscow. 176p.

0732 USSR All Union Research Institute Of The Causes And Prevention Of Crime *Juvenile Crime In The Soviet Union.* Moscow: The Novosti Press Agency, 1976. This publication presents estimates of juvenile crime rate in the USSR, and argues that a key factor in delinquency prevention is the family. 5p.

0733 Vorontsov, Boris; Gukovskaya, Natalya & Melnikova, Evelina Juvenile Delinquency In Town And Country, pp 73-80 in USSR Academy Of Sciences (ed.) *Social Sciences Today.* Moscow, Russia: International Social Defence Society, 1981. This research found some similarity between the rural-urban rates but also more incidents of robbery and robbery with violence in towns and more adult participation in juveniles' offenses in the countryside.

0734 Zeldes, Ilya Juvenile Delinquency In The USSR: A Criminological Survey, *International Journal Of Comparative And Applied Criminal Justice* 4:15-28, 1980. Statistics on juvenile delinquency in the USSR including the social and demographic characteristics of juvenile delinquents and Soviet methods of preventing delinquency are described in this article.

0735 Zeldes, Ilya Some Data Concerning Female Criminality In The USSR, *International Journal Of Comparative And Applied Criminal Justice*

2:171-176, 1978. Demographic factors' role in female criminality, females' tendency to be recidivists who start their criminal careers while young are discussed by the author.

0736 Zhiritskaia, I. G. The Family-Type Children's Home, *The Soviet Review* 31:81-85, 1990. Statistics on the number of children in the various institutions in the USSR and a critique of the staff, facilities, and programs are provided.

0737 Zinchuk, E. G. & Karpukhin, Iu G. Juvenile Crimes Of Greed, *Russian Education And Society* 37:62-77, 1995. Based on interviews with enforcement officials and files of juveniles, this article argues that rising juvenile crime is fostered by declining standards of living, the growth of inflation and unemployment, as well as declining levels of morality, administrative prohibitions, and punitive practices by law enforcement.

Saudi Arabia

0738 Al Romaih, Yousel Ahmed *Social Control And Delinquency In Saudi Arabia.* Ann Arbor, Michigan: University Microfilms International, 1993. Based on a sample of high school students, youths institutionalized for serious offenses, and youth institutionalized for status offenses, this study sheds light on the problem of juvenile delinquency in Saudi Arabia. 127p.

0739 Kara, Mustafa Social Control In Arab Societies, pp 151-157 in Kubota, Yo (ed.) *International Review Of Criminal Policy: Special Double Volume On Juvenile Justice In International Perspective.* New York: United Nations Centre for Social Development and Humanitarian Affairs, 1990. This article describes the place of youth in Arab society and social control factors such as family, school, and religious beliefs.

Senegal

0740 Diop, Momar-Coumba & Faye, Ousseynou Dakar: Youth, Authorities, And Associates (Dakar: Les Jeunes, Les Autorités Et Les Associations), pp 147-213 in Hérault, Georges & Adesanmi, Pius (eds.) *Youth, Street Culture And Urban Violence In Africa: Proceedings Of The International Symposium In Abidjan 5-7 May, 1997 (Jeunes, Culture De La Rue Et Violence Urbaine En Afrique: Actes Du Symposium International D'Abidjan 5-7 Mai 1997).* Ibadan, Nigeria: French Institute for Research in Africa, 1997. This chapter reports the results of a study of street gangs in Dakar and provides some official statistics on increases in youth crime. French with English summary.

Singapore

0741 Lau, Fong Mak A Typological Analysis Of Juvenile Delinquent Activities, *Journal Of Social Science* 23:39-46, 1975. To determine whether juveniles who engage extensively in one type of crime will also engage in other or all types of crime, a self-report questionnaire was administered to boys in Singapore.

Slovakia

0742 Matúšová, Silvia Bullying And Violence In The Slovakian School, pp 85-109 in Ohsako, Toshio (ed) *Violence At School: Global Issues And Interventions*. Paris, France: United Nations Educational, Scientific and Cultural Organization, 1997. This chapter provides and extensive description of some aspects of violence in Slovakian schools.

Slovenia

0743 Dekleva, Bojan Juvenile Delinquent Gangs And Their Structure (Mladoletniške Prestopniške Združbe In Njihova Sestava), *Revija Za Kriminalistiko In Kriminologijo* 34:39-48, 1983. Using court data from Ljubljana, this study examined the structure of juvenile delinquent gangs. Slovene with English summary.

0744 Mesko, Gorazd; Lobnikar, Branko, Pagon, Milan & Dekleva, Bojan Slovenia, pp 133-143 in Hoffman, Allan M. & Summers, Randal W. (eds.) *Teen Violence: A Global View*. Westport, Connecticut: Greenwood, 2001. This chapter of the anthology describes teen violence in Slovenia, and societal reaction to it.

0745 Tomori, Martina Autoaggressive Behavior In Adolescents (Avtoagreviuno Vedenje Pri Mladostnikih), *Revija Za Kriminalistiko In Kriminologijo* 34:310-318, 1983. This study found that autoaggressive behavior in juveniles develops more frequently in those who grow up in unfavorable family conditions, manifest symptoms of disturbance of central nervous system coordination function. Slovene with English summary.

South Africa

0746 Dissel, Amanda Youth, Street Gangs And Violence In South Africa, pp 405-411 in Hérault, Georges & Adesanmi, Pius (eds.) *Youth, Street Culture And Urban Violence In Africa: Proceedings Of The International Symposium In Abidjan 5-7 May, 1997 (Jeunes, Culture De La Rue Et Violence Urbaine En Afrique: Actes Du Symposium International*

D'Abidjan 5-7 Mai 1997). Ibadan, Nigeria: French Institute for Research in Africa, 1997. This brief chapter offers a discussion of youth and their inolvement in street gangs in South Africa.

0747 Naude, Beaty South Africa, pp 145-158 in Hoffman, Allan M. & Summers, Randal W. (eds.) *Teen Violence: A Global View*. Westport, Connecticut: Greenwood, 2001. In this chapter the author argues that teen violence in South Africa results from socio-economic conditions.

0748 Osaghae, Eghosa E. Umtata: A Clearing House For Delinquents In South Africa, pp 215-246 in Hérault, Georges & Adesanmi, Pius (eds.) *Youth, Street Culture And Urban Violence In Africa: Proceedings Of The International Symposium In Abidjan 5-7 May, 1997 (Jeunes, Culture De La Rue Et Violence Urbaine En Afrique: Actes Du Symposium International D'Abidjan 5-7 Mai 1997)*. Ibadan, Nigeria: French Institute for Research in Africa, 1997. This study focuses on street youths in Umtata, South Africa and discusses some ways to address problems relating to street culture. English with French summary.

0749 Pinnock, Don & Douglas-Hamilton, Mara Rituals, Rights, And Tradition: Rethinking Youth Programs In South Africa, pp 307-341 in Hazlehurst, Kayleen & Hazlehurst, Cameron (eds.) *Gangs And Youth Subcultures: International Explorations*. New Brunswick, New Jersey: Transaction, 1998. This chapter describes how youth gangs have become an alternative "right of passage" for some groups in South Africa and how organized programs may serve as a way of deflecting youths from gang involvement.

South Korea

0750 Axenroth, Joseph B. Social Class And Delinquency In Cross-Cultural Perspective, *Journal Of Research In Crime And Delinquency* 20:164-182, 1983. This study of students in Seoul, Korea showed that even though lower socioeconomic status remained associated with delinquency, access to the regular school system reduced delinquency among lower-class boys.

0751 Cho, Byung In & Chang, Richard J. The Youth Crime Problems In The Republic Of Korea, *International Journal Of Comparative And Applied Criminal Justice* 16:301-316,1992. Articles describes how delinquency rates are related to recent changes in South Korea.

0752 Japan Ministry Of Justice Research And Training Institute Republic Of Korea, pp 25-29 in United Nations Asia And Far East Institute (ed.) *Asia Crime Report No.1*. Tokyo, Japan: UNAFEI, 1993. Chapter provides some official data on juvenile delinquency rates in South Korea.

0753 Jung-Sok, Yun Urbanization And Juvenile Delinquency In South Korea, pp 181-192 in United Nations Asia And Far East Institute (ed.) *Report for 1993 And Resource Material Series No.* 45. Tokyo, Japan: UNAFEI, 1994. This chapter provides a discusses of the impact of urbanization, on the nature as well as the and extent of delinquency in South Korea.

0754 Yoon, Ho Lee An Integration And Elaboration Of Theory To Explain The Delinquency Of Korean Boys, *International Journal Of Comparative And Applied Criminal Justice* 14:25-38, 1990. In an attempt to test causal theories of delinquent behavior, this study found that low attachment to school is a precusor of delinquency among 11th grade male students in South Korea.

Spain

0755 Andrieu-Sanz, Rosa & Vasquez-Anton, Karmele Young Women Prostitutes In Bilbao: A Description And Interpretation, pp 70-79 in Cain, Maureen (ed.) *Growing Up Good: Policing the Behavior of Girls in Europe*. Newbury Park, California: Sage, 1989. This chapter provides a descriptive study of the youthful female prostitutes in a major city in Spain.

0756 Barberet, Rosemary; Rechea-Alberola, Cristina & Montañés-Rodriguez, Juan Self-Reported Juvenile Delinquency In Spain, pp 238-266 in Junger-Tas, Josine; Terlouw, Gert-Jan & Klein, Malcolm W. (eds.) *Delinquent Behavior Among Young People In The Western World: First Results Of The International Self-Report Delinquency Study*. Amsterdam/New York: Kugler, 1994. Chapter reports the findings of a self-reported delinquency survey carried out in Spain.

0757 Canivell, Joaquin Martin Juvenile Delinquency In Spain, pp 51-56 in United Nations Crime Prevention And Criminal Justice Program International Scientific And Professional Advisory Council (ed.) *Juveniles And Delinquency*. Milan, Italy, 1995. Chapter offers some general comments on delinquent behavior and juvenile justice in Spain.

0758 Canteras, Murillo Andrés *Female Delinquency In Spain (Delincuencia Femenina En España)*. Madrid: Ministerio De Justicio, 1990. This volume provides an anlaysis of the history, evolution, and backgrounds of female delinquents in Spain. 805p. Spanish.

0759 Costa, Pere Oriol; Perez, Tornero José Manuel & Tropea, Fabio *Urban Tribes: The Anxiety Of Youngsters For Identity: Self Preservation Through The Use Of Violence (Tribus Urbanas: El Ansia De Identidad*

Juvenil: Entre El Culto A La Imagen Y La Autoafirmación A Traves De La Violencia). Barcelona, Spain: Ediciones Paidos, 1996. Based on a study of Spanish youth subcultures, this book describes the Skinhead movement in Barcelona and describes how it might be related to football hooliganism. Spanish. 246p.

0760 Diaz, Amelia; Belena, Angela & Baguena, María José The Role Of Gender In Juvenile Delinquency – Personality And Intelligence, *Personality & Individual Differences* 16:309-324, 1994. Th research reported here explored various dimensions of personality among male and female delinquents and non-delinquents in Valencia, Spain.

0761 García-Perales, Javier Spain, pp 159-168 in Hoffman, Allan M. & Summers, Randal W. (eds.) *Teen Violence: A Global View*. Westport, Connecticut: Greenwood, 2001. This chapter of the anthology on violence offers a description of teen violence in Spain.

0762 Maquieira, Virginia Growing Up in Madrid, pp 38-54 in Cain, Maureen (ed.) *Growing Up Good: Policing The Behavior Of Girls In Europe*. Newbury Park, California: Sage, 1989. This is a discussion on Spanish adolescents' identities, concept of "we"and "they," and critical view of the adult world.

0763 Osuna, Eduardo; Alarcon, Concepcion & Luna, Aurelio Family Violence As A Determinant Factor In Juvenile Maladjustment, *Journal Of Forensic Sciences* 37:1633-1639, 1992. Based on a sample of boys and girls from a training school in Murcia, Spain, this study focused on the importance of family conflict in the genesis of social maladjustment among young people.

0764 Osuna, Eduardo; Alarcon, Concepcion & Luna, Aurelio Personality Traits In Juvenile Maladjustment, *Journal Of Forensic Sciences* 37:228-236, 1992. This study sought to identify the role of various personality traits in the social integration problems of maladjusted young people in Spain.

0765 Otero-Lopez, José Manuel; Luengo, Martin Ángeles; Miron-Rodondo, Lourdes; Carrillo-De-La-Piña, María Teresa & Ronano-Triñanes, Estrella An Empirical Study Of The Relations Between Drug Abuse And Delinquency Among Adolescents, *British Journal Of Criminology* 34:459-478, 1994. This study based on a self-report survey of public school students in Galicia, Spain tests the causal relationship between delinquency and drug abuse.

0766 Rechea, Cristina; Barberet, Rosemay & Moñtanés, Juan & Arroyo, Luis *Juvenile Delinquency In Spain*. Madrid, Spain: Spanish Ministry of Justice and Interior, 1995. Document reports the results of a self-report survey conducted as part of the international self-report delinquency study. 104p. Appendix.

0767 Romero, Estrella; Luengo, M. Ángeles & Sobral, Jorge Personality And Antisocial Behaviour: Study Of Temperamental Dimensions, *Personality And Individual Differences* 31:329-348, 2001. This study examining relationships between self-reported antisocial behavior and a number of temperament variables confirms that these variables are closely associated with self-reported behavior.

0768 Romero, Estrella; Sobral, Jorge; Luengo, M. Ángeles & Marzoa, José Values And Antisocial Behavior Among Spanish Adolescents, *The Journal Of Genetic Psychology* 162:20-40, 2001. In this study of self-reported antisocial behavior, it was found that such conduct is related to numrous temperament variables the authors studied.

St. Lucia

0769 Bruner, Victoria St. Lucia, pp 119-131 in Hoffman, Allan M. & Summers, Randal W. (eds.) *Teen Violence: A Global View*. Westport, Connecticut: Greenwood, 2001. Describes the socioeconomic factors that contribute to teen violence and the need to educate the public and the government of the need to improve the lot of women and children.

Sweden

0770 Adler, H.; Frisk, M. & Lidberg, L. Severe Delinquency In Young People – Background Factors And Characterizing Features, *Nordic Journal Of Psychiatry* 49:263-274, 1995. This study of 127 young criminals sought to determine if there were individual and social background characteristics and early symptoms of behavioral disorder.

0771 Andersson, Jan Continuity In Crime: Sex And Age Differences, *Journal Of Quantitative Criminology* 6:85-100, 1990. Following a cohort of 15,117 individual males and females, this study tried to predict continuity in serious crime from several dimensions.

0772 Andersson, Tommy; Magnusson, David & Wennberg, Peter Early Aggressiveness And Hyperactivity As Indicators Of Adult Alcohol Problems And Criminality: A Prospective Longitudinal Study Of Male Subjects, *Studies On Crime And Crime Prevention* 6:7-20, 1997. This study tries to establish the relationship of the occurrence of early aggressiveness and hyperactivity to later alcohol problems and criminality.

0773 Andersson, Tommy; Mahoney, Joseph L.; Wennberg, Peter; Kühlhorn, Eckart & Magnusson, David The Co-Occurrence Of Alcohol Problems And Criminality In The Transition From Adolescence To Young Adulthood: A Prospective Longitudinal Study Of Young Men, *Studies On Crime And Crime Prevention* 8:169-188, 1999. Using self-report and official data, this study sought to determine if alcohol problems were predicted by criminality in adolescence and young adulthood.

0774 Dalteg, Arne & Levander, Sten Twelve Thousand Crimes By 75 Boys: A 20-Year Follow-Up Study Of Childhood Hyperactivity, *Journal of Forensic Psychiatry* 9:39-57, 1998. This document reports an assessment of attention deficit hyperactivity disorder among advanced delinquents who were treated at a Borstal unit in Sweden.

0775 Duner, Anders & Haglund, Bo *Teenage Boys And Delinquency: Knowledge, Attitudes And Behavior*. Stockholm, Sweden: Swedish Studies on juvenile delinquency, Sweden National Council for Crime Prevention, 1976. This document reports results from a study of Swedish boys to gauge their delinquency involvement, their attitudes, and their knowledge of the law and criminal justice system. 27p.

0776 Durrant, Joan E. Trends In Youth Crime And Well-Being Since The Abolition Of Capital Punishment In Sweden, *Youth And Society* 31:437-455, 2000. According to the author, the rates of a variety of misbehaviors among Swedish youths decreased after the abolition of capital punishment.

0777 Estrada, Felipe The Development Of Juvenile Delinquency In Sweden (Ungdomsbrottslighetens Utveckling I Sverige), *Nordisk Tidsskrift For Kriminalvidenskab* 84:153-169, 1997. This study found that property crimes among juveniles were either constant or decreased among Swedish juveniles. Swedish.

0778 Friday, Paul C. Delinquency In Sweden: Current Trends And Theoretical Implications, *International Journal Of Comparative And Applied Criminal Justice* 16:231-246, 1992. Article describes forms and trends of delinquency in Sweden, and suggests that a small number of youths are responsible for increasing numbers of offenses.

0779 Fry, Lincoln, J. Drug Abuse And Crime In A Swedish Birth Cohort, *British Journal Of Criminology* 25:46-59, 1985. The author traces the trajectory of drug-use, arrests, and criminal careers of male and female Swedish youth.

0780 Goldsmith, Robert W.; Throfast, Gunilla & Nilsson, Pär-Eric Situational Effects On The Decisions Of Adolescent Offenders To Carry Out Delinquent Acts. Relations To Moral Reasoning, Moral Goals, And Personal Constructs, pp 81-102 in Wegener, Hermann; Lösel, Friedrich & Haisch, Jochen (eds.) *Criminal Behavior And The Justice System: Psychological Perspectives*. New York: Springer-Verlag, 1989. This chapter is about a study of moral development levels and delinquent behavior among Swedish youths.

0781 Janson, Carl-Gunnar *Delinquency Among Metropolitan Boys*. Stockholm, Sweden: Department of Sociology, Stockholm University, 1982. This document reports results from Project Metropolitan, a longitudinal delinquency study of a cohort of 15,117 boys and girls in Stockholm, Sweden. 40p.

0782 Janson, Carl-Gunnar & Wikström, Per-Olof H. Growing Up In A Welfare State: The Social Class-Offending Relationship, pp 191-215 in Blau, Zena Smith & Hagan, John (ed.) *Current Perspectives On Aging And The Life Cycle: Delinquency And Disrepute In The Life Course, Vol. 4*. Greenwich, Connecticut: JAI Press, 1995. This study investigated if and how the social situations and behaviors of Scandinavian metropolitan adolescents and young adults reflected their social origins, resources, and childhood experiences.

0783 Korpilahti, Marja *Child Abuse In Finland And Sweden (Barnmisshandel I Finland Och Sverige)*. Helsinki, Finland: Rittspolitiska Forskningsinstitutet, 1981. This report discusses child battering and the known incidence of child battering, and the methods of dealing with it including legislation in Finland and Sweden. 71p.

0784 Långström, Niklas & Lindblad, Frank Young Sex Offenders: Background, Personality, And Crime Characteristics In A Swedish Forensic Psychiatric Sample, *Nordic Journal Of Psychiatry* 54:113-120, 2000. The findings of this research support the idea that experiences and models from abroad can be applied to assessment and treatment procedures for offenders in Sweden and other Nordic countries.

0785 Lie, Nils Boys Who Became Offenders: A Follow-Up Study Of 2,203 Boys Tested With Projective Methods, *Acta Psychiatrica Scandinavica* 77:7-122, 1988. This study investigated the relationships between emotional characteristics in childhood, and emotional disorder and social adjustment problems in in adulthood.

0786 Lindström, Peter Patterns Of School Crime: A Replication And Empirical Extension, *British Journal Of Criminology* 37:121-130, 1997. This article reports the extent, nature, and distribution of school crime in Stockholm, Sweden.

0787 Lindström, Peter Family Interaction, Neighborhood Context And Deviant Behavior: A Research Note, *Studies On Crime And Crime Prevention* 5:113-119, 1996. Using self-report data, this study addresses the question of whether youths with similar family relations have different risks of delinquency depending on the neighborhood they live in.

0788 Lindström, Peter *School Context And Delinquency*. Stockholm, Sweden: University of Stockholm, 1995. In this study of 500 Stockholm school boys, the author examines whether police-recorded delinquency is affected by the social class structure and theacademic balance of the student body. 60p.

0789 Lindström, Peter *School And Delinquency In A Contextual Perspective*. Stockholm, Sweden: National Council for Crime Prevention, 1993. This study examines whether social problem behaviors among youths are influenced by the social context of school, when individual characteristics have been taken into account. 200p. Appendix.

0790 Mahoney, Joseph L. & Stattin, Hakån Leisure Activities And Adolescent Antisocial Behavior: The Role Of Structure And Social Context, *Journal Of Adolescence* 23:113-127, 2000. Using a sample of 14-year olds and their parents, this study sought to assess the relationship be tween leisure and other activities and delinquency.

0791 Martens, Peter L. Parental Monitoring And Deviant Behavior Among Juveniles, *Studies On Crime And Crime Prevention* 6:224-244, 1997. This article reports findings from a study of the different aspects of parental supervision as perceived by 8th graders in neighboring municipalities in southwestern Sweden.

0792 Olofsson, Birgitta *On Delinquency And Conformity Among School Boys*. Stockholm, Sweden: Swedish Studies on Juvenile Delinquency, Sweden, National Council for Crime Prevention, 1976. This is a report based on a longitudinal study of boys attending the ninth grade in a Stockholm high school. 15p.

0793 Peltoniemi, Teuvo Child Abuse And Physical Punishment Of Children In Finland, *Child Abuse And Neglect* 7:33-36, 1983. The findings of a poll on family violence that included attitudes toward child abuse and physical punishment of children in Finland and Sweden are reported in this article.

0794 Sarnecki, Jerzy Juvenile Delinquency In Sweden, pp 11-25 in 41 in Snare, Annika (ed.) *Youth Crime And Justice, Vol. 12*. Oslo, Norway: Norwegian University Press, 1991. Reprinted with minor changes from National Council for Crime Prevention, 1981 pamphlet, this chapter describes the nature of delinquency in Sweden.

0795 Sarnecki, Jerzy Delinquent Networks In Sweden, *Journal Of Quantitative Criminology* 6:31-50, 1990. Following a cohort of 575 youths, this study found that the strong the connection to a delinquent network, the greater the involvement of youths in delinquent behavior.

0796 Sarnecki, Jerzy Self-Reported And Recorded Data On Drug Abuse And Delinquency On 287 Men In Stockholm, pp 107-130 in Klein, Malcolm W. (ed.) *Cross-National Research In Self-Reported Crime And Delinquency,* Dordrecht, The Netherlands: Kluwer, 1989. This study reports findings from a longitudinal investigation of Swedish males surveyed at various ages up to their early 40s.

0797 Sarnecki, Jerzy *Juvenile Delinquency In Sweden: An Overview.* Stockholm, Sweden: National Council for Crime Prevention, 1989. This provides a brief examination of juvenile delinquency in Sweden. 20p.

0798 Sarnecki, Jerzy *Delinquent Networks*. Stockholm, Sweden: Swedish National Council for Crime Prevention, 1986. This report contends that the social orientation of delinquency decreases as juveniles grow older and that rather than being a profession, delinquency is a way of relating to other deviants. 184p.

0799 Smith, William R. *Social Structure, Family Structure, Child Rearing, And Delinquency: Another Look.* Stockholm, Sweden: Department of Sociology, University of Stockholm, 1991. This study examines the effects of social structure, family structure, family socialization, and the child's educational adaptations on delinquency. 135p.

0800 Stattin, Hakån & Magnusson, David Onset Of Official Delinquency: Its Co-Occurrence In Time With Educational, Behavioral, And Interpersonal Problems, *British Journal Of Criminology* 35:417-449, 1995. Using a sample of Swedish boys, this study sought to determine if the age at official delinquency is associated with school and other behavioral problems.

0801 Stattin, Hakån & Klackenberg-Larsson, Ingrid Early Language And Intelligence Development And Their Relationship To Future Criminal Behavior, *Journal Of Abnormal Psychology* 102:369-378, 1993. This research focused on the relationship between intelligence and recorded criminality among Stockholm males and females.

0802 Stattin, Hakån & Magnusson, David Stability And Change In Criminal Behaviour Up To Age 30, *British Journal Of Criminology* 31:327-346, 1991. This study on stability and change in criminal behavior found that diverse adult criminal behavior is preceded by a spread of offenses of different types in adolescence.

0803 Stattin, Hakån & Magnusson, David Criminal Activity At Different Ages: A Study Based On A Swedish Longitudinal Population, *British Journal Of Criminology* 29:368-385, 1989. This article based on longitudinal data regarding students from age 10, analyses the age at first conviction, types of crimes at different ages and sanctions received.

0804 Stattin, Hakån & Magnusson, David The Role Of Early Aggressive Behavior In The Frequency, Seriousness, And Types Of Later Crime, *Journal Of Consulting And Clinical Psychology* 57:710-718, 1989. This study focused on the interaction between aggressive behavior at early school age and later delinquent activities.

0805 Stattin, Hakån *Delinquency As Related To Parents' Preferences For Their Child's Gender.* Stockholm, Sweden: University of Stockholm, 1989. This study found that the prevalence of registered delinquency through age 20 was about twice as high for children whose parents had wanted a child of the opposite sex. 7p.

0806 Timms, Duncan W. G. *Individual Characteristics, Parental Ideology And Mental Health In Adolescence.* Stockholm, Sweden: Department of Sociology, University of Stockholm, 1991. This publication focuses on the relationship between certain individual characteristics and behaviors of a group of boys in early adolescence and their mental health in early adulthood and the childrearing behavior and attitudes of their parents. 78p.

0807 Torstensson, Marie Female Delinquents In A Birth Cohort: Test Of Some Aspects Of Control Theory, *Journal Of Quantiative Criminology* 6:101-115, 1990. This study found that delinquency varies with the strength of the social bond but predicting delinquency from know this information is limited.

0808 Torstensson, Marie *Drug-Abusers In A Metropolitan Cohort.* Stockholm, Sweden: University of Stockholm, Department of Sociology, 1987. This volume is based on a research on delinquency and drug abuse among Swedish youths. 206p.

0809 Van Hofer, Hanns Criminal Behavior And Youth In Sweden: A Long-Term Perspective, *Journal Of Scandinavian Studies In Criminology And Crime Prevention* 1:56-72, 2000. Using diverse official statistical evidence that does not support the public perception, this study evaluates the perception in Sweden that youth crime is on the rise.

0810 Van Hofer, Hanns; Leuke, Leif & Thorsson, Ulf Criminality Among 13 Swedish Birth Cohorts, *British Journal Of Criminology* 23:263-269, 1983. In this study of serious crimes, the authors traced the criminal careers of a cohort of Swedes from age 15 for over a period of seven years.

0811 Wikström, Per-Olof H. Housing Tenure, Social Class And Offending: The Individual-Level Relationship In Childhood And Youth, *Criminal Behaviour And Mental Health* 1:69-89, 1991. The author explores the individual-level relationship between housing and offending among youths.

0812 Wikström, Per-Olof H. Age And Crime In A Stockholm Cohort, *Journal Of Quantitative Criminology* 6:61-84, 1990. Based on data from a cohort of youths followed through young adulthood, this study reports information on the age-crime relationship.

0813 Wikström, Per-Olof H. *Patterns Of Crime In A Birth Cohort: Age, Sex, And Social Class Differences.* Stockholm, Sweden: Department of Sociology, University of Stockholm, 1987. In this study examining patterns of youth and young adulthood crime in a Stockholm cohort of 15,117 males and females, nearly one-fifth of the cohort members had records for a crime, and more than 10% had records as repeat offenders. 80p.

Switzerland

0814 Aebi, Marcelo F. Disrupted Family And Criminality: The Swiss Case (Famille Dissociée Et Criminalité: Le Cas Suisse) *Kriminologisches Bulletin De Criminologie* 23:53-80, 1997. This study of family disruption and its impact on delinquency examines the data from the Swiss International Self-Report Delinquency Study. French.

0815 Gesseney, Eliane & Maret, Daphnée Self-Reported Juvenile Delinquency In Switzerland And Leisure (La Délinquance Juvénile Autorepotée En Suisse Et La Sphère Des Loisirs), *Kriminologisches Bulletin De Criminologie* 23:35-51, 1997. The Swiss data from the International Self-Report Delinquency Study is examined to test the relationship between juvenile delinquency and leisure activity of both male and female youths. French.

0816 Haesler, Walter T. Juvenile Delinquency In Switzerland, *Eurocriminology* 11:133-150, 1997. Focusing on decreasing rates of Swiss delinquency, this article provides an overview of juvenile delinquency in Switzerland.

0817 Killias, Martin & Rabasa, Juan Weapons And Athletic Constitution As Factors Linked To Violence Among Male Juveniles: Findings From The

Swiss Self-Reported Delinquency Project, *British Journal Of Criminology* 37:446-457, 1997. Based on data from Swiss males ages 14-21, this study examined the relationship between violenc and weapons and youths' physical fitness.

0818 Killias, Martin; Villettaz, Patrice & Rabasa, Juan Self-Reported Juvenile Delinquency In Switzerland, pp156-187 in Junger-Tas, Josine; Terlouw, Gert-Jan & Klein, Malcolm W. (eds.) *Delinquent Behavior Among Young People In The Western World: First Results Of The International Self-Report Delinquency Study.* Amsterdam/New York: Kugler, 1994. This chapter summarizes the findings of an international self-report survey on Swiss youths' self-reported delinquency involvement.

0819 Vazsonyi, Alexander T. & Killias, Martin Immigration And Crime Among Youth In Switzerland, *Criminal Justice And Behavior* 28:329-366, 2001. In this study of rates and predictors of deviance among Swiss youth, it was found that second-generation immigrant male youth were more deviant than other Swiss adolescents.

Taiwan

0820 Doerner, William G. & Tsai, Te Hui Child Maltreatment And Juvenile Delinquency In Taiwan, *International Journal Of Comparative And Applied Criminal Justice* 14:225-238, 1990. This study exploring attitudes toward child maltreatment and juvenile delinquency in Taiwan found that respondents exhibited a high degree of consensus in evaluations of the seriousness of various kinds of maltreatment.

0821 Sheu, Chuen Jim Juvenile Delinquency In The Republic Of China: A Chinese Empirical Study Of Social Control Theory, *International Journal Of Comparative And Applied Criminal Justice* 12:59-71, 1988. In examining increasing delinquency in the Republic of China, the author argues that social control theory was the most appropriate in explaining the origin of and the increase in delinquency.

Thailand

0822 Quicker, John C. Thailand, pp 169-181 in Hoffman, Allan M. & Summers, Randal W. (eds.) *Teen Violence: A Global View.* Westport, Connecticut: Greenwood, 2001. This chapter briefly reviews school gang rivalries, drug problems and the response of the system in Thailand.

0823 Tori, Christopher D. & Emavardhana, Tipawadee The Psychology Of Thai Delinquent Youth: A Study Of Self-Perception, Ego Defenses, And Personality Traits, *International Journal Of Offender Therapy And Com-*

parative Criminology 42:305-318, 1998. In this study of the mental and emotional functioning of delinquent adolescents in Thailand, it was found that girls, compared to boys, had better social skills and were more aware of their emotions.

Trinidad and Tobago

0824 Deosaran, Ramesh & Chadee, Derek Juvenile Delinquency In Trinidad And Tobago: Challenges For Social Policy And Caribbean Criminology, *Caribbean Journal Of Criminology And Social Psychology* 2:36-83, 1997. This study examines the social backgrounds and psychological dispositions of 486 juveniles under detention in Trinidad and Tobago.

Turkey

0825 Gunçe, Gülseren & Konanç-Onur, Esin Child Abuse In Turkey, pp 135-150 in Leavitt, Jerome E. (ed.) *Child Abuse And Neglect: Research And Innovation*. Hague, The Netherlands: Martinus Nijhoff, 1983. The authors review the literature on child abuse and various research findings on children in need of protection and on juvenile delinquency in Turkey.

0826 Human Rights Watch *Nothing Unusual: The Torture Of Children In Turkey*. New York, New York, 1991. This document examines the international laws and evidence regarding torture and detention of children aged 13-17 in Turkey.

0827 Ulugtekin, Sevda Family Background And Resocialization Of Turkish Delinquents, *International Journal Of Offender Therapy And Comparative Criminology* 33:27-35, 1989. The interaction between family socialization and delinquency among Turkish boy was the focus of this inquiry.

United Kingdom

0828 Abrahams, Caroline & Mungall, Roddy *Runaways: Exploding The Myths—An Evaluative Report*. London, United Kingdom: Police Foundation, National Children's Home and the Metropolitan Police, 1992. This research found that there are an estimated 43,000 13-16 year olds who had runaway at least once during the year that involved more than 100,000 incidents in 1990 in England and Scotland. 39p. Appendix.

0829 Allsopp, John F. & Feldman, M. Philip Personality And Anti-Social Behaviour In School Boys, *British Journal Of Criminology*, 16:337-351, 1976. This psychological study of personality among 11-16 year old boys in the United Kingdom includes some self-reported delinquency items.

0830 Al-Talib, Nadhim I. & Griffin, Christine Labeling Effect On Adolescents' Self-Concept, *International Journal Of Offender Therapy And Comparative Criminology* 38:47-57, 1994. This report, based on research in Birmingham, United Kingdom, investigating labeled and unlabeled juvenile delinquents' self-concept found support for labeling theory and a significant difference between the two groups.

0831 Bailey, S. M.; Thornton, L. & Weaver, A. B. The First 100 Admissions To An Adolescent Secure Unit, *Journal of Adolescence* 17:207-220, 1994. This study of the clinical, individual and family background characteristics of the first 100 adolescents admitted to an adolescent secure unit in Manchester found that the recent major offense, posing a risk to others upon admission, and being from a secure facility were predictors of future delinquent behavior.

0832 Bailey, Susan Adolescents Who Murder, *Journal Of Adolescence*19:19-39, 1996. Besides a description of a 5-year cohort of 20 adolescent murderers in England and Wales, the author reviews the etiology of delinquency, assessment, treatments and outcomes and the juvenile justice process.

0833 Baker, Anthony W. & Duncan, Sylvia P. Child Sexual Abuse: A Study Of Prevalence In Great Britain, *Child Abuse And Neglect* 9:457-467, 1985. This national survey in England provides details on the number of sexually abused and those abused as children.

0834 Balding, John; Regis, David & Wise, Anne *Cash And Carry? Young People, Their Friends, And Offensive Weapons*. Exeter, United Kingdom: Schools Health Education Unit, University of Exeter, 1996. This is a 1995-1996 survey of weapon carrying, friends who carry weapons, and type of weapon carried; bullying and fear of crime, and the use of drugs, alcohol and tobacco among 5,000 youths aged 14-15 years. 79p.

0835 Baldwin, Steve *Alcohol Education And Young Offenders: Medium and Short Term Effectiveness of Educational Programs*, New York & Berlin: Springer-Verlag, 1991. This psychological quasi-experimental and evaluative replication study on the effectiveness of alcohol education courses in the United Kingdom concludes that the effect was limited but and younger clients and those under behavioral/counseling reduced their heavy drinking and offending. 152p.

0836 Ball, Caroline & Connolly, Jo Educationally Disaffected Young Offenders, *British Journal Of Criminology* 40:594-616, 2000. This research describes the impact of youth justice agencies' supervision and pre-sentence school-based reports on the educational situation and reoffending behavior of truants who were defendants and others.

0837 Barclay, Gordon C. & Turner, David Recent Trends In Official Statistics On Juvenile Offending In England And Wales, pp 75-85 in Booth, Tim (ed.) *Juvenile Justice In The New Europe.* Sheffield, United Kingdom: Joint Unit for Social Services Research, Sheffield University, 1991. Home Office statistics reveal that changes in the handling of young offenders as much as their offense behavior account for the recent trends in juvenile criminality.

0838 Barker, Martin & Petley, Julian (eds.) *Ill Effects: The Media/Violence Debate.* London, United Kingdom; Routledge, 1997. The articles in this anthology on media and children include discussions of legal issues and impact of the media on behavior. 171p.

0839 Barrett, David (ed.) *Child Prostitution In Britain: Dilemmas And Practical Responses.* London, United kingdom: Children's Society, 1997. This volume contains nine articles on various issues such as policing underage prostitution, the legal context of child prostitution, health professionals' response to it, street views of child prostitution, causes, political response and new forms of child prostitution in Britain. 192p. Appendix.

0840 Batta, I. D.; McCulloch, J. W. & Smith, N. J. A Study Of Juvenile Delinquency Amongst Asians And Half-Asians, *British Journal Of Criminology* 15:32-42, 1975. When comparing the rates and types of delinquent behavior among Asians, half-Asians, and "other" juveniles in Bradford it was found that the half-Asian youths had five times the rates of juvenile delinquency than the Asian youngsters and double the rates of others.

0841 Berg, Ian Features Of Children Taken To Juvenile Court For Failure To Attend School, *Psychological Medicine* 8:447-453, 1978. Social reports regarding the behavior, school, family, and previous involvement with social work agencies in 84 truancy cases from Leeds' juvenile court were examined for prior antisocial and other problem behavior.

0842 Boswell, Gwyneth R. Criminal Justice And Violent Young Offenders, *Howard Journal* 37:148-160, 1998. In studying the characteristics of a group of serious juvenile offenders sentenced to an indeterminate period of detention in the United Kingdom found that 91% of the young offenders report childhood trauma of abuse or loss while 34% reported both leading the author to conclude that such a double trauma in childhood might be factor in the development of violent offenders.

0843 Boswell, Gwyneth *Young And Dangerous: The Backgrounds And Careers Of Sec-tion 53 Offenders*. Aldershot, United Kingdom: Avebury, 1996. Two studies, one examining the custodial experiences and developmental needs of 25 young offenders from various detention facilities and the second assessing the prevalence of abuse and loss in the lives of "Section 53" offenders given indeterminate detention, suggest a close link between serious violent criminal behavior and degree of loss and/or abuse in their earlier lives. 167p.

0844 Bowling, Benjamin; Graham, John & Ross, Alec Self-Reported Offending Among Young People In England And Wales, pp 42-64 in Junger-Tas, Josine; Terlouw, Gert-Jan & Klein, Malcolm W. (eds.) *Delinquent Behavior Among Young People In The Western World: First Results Of The International Self-Report Delinquency Study*. Amsterdam/New York: Kugler, 1994. This chapter reports the findings from a self-reported delinquency survey of 14-21 year olds that was carried out in England and Wales.

0845 Brown, B. J.; Druce, N. R. & Sawyer, C. E. Individual Differences And Absconding Behaviour, *British Journal Of Criminology* 18:62-78, 1978. Psychometric evaluations of boys from a regional assessment center were the focus of this inquiry that found a relationship between temperament and running away.

0846 Buckingham, David Electronic Child Abuse? Rethinking The Media's Effects On Children pp 32-47 in Barker, Martin & Petley, Julian (eds.) *Ill Effects: The Media/Violence Debate*, London, United Kingdom, 1997. The author of this chapter discusses academic research, public debate and regulation, definition of and discourse on effects, and children as active audiences of media.

0847 Burke, Roger & Sunley, Ros Post-Modernism And Youth Subcultures In Britain In The 1990's, pp 35-66 in Hazlehurst, Kayleen & Hazlehurst, Cameron (eds.) *Gangs And Youth Subcultures: International Explorations*. New Brunswick, New Jersey: Transaction, 1998. This chapter provides and review of various theories of youth subcultures in Britain.

0848 Burke, Roger & Sunley, Ros *"Hanging Out" In The 1990s: Young People And The Postmodern Condition*. Leicester, United Kingdom: Scarman Centre for the Study of Public Order, University of Leicester, 1996. This essay is an overview of youth subculture theories of the Chicago School and the 1970s' neo-Marxist version in a discussion of social change and working class youthful misconduct in Birmingham. 29p.

0849 Burr, Angela Chasing The Dragon: Heroin Misuse, Delinquency And Crime In The Context Of South London Culture, *British Journal Of*

Criminology 27:333-357, 1987. Based on participant observation, the author found that various sociocultural factors such as prior use and being part of the "skag" subculture affect drug use and delinquency.

0850 Burrows, John; Shapland, Joanna & Wiles, Paul Arson In Schools: Its Impact And Implications For Prevention, *International Journal Of Risk Security And Crime Prevention* 1:89-102, 1996. This study of the prevalence and implications of arson in schools reported that 1 out of 8 schools in United Kingdom experienced arson or suspected arson during the year and the most likely arsonist was a student or local youth.

0851 Burrows, John; Shapland, Joanna & Wiles, Paul *Arson In Schools*. London, United Kingdom: Arson Prevention Bureau, 1993. The prevalence of arson in United Kingdom's schools and the various preventive measures taken are the subject of this report. 88p. Appendix.

0852 Campbell, Anne Self-Reported Delinquency And Home Life: Evidence From A Sample Of British Girls, *Journal of Youth And Adolescence* 16:167-177, 1987. This study of self-reported delinquency among British girls focused on the relationship of family variables and the girls' delinquency.

0853 Campbell, Anne Self-Report Of Fighting By Females: A Preliminary Study, *British Journal Of Criminology* 26:28-46, 1986. The admission of institutionalized and normal juveniles and adult females in prison to fighting with another female within the past year leads the author to conclude that such self-report reveals the pervasiveness of female aggression that official statistics do not.

0854 Carlen, Pat *Jigsaw: A Political Criminology Of Youth Homelessness*. Buckingham, United Kingdom: Open University Press, 1996. This article discusses the nature and impact of homelessness among youth in its current sociopolitical context preceded by ignoring the needs of youth population in the 1980s while increasing greater controls, and increasingly harsher punishments in United Kingdom in the 1990s. 162p.

0855 Clarke, R. V. G. *Tackling Vandalism*. London, United Kingdom: Her Majesty's Stationery Office, 1978. This report on three studies of the vandalism claims that building design in public housing enables vandalism in these "housing estates" in Manchester found that many boys self-report minor vandalism but only a minority were seriously involved in this behavior.

0856 Commission Of Children And Violence *Children And Violence: Report Of The Gulbenkian Foundation Commission*. London, United Kingdom,

1995. This report reviews the extent of violence involving children and reasons why children become violent, and included is a discussion of the violent conflict in Northern Ireland. 313p.

0857 Cookson, Hazel M. Alcohol Use And Offense Type In Young Offenders, *British Journal Of Criminology* 32:352-360, 1992. When alcohol use and offense type of convicted 17-21 year old males in Young Offender Institutions in England were surveyed, it was found that there was a significant association between habitual drunkenness and self-reported delinquency, and between alcohol imbibing and violent offense.

0858 Coote, Anna (ed.) *Families, Children And Crime*. London, United Kingdom: Insti-tute for Public Policy Research, 1994. The articles in this anthology address issues such as "families, gender and crime", "evidence, ideas and policy", "working with offenders" and "working with families and children."147p.

0859 Corby, Brian *Child Abuse: Towards A Knowledge Base*. Buckingham, United Kingdom: Open University Press, 1993. This volume offers an extensive discussion of diverse topics relating to children in the United States and Great Britain. 195p.

0860 Core, Dianne & Harrison, Fred *Chasing Satan: An Investigation Into Satanic Crimes Against Children*. London, United Kingdom: Gunter Books, 1991. The authors investigate satanic crimes committed against children in Great Britain in order to raise public awareness of crimes that authorities, they feel, have tended to deny or disbelieve such crimes. 183p.

0861 Danson, Linda & Soothill, Keith Child Murder And The Media: A Study Of The Reporting Of Child Murder In "The Times" 1887-1990, *Journal Of Forensic Psychiatry* 7:495-503, 1996. This study focused on the coverage of murders of children in the United Kingdom by "The Times" from 1890 to 1990 at 5-yearly intervals.

0862 De Li, Spencer Legal Sanctions And Youths' Status Achievement: A Longitudinal Study, *Justice Quarterly* 16:377-401, 1999. This test of labeling theory and the need for integrating the life course perspective found that legal sanctions decreased the likelihood of high status achievement thereby increasing youths' involvement in delinquent behavior.

0863 Devlin, Angela *Criminal Classes: Offenders At School*. Winchester, United Kingdom: Waterside, 1995. In a study of the relationship between school failure and future criminal behavior, it was found that many offenders report having been subject to bullying, abuse and dysfunctional relationships that led to school problems such as truancy. 189p.

0864 Dobash, Russell P.; Dobash, R. Emerson; Ballintyne, Scott; Schumann, Karl; Kaulitzki, Reiner & Garth, Hans-Werner Ignorance And Suspicion: Young People And Criminal Justice In Scotland And Germany, *British Journal Of Criminology* 30:306-320, 1990. This study compares young people's contacts with and perceptions of criminal justice in the two countries. In both, contacts with authorities were described in negative terms by youths and had negative impact on subsequent behavior among them.

0865 Dyson, Graham P.; Power, Kevin G. & Wozniak, Edward Problems With Using Official Records From Young Offender Institutions As Indices Of Bullying, *International Journal Of Offender Therapy And Comparative Criminology* 41:121-138, 1997. Scottish official records were analyzed from five young offender institutions in an attempt to ascertain their reliability as a measure of bullying among inmates.

0866 Eley, Thalia C. & Lichtenstein, Paul Sex Differences In The Etiology Of Aggressive And Nonagressive Antisocial Behavior: Results From Two Twin Studies, *Child Development* 70:155-168, 1999. This study of British and Swedish twins reveals genetic factors in anti-social aggressive behavior and a sex difference in non-aggressive anti-social behavior leading the authors to conclude that the former is heritable while the latter is affected by shared environment.

0867 Emler, Nicholas & Reicher, Stephen *Adolescence And Delinquency: The Collective Management Of Reputation*. Oxford, United Kingdom: Blackwell, 1995. The authors argue that the central task of adolescence is defining one's place in society that involves the negotiation of one's reputation by committing or abstaining from delinquency within the collective character of adolescent behavior. 267p.

0868 Emms, T. W.; Povey, R. M. & Clift, S. M. The Self-Concepts Of Black And White Delinquents, *British Journal Of Criminology* 26:385-393, 1986. Difference between the self-concepts of black and white offenders was found to not be statistically signifcant by these researchers.

0869 Evans, David J. *Geographical Perspectives On Juvenile Delinquency*. Westmead, United Kingdom: Gower Publishing Company, 1980. Using offender data for the city of Cardiff, the author examines spatial, ecological, and behavioral approaches to the study of delinquency. 132 p.

0870 Farrington, David P.; Lambert, Sandra & West, Donald J. Criminal Careers Of Two Generations Of Family Members In The Cambridge

Study In Delinquent Development, *Studies On Crime And Prevention* 7:85-106, 1998. This longitudinal research on the criminal careers of a sample up to age 40 and their biological parents, their full brothers, sisters, wives, and cohabitees found that offending is less concentrated in the teenage years but more persistent throughout life, and the significant differences exists between generations and not gender groups.

0871 Farrington, David P. Early Predictions Of Violent And Non-Violent Youthful Offending, *European Journal On Criminal Policy And Research* 5:51-66, 1997. Summarizes the Cambridge study of self-reported criminality and conviction records, violent and non-violent offending, and the attempt at predicting future criminality of youth.

0872 Farrington, David P. *Understanding And Preventing Youth Crime.* York, United Kingdom: Joseph Rowntree Foundation, 1996. This is a summary of current information on youth crime in England in Wales, risk factors in juvenile delinquency that can be modified, preventing youth crime, and priorities for research and development. 43p.

0873 Farrington, David P. The Development Of Offending And Antisocial Behaviour From Childhood: Key Findings From The Cambridge Study In Delinquent Development, *Journal Of Child Psychology And Psychiatry* 36:929-964, 1995. This article reports on the longitudinal study of a cohort of London boys from age 8 to 32.

0874 Farrington, David P. Early Developmental Prevention Of Juvenile Delinquency, *Criminal Behavior And Mental Health* 4:209-227, 1994. This assessment of delinquency prevention in England list poor parental supervision as the most important family risk factors along with harsh and erratic parental discipline besides teenage pregnancy, substance use in pregnancy and perinatal complications such as low birth-weight, high impulsivity and low intelligence.

0875 Farrington David P. & West, Donald J. Criminal, Penal And Life Histories Of Chronic Offenders: Risk And Protective Factors And Early Identification, *Criminal Behavior And Mental Health* 3:492-523, 1993. This study of penal history found that the most important childhood risk factors of chronic criminality were troublesome and daring behavior, having a delinquent sibling or a convicted parent, and almost all of those studied were sent to a penal institution at some stage although most claim that such detention had no effect on their recidivism.

0876 Farrington, David P. & Burrows, John N. Did Shoplifting Really Decrease? *British Journal Of Criminology* 33:57-69, 1993. Explaining the decreasing number of juvenile shoplifting incidents in Great Britain during 1985-1989, the authors conclude that this was due to the informal manner in which increasing numbers of shoplifters were dealt with by the police thereby unaccounted for in the official data.

0877 Farrington, David P. Trends In English Juvenile Delinquency And Their Explanation, *International Journal Of Comparative And Applied Criminal Justice* 16:151-163, 1992. This summary and interpretation of trends in recorded juvenile delinquency in England and Wales between 1961-1989 argues that the recent fall in the juvenile crime rate is an artifact of unrecorded warnings.

0878 Farrington, David P. Long-Term Prediction Of Offending And Other Life Outcomes, pp. 26-37 in Wegener, Hermann; Lösel, Friedrich & Haisch, Jochen (eds.) *Criminal Behavior And The Justice System: Psychological Perspectives*, New York, New York: Springer-Verlag, 1989. Summaries of the Cambridge longitudinal study and the author's various prediction studies are the focus of this article.

0879 Farrington, David P. Early Predictors Of Frequent Delinquent Behavior (Les Signaux Précoces De S'Agir Délinquant Fréquent), *Criminologie* 19:9-31, 1986. The author concludes that harsh and erratic parental discipline and parental conflict along with childhood antisocial behavior, criminal parents and siblings, social deprivation, low intelligence and attainment are excellent predictors of offending in general but fail to delineate between high and low rate adolescent offenders. French with English summary.

0880 Farrington, David P. Predicting Self-Reported And Official Delinquency, pp 150-173 in Farrington, David & Tarling, Roger (eds.) *Prediction In Criminology*. Albany, New York: State University of New York Press, 1985. This analysis of longitudinal data to predict offense behavior concludes that identifying a group with much more than a 50% chance of delinquency or identifying more than 50% of the delinquents is difficult while it may be possible to predict persistent or chronic offending.

0881 Farrington, D. P. The Life Span Of Criminal Behaviour: What Do We Know, *Forum On Correctional Research* 5:6-9, 1993. This paper reports that most individual's offending behavior peaks at 17 with about 16 offenses per 100 males studied in the Cambridge, England study of development and delinquency.

0882 Forsyth, Alasdair & Barnard, Marina Preferred Drinking Locations Of Scottish Adolescents, *Health And Place* 6:105-115, 2000. The results of a research into the alcohol use by juveniles indicates a continuum of drinking styles between low-risk and high-risk circumstances.

0883 Foster, Janet & Hope, Timothy *Housing, Community And Crime: The Impact Of The Priority Estates Project.* London, United Kingdom: Her Majesty's Stationery office, 1993. This evaluation using diverse data sources from London borough elaborates on crime and delinquency and community life in public housing projects in the United Kingdom. 119p.

0884 Gibson, Evelyn *Homicide In England And Wales.* London, United Kingdom: Her Majesty's Stationery Office, 1985. This report on the numbers, victims and perpetrators of murders in England and Wales includes data on youthful offenders as well.

0885 Gill, Owen Urban Stereotypes And Delinquent Incidents, *British Journal Of Criminology* 16:321-336, 1976. This descriptive study narrates confrontations involving boys and the police in the Luke Street neighborhood of London, United Kingdom.

0886 Gilmour, Alan *Innocent Victims: The Question Of Child Abuse.* London, United Kingdom: Michael Joseph, 1989. This is a discussion of child abuse, its causes, and what constitutes abuse—physical, sexual and emotional abuse and neglect, and includes a discussion of protection for children and prevention of abuse. 198p.

0887 Goodey, Jo Examining The 'White Racist/Black Victim' Stereotype, *International Review Of Victimology* 5:235-256, 1998. Based on a study of the impact of race and racism on boys' fear of crime, the author concludes that the emergence of a "new" Asian male assertiveness frequently translating into aggression toward other racial groups should be viewed in the larger context of white racism and not limited to Islamophobia, power, powerlessness, and masculinity.

0888 Goodey, Jo Understanding Racism And Masculinity: Drawing On Research With Boys Aged Eight To Sixteen, *International Journal Of The Sociology Of Law* 26:393-418, 1998. The author explores the racism experienced by his sample of Asian, Afro-Caribbean and white boys in Sheffield in the context of marginalization of racial groups, racism and masculinity in mainstream criminology.

0889 Gow, James & Peggrem, Alan *Car Crime Culture? A Study Of Motor Vehicle Theft By Juveniles.* Cardiff, United Kingdom: Bernardo's Research & Development, 1991. This report on juvenile car thefts in three south Wales counties found that the youths stole a particular high-performance car, mainly from parking lots during late evening or early morning hours and, on impulse and for the excitement of the activity. 11p. Appendix.

0890 Huff, Graham & Collinson, Frances Young Offenders, Gambling And Video Game Playing, *British Journal Of Criminology* 27:401-410, 1987. In interviews with adolescent under custody in Feltham, the authors found that gamblers, compared with video-game players, were a more homogeneous group and have fewer problems, and a fifth of those interviewed engaged in illegal behavior to finance their habit.

0891 Graham, John & Bowling, Benjamin *Young People And Crime*. London, United Kingdom: Research and Statistics Department, Home Office, 1996. This self-reported delinquency survey of a national sample of 1,721 and a booster sample of 808 minority ethnic 14-25 year olds in England and Wales found that youthful illegality was widespread and a large numbers of youths committed a wide variety of property and violent offenses. 142p.

0892 Graham, John *Amusement Machines: Dependency And Delinquency*. London, Unit-ed Kingdom: Her Majesty's Stationery Office, 1988. This report of youths' involvement with amusement machines concludes that the small magnitude of the problem did not warrant legislation. 48p. Appendix.

0893 Great Britain Home Affairs Committee *Juvenile Offenders*. London, United Kingdom: Her Majesty's Stationery Office, 1993. Besides describing aspects of juvenile offending, causes of delinquency and justice system treatment in Great Britain, this document provides statistics on the incidence and trends in juvenile illegality. 444p.

0894 Great Britain Home Office Standing Conference On Crime Prevention *Report Of The Working Group On Juvenile Crime*. London, United Kingdom, 1987. This report on juvenile crime in England reports that many juveniles involved in illegality most of which is minor, juvenile crime rates are higher in inner city neighborhoods, and four times as many boys as girls were processed for criminal conduct, and less than 5 percent of the known juvenile delinquents were processed for crimes of violence. 45 p.

0895 Grubin, Don *Sex Offending Against Children: Understanding The Risk*. London, United Kingdom: Home Office, Policing and Reducing Crime Unit, 1998. Drawing upon published studies in the 1990s, this document reviews the nature and extent of child sexual abuse in United Kingdom. 56p.

0896 Hagan, John & Palloni, Alberto The Social Reproduction Of A Criminal Class In Working-Class London, Circa 1950-1980, *American Journal Of Sociology* 96:265-299, 1990. This analysis found that labeling of parents and sons had an intergenerational interaction effect for subsequent illegal behavior particularly among younger, previously delinquent adolescent males.

0897 Hagell, Ann & Newburn, Tim Family And Social Context Of Adolescent Re-Offenders, *Journal Of Adolescence* 19:5-18, 1996. Recidivists reveal a high level of family disruption in a variety of living arrangements, and although most claim good relationships with their mothers and report strong social ties with friends and peers, report heavy use of drugs and alcohol.

0898 Hagell, Ann & Newburn, Tim *Persistent Young Offenders*. London, United Kingdom: Policy Studies Institute, 1994. This study of persistent juvenile delinquency in Great Britain estimates the numbers of young offenders and provides a portrait of their backgrounds such as criminal, education and family history, welfare and drug use, and the type and numbers of offenses committed by them, and the criminal justice system's handling of them. 136p. Appendix.

0899 Hagell, Ann & Newburn, Tim *Young Offenders And The Media: Viewing Habits And Preferences*. London, United Kingdom: Policy Studies Institute, 1994. This policy paper concludes that the television viewing habits of juvenile offenders and their non-offending peers in the United Kingdom were not different. 105p.

0900 Haines, Kevin & Drakeford, Mark *Young People And Youth Justice*. London, United Kingdom: Macmillan, 1998. The author emphasizes the need to maintain a separate justice system for young people and stresses the need to treat juvenile delinquents as children first and then as lawbreakers while safeguarding their rights within the international rules and conventions. 288p.

0901 Harbison, J.; Jardine, E. & Curran, J. D. The Use Of The Jesness Inventory With Northern Ireland Populations, *British Journal Of Criminology* 18:387-390, 1978. Five of the Jesness scales clearly differentiated the normal school group from the delinquent samples while several other scales were less consistent in discriminating, and three scales showed no difference between the groups.

0902 Hartless, Julie M.; Ditton, Jason; Nair, Gwyneth & Phillips, Samuel More Sinned Against Than Sinning: A Study Of Young Teenagers' Experience Of Crime, *British Journal Of Criminology* 35:114-133, 1995. Based on a survey of youths attending an inner city school in Glasgow, Scotland, this study examines their crime experiences, as both victims and perpetrators.

0903 Higgins, Kathryn & McElrath, Karen The Trouble With Peace: The Cease-Fires And Their Impact On Drug Use Among Youth In Northern Ireland, *Youth And Society* 32:6-28, 2000. The impact of Northern Ireland's conflict on youth people's health and consequent drug use is the theme of this discussion.

0904 Hollin, Clive R. & Swaffer, Tracey Social Functioning And Delinquency: A Return To Basics, *Journal Of Adolescence* 16:205-210, 1993. In study of 20 15-20 year old male offenders in residence at a youth treatment service in United Kingdom found an association between social cognition and social performance but not any difference between sex-offenders and others.

0905 Holman, Bob *Children & Crime*. Oxford, United Kingdom: Lion Publishing, 1995. The author explores juvenile crime using case histories as examples to examine the nature of crime, explanations for delinquency, and strategies for preventing youthful involvement in criminal activities—all aimed at laypersons wishing to work with troubled youth. 221p.

0906 Hope, Timothy Conflicting Forces: Changing The Dynamics Of Crime And Community On A "Problem" Estate, *British Journal Of Criminology* 32:488-504, 1992. Using Victimization and household surveys, observations and interviews, this study explores the effect of public housing on crime and delinquency in the community in Northern England.

0907 Howard League *Child Offenders: UK & International Practice*. London, United Kingdom: The Howard League for Penal Reform, 1995. This report on juvenile delinquents has eight short pieces on topics varying from media and political interest in youth crime in the United Kingdom, and the common law concept of *doli incapax*. 61p.

0908 Hundleby, John D. Personality And The Prediction Of Delinquency And Drug Use, *British Journal Of Criminology* 26:129-146, 1986. In a study of public school and training school boys, the author found drug use was predicted by extraversion while various indices of recidivism were poorly predicted.

0909 Hunter, John A. Jr. & Becker, Judith V. The Role Of Deviant Sexual Arousal In Juvenile Sexual Offending, *Criminal Justice And Behavior* 21:132-149, 1994. The author concludes that juvenile sex offenders, unlike the adult sex offenders, are a diverse group.

0910 Jaffe, Peter & Thompson, Judy Family Consultant Service With The London Police Force—A Description, *Canadian Police College Journal*

3:115-125, 1979. According to the data from this research, about a third of domestic crises that it deals with in London, England involve juveniles who are runaways or exhibit behavior problems.

0911 James, A. C. & Neil, P. Juvenile Sexual Offending: One-Year Period Prevalence Study Within Oxfordshire, *Child Abuse And Neglect* 20:477-485, 1996. This study found official juvenile sexual offense prevalence rate to be 1.5 per 1,000 males aged 12 to 17, and that sexually abusive male youths had a family history of neglect as well as physical and/or sexual abuse.

0912 James, Allison & Jenks, Chris Public Perceptions Of Childhood Criminality, *British Journal Of Sociology* 47:315-331, 1996. This essay examines the sociological contexts—of traditional and present conceptions of the child and their social and moral implications in views of innocence and dependency, the public's reaction to mass media reports of children murdered by children.

0913 James, Oliver *Juvenile Violence In A Winner-Loser Culture: Socio-Economic And Familial Origins Of The Rise In Violence Against The Person*. London, United Kingdom: Free Association Books, 1995. In examining the role of inequality in the crime statistics ofUnited kingdom during 1987-1994, the author found a 40% increase in male juvenile violence and argues that income inequality combined with false hopes for equal opportunities, lack of welfare support for the disadvantaged, and poor job quality are the root causes. 171p.

0914 Jenkins, Philip *Intimate Enemies: Moral Panics In Contemporary Great Britain*. New York, New York: Aldine de Gruyter, 1992. Investigation of the 1980s moral panics in Great Britain revealed that an existing phenomenon such as sexual abuse of children, Satanists, and serial murder, was suddenly discovered and exaggerated rousing widely-held fears of changes in British society and national identity thereby providing political campaign issues. 262p.

0915 Kilpatrick, Rosemary; Trew, Karen & Young, Valerie Juvenile Crime In Northern Ireland: Psychological Research And Social Policy, *Irish Journal Of Psychology* 16:356-365, 1995. This literature review identifies themes in research relating to crime and antisocial behavior among young people in Northern Ireland.

0916 Knight, B. J. & West, D. J. Temporary And Continuing Delinquency, *British Journal Of Criminology* 15:43-50, 1975. Using data from Cambridge study on delinquency development of 411 working class London boys, this article reports on those factors that delineate boys who continue to be law violators at 18 and 19 years of age.

0917 La Fontane, J. S *The Extent And Nature Of Organised And Ritual Abuse: Research Findings*. London, United Kingdom: Her Majesty's Stationery Office, 1994. The author investigates the prevalence and nature of organized and ritual satanic sexual abuse of children. 36p. Appendix.

0918 Lee, Mark & O'Brien, Rachel *The Game's Up: Redefining Child Prostitution*. London, United Kingdom: The Children's Society, 1995. This report criticizes the inappropriate and inadequate responses to the sexual exploitation of vulnerable children and young people in England and Wales, and increase constructive analysis of the factors that lead to prostitution by young people. 81p.

0919 Lewis, Christopher Juvenile Delinquents In England And Wales: Social, Judicial And Statistical Backgrounds (Jugendliche Straftäter In England Und Wales: Soziale, Gesetzliche Und Statistische Hintergründe) pp 51-58 in Friedrich Ebert Stiftung (ed.) *Child And Juvenile Delinquency In Germany (Kinder- Und Jugendkriminalität In Deutschland)*. Berlin, Germany: Friedrich Ebert Stiftung, 1996. This chapter offers a statistical profile of delinquent youths, their behavior and processing in England and Wales. German.

0920 Liddle, Mark *Wasted Lives*. London, United Kingdom: National Association for the Care and Resettlement of Offenders, 1998. This report on the male youths in prisoners in the United Kingdom during 1997 draws from files their characteristics including those between 15-17, life histories, and the cost of their imprisonment. 76p.

0921 Liebling, Alison *Suicide In Prison*. London & New York: Routledge, 1992. Besides exploring the previous research, this study of four young offender facilities in England and Wales collected data using diverse methods to provide profiles, male/female differences and details on the onset of suicidal crisis among these young offenders. 273p.

0922 Loader, Ian; Girling, Evi & Sparks, Richard Narratives Of Decline: Youth, Disorder And Community In An English 'Middletown,' *British Journal Of Criminology* 38:388-403, 1998. This research describes how adult residents of a medium-sized, moderately affluent low-crime rate English town interpret and respond to teenagers' incivilities and the contradiction between their acknowledged obligations to troublesome local adolescents and their punitive, exclusionary statements about "youth in general."

0923 Maden, Tony; Swinton, Mark & Gunn, John Gambling In Young Offenders, *Criminal Behavior And Mental Health* 2:300-308, 1992. The authors of this study of gambling among young offenders argue that gambling, other behavioral disorders and recidivism have common origins, and found that 12% who identified themselves as excessive gamblers had more criminality than non-gamblers, had been in care or in children's homes, and have had psychiatric treatment.

0924 Mawby, R. I. The Victimization Of Juveniles: A Comparative Study Of Three Areas Of Publicly Owned Housing In Sheffield, *Journal Of Research In Crime And Delinquency* 16:98-113, 1979. When self-reported victimization of juveniles in Sheffield, England was examined, the rate of victimization was quite extensive, sex and offender status were associated with being a victim, but only a small proportion were reported to the police.

0925 Mawby, R. I.; McCulloch, J. W. & Batta, I. D. Crime Amongst Asian Juveniles In Bradford, *International Journal Of Sociology Of Law* 7:297-306, 1979. Data on boys and girls of Pakistani-Indian origin, and others who were cautioned, prosecuted and found guilty, demonstrates that the Asian youths tend to be less delinquent than non-Asian youths.

0926 Mawby, Rob Sex And Crime: The Results Of A Self-Report Study, *British Journal Of Sociology* 31:525-543, 1980. Questionnaire survey of boys and girls from a school in Sheffield when examined reveal that the delinquency of girls, despite a narrowing of the sex differences in recorded crime statistics, were more likely to be truancy while boys were more likely to commit crimes.

0927 Maxim, Paul S. Cohort Size And Juvenile Delinquency In England And Wales, *Journal Of Criminal Justice* 14:491-499, 1986. Reported crime was used to analyze the relationship between fluctuations in cohort size and rates of conviction found that the rates of convictions is related to cohort size for the first few cohorts, while caution rates co-vary with cohort size for latter two-thirds.

0928 McCullough, Dave; Schmidt, Tanja & Lockhard, Bill *Car Theft In Northern Ireland: Recent Studies On A Persistent Problem.* Belfast: Extern Organization, 1990. This report examines the problem of joyriding in West Belfast, Northern Ireland. 40p.

0929 McGurk, B. J.; McEwan, A. W. & Graham, F. Personality Types And Recidivism Among Young Delinquents, *British Journal Of Criminology* 21:159-165, 1981. In a sample of youths in a reception center, the authors found recidivism is related to personality types that they divided into anxious, normal, disturbed and truculent.

0930 McMurran, Mary & Hollin, Clive R. *Young Offenders And Alcohol-Related Crime: A Practitioner's Guidebook.* Chichester, United Kingdom: John Wiley & Sons, 1993. Summarizes the various cognitive-behavioral treatment programs for alcohol abusing juvenile offenders with some chapters devoted to understanding behavior, youthful offending and drinking, alcohol education and lifestyle modification. 195p.

0931 McMurran, Mary & Hollin, Clive R. Drinking And Delinquency: Another Look At Young Offenders And Alcohol, *British Journal Of Criminology* 29:386-394, 1989. Males 15-21 in a Leicester young offender institution were interviewed to examine the relationship between alcohol abuse and involvement in illegal behavior.

0932 McNally, Roger B. Homicidal Youth In England And Wales 1982-1992: Profile And Policy, *Psychology Crime And Law* 1:333-342, 1995. After studying profiles of homicidal youths below 17 in England and Wales, this article argues that such violence is highly correlated with cultural male socialization and antisocial personality, and dysfunctional family facilitates the early onset of aggression and recommends support for family stability, parenting skills and violence reduction programs.

0933 McQuoid, Joan The ISRD Study - Self-Report Findings From N. Ireland, *Journal Of Adolescence* 19:95-98, 1996. Article summarizes one of the large-scale surveys of self-reported delinquency in Northern Ireland.

0934 McQuoid, Joan The Self-Reported Delinquency Study In Belfast, Northern Ireland, pp 65-101 in Junger-Tas, Josine; Terlouw, Gert-Jan & Klein, Malcolm W. (eds.) *Delinquent Behavior Among Young People In The Western World: First Results Of The International Self-Report Delinquency Study.* Amsterdam/New York: Kugler, 1994. Chapter reports findings from a self-reported delinquency survey carried out in Belfast, Northern Ireland.

0935 McQuoid, Joan *Self-Reported Delinquency: A Pilot Study.* Belfast, Northern Ireland: The Extern Organisation, 1992. This report describes a pilot study of self- reported delinquency in Northern Ireland whose findings cover participation, frequency, age of onset, offending during the last year and nature of offending; and characteristics such as age, education, gender, location, accomplices, and detection. 41p. Appendix.

0936 McWilliams, Monica Gendered Responses To Crime In Northern Ireland, pp 50-64 in Coote, Anna (ed.) *Families, Children And Crime.*

London, United Kingdom: Institute for Public Policy Research, 1994. This chapter seeks to add to the discussion on masculinity and crime by illustrating the ways in which responses to crime are also gendered.

0937 Measham, Fiona; Newcombe, Russell & Parker, Howard The Normalization Of Recreational Drug Use Among Young People In Northwest England, *British Journal Of Sociology* 45:287-312, 1994. A self-reported drug-use survey of a cohort of 14-15 year olds, this study reports that over half of those surveyed admit to having been offered and having tried drugs with highest lifetime prevalence for cannabis users.

0938 Minty, Brian Public Care Or Distorted Family Relationships: The Antecedents Of Violent Crime, *Howard Journal* 27:172-187, 1988. In a sample of northern England inner-city boys who were followed up to an average age of 30, it was found that 26% had been convicted for an offense against a person, and the length of time in health service care, past juvenile delinquency, conduct disorder, distorted relationships in their family of origin are all inversely related to their illegality.

0939 Minty, Brian *Child Care And Adult Crime*. Manchester, United Kingdom: Manches-ter University Press, 1987. This 20-year follow-up of a cohort of male children from socially disadvantaged areas found that those who were admitted to care early and stayed the longest had more criminal histories into adulthood. 232p. Appendix.

0940 Monck, Elizabeth & New, Michelle *Report Of A Study Of Sexually Abused Children And Adolescents, And Of Young Perpetrators Of Sexual Abuse Who Were Treated In Voluntary Agency Community Facilities*. London, United Kingdom: Her Majesty's Stationery Office, 1996. This document reports the results from a self-report survey that included youths in a treatment program as well as surveys of their parents and teachers. 99p.

0941 Moore, Jack B. *Skinheads Shaved For Battle: A Cultural History Of American Skinheads*. Bowling Green, Ohio: Bowling Green State University Press, 1993. The English origins and American adaptation of the 20th century skinhead movement is the center of this discussion. 217p.

0942 Nagin, Daniel S.; Pogarsky, Greg & Farrington, David P. Adolescent Mothers And The Criminal Behavior Of Their Children, *Law And Society Review* 31:137-162, 1997. This article from the Cambridge Study in Delinquent Development reports that children born to adolescent mothers are at greater risk of criminality.

0943 Nagin, Daniel S. & Farrington, David P. The Onset And Persistence Of Offending, *Criminology* 30:501-524, 1992. This study assesses the need for and focus of developmental theories of crime by exploring if the age of onset of criminal behavior has an impact on subsequent behavior, the determinants of onset and age, and any differences in continued offending behavior.

0944 National Children's Bureau Information Service *Community Home Schools Gazette* 71:196-198, 1977. This is a brief review of research on the prevalence of, explanations of juvenile misconduct, and official reaction to it in the United Kingdom.

0945 Nelson, Amanda L.; Bromley, Rosemary D. F. & Thomas, Colin J. The Geography Of Shoplifting In A British City: Evidence From Cardiff, *Geoforum* 27:409-423, 1996. Examination of the police crime records, the spatial and temporal distribution of shoplifting in central Cardiff, Wales in 1993 revealed that offenders were disproportionately males from the younger age groups.

0946 Newing, J. F. A Police Perspective, *Royal Society Of Health Journal* 1:9-14, 1976. According to the authors, the 5.2 million of the 10-16 year old juveniles in England and Wales who are 12.6% of the total potential criminal population, are over-represented from 1969-1974 in all categories of indictable crimes except fraud and forgery, with 15.1% in crimes of violence against the person, 12.1% in criminal damage, 59% in theft, and 37% in burglary.

0947 Osborn, S. G. & West, D. J. Conviction Records Of Fathers And Sons Compared, *British Journal Of Criminology* 19:120-133, 1979. Data from a study in delinquency development found that fathers with a conviction record of any sort than fathers with no such record, tend to have a delinquent son, while fathers with multiple convictions compared with those with just one conviction were only moderately more likely to have a delinquent son.

0948 Ouston, Janet Delinquency, Family Background And Educational Attainment, *British Journal Of Criminology* 24:2-26, 1984. In her study of inner-London secondary school boys and girls, the author found that delinquency is related to parental occupation, ethnicity, school attendance, IQ score and teacher's report of behavior, an that overall girls had a lower delinquency rate.

0949 Painter, Kate *An Evaluation Of Public Lighting As A Crime Prevention Strategy With Special Focus On Women And Elderly People*. Manchester, United Kingdom: University of Manchester, 1991. This household and pedestrian survey in Hammersmith and Fulham boroughs focused on the impact of variations in lighting on vandalism and youth hangouts, and reports some reduction in crime, but an increased sense of safety. 182p.

0950 Parker, Howard & Measham, Fiona Pick 'n Mix: Changing Patterns Of Illicit Drug Use Amongst 1990's Adolescents, pp 22-28 in Martin, Carol (ed.) *Dealing With Drugs: A New Philosophy?* London, United Kingdom: Institute for Study and Treatment of Delinquency, 1995. Based on a self-report delinquency study of boys and girls, this research concludes that irrespective of social class differences, 71% of the youth report having been offered drugs and 47% admit to having tried drugs.

0951 Parker, Howard J. *View From The Boys: A Sociology Of Down-Town Adolescents*. Aldershot, United Kingdom: Gregg Revivals, 1992. This study of occasionally delinquent adolescents of downtown Liverpool examines the network members' perceptions, beliefs, and behavior, and concludes that delinquent styles varied over time and place and related to age, opportunity, contingency and personal experience. 237p.

0952 Parry, Phil Juveniles, pp 210-226 in Stockdale, Eric & Casale, Sylvia (eds.) *Criminal Justice Under Stress*. London, United Kingdom, 1992. Juvenile justice is the focus of this article covering diversion, the juvenile court, sentencing, custody and its alternatives in United Kingdom.

0953 Petley, Julian Going Public With Children And Violence, pp 152-156 in Barker, Martin & Petley, Julian (eds.) *Ill Effects: The Media/Violence Debate*, London, United Kingdom: Routledge, 1997. Reports on research findings on 78 British offenders and 500 school children of 10-16 years of age.

0954 Pfeffer, Karen; Cole, Bankole & Dada, Kayode British And Nigerian Adolescents' Lay Theories Of Youth Crime, *Psychology Crime And Law* 3:21-35, 1996. This study of British and Nigerian youths' different explanations for the causes of juvenile crime found that the British youths' explanations of youthful criminality were personal while their Nigerian counterparts provided situational explanations.

0955 Phillips, Brian *Patterns Of Juvenile Crime*. London, United Kingdom: Peel Press, 1978. Police files on juveniles responsible for indictable offenses in Torbay when examined for their origins, backgrounds, criminality and its place of occurrence, and their victims shows that the majority of all offenders were from the two lowest social classes. 101p.

0956 Pitts, John & Smith, Philip *Preventing School Bullying*. London, United Kingdom: Police Research Group, Home Office, 1995. This evaluation of bullying prevention-projects in two high-crime public housing area schools, found that after two years the levels of bullying had decreased in three of the four schools but remained at the same level as in London secondary schools. 74p. Appendix.

0957 Powis, Beverly; Griffiths, Paul & Gossop, Michael Drug Use And Offending Behaviour Among Young People Excluded From School, *Drugs Education Prevention and Policy* 5:245-256, 1998. Exploring the levels of drug use and offending behavior in a sample of youths excluded from school, this research concludes that nearly all report having that they committed a crime.

0958 Prins, Herschel *Fire Raising: Its Motivation and Management*, London, United Kingdom: Routledge, 1994. History and anthropological context of arson, its prevalence, legal aspects, arsonists both youthful and adult, their motivations, management are some of the topics covered. 111p.

0959 Rawstorne, Shirley England And Wales, pp 33-46 in Hoffman, Allan M. & Summers, Randal W. (eds.) *Teen Violence: A Global View*. Westport, Connecticut: Greenwood, 2001. Chapter describes the nature and extent of teen violence in England and Wales and official responses to it.

0960 Richardson, G.; Graham, F. & Bhate, S. R. A British Sample Of Sexually Abusive Adolescents: Abuser And Abuse Characteristics, *Criminal Behavior And Mental Health* 5:187-208, 1995. The authors describe the background characteristics and behavior of 100 British sexually abusive male adolescents aged 11-18 who resemble North American abuser and exhibit similar abuse characteristics, and the etiology of their behavior, and the management and treatment of sexually abusive behavior among British adolescents.

0961 Riley, David & Shaw, Margaret *Parental Supervision And Juvenile Delinquency*. London, United Kingdom: Her Majesty's Stationery Office, 1985. This report on a nationwide English survey of 14-15 year olds and their parents indicates that parents and their children are in agreement over how they should behave, although girls are more closely supervised than boys. 91p.

0962 Robins, David *Tarnished Vision: Crime And Conflict In The Inner City*. Oxford, United Kingdom: Oxford University, 1992. The story of the founding of a utopian community organization by former street robbers to revive an impoverished inner city neighborhood in 1980s in England, and the factors in its demise is narrated in this book. 142p.

0963 Rowe, David C. & Farrington, David P. The Familial Transmission Of Criminal Convictions, *Criminology* 35:177-201, 1997. This study of familial relationship of criminality reveals, that criminal convictions in a parent increased the risk of convictions in a child irrespective of the mediating effect of family environment variables.

0964 Rutter, Michael; Giller, Henri & Hagell, Ann *Antisocial Behavior By Young People*. Cambridge, United Kingdom: Cambridge University Press, 1998. The thirteen chapters in this book address the issues in juvenile crime data collection, coding and description, the variety in adolescent antisocial behavior and its causes, the process from juvenile delinquency to adult criminality, early treatment, and prevention.

0965 Samuel, Elaine & Tisdall, Kay Female Offenders In Scotland: Implications For Theory, pp 102-130 in Asquith, Stewart (ed.) *Children And Young People In Conflict With The Law*. London, United Kingdom: Jessica Kingsley, 1996. This chapter provides data on adult and juvenile offenders in Scotland, the differential treatment boys and girls receive in the juvenile justice system along with a discussion of the theoretic implications of these data.

0966 Shapland, Joanna M. Self-Reported Delinquency In Boys Aged 11 To 14, *British Journal Of Criminology* 18:255-266, 1978. This longitudinal study of boys from a public housing project found that self-admission and police records were examined, most often delinquent acts were committed in the company of other boys and the delinquent behavior reflected age-related pattern of adolescent group activities.

0967 Shaw, Margaret & Riley, David Working Towards Clearer Definition: A National Self-Report Study Of Teenage Boys And Girls In England And Wales, pp 67-88 in Klein, Malcolm W. (ed.) *Cross-National Research In Self-Reported Crime And Delinquency*. Dordrecht, The Netherlands: Kluwer, 1989. This is a report of the findings from a self-report survey conducted in England and Wales during 1982.

0968 Slobodian, Paul J. & Browne, Kevin D. Car Crime As A Developmental Career: An Analysis Of Young Offenders In Coventry, *Psychology Crime And Law* 3:275-286, 1997. This study of juveniles involved in car crimes in Coventry found that the mean age of a first criminal offender was lower than for a car-related offense indicating that criminal careers began with non-car related crimes, and evolved over several stages.

0969 Smith, David James Beyond All Reason: The Crime That Shocked The World - The Story Of Two British Ten-Year Old Killers And Their Three-Year Old Victim. New York, New York: Donald I. Fine, 1994. This book chronicles the murder of a 3-year old British child by two 10-year old boys, events leading to the murder and explanation of the youths' behavior, and public reaction. 245p.

0970 Smith, David Juvenile Delinquency In Britain In The First World War, pp 119-145 in Knafla, Louis A. (ed.) *Criminal Justice History: An International Annual, Vol. 2*. Westport, Connecticut: Meckler, 1990. This discussion on Britain's panic about juvenile delinquency during World War I argues that views of rising juvenile delinquency as a male phenomenon shifted the focus to boys, thereby creating the distinction between male and female delinquency, and contributed to gender identities based on the myths of masculinity and domesticity, while burdening the mothers of unruly boys to provide them a stable family life in the national interest.

0971 Smith, N. J.; Batta, I. D. & McCulloch, J. W. A Comparison By Color Of Boys In A Classifying School, *Probation Journal*, 22:87-91 & 116-121, 1975. This research found that delinquency among colored juveniles is neither qualitatively nor quantitatively a serious problem, but that half-colored children, in terms of delinquency and deprivation, constitute a higher risk group.

0972 Stewart, Gill & Stewart, John *Social Circumstances Of Younger Offenders Under Supervision*. London, United Kingdom: Association of Chief Officers of Probation, 1993. This study of offenders from seven probation areas in Great Britain includes relationships among social and economic circumstances, offense behavior, and probation of youthful offenders and. 94p.

0973 Stott, D. H. & Wilson, D. M. The Adult Criminal As Juvenile, *British Journal Of Criminology* 17:47-57, 1977. The authors follow-up adolescence to adulthood criminal perpetrators, and conclude that personal instability in conjunction with social environment influence criminality among a special group of individuals who begin their delinquencies in childhood and continue at least until early adulthood.

0974 Tarling, Roger *Analyzing Offending: Data, Models And Interpretations*. London, United Kingdom: Her Majesty's Stationery Office, 1993. This research on criminal careers of offenders found that most of the crime is committed primarily by males and peaks at age 18. 203p. Appendix.

0975 Trasler, Gordon Delinquency, Recidivism And Desistance, *British Journal Of Criminology* 19:314-322, 1979. This is a critique of behavior modification using token economies to deal with juvenile delinquency.

0976 Trivizas, Eugene Offences And Offenders In Football Hooliganism, *British Journal Of Criminology* 20:276-288, 1980. Examines football hooliganism and concludes that public stereotype of juveniles as the culprits has no basis in police statistics.

0977 Tutt, Norman (ed.) *Violence*. London, United Kingdom: Her Majesty's Stationery Office, 1976. This "how to" volume based on seminars on violence in juvenile correctional institutions describes the problem, its nature and causes, and possible ways of helping staff deal with it. 278 p.

0978 UK Audit Commission *Misspent Youth: Young People And Crime (Summary Report)*. Abingdon, United Kingdom: Bookpoint, 1996. This report on the nature of British youth crime describes how young offenders once apprehended are dealt with, and measures the local agencies can take to prevent and reduce such youthful misconduct. 35p.

0979 Wadsworth, M. E. J. Delinquency In A National Sample Of Children, *British Journal Of Criminology* 15:167-174, 1975. This large-scale study of boys in England and Wales found class difference in overall incidence and age at first offense.

0980 Walsh, D. P. *Shoplifting*. New York, New York: Holmes and Meier, 1978. Reports on shoplifting data in United Kingdom, and concludes that most offenders in shoplifting were either minors or those who had not committed any other type of crime. 124p.

0981 Walshe-Brennan, K. S. Trends In Juvenile Crime, *Royal Society Of Health Journal* 1:6-9, 1976. According to the author, juvenile crime in Great Britain has been rising since 1961, with an increasing number of murders committed by children and adolescents, and girls increasingly playing a larger part while increasing age does not seem to decrease this aggression in either sex.

0982 Walshe-Brennan, Kieran Social And Biological Aspects Of Delinquency, *Probation Journal* 22:77-86, 1975. Data on social and biological characteristics of a sample of English young offenders and a matched control group of mentally handicapped subjects showed that there were more delinquent juveniles in the former group than in the control group, and more of the parents of the delinquents had criminal records and impaired relationships.

0983 Washbrook, R. A. H. Neuroticism And Offenders, *International Journal Of Offender Therapy And Comparative Criminology* 25:122-129, 1981. A group of male juvenile inmates with prior offense history and a group of male juvenile non-offenders in Great Britain when compared for neurotic and social factors indicate that the former are more neurotically disturbed and more socially maladjusted than the non-offenders.

0984 Webster, Colin The Construction Of British 'Asian' Criminality, *International Journal Of The Sociology Of Law* 25:65-86, 1997. This 6-year longitudinal study of delinquency and victimization among Pakistani, Bangladeshi and white youths focused on the evolution of popular and public construction of young male Asian criminality.

0985 Weinberger, Barbara Policing Juveniles: Delinquency In Late Nineteenth And Early Twentieth Century Manchester, pp 43-55 in Knafla, Louis A. (ed.). *Criminal Justice History: An International Annual, Vol. 14*. Westport, Connecticut: Greenwood, 1994. Thi study of delinquency in late nineteenth- and early twentieth-century Manchester focuses on the processes and phenomena of the middle-class reformist enterprises targeting juveniles.

0986 Werner, Eric Psychological And Ethnic Correlates Of Inter-Personal Maturity Among Delinquents, *British Journal Of Criminology* 15:51-68, 1975. This research ison developmental stages and interpersonal maturity among 934 juvenile delinquents of diverse ethnic backgrounds.

0987 West, D. J. *Male Prostitution: Gay Sex Services In London*. London, United Kingdom: Duckworth, 1992. Based on interviews with male youths at a drop-in day center in London and street workers and employees in the sex industry, this study describes the male sex industry in London with proposals for controlling the "trade." 358p.

0988 West, Donald The Politicization Of Delinquency, pp 5-20 in Farrington, David & Gunn, John (eds.) *Reactions To Crime: The Public, The Police, Courts, And Prisons*. Chichester, United Kingdom: John Wiley, 1985. This essay is on juvenile delinquency and the politics of social control in general, and in United Kingdom in particular.

0989 Wilczynski, Ania Risk Factors For Parental Child Homicide, Results Of An English Study, *Current Issues In Criminal Justice* 7:193-222, 1995. This article provides a detailed profile of the common background "risk" factors in cases of filicide.

0990 Wiles, Paul Ghettoization In Europe? *European Journal On Criminal Policy & Research* 1:52-69, 1993. This article raises the issues related to crime and ethnic immigrants in various European countries, with reference to the United Kingdom.

0991 Williams, Joanne M. & Dunlop, Lillian Pubertal Timing And Self-Reported Delinquency Among Male Adolescents, *Journal Of Adolescence* 22:157-171, 1999. Based on a sample of 13-15 year old boy, this self-reported survey found a wide range of delinquency in adolescent youths.

0992 Wilson, Harriet Parental Supervision Re-examined, *British Journal Of Criminology* 27:275-301, 1987. A follow-up study of West Midlands families revealed that lack of parental supervision, economic deprivation, family criminality, failure at school were important factors in antisocial and delinquent forms of behavior.

0993 Wilson, Harriet Parental Supervision: A Neglected Aspect Of Delinquency, *British Journal Of Criminology* 20:203-235, 1980. This self-reported delinquenc and teacher ratings of children in inner-city and suburban areas in Britain compares background variables such as parental supervision and social handicap on young people's delinquency.

0994 Wilson, Harriet Juvenile Delinquency, Parental Criminality And Social Handicap, *British Journal Of Criminology* 15:241-250, 1975. Among the children of families who were clients of social service department, it was found that social handicaps such as father's occupation, family size, adequacy of the school, parental criminality and child rearing practices were related to juvenile delinquency.

0995 Wright, Barry; McKenzie, Immanuel & Stace, Joanna Adult Criminality In Previously Hospitalized Child Psychiatric Patients: With Particular Reference To Girls And The Use Of ICD-10 Diagnoses, *Criminal Behavior And Mental Health* 8:19-38, 1998. This study found that the important factors for both boys and girls were parental criminality and a diagnosis of conduct disorder, and boys' large family size and girls' previous experience "under-care."

0996 Yeoman, Tim & Griffiths, Mark Adolescent Machine Gambling And Crime, *Journal Of Adolescence* 19:183-188, 1996. In this survey examining the relationship between criminal activity and gaming machine use among children and adolescents, it was found that approximately four percent of juvenile crime was associated with gaming machine use.

United States

0997 Agnew, Robert & Brezina, Timothy Relationship Problems With Peers, Gender, And Delinquency, *Youth & Society* 29:84-111, 1997. This longitudinal survey of male and female students found that interpersonal strain predicted girls' delinquency, and was even more important in boys' delinquency.

0998 Agnew, Robert & Cullen, Francis T. A New Test Of Classic Strain Theory, *Justice Quarterly* 13:681-704, 1996. This report of the results from a research testing one of the main aspects of classic strain theory found support for the argument that dissatisfaction with monetary status is related to income-generating crime and drug use among juveneiles.

0999 Agnew, Robert Determinism, Indeterminism, And Crime: An Empirical Exploration, *Criminology* 33: 83-109, 1995. The author tested an empirical model of the factors that foster freedom of action and choice, and their ability to predict the amount of variation in crimes of individuals or groups of similar individuals.

1000 Agnew, Robert Delinquency And The Desire For Money, *Justice Quarterly* 11:411-427, 1994. Using data from the Youth In Transition survey, this report examined if delinquency is related to the gap between monetary goals and achievements but found only a weak relationship.

1001 Agnew, Robert The Techniques Of Neutralization And Violence, *Criminology* 32:555-580, 1994. Analysis of data from the second and third waves of the National Youth Survey reveal that only a small proportion of adolescents express general approval of, or indifference to, violence.

1002 Agnew, Robert Why Do They Do It? An Examination Of The Intervening Mechanisms Between "Social Control" Variables And Delinquency, *Journal Of Research In Crime And Delinquency* 30:245-266, 1993. In this critique, an examination of the intervening mechanisms between social control variables and delinquency suggests that low attachment, commitment and belief lead to an increase in anger and frustration and to an increased likelihood of association with delinquent peers.

1003 Agnew, Robert Foundation For A General Strain Theory Of Crime And Delinquency, *Criminology* 30:47-88, 1992. Arguing that strain has a central role in explanations of crime and delinquency, the author presents a general strain theory of crime and delinquency with remedies for the criticisms of earlier strain theories.

1004 Agnew, Robert & White, Helene Raskin An Empirical Test Of General Strain Theory, *Criminology* 30: 475-499, 1992. This study tests Agnew's general strain theory of crime and delinquency.

1005 Agnew, Robert The Interactive Effects of Peer Variables On Delinquency, *Criminology* 29:47-72, 1991. Drawing on relevant theory and research, it is argued that the impact of delinquent peers on delinquency is conditioned by (1) attachment to peers, (2) time spent with peers, and (3) the extent of peers' delinquency.

1006 Agnew, Robert The Origins Of Delinquent Events: An Examination Of Offender Accounts, *Journal Of Research In Crime And Delinquency* 27:267-294, 1990. Based on an examination of delinquents' explanations for their offense beahviors, the author argues that different crimes are committed by adolescents for different reasons.

1007 Agnew, Robert Adolescent Resources And Delinquency, *Criminology* 28:535-566, 1990. In this analysis of data from surveys of adolescents delinquency, resources, and predisposition to delinquency, it was found that, in most cases, resources are positively related to delinquency when the predisposition for delinquency is high.

1008 Akers, Ronald Delinquent Behavior, Drugs, And Alcohol. What Is The Relationship? *Today's Delinquent* 3:19-47, 1984. The author reviews the literature, arrest, and court data to describe the trends in delinquent behavior, specifically adolescent substance abuse, drinking and smoking and their social correlates.

1009 Altschuler, David M. & Brounstein, Paul J. Patterns Of Drug Use, Drug Trafficking, And Other Delinquency Among Inner-City Adolescent Males In Washington, D.C., *Criminology* 29:589-622, 1991. This research examined the relationship between crime and drug procurement, the role of drug use in committing crimes and the factors that distinguish drug users from others in terms the levels of involvement in drug trafficking and of criminal activity.

1010 Ambert, Anne-Marie The Effect Of Male Delinquency On Mothers And Fathers: A Heuristic Study, *Sociological Inquiry* 69:621-640, 1999. This study found that mothers compared to fathers, were more affected when their sons engage in difficult and delinquent behaviors.

1011 American Humane Association *National Analysis Of Official Child Neglect And Abuse Reporting: An Executive Summary*. Englewood, Colorado, 1978. The feasibility of systematically gathering data on the nature, reported incidence, and characteristics of child maltreatment, the sources of reporting, and the actions taken by receiving agencies was examined in this study. 12p.

1012 Anderson, Bobbi Jo; Holmes, Malcolm D. & Ostresh, Erik Male And Female Delinquents' Attachments And Effects Of Attachments On Severity Of Self-Reported Delinquency, *Criminal Justice And Behavior* 26:435-452, 1999. This study examines the differences in boys' and girls' level of attachment to parents, peers, and school and the effects of the various attachments on the severity of boys' and girls' self-reported delinquency.

1013 Arizona Legislative Council Joint Juvenile Justice Committee *The Serious Juvenile Offender: Violent And/Or Repeat Delinquent Acts Rev. Ed*. Phoenix, Arizona, 1980. This document reveals that the proportion of serious juvenile offenders in the total population is comparatively small. 50p.

1014 Austin, Roy L. Recent Trends In Official Male And Female Crime Rates: The Convergence Controversy, *Journal Of Criminal Justice* 21:447-466, 1993. In evaluating earlier research on male and female arrest rates, this study found the convergence in arrest rates was greater for juveniles than it was for adults.

1015 Austin, Roy L. Race, Female Headship, And Delinquency: A Longitudinal Analysis, *Justice Quarterly* 9:585-607, 1992. This study found no significant relationship between female headship among either black or white juveniles for total Index Crimes, or any of the Index Crimes.

1016 Ayers, Charles D.; Williams, James Herbert; Hawkins, J. David. Peterson, Peggy L.; Catalano, Richard F. & Abbott, Robert D. Assessing Correlates Of Onset, Escalation, De-escalation And Desistance Of Delinquent Behavior, *Journal Of Quantitative Criminology* 15:277-306, 1999. This longitudinal study of 566 adolescents assesses the value of social developmental risk and protective factors in distinguishing among groups of adolescents continuing, deescalating, and desisting delinquency.

1017 Baba, Yoko Vietnamese Gangs, Cliques And Delinquents, *Journal Of Gang Research* 8:1-20, 2001. Data from detainees at juvenile centers were used to compare and contrast gang and non-gang related involvement of Vietnamese youths in various illegal activities.

1018 Baccaglini, William F. & Marshall, Eunice *A Summary Of Arrest Rate Trends: 1977-1983*. Albany, New York: New York State Division for Youth, 1984. This report is on juvenile arrest rates for 1977-1983 in New York State, New York City, and the rest of the state excluding New York City. 20 p.

1019 Badey, James R. *Dragons And Tigers*. Loomis, California: Palmer Enterprises, 1988. This is a guidebook for law-enforcement personnel on Asian Youth gangs and their various illegal activities. 176p.

1020 Bahr, Stephen J.; Hawks, Ricky D. & Wang, Gabe Family And Religious Influence On Adolescent Substance Abuse, *Youth & Society* 24:443-465, 1993. The authors found that the level of peer drug use was the most directly and strongly related variable in substance abuse when parental monitoring, family drug use, family cohesion and religiosity were controlled.

1021 Baker, Keith; Pollack, Marcus & Kohn, Imre Violence Prevention Through Informal Socialization: An Evaluation Of the South Baltimore Youth Center, *Studies On Crime & Crime Prevention* 4:61-85, 1995. A violence, substance abuse and delinquency prevention program in Balttimore is evaluated in this research.

1022 Bankston III, Carl L. Youth Gangs And The New Second Generation: A Review Essay, *Aggression And Violent Behavior* 3:35-45, 1998. The author reviews the various theories of delinquent behavior within the socio-political context of changes in immigration law.

1023 Barnes, Grace M.; Welte, John W.; Hoffman, Joseph H. & Dintcheff, Barbara A. Gambling And Alcohol Use Among Youth - Interrelations With Depressive Symptoms And Delinquent Behaviors, *Addictive Behaviors* 24: 749-767, 1999. Data from two household samples of youth in the Buffalo, New York area revealed that impulsivity, moral disengage ment, and delinquency predicted alcohol consumption and gambling.

1024 Baron, Stephen W. & Hartnagel, Timothy F. Street Youth And Criminal Violence, *Journal Of Research In Crime And Delinquency* 35:166-192, 1998. The authors examine the roles of various sub-cultural, economic, and victimization factors in the violent behavior of male homeless street youths.

1025 Baron, Stephen W.; Hartnagel, Timothy F. Attributions, Affect, And Crime: Street Youths' Reactions To Unemployment, *Criminology* 35:409-434, 1997. Familial, school, labor market and street factors' role in the criminality of 200 homeless male street youths is examined in this article.

1026 Barriga, Alvaro Q.; Landau, Jennifer R.; Stinson, Bobby L. I.; Liau, Albert K. & Gibbs, John C. Cognitive Distortion And Problem Behaviors In Adolescents, *Criminal Justice And Behavior* 27:36-56, 2001. This study compares incarcerated male and female delinquents and a sample of high school students' self-serving and self-debasing cognitive distortions and their specific impact on externalizing and internalizing problem behaviors.

1027 Bartollas, Clemens Runaways At The Training Institutions In Central Ohio, *Canadian Journal Of Criminology* 17:221-235, 1975. Both white and African-American boys in a maximum-security institution were interviewed for a profile of the runaways' personality problems.

1028 Bartusch, Dawn R. Jeglum; Lynam, Donald R.; Moffitt, Terrie E. & Silva, Phil A. Is Age Important? Testing A General Versus A Developmental Theory Of Antisocial Behavior, *Criminology* 35:13-48, 1997. Competing hypotheses derived from Gottfredson and Hirschi's general theory and Moffitt's developmental theory of anti-social behavior are tested in this research.

1029 Battin, Sara R.; Hill, Karl G.; Abbott, Robert D.; Catalano, Richard F. & Hawkins, J. David The Contribution Of Gang Membership To Delinquency Beyond Delinquent Friends, *Criminology* 36:93-115, 1998. Data from the Seattle Social Development Project on the delinquency involvement of gang members, non-gang youths with delinquent friends, and non-gang youths who did not have delinquent friends are compared.

1030 Becker, Judith; Cunningham-Rathner, Jerry & Kaplan, Meg S. Adolescent Sexual Offenders: Demographics, Criminal And Sexual Histories, And Recommendations For Reducing Future Offenses, *Journal Of Interpersonal Violence* 1:431-445, 1986. This is a study of prior arrest and type of sexual crime of 13-19 year old American adolescent boys who were charged/convicted of sexual crimes.

1031 Belkin, Alison M. (ed.) *The Criminal Child.* Dubuque, Iowa: Kendall/Hunt, 1978. Besides providing a general focus on the juvenile offender and the response of the juvenile justice system to juvenile crime, the seventeen essays of this volume address causes of delinquency, the treatment of offenders, and alternatives. 183p.

1032 Benda, Brent B. & Corwyn, Robert Flynn A Test Of The Validity Of Delinquency Syndrome Construct In A Homogeneous Sample, *Journal Of Adolescence* 23:497-511, 2000. The authors report that social control elements account for more variance than either social learning or sociodemographic factors in the delinquency of adoles-cents who regularly attended Protestant denominational churches.

1033 Benda, Brent B. An Examination Of Reciprocal Relationship Between Religiosity And Different Forms Of Delinquency Within A Theoretical Model, *Journal Of Research In Crime And Delinquency* 34:163-186, 1997. This study of adolescents from six public high schools fail to support the argument that property crimes, crimes against persons, and use of alcohol and other drugs are the behavioral manifestations of an interrelated constellation of delinquency.

1034 Benda, Brent B. The Effect Of Religion On Adolescent Delinquency Revisited, *Journal Of Research In Crime And Delinquency* 32:446-466, 1995. This examination of the effects of religiosity found few real differ ences in its effects on various forms of juvenile delinquent behavior.

1035 Bernard, Thomas J. Juvenile Crime And The Transformation Of Juvenile Justice: Is There A Juvenile Crime Wave? *Justice Quarterly* 16:337-356, 1999. This study on the official statistics of the Uniform Crime Reports and the National Crime Victimization Survey found that among the many conflicting trends, overall juvenile crime has declined by about one-third over the last twenty years amid recent increases in juvenile homicides, and the author argues that the latter does not justify a whole sale transformation of juvenile justice.

1036 Bessant, Judith From Sociology Of Deviance To Sociology Of Risk - Youth Homelessness And The Problem Of Empiricism, *Journal Of Criminal Justice* 29:31-43, 2001. The author argues that risk-based research and its capacity to predict the risk young people present to themselves and others assumes expertise on the part of researchers on homeless youth while de-legitimizing young people's ability to frame their problems in different ways.

1037 Boyd, Norma Jeanne; Hagan, Michael & Cho, Meg E. Characteristics Of Adolescent Sex Offenders: A Review Of The Research, *Aggression And Violent Behavior* 5:137-146, 2000. This is a review of the literature on juvenile sex-offenders.

1038 Braga, Anthony A.; Piehl, Anne M. & Kennedy, David M. Youth Homicide In Boston: An Assessment Of Supplementary Homicide Report Data, *Homicide Studies* 3:277-299, 1999. The authors compared the Supplementary Homicide Report on gun and knife victims and the data from the Boston Gun Project on victims below age 21.

1039 Brener, Nancy D.; Simon, Thomas R. & Krug, Etienne G. Recent Trends In Violence-Related Behaviors Among High School Students In The United States, *Journal Of The American Medical Association* 282:440-446, 1999. Using data from the nationally representative Youth Risk Behavior Surveys, the authors examine the trends in non-fatal violent behaviors such as fighting and weapon carrying among adolescents in the United States.

1040 Brezina, Timothy Delinquency, Control Maintenance, And The Negation Of Fatalism, *Justice Quarterly* 17:779-807, 2000. In explaining the malicious and non-utilitarian character of much delinquent behavior, the author argues that delinquency is a symbolic statement of personal independence, in particular a functional device or maneuver that enables youths to maintain a sense of personal control given adult impositions.

1041 Brezina, Timothy Delinquent Problem-Solving: An Interpretive Framework For Criminological Theory And Research, *Journal Of Research In Crime And Delinquency* 37:3-30, 2000. The author advocates the idea that delinquency be interpreted as a form of problem-solving behavior in response to the pressures of adolescence.

1042 Brezina, Timothy Teenage Violence Toward Parents As An Adaptation To Family Strain: Evidence From A National Survey Of Male Adolescents, *Youth And Society* 30:416-444, 1999. This study investigated, gender, violence toward parents, parental aggression, and family strain.

1043 Brezina, Timothy Adolescent Maltreatment And Delinquency: The Question Of Intervening Processes, *Journal Of Research In Crime And Delinquency* 35:71-99, 1998. National survey data are used to assess the competing explanations of research findings that attribute higher levels of delinquency to adolescent maltreatment.

1044 Brezina, Timothy Adapting To Strain: An Examination Of Delinquent Coping Responses, *Criminology* 34:39-60, 1996. This study concludes that delinquency enables adolescents to minimize the negative emotional consequences of strain.

1045 Britt, C. L. Crime And Unemployment Among Youths In The United States, 1958-1990, *American Journal Of Economics And Sociology* 53:99-110, 1994. This time-series analysis of the relationship of crime and unemployment among 16-19 year old American youths found an association between crime and the annual change in the rate of youth unemployment.

1046 Broidy, Lisa M. Direct Supervision And Delinquency: Assessing The Adequacy Of Structural Proxies, *Journal Of Criminal Justice* 23:541-554, 1995. The results of this research confirm Wells and Rankin's contention that family structural measures are inadequate measures of specific family supervisory functions.

1047 Brown, Marjorie E. Teenage Prostitution, *Adolescence* 14:665-680, 1979. This review of the literature identifies the various social conditions and experiences that predispose and motivate adolescent girls into prostitution and determine the response of the juvenile justice system to them.

1048 Brown, Richard Maxwell American Violence, American Values, And Childhood Games, pp 171-177 in Chiland, Colette & Young, J. Gerald (eds.) *Children And Violence*. Northvale, New Jersey: Jason Aronson, 1994. This chapter offers a brief discussion of how violence is perpetuated by the features of American culture.

1049 Brownfield, David & Thompson, Kevin Attachment To Peers And Delinquent Behaviour, *Canadian Journal Of Criminology* 33:45-60, 1991. This study of self-reported delinquency and attachment to peers found only moderate relationship between the two, but peer involvement in delinquency was strongly related to the youth's own delinquency.

1050 Bruce, Marino A. Inequality And Delinquency: Sorting Out Some Class And Race Effects, *Race And Society* 2:133-148, 2000. This assessment of the degree to which structural, family, and peer factors influence alcohol use and fighting, raises doubts on culture-based assumptions of the theoretical bases of the linkages between race, class, and delinquency and of much of the research in this area.

1051 Buka, Stephen & Earls, Felton Early Determinants Of Delinquency And Violence, *Health Affairs* 31:46-64, 1993. This paper on risk factors in later delinquency and violence present prior to school age concludes that population based efforts in education and health should be expanded in reducing anticipated violent behavior.

1052 Burquest, Bret The Violent Girl, *Adolescence* 16:749-764, 1981. Violent crimes by female American juveniles is the focus of this research based on available data.

1053 Bute, Joseph Practicing From Theory: Work With Youths And Reflections On Radical Criminology, *Crime & Delinquency* 27:106-121, 1981. A description of a number of economic and social conditions confronting youths in the United States are followed by a discussion of conditions in lower-income urban communities and the effects of such economic and social pressures on youthful conduct.

1054 Butts, Jeffrey A. & Snyder, Howard N. *The Youngest Delinquents: Offenders Under Age 15*. Washington, D.C.: US Office of Juvenile Justice and Delinquency Prevention, 1997. Based on data collected from reported crime records and the National Juvenile Court Data Archive, this research describes American offenders below 15 and the juvenile court's response to them. 111p.

1055 Bytheway, Bill The Statistical Association Between Social Class And Self-Reported Delinquency, *International Journal Of Criminology And Penology* 3:243-251, 1975. The author summarizes the findings from research on social class and delinquency.

1056 Calhoun, Georgia B.; Glaser, Brian A.; Stefurak, Tres & Bradshaw, Catherine P. Preliminary Validation Of The Narcissistic Personality Inventory—Juvenile Offender, *International Journal Of Offender Therapy And Comparative Criminology* 44:564-580, 2000. The authors, examining the relationship between self-esteem and delinquent behavior suggest that pathological narcissism, characterized by a grandiose self-image and interpersonal exploitation, may be a factor in the etiology of juvenile delinquency.

1057 California Legislature Joint Committee On Fire Police Emergency And Disaster Services *Juvenile Arson And Firesetting: A Growing Problem*. Sacramento, California, 1984. This report offers a brief review of various elements of juvenile arson and includes classification of firesetters, the available statistical data on juvenile arsonists, and their treatment. 126 p.

1058 Calvin, Allen D. Unemployment Among Black Youths, Demographics, And Crime, *Crime & Delinquency* 27:234-244, 1981. The author argues that a number of assumptions regarding race, economics, and youth crime are based on incorrect data or faulty interpretation.

1059 Campbell, Anne Girls' Talk: The Social Representation Of Aggression By Female Gang Members, *Criminal Justice And Behavior* 11:139-156, 1984. This article provides descriptions of verbal fights girls affiliated with various gangs engage in.

1060 Campbell, Anne *Girls In The The Gang: A Report From New York City.* New York, New York: Basil Blackwell, 1984. In this study of three gangs in New York city, the author elucidates the life-styles, aspirations, and behaviors of women aged 16-30 affiliated with these gangs. 277p.

1061 Campbell, Anne *Girl Delinquents*. New York, New York: St. Martin's Press, 1981. The the politics of subjectivity and the application of second-rate theories to explain the delinquency of girls, the problem of defining girl delinquents, involvement in shoplifting, and their imitation of male delinquents, aggression, are among the issues addressed by this book. 266p.

1062 Canada, Geoffrey *Fish Stick Knife Gun: A Personal History Of Violence In America*. Boston, Massachusetts: Beacon, 1995. This is an autobiography of the author's young, violent life in an American inner city.

1063 Capaldi, Deborah & Patterson, Gerald R. Can Violent Offenders Be distinguished From Frequent Offenders: Prediction From Childhood To Adolescence, *Journal Of Research In Crime And Delinquency* 33:206-231, 1996. Both violent and non-violent Oregon juvenile male arrestees were the subject of this self-report study.

1064 Caputo, Alicia A.; Frick, Paul J. & Brodsky, Stanley L. Family Violence And Juvenile Sex Offending: The Potential Mediating Role Of Psychopathic Traits And Negative Attitudes Toward Women, *Criminal Justice And Behavior* 26:338-356, 1999. A comparison of juvenile sex and other offenders for the degree of violence against women witnessed in their families origin indicated that their family domestic violence was related to sex offenses and also to contact offenses in general.

1065 Cassetty, Judith The Family And Delinquency: A Critique, *Today's Delinquent* 4:55-67, 1985. This critique focuses on the effect of sociodemographics and structural factors on juvenile delinquency.

1066 Cattarello, Anne M. Community-Level Influences On Individuals' Social Bonds, Peer Associations, And Delinquency: A Multilevel Analysis, *Justice Quarterly* 17:33-60, 2000. The authors contention in this article is that the social disorganization theory of Shaw and McKay can be applied to explain micro-level variation in social bonds, peer associations, and delinquency.

1067 Cernkovich, Stephen A. & Giordano, Peggy C. School Bonding, Race, And Delinquency, *Criminology* 30:261-291, 1992. This paper describes the manner, particularly in the delinquent involvement of African-American youths, in which school bonding affects delinquent conduct.

1068 Cheatwood, Derral & Block, Kathleen J. Youth And Homicide: An Investigation Of The Age Factor In Criminal Homicide, *Justice Quarterly* 7:265-292, 1990. Homicide data is used to examine if getting tougher on juveniles is justified or not, and the author concludes that the data do not support such a policy.

1069 Chesney-Lind, Meda & Paramore, Vickie V. Are Girls Getting More Violent? Exploring Juvenile Robbery Trends, *Journal Of Contemporary Criminal Justice* 17:142-166, 2001. In examining robbery trends, the writers argue that the aggression of girls can only be understood in terms of the interpersonal and institutionalized nature of a patriarchal society.

1070 Chesney-Lind, Meda & Hagedorn, John M. (eds.) *Female Gangs In America: Essays On Girls, Gangs And Gender*. Chicago, Illinois: Lakeview, 1999. This anthology of 19 articles deals with various historic and geographic aspects of girls and their membership in gangs. 353p.

1071 Chesney-Lind, Meda; Rockhill, Anna; Marker, Nancy & Reyes, Howard Gangs And Delinquency: Exploring Police Estimates Of Gang Membership, *Crime Law And Social Change* 21:201-228, 1994. This study sought to determine the validity of police estimates of gang membership in Honolulu.

1072 Chiland, Colette & Young, J. Gerald *Children And Violence*. Northvale, New Jersey: Jason Aronson, 1993. This book has 12 articles that discus diverse aspects of human violence, violence in family and social environment of neighborhood and culture affecting children's lives and behavior. 217p.

1073 Cochran, John K. & Akers, Ronald L. Beyond Hellfire: An Exploration Of The Variable Effects Of Religiosity On Adolescent Marijuana And Alcohol Use, *Journal Of Research In Crime And Delinquency* 26:198-225, 1989. The original Hellfire hypothesis is evaluated using self-reported data on marijuana and alcohol use among a sample of female and male adolescents from the 7th through the 12th grades.

1074 Cook, Linda S. Adolescent Addiction And Delinquency In The Family System, *Issues in Mental Health Nursing* 22:151-157, 2001. This is an examination of addiction and delinquent behaviors within the framework of family systems theory.

1075 Cook, Philip J. & Laub, John H. The Unprecedented Epidemic In Youth Violence, pp 27-64 in Tonry, Michael & Moore, Mark H. (eds.) *Youth Violence*. Chicago, Illinois: University of Chicago Press, 1998. This analysis of the role of juveniles in criminal violence documents trends in arrest rates since the 1960s in the United States.

1076 Corby, Brian *Child Abuse: Towards A Knowledge Base*. Buckingham, United Kingdom: Open University Press, 1993. The author offers an extensive discussion of diverse topics relating to child abuse in the United States and Great Britain. 195p.

1077 Costello, Barbara J. & Vowell, Paul R. Testing Control Theory And Differential Association: A Reanalysis Of The Richmond Youth Project Data, *Criminology* 37:815-742, 1999. This is a discussion of the various problems in Matsueda's specifications of control theory and reanalyzing the data from the Richmond Youth Project arrived at different conclusions.

1078 Cottle, Cindy C.; Lee, Ria J. & Heilbrun, Kirk The Prediction Of Criminal Recidivism In Juveniles: A Meta-Analysis, *Criminal Justice And Behavior* 28:367-394, 2001. This meta-analysis of 23 studies to identify risk factors that best predict juvenile recidivism found offense history to be the strongest predictor of re-offending along with family problems, ineffective use of leisure time, delinquent peers, conduct problems, and non-severe pathology.

1079 Currie, Elliott *Dope And Trouble: Portraits Of Delinquent Youths*. New York, New York: Pantheon, 1991. Interviews of male and female youths awaiting placement leads the author to conclude that these juvenile delinquents are over-socialized rather than under-socialized. 352p.

1080 Curry, G. David Self-Reported Gang Involvement And Officially Recorded Delinquency, *Criminology* 38:1253-1274, 2000. This research based on Chicago Police Department information over a five-year period found gang involvement in early adolescence is linked to offending.

1081 Curry, G. David Female Gang Involvement, *Journal Of Research In Crime And Delinquency* 35:100-118, 1998. This review of female gang involvement identifies three central themes—changes in the magnitude of the problem, the need for a feminist perspective, and the degree to which membership can be a form of liberation.

1082 Curry, G. David & Spergel, Irving A. Gang Involvement And Delinquency Among Hispanic And African-American Adolescent Males, *Journal Of Research In Crime And Delinquency* 29:273-291, 1992. This survey of Hispanic and African-American males at four Chicago inner-city schools sought to create incremental measures of gang involvement and delinquency.

1083 Curry, John P.; Autry, Bess & Harris, Harold J. Structural Family Assessment With Status Offenders, *Corrective And Social Psychiatry And Journal Of Behavior Technology Methods And Therapy* 26:39-44, 1980. Components of a "normal" family structural assessment in treating status offenders along with three clinical cases involving status offenders and their families are described in this article.

1084 Dahlberg, Linda L. Youth Violence In The United States: Major Trends, Risk Factors, And Prevention Approaches, *American Journal Of Preventive Medicine* 14:259-272, 1998. The major trends in juvenile homicides, the key risk variables in adolescent violence, and the current prevention efforts to reduce youth violence are the subject of this paper.

1085 Damphousses, Kelly R. & Crouch, Ben M. Did The Devil Make Them Do It? An Examination Of The Etiology Of Satanism Among Juvenile Delinquents, *Youth & Society* 24:204-227, 1992. Youthful Satanism and its manifestations are the focus of this study.

1086 Danser, Kenneth R. & Laub, John H. *Analysis Of National Crime Victimization Survey Data To Study Serious Delinquent Behavior Monograph Four: Juvenile Criminal Behavior And Its Relation To Economic Conditions.* Washington, D.C. National Institute for Juvenile Justice and Delinquency Prevention, 1981. When analyzed, quarterly offense data from the National Crime Survey 1973-1978 do not affirm any effect of economic conditions on criminal behavior. 116p.

1087 Davies, Patrick T. & Windle, Michael Interparental Discord And Adolescent Adjustment Trajectories: The Potentiating And Protective Role Of Intrapersonal Attributes, *Child Development* 72:1163-1178, 2001. In a study of adolescent-mother dyads involving elevated marital discord, those youths with behavior problem histories and depressive symptoms initially seem less vulnerable but exhibit persistence of their behavior problems.

1088 Dawes, Michael A.; Dorn, Lorah D.; Moss, Howard B.; Yao, J. K.; Kirisci, Levent; Ammerman, Robert T. & Tarter, Ralph E. Hormonal And Behavioral Homeostasis In Boys At Risk For Substance Abuse, *Drug And Alcohol Dependence* 55:165-176, 1999. This study found boys' risk of substance abuse was associated with concentrations for testosterone, dihydrotestosterone, salivary cortisol, parental personality, and peer dysfunction.

1089 Dawley, David *A Nation Of Lords. 2 Ed.* Prospect Heights, Illinois: Waveland Press, 1992. The author reports on his interviews with members of Chicago's African-American gangs of 1950s and 1960. 205p

1090 Decker, Scott H. & Curry, G. David. Addressing Key Features Of Gang Membership: Measuring The Involvement Of Gang Members, *Journal Of Criminal Justice* 28:473-482, 2000. Four dimensions of gang membership are examined in this study of youths in St. Louis, Missouri.

1091 Decker, Scott H.; Bynum, Tim & Weisel, Deborah. A Tale Of Two Cities: Gangs As Organized Crime Groups, *Justice Quarterly* 15:395-425, 1998. This article addresses the extent to which street gangs are becoming organized crime groups.

1092 Dembo, Richard & Williams, Linda The Generality Of Deviance: Replication Of A Structural Model Among High-Risk Youths, *Journal Of Research In Crime And Delinquency* 29:200-216, 1992. The authors tested a structural equation model indicating that each deviant behavior is a manifestation of a general tendency toward deviance.

1093 Devlin, Rachel Female Juvenile Delinquency And The Problem Of Sexual Authority In America, *Yale Journal of Law And The Humanities* 9:147-182, 1997. Using on case histories, this article discusses social control of young female sexual conduct, and the relationship between fathers and daughters who become delinquent.

1094 Dishion, Thomas J.; McCord, Joan & Poulin, François When Interventions Harm: Peer Groups And Problem Behavior, *American Psychologist* 54:755-764, 1999. The impact of deviancy training peer reinforcement of high-risk youth groups is the focus of this analysis of data from Cambridge-Somerville Youth Study.

1095 Doleschal, Eugene & Newton, Anne The Violent Juvenile, *Criminal Justice Abstracts*, 10:539-546, 1978. This paper argues that the media images of waves of youthful violence in the United States are not supported by data on reported crime, victimization surveys, or self-report surveys, and includes an annotated bibliography from 1970-1978.

1096 Dornbusch, Stanford M.; Erickson, Kristan G.; Laird, Jennifer & Wong, Carol A. The Relation Of Family And School Attachment To Adolescent Deviance In Diverse Groups And Communities, *Journal Of Adolescent Research* 16:396-422, 2001. This study on reducing five forms of adolescent deviance found that with increased attachments to the family and school, the overall frequency, prevalence and intensity of deviant involvement decreased irrespective of community or gender.

1097 Dukes, Richard L. & Stein, Judith A. Effects Of Assets And Deficits On The Social Control Of At-Risk Behavior Among Youth: A Structural Equations Approach, *Youth & Society* 32:337-359, 2001. The findings of this research on deviant drug use, delinquency, truancy, and weapons possession were consistent with control theory among subgroups of young men and women in both middle school and high school who were the subject of an investigation of the protective effects of personal and social assets and risk effects of personal deficits.

1098 Dukes, Richard L.; Martinez, Rubén O. & Stein, Judith A. Precursors And Consequences Of Membership In Youth Gangs, *Youth & Society* 29:139-165, 1997. The authors found that low self-esteem, perceived academic disability, drug use, greater fear of harm and being armed precede gang membership among secondary school students.

1099 Dunford, Franklyn W. & Elliott, Delbert S. Identifying Career Offenders Using Self-Reported Data, *Journal Of Research In Crime And Delinquency* 21:57-86, 1984. Data from a national youth panel self-report study were used to develop a career offender typology, demonstrating that self-report techniques can identify more career offenders than can official data.

1100 Durant, Robert H.; Getts, Alan G.; Cadenhead, Chris & Woods, Elizabeth R. The Association Between Weapon Carrying And The Use Of Violence Among Adolescents Living In And Around Public Housing, *Journal Of Adolescent Health* 17:376-380, 1995. This study found that the lower socioeconomic status black adolescents who carried, compared to those who did not carry, weapons in this sample were more likely to engage in violent behaviors.

1101 Duxbury, Elaine B. Violence By Youth; Violence Against Youth, *American Behavioral Scientist* 23:667-680, 1980. This discussion on the incidence of violence among young people and their victimization by other youths suggests that public perceptions overestimate the former and under-realize the latter.

1102 Edwards, Dan W.; Roundtree, George A.; Shaffer, C. Edwards & Irwin, Emmitt Comparative Analysis Of Runaways And Non-

Runaway/Ungovernable Delinquents In A Family Court, *Journal Of Crime And Justice* 5:35-46, 1982. This study to identify biographic and demographic variables differentiating runaways and non-runaways found that the majority were from middle-class families, and the oldest, oldest female, and middle child are most prone to run away, and that runaways compared to non-runaways, are more likely to become delinquent.

1103 Edwards, Willie J. Predicting Juvenile Delinquency: A Review Of Correlates And A Confirmation By Recent Research Based On An Integrated Theoretical Model *Justice Quarterly* 9:553-583, 1992. This study used a multi-theory model to explain juvenile delinquency to conclude that differential association and anomie theory contributed most to the model.

1104 Elliott, Delbert S.; Wilson, William Julius; Huizinga, David & Sampson, Robert J. The Effects Of Neighborhood Disadvantage On Adolescent Development, *Journal Of Research In Crime And Delinquency* 33:389-426, 1996. Mechanisms and processes of neighborhood disadvantage that affect adolescent developmental outcomes are identified by the authors.

1105 Elliott, D. S.; Huizinga, D. & Menard, S. *Multiple Problem Youths: Delinquency, Subsance Abuse, And Mental Health Problems.* New York, New York: Springer-Verlag, 1989. This study expands on the original National Youth Survey research with an extensive analysis of serious delinquency and its causes. 266p.

1106 Elliott, Delbert S. & Morse, Barbara J. Delinquency And Drug Use As Risk Factors In Teenage Sexual Activity, *Youth & Society* 21:32-60, 1989. This is a study of the interaction among substance use, sexual activity, and delinquency.

1107 Elliott, Delbert S.; Huizinga, David & Morse, Barbara Self-Reported Violent Offending: A Descriptive Analysis Of Juvenile Violent Offenders And Their Offending Careers, *Journal Of Interpersonal Violence* 1:472-514, 1986. This description of the self-reported violent offenders from the National Youth survey concludes that offending increases and becomes diversified with time.

1108 Elliott, Delbert S. & Huizinga, David Social Class And Delinquent Behavior In A National Youth Panel, *Criminology* 21:149-177, 1983. The results of this study indicate substantial class differences in both the prevalence and incidence of serious crime among American adolescents.

1109 Elliott, Delbert S.; Ageton, Suzanne S.; Huizinga, David ; Knowles, Brian A. & Canter, Rachelle J. *The Prevalence And Incidence Of Delinquent Behavior: 1976-1980.* Boulder, Colorado: Behavioral Research

Institute, 1983. This report describes the prevalence and incidence of various delinquent behaviors among subpopulations of American adolescents of variying age, sex, race, social class, and residential location. 568p.

1110 Empey, LaMar T. The Family And Delinquency, *Today's Delinquent* 4:5-46, 1985. History of childhood, delinquency in the nineteenth and twentieth centuries, invention of the juvenile court, various theories of delinquency and the evidence on impact of school, broken homes and other family variables, official versus self-reported delinquency, transition to adulthood are topics covered in this article.

1111 Entner Wright, Bradley R.; Caspi, Avshalom; Moffitt, Terrie E.; Miech, Richard A. & Silva, Phil A. Reconsidering The Relationship Between SES And Delinquency: Causation But Not Correlation, *Criminology* 37:175-194, 1999. This article address the question of theories of crime linking low levels of socioeconomic status to high levels of delinquency that empirical studies have consistently found to be weak or nonexistent in various self-reported delinquency studies.

1112 Esbensen, Finn-Aage & Winfree, L. Thomas Jr. Race And Gender Differences Between Gang And Nongang Youths: Results From A Multisite Survey, *Justice Quarterly* 15:505-526, 1998. This is an analysis of gang affiliation from a multi-site survey of eighth grade students in schools located across the United States.

1113 Esbensen, Finn-Aage; Deschenes, Elizabeth Piper A Multisite Examination Of Youth Gang Membership: Does Gender Matter? *Criminology* 36:799-827, 1998. Descriptions of gang membership among a cross-section of American eighth grade students and the differences in the attitudes of boys and girls associated with gang membership are the focus of this research.

1114 Esbensen, Finn-Aage & Huizinga, David Gangs, Drugs, And Delinquency In A Survey Of Urban Youth, *Criminology* 31:565-590, 1993. The author analyzes the prevalence and demographic composition of gangs in one city, the temporal relationship between criminal offending and gang membership, and the degree to which gang members are involved in illegal activities, and found that gang members were active in all types of delinquency.

1115 Esbensen, Finn-Aage & Huizinga, David Juvenile Victimization And Delinquency, *Youth & Society* 23:202-228, 1991. Interviews with youths from "high-risk" neighborhoods were examined for incidents of victimization and reported delinquency.

1116 Evans, Willaim P.; Fitzgerald, Carla; Weigel, Dan & Chvilicek, Sarah Are Rural Gang Members Similar Their Urban Peers? Implications For Rural Communities, *Youth & Society* 30:267-282, 1999. This self-report study of 12th graders in Nevada found no difference in either gang-membership or pressure to join one, but gender-related rural-urban differences do exist.

1117 Fagan, Jeffrey & Pabon, Edward Contributions Of Delinquency And Substance Use To School Dropout Among Inner-City Youths, *Youth & Society* 21:306-354, 1990. Patterns of substance abuse and delinquency were found to be related to dropping out of school among youths in six inner-city communities.

1118 Fagan, Jeffrey The Social Organization Of Drug Use And Drug Dealing Among Urban Gangs, *Criminology* 27:633-670, 1989. Drug-crime relationships of urban gangs' involvement in drug dealing and consequent increase in violence among gangs were the focus of this study which found that dealing was varied, although all gang types had high involvement in drug use.

1119 Farnworth, Margaret Male-Female Differences In Delinquency In A Minority-Group Sample, *Journal Of Research In Crime And Delinquency* 21:191-212, 1984. In testing the efficacy of same etiological explanations of male/female delinquency and gender's indirect influence on delinquency through its relationship within family and school, the author found the results differed depending on the type of delinquency involved.

1120 Farrell, Ronald A. & Nelson, James F. A Sequential Analysis Of Delinquency, *International Journal Of Criminology And Penology* 6:255-268, 1978. This test of the Farrell-Morrione model of delinquency causation offers support, and suggests that delinquent behavior is a result of association with delinquent groups and such association is a consequence of perceived societal rejection.

1121 Farrington, David P.; Jolliffe, Darrick; Loeber, Rolf; Stouthamer-Loeber, Magda & Kalb, Larry M. The Concentration Of Offenders In Families, And Family Criminality In The Prediction Of Boys' Delinquency, *Journal Of Adolescence* 24:579-596, 2001. This study focused on the concentration of offending in families, and criminality among three generations of relatives.

1122 Farrington, David P.; Loeber, Rolf; Stouthamer-Loeber, Magda; Van Kammen, Welmoet B. & Schmidt, Laura Self-Reported Delinquency And A Combined Delinquency Seriousness Scale Based On Boys, Mothers, And Teachers: Concurrent And Predictive Validity For African-Americans And Caucasians, *Criminology* 34:493-517, 1996. This paper is based on the combined delinquency seriousness scores for the middle sample and oldest sample of the Pittsburgh Youth Study on self-reported delinquency.

1123 Ferdinand, Theodore N. Juvenile Crime In Nineteenth Century Boston: A Developmental Paradigm, pp 577-598 in Hess, Albert G. & Clement, Priscilla F. (eds.) *History Of Juvenile Delinquency: A Collection Of Essays On Crime Committed By Young Offenders, In History And In Selected Countries Volume II.* Aalen, Germany: Scientia Verlag, 1993. This chapter discusses criminality among 1800's Boston juveniles with present-day developing countries.

1124 Ferns, William J.; Dologite, Dorothy G.; Mockler, Robert J. & Pfeffer, Robert S. An Expert System For Juvenile Delinquent Disposition Advisement, *Applied Artificial Intelligence* 20:329-352, 1996. This article reports on the development of the Juvenile Delinquent Disposition Advisor which was tested by Family Court attorneys with actual cases involving juveniles who were receptive to the assistance of this expert.

1125 Figueira-McDonough, Josefina Community Structure And Female Delinquency Rates: A Heuristic Discussion, *Youth & Society* 24:3-30, 1992. The interactions of delinquency, gender and ecology are the subject of this analysis.

1126 Figueira-McDonough, Josefina Feminism And Delinquency, *British Journal Of Criminology* 24:325-342, 1984. A variety of factors in delinquency, including the feminist orientations of girls, were assessed by this investigation of male and female youths.

1127 Figueira-McDonough, Josefina A Reformulation Of The 'Equal Opportunity' Explanation Of Female Delinquency, *Crime & Delinquency* 26:333-343, 1980. The author argues that given similar conventional opportunities, both males and females will engage in identical, illegal behavior.

1128 Fingerhut, Lois A.; Ingram, Deborah D. & Feldman, Jacob J. Homicide Rates Among US Teenagers And Young Adults: Differences By Mechanism, Level Of Urbanization, Race, And Sex, 1987 Through 1995. *Journal Of The American Medical Association* 280:423-427, 1998. This study examines trends in homicides for persons of age 15-24 in the United States.

1129 Fingerhut, Lois A. *Firearm Mortality Among Children, Youth, And Young Adults 1-34 Years Of Age, Trends And Current Status: United States, 1985-90*. Washington, D.C.: US National Center for Health Statistics, 1993. This document is a revision of 1985-88 data on firearm mortality among persons of age 1-34 in the United States. 20p.

1130 Fingerhut, Lois A.; Ingram, Deborah D. & Feldman, Jacob J. Firearm And Nonfirearm Homicide Among Persons 15 Through 19 Years Of Age: Differences By Level Of Urbanization, United States, 1979 Through 1989. *Journal Of The American Medical Association* 267:3048-3053, 1992. This study compares firearm and other homicides among 15-19-year olds in the United States.

1131 Fingerhut, Lois A.; Ingram, Deborah D. & Feldman, Jacob J. Firearm Homicide Among Black Teenage Males In Metropolitan Counties: Comparison Of Death Rates In Two Periods, 1983 Through 1985 And 1987 Through 1989. *Journal Of The American Medical Association* 267:3054-3058, 1992. This study sought to identify counties that had experienced a significant increase over the times studied, or had higher or lower rates of homicide for male African-Americans.

1132 Fleisher, Mark S. *Beggars And Thieves: Lives Of Urban Street Criminals*. Madison, Wisconsin: University of Wisconsin Press, 1995. The author provides an ethnographic account of Seattle delinquent gang members, their families, peers and social networks. 332p.

1133 Flowers, Ronald Barri *Children And Criminality: The Child As Victim And Perpetrator*. New York, New York: Greenwood, 1986. The third section of this book deals with the juvenile offender, etiological features, social and other factors in delinquency, the problem and control of juvenile delinquency. 223p.

1134 Foglia, Wanda D. Perceptual Deterrence And The Mediating Effect Of Internalized Norms Among Inner-City Teenagers, *Journal Of Research In Crime And Delinquency* 34:414-442, 1997. This is a study of the relationship of mediating norms between social sanctions and perceived risk of arrest and delinquency among a sample of inner-city high school students.

1135 Fox, James Alan *Trends In Juvenile Violence: A Report To The United States Attorney General On Current And Future Rates Of Juvenile Offending*. Washington, D.C.: US Bureau of Justice Statistics, 1996. This study examines increases in juvenile homicide and other violent offenses in the United States, and projects continued increase in offending rates under worsening economic and social conditions. 15p.

1136 Frank, Ove Statistical Estimation Of Co-Offending Youth Networks, *Social Networks* 23:203-214, 2001. This article deals with statistical network models and the structure of co-offending youth networks in estimates of joint participation in crime.

1137 French, Laurence A Cultural Perspective Toward Juvenile Delinquency, *International Journal Of Comparative And Applied Criminal Justice* 1:111-121, 1977. While assessing and comparing the prevalence of adolescent marginality in the United States with four traditional folk societies—the Nuer, Hopi, Keraki Indians, and Arunta cultures, the author argues that deviance and delinquency are a consequence of social structural factors reflecting the interplay of ambiguous normative expectations and the development of unacceptable behavioral adaptations.

1138 French, Warren A. *National Research Report On Shoplifting 1980 1981*. Atlanta, Georgia: National Coalition to Prevent Shoplifting, 1981. This is a report on surveys of students' attitudes toward shoplifting and self-reported involvement in it, and includes a reported incidence of such behavior. 20p.

1139 Gable, Richard J. Juvenile Delinquency Research: Truths, Myths And Hopes, *Today's Delinquent* 1:39-55, 1982. The author provides an overview of research on violent juvenile offenders, discusses the issues of predicting who becomes one, who remains the habitual offender, and the juvenile justice system's role in creating career criminals and effective rehabilitation.

1140 Garbarino, James & Kostelny, Kathleen Children And Violence Trauma In The American War Zone, pp 92-101 in Asquith, Stewart (ed.) *Children And Young People In Conflict With The Law*. London, United Kingdom: Jessica Kingsley, 1996. This chapter describes children growing up in war zones , and areas with high rates of violence in American cities.

1141 Gardner, LeGrande & Shoemaker, Donald J. Social Bonding And Delinquency: A Comparative Analysis, *Sociological Quarterly* 30:481-499, 1989. This is report based on urban and rural Virginia students and includes some Japanese data.

1142 Gardner, Sandra *Street Gangs*. New York, New York: Franklin Watts, 1983. This is a journalistic report of street gangs, their codes, their crimes and community efforts to curtail them in American urban milieu. 128p.

1143 Garnier, Helen E. & Stein, Judith A. Values And The Family Risk And Protective Factors For Adolescent Problem Behaviors, *Youth & Society* 30:89-120, 1998. In this 18-year longitudinal study of Euro-American families, it was found that counter-culture identity protected adolescents against hard drug use, and traditional maternal values protected against problem behavior while humanistic-egalitarian values protected against delinquency but had increased risk of drug use.

1144 Gibbons, Don C. Juvenile Delinquency: Can Social Science Find A Cure? *Crime And Delinquency* 32:2:186-204, 1986. The author discusses the implications of research findings on etiology and intervention in the United States, and highlights the importance of developing theory and research integrating the experiences of justice system participants.

1145 Gibbs, John J.; Giever, Dennis & Martin, Jamie S. Parental Management And Self-Control: An Empirical Test Of Gottfredson And Hirschi's General Theory, *Journal Of Research In Crime And Delinquency* 35:40-70, 1998. A self-report instrument that included a parental management scale, a self-control scale and measures of deviance were employed by the authors to test Gottfredson and Hirschi's general theory.

1146 Gillis, A. R. & Hagan, John Delinquent Samaritans: Network Structure, Social Conflict, And The Willingness To Intervene, *Journal Of Research In Crime And Delinquency* 27:30-51, 1990. Results of this test of whether or not delinquents are asocial and amoral indicate that in situations of conflict, delinquents show more loyalty than other juveniles to family and friends.

1147 Goldschmidt, Lidush; Day, Nancy L. & Richardson, Gale A. Effects Of Prenatal Marijuana Exposure On Child Behavior Problems At Age 10, *Neurotoxicology And Teratology* 22:325-336, 2000. This study of the effects of prenatal marijuana exposure on children's behavior problems at age 10 found that prenatal marijuana use was significantly related to increased symptoms of hyperactivity, impulsivity, inattention, externalizing of problems as well as increased delinquency.

1148 Gottfredson, Gary D. Schooling And Delinquency, pp 424-469 in Martin, Susan E.; Sechrest, Lee B. & National Research Council Panel On Research On Rehabilitative Techniques (eds.) *New Directions In The Rehabilitation Of Criminal Offenders*. Washington D.C.: National Academy Press, 1981. This chapter offers a summary on the interactions among crime, social class, ability, school performance and delinquency.

1149 Ousey, Graham C. Deindustrialization, Female-Headed Familes, And Black And White Juvenile Homicide Rates, 1970-1990, *Sociological Inquiry* 70:391-419, 2000. The interactions among declining manufacturing and increased rates of female-headed households, race, and homicide rates are examined in this article.

1150 Graham, Nanette The Influence Of Predictors On Adolescent Drug Use: An Examination Of Individual Effects, *Youth & Society* 28:215-235, 1996. Among this sample of Charleston, South Carolina adolescents it was found that for both white and African-American participants negative misconduct and attitude favoring drug use were good predictors of adolescent drug use.

1151 Gray-Ray, Phyllis & Ray, Melvin C. Juvenile Delinquency In The Black Community, *Youth & Society* 22:67-84, 1990. African-American urban male youths from several states participated in this study of family control and delinquency.

1152 Greenbaum, Paul E.; Brown, Eric C. & Friedman, Robert M. Alcohol Expectancies Among Adolescents With Conduct Disorder: Prediction And Mediation Of Drinking, *Addictive Behaviors* 20:321-333, 1995. This study examining alcohol expectancies among adolescents with conduct disorder concludes that expectancies of enhanced social and cognitive behavior had the strongest association with alcohol use and were signify cant univariate predictors of drinking.

1153 Greene, Kathryn; Krcmar, Marina; Walters, Linda H.; Rubin, Donald L.; Hale, Jerold & Hale, L. Targeting Adolescent Risk-Taking Behaviors: The Contributions Of Egocentrism And Sensation-Seeking, *Journal Of Adolescence* 23:439-461, 2000. This study sampled adolescents and college students to assess the relationship between risk-taking behavior and egocentrism and sensation-seeking.

1154 Greve, Werner Imprisonment Of Juveniles And Adolescents: Deficits And Demands For Developmental Research, *Applied Developmental Science* 5:21-36, 2001. This article reviews current knowledge about the development of juvenile delinquency and the literature on the effects of imprisonment in general, and concludes that the psychological effects of imprisonment on juveniles and adolescents is still unknown.

1155 Griffiths, Curt T. & Nance, Margit *The Female Offender: Selected Papers From an International Symposium*. Vancouver, Canada: Simon Fraser University Criminology Research Center, 1980. Female criminality and the treatment of female juvenile and adult offenders are some of the topics the authors address. 331p.

1156 Groeneveld, Lyle P; Short, James F. & Thoits, Peggy *Design Of A Study To Assess The Impact Of Income Maintenance On Delinquency: Final Report*. Menlo Park, California: SRI International, 1979. This study based on data from the Seattle and Denver Income Maintenance Experiments and other sources focused on the effect of income maintenance experiments on juvenile delinquency and found no consistent pattern in the levels of delinquency of experimental-control groups. 79p Appendix.

1157 Groth, Nicholas A.; Longo, Robert E. & McFadin, J. Bradley Undetected Recidivism Among Rapists And Child Molesters, *Crime & Delinquency* 28:450-458, 1982. The authors' study of convicted rapists and child molesters reveals that many ot them usually commit their first offense as adolescents.

1158 Gruber, Enid & Machamer, Anne Marie Risk Of School Failure As An Early Indicator Of Other Health Risk Behavior In American High School Students, *Health, Risk & Society* 2:59-68, 2000. This study treating educational risk factors as indicators of other risk behavior in adolescence suggests that health risk exposure increases with increased educational risk, and the latter is a significant predictor of other health risk behaviors when the effects of grade level, gender, ethnicity, and average grades were controlled.

1159 Hagan, J. & Kay, F. Gender And Delinquency In White-Collar Families: A Power-Control Perspective, *Crime & Delinquency* 36:391-407, 1990. From a power-control perspective, this study addresses white-collar delinquency such as youthful violations of patents and copyrights through the copying of audio-/videotapes and computer software.

1160 Hanke, Penelope J. Putting School Crime Into Perspective: Self-Reported School Victimizations Of High School Seniors, *Journal Of Criminal Justice* 24:207-226, 1996. Analyzing data from a 1988 survey, the author found that the most common personal crimes in the school setting were threats not involving weapons or injury, and most students did not report such experiences, and were victimized a single time.

1161 Harris, Philip W. & Jones, Peter R. Differentiating Delinquent Youths For Program Planning And Evaluation, *Criminal Justice And Behavior* 26:403-434, 1999. The authors describe their treatment-relevant typologies of juveniles using a continuing system of information.

1162 Hartwell, Stephanie W. Juvenile Delinquency And The Social Development Model: The Retrospective Accounts Of Homeless Substance Abusers, *Criminal Justice Policy Review* 11:217-233, 2000. The life history accounts of 31 men who are currently homeless drug addicts are examined to find the relationship between early illicit drug exposure, delinquency, and subsequent adult experience.

1163 Hashima, Patricia Y. & Finkelhor, David Violent Victimization Of Youth Versus Adults In The National Crime Victimization Survey, *Journal Of Interpersonal Violence* 14:799-820, 1999. This study compares the violent victimization of juveniles who, more so than adults, tend to be victims of violent crimes and to suffer from crime-related injuries.

1164 Hawaii Budget And Finance Department *Crime In Hawaii: Perspectives In Early Prevention*. Honolulu, Hawaii, 1980. This is a report on the results of a series of studies on the extent and important aspects of delinquency and youth crime, some correlates of the delinquency rates, and an overview of some of the more important problems in developing effective prevention and control services. 305p.

1165 Hay, Carter An Exploratory Test Of Braithwaite's Reintegrative Shaming Theory, *Journal Of Research In Crime And Delinquency* 38:132-153, 2001. This research testing Braithwaite's reintegrative shaming theory revealed a partial support for the theory, and found an enduring negative effect of shaming on predatory delinquency.

1166 Heck, Carry & Walsh, Anthony The Effects Of Maltreatment And Family Structure On Minor And Serious Delinquency, *International Journal Of Offender Therapy And Comparative Criminology* 44:178-193, 2000. This study on the effects of maltreatment on serious violent and property delinquency as well as on minor misbehavior among white, male delinquents found that maltreatment was found to be significant in delinquency, although the variables' impact differed based on the type of delinquency.

1167 Heide, Kathleen M. Parents Who Get Killed And The Children Who Kill Them, *Journal Of Interpersonal Violence* 8:531-544, 1993. On the basis of FBI homicide reports, the author describes homicides of parents by their children, the characteristics of offenders and victims, and suggests that there is lack of evidence in claims of increased youth involvement in such killings.

1168 Heide, Kathleen M. Juvenile Involvement In Multiple Offender And Multiple Victim Parricides, *Journal Of Police And Criminal Psychology* 9:53-64, 1993. This investigation on the involvement of juveniles in multiple-offender and/or multiple-victim parricide reports that in the United States only 45 fathers, 19 mothers, 14 stepfathers and 1 stepmother were slain by 2 or more offenders with at least a minor son or daughter, and elaborates on the limitations of the FBI data.

1169 Heimer, Karen & De Coster, Stacy The Gendering Of Violent Delinquency, *Criminology* 37:277-317, 1999. This study claims that differences in cultural practices and structural positions combine to influence violent delinquency in different ways across gender as well as account for the observed gender gap in violent delinquency.

1170 Heimer, Karen Gender, Interaction, And Delinquency – Testing A Theory Of Differential Social Control, *Social Psychology Quarterly* 59:39-61, 1996. This interactionist explanation of gender differences in the processes that lead to juvenile delinquency found supported for both females' and males' behavior and help explain differences in the genesis of delinquency of boys and girls.

1171 Henry, David B.; Tolan, Patrick H. & Gorman-Smith, Deborah Longitudinal Family And Peer Group Effects On Violence And Nonviolent Delinquency, *Journal Of Clinical Child Psychology* 30:172-186, 2001. This study concludes that peers' violence, and not nonviolent delinquency, predicted individual violence and nonviolent delinquency while family types predicted peer deviance, individual violence and delinquency.

1172 Herrenkohl, Todd I.; Huang, Bu; Kosterman, Rick & Hawkins, J. David A Comparison Of Social Development Processes Leading To Violent Behavior In Late Adolescence For Childhood Initiators And Adolescent Initiators Of Violence, *Journal Of Research In Crime And Delinquency* 38:45-63, 2001. This study used data from the Seattle Social Development Project to compare the developmental mechanisms that predict violence at age 18 of those with childhood violence behavior and those with adolescence violence.

1173 Herrenkohl, Todd I.; Maguin, Eugene; Hill, Karl G.; Hawkins, J. David; Abbott, Robert D. & Catalano, Richard F. Developmental Risk Factors For Youth Violence, *Journal Of Adolescent Health* 26:176-186, 2000. The authors replicated earlier research on risk factors in youth violence to explore the effects of other developmental problem behavior that increase risk of violent behavior.

1174 Herrera, Veronica M. & McCloskey, Laura Ann Gender Differences In The Risk For Delinquency Among Youth Exposed To Family Violence, *Child Abuse And Neglect* 25:1037-1051, 2001. This research on gender differences in adolescent delinquency and childhood exposure to both marital violence and physical child abuse concluded that although boys and girls share similar family risk factors for delinquency, girls are more likely to be arrested for violent offenses involving child physical abuse.

1175 Hill, Karl G.; Howell, James C.; Hawkins, J. David & Battin-Pearson, Sara R. Childhood Risk Factors For Adolescent Gang Membership: Results From The Seattle Social Development Project, *Journal Of Research In Crime And Delinquency* 36:300-322, 1999. This study uses longitudinal data to predict adolescent gang membership from variables measured in childhood.

1176 Hindelang, Michael J. & McDermott, M. Joan *Analysis Of National Crime Victimization Survey Data To Study Serious Delinquent Behavior, Monograph Two: Juvenile Criminal Behavior: An Analysis Of Rates And*

Victim Characteristics. Washington, D.C.: National Institute for Juvenile Justice and Delinquency, 1981. Victimization data from a National Crime Survey were used to study the rates of offending attributable to offenders of particular demographics, offender age-based variations in rates of victimization of persons of particular demographic characteristics, and similarities and dissimilarities of the demographic characteristics of offenders and victims. 124p.

1177 Hindelang, Michael J.; Hirschi, Travis & Weis, Joseph G. *Measuring Delinquency*. Beverly Hills, California: Sage, 1981. This volume examines the location of systematic bias in the measurement of delinquency in the literature on delinquency measurement and analyzes the results of a quasi-experimental study of conditions affecting the reliability and validity of self-report procedures. 248p.

1178 Hindelang, Michael J.; Hirschi, Travis & Weis, Joseph G. Correlates Of Delinquency: The Illusion Of Discrepancy Between Self-Report And Official Measures, *American Sociological Review* 44:995-1014, 1979. The authors argue that current evidence on the issue of crime measurement is sufficient to resolve many of the apparent inconsistencies among various measures of criminality.

1179 Hinkle, William J. & Stuart, Henry (eds.) School Violence, *Annals Of The American Academy Of Political And Social Science* 567:8-208, 2000. This special issue of the journal has seven papers and reviews focusing on the extent and causes of school violence.

1180 Hirschi, Travis & Gottfredson, Michael Age And The Explanation Of Crime, *American Journal Of Sociology* 89:522-84, 1983. The authors argue that criminologists are misguided in current conceptions of the effect of age and its implications for research and theory.

1181 Hockaday, Cathy; Crase, Sedahlia Jasper; Shelley, Mark C. & Stockdale, Dahlia F. A Prospective Study Of Adolescent Pregnancy *Journal Of Adolescence* 23:423-438, 2000. Studying the characteristics of adolescent pregnancy in a pregnant and comparison group of adolescents females, this research concluded that pregnancy in white adolescents was more often predicted by wishes for higher education but lower educational expectations, desire to have sex at a younger age and more children.

1182 Hoffmann, John P. & Cerbone, Felicia Gray Stressful Life Events And Delinquency Escalation In Early Adolescence, *Criminology* 37:343-373, 1999. This article describes and examines one potential pathway of delinquency escalation, stressful life events, in early and mid-adolescence.

1183 Hoffmann, John P. & Su, S. Susan The Conditional Effects Of Stress On Delinquency And Drug Use: A Strain Theory Assessment Of Sex Differences, *Journal Of Research In Crime And Delinquency* 34:46-78, 1997. Agnew's general strain model is elaborated by assessing the sex-specific effects of stressful life events on delinquency and drug use in a structural equation model that indicated few important sex differerences among females and males.

1184 Hoffman, Allan M. (ed.) *Schools, Violence, And Society*. Westport, Connecticut: Praeger, 1996. The 20 articles of this volume are organized under four topics - the problem of school violence, its causes, legal and related issues in school security, and toward a less violent school environment - in this anthology addressing various issues on school violence in the United States. 357p.

1185 Howell, James C. Recent Gang Research: Program And Policy Implications, *Crime & Delinquency* 40:495-515, 1994. This paper reviews and analyzes existing knowledge of and literature on gangs in the United States, and the factors in increasing youth violence.

1186 Hoyt, Dan R.; Ryan, Kimberly D. & Cauce, Ana Mari Personal Victimization In A High-Risk Environment: Homeless And Runaway Adolescents, *Journal Of Research In Crime And Delinquency* 36:371-392, 1999. By controlling for proximity, this study examined in detail the potential effects of exposure, victim attractiveness, and guardianship.

1187 Huang, Bu; White, Helene R.; Kosterman, Rick; Catalano Richard F. & Hawkins, J. David Developmental Associations Between Alcohol And Interpersonal Aggression During Adolescence, *Journal Of Research In Crime And Delinquency* 38:64-83, 2001. Yearly data from 808 males and females from the Seattle Social Development Project were explored for any associations between alcohol use and interpersonal aggression from early to late adolescence.

1188 Huff, C. Ronald (ed.) *Gangs In America*. London, United Kingdom: Sage, 1990. There are 14 chapters organized under such topics as social-anthropological perspective, defining and measuring gang violence, diffusion, diversity and drugs in this collection about American gangs. 351p.

1189 Huizinga, David H. & Menard, Scott Delinquency And Drug Use: Temporal And Developmental Patterns, *Justice Quarterly* 6:419-455, 1989. This study examining the short and long-term relationships among alcohol, illegal drug use and delinquency concludes that substance use and serious delinquency are developmental rather than causal.

1190 Hurst, Hunter (ed.) Serious Crime By Juveniles, *Today's Delinquent* 1:5-68, 1982. This special issue focuses on serious crime by juveniles including data that suggest that the rate of violent crime in the United States decreased between 1973 and 1979, and that juvenile violent crimes compared to those of adults were less serious in terms of physical harm and economic loss, new mandates on criminal court processing of juvenile offenders, prediction research, and revival of retribution in juvenile justice.

1191 Jackson, Pamela Irving Crime, Youth Gangs, And Urban Transition: The Social Dislocations Of Postindustrial Economic Development, *Justice Quarterly* 8:379-397, 1991. This discussion of the impact of economic changes and population shifts on youth crime and gangs concludes that increasing crime and youth gangs are uniniiended consequences of post-industrial development.

1192 Janeksela, Galan M. Juvenile Attitudes Toward The Police: Theory And Application, *International Journal Of Comparative And Applied Criminal Justice* 23:313-329, 1999. The author discusses the relationship between attitudes toward authority and delinquent behavior.

1193 Janeksela, Galan M. Deviants Have Bad Attitudes, *International Journal Of Criminology And Penology* 5:337-347, 1977. This article reviews studies on the interactions of attitudes and delinquent behavior and concludes that attitudes are not closely related to behavior.

1194 Jang, S. J. & Krohn, M. D. Developmental Patterns Of Sex Differences In Delinquency Among African American Adolescents: A Test Of The Sex-Invariance Hypothesis, *Journal Of Quantitative Criminology* 11:195-222, 1995. In testing the hypothesis that sex differences in delinquency are invariant over developmental stages of adolescence, this study found that sex differences in delinquency rather than remain constant, tend to vary as the subjects grow older.

1195 Jang, Sung Joon & Smith, Carolyn A. A Test Of Reciprocal Causal Relationships Among Parental Supervision, Affective Ties, And Delinquency, *Journal Of Research In Crime And Delinquency* 34:307-336, 1997. Using panel data from a representative sample of 838 urban adolescents, the authors tested the hypothesis that parenting and delinquency are related.

1196 Jang, Sung Joon Age-Varying Effects Of Family, School, And Peers On Delinquency: A Multilevel Modeling Test Of Interactional Theory, *Criminology* 37:643-685, 1999. This study tests hypotheses about the age-varying effects of attachment to parents, commitment to school, and association with delinquent peers on delinquency.

1197 Jarjoura, G. Roger & Triplett, Ruth A. Delinquency And Class: A Test of the Proximity Principle, *Justice Quarterly* 14:763-792, 1997. This study aiming to clarify the class-crime relationship found that youths' expected educational attainment and experiences mediate the effect of social class on delinquent behavior.

1198 Jarjoura, G. Roger The Conditional Effect Of Social Class On The Dropout-Delinquency Relationship, *Journal Of Research In Crime And Delinquency* 33:232-255, 1996. Results of this analysis support the proposition that middle-class compared to lower class dropouts, are more likely to engage in delinquency as a consequence of dropping out.

1199 Jarjoura, G. Roger Does Dropping Out Of School Enhance Delinquent Involvement?: Results From A Large-Scale National Probability Sample, *Criminology* 31:149-172, 1993. This study of the relationship between dropping out of school and later involvement in delinquency indicates that the effect of dropping out of school on later offending is more complicated than previously believed.

1200 Jaros, Kenneth J. (ed.) *Violence As A Public Health Problem: Developing Culturally Appropriate Prevention Strategies For Adolescents And Children*. McClean, Virginia: National Maternal & Child Health Clearinghouse, 1992. This report is on on violence, African-American youth, and the juvenile justice system.

1201 Jenkins, Patricia H. School Delinquency And The School Social Bond, *Journal Of Research In Crime And Delinquency* 34:337-367, 1997. Data from a sample of 754 middle school students, are examined for the independent effects of components of school and social bond on school crime, school misconduct, and school nonattedance.

1202 Jensen, Gary F. *Sociology Of Delinquency*. Beverly Hills, California: Sage, 1981. This anthology of 9 chapters deals with criminological theories and critical criminology as well as deviance, peers and self-reported delinquency, arrests, and correction in the United States and abroad. 144p.

1203 Jenson, Jeffrey M. & Howard, Matthew O. Hallucinogen Use Among Juvenile Probationers: Prevalence And Characteristics, *Criminal Justice And Behavior* 26:357-372, 1999. Based on a sample of juvenile probationers, this study assessed the prevalence of hallucinogen use, identified differences between lifetime hallucinogen users and nonusers, and evaluated variables predicting age at onset and lifetime frequency of use.

1204 Joe, Karen A. & Chesney-Lind, Meda 'Just Every Mother's Angel': An Analysis Of Gender And Ethnic Variations In Youth Gang Membership, *Gender And Society* 9:408-431, 1995. This study sought to determine why boys and girls from varied ethnic backgrounds joined gangs.

1205 Joe-Laidler, Karen A. & Hunt, Geoffrey Violence And Social Organization In Female Gangs, *Social Justice* 24:148-169, 1997. Self-identified female and male gang members were surveyed in this ethnographic study of gang violence.

1206 Johnson, Byron R.; Jang, Sung Joon; Larson, David B. & De Li, Spencer Does Adolescent Religious Commitment Matter? A Reexamination Of The Effects Of Religiosity In Delinquency, *Journal Of Research In Crime And Delinquency* 38:22-44, 2001. This is a study on the relevance of religiosity to the etiology of delinquency tested whether the effects of religiosity on delinquency are spurious or completely indirect via social bonding, social learning, and socio-demographic variables.

1207 Johnson, Byron R.; De Li, Spencer; Larson, David B. & McCullough, Michael A. Systematic Review Of The Religiosity And Delinquency Literature: A Research Note, *Journal Of Contemporary Criminal Justice* 16:32-52, 2000. This is an assessment and systematic review of religion-delinquency literature that demonstrates that the relationship is neither disparate nor contradictory as previous studies have suggested.

1208 Johnson, David R. & Scheuble, Laurie K. Gender Bias In The Disposition Of Juvenile Court Referrals: The Effects Of Time And Location, *Criminology* 29:677-700, 1991. When models predicting more punitive decisions of female offenders as well as models predicting greater leniency for female offenders were tested, findings reveal that greater punishment for girls compared to boys were meted out only in cases involving repeat offenders who had committed more serious crimes.

1209 Jussim, Lee & Osgood, D. Wayne Influence And Similarity Among Friends: An Integrative Model Applied To Incarcerated Adolescents, *Social Psychology Quarterly* 52:98-112, 1989. The authors propose a causal model for identifying interpersonal relations on delinquency and illustrate it through a study of delinquent values among pairs of male adolescents incarcerated in four institutions.

1210 Kakar, Suman Child Abuse And Juvenile Delinquency: A Prospective Study, *Australian And New Zealand Journal Of Criminology* 29:47-57, 1996. This Florida study found that abused children more often were referred for personal and status offenses than property offenses.

1211 Kandel, Denise & Davies, Mark Friendship Networks, Intimacy, And Illicit Drug Use In Young Adulthood: A Comparison Of Two Competing Theories, *Criminology* 29:441-470, 1991. The authors compare social control and cultural deviance theories and suggest that illicit drug use is positively associated with intimacy among members of male friendship networks irrespective of level of confiding or interaction.

1212 Kaplan, Howard B. & Fukurai, Hiroshi Negative Social Sanctions, Self Rejection, And Drug Use, *Youth & Society* 23:275-298, 1992. The findings from this sample support labeling theory in that negative sanctions experienced in earlier deviance are associated with later deviant behavior.

1213 Kaplan, Howard B. & Liu, Xiaoru A Longitudinal Analysis Of Mediating Variables In The Drug Use-Dropping Out Relationship, *Criminology* 32:415-440, 1994. This longitudinal study assesses various models of the relationship between antecedent drug use among young people and later dropping out of school.

1214 Katuer, Tara L. Moral Reasoning, Perceived Competence, And Adolescent Engagement In Risky Activity, *Journal Of Adolescence* 23:599-604, 2000. This self-report study focused on the relationships among moral reasoning, perceived competence, scholastic achievement and delinquent behavior.

1215 Kaufman, Jeanne G. & Widom, Cathy Spatz Childhood Victimization, Running Away, And Delinquency, *Journal Of Research In Crime And Delinquency* 36:347-370, 1999. The authors studied the interaction among childhood victimization, running away, and delinquency, and whether running away serves to mediate or moderate these relationships.

1216 Kelley, Thomas M. A Critique Of Social Bonding And Control Theory Of Delinquency Using The Principles Of Psychology Of Mind, *Adolescence* 31:321-337, 1996. This article examine the major assumptions of social bonding and control theories of delinquency within the frame work of the refined principles of psychology of mind in explaining the comparative amount of both deviant and conforming behavior of youthful offenders.

1217 Kennedy, David M.; Braga, Anthony A. & Piehl, Anne M. The (Un)known Universe: Mapping Gangs And Gang Violence In Boston, Weisburd, David & McEwen, Tom (eds.) *Crime Mapping And Crime Prevention*. Monsey, New York, New York: Criminal Justice Press, 1997. This article discusses the problem of mapping gang crime in a community using police information about gangs and their localities of operation as a main data source on which to base the maps.

1218 Kerpelman, Jennifer L. & Smith, Sondra L. Adjudicated Adolescent Girls And Their Mothers: Examining Identity Perceptions And Processes, *Youth & Society* 30:313-347, 1999. In the authors' interviews of adjudicated adolescent daughters, it was found their interactions with their mothers both promoted and impeded their identity development.

1219 Kim, Julia Yun Soo; Fendrich, Michael & Wislar, Joseph S. The Validity Of Juvenile Arrestees' Drug Use Reporting: A Gender Comparison, *Journal Of Research In Crime And Delinquency* 37:419-432, 2000. The validity of gender differences in admissions of drug use among juvenile arrestees is examined.

1220 Kingree, J. B.; Braithwaite, Ronald & Woodring, Tammy Psychosocial And Behavioral Problems In Relation To Recent Experience As A Runaway Among Adolescent Detainees, *Criminal Justice And Behavior* 28:190-205, 2001. This study of psychosocial and behavioral problems and recent experience as a runaway found that recent experience as a runaway was common, and detainees who had recently run away reported more psychosocial and behavioral problems than those who were not runaways.

1221 Klemke, Lloyd W. Reassessment Of The Adolescent Crime Wave Model, *California Sociologist* 1:183-192, 1978. In this test of the Adolescent Crime Wave model of juvenile delinquency, there was support for a Declining Adolescent Crime model of youths' involvement in crime that began and peaked in preadolescence and decreased during adolescence.

1222 Knight, Karen Witchcoff & Tripodi, Tony Societal Bonding And Delinquency: An Empirical Test Of Hirschi's Theory Of Control, *Journal Of Offender Rehabilitation* 23:117-129, 1996. This survey of youths detained in a juvenile center confirms part of Hirschi's contention that delinquent youths appear to identify with a delinquent subculture favoring delinquency.

1223 Kratcoski, Peter C. Child Abuse And Violence Against The Family, *Child Welfare* 61:435-444, 1982. This study concludes that regardless of the specific incident that triggered the violent behavior of the delinquents studied, those who had abused their parents tended to come from families

1224 Krisberg, Barry Themes of Violence And Gang Youth, *International Annals Of Criminology* 18:9-18, 1979:1980. Observations of and interviews with 22 Philadelphia youth gang leaders leads the author to conclude that violence was inextricably intertwined with the lives and self-concepts exhibited by these youths.

1225 Krohn, Marvin D.; Akers, Ronald L.; Radosevich, Marcia & Lanza-Kaduce, Lonn Social Status And Deviance: Class Context Of School, Social Status, And Delinquent Behavior, *Criminology* 18:303-318, 1980. The relationship between social class and four measures of deviance in American schools with predominantly upper-middle-class, middle-class, and working-class students suggests that social class does not seem to be an important predictor of juvenile delinquency.

1226 Kruttschnitt, Candace & Dornfield, Maude Will They Tell? Assessing Preadolescents' Reports Of Family Violence? *Journal Of Research In Crime And Delinquency* 29:136-147, 1992. The Conflict Tactics Scale was employed to examine the concurrent validity and reliability of youth reports of victimization and observation of spousal violence in their family.

1227 LaGrange, Randy L. & White, Helene Raskin Age Differences In Delinquency: A Test Of Theory, *Criminology* 23:19-45, 1985. This study tests an integrated model of delinquency based on a modified version of Hirschi's control theory.

1228 LaGrange, Randy L. & Ferraro, Kenneth F. Assessing Age And Gender Differences In Perceived Risk And Fear Of Crime, *Criminology* 27:697-720, 1989. This article is about age and gender differences in perceived risk and fear of crime and how the measurement of the latter greatly shapes the results of research on fear of crime.

1229 Lahey, Benjamin B.; Gordon, Rachel A. & Loeber, Rolf; Stouthamer-Loeber, Magda & Farrington, David P. Boys Who Join Gangs: A Prospective Study OF first Gang Entry, *Journal Of Abnormal Child Psychology* 27:261-276, 1999. This study of African-American and white boys attempted to replicate earlier research on predicting future gang involvement.

1230 Landsheer, Johannes & Hart, Harm T. Age And Adolescent Delinquency: The Changing Relationship Among Age, Delinquent Attitude, And Delinquent Activity, *Criminal Justice And Behavior* 26:373-388, 1999. This study investigating the relationship between attitudes toward delinquent activities and levels of delinquent activity found that youths with a strictly non-permissive attitude showed a low and stable level of delinquency at every age.

1231 Larzelere, Robert E. & Patterson, Gerald R. Parental Management: Mediator Of The Effect Of Socioeconomic Status On Early Delinquency, *Criminology* 28:301-324, 1990. Results of this research testing if the effect of socioeconomic status on delinquency in early adolescence could be mediated entirely by parental management skills supported theories emphasizing the effects of parental control on delinquency.

1232 Lasley, James R. Age, Social Context, And Street Gang Membership: Are 'Youth' Gangs Becoming 'Adult' Gangs?, *Youth & Society* 23:434-451, 1992. The issue of the age-composition of gangs and the ecological deterioration of inner cities is the focus of this discussion.

1233 Lattimore, Pamela K.; Linster, Richard L. & MacDonald, John M. Risk Of Death Among Serious Young Offenders, *Journal Of Research In Crime And Delinquency* 34:187-209, 1997. Analyzing the mortality data gathered from California Vital Statistics on more than 4,000 youth paroled by the California Youth Authority, this study found that homicide was the dominant cause of early death among them.

1234 Lauritsen, Janet L. Sibling Resemblance In Juvenile Delinquency: Findings From The National Youth Survey, *Criminology* 31:387-410, 1993. This study found that family functioning was the only variable accounting for a small proportion of resemblance in offending behavior of siblings.

1235 Lauritsen, Janet L.; Laub, John H. & Sampson, Robert J. Conventional And Delinquent Activities: Implications For The Prevention Of Violent Victimization Among Adolescents, *Violence And Victims* 7:91-108, 1992. The Authors' findings on the relationships between activity involvement and the risk of assault and robbery victimization among adolescents suggest that while individual-level theories of victimization are not necessary, lifestyle theories must be supplemented with theories of offending behavior.

1236 Lauritsen, Janet L.; Sampson, Robert J.& Laub, John H. The Link Between Offending And Victimization Among Adolescents, *Criminology* 29:265-292, 1991. The authors, in examining the effect of delinquent lifestyles on the criminal victimization of teenagers and young adults, argue that victimization patterns of youths have to be understood within the milieu of their criminal and deviant activities.

1237 Lawrence, Janet S. & Shireman, Charles H. *The Findings Of Self-Report Studies Of Juvenile Misbehavior: A Summary*. Chicago, Illinois: University of Chicago Center for the Assessment of Alternatives to Juvenile Justice Processing, 1980. This review of 70 self-report studies concludes that boys' delinquency exceeds that of girls by two to one, and not four to one as suggested by arrest statistics. 50p.

1238 Lee, E. Ross School Environment, Self-Esteem, And Delinquency, *Journal Of Criminal Justice* 23:555-567, 1995. This study of self-esteem, racial-esteem, school commitment, and delinquency found, compared to racially homogeneous schools, higher rates of self-reported delinquency in the equally mixed school environment.

1239 Lee, Yoon Ho Acculturation And Delinquent Behavior: The Case Of Korean American Youths, *International Journal Of Comparative And Applied Criminal Justice* 22:273-292, 1998. This study investigated the acculturation and delinquent behavior of ethnic Korean juveniles in America.

1240 Lemmon, John H. How Child Maltreatment Affects Dimensions Of Juvenile Delinquency In A Cohort Of Low-Income Urban Youths, *Justice Quarterly* 16:357-376, 1999. Examining the relationship of socio-demographic factors and maltreatment's effects on delinquency, the author concludes that maltreatment significantly affected the initiation into and continuation of delinquency.

1241 Lewis, Dorothy Otnow; Pincus, Jonathan H.; Bard, Barbara; Richardson, Ellis; Prichep, Leslie; Feldman, Marilyn & Yeager, Catherine Neuropsychiatric, Psychoeducational, And Family Characteristics Of 14 Juveniles Condemned To Death In The United States, *American Journal Of Psychiatry* 145:584-589, 1988. This study describes the bio-psychosocial characteristics of 14 juveniles sentenced to death in 4 American states during 1986-1987.

1242 Lewis, Dorothy Otnow; Shanok, Shelley S. & Balla, David Parents Of Delinquents, pp 265-292 in Lewis, Dorothy Otnow (ed.) *Vulnerabilities To Delinquency*. New York, New York: SP Medical and Scientific Books, 1981. This article discusses the psychosocial state of parents and its consequences to the delinquent behavior of their children.

1243 Leiber, Michael J. & Wacker, Mary Ellen Ellyson A Theoretical And Empirical Assessment Of Power-Control Theory And Single-Mother Families, *Youth & Society* 28:317-350, 1997. The authors found that peers and age were good predictors of delinquent behavior that increased with delinquent peer association particularly among girls, but when all other variables were controlled, overall no gender difference in delinquency was observed.

1244 Lieber, Michael; Farnworth, Margaret; Jamieson, Katherine M. & Nalla, Mahesh K. Bridging The Gender Gap In Criminology: Liberation And Gender-Specific Strain Effects On Delinquency, *Sociological Inquiry* 64:56-68, 1994. This research on male and female delinquents concludes that "strain" is consistently and positively related to delinquency while "liberation" is not related to female delinquency.

1245 Lipton, Wendy L. & Smith, M. Dwayne Explaining Delinquent Involvement: A Consideration Of Suppressor Effects, *Journal Of Research In Crime And Delinquency* 20:199-213, 1983. Using data from the Youth in Transition study, this report attempts to demonstrate the importance of suppressor effects in delinquency research.

1246 Liu, Xiaoru & Kaplan, Howard B. Explaining The Gender Difference In Adolescent Delinquent Behavior: A Longitudinal Test Of Mediating Mechanisms, *Criminology* 37:195-215, 1999. The extent to which mediating mechanisms account for the gender difference in delinquency was tested on a sample of adolescents studied during three points in their lives.

1247 Lizotte, Alan J. & Tesoriero, James M. Patterns Of Adolescent Firearms Ownership And Use, *Justice Quarterly* 11:51-74, 1994. This study on how youths come to acquire and use guns has implications for understanding juveniles' use of guns to engage in delinquency.

1248 Loeber, Rolf; Wei, Evelyn; Stouthamer-Loeber, Magda; Huizinga, David & Thornberry, Terence P. Behavioral Antecedents To Serious And Violent Offending: Joint Analyses From The Denver Youth Survey, Pittsburgh Youth Study And The Rochester Youth Development Study, *Studies In Crime And Crime Prevention* 8:245-264, 1999. This longitudinal developmental study focused on the age-of-onset from less serious problem behavior and delinquency in overt to covert pathways.

1249 Loeber, Rolf & Snyder, Howard N. Rate Of Offending In Juvenile Careers: Findings Of Constancy And Change In Lambda, *Criminology* 28:97-110, 1990. Changes in the rate of offending in a sample of American males between ages 8 and 17 in this study leads to the conclusion that the rate of offending by active offenders was not related to age at first offense and was constant at each age level.

1250 Loeber, Rolf & Waller, Danette Artefacts In Delinquency Specialisation And Generalisation Studies, *British Journal Of Criminology* 28:461-477, 1988. The methodological nuances of possible response categories in delineating the incidence of self-reported general versus specialized delinquency were tested in this investigation.

1251 Loeber, Rolf & Dishion, Thomas J. Multiple Gating: A Multistage Assessment Procedure For Identifying Youths At Risk For Delinquency, *Journal Of Research In Crime And Delinquency* 21:7-32, 1984. This research presenting a multistage device to screen delinquents from non-delinquents concludes that the device was useful.

1252 Longo, Robert E. & Groth, Nicholas A. Juvenile Sexual Offenses Of Adult Rapists And Child Molesters, *International Journal Of Offender Therapy And Comparative Criminology* 27:150-155, 1983. Florida and Connecticut their progression from adolescent to adult non-contact voyeurism and exhibitionism to serious sexual assault behavior is the subject of this study.

1253 Lotz, Roy & Lee, Leona Sociability, School Experience And Delinquency, *Youth & Society* 31:199-223, 1999. The conclusion of this study is that sociability was a strong predictor of delinquency while negative school experience as a predictor of delinquency is valid only among white youths.

1254 Louis Harris And Associates, Inc. *Between Hope And Fear: Teens Speak Out On Crime And The Community*. New York, New York, 1996. This survey based on interviews with students in grades 7 through 12, examines young people's experiences with violence and crime in the United States. 208p Appendix.

1255 Ludwig, Kristin B. & Pittman, Joe F. Adolescent Prosocial Values And Self-Efficacy In Relation To Delinquency, Risky Sexual Behavior, And Drug Use, *Youth & Society* 30:461-482, 1999. In this study it was found that males were more likely than females to engage in various forms of misbehavior.

1256 Lukin, Penny R. Recidivism And Changes Made By Delinquents During Residential Treatment, *Journal Of Research In Crime And Delinquency* 18:101-112, 1981. This study investigated the relationship of changes in juvenile offenders' behavior during residential treatment and recidivism.

1257 Lund, N. L. & Salary, H. M. Measured Self-Concept In Adjudicated Juvenile Offenders, *Adolescence* 15:65-74, 1980. When patterns of self-concept scores of noninstitutionalized, adjudicated juvenile offenders and a sample of randomly selected juveniles with no prior offense record were compared, their average scores differed on strength of ego, self-control, and tendency to act out.

1258 Lyerly, Robert R. & Skipper, James K. Differential Rates Of Rural-Urban Delinquency: A Social Control Approach, *Criminology* 19:385-399, 1981. This article reports significantly less delinquent activity among rural than the urban sample of youths.

1259 Matza, David *Delinquency And Drift*. New Brunswick, New Jersey: Transaction, 1989. This book covers a wide spectrum of topics and presents a theory of delinquency based on the concept of drift. 199p.

1260 Mazerolle, Paul & Maahs, Jeff General Strain And Delinquency: An Alternative Examination Of Conditioning Influences, *Justice Quarterly* 17:753-778, 2000. This article addresses the key assumptions of Agnew's general strain theory that various factors affect impact of strain on delinquency.

1261 Mazerolle, Paul Delinquent Definitions And Participation Age: Assessing The Invariance Hypothesis, *Studies On Crime And Crime Prevention* 6:151-167, 1997. The author concludes that trivial delinquent behavior is invariant among different age groups, while serious offense behavior varies by age.

1262 Macmillan, Ross Adolescent Victimization And Income Deficits In Adulthood: Rethinking The Costs Of Criminal Violence From A Life-Course Perspective, *Criminology* 38:553-587, 2000. In assessing both the impact of crime on individuals and evaluating the feasibility and utility of various crime prevention, crime control, and criminal justice policies, the importance of estimating the financial costs of criminal violence to victims is highlighted by the author.

1263 Mann, Fredrica; Friedman, C. Jack & Friedman, Alfred S. Characteristics Of Self-Reported Violent Offenders Versus Court Identified Violent Offenders, *International Journal Of Criminology And Penology* 4:69-87, 1976. The violent behavior and characteristics of self-reported violent and official violent offenders are compared.

1264 Marshall, Ineke Haen & Webb, Vincent J. Self-Reported Delinquency In A Midwestern American City, pp 319-342 in Junger-Tas, Josine; Terlouw, Gert-Jan & Klein, Malcolm W. (eds.) *Delinquent Behavior Among Young People In The Western World: First Results Of The International Self-Report Delinquency Survey*. Amsterdam/New York: Kugler, 1994. This chapter reports the findings from a self-reported delinquency survey carried out in Omaha, Nebraska.

1265 Mason, W. Alex & Windle, Michael Delinquency Risk As A Function Of Number Of Early Onset Problem Behaviors, *International Journal Of Offender Therapy And Comparative Criminology* 45:436-448, 2001. This research found that the number of problem behaviors explained a significant, but small, variance in self–reported frequency of delinquency.

1266 Matsueda, Ross L. & Anderson, Kathleen The Dynamics Of Delinquent Peers And Delinquent Behavior, *Criminology* 36:269-308, 1998. This is an analysis of the reciprocal relationship between delinquent peer associations and delinquent behavior that foster future delinquency, increased delinquency and likelihood of associating with delinquent peers.

1267 Mayeda, David Tokiharu; Chesney-Lind, Meda & Koo, Jennifer Talking Story With Hawaii's Youth: Confronting Violent And Sexualized Perceptions Of Ethnicity And Gender, *Youth & Society* 33:99-128, 2001. Using focus groups, this study sought to examine the role of gender in the lives of young people and how this related to delinquent behavior.

1268 Mays, G. Larry.; Fuller, Kathy & Winfree, L. Thomas Jr. Gangs And Gang Activity In Southern New Mexico: A Descriptive Look At A Growing Rural Problem, *Journal Of Crime And Justice* 17:25-44, 1994. The authors surveyed 373 New Mexico rural male and female school youths who were gang members and their delinquent activities.

1269 McBroom, James R. Correlates Of Alcohol And Marijuana Use Among Junior High School Students: Family, Peers, School Problems, And Psychosocial Concerns, *Youth & Society* 26:54-68, 1994. This multidisciplinary self-report of 7th and 8th graders found that abstainers, compared to substance users, had families and friends who are not users of alcohol and marijuana, and are less likely to exhibit school and psychological problems.

1270 McCarthy, Bill; Hagan, John & Woodward, Todd S. In the Company Of Women; Structure And Agency In Revised Power-Control Theory Of Gender And Delinquency, *Criminology* 37:761-788, 1999. Testing the power-control theory, the authors conclude that mothers in patriarchal families have a positive role in lowering delinquency.

1271 McCord, Joan Family Relationships, Juvenile Delinquency, And Adult Criminality, *Criminology* 29:397-418, 1991. This research suggests that maternal behavior influences juvenile delinquency and adult criminality while paternal interaction within the family has a more direct influence on adult criminality.

1272 McDermott, M. Joan & Hindelang, Michael J. Analysis Of National Crime Victimization Survey Data To Study Serious Delinquent Behavior. Monograph One. *Juvenile Criminal Behavior In The United States: Its Trends And Patterns.* Washington, D.C.: National Institute for Juvenile Justice and Delinquency Prevention, 1981. National Crime Survey victimization data are used to examine trends and patterns in the criminal behavior of juveniles below 18 years, youthful offenders 18-20 years old, and adults over 21. 110p.

1273 McGarvey, E. L.; Canterbury, R. J. & Waite, D. Delinquency And Family Problems In Incarcerated Adolescents With And Without A History Of Inhalant Use, *Addictive Behaviors* 21:537-542, 1996. In this study of incarcerated adolescents, it was found that inhalants were used by significantly more non-minority than minority youth, and in both groups family problems and delinquent behaviors were higher among those with a history of inhalant use than non-users.

1274 McPartland, James M. & McDill, Edward L. (eds.) *Violence In Schools: Perspectives, Programs, And Positions*. Lexington, Massachusetts, 1977. The papers in this anthology, presented at a conference focusing on school violence conducted by the Council for Educational Development and Research, offer a number of perspectives and insights into the problem of school violence and ways to combat it. 185p.

1275 Mears, Daniel P.; Ploeger, Matthew & Warr, Mark Explaining The Gender Gap In Delinquency: Peer Influence And Moral Evaluations Of Behavior, *Journal Of Research In Crime And Delinquency* 35:251-266, 1998. This article focuses on the issues of gender as one of the strongest correlates of delinquent behavior as some have called for gender-specific theories of delinquency while others argue that males and females are differentially exposed to or differentially affected by the same criminogenic conditions.

1276 Menard, Scott & Huizinga, David Changes In Conventional Attitudes And Delinquent Behavior In Adolescence, *Youth & Society* 26:23-53, 1994. This study of criminological and social psychological theories found that the influence of conventional beliefs on illegal behavior has an indirect effect on delinquent behavior that is mediated by exposure to delinquent peers.

1277 Miller, Jody & Brunson, Rod K. Gender Dynamics In Youth Gangs: A Comparison Of Males' And Females' Accounts, *Justice Quarterly* 17:419-448, 2000. Based on interviews with gang members in St. Louis, this paper compares male and female perspectives on the gender dynamics in street gangs.

1278 Miller, Walter B. *Violence By Youth Gangs And Youth Groups As A Crime Problem In Major American Cities: A Summary Report*. Washington, D. C.: US National Institute for Juvenile Justice and Delinquency Prevention, 1976. This volume reports on a nation-wide study that examined the nature and extent of youth gang violence in twelve major cities. 16p.

1279 Minor, Kevin I. & Elrod, Preston The Effects Of A Probation Intervention On Juvenile Offenders' Self-Concepts, Loci Of Control, And Perceptions Of Juvenile Justice, *Youth & Society* 25:490-511, 1994. This study focuses on a variety of attitudinal and perceptual variables from a sample of probationers from a Michigan juvenile court.

1280 Moore, Jack B. *Skinheads Shaved For Battle: A Cultural History Of American Skinheads*,. Bowling Green, Ohio: Bowling Green State University Press, 1993. The English origins and American adaptation of the 20th century skinhead movement is the focus of this discussion. 217p.

1281 Morash, Merry & Chesney-Lind, Meda A Reformation And Partial Test Of The Power Control Theory Of Delinquency, *Justice Quarterly* 8:347-377, 1991. This paper assesses the conceptual framework of power control theory and its revised model, and concludes that aspects of the theory are not supported by the research evidence.

1282 Morash, Merry Gender, Peer Group Experiences, And Seriousness Of Delinquency, *Journal Of Research In Crime And Delinquency* 23:43-67, 1986. In this study, the author tests the extent to which peer groups mediate the effects of gender on both personal aggressive and property delinquency.

1283 Morash, Merry Gangs, Groups And Delinquency, *British Journal Of Criminology* 23:309-335, 1983. This study found that regardless of gender, the conduct of peers has greater impact on individual offending.

1284 Nagin, Daniel S. & Land, Kenneth C. Age, Criminal Careers, And Population Heterogeneity: Specification And Estimation Of A Nonparametric, Mixed Poisson Model, *Criminology* 31:327-363, 1993. This research indicates that the individual average offense rate varies on the basis of observable individual-level characteristics as well as unoberv-able heterogeneity among individuals.

1285 Nagin, Daniel S. & Farrington, David P. The Onset And Persistence Of Offending, *Criminology* 30:501-525, 1992. The authors argue that developmental theories of crime need more attention in criminology since there is ample evidence that covariates of onset change with age, and that there are differences in the covariates of onset and of the continued of offending.

1286 Nagin, Daniel S. & Farrington, David P. The Stability Of Criminal Potential From Childhood To Adulthood, *Criminology* 30:235-260, 1992. This study examines two interpretations of the positive association between past and future criminal behavior: prior participation increases likelihood of future participation, and there are stable but unmeasured differences in criminal potential across the population.

1287 Nagin, Daniel S.& Paternoster, Raymond On The Relationship of Past And Future Participation In Delinquency, *Criminology* 29:163-190, 1991. The authors examine alternative interpretations of the positive association between past and future delinquency and criminality.

1288 National Center For The Assessment Of Alternatives To Juvenile Justice Processing *Young Women And The Juvenile Justice System: An Examination Of National Data And Summaries Of Fourteen Alternative Programs.* Chicago, Illinois: University of Chicago School of Social Service Administration, 1980. In examining differential processing of young male and female offenders by the juvenile justice system, the data does not support the belief that female juvenile crime, relative to that of male juveniles, is increasing dramatically in either frequency or seriousness. 110p.

1289 National Gang Crime Research Center The Facts About Female Gang Members, *Journal of Gang Research* 4:41-59, 1997. Data from various states and correctional facilities on 10,000 plus detained juveniles reveals that females were less likely to be gang members, fire at the police, or be leaders but they are more likely to have been sexually abused, come from father-only homes, join gangs while in incarceration, quit their violent behavior when tried as adults.

1290 National Juvenile Justice System Assessment Center *A National Assessment Of Serious Juvenile Crime And The Juvenile Justice System: The Need For A Rational Response.* Sacramento, California: American Justice Institute, 1979. This volume synthesizes existing information on serious juvenile crime in the United States , the patterns and trends of serious juvenile crime, the spatial distribution, contexts, and settings of serious juvenile crime, and the characteristics of juveniles arrested and adjudicated for serious offenses. 440p.

1291 Neapolitan, Jerry Parental InfluencesOn Aggressive Behavior: A Social Learning Approach, *Adolescence* 16:831-840, 1981. This self-report questionnaire testing social learning theory measured the incidence of violent or aggressive juvenile and parental behavior and the role of parents in increasing juvenile aggression by physical punishment and encouraging and supporting such behavior.

1292 Nevares, Dora; Wolfgang, Marvin E.; Tracy, Paul E. & Aurand, Steven *Delinquency In Puerto Rico.* Westport, Connecticut: Greenwood, 1990. This is a report on the longitudinal study of court and police records of a 1970 male and female birth cohorts' delinquency in Puerto Rico.

1293 Nielsen, Marianne O.; Zion, James W. & Hailer, Julie A. Navajo Nation Gang Formation And Intervention Initiatives, pp 141-164 in Hazlehurst,

Kayleen & Hazlehurst, Cameron (eds.) *Gangs And Youth Subcultures: International Explorations*. New Brunswick, New Jersey: Transaction, 1998. Focusing on the Navajo Nation, this chapter describes gangs and gang formation among Native American youths.

1294 Norland, Stephen; Wessel, Randall C. & Shover, Neal Masculinity And Delinquency, *Criminology* 19:421-433, 1981. Based on a self-report survey on the relationship between stereotyped masculine characteristics and adolescent delinquency, this study contradicts previous research emphasizing adoption of masculine characteristics among female delinquents.

1295 O'Connor, B. P. & Dvorak, T. Conditional Associations Between Parental Behavior And Adolescent Problems: A Search For Personality–Environment Interactions, *Journal Of Research In Personality* 35:1-26, 2001. This is a study on the dynamics of parenting behaviors, types, resiliency, personality characteristics of respondents, and internalizing and externalizing problems of a sample of 14-21 year-olds.

1296 Oliver, Marilyn Tower *Gangs: Trouble In The Streets-Issues In Focus*. Springfield, New Jersey: Enslow, 1995. This volume provides a journalistic view of history, definitions and problems of gangs, girls in gangs, gang life, and gangs and criminal life in the United States. 128p.

1297 Opinion Research Corporation *Public Attitudes Toward Youth Crime*. Minneapolis, Minnesota: The University of Minnesota School of Social Work, and the Field Institute, 1982. A telephone survey of a national probability sample of adults in private households found that 71% agreed that the main purpose of the juvenile justice system should be to treat and rehabilitate rather than to punish. 17p.

1298 Osgood, D. Wayne & Chambers, Jeff M. Social Disorganization Outside The Metropolis: An Analysis Of Rural Youth Violence, *Criminology* 38: 81-115, 2000. This study analyzes the community structural correlates, such as social disorganization, of violence related arrest rates of juveniles in non-metropolitan counties of Florida, Georgia, South Carolina and Nebraska.

1299 Osgood, D. Wayne, O'Malley, Patrick M.; Bachman, Jerald G. & Johnston, Lloyd D. Time Trends And Age Trends In Arrests And Self-Reported Illegal Behavior *Criminology* 27:389-417, 1989. This study compares national estimates of time and age trends based on self-reported illegal behavior and corresponding arrest data for a sample of 17-23 yearolds in the United States.

1300 Osgood, D. Wayne *Drugs, Alcohol, And Adolescent Violence*. Boulder, Colorado: University of Colorado, Center for the Study and Prosecution of Violence, 1995. This study examined the relationship between alcohol and drug-related intoxication and the occurance of violent behavior among adolescents. 59p.

1301 Osgood, D. Wayne; Johnston, Lloyd D.; O'Malley, Patrick M. & Bachman, Jerald G. The Generality Of Deviance In Late Adolescence And Early Adulthood, *American Sociological Review* 53:81-93, 1988. This study about heavy alcohol and marijuana use, the use of other illicit drugs, dangerous driving and other criminal behavior was carried out among a nationally representative sample of American high school students.

1302 Padon, Edward; Rodriguez, Orlando & Gurin, Gerald Clarifying Peer Relations And Delinquency, *Youth & Society* 24:149-165, 1992. This study of New York City Puerto Rican youths examined peer relations and delinquency involvement.

1303 Paschall, Mallie J.; Ornstein, Miriam L. & Flewelling, Robert L. African American Male Adolescents' Involvement In The Criminal Justice System: The Criterion Validity Of Self-Report Measures In A Prospective Study, *Journal Of Research In Crime And Delinquency* 38:174-187, 2001. This study examined the criterion validity of self-report measures of involvement in the criminal justice system and delinquent behavior in a cohort of African-American male adolescents.

1304 Pasternack, Robert & Lyon, Reid Clinical And Empirical Identification Of Learning Disabled Juvenile Delinquents, *Journal Of Correctional Education* 33:7-13, 1982. The relationship between learning disabilities and delinquency among 'normal' school population and juvenile delinquents in detention facilities of New Mexico was the subject of this study.

1305 Paternoster, Raymond & Brame, Robert The Structural Similarity Of Processes Generating Criminal And Analogous Behaviors, *Criminology* 36: 633-669, 1998. This study to test the association between self-control and self-reported involvement in crime and analogous behaviors found that although self-control was linked to both types of behavior, other factors also seem to affect such behaviors.

1306 Paternoster, Raymond & Brame, Robert Multiple Routes To Delinquency? A Test Of Developmental And General Theories Of Crime, *Criminology* 35:49-84, 1997. This study examining the general theory of Gottfredson and Hirschi and developmental theory of crime found that neither is adequate in explaining the criminal behavior of youth.

1307 Paternoster, Raymond & Mazerolle, Paul General Strain Theory And Delinquency: A Replication And Extension, *Journal Of Research In Crime And Delinquency* 31:235-263, 1994. This test of strain theory indicates that several dimensions of general strain are positively associated with involvement in a wide range of delinquent acts.

1308 Paternoster, Raymond Decisions To Participate In And Desist From Four Types Of Common Delinquency: Deterrence And The Rational Choice Perspective, *Law & Society Review* 23:7-40, 1989. The author concludes that the decision to offend or not is affected by interpretations of sanctions and perceptions of certain punishment.

1309 Perez, Deanna M. Ethnic Differences In Property, Violent, And Sex Offending For Abused And Nonabused Adolescents. *Journal Of Criminal Justice* 29:407-417, 2001. From the evidence of this study, the author concludes that a history of physical abuse or sexual victimization significantly increased the likelihood of juvenile delinquents' involvement in property, violent, and sexual offending.

1310 Perrone, Paul A. & Chesney-Lind, Meda Media Presentations Of Juvenile Crime In Hawaii: Wild In The Streets, *Crime Trend Series* 6:1-11, 1998. This study compared data on juvenile crime in Hawaii with its presentation in the media and found that the media focus on juvenil crime did not reflect any substantial actual increase in such behavior.

1311 Petee, Thomas A.; Kowalski, Gregory S. & Duffield, Don W. Crime, Social Disorganization, And Social Structure: A Research Note On the Use of Interurban Ecological Models, *American Journal Of Criminal Justice* 19:117-132, 1994. The author applied Shaw and McKay's classic concept of social disorganization to analyze official crime data and population figures of 682 statistical areas in the United States.

1312 Piquero, Alex R. & Chung, He Len On The Relationships Between Gender, Early Onset, And The Seriousness Of Offending, *Journal Of Criminal Justice* 29:189-206, 2001. Data on subjects' participating in the Philadelphia Collaborative Perinatal Project and their criminal history records from the Philadelphia Police Department suggest that onset before age fourteen and is predictive of serious offending by age eighteen, with the earliest onset ages relating to the most serious patterns of delinquency.

1313 Piquero, Alex; Paternoster, Raymond; Mazerolle, Paul; Brame, Robert & Dean, Charles W. Onset Age And Offense Specialization, *Journal Of*

Research In Crime And Delinquency 36:275-299, 1999. This is an analysis of the age at which people begin to offend and the variety of offenses they engage in.

1314 Ploeger, Matthew Youth Employment And Delinquency: Reconsidering A Problematic Relationship, *Criminology* 35:659-675, 1997. In explaining the consistently positive correlation between employment and delinquency, this analysis found that selection bias explained much of the association, and parental influence and exposure to delinquent peers also correlated to delinquency.

1315 Poulin, François; Dishion, Thomas J. & Burraston, Bert 3-Year Iatrogenic Effects Associated With Aggregating High-Risk Adolescents In Cognitive-Behavioral Preventive Interventions, *Applied Developmental Science* 5:214-224, 2001. This article on the 3-year outcomes of a preventive intervention program with high-risk youth revealed the intervention caused increased self-reported smoking as well as teacher reported delinquency.

1316 Poulin, François; Dishion, Thomas J.; Kavanagh, Kate & Kiesner, Jeff The Prevention Of Adolescent Behavior Problems: The Adolescent Transition Program (La Prévention Des Problèmes De Comportement À L'Adolescence: Le Adolescent Transition Program), *Criminologie* 31:67-86, 1998. This report is on a school-based pilot study in northwest United States to modify parents' behavior by changing parenting strategies. French with English summary.

1317 Preski, Sally & Shelton, Deborah The Role Of Contextual, Child, And Parent Factors In Predicting Criminal Outcomes In Adolescence, *Issues In Mental Health Nursing* 22:197-205, 2001. This test of variable that would predict child maltreatment and the serious criminal behavior of youth found that those who had been exposed to community violence or who had a mother with mental illness were four times as likely to commit serious crimes.

1318 Rankin, Joseph H. & Wells, L. Edward The Effect Of Parental Attachments And Direct Controls On Delinquency, *Journal Of Research In Crime And Delinquency* 27:140-165, 1990. The issue of whether direct parental controls on delinquency are conditional upon the level of indirect parental controls is addressed by this study.

1319 Rankin, Joseph H. & Kern, Roger Parental Attachments And Delinquency, *Criminology* 32:495-516, 1994. Evidence from this study shows that children who have a strong attachment to both parents, compared to those children who are strongly attached to only one parent, tend to have a lower probability of self-reported delinquency.

1320 Rapp-Paglicci, Lisa A. & Wodarski, John S. Antecedent Behaviors Of Male Youth Victimization: An Exploratory Study, *Deviant Behavior* 21:519-536, 2000. The authors argue that their findings confirm violent victimization theories of lifestyle-routine activities and risky behavior among their sample of violently victimized male youths.

1321 Rathus, Spencer A. & Siegel, Larry J. Psychopathic Deviation Among Female Suburban Adolescents, *Criminology* 19:455-460, 1981. Using self-reported delinquency and MMPI surveys, this study indicates that girls who scored high on the psychopathic tendency exhibit low self-esteem, personality disorders, report family and residential disruptions, and a variety of delinquent experiences.

1322 Rice, Berkeley The New Gangs Of China Town, *Psychology Today*, 10:60-64,69, 1977. This is an exposition on the historic, socioeconomic and cultural factors that have given rise to the new gangs of Chinese enclaves in urban America in general, and New York's China Town in particular.

1323 Richards, Pamela Quantitative And Qualitative Sex Differences In Middle-Class Delinquency, *Criminology* 18:453-470, 1981. When this self-reported survey of junior and senior high school students in an affluent suburb of a large Midwestern American city examined sex differences in middle-class juvenile delinquency, there was little evidence of marked differences in the delinquent activities of girls and boys.

1324 Rodriguez, Luis J. Hearts And Hands: A New Paradigm For Work With Youth And Violence, *Social Justice* 24:7-20, 1997. This article discusses alternative ways of engaging youth to deal with the problem of violence.

1325 Roeber, R. & Dishion, T. Early Predictors Of Male Delinquency: A Review, *Psychological Bulletin* 94: 68-99, 1983. This review of prediction studies on delinquency concludes that the principal predictors of delinquency are the parents' criminality and family management and techniques, and the child's conduct problems and poor academic performance.

1326 Rosenbaum, Jill Leslie & Lasley, James R. School, Community Context, And Delinquency: Rethinking The Gender Gap, *Justice Quarterly* 7:493-513, 1990. This study examined the role of gender and community context in the relationship between school factors and delinquency.

1327 Rosenbaum, Jill Leslie & Prinsky, Lorraine The Presumption Of Influence: Recent Responses To Popular Music Subcultures, *Crime & Delinquency* 37:528-535, 1991. This discussion on the juvenile justice system in California describes current approaches to dealing with teenagers who are part of the 'punk' and 'heavy metal' subculture.

1328 Rosenberg, Marsha F. & Anthony, James C. Aggressive Behavior And Opportunities To Purchase Drugs, *Drug And Alcohol Dependence* 63:245-252, 2001. This study found that it is five times more likely that most aggressive youths were offered drugs for purchase, although this association was attenuated when their of delinquency was taken into account.

1329 Ross, Lee E. Blacks Self-Esteem And Delinquency: It's Time For A New Approach, *Justice Quarterly* 9:609-624, 1992. This article reviews the role of race in explaining self-esteem and delinquency, and raises questions about this relationship and how it is measured.

1330 Rowe, David C. & Osgood, D. Wayne Heredity And Sociological Theories Of Delinquency: A Reconsideration, *American Sociological Review* 49:526-540, 1984. The covariation in their sample of twins' delinquent behavior and association with delinquent peers, according to the authors, demonstrates the value of a behavioral genetic analysis for developing social theory.

1331 Rowe, David C. & Gulley, Bill L. Sibling Effects On Substance Use And Delinquency, *Criminology* 30:217-235, 1992. This study investigated sibling's warmth, conflict and frequency of contact with mutual friends, and sibling effects on delinquency and substance abuse.

1332 Rowley, M. S. Recidivism Of Juvenile Offenders In A Diversion Restitution Program (Compared To A Matched Group Of Offenders Processed Through Courts), pp 217-225 in Galaway, Burt & Hudson, Joe (eds.) *Criminal Justice, Restitution, And Reconciliation.* Monsey, New York: Criminal Justice Press, 1990. The author found significantly lower recidivism and seriousness of subsequent offending among 16-17 year-olds under diversion.

1333 Rubel, Robert J. (ed.) Crime And Violence In Public Schools: Emerging Perspectives Of The 1980s, *Contemporary Education* 52:5-49, 1980. In this special issue of seven articles on crime and violence in public schools in the United States, the status of American schools and strategies for crime and vandalism prevention are the discussed.

1334 Samaniego, Roxana Y. & Gonzales, Nancy A. Multiple Mediators Of The Effects Of Acculturation Status On Delinquency For Mexican

American Adolescents, *American Journal Of Community Psychology* 27:189-210, 1999. Using the National Youth Survey scale of self-reported delinquency among Mexican American youths, this study explored the mediating effects of family conflict, peer hassle, inconsistent discipline and maternal mentoring.

1335 Saner, Hilary & Ellickson, Phyllis Concurrent Risk Factors For Adolescent Violence, *Journal Of Adolescent Health* 19:94-103, 1996. This examination of the risk and protective factors for violent behavior of a sample of high-school age adolescents drawn from the general population confirmed that risk factors related to demographic, environmental, and behavioral domains contribute to involvement in a variety of violent behaviors.

1336 Sankey, M. & Huon, G. F. Investigating The Role Of Alienation In A Multicomponent Model Of Juvenile Delinquency, *Journal Of Adolescence* 22:95-107, 1999. This survey of male and female juveniles to study the association between dimensions of alienation and delinquency identifies several salient pathways to delinquency.

1337 Schwendinger, Herman & Schwendinger, Julia When The Study Of Delinquent Groups Stood Still: In Defense Of A Classical Tradition, *Critical Criminology* 8:5-38, 1997. The authors critique Freudian and Neo-Freudian social control perspectives on delinquent groups.

1338 Schwendinger, Herman & Schwendinger, Julia *Adolescent Subcultures And Delinquency*. New York, New York: Praeger, 1985. The authors present "integration" as a concept in understanding delinquency and subculture formation. 329p.

1339 Seydlitz, Ruth Compared To What? Delinquent Girls And The Similarity And Difference Issue, pp 133-165 in Culliver, Concetta C. (ed.) *Female Criminality: The State Of The Art*. New York, New York: Garland, 1993. Analysis of data from male and female adolescents from the National Youth Survey shows support for social control theory.

1340 Seydlitz, Ruth Complexity In The Relationships Among Direct And Indirect Parental Controls And Delinquency, *Youth & Society* 24:243-275, 1993. Results of this anaysis based on National Youth Survey found complex curvilinearity in the relationships between parental controls and delinquency than current theories suggest.

1341 Seydlitz, Ruth The Effects Of Age And Gender On Parental Control And Delinquency, *Youth & Society* 23:175-201, 1991. National survey data were analyzed to assess the impact of age and gender on parental control and delinquent behavior.

1342 Shannon, Lyle W. *Alcohol And Drugs, Delinquency And Crime: Looking Back To The Future*. New York, New York: St. Martin's, 1998. Research on the relationship between delinquency/crime and alcohol and drug use in the United States found that sex, age, residence, cohort and time period related to opportunity structure determined rates and patterns of delinquency/crime. 204p.

1343 Shelden, Randall G. & Chesney-Lind, Meda Gender And Race Differences In Delinquency Careers, *Juvenile And Family Court Journal* 44:73-90, 1993. A cohort of youths was followed for seven years to investigate variations in delinquent careers by race and gender.

1344 Sheley, Joseph F.; McGee, Zina T. & Wright, James D. Gun-Related Violence In And Around Inner-City Schools, *American Journal Of Diseases Of Children* 146:677-682, 1992. This study predicting victimization of inner-city high-school students who were subject to actual firearm attack or threatened with one included the gender, number of siblings, exposure to violence outside of school, and personal violence-related attributes.

1345 Shichor, David & Kelly, Delos H. (eds.) *Critical Issues In Juvenile Delinquency*. Lexington, Mass: Lexington Books, 1980. This volume contains articles addressing the major issues in juvenile delinquency and juvenile justice. 347p.

1346 Shover, Neal; Norland, Stephen; James, Jennifer & Thornton, William E. Gender Roles And Delinquency, *Social Forces* 58:162-175, 1979. This self-reported delinquency survey of a sample of public school students found that the opportunity theory had considerably more empirical support than others, although the findings varied somewhat for property offenses and aggression.

1347 Silverman, Robert A.; Riedel, Marc & Kennedy, Leslie W. Murdered Children: A Comparison Of Racial Differences Across Two Jurisdictions, *Journal Of Criminal Justice* 18:401-416, 1990. Most of the official homicide data reported in this article deal with children as victims.

1348 Simons-Morton, Bruce G.; Crump, Aria Davis; Haynie, Demose L. & Saylor, Keith E. Student-School Bonding And Adolescent Problem Behavior, *Health Education Research* 14:99-107, 1999. This survey data from seven middle schools in one United States school district support the conclusion that school bonding is associated with problem behavior.

1349 Simons, Ronald L.; Wu, Chyi-In; Lin, Kuei-Hsiu; Gordon, Leslie & Conger, Rand D. A Cross-Cultural Examination Of The Link Between Corporal Punishment And Adolescent Antisocial Behavior, *Criminology* 38:47-79, 2000. When a measure of corporal punishment controlling for earlier behavior problems and other dimensions of parenting was tested, it was found that level of parental warmth/control was the strongest predictor of adolescent conduct problems.

1350 Simons, Ronald L.; Johnson, Christine; Conger, Rand D. & Elder, Glen Jr. A Test Of Latent Trait Versus Life-Course Perspectives On The Stability Of Adolescent Antisocial Behavior, *Criminology* 36:217-243, 1998. This longitudinal study of 179 boys and their parents used to test hypotheses based on latent trait and life-course theories largely supported this theoretical view.

1351 Simons, Ronald L.; Wu, Chyi-In; Conger, Rand D.; Lorenz, Frederick O. Two Routes To Delinquency: Differences Between Early And Late Starters In The Impact Of Parenting And Deviant Peers, *Criminology* 32:247-276, 1994. Hypotheses concerning different determinants of the criminal justice system involvement of adolescents who demonstrate early versus late onset of delinquency were tested.

1352 Simons, Ronald L. & Gray, Phyllis A. Perceived Blocked Opportunity As An Explanation Of Delinquency Among Lower-Class Black Males: A Research Note, *Journal Of Research In Crime And Delinquency* 26:90-101, 1989. In testing the idea that the relationship between perceived occupational opportunity and delinquency would be strong for lower-class African-Americans, somewhat less for lower-class whites and small for higher-status whites and African-Americans, it was found that a moderate relationship exists between perceived occupational opportunities and delinquency for lower-class African-Americans.

1353 Simpson, Sally S. & Elis, Lori Doing Gender: Sorting Out The Caste And Crime Conundrum, *Criminology* 33:47-81, 1995. In this exploration of the link between social structures and crime variation by gender and race -- if factors related to violent and property delinquency operate in similar ways for males and females as well as for African-americans and whites—found that across the board, peers generally produced greater involvement in delinquency.

1354 Singer, Mark I.; Miller, David B.; Shenyang, Guo; Flannery, David J.; Frierson, Tracy & Slovak, Karen Contributors To Violent Behavior Among Elementary And Middle School Children, *Pediatrics* 104:878-884, 1999. The relative impact of demographics, television viewing, parental monitoring and exposure to violence among students in several public schools concludes that parental supervision and exposure to violence were the most important factors in American delinquency.

1355 Singer, Simon I.; Levine, Murray & Jou, Susyan Heavy Metal Music Preference, Delinquent Friends, Social Control, And Delinquency, *Journal Of Research In Crime And Delinquency* 30:317-329, 1993. The results of this study on the relationship between a preference for heavy metal music and delinquency support the hypothesis that heavy-metal music has an effect on delinquency when parental control is low.

1356 Smith, Carolyn; Lizotte, Alan J.; Thornberry, Terence P. & Krohn, Marvin D. Resilient Youth: Identifying Factors That Prevent High-Risk Youth From Engaging In Delinquency And Drug Use, pp 217-247 in Blau, Zena Smith & Hagan, John (eds.) *Current Perspectives On Aging And The Life Cycle*: *Delinquency And Disrepute In The Life Course, Vol. 4*. Greenwich, Connecticut: JAI Press, 1995. This chapter reports the results from the Rochester Youth development Study on the relationship among social origins, resources, and childhood experiences of a group of metropolitan American youths.

1357 Smith, Carolyn & Thornberry, Terence P. The Relationship Between Childhood Maltreatment And Adolescent Involvement In Delinquency, *Criminology* 33:451-482, 1995. This study on the magnitude of the relationship between early child maltreatment and more extensive measurement of the impact of maltreatment on later delinquency focused on the possibility of spuriousness in this relationship.

1358 Smith, Charles P.; Alexander, Paul S. & Thalheimer, Donald J. *A National Assessment Of Serious Juvenile Crime And The Juvenile Justice System: The Need For A Rational Response. Volume IV*: *Economic Impact*. Washington, D.C.: US National Institute for Juvenile Justice and Delinquency Prevention, 1979. This volume address the direct and indirect economic impact of serious crime by juveniles in the United States. 240p.

1359 Smith, Douglas A. & Brame, Robert On The Initiation And Continuation Of Delinquency, *Criminology* 32:607-630, 1994. The authors conclude that there are many similarities and some differences between models for initiation and continuation of delinquency.

1360 Smith, Douglas A.; Visher, Christy A. & Jarjoura, G. Roger Dimensions Of Delinquency: Exploring The Correlates Of Participation, Frequency, And Persistence Of Delinquent Behavior, *Journal Of Research In Crime And Delinquency* 28:6-32, 1991. This discussion focus on the theoretical, analytic, and empirical isues in the debate on the relationship among similar and different factors to participation, persistence in, and frequency of delinquency.

1361 Snyder, Howard N. & Sickmund, Melissa *Juvenile Offenders And Victims: A Focus On Violence.* Washington, D.C: US Office of Juvenile Justice and Delinquency Prevention, 1994. The literture and data on juvenile offense behavior, victimization, and the juvenile justice system is reviewed. 33p.

1362 Snyder, Howard N. *Arrests Of Youth 1990.* Washington, D.C.: US Office of Juvenile Justice and Delinquency Prevention, 1992. This document on arrests and long-term arrest trends of minors under 18 provides offense rates and offense/offender characteristics. 12p.

1363 Snyder, Howard N. & Nimick, Ellen H. City Delinquents And Their Country Cousins, *Today's Delinquent* 2:45-69, 1983. Using Uniform Crime Report data, the authors analyze urban-rural delinquency, its nature, extent, clearance rates, court case loads, with data on status offenses.

1364 Snyder, Howard N. Violent Juvenile Crime: The Problem In Perspective, *Today's Delinquent* 1:7-24, 1982. This is a critical analysis of the National Crime Survey and FBI crime data describing the nature and character of juvenile violence.

1365 Soderstrom, Irina R.; Castellano, Thomas C. & Figaro, Heather R. Measuring "Mature Coping" Skills Among Adult And Juvenile Offenders: A Psychometric Assessment Of Relevant Instruments, *Criminal Justice And Behavior* 28:300-328, 2001. This investigation of the psychometric properties of various scales measuring Robert Johnson's construct of mature coping demonstrates its factor validity, internal consistency and reliability.

1366 Sommers, Ira & Baskin, Deborah R. Factors Related To Female Adolescent Initiation Into Violent Street Crime, *Youth & Society* 25: 468-489, 1994. This study sought to investigate how female juveniles become involved in violent street crimes.

1367 Sondheimer, Diane L. Young Female Offenders: Increasingly Visible Yet Poorly Understood, *Gender Issues* 19:79-90, 2001. This article on the growing literature on and increasing rates of female delinquency discusses the implications of findings for future research, public policy, and practice.

1368 Song, John Huey-Long; Dombrink, John & Geis, Gilbert Lost In The Melting Pot: Asian Youth Gangs In The United States, *Gang Journal* 1:1-12, 1992. In this review of the applicability of conventional criminological theories in understanding the structure and behavior of Chinese and Vietnamese youth gangs in the United States, the author wants to include the failure of Asian immigrant youths to cope satisfactorily with issues of identity and their reaction to law enforcement tactics.

1369 Sorensen, Erik & Johnson, Eric Subtypes Of Incarcerated Delinquents Constructed Via Cluster Analysis, *Journal Of Child Psychology And Psychiatry* 37:293-303, 1996. In this research, using the MMPI and Jesness Inventory to categorize and identify juvenile delinquents with homogeneous personality characteristics, it was found that the approach more accurately classified offenders compared to previous systems.

1370 Stark, Rodney & Kent, Lori Religion And Delinquency: The Ecology Of A "Lost" Relationship, *Journal Of Research In Crime And Delinquency* 19:4-24, 1982. The authors argue that variations in the religious ecology of communities results in conflicting findings regarding delinquency and religious commitment.

1371 Stark, Rodney; Kent, Lori & Finke, Roger Sports And Delinquency, pp 115-124 in Gottfredson, Michael R. & Hirschi, Travis (eds.) *Positive Criminology*. Newbury Park, California: Sage, 1987. This reanalysis of data on tenth grade boys focused on the relationship between sports participation and delinquency.

1372 Steffensmeier, Darrell J. & Steffensmeier, Renee H. Trends In Female Delinquency: An Examination Of Arrest, Juvenile Court, Self-Report, *Criminology* 18:62-85, 1980. National arrest and juvenile court, self-report, and field observational data were combined in an evaluation of the changing nature of female delinquency to conclude that there is a negligible or non-existent effect of the women's movement on female delinquency.

1373 Stein, Nancy; Katz, Susan Roberta; Mendez, Esther & Shick, Shelley Losing A Generation: Probing The Myths And Realities Of Youth And Violence, *Social Justice* 24:1-5, 1997. The authors debunk the idea that youth and violence are synonymous.

1374 Strasburg, Paul A. *Violent Delinquents*. New York, New York: Ford Foundation, 1977. This volume reports the findings of a study of juvenile violence in the United States that examined arrest data, self-report surveys, cohort studies, and a Vera Foundation study of juvenile crime. 375p.

1375 Sullivan, Mercer Developmental Transitions In Poor Youth: Delinquency And Crime, pp 141-164 in Graver, Julia; Brooks-Gunn, Julia & Peterson, Anne C. (eds.) *Transitions Through Adolescence: Interpersonal Domains And Context*. Mahwah, New Jersey: Lawrence Erlbaum, 1996.

This review explores the continuities and discontinuities in the progression from early childhood antisocial behavior and juvenile delinquency to adult criminality.

1376 Sullivan, Mercer L. *Getting Paid: Youth Crime And Work In The Inner City*. Ithaca, New York: Cornell University Press, 1989. This book reports the results of a study of youth employment and delinquency in an inner-city setting. 275p.

1377 Sullivan, Mercer L. *Youth Crime And Employment Patterns In Three Brooklyn Neighborhoods*. New York, New York: Vera Institute of Justice, 1984. This is based on the findings of the Employment and Crime Project's ethnographic studies of the relationships between work and crime involvement of "high-risk" youths in three neighborhoods of Brooklyn, New York. 343p.

1378 Sullivan, Mercer L. Youth Crime: New York's Two Varieties, *New York Affairs* 8:31-48, 1983. This two-year study sought to determine the reality of youthful crime by tracing the experiences of three groups of youths, one in each of three low-income neighborhoods in Brooklyn, New York.

1379 Sulton, Anne (ed.) *African American Perspectives On Crime Causation, Criminal Justice Administration And Crime Prevention*. Englewood, Colorado: Sulton Books, 1994. This anthology of fifteen articles has six chapters dealing with African-American juvenile delinquency and its causes. 220p.

1380 Summers, Ira & Baskin, Deborah R. Factors Related To Female Adolescent Initiation Into Violent Street Crime, *Youth & Society* 25:468-489, 1994. The involvement and development of adolescent girls' violent street crimes is the focus of this research.

1381 Takata, Susan R. & Zevitz, Richard G. Divergent Perceptions Of Group Delinquency In A Midwestern Community: Racine's Gang Problem, *Youth & Society* 21:282-305, 1990. In this study, the authors tried to delineate among the perceptions of adults regarding the gang problem in a Midwestern community.

1382 Taylor, Dorothy L.; Biafora, Frank A. Jr. & Warheit, George J. Racial Mistrust And Disposition To Deviance Among African American, Haitian, And Other Caribbean Island Adolescent Boys, *Law And Human Behavior* 18:291-303, 1994. This study of males from middle-schools in Miami, Florida found racial mistrust was related to a disposition to engage in delinquency, although no significant differences in the delinquency proclivity of African-American, Haitian, or other Caribbean

Island black adolescents was found to exist.

1383 Taylor, Leah The Family As An Adaptable And Enduring Social Unit, *Today's Delinquent* 4:69-97, 1985. Using case studies as examples, the author portrays juvenile delinquency as a symptom of post-industrial stresses on and variation in the family.

1384 Teichner, Gordon; Golden, Charles J.; Crum, Thomas A.; Azrin, Nathan H.; Donohue, Brad & Van Hasselt, Vincent B. Identification Of Neuropsychological Subtypes In A Sample Of Delinquent Adolescents, *Journal Of Psychiatric Research* 34:129-132, 2000. This research used Hierarchical Cluster Analysis to identify four different clusters of neurological dysfunctions among delinquent youths that the authors claim contributes to their delinquency.

1385 Terrell, Francis & Taylor, Jerome Self Concept Of Juveniles Who Commit Black On Black Crimes, *Corrective And Social Psychiatry And Journal Of Behavior Technology Methods And Therapy* 26:107-109, 1980. The relationship between the self-concepts of African-American juveniles, their crimes, and their African-American victims, reveals that those youths who committed property crimes, compred to those who committed crimes against another Afrcian-American person, had a higher global and black self-concept which accounted for more of the difference in the type of crimes committed.

1386 Terrell, Nathaniel Eugene Aggravated And Sexual Assaults Among Homeless And Runaway Adolescents, *Youth & Society* 28:267-290, 1997. Based on interview and survey data, this study attempted to assess the incidence of assaults on homeless and runaway youths.

1387 Thornberry, Terence P. (ed.) *Developmental Theories Of Crime And Delinquency*. New Brunswick, New Jersey: Transaction, 1997. This volume of eight articles focuses on various dimensions of developmental approaches to delinquent behavior. 359p.

1388 Thornberry, Terence P.; Lizotte, Alan J.; Krohn, Marvin D.; Farnworth, Margaret & Jang, Sung Joon Delinquent Peers, Beliefs, And Delinquent Behavior: A Longitudinal Test Of Interactional Theory, *Criminology* 32:47-84, 1994. Three theoretical models of the interrelations among delinquent beliefs, delinquent behavior, and associations with delinquent peers when tested suggest that associating with delinquent peers leads to increased delinquency which in turn, leads to increased associations with delinquent peers.

1389 Thornton, William E. & James, Jennifer Masculinity And Delinquency Revisited, *British Journal Of Criminology* 19:225-241, 1979. This self-report study of boys and girls in the Nashville, Tennessee area focused on the relationships among gender, role expectations of self and of others, and juvenile delinquency.

1390 Tibbetts, Stephen G. & Piquero, Alex R. The Influence Of Gender, Low Birth Weight, And Disadvantaged Environment In Predicting Early Onset Of Offending: A Test Of Moffitt's Interactional Hypothesis, *Criminology* 37:843-877, 1999. This analysis is based on a model predicting that early offending is caused by an interaction between increased risk for neuropsychological disorders and disadvantaged childhood environments.

1391 Tittle, Charles R. & Meier, Robert F. Specifying The SES/Delinquency Relationship By Social Characteristics Of Contexts, *Journal Of Research In Crime And Delinquency* 28:430-455, 1991. This study could not identify any aspect of the social context that can consistently predict delinquency from individuals' socioeconomic status.

1392 Towberman, Donna B. Psychosocial Antecedents Of Chronic Delinquency, *Journal Of Offender Rehabilitation* 21:151-164, 1994. This study sought to assess the impact of family functioning and bonding on prior and current offense behavior.

1393 Tracy, Paul E.; Wolfgang, Marvin E. & Figlio, Robert M. *Delinquency Careers In Two Birth Cohorts*. New York, New York: Plenum Press, 1990. This volume reports findings of a 1977 longitudinal study examining the delinquency history of a cohort of males born in 1958 residing in Philadelphia through age 17. 308p.

1394 Triplett, Ruth & Myers, Laura B. Evaluating Contextual Patterns Of Delinquency: Gender-Based Differences, *Justice Quarterly* 12:59-84, 1995. This study examining gender-related differences in offense patterns for specific types of crime found that the more serious the offense, the greater the contextual differences by gender.

1395 Tygart, Clarence E. Strain Theory And Public School Vandalism: Academic Tracking, School Social Status, And Students' Academic Achievement, *Youth & Society* 20:106-118, 1988. The effect of academic achievement, school status and track-ing on vandalism is explored in this study.

1396 Uggen, Christopher & Janikula, Jennifer Volunteerism And Arrest In Transition To Adulthood, *Social Forces* 78:331-362, 1999. In this study of adolescents in Youth Development Study, the authors found an inverse relationship between volunteer-work and criminal behavior.

1397 US Office Of Juvenile Justice And Delinquency Prevention *1996 National Youth Gang Survey*. Washington, D.C., 1999. This 1996 survey examines the prevalence of American youth gangs, the numbers of gangs and members, gang demographics, gang migration, and gang drug distribution and crime involvement. 75p.

1398 US Senate Committee On The Judiciary International Narcotics Control Caucus *Facing The Future—The Rise Of Teen Drug Abuse And Teen Violence*. Washington, D.C., 1995. This report to the United States senate presents evidence of teenage drug abuse between 1995 - 2020, teen violence, and the new dangers posed by the drugs rohypnol and ketamine, and the congressional drug budget cuts. 87p.

1399 Van Houten, Therese & Golembiewski, Gary *Adolescent Life Stress As A Predictor Of Alcohol Abuse And/Or Runaway Behavior*. Washington, D.C.: National Youth Alternatives Project, 1978. This study on whether alcohol abuse and running away are responses to or to escape from stress found positive correlations among adolescent alcohol-abuse, running away, and parental alcohol abuse. 116 p.

1400 Vazsonyi, Alexander T. Family Socialization And Delinqeuncy In The United States And Switzerland, *European Journal On Criminal Policy And Research* 4:81-100, 1996. This article reports on differences between Swiss and American socialization practices and delinquency rates in two countries.

1401 Vazsonyi, Alexander T.; Vesterdal, Wendy J.; Flannery, Daniel J. & Belliston, Sara The Utility Of Child Self-Reports And Teacher Ratings In Classifying Children's Official Delinquency Status, *Studies On Crime And Crime Prevention* 8:225-244, 1999. This article is on the usefulness of self-reported delinquency versus teacher classification in identifying youths as being at high-risk of becoming delinquent.

1402 Velard, Albert J. Do Delinquents Really Drift, *British Journal Of Criminology* 18:23-39, 1978. The author interviewed 40 court-certified Illinois juvenile delinquents to test Matza's theory of delinquent subculture.

1403 Velmer, S. Burton Jr.; Evans, T. David; Kethineni, Sesha R.; Cullen, Francis T.; Dunaway, R.Gregory & Payne, Gary L. The Impact Of Parental Controls On Delinquency, *Journal Of Criminal Justice* 23:111-126, 1995. The data from this self-report survey of high school youths revealed that direct control was inversely related to delinquent involvement, even after ontrolling for the effects of a range of theoretically salient variables, and that the relationship was stronger and more consistent for males compared to female respondents.

1404 Ven, Thomas M.Vander; Cullen, Francis T.; Carrozza, Mark A. & Wright, John Paul Home Alone: The Impact Of Maternal Employment On Delinquency, *Social Problems* 48: 236-257, 2001. Using data from the National Longitudinal Survey of Youth, this study found that the characteristics of maternal work have relatively little or no influence on delinquency, but had a complex albeit slight indirect effect via the "supervision" factor.

1405 Vigil, James Diego & Yun, Steve Chong Vietnamese Youth Gangs In The Context Of Multiple Marginality And The Los Angeles Youth Gang Phenomenon, pp 117-140 in Hazlehurst, Kayleen & Hazlehurst, Cameron (eds.) *Gangs And Youth Subcultures: International Explorations.* New Brunswick, New Jersey: Transaction, 1998. Besides describing the various youth gangs in the Los Angeles area, this chapter offers an extensive discussion of the unique aspects of Vietnamese youth gangs in the American milieu.

1406 Visher, Christy A.; Lattimore, Pamela K. & Linster, Richard L. Predicting The Recidivism Of Serious Youthful Offenders Using Survival Models, *Criminology* 29:329-366, 1991.The authors conclude that the re-arrest probability for violent juvenile offenders can be predicted from prior criminal history, institutional behavior, and personal background characteristics considered together.

1407 Vitaro, Frank ; Brendgen, Mara & Tremblay, Richard E. Preventive Intervention: Assessing Its Effects On The Trajectories Of Delinquency And Testing For Mediational Processes, *Applied Developmental Science* 5: 201-213, 2001. The growth-curve analysis used in this study found, that when compared with the control group, the prevention group level of delinquency was lower due to the effect of a prevention program during a developmental chain of events from ages 13-16.

1408 Vowell, Paul R. & May, David C. Another Look At Classic Strain Theory: Poverty Status, Perceived Blocked Opportunity, And Gang Membership As Predictors Of Adolescent Violent Behavior, *Sociological Inquiry* 70:42-60, 2000. This study examined correlations among violent behavior, gang membership, poverty status, and perceptions of blocked opportunity.

1409 Wallace, John M.; Forman, Tyrone A.; Guthrie, Barbara J.; Bachman, Jerald G.; O'Malley, Patrick M. & Johnston, Lloyd D. The Epidemiology Of Alcohol, Tobacco And Other Drug Use Among Black Youth, *Journal Of Studies On Alcohol* 60:800-809, 1999. Data on a nationwide sample of about 25,000 African American high school students in the project 'Monitoring the Future' found that about 25% had used marijuana while less than 2% had used cocaine.

1410 Warr, Mark Life-Course Transitions And Desistance From Crime, *Criminology* 36:183-216, 1998. This study used control theory in interpreting Sampson and Laub's findings, but found evidence that life-course transitions affect criminal behavior by changing relations with delinquent peers.

1411 Warr, Mark Organization And Instigation In Delinquent Groups, *Criminology* 34:11-38, 1996. This study, focusing on the identity and role of instigators in delinquent groups, found that the roles offenders adopt are determined by the individual charac-teristics and the situational interaction of the group.

1412 Warr, Mark Age, Peers, And Delinquency, *Criminology* 31:17-40, 1993. When peer influence was controlled, the effects of age on self-reported delinquency became insignificant in this test of differential association theory explaining the age distribution of crime and peer relations that changed dramatically over the age span in much the same pattern as did crime itself.

1413 Warr, Mark & Stafford, Mark The Influence Of Delinquent Peers: What They Think Or What They Do? *Criminology* 29:851-866, 1991. This research found that although peer attitudes affect delinquency, greater is the effect of peers' behavior.

1414 Waters, Tony *Crime And Immigrant Youth*. Thousand Oaks: California: Sage, 1999. The author uses immigrants' records to explore why youthful criminality occurs in some immigrant groups and not the others. 233p.

1415 Wells, L. Edward & Rankin, Joseph H. Juvenile Victimization: Convergent Validation Of Alternative Measurements, *Journal Of Research In Crime And Delinquency* 32:287-307, 1995. The authors argue that crime victim surveys are a valuable supplement to official measures of serious juvenile crime in that they provide a more complete picture of street crime levels as well as a more dynamic view of crime as interactions between offenders and victims.

1416 Wells, L. Edward Self-Enhancement Through Delinquency: A Conditional Test Of Self-Derogation Theory, *Journal Of Research In Crime And Delinquency* 26:226-252, 1989. Results of this study show a curvilinear interaction in self-enhancement by delinquent acts among youths with high need for self-esteem, and occasionally in this sample had enhancing effects among persons with very high self-esteem.

1417 Wells, L. Edward & Rankin, Joseph H. The Broken Homes Model Of Delinquency: Analytic Issues, *Journal Of Research In Crime And Delinquency* 23:68-93, 1986. This article aims at a conceptual/theoretical framework to be used in the empirical analysis of the relaltionship between broken homes and delinquency.

1418 Welsh, Ralph S. Delinquency, Corporal Punishment, And The Schools, *Crime & Delinquency* 24:336-354, 1978. Linking delinquent aggression to the severity of parental discipline, the author argues that existing data do not substantiate that parental over-permissiveness produces youth crime, and wants to discourage corporal punishment as a socially acceptable child-rearing technique.

1419 Welsh, Wayne N. United States, pp 183-200 in Hoffman, Allan M. & Summers, Randal W. (eds.) *Teen Violence: A Global View*. Westport, Connecticut: Greenwood, 2001. This chapter describes the nature and extent of teen violence and responses to it in the United States.

1420 Welsh, Wayne N.; Greene, Jack R. & Jenkins, Patricia H. School Disorder: The Influence Of Individual, Institutional, And Community Factors, *Criminology* 37:73-115, 1999. Drawing upon control theory, school climate theory, and social disorganization theory this study examined the relative influence of individual, institutional, and community factors on misconduct of students in Philadelphia middle schools.

1421 Welsh, Wayne N.; Stokes, Robert & Greene, Jack R. A Macro-Level Model Of School Disorder, *Journal Of Research In Crime And Delinquency* 37:243-283, 2000. This article examines the effect of major institutional and community factors on school disorder in Philadelphia.

1422 Werner, Eric Psychological And Ethnic Correlates Of Interpersonal Maturity Among Delinquents, *British Journal of Criminology* 15:51-68, 1975. The author reports that his research found no difference between the interpersonal maturity of the 934 white and non-white delinquents he studied in California.

1423 Wertlieb, Ellen C. Juvenile Delinquency And The Schools: A Review Of The Literature, *Juvenile And Family Court Journal* 33:15-24, 1982. The author concludes that the defects of the educational system seem to lead America's youths toward alienation because of the schools' failure to adapt to the recent transitions in society.

1424 Whitbeck, Les B.; Conger, Rand D.; Simons, Ronald L. & Kao, Meei-Ying Minor Deviant Behaviors and Adolescent Sexual Activity, *Youth*

& Society 25:24-37, 1993. This study of 7th grade boys and girls argues that adolescent deviance, such as age-related sexual activity due to peer association, is an early adoption of adult behavior.

1425 White, Helene Raskin Early Problem Behavior And Later Drug Problems, *Journal Of Research In Crime And Delinquency* 29:412-429, 1992. The findings of this study of the relationship between problem behaviors of adolescents and the persistence of problem behaviors in young adulthood, suggest that problems vary by gender and age.

1426 White, Helene Raskin; Pandina, Robert J. & LaGrange, Randy L. Longitudinal Predictors Of Serious Substance Use And Delinquency, *Criminology* 25:715-740, 1987. This study tests the validity of a common-cause model in explaining both serious substance use and serious delinquent behavior.

1427 White, Helene Raskin; Labouvie, Erich W. & Bates, Marsha E. The Relationship Between Sensation Seeking And Delinquency: A Longitudinal Analysis, *Journal Of Research In Crime And Delinquency* 22:197-211, 1985. This study sought to determine the relationship between self-reported delinquency and sensation seeking.

1428 White, Jennifer L.; Moffitt, Terrie E..; Earls, Felton; Robins, Lee & Silva, Phil A. How Early Can We Tell? Predictors Of Childhood Conduct Disorder And Adolescent Delinquency, *Criminology* 28:507-534, 1990. This study of a variety of characteristics of pre-school children in predicting antisocial outcomes found that having preschool behavior problems was the single best predictor of antisocial disorders at age 11.

1429 Widom, Cathy Spatz & Katkin, Faith S. Multivariate Analysis Of Personality And Motivation In Female Delinquents, *Journal Of Research In Crime And Delinquency* 20:277-290, 1983. The authors examining hypotheses concerning the personality, background, and motivations for female delinquency conclude that multiple factors contribute to delinquent behavior among females.

1430 Wikström, Per-Olof H. & Loeber, Rolf Do Disadvantaged Neighborhoods Cause Well-Adjusted Children To Become Adolescent Delinquents? A Study Of Male Juvenile Serious Offending, Individual Risk And Protective, *Criminology* 38:1109-1142, 2000. This is an analysis of the relationship between type of neighborhood, socioeconomic context, individual characteristics and serious offending among Pittsburgh's male juveniles.

1431 Williams, James Herbert; Ayers, Charles D.; Abbott, Robert D.; Hawkins, J. David & Catalano, Richard F. Racial Differences In Risk Factors For Delinquent And Substance Use Among Adolescents, *Social Work Research* 23:241-256, 1999. This is a prediction study of risk factors in the delinquency and substance abuse among 567 Seattle, Washington youngsters.

1432 Williams, R. Alan & Hollis, Helen M. Health Beliefs And Reported Symptoms Among A Sample Of Incarcerated Adolescent Females - Are They Impulsive? *Journal Of Adolescent Health* 24:21-27, 1999. This study compares the rates of physical complaints, health attitudes, and treatment seeking of an incarcerated sample to a normative sample and concludes that the frequency, variety and emotional distress of the detainees highlights the need for integrated of physical and mental health services within juvenile facilities.

1433 Windle, M. A Latent Growth Curve Model Of Delinquent Activity Among Adolescents, *Applied Developmental Science* 4:193-207, 2000. To examine age-related adolescent delinquent activity, the author used Latent Growth Curve modeling of a four-wave longitudinal data.

1434 Winfree, L. Thomas Jr.; & Griffiths, Curt T. & Sellers, Christine S. Social Learning Theory, Drug Use, And American Indian Youths: A Cross-Cultural Test, *Justice Quarterly* 6:395-417, 1989. This research examined the link between key constructs of social learning theory and self-reported delinquent behavior on a census of rural American Indian and Caucasian youths.

1435 Winfree, L. Thomas Jr.; Mays, G. Larry. & Bäckström, Teresa Vigil Youth Gangs And Incarcerated Delinquents: Exploring The Ties Between Gang Membership, Delinquency, And Social Learning Theory, *Justice Quarterly* 11: 229-256, 1994. This study on the relationships among youth gang membership, youthful misconduct and social learning theory found that neither gang membership nor variables of social learning theory had uniform effect on all forms of self-reported delinquency.

1436 Winfree, L. Thomas Jr.; Bäckström, Teresa Vigil & Mays, G. Larry Social Learning Theory, Self-Reported Delinquency, And Youth Gangs: A New Twist On A General Theory Of Crime And Delinquency, *Youth And Society* 26:147-177, 1994. In investigating the interactions among gangs and gang activity, social reinforcers and punishers, and differential associations related to self-reported gang involvement and delinquency, the authors conclude that "group-context" offending was related to both social learning theory and gang membership.

1437 Wolfgang, Marvin E. Transitions Of Crime In The Aging process, pp 141-154 in Blau, Zena Smith (ed.) *Current Perspectives On Aging and the Life Cycle*. Greenwich, Connecticut: JAI Press, 1995. The persistence of criminal involvement over the course of changing life-cycle among two Philadelphia cohorts are analyzed by the author.

1438 Wolfgang, Marvin E.; Thornberry, Terence P. & Figlio, Robert M. *From Boy To Man, From Delinquency To Crime*. Chicago, Illinois: University of Chicago Press, 1987. This study traces the adult criminal careers of a random sample of the 1945 Philadelphia birth cohort. 221p.

1439 Wolfgang, Marvin E. Delinquency In Two Birth Cohorts, *American Behavioral Scientist* 27:75-86, 1983. This article presents selected findings and their implications for policy from a cohort study of delinquents in Philadelphia.

1440 Wolfgang, Marvin E. The Sociology Of Aggression - Crime And Violence, *Australian And New Zealand Journal Of Forensic Sciences* 11:3-32, 1978. This is a report on the findings of the author's longitudinal Philadelphia cohort study of male juvenile delinquents.

1441 Wooden, Wayne S. *Renegade Kids, Suburban Outlaws: From Youth Culture To Delinquency*. Belmont, California: Wadsworth, 1995. The subject of this publication is the evolution of troubled youths in American suburbs from harmless youth sub-cultural behaviors to serious illegality with some comparisons with New Zealand research on youthful deviance. 248p.

1442 Wright, John Paul; Cullen, Francis T.; Agnew, Robert S. & Brezina, Timothy "The Root Of All Evil"? An Exploratory Study Of Money And Delinquent Involvement, *Justice Quarterly* 18:239-268, 2001. This research tested strain theory arguing that the possession of monetary resources facilitates goal achievement thereby reducing the likelihood of offending behavior.

1443 Wright, John Paul; Cullen, Francis T. & Miller, Jeremy T. Family Social Capital And Delinquent Involvement, *Journal Of Criminal Justice* 29:1-9, 2001. Drawing on Coleman's perspective, the authors studied family "investment" in youth that produce personal and social capital inhibiting misbehavior and found that family investment in their young indeed reduces delinquency across time, moderates the effects of misbehaviorand is associated with general positive effects across the life course.

1444 Wright, John Paul & Cullen, Francis T. Juvenile Involvement In Occupational Delinquency, *Criminology* 38:863-896, 2000. This study examining the work-place criminality of juveniles found evidence of the influence of peers on such behavior.

1445 Wright, John Paul & Cullen, Francis T. Working While In School And Delinquent Involvement: Implications For Social Policy, *Crime & Delinquency* 43:203-221, 1998. This study explored the relationship between labor market participation and delinquency among high-school students.

1446 Yin, Zenong; Katims, David S. & Zapata, Jesse T. Participation In Leisure Activities And Involvement In Delinquency By Mexican American Adolescents, *Hispanic Journal Of Behavioral Sciences* 21:170-185, 1999. This study of the association between participation in the type of leisure activity and delinquent behavior among low socioeconomic status middle and senior high-school Mexican American adolescents, indicates that a greater delinquency involvement was significantly associated with increased participation in unsupervised socialization with friends and less frequent participation in organized leisure, sport activities, and at home activities.

1447 Zhang, Lening & Messner, Steven F. The Effects Of Alternative Measures Of Delinquent Peers On Self-Reported Delinquency, *Journal Of Research In Crime And Delinquency* 37:323-337, 2000. This examination of two alternative measures of delinquent peers indicates that parental and adolescent reports of delinquent peers vary, and while the measure of delinquent peers based on parental reports is related to subsequent self-reported delinquency, the measure based on adolescents' reports has no such effect.

1448 Zhang, Lening; Wieczorek, William F. & Welte, John W. The Impact Of Age Of Onset Of Substance Use On Delinquency, *Journal Of Research In Crime And Delinquency* 34:253-268, 1997. The authors developed a model to examine the link between age of onset of substance use and delinquency.

1449 Zhang, Lening; Welte, John W. & Wieczorek, William F. Youth Gangs, Drug Use, And Delinquency, *Journal Of Criminal Justice* 27:101-109, 1999. This study on the relationship among youth gangs, drug use, and delinquency found that prior delinquency significantly affects gang membership, while prior drug use has no effect on gang membership, and although its effect on subsequent delinquency is fairly modest, membership has an effect on subsequent delinquency and drug use.

1450 Ziedenberg, Jason & Schiraldi, Vincent *Runaway Juvenile Crime? The Context Of Juvenile Arrests In America*. Washington, D.C.: Justice Policy Institute, 1998. An analysis of 1998 data on juvenile arrests from the US Federal Bureau of Investigation reveals that there is a decrease in juvenile violent crime rate and juvenile arrests for homicide, but youths were arrested six times more frequently for petty crimes compared to the four most serious crimes. 10p. Appendix.

1451 Zimet, Gregory D.; Sobo, Elisa J.; Zimmerman, Tenna; Jackson, Joann; Mortimer, Joan; Yanda, Carlyn P. & LaZebnik, Rina Sexual Behavior, Drug Use, And AIDS Knowledge Among Midwestern Runaways, *Youth & Society* 26:450-462, 1995. This study focused on the sexual behavior, drug use and AIDS knowledge among a sample of Cleveland, Ohio runaways.

1452 Zimring, Franklin E. American Youth Violence: Issues And Trends, pp 67-108 in Morris, Norval & & Tonry, Michael (eds.) *Crime And Justice: An Annual Review Of Research, Vol. 1*. Chicago, Illinois: The University of Chicago Press, 1979. This review of trends in violent youth crime in the United States during the 1960s and 1970s notes that the data are more ambiguous than the current debate about "cracking down" on juvenile violence, or identifying and isolating hard-core or young career offenders, acknowledges.

1453 Zimring, Franklin E. *Kids, Guns, And Homicide: Policy Notes On An Age-Specific Epidemic*. Berkeley, California: Earl Warren Legal Institute, School of Law, University of California, 1996. This review of the increasing juvenile firearms use since 1985 argues against unrestrained punitive prohibition, and concludes that the policy toward youth gun ownership may have to be less efficient at deterring and preventing gun use by juveniles. 25p.

1454 Zingraff, Matthew T.; Leiter, Jeffrey; Myers, Kristen A. & Johnsen, Matthew C. Child Maltreatment And Youthful Problem Behavior, *Criminology* 31:173-202, 1993. This article examines the extent of juvenile misconduct and specific types of juvenile offenses that maltreated children are at risk of committing.

1455 Zolondek, Stacey C.; Abel, Gene G.; Northey, William F. Jr. & Jordan, Alan D. The Self-Reported Behaviors Of Juvenile Sexual Offenders, *Journal Of Interpersonal Violence* 16:73-85, 2001. Possible sex-related misbehavior of males under 18 was evaluated and their relevance for the assessment and treatment of juvenile sexual offenders are discussed.

Yugoslavia (Former)

1456 Dekleva, Bojan Juvenile Delinquency Gangs And Their Structure (Mladoletniške Prestopniške Združbe In Njihova Sestava), *Revija Za Kriminalistiko In Kriminologijo* 34:39-48, 1983. This study examined the structure of delinquent gangs processed by a court in Ljubljana. Slovene with English summary.

1457 Selih, Alenka Disorganization Of The Family And Its Influence On Juvenile Delinquency (Dezorganizacija Druzine In Njen Vpliv Na Mi-adinsko Prestopnistvo), *Revija Za Kriminalistiko In Kriminologijo* 22:251-257, 1971. The article deals with the role of the family in juvenile delinquency and reviews developments in modern family life and delinquency. Slovene with English summary.

1458 Tomori, Martina Autoaggressive Behavior In Adolescents (Avtoagreviuno Vedenje Pri Mladostnikih) *Revija Za Kriminalistiko In Kriminologijo* 34:310-318, 1983. In this study the author found that juvenile aggressive behavior is correlated with unfavorable family conditions, as well as various central nervous system and personality disorders. Slovene with English summary.

Zaire

1459 Biaya, Tshikala K. Kinshasa: Anomie, Atmosphere And Violence (Kinshasa: Anomie, 'Ambiance' Et Violence), pp 329-382 in Hérault, Georges & Adesanmi, Pius (eds.) *Youth, Street Culture And Urban Vioilence In Africa: Proceedings Of The International Symposium at Abidjan 5-7 May, 1997(Jeunes, Culture De La Rue Et Violence Urbaine En Afrique: Actes Du Symposium International D'Abidjan 5-7 Mai, 1997)*. Ibadan, 1997. This chapter describes street gangs and youthful criminality in Kinshasa. French with English Summary.

1460 Kabena-Basue, Kabundi The Zaire Juvenile Law And Alternative Measures To Institutional Confinement: The Actuality (Le Droit Zaïrois Des Mineurs Et Les Mesures Alternatives À L'Internement Institutionnel: Où En Est-on? *Revue Internationale De Criminologie Et De Police Technique* 40:448-459, 1987. This is a critique of the institutionalization of street children in Zaire. French.

Multi-National

1461 Anti Defamation League Of B'nai B'rith *The Skinhead International: A Worldwide Survey Of Neo-Nazi Skinheads*. New York, New York, 1995. This study of the international Skinhead phenomenon shows that the neo-Nazi Skinhead movement is active in 33 countries on 6 continents. 89p.

1462 Arnett, Jeffrey Jensen & Jensen, Lene Arnett Socialization And Risk Behavior In Two Countries: Denmark And The United States, *Youth And Society* 26:3-22, 1994. This study concludes that American youths exhibited higher rates of risk behavior in automobile driving and minor criminal behavior while the Danish youths had higher rates of driving a bicycle or moped while intoxicated and of sexual intercourse.

1463 Aromaa, Kauko Finland, Sweden And Norway: Increasing Concern In A Relatively Stable Situation (Finnland, Schweden Und Norwegen: Zunehmende Besorgnis Bei Relativ Stabiler Lage), pp 59-64 in Friedrich Ebert Stiftung (ed.) *Child And Juvenile Delinquency In Germany (Kinder- Und Jugendkriminalität In Deutschland).* Berlin, Germany: Friedrich Ebert Stiftung, 1996. Discusses juvenile delinquency in Norway, Finland and Sweden, and the official reaction to it.

1464 Bennett, Richard R. & Basiotis, P. Peter Structural Correlates Of Juvenile Property Crime: A Cross-National, Time-Series Analysis, *Journal Of Research In Crime And Delinquency* 28:262-297, 1991. This study used fixed effect, pooled, time-series analyses over a 25-year time period to evaluate a structural model of juvenile delinquency in a sample of 29 countries.

1465 Boehnke, Klaus & Bergs-Winkels, Dagmar Juvenile Delinquency Under Conditions Of Rapid Social Change, *Sociological Forum* 17:57-79, 2002. In analyzing data from samples drawn in Germany, Poland, Russia, Slovakia, Hungary, Czechoslovakia and Greece this study found that the extent to which adolescents engaged in prodelinquent peer activities depends largely on the cultural context.

1466 Boyer, Debra & James, Jennifer Juvenile Prostitution, pp 99-117 in Griffiths, Curt T. & Nance, Margit (eds.) *The Female Offender: Selected Papers From An International Symposium.* Vancouver, British Columbia: Simon Fraser University Criminology Research Center, 1980.The authors discuss the various causes of juvenile prostitution of deprived and disadvantaged, physical and sexual abuse and the affluent and over-indulged girls.

1467 Brake, Michael *Comparative Youth Culture: The Sociology Of Youth Culture And Youth Subculture In America, Britain And Canada.* London, United Kingdom: Routledge & Kegan Paul, 1985. The author views both male and female cultures and subcultures as a consequence of the differential historic, social structural factors such as the economic climate and ethnic minorities in each of the three countries. 198p.

1468 Brillon, Yves The Effect Of Development On Criminality In Africa (Les Incidences Du Developpement Sur La Criminalite Africaine), *International Annals Of Criminology* 24:23-38, 1986. This article discusses how economic development has impacted crime and juvenile delinquency in African countries.

1469 Campbell, Anne & Muncer, Steven Them And Us: A Comparison Of The Cultural Context Of American gangs And British Subcultures, *Deviant Behabior* 10:3:271-288, 1989. The author while comparing American street gangs' history, geography, educational experiences, structure and implicit ideologies with the post World war II British immigrant waves and subcultures, argues that the form of social deviance depends on the sociocultural milieu in which it occurs.

1470 Caspi, Avshalom; Moffitt, Terrie E.; Silva, Phil A.; Stouthamer-Loeber, Magda; Krueger, Robert F. & Schumtte, Pamela S. Are Some People Crime-Prone? Replications Of The Personality-Crime Relationship Across Countries, Genders, Races, And Methods, *Criminology* 32:163-195, 1994. This study examined the relations between personality traits and crime in New Zealand and Pittsburgh, United States.

1471 Chiland, Colette & Young, J. Gerald *Children And Violence*. Northvale, New Jersey: Jason Aronson, 1993. This anthology offers diverse articles on violence relating to children in countries around the world. 217p.

1472 Corrado, Raymond R.; Roesch, Ronald; Hart, Stephen D. & Gierowski, Jozef K. *Multi-problem Violent Youth: A Foundation For Comparative Research On Needs Interventions And Outcomes*. Washington D.C.: Kluwer, 2002. Of the four parts of this anthology, part III has five comparative chapters and the remainder of the book has numerous implications of value in comparative research.

1473 Donovan, Keith *Hidden From View: An Analysis Of The Problems Of Young Male Prostitutes In Order To Formulate An Effective Interagency Approach*. London, United Kingdom: Police Requirements Support Unit, Home Office, 1991. Based on data drawn from four British cities and six cities in Denmark, the Netherlands, Germany, and France, this investigation of prostitution among male adolescents and police response to the problem produced 16 recommendations. 109p. Appendix.

1474 Estrada, Felipe Juvenile Crime Trends In Postwar Europe, *European Journal On Criminal Policy & Research* 7:23-42, 1999. This article includes some information on delinquency and youth crime trends in the post-second world war countries of Europe.

1475 European Committee On Crime Prevention *Social Change And Juvenile Delinquency*. Strasbourg, France: Council of Europe, 1979. This publication discusses the various aspects of urbanization and social change on the illegal behavior of youths in Western European countries. 147p.

1476 European Committee On Crime Problems *European Sourcebook Of Crime and Criminal Justice Statistics*. Strasbourg, France: Council Of Europe, 1999. This document provides general crime and criminal justice statistics and juvenile data on European Union countries, the Balkans and

Central European countries. 208p.

1477 Evans, Robert C.; Copus, Gary & Sullenberger, Thomas A Cross-Cultural Comparison Of The Self-Concepts Of Imprisoned Young Offenders By Country, Race, And Parental Status, *International Journal Of Comparative And Applied Criminal Justice* 20:157-176, 1996. This research found that self-concept scores were lower among American juvenile offenders compared to normal subjects both in the United Kingdom and the United States.

1478 Eve, Raymond A. & Cassani, Ursula The Etiology Of Juvenile Delinquency: The United States And Switzerland Compared. *International Journal Of Comparative And Applied Criminal Justice* 8:163-174, 1984. This paper seeks to explain the sources of the differences in rates of juvenile misconduct between the United States and Switzerland, with a discussion of differences in measurement.

1479 Ferdinand, Theodore N. A Brief History Of Juvenile Delinquency In Boston And A Comparative Interpretation, *International Annals Of Criminology* 24:59-81, 1986. Besides presenting a history of delinquency in Boston, Massachusetts this study describes how parallel developments in modern times impact on delinquency rates in China, Latin America, Africa, and Japan.

1480 Ferrell, Jeff Urban Graffiti: Crime, Control, And Resistance, *Youth And Society* 27:73-92, 1995. This four-year descriptive study deals with the dynamic processes of youthful graffiti writing in various urban milieus of the world as alternative socioeconomic resistance and undermining of segregation and social control by authorities.

1481 Finckenauer, James O. Two Worlds Of Deviance: Russia And The United States, pp 193-206 in White, Susan O. (ed.) Handbook Of Youth And Justice. New York, New York: Kulwer/Plenum, 2001. A sample of Moscow school youth's perceptions of their peers' impact on deviance and some statistics on the nature and trends in delinquency as well as the unique Russian experience and responses are presented along with a comparative overview of the two countries' juvenile justice approaches.

1482 Fingerhut, Lois A. & Kleinman, Joel C. *Firearm Mortality Among Children And Youth*. Washington, D.C.: US National Center for Health Statistics, 1989. This is a report on the contribution of firearms to childhood mortality from homicide, suicide and unintentional injury in Canada besides the 50 American states, the District of Columbia, England and Wales, Germany, Japan and Sweden. 6p.

1483 Fingerhut, Lois A. & Kleinman, Joel C. International And Interstate Comparisons Of Homicide Among Young Males, *Journal Of The American Medical Association* 263:3929-3295, 1990. This article compares homicide rates for young males in developing and developed countries, and across the United States.

1484 Friday, Paul C. & Hage, Jerald Youth Crime In Postindustrial Societies, *Criminology* 14:347-367,1976. This article links increases in youth-crime rates to postindustrial socio-economic development across the world.

1485 Friederich Ebert Stiftung (ed.) *Criminality Of Children And Youths In Germany (Kinder-Und Jugendkriminalität In Deutschland)*. Berlin, Germany: Friederich Ebert Stiftung, 1996. This volume contains 16 chapters from presentations given at a conference on various aspects of delinquency in Germany and other (mostly European) countries. German. 128p.

1486 Gartner, Rosemary The Victims Of Homicide: A Temporal And Cross-National Comparison, *American Sociological Review* 55:92-106, 1990. This article includes also data on juvenile perpetrators and victims.

1487 Hamm, Mark S. Conceptualizing Hate Crime In A Global Context, pp 173-194 in Hamm, Mark S. (ed.) *Hate Crime: International Perspective On Causes And Control*. Cincinnati, Ohio: Anderson, 1994. The author concludes that hate crimes are an international racist movement among young people and describes several case studies to support this argument. 202p.

1488 Hagan, John The New Sociology Of Crime And Inequality In America, *Studies On Crime And Crime Prevention* 3:7-23, 1994. This theoretical review is on the relationship among inequality, minorities, low-income groups and crime among youths and others in Canada, Great Britain, and United States.

1489 Hartjen, Clayton A. & Kethineni, Sesha *Comparative Delinquency: India And The United States*. New York: Garland, 1996. In addition to an analysis of offense behavior, this volume presents information on post 1986 developments in juvenile law and justice in India and the United States. 228p. Appendix.

1490 Hartjen, Clayton A. & Kethineni, Sesharajani Culture, Gender, And Delinquency: A Study Of Youths In The United States And India, *Women And Criminal Justice* 5:37-69, 1993. Comparing the impact of gender on official and self-reported delinquency rates in the United States and India, this study reports differences in self-reported offense rates across countries as well as across genders.

1491 Hartjen, Clayton A. & Priyadarsini, S. *Delinquency In India: A Comparative Analysis.* New Brunswick, New Jersey: Rutgers University Press, 1984. This study of delinquency in India in comparison with Western nations, focuses on the extent and distribution of delinquency in the state of Tamil Nadu, the reactions of the Indian public toward delinquency, and the judicial and correctional treatment of youths accused of delinquency. 252p.

1492 Hartjen, Clayton A. Crime And Development: Some Observations On Women And Children In India, *International Annals Of Criminology* 24:39-57, 1986. The arrest frequencies and distributions for nine serious crimes in the Unied States and India are compared.

1493 Hedin, Diane; Wolfe, Howard & Arneson, Janis *Youth's Views On Reputations & Delinquency: Minnesota Youth Poll #5.* St. Paul, Minnesota: Center for Youth Development and Research, 1979. This survey provides information on the opinions of youths in Minnesota and Ireland, regarding their experiences with and values regarding such issues as youth rights, health, career aspirations, drug and alcohol abuse, education, crime and delinquency, and government. 75p.

1494 Huesmann, L. Rowell & Eron, Leonard D. (eds.) *Television And The Aggressive Child: A Cross-National Comparison* Hillsdale, New Jersey: Lawrence Erlbaum, 1986. Based on interviews with children, parents, peers, and school officials in Australia, Finland, Israel, Poland, and the United States, the authors discuss the contribution of media violence to aggression.

1495 Huesmann, L. Rowell; Lagerspetz, Kristi & Eron, Leonard D. Intervening Variables In The T.V. Violence-Aggression Relation: Evidence From Two Cities, *Developmental Psychology* 20:746-775, 1984. Samples of children in the United States and Finland were interviewed and tested in each of 3 years in an overlapping longitudinal design to investigate the impact of television violence on behavior. 314p.

1496 Igbinovia, Patrick Perspectives On Juvenile Delinquency In Africa, *Journal Of Juvenile Law* 9:12-35, 1985. This review of the literature asserts that juvenile crime is increasing in African countries.

1497 International Criminal Police Organization Trends In Juvenile Delinquency, 1982-1985. Strasbourg, France: Secretariat Publication, 1992. Presents data on gender, age and offense types from various countries. 236p.

1498 International Criminal Police Organization *International Crime Statistics*. Strasbourg, France: Secretariat Publication, 1996. The total population, crimes known to the police, offenders' gender, age etc. for all countries from Andorra to Zimbabwe are provided in this publication. 120p. English, French, Spanish & Arabic.

1499 Ireland, Kevin *'Wish You Weren't Here': The Sexual Exploitation Of Children And The Connection With Tourism And International Travel.* London, United Kingdom: Save the Children, 1993. This study describes the sexual exploitation and abuse of Asian children by tourists and international travelers, and some case studies from Philippines, Sri Lanka and Thailand are provided. 82p.

1500 Jensen, Gary F. *Sociology Of Delinquency*. Beverly Hills, California: Sage, 1981. This anthology of 9 chapters deals with deviance, peers and self-reported delinquency, arrests, and corrections in several countries including the United States, Papua New Guinea, and India. 144p.

1501 Joutsen, Matti From Theory To Research, To Policy: Nordic Developments In The Prevention And Control Of Juvenile Crime, *Eurocriminology* 2:115-127, 1988. Current research on youth crime in Denmark, Finland, Norway and Sweden is surveyed in this article.

1502 Junger-Tas, Josine Recent Trends In Juvenile Delinquency And Juvenile Justice, pp 1-19 in Junger-Tas, Josine; Boendermaker, Leonieke & Van Der Laan, Peter H. (eds.) *The Future Of The Juvenile Justice System (L'Avenir Du Système Pénal Des Mineurs)*. Leuven, Belgium: Acco, 1991. This essay provides a brief update on trends in juvenile offense behavior during the decades up to 1990, mostly in Europe.

1503 Junger-Tas, Josine & Van Kesteren, J. N. *Bullying And Delinquency In A Dutch School Population*. Hague, The Netherlands: Kugler, 1999. This volume presents results from a self-reported study of the correlates of problem behaviors, such as delinquency and bullying, among Dutch 9-16 years olds along with Japanese, Norwegian, English and Washington State youths. 107p.

1504 Junger-Tas, Josine Youth And Violence In Europe, Studies On Crime And Crime Prevention 5:31-58, 1996. The author discusses the involvement of youth in deviance, violence and crime in the European context of immigration, emerging diversity and the underclass.

1505 Killias, Martin & Ribeaud, Denis Drug Use And Crime Among Juveniles: An International Perspective, *Studies On Crime And Crime Prevention* 8:189-209, 1999. Using international data on self-reported drug use from 12 countries, this article reports a number of correlates of drug use and other youthful criminality.

1506 Klein, Malcolm W. Gangs In The United States And Europe, *European Journal On Criminal Policy And Research* 4:63-80, 1996. This article discusses the findings of research on street gangs in the United States, Sweden, the Netherlands, and Germany.

1507 Klein, Malcolm W. Offence Specialization And Versatility Among Juveniles, *British Journal Of Criminology* 24:185-194, 1984. This article presents a summary table of research showing the types of data, sample, and mode of analysis used to assess specialization of offense progression among juveniles.

1508 Korem, Dan *Suburban Gangs: The Affluent Rebels*. Richardson, Texas: International Focus Press, 1994. The absence of protective factors leading to the development of the youth gang phenomenon in the United States and Europe is the focus of this book. 279p.

1509 Korpilahti, Marja *Child Battering In Finland And Sweden (Barnmisshandel I Finland Och Sverige)*. Helsinki, Finland: Rittspolitiska Forskningsinstitutet, 1981. This report discusses Finnish and Swedish child battering and the known incidence of child battering, and the methods, including legislation, for dealing with it. 71p.

1510 Kyvsgaard, Britta The Decline In Child And Youth Criminality: Possible Explanations Of An International Trend, pp 26-41 in Snare, Annika (ed.) *Youth Crime And Justice, Vol. 12*. Oslo, Norway: Norwegian University Press, 1991. This chapter traces and speculates on the reasons for reductions in youth crime, especially in Scandinavian countries during the 1970s and 1980s. Also found in Hackler, Jim (ed.) *Official Responses To Problem Juveniles: Some International Reflections*. Euskadi, Spain: The Oñati International Institute for the Sociology of Law, 1991.

1511 Lalor, Kevin J. Street Children: A Comparative Perspective, *Child Abuse And Neglect* 23: 759-770, 1999. This paper examines the findings from recent studies of street children in Ethiopia and Latin America.

1512 Marguerat, Yves Path Without Escape: Reflections On The Future Of Street Children (Rue Sans Issue: Réflexions Sur Le Devenir Des Enfants De La Rue), pp 383-396 in Hérault, Georges & Adesanmi, Pius (eds.) *Youth, Street Culture And Urban Violence In Africa: Proceedings Of The International Symposium In Abidjan 5-7 May, 1997 (Jeunes, Culture De La Rue Et Violence Urbaine En Afrique: Actes Du Symposium International D'Abidjan 5-7 Mai 1997)*. Ibadan, Nigeria: French Institute for

Research in Africa, 1997. This general discussion of the problem of street children in African and Asian countries focuses on their situation and what may happen to them. French.

1513 Martin, Robert G. & Conger, Rand D. A Comparison Of Delinquency Trends: Japan And The United States, *Criminology*, 18:53-61, 1980. This paper assesses trends in the juvenile crime rates for Japan and the United States from 1960 to 1974.

1514 Mukherjee, Satyanshu K. *Age And Crime*. Phillip, Australia: Australian Institute of Criminology, 1983. Examining data collected for the past twenty years in Australia, the United Kingdom, and the United States, this research evaluates the claim that juveniles are committing more serious violent and property crimes than ever before. 79p.

1515 Mukherjee, Satyanshu K.; Walker, John R.; Psaila, Trish; Scandia, Anita & Dagger, Dianne *The Size Of The Crime Problem In Australia*. Phillip, Australia: Australian Institute of Criminology, 1987. Focusing on Australia generally, this report presents comparative data on juvenile crime for the United Kingdom, Canada, West Germany, the United States, and New Zealand. 111p.

1516 Murray, John P. *Television And Youth: 25 Years Of Research And Controversy*. Stanford, Washington: Boys Town Center for the Study of Youth Development, 1980. This volume summarizes research, provides a bibliography on, and comments on the impact of television violence on youth in America and Europe.

1517 O'Donoghue, Joseph Violence In Schools, pp 101-108 in Adler, Lenore Loeb & Denmark, Florence L. (eds.) *Violence And The Prevention Of Violence*. Westport, Connecticut: Praeger, 1995. The author has a summary of Japanese school violence research along with a discussion of school violence in the United States.

1518 Palidda, Salvatore (ed.) *Immigrant Delinquency*. Brussels, Belgium: European Commission, 1997. The Contributors of twelve papers explore deviance and crime among migrants in Europe, discuss immigration and crime in cross-national perspectives, and in national studies of Belgium, France, Germany, Greece, Italy and the United Kingdom. 270p.

1519 Pearson, Geoffrey Youth, Crime And Society, pp 1161-1206 in Maguire, Mike; Morgan, Rod & Reiner, Robert (eds.) *The Oxford Handbook of Criminology*. Oxford, United Kingdom: Clarendon, 1994. Discussing the British and North American history and traditions regarding youth crime, the author also addresses youth subcultures, youth crime, and social structural factors relating to delinquency.

1520 Pfeffer, Karen; Cole, Bankole & Dada, Kayode British And Nigerian Adolescents' Lay Theories Of Youth Crime, *Psychology Crime And Law* 3:21-35, 1996. This study of British and Nigerian youths' different explanations for the causes of juvenile crime found that the British youths' explanations of youthful criminality were personal while their Nigerian counterparts provided situational explanations.

1521 Pfeiffer, Christian Juvenile Crime And Violence In Europe, pp 255-328 in Tonry, Michael (ed.) *Crime And Justice: A Review Of Research, Vol. 23*. Chicago, Illinois: University of Chicago Press, 1998. Increasing youth violence since the early to mid-1980s in 10 European countries--England and Wales, Sweden, Germany, the Netherlands, Italy, Austria, France, Denmark, Switzerland and Poland --is examined in this chapter.

1522 Priyadarsini, S. & Hartjen, Clayton A. Legal Control And Alcohol In The United States And India, *The International Journal Of The Addictions*, 17:1099-1106, 1982. Based on available and survey data, the authors compare the arrest rates in the two countries as indicative of public concern regarding illegal, youthful alcohol consumption.

1523 Renvoize, Jean *Innocence Destroyed: A Study Of Child Sexual Abuse*. London, United Kingdom: Routledge, 1993. Based on interviews with victims and professionals and data from Australia, Britain, and North America, this volume provides an overview of the extent and effects of child sexual abuse. 181p.

1524 Rosenberg, Tina *Children Of Cain: Violence And The Violent In Latin America*. New York, New York: Penguin Books, 1991. In discussing violence and the perpetrators of violence in Latin America, the author includes a discussion of juveniles in Columbia, Argentina, Peru, El Salvador, Nicaragua and Chile. 394p.

1525 Salas, Liliana Mayorga Violence And Aggression In The Schools Of Colombia, El Salvador, Guatemala, Nicaragua And Peru, pp 110-127 in Ohsako, Toshio (ed.) *Violence At School: Global Issues And Interventions*. Paris, France: United Nations Educational, Scientific and Cultural Organization, 1997. This chapter provides a discussion of violence in schools in Latin American countries and some of the factors that may promote it.

1526 Sandhu, Harjit S. Low Rates Of Delinquency And Crime In India. *Indian Journal Of Criminology* 15:9-16, 1987. This study compares Indian and American crime rates from 1971 to 1978. The rate of juvenile crime was 188 in India compared to 4,116 in the United States.

1527 Sereny, Gitta *The Invisible Children: Child Prostitution In America, West Germany And Great Britain*. New York, New York: Knopf, 1985. A journalist describes the life histories of child prostitutes in the United States, West Germany and Great Britain. 254p.

1528 Silverman, Robert A.; Riedel, Marc & Kennedy, Leslie W. Murdererd Children: A Comparison Of Racial Differences Across Two Jurisdictions, *Journal Of Criminal Justice* 18:401-416, 1990. This study compared murder rates of children in Illinois, United States and Ontario, Canada.

1529 Sprott, Jane B. & Snyder, Howard N. A Comparison Of Youthful Delinquency In Canada And The United States (Une Comparaison De La Délinquance Des Jeunes Au Canada Et Aux États-Unis), *Criminologie* 32:2:55-82, 1999. After examining youth crime, differential arrest, diversion, and court processing rates in Canada and the United States, this study concludes that serious crimes involving juvenile violence have increased. French with English summary.

1530 Stamatel, Janet P.; Arato, Nora & Dunn, Christopher S. The 'Americicanization' Of Juvenile Delinquency? A Comparison Of Hungary, Poland And The United States, *Security Journal* 11:243-253, 1998. The pervasiveness of American social influence is used to explain juvenile delinquency in the transitional countries of Hungary and Poland.

1531 United Nations Social Defence Research Institute *Juvenile Social Maladjustment And Human Rights In The Context Of Urban Development*. Rome, Italy: Fratelli Palombi Editori, 1984. This cross-national study examines if high rates of juvenile social maladjustment are associated with rapid urbanization focusing on Bogota, Colombia; Bombay, India; Dakar, Senegal; Lagos, Nigeria and San Jose, Costa Rica. 540p.

1532 Utting, David; Bright, Jon & Henricson, Clem *Crime And The Family: Improving Child-Rearing And Preventing Delinquency*. London, United Kingdom: Family Policy Studies Centre, 1993. This examination of the relationship between juvenile delinquency and the family and its implications for crime prevention is based on research conducted in Great Britain and the United States. 84p.

1533 Van Der Werf, Cornelia & Block, Carolyn Rebecca Initiation Into And Continuation of Criminal Careers: Results Of A Dutch Research (Initiation Et Continuation D'Une Carrière Criminelle: Résultats D'Une Recherche Hollandaise), pp 279-292 in Killias, Martin (ed.) *Recidivism And Rehabilitation (Rückfall Und Bewährung/Récidive Et Réhabilitation).*

Zurich, Switzerland: Verlag Rüegger, 1992. The authors use arrest, judicial contacts and other official data in a time series analyis to examine the recidivism of young Dutch offenders for 6 years. French.

1534 Van Dijk, Jan J. M. Determinants Of Crime, pp 32-53 in Kangaspunta, Kristiina; Joutsen, Matti & Ollus, Natalia (eds.) *Crime And Criminal Justice Systems In Europe And North America 1990-1994*. Helsinki, Finland: HEUNI, 1998. Reports on the upward trend of juvenile violent crime in European Union member countries; while attributing some of these to the lifestyle of young in general and the strain urban ethnic youths face.

1535 Vaz, Edmund W. & Casparis, John A Comparative Study Of Youth Culture And Delinquency: Upper Middle-Class Canadian And Swiss Boys, pp 56-77 in Shelley, Louise I. (ed.) *Readings In Comparative Criminology*. Carbondale, Illinois: Southern Illinois University Press, 1981. This chapter presents a cross-cultural analysis of self-reported delinquency and factors that may influence it among upper middle-class Canadian and Swiss boys.

1536 Vazsonyi, Alexander T. Family Socialization And Delinqeuncy In The United States And Switzerland, *European Journal On Criminal Policy And Research* 4:81-100, 1996. This article reviews research on socialization differences among nations and reports the results of a self-report study form Switzerland and the United States showing that differences in socialization between youth in the two countries is related to differences in their rates of delinquency.

1537 Vazsonyi, Alexander T.; Pickering, Lloyd E.; Junger, Marianne & Hessing, Dick An Empirical Test Of A General Theory Of Crime: A Four-Nation Comparative Study Of Self-Control And The Prediction Of Deviance, *Journal Of Research In Crime And Delinquency* 28:91-131, 2001. This study examined psychometric properties and their relationship to deviance on representative samples of youths from Hungary, the Netherlands, Switzerland, and the United States.

1538 Walshe-Brennan K. S. Trends In Juvenile Crime, *Royal Society Of Health Journal* 1:6-9, 1976. This is a brief report on increases in juvenile crime since 1961 in Great Britain, Germany, France and Italy.

1539 Walter, Michael & Fischer, Wolfgang Juvenile Delinquency Structures And Forms Of Dealing With It In Budapest And *Hamburg, International Journal Of Offender Therapy And Comparative Criminology* 33:1-20, 1989. Using official crime statistics for the years 1974-1983, this study compares reates of juvenile delinquency in Budapest and Hamburg.

1540 Wiegman, O.; Kuttschreuter, M. & Baarda, B. *Television Viewing Related To Aggressive And Prosocial Behavior*. Hague, The Netherlands: Foundation for the Educational Research in the Netherlands, 1985. This volume reports the findings of simultaneous research in Australia, Finland, Israel, Poland, and the United States on the effects of television viewing on children's aggressive behavior. 191p.

1541 Wilson, Paul R. *Murder Of The Innocents: Child-Killers And Their Victims*. Adelaide, Australia: Rigby, 1985. This book includes data and information on Canada, the United States, Australia, and the United Kingdom regarding how they respond to juveniles as offenders and victims.

1542 Wong, Dennis S. W. Pathways To Delinquency In Hong Kong And Guangzhou (South China), *International Journal Of Adolescence And Youth* 10:91-115, 2001. Based on interviews with delinquents in Hong Kong and Guangzhou, this study attempts to assess various etiological theories for explaining delinquent behavior.

1543 Yokoyama, Minoru Change Of Characters Of Juvenile Delinquents: Comparative Study Of Japan And South Korea, *Japanese Journal Of Sociological Criminology* 12:141-157, 1987. The author compares trends in juvenile delinquency and social control in Japan and South Korea during 1960s to 1980s.

1544 Zapatero, Luis Arroyo (ed.) Studies In Criminology I (Estudios De Criminologiá I). Cuenca, Spain: Tarancón. This anthology of 16 articles includes an international selfreported delinquency study from Albacete, Spain and Omaha, Nebraska, Italian legislation pertaining to personal consumption of drugs and some data on drug use including that of juveniles, application of clinical sociology in delinquency prevention, psychological aspects of child abuse in Spain, the myths and realities of the problem of drug addiction in Latin America and in diverse countries of the world. 261p. Spanish.

JUSTICE

The references included in this section broadly cover topics typically within the scope of "criminal justice." These include publications on and issues of law; the organization, nature, operation of, and problems related to juvenile justice agencies, from police and law enforcement, to courts and the judiciary, to penal and other corrections. Specific references focus on court processing and sentencing, including disparities in sentencing due to race, ethnicity or minority status; diversion, restitution, community service and other non-penal, intermediate and alternative sanctions; probation and parole, the impact of juvenile justice processing on juveniles and their families, preventive measures (such as curfew education and treatment programs, family group counseling, and the like) are also included in this section. References on laws regarding juveniles in various countries are also included along with court decisions that significantly impacted the processing and treatment of offenders.

Afghanistan

1545 Kakar, M. A. & Payam, M. A. Afghanistan: Notes On The Juvenile Justice System, pp 129-139 in United Nations Social Defence Research Institute (ed.) *Juvenile Justice An International Survey*. Rome, Italy, 1976. A brief description of the organization and procedures of the juvenile justice system of Afghanistan is provided in this chapter.

Argentina

1546 David, Pedro R. Argentina, pp 1-34 in Stewart, V. Lorne (ed.) *Justice And Troubled Children Around The World, Vol.2*. New York, New York:

New York University Press, 1981. The private and government efforts to cope with poverty and other social environmental weakness in Argentina and their negative impact on children are described with implications for understanding offense rates and patterns.

1547 David, Pedro R. Juvenile Justice In Argentina, pp 6-10 in Friday, Paul C. & Stewart, V. Lorne (eds.) *Youth Crime And Juvenile Justice: International Perspectives*. New York, New York: Praeger, 1977. This brief chapter offers a concise overview of the law and juvenile justice system in Argentina.

Australia

1548 Alder, Christine (ed.) *Juvenile Crime And Juvenile Justice*. Griffith, Australia: Australian Institute of Criminology, 1998. This volume of eight essays concerns diverse aspects of juvenile crime and justice in Australia. 86p.

1549 Alder, Christine M. Passionate And Willful Girls: Confronting Practices, *Women And Criminal Justice* 9:81-101, 1998. Focusing primnarily on the Australian experience, this article questions our contemporary understandings of girlhood, especially those ideas relating to sexuality and independence that are the bases of judicial practices in dealing with female delinquents.

1550 Alder, Christine & Baines, Margaret *And When She Was Bad? Working With Young Women In Juvenile Justice & Related Areas*. Hobart, Australia: National Clearinghouse for Youth Studies, 1996. This volume on female delinquency is concerned with justice issues, such as the Queensland's juvenile justice system, family group conferences, various sanctions for young women, and Australian vocational training system for young women. 109p.

1551 Alder, Christine Policing Youth Homelessness In Australia, pp 377-386 in Hackler, Jim (ed.) *Official Responses To Problem Juveniles: Some International Reflections*. Euskadi, Spain: The Oñati International Institute for the Sociology of Law, 1991. Drawing upon a study of homeless youth, this chapter provides some details on the violence experienced by homeless young people in Australia at the hands of the police.

1552 Alder, Christine Victims Of Violence: The Case Of Homeless Youth, *Australian And New Zealand Journal Of Criminology* 24:1-14, 1991. Based on interviews with homeless youths to explore the nature and extent of violent victimization since their leaving home, the author found that almost two-thirds of the youths interviewed had been physically assaulted, and half had been sexually assaulted.

1553 Antrum, Michael Frisky Business: Police Search Powers And Young People, *Current Issues In Criminal Justice* 10:197-201, 1998. This article discusses special precautions that the police in New South Wales must follow in searching young people.

1554 Atkinson, Lynn Juvenile Justice In Australia, pp 29-53 in Winterdyk, John A. (ed.) *Juvenile Justice Systems: International Perspectives*. Toronto: Canadian Scholars' Press, 1997. Reviews the history and operations of the juvenile justice system, its transition from welfare to due process orientation, the Aboriginal youths in the juvenile justice system with numerous graphic and tabular presentations of official data.

1555 Atkinson, Lynn *Detaining Aboriginal Juveniles As A Last Resort: Variations From The Theme*. Canberra, Australia: Australian Institute of Criminology, 1996. This review presents demographic information on and data on trends in the number of indigenous juveniles in detention. 6p.

1556 Atkinson, Lynn & Gerull, Sally-Anne (eds.) *National Conference On Juvenile Detention*. Canberra, Australia: Australian Institute of Criminology, 1994. Proceedings of a 1993 conference held in Australia, this volume examines if confinement in a detention center is the best alternative for young offenders. 220p.

1557 Atkinson, Lynn & Gerull, Sally-Anne (eds.) *National Conference On Juvenile Justice*. Canberra, Australia: Australian Institute of Criminology, 1993. This volume of the proceedings of the 1992 National Conference on Juvenile Justice in Australia explores the shift from a welfare/rehabilitation model to a due process and multi-dimensional responses in processing and a presents a discussion of various juvenile justice issues. 477p.

1558 Australia Law Reform Commission *Sentencing*. Canberra, Australia: Australian Government Publishing, 1988. Assesses sentencing statutes and practices including juvenile sentencing in the Australian federal and capital territory jurisdictions, and recommends decreased custodial sentences and increased non-custodial measures such as fines and civil enforcement. 203p.

1559 Australian Capital Territory Corrections Review Committee *Paying The Price: A Review Of Adult Corrective Services And Juvenile Justice In The A.C.T.* Canberra, Australia, 1991. This review of juvenile and adult correctional justice services includes pre-trial and pre-sentencing options, such as community-based programs, the role of volunteers in corrections, custodial facilities, mentally ill or mentally disabled offenders, improving services to inmates, research and evaluation, and administration of services. 188p.

1560 Baines, Margaret & Alder, Christine Are Girls More Difficult To Work With? Youth Workers' Perspectives In Juvenile Justice And Related Areas, *Crime & Delinquency* 42:467-485, 1996. This study found that nearly all youth workers concurred that work with young women involved dealing with their verbal aggression with its highly personal overtones.

1561 Baker, Eric Assessing And Managing Allegations Of Child Sexual Abuse: An Australian Perspective, *Family And Conciliation Courts Review* 35:293-299, 1997. The author discusses the procedures involved in assessing and managing allegations of child sexual abuse in Australian courts and focuses on the issues of parental access to the child, custodial change, and the child's welfare.

1562 Ban, Paul Implementing And Evaluating Family Group Conferences With Children And Families In Victoria Australia, pp 140-151 in Hudson, Joe; Morris, Allison & Maxwell, Gabrielle (eds.) *Family Group Conferences: Perspectives On Policy & Practice.* Annandale, Australia: Criminal Justice Press, 1996. This chapter describes the implementation and an evaluation of the Family Group Conference program at two institutions.

1563 Beresford, Quentin & Omaji, Paul Preventing Aboriginal Juvenile Crime, pp 141-149 in Sirr, Peter (ed.) *Crime Prevention -- Everybody's Business. Proceedings Of A Conference 27 & 28 April, 1995.* East Perth, Australia: Crime Prevention Council Of Australia, 1995. This chapter offers a brief discussion of programs designed to prevent Aboriginal juvenile crime in Australia.

1564 Bessant, Judith & Hil, Richard Parenting On Trial: State Wards' And Governments' Accountability In Australia, *Journal Of Criminal Justice* 26:145-157, 1998. This article asserts that Australian legislation authorizing courts to penalize parents for their children's offending contrasts with provisions exempting the state from the same liability when children in custody offend.

1565 Blagg, Harry & Braithwaite, John A Just Measure Of Shame? Aboriginal Youth And Conferencing In Australia, *British Journal Of Criminology* 37:481-501, 1997. The limits of "re-integrative shaming" and family-group conferencing, that are the bases of the popular Australian Wagga Wagga juvenile justice model, and its limitations in reducing the overrepresentation of Aboriginals in custody are discussed.

1566 Borowski, Allan & Murray, James M. *Juvenile Delinquency In Australia*. North Ryde, Australia: Methuen, 1985. The articles of this anthology cover dimensions and causes of and policy responses to the juvenile offender, laws regarding juveniles, programs for dealing with offender, and the future of Australian juvenile delinquency. 438p.

1567 Braithwaite, John & Mugford, Stephen Conditions Of Successful Reintegration Ceremonies: Dealing With Juvenile Offenders, *British Journal Of Criminology* 34:139-171, 1994. This article argues that the innovation of community conferences in New Zealand and Australia has two structural features that are conducive to reintegrative shaming: selection of the people who respect and care most about the offender as conference participant, and confrontation with victims.

1568 Broadhurst, Roderic & Loh, Nini The Phantom Of Deterrence: The Crime (Serious And Repeat Offenders) Sentencing Act, *Australian And New Zealand Journal Of Criminology* 26:251-271, 1993. Analyzes the deterrent effects of Western Australia's Crime (Serious and Repeat Offenders) Sentencing Act 1992, which increased penalties for "high-risk" juvenile offenders.

1569 Brown, Mark & Polk, Kenneth Taking Fear Of Crime Seriously: The Tasmanian Approach To Community Crime Prevention, *Crime &Delinquency* 42:398-420, 1996. This article summarizes crime-prevention via integrative techniques of restorative justice and community enhancement respectively in family group conferences and community service sentencing.

1570 Burrows, Gerard Glue Sniffing: The Psychosocial Context *Australian And New Zealand Journal Of Criminology* 16:163-171, 1983. Using age and sex data from an adolescent mental health clinic, this research confirms that predominantly 13-15 year olds are engaged in glue-sniffing behavior.

1571 Cain, Michael *The Children's Court*. Sydney, Australia: Judicial Commission of New South Wales, 1991. General patterns and characteristics in sentencing of juveniles in the Children's Court in New South Wales since implementation of the Sentencing Act are described. 6p.

1572 Cairns, Bernard C. Social Background Investigations For The Children's Court, *Australian And New Zealand Journal Of Criminology* 9:109-122, 1976. This article describes the social background report conducted for the Tasmanian children's courts following the 1960 Child Welfare Act.

1573 Carney, Terry Reforming Child Welfare: Diverting By-Ways On The Road To Utopia? *Australian And New Zealand Journal Of Criminology* 18:237-256, 1985. Using the social policy agencies in Victoria, Australia as a case study, the author addresses their role in child welfare legislation and practice.

1574 Carney, Terry Young Offenders And State Intervention: Issues Of Control And Support For Parents And Young People, *Australian And New Zealand Journal Of Criminology* 22:22-39, 1989. The Children and Young Persons Bill 1988 is discussed as an example of the tensions between welfare versus justice, and support versus control measures in state intervention of youthful offenders

1575 Carrington, Kerry *Offending Girls*. St Leonards, Australia: Allen and Unwin, 1993. Based on records and observations of children's courts, this study explores the policing of youth culture and how, upon referral from the principal channeling agents such as the school, and the family, female delinquency is "manufactured" by the Australian juvenile justice authorities. 173p.

1576 Carrington, Kerry Truancy, Schooling, And Juvenile Justice: "She Says She Hates School", *Australian And New Zealand Journal Of Criminology* 23:259-268, 1990. From the case histories of New South Wales truant girls' interaction with school authorities and juvenile justice agencies, the author warns against translating truancy into delinquency, and its negative impact on youths, their families and community, particularly the Aboriginals and working class youths.

1577 Cashmore, Judy & Bussey, Kay Judicial Perceptions Of Child Witness Competence, *Law And Human Behavior* 20:313-334, 1996. The authors present a survey of fifty magistrates and judges in New South Wales, Australia on their judicial beliefs, concerns, and practices related to child witnesses.

1578 Cashmore, Judy The Prosecution Of Child Sexual Assault: A Survey Of NSW DPP Solicitors, *Australian And New Zealand Journal Of Criminology* 28:32-54, 1995. Changes facilitating the acceptance of children's evidence in prosecuting child sexual assault in New South Wales, Australia are explored.

1579 Chan, Janet Crime Prevention And The Lure Of Relevance A Response To Adam Sutton, *Australian And New Zealand Journal Of Criminology* 27:21-24, 1994. This article is a critique of Adam Sutton's view regarding the threat and promises of new developments in crime prevention ignors the dangers of the structural issues in social control.

1580 Chapman, M. Philippa A Re-Education Program For Acting-Out Adolescent Girls In A Residential Setting, *Australian And New Zealand Journal Of Criminology*, 8:163-167, 1975. Describes her eight-year experience in an institution for disturbed 12-16 year old girls in Hobart, Tasmania and recommends diversified treatment approaches.

1581 Chappell, Duncan Juvenile Justice In Australia: Issues And Changes, pp 121-144 in Corrado, Raymond R.; LeBlanc, Marc & Trépanier, Jean (eds.) *Current Issues In Juvenile Justice*. Toronto, Canada: Butterworths, 1983. This paper attempts to update Canadian audience of some recent developments in Australian juvenile justice.

1582 Clunies-Ross, Janet & Foreman, Lynne Deviance Or Deprivation - The Dilemma Of Identification, pp 163-169 in Chappell, Duncan & Wilson, Paul (eds.) *The Australian Criminal Justice System, 2nd Ed.* Chatswood, Australia: Butterworths, 1977. Discusses the philosophical and practical issues involved in identifying, labeling, and processing some young people as deviant.

1583 Costigan, Phil A Youth Based Community Initiative-The Juvenile Advocacy Service, pp 113-117 in McKillop, Sandra & Vernon, Julia (eds.) *The Police And The Community*. Canberra, Australia: Australian Institute of Criminology, 1991. This volume describes the development of a youth advocacy program with parents' support to implement reforms of the juvenile justice system and administration, police relations, and cooperation among government and nongovernmental agencies in Queensland.

1584 Coumarelos, Christine & Weatherburn, Don Targeting Intervention Strategies To Reduce Juvenile Recidivism, *Australian And New Zealand Journal Of Criminology* 28:55-72, 1995. This critique of labeling theory argues that there is a lack of evidence regarding the criminogenic impact of formal process of Australia's community-based restorative sanctions for repeat juveniles offenders.

1585 Coumarelos, Christine *Juvenile Offending: Predicting Persistence And Determining The Cost-Effectiveness Of Interventions*. New South Wales, Australia: New South Wales Bureau of Crime Statistics and Research, 1994. This study concludes that it is more cost- effective to intervene after a juvenile has had several court appearances than early in the youth's criminal career. 39p.

1586 Cunneen, Chris Criminology, Genocide And The Forced Removal Of Indigenous Children From Their Families, *Australian And New Zealand*

Journal Of Criminology 32:124-138, 1999. This is a report and critique of the roles criminologists had in the inquiry on the children of Torres Strait Islanders who were institutionalized, and came to be known as the Stolen Generation.

1587 Cunneen, Chris Community Conferencing And The Fiction Of Indigenous Control, *Australian And New Zealand Journal Of Criminology* 30:292-311, 1997. This article offers a critique of the use of family group conferencing for young people given its impact on indigenous communities, in various Australian jurisdictions.

1588 Cunneen, Chris & White, Rob Masculinity And Juvenile Justice, *Australian And New Zealand Journal Of Criminology* 29:69-73, 1996. This article argues that notions of masculinity are useful in explaining offending behavior as well as the responses to it by the juvenile justice agencies.

1589 Cunneen, Chris & White, Rob *Juvenile Justice: An Australian Perspective.* Melbourne, Australia: Oxford University Press, 1995. This book describes juvenile justice in Australia including history and theory, the dynamics of the juvenile justice system and the state, punishment and crime prevention. 296p.

1590 Cunneen, Chris *Report Commissioned By The National Inquiry Into Racist Violence: A Study Of Aboriginal Juveniles And Police Violence.* Sydney, Australia: Institute of Criminology, Sydney University, 1990. Interviews of male and female youths in detention centers found that incidence of alleged police assault was widespread, although few of these juveniles made any official complaints. 64p.

1591 Dalton, Vicki *Australian Deaths In Custody & Custody-Related Police Operations 1996.* Griffith, Australia: Australian Institute of Criminology, 1997. Although most of the deaths in custody from 1980-1989 in Australia involved adults, juveniles are included in this analysis of official records. 65p.

1592 Doherty, Justine *Aboriginal People And The Criminal Justice System: Comparison Of Aboriginal And Non-Aboriginal Contact With The South Australian Juvenile Justice System, 1997.* Adelaide, Australia: South Australian Attorney General's Department, 1999. This review of official data indicates that among those who come into contact with the juvenile justice system there is a disproportionate and harsher handling of 10-17 year old Aboriginal youths.

1593 Doyle, Stephanie Educational Options For 'At Risk' Youth, pp 195-204 in Sirr, Peter (ed.) *Crime Prevention -- Everybody's Business.*

Proceedings Of A Conference 27 & 28 April, 1995. East Perth, Australia: Crime Prevention Council Of Australia, 1995. This chapter presents an overview of various Australian educational programs for juveniles who are "at risk" of becoming delinquents.

1594 Duggan, Vaughn Youth Training Centres In Victoria, pp 155-164 in McKillop, Sandra (ed.) *Keeping People Out Of Prison*. Canberra, Australia: Australian institute of Criminology, 1991. This chapter describes a variety of strategies for keeping young people out of prison by establishing youth training centers in Australia.

1595 Finlay, Marjorie Breaking The Barriers And Embracing "You" (Youth Options Unlimited) pp 115-120 in Sirr, Peter (ed.) *Crime Prevention -- Everybody's Business. Proceedings Of A Conference 27 & 28 April, 1995*. East Perth, Australia: Crime Prevention Council Of Australia, 1995. This chapter offers a brief description of the Youth Options Unlimited program initiated in partnership with Balcatta Community Corrections.

1596 Freckelton, Ian Child Sexual Abuse Accommodation Evidence: The Travails Of Counterintuitive Evidence In Australia And New Zealand, *Behavioral Sciences And The Law* 15:247-283, 1997. The author reviews the responses of sexually abused Australian and New Zealand children to their assaults.

1597 Freiberg, Arie Abolish Children's Courts? Juveniles, Justice And Sentencing, *Current Issues In Criminal Justice* 4:240-262, 1993. This articles offers a critique and assessment of the idea of separate systems of justice for juveniles.

1598 Gale, Fay; Naffine, Ngaire & Wundersitz, Joy *Juvenile Justice: Debating The Issues*. St. Leonards, Australia: Allen & Unwin, 1993. This anthology covers diverse Australian youthful offender issues ranging from theories, philosophical perspectives, statistical figures, policing, informal processing, to the courts. 185p. Appendix.

1599 Gale, Fay & Wundersitz, Joy The Operation Of Hidden Prejudice In Pre-Court Procedures: The Case Of Australian Aboriginal Youth, *Australian And New Zealand Journal Of Criminology* 22:1-21, 1989. This study of by Screening Panel treatment of youths found that Aboriginal youths living westernized lifestyles in the city appear to be treated worse than white youths who occupy the very bottom rung of the social ladder.

1600 Gale, Fay & Wundersitz, Joy Police And Black Minorities: The Case Of Aboriginal Youth In South Australia, *Australian And New Zealand*

Journal Of Criminology 20:78-94, 1987. This research found that although the young Aborigines experienced disproportionately high rates of arrest, there was no statistical evidence to indicate that police overtly discriminate against them on racial grounds at the point of arrest.

1601 Gallagher, Patricia & Poletti, Patrizia *Sentencing Disparity And The Ethnicity Of Juvenile Offenders* Sydney, Australia: Judicial Commission of New South Wales, 1998. In analyzing court files, the authors conclude that Aboriginal and Torres islander juvenile offenders received inconsistent, and often harsher, sentences while Anglo Australians were treated favorably. 43p.

1602 Gamble, Helen Decision-Making In The Children's Courts Of Sydney, *Australian And New Zealand Journal Of Criminology* 9:187-206, 1976. Based on a study of decision-making in three children's courts in Sydney, this research concludes that the magistrates do not always agree with the officers' recommendations, but do use the social background reports in deciding appropriate "orders"/sentences.

1603 Gliksman, Michael Gender-Based Differences In The Treatment Of Young Offenders By The Police And The Children's Court In New South Wales, Australia, *Medicine Science And The Law* 37:165-169, 1997. Police and juvenile justice data of both males and females indicate that court and police statistics do reflect a form of selection bias in which male offenders are over-represented relative to their actual offending behavior.

1604 Goodwin, Alix *Child Sexual Assault: The Court Response II.* New South Wales, Australia: New South Wales Bureau of Crime Statistics and Research, 1989. Examination of all indictable cases for information on victims, offenders, processing and sanction in cases of sexual assault of victims under 18 in New South Wales found that most defendants received non-custodial sanctions. 155p. Appendix.

1605 Hackett, Peter Juvenile Corrections, pp 109-112 in Biles, David (ed.) *Current Australian Trends In Corrections* Annandale, Australia: Federation, 1988. This volume offers a description of the New South Wales Department of Youth and Community services, its sentencing policies under the Child Welfare Act, and various sentencing programs.

1606 Hackler, Jim *The Possible Overuse Of Not Guilty Pleas In Juvenile Justice*. Alberta, Canada: Centre for Criminological Research, University of Alberta, 1991. This volume argues that instead of protecting the rights of minors, not-guilty pleas may negatively impact the children and juveniles will be better served by appointed attorneys. 16p.

1607 Hackler, Jim Two Strategies For Defending Juveniles In Australia: Which Does The Least Damage? pp 175-188 in Hackler, Jim (ed.) *Official Responses To Problem Juveniles: Some International Reflections.* Euskadi, Spain: The Oñati International Institute for the Sociology of Law, 1991. The value of "not guilty" pleas versus carefully prepared dispositional options in children's court in Australia is the focus of this chapter.

1608 Halstead, Boronia (eds.) *Youth Crime Prevention: Proceedings Of A Policy Forum Held 28 And 29 August 1990.* Canberra, Australia: Australian Institute of Criminology, 1991. This is the proceedings of a 1990 conference that includes some 20 presentations on youth crime prevention and treatment issues in Australia. 258p.

1609 Hancock, Linda The Myth That Females Are Treated More Leniently Than Males In The Juvenile Justice System, *Australian And New Zealand Journal Of Criminology* 16:4-13, 1980. An analysis of the definition and processing of delinquents indicates that police decisions based on legal versus moral grounds has definite consequences for their processing, decisions and appears to be related to variations in gender, and social class.

1610 Harding, Richard W. (eds.) *Repeat Juvenile Offenders: The Failure Of Selective Incapacitation In Western Australia.* Nedlands, Australia: Crime and Research Centre, University of Western Australia, 1995. This volume has ten chapters that deal with the Young Offenders Act of 1994 and discusseshow repeat juvenile offenders are dealt with under this law. 167p.

1611 Harding, Richard W.; Broadhurst, Roderic; Ferrante, Anna & Loh, Nini *Aboriginal Contact With The Criminal Justice System And The Impact Of The Royal Commission Into The Aboriginal Deaths In Custody.* Sydney, Australia: Hawkins, 1995. Data on police arrests of persons by age, gender, and Aboriginal/non-Aboriginal status, statistics on the young Aborigines, the Australian children's court, and the juveniles in detention are included. 144p.

1612 Harding, Richard *Administration Of Criminal Justice In The A.C.T.* Phillip, Australia: Australian Institute of Criminology, 1984. Issues related to policing, the courts, and the treatments for juvenile and adult offenders in Australian Capital Territory are discussed. 68p.

1613 Hayes, Hennessey; Prenzler, Tim & Wortley, Richard *Making Amends: Final Evaluation Of The Queensland Community Conferencing Pilot.* Brisbane, Australia: Queensland Department of Justice, 1998. This evaluation of three pilot programs in community conferencing found evidence of success in cost, reparation, and participation levels, although there were increasing numbers of juveniles appearing in the Children's courts. 82p.

1614 Hazlehurst, Kayleen M. (ed.) *Justice Program For Aboriginal And Other Indigenous Communities: Australia, New Zealand, Canada, Fiji, Papua New Guinea.* Canberra, Australia: Australian institute of criminology, 1985. This document has a brief description of the Youth Aid Section, and the role of Youth Aid Officers.

1615 Hidden, Peter; Campbell, M. & Ford, Joe The Sentencing Act 1989, *Current Issues In Criminal Justice* 3:285-348, 1992. In this special issue of the journal, eight papers address the Sentencing Act 1989 in New South Wales, Australia and includes besides the children's court, the history of the law, its impact on the prison population, and criminal justice administration.

1616 Hood, Mary & Boltje, Christopher The Progress Of 500 Referrals From The Child Protection Response System To The Criminal Court, *Australian And New Zealand Journal Of Criminology* 31:182-195, 1998. Five hundred reports of child abuse in South Australia were followed from the initial report, contact with a child welfare system, the intervention process, to criminal prosecution found that only a quarter of the cases substantiated at the welfare/health level were prosecuted in criminal courts, and only 17% of them had convictions.

1617 Houghton, Stephen; Carroll, Annemaree & Shier, John A Wilderness Program For Young Offenders In Western Australia, *Journal Of Offender Rehabilitation*, 24: pp 183-202, 1996. This article reports on a camp organized by the police that experienced increasing attendance as the camp progressed to more challenging levels when both the sponsors and participants had similar physical, interpersonal skills and career goals.

1618 Howlett, Christine Cultures Of Institutional Violence: Deaths In Juvenile Detention, pp 24-35 in Bessant, Judith; Carrington, Kerry & Cook, Sandy (eds.) *Culture Of Crime And Violence: The Australian Experience.* Bundoora, Australia: La Trobe University Press, 1995. This chapter seeks to provide insights into the complexities of the circumstances surrounding the deaths of children in Australian juvenile detention facilities.

1619 James, Stephen & Polk, Kenneth Policing Youths: Themes And Directions, pp 41-62 in Chappell, Duncan & Wilson, Paul (eds.) *Australian Policing: Contemporary Issues* Sydney, Australia: Butterworths, 1989. This chapter presents a dscussion of police discretionary behavior in deciding who gets their attention, predicting who the trouble-makers are and its consequences, and policing marginal youth in public milieu.

1620 Kraus, J. & Bowmaker, B. How Delinquent Are The Delinquents? - A Study Of Self-Reported Offences, *Australian And New Zealand Journal Of Criminology* 15:163-169, 1982. This self-reported study of deviance among convicted male youths in Australia found that minor offenses were under- and un-reported and only a small fraction of the actual infractions are apprehended and convictions obtained.

1621 Kraus, J. On The Consistency Of Court Dispositions In The Juvenile Criminal Justice System, *Australian Journal Of Social Issues* 16:285-296, 1981. An analysis of 13,919 cases from the Australian Children's Court during a two-year period shows that the urban courts were more lenient than were country courts, and that country courts in general were more lenient than country courts in areas with a high Aboriginal concentration.

1622 Kraus, J. Police Caution Of Juvenile Offenders: A Research Note, *Australian And New Zealand Journal Of Criminology* 14:91-94, 1981. In comparing recidivism of Australian youths, those who received a police caution vs. those adjudicated in Children's Court, the author found that a significantly larger number of children dealt with by the children's court were recidivists, although they did not differ in either the intensity or the seriousness of recidivism.

1623 Kraus, J. On The Adult Criminality Of Male Juvenile Delinquents, *Australian And New Zealand Journal Of Criminology* 14:157-164, 1981. This study of higher criminal courts in New South Wales revealed that those offenders with prior commitment to juvenile institutions, and those who were juvenile delinquents, were more likely to be adult offenders as well.

1624 Kraus, J. Remand In Custody As A Deterrent In Juvenile Jurisdiction, *British Journal Of Criminology* 18:285-289, 1978. Data on recidivism found that significantly more juveniles re-offend after pretrial detention although no differences in the frequency, pattern, and seriousness of offending were found between the recidivists and those sent home before trial which suggests that there is no pragmatic justification for the use of pretrial detention for male juvenile offenders.

1625 Kraus, J. Children's Court Policy In New South Wales, pp 170-178 in Chappell, Duncan & Wilson, Paul (eds.) *The Australian Criminal Justice System, 2nd Edition*. Chatswood, Australia: Butterworths, 1977. Data on sentences from the Department of Child Welfare indicates that use of various sentences of institutionalization have decreased, while fines and admonishments were being used increasingly irrespective of type of offense of the age of the juvenile.

1626 Kraus, J. Do Existing Penal Measures "Reform" Juvenile Offenders? *Australian And New Zealand Journal Of Criminology* 10:217-222, 1977. The author concludes from a survey of secondary school and institutionalized males in New South Wales that knowledge and fear of legal consequences do not function as a deterrent.

1627 Kraus, Jonathan Decision Process In Children's Court And The Social Background Report, *Journal Of Research In Crime And Delinquency* 12:17-29, 1975. This study of the Australian Children's Courts' decision to sentence male juvenile offenders found that most weight is attached to the Child Welfare Officer's recommendation in sentencing and if no recommendation is made, the number of the offender's previous court appearances had significant impact.

1628 Lawrence, Jeanette & Hore, Philippa Greedy, Needy, Or Troubled? High School And University Students' Natural And Induced Views Of Shop Stealers, *Australian And New Zealand Journal Of Criminology* 26:59-71, 1993. Study of Melbourne male and female students' attitude toward shoplifters reveals that the younger students tend to be harsher while their female and older classmates exhibit greater understanding of the shoplifters.

1629 Lawrence, Jeanette A. & Homel, Ross J. Sentence And Offender Factors As Sources Of Discrimination In Magistrates' Penalties For Drinking Drivers, *Social Justice Research* 5:385-413, 1992. This study found that judges who sentenced drunk drivers in an Australian city responded to offender characteristics in that their treatment of youthful offenders and women than men under age 56 were more harsh.

1630 Lees, Rod The Inter-Departmental Committee On Crime Prevention Working Party, pp 199-203 in McKillop, Sandra & Vernon, Julia (eds.) *The Police And The Community*. Canberra, Australia: Australian Institute of Criminology, 1991. Thiv volume descrives the cooperative efforts of diverse departments of education, training and industrial relations, family services, Aboriginal and islander affairs, police, health, housing, local governments, attorney generals, ethnic affairs, corrective services and others involved in the delivery of services to and regulation of youths.

1631 Loftus, A. P. T. Factors Associated With Juvenile Court Orders, *Australian And New Zealand Journal Of Criminology* 8:215-220, 1975. This study observed that the juvenile court magistrate does make an attempt to tailor the court order to the needs of the child by making the probation officer in loco parent and remedy the domestic problems of affection, disciplinary or supervisory parental dysfunctions.

1632 Luke, Garth Gaol As A Last Resort: The Situation For Juveniles, pp 247-254 in Findlay, Mark & Hogg, Russell (eds.) *Understanding Crime And Criminal Justice*. North Ryde, Australia: Law Book Company, 1988. An examination of the sentencing of young people appearing before the Children's Courts in New South Wales found that there were large sentencing differences among courts.

1633 Maher, Lisa; Dixon, David & Swift, Wendy *Anh Hai: Young Asian Background People's Perceptions And Experiences Of Policing*. Sydney, Australia: Faculty of Law, University of New South Wales, 1997. This study concludes that youths of Asian-background were often treated with racism, hostility, routine harassment, intimidation, mistreatment, detention and search without clear legal authority in a denigrating, offensive, questionable and sometimes unlawful manner particularly in instances of seizure of drugs and money. 68p.

1634 Maley, Kevin School-based Community Policing-Northern Territory, pp 127-131 in McKillop, Sandra & Vernon, Julia (eds.) *The Police And The Community*. Canberra, Australia: Australian Institute of Criminology, 1991. The author narrates how opposition to a prevention pilot program in Darwin from the police, teachers, unions and school councils was handled.

1635 Mason, G. & Wilson, P. Sport, Recreation And Juvenile Crime: An Assessment Of The Impact Of Sport And Recreation Upon Aboriginal And Non-Aboriginal Youth Offenders Canberra, Australia: Australian Institute of Criminology, 1988. This volume discusses preventing juveniles crime in Australia by offering sports and recreation programs, such as wilderness and survival camps. 183p. Appendix.

1636 Maunders, David; Liddell, Max; Liddell, Margaret & Green, Sue *Young People Leaving Care And Protection*. Hobart, Australia: Australian Clearinghouse for Youth Studies, 1999. This volume reviews data confirming the failure of diverse governmental agencies in assuring the transition of institutionalized youths into independent living. 95p.

1637 McKillop, Sandra (ed.) *Aboriginal Justice Issues*. Canberra, Australia: Australian Institute of Criminology, 1993. Reports the proceedings of a 1992 conference on Australian criminal justice system issues involving Aboriginal juveniles. 229p.

1638 Merrill, Jackson The Perceived Behavior Of Parents By Children In Moral Dilemmas; Implications For Parents And Educators, *Australian And New Zealand Journal Of Criminology* 12:17-23, 1979. A sample of boys and girls were asked about their perceptions of their parent's reactions to stealing, and reveals that parental handling of female juveniles is different from that of males.

1639 Moore, David & Forsythe, Lubica *A New Approach To Juvenile Justice: An Evaluation Of Family Conferencing In Wagga Wagga*. Wagga Wagga, Australia: Center for Rural Social Research, Charles Sturt University, 1995. This study evaluating a family group conferencing program for juvenile offenders in Wagga Wagga, Australia found that data on police contacts do not reveal "net widening" of the program, and the rate of re-arrest of youths who attended a family conference decreased. 318p.

1640 Moore, David B. Shame, Forgiveness, And Juvenile Justice, *Criminal Justice Ethics* 12:3-25, 1993. This essay describes the Family Group Conference approach to dealing with juvenile offenders, discusses its overall implications.

1641 Mukherjee, Satyanshu K. & Walker, John R. *The Size Of The Crime Problem In Australia*. Phillip, Australia: Australian Institute of Criminology, 1987. Using official and crime victim survey data, this study concludes that juveniles were over-represented in arrests for breaking and entering, stealing, and vehicle theft. 111p.

1642 Mukherjee, Satyanshu; Carcach, Carlos & Higgins, Karl *Juvenile Crime And Justice: Australia 1997*. Griffith, Australia: Australian Institute Of Criminology, 1997. Covers topics such as juveniles and the law, juveniles' educational and labor-force participation, statistics on juvenile offenders in various Australian regions, and juveniles in various correctional institutions. 86p.

1643 Muncie, John & Coventry, Garry Punishment In The Community And The Victorian Youth Attendance Order: A Look Into The Future, *Australian And New Zealand Journal Of Criminology* 22:179-190, 1989. Assessing reforms in the juvenile justice system in Victoria, this study concludes that magistrates have used the new power to exert greater control over minor offenders rather than the more serious ones.

1644 Murphy, Shane & Lawrie, Sandra Community-Based Programs For Young People, pp 145-154 in McKillop, Sandra (eds.) *Keeping People Out Of Prison: Conference Proceedings*. Canberra, Australia: Australian Institute Of Criminology, 1991. This chapter describes the Barwon Youth Support Unit operating in Victoria as being a model to be used for community based corrections for juveniles in Australia.

1645 Murray, Gwenn; Homel, Ross; Wimshurst, Kerry; Prenzler, Tim & O'Connor, Ian *A Framework For Evaluating Community-Based Juvenile Crime Prevention Programs.* Queensland, Australia: Centre for Crime Policy and Public Safety, 1993. This report has a framework for evaluating community-based programs for the prevention of juvenile crime focusing on trends, changes, and local options. 45p.

1646 Naffine, Ngaire & Wundersitz, Joy Trends In Juvenile Justice, pp 235-252 in Chappell, Duncan & Wilson, Paul (eds.) *The Australian Criminal Justice System: The Mid 1990s.* Sydney, Australia: Butterworths, 1994. Chapters in this anthology provides a broad overview of the current status of territory laws and juvenile judicial processing in Australia.

1647 Naffine, Ngaire & Wundersitz, Joy Lawyers In The Children's Court: An Australian Perspective, *Crime & Delinquency* 37:374-392, 1991. This study found a considerable gap between the philosophies of justice and the actual workings of the system based on evidence of informal agreements and bureaucratic shortcuts resorted to by the lawyers for the best possible deal prior to judicial hearing in the children's court in South Australia.

1648 Naffine, Ngaire; Wundersitz, Joy & Gale, Fay Back To Justice For Juveniles: The Rhetoric And Reality Of Law Reform, *Australian And New Zealand Journal Of Criminology* 23:192-205, 1990. The author argues that the rhetoric of adversarial justice and the due process model is incompatible with the reality of the routine admission of guilt in juvenile trials.

1649 Naffine, Ngaire Towards Justice For Girls: Rhetoric And Practice In The Treatment Of Status Offenders, *Women And Criminal Justice* 1:3-19, 1989. This study concludes that both in rhetoric and practice, the courts in South Australia allow boys to explore their sexuality with impunity while girls are brought under the state's protection.

1650 New South Wales Ombudsman *Policing Public Safety.* Sydney, Australia: Report under S.6 of the Crime Legislation Amendment (Police and Public Safety) Act 1998, 1999. Drawing on police files, citizen complaints, and court records, this report concludes that young people, particularly of Aboriginal and of Torres Island origins, were searched more often for hidden weapons, disproportionately harassed and notified by the police. 380p.

1651 New South Wales Youth Justice Project *Kids In Justice: A Blueprint For The 90s.* Sydney South, Australia: The Law Foundation of New

South Wales, 1990. Reviews the juvenile justice system, the social context of juvenile crime and juvenile justice, issues of territory, equity, and family, rights and responsibilities in juvenile justice, policing of youth, community-based corrections, and detention centers in New South Wales. 334p.

1652 Newman, Kenneth Juvenile Offender Divisionary Programs In The Northern Territory, pp 135-144 in McKillop, Sandra (ed.) *Keeping People Out Of Prison: Conference Proceedings*. Canberra, Australia: Australian Institute Of Criminology, 1991. This chapter offers an extensive discussion of various diversion programs and sentencing options for juvenile couts in Australia.

1653 Newman, Kingsley Juvenile Justice In South Australia: In Need Of A Tune Up Or A Complete Overhaul? pp 279-294 in Hackler, Jim (ed.) *Official Responses To Problem Juveniles: Some International Reflections*. Euskadi, Spain: The Oñati International Institute for the Sociology of Law, 1991. Chapter debates the potential problems faced by creation of the "two panel diversion" system for juvenile offenders in South Australia.

1654 Nichols, Helen South Australia, pp 141-174 in Stewart, V. Lorne (ed.) *Justice And Troubled Children Around The World, Vol. 3*. New York: New York University Press, 1981. This chapter provides an extensive discussion of welfare programs for juveniles, laws, and the structure and operation of the juvenile justice system in South Australia.

1655 O'Connor, Ian & Callahan, Mary Youth, The Law And legal Services: Patterns Of Legal Need, *Australian And New Zealand Journal Of Criminology* 21:5-19, 1988. A survey of youths in custody found that they had very limited knowledge of their rights and recourses in criminal justice, child welfare and educational systems, or consumer and labor markets.

1656 Ogilvie, Emma Masculine Obsessions: An Examination Of Criminology, Criminality And Gender, *Australian And New Zealand Journal Of Criminology* 29:205-226, 1996. This article discusses gendering of criminality and the consequent differential treatment by the justice system, although this traditional approach fails to explain female criminality.

1657 O'Malley, Pat Responsibility And Crime Prevention: A Response To Adam Sutton, *Australian And New Zealand Journal Of Criminology* 27:21-24, 1994. This paper presents a response to Adam Sutton's view that on the threat and promises of the new developments in crime prevention and argues that his view neglects the dangers of ignoring the structural issues in social control.

1658 O'Malley, Pat; Coventry, Garry & Walters, Reece Victoria's `Day In Prison Program': An Evaluation And Critique, *Australian And New Zealand Journal Of Criminology* 26:171-183, 1993. Evaluates a pilot program for delinquents' "Day in Prison" in Victoria and concludes that there is no reliable evidence to indicate the crime prevention effect of this program.

1659 Owston, Doug Correctional Programmes For Juveniles And Young People, pp 119-125 in Biles, David (eds.) *Current Australian Trends In Corrections*. Annandale, Australia: Federation Press, 1988. This chapter provides a brief, but extensive, listing of correctional programs for juveniles and young people in Australia.

1660 Parker, Ann L. & Mohr, Philip B. Police Opinions On The Deployment Of Civilian Youth Development Officers, *International Journal Of Police Science And Management*, 3:19-24, 2000. A survey of police officers' opinions shows support on the part of officers for the Youth Development Office.

1661 Pasmore, Joe & Walker, John *A Computer Forecasting Model For Predicting Requirements For Beds In Secure Custody Juvenile Corrections Institutions*. Phillip, Australia: Australian Institute of Criminology, 1989. Describes the computer-assisted forecasting model developed to predict, anticipated population and governmental policy changes, the numbers of youths likely to be held in secure detention by the year 2000 in Australia, 74p. Appendix.

1662 Petrie, Simon; Berry, Paul & Smith, Richard Juvenile Delinquency And The Labyrinth Of Services: A Case Study, *Australian And New Zealand Journal Of Criminology* 13:52-60, 1980. This paper examines the possible points of breakdown and conflict in the coordination of services, and the relative contributions of health, welfare, education, and police agencies.

1663 Polk, Ken A Community And Youth Development Approach To Youth Crime Prevention, pp 185-199 in O'Malley, Pat & Sutton, Adam (eds.) *Crime Prevention In Australia* Sydney, Australia: Federation, 1997. In this chapter the author highlights the importance of local initiative in developing appropriate youth crime prevention programs.

1664 Potas, Ivan; Vining, Aidan & Wilson, Paul *Young People And Crime: Costs And Prevention*. Canberra, Australia: Australian Institute of Criminology, 1990. This volume provides estimates of the costs of juvenile justice in Australia and evaluates data on benefits derived from expenditures on juvenile justice prevention and treatment. 82p. Appendix.

1665 Prenzler, Tim & Hayes, Hennessey Victim-Offender Mediation And The Gatekeeping Role Of Police, *International Journal Of Police Science And Management* 2:17-32, 1999. Multiple sources and techniques were used in evaluating community conferencing, and the police discretionary role in referrals for restoration.

1666 Pritchard, Bob What Do We Do With Young Offenders?, pp 155-160 in Sirr, Peter (ed.) *Crime Prevention -- Everybody's Business. Proceedings Of A Conference 27 & 28 April, 1995.* East Perth, Australia: Crime Prevention Council Of Australia, 1995. This chapter discusses the importance of society's role in facilitating juvenile delinquents who want to change.

1667 Queensland Criminal Justice Commission *The Inala Community And Police Network: An Evaluation.* Brisbane, Australia, 1995. Evaluates a community-policing project that primarily provides activities and strategies for Aboriginal Inala youth in Queensland. 57p. Appendix.

1668 Rafter, Nicole Hahn (ed.) *Encyclopedia Of Women And Crime.* Phoenix, Arizona: Oryx, 2000. This document has an alphabetical listing of 240 entries with numerous short notes on juvenile delinquency and age, drugs, alcohol, class, race, peers and family conflict, and an Aistralian female gang. 361p.

1669 Read, Hilary & Alder, Christine Job Retention: Employment Problems Of Youth From Youth Training Centers, *Australian And New Zealand Journal Of Criminology* 21:67-80, 1988. Interviews with a small group of adolescent youths released into employment by a Youth Training Center in Australia reveal the effects of the following six factors as the most important in job retention: type of job, support; emotional and personality problems, effects of institutionalization, stigma, and peers.

1670 Reddrop, Susan *Outdoor Programs For Young Offenders In Detention: An Overview.* Hobart, Australia: National Clearinghouse for Youth Studies, 1997. This manual on outdoor programming for young offenders in a detention center outlines an outdoor program, the most common program components and its benefits, research evidence and its limitations, models and strategies, adaptations for special youthful offenders, and evaluation mechanisms. 228p.

1671 Richards, Ian & Sullivan, Ann Psychotherapy For Delinquents? *Journal Of Adolescence* 19:63-73, 1996. This study presents the results of psychotherapy consultation service for delinquents.

1672 Robertson, Don Streets Ahead -- The Rhetoric And Reality Of Youth Participation In Neighbourhood Crime Control And Prevention -- A Case Study, pp 465-471 in Biles, David & Vernon, Julia (eds.) *Private Sector And Community Involvement In The Criminal Justice System*. Canberra, Australia: Australian Institute of Criminology, 1994. This chapter provides a description of diversion programs in two localities in Australia.

1673 Royal Commission *Royal Commission Into Aboriginal Deaths In Custody: Regional Report Of Inquiry In New South Wales, Victoria And Tasmania*. Canberra, Australia: Australian Government Publishing Service, 1991. This volume covers juvenile detention and their encounters with the police, separating justice from welfare, bail and the institutions, parental control and prevention by means of employment and leisure activities within the larger context of the treatment of Aboriginals in custody. 438p.

1674 Russo, Laura Date Rape: The Hidden Crime, *Trends And Issues Australian Institute Of Criminology* 157:1-6, 2000. Discusses various judicial, legislative responses and prevention strategies that should be directed toward adolescents and young people.

1675 Sanson-Fisher, R.; Woollacott, H. & Mulligan, B. Knowledge Of The Law: The Disadvantaged Delinquent? *Australian And New Zealand Journal Of Criminology* 13:204-214, 1980. This research showed that non-offenders were significantly less delinquent than the institutionalized group, and scored better on the questions relating to their knowledge of their rights.

1676 Sarre, Rick Family Conferencing As A Juvenile Justice Strategy, *Justice Professional*, 11:259-296, 1999. This review highlights the South Australian experience in family conferencing involving juvenile delinquents that considers the social milieu of delinquents in dispensing juvenile justice.

1677 Sarri, Rosemary & Bradley, Patrick W. Juvenile Aid Panels: An Alternative To Juvenile Court Processing In South Australia, *Crime & Delinquency* 26:42-62, 1980. This is a comparative analysis that found that the rate of reappearance of youths processed through the panels, and that of youths processed through the court, were essentially similar.

1678 Sarri, Rosemary C. Juvenile Aid Panels: The Australian Approach To Juvenile Diversion, pp 105-125 in Brantingham, Patricia L. & Blomberg, Thomas G. (eds.) *Courts And Diversion: Policy And Operations Study*.

Beverly Hills, California: Sage, 1979. A longitudinal study of young persons in South Australia concludes that instead of diversion, a large number of minor offenders and status offenders were still being processed through the courts.

1679 Schneider, Hans Joachim Life In Societal No-Man's Land: Aboriginal Crime In Central Australia, *International Journal Of Offender Therapy And Comparative Criminology* 36:5-19, 1992. This article discusses the cultural conflicts in using white-people's definitions of delinquency and criminality.

1680 Semple, Des Juvenile Justice In Western Australia, pp 113-125 in Biles, David (ed.) *Current Australian Trends In Corrections*. Annandale, Australia: Federation, 1988. In this chapter, the author discusses the high rate of Aboriginal youths' encounters with the juvenile justice system in all of Australia and its various states and territories reflecting the integration of welfare and justice functions, and argues in favor of separating the two.

1681 Seymour, John Australia, pp 1-19 in Shoemaker, Donald J. (ed.) *International Handbook On Juvenile Justice*. Westport, Connecticut: Greenwood, 1996. This chapter offers an extensive discussion of the juvenile justice system of Australia.

1682 Seymour, John *Dealing With Young Offenders*. North Ryde, Australia: Law Book Company, 1988. Two parts of this volume present a legal guide on Australian procedures for dealing with young offenders. 495p. Appendix.

1683 Seymour, John Dealing With young Offenders: The Report Of The Australian Law Reform Commission, *Australian And New Zealand Journal Of Criminology* 15:245-254, 1982. This chaper offers a concise summary of the Commission's recommendations for police and court procedures regarding young offenders.

1684 Seymour, John *Juvenile Justice In South Australia*. Sydney, Australia: The Law Book Company, 1982. This book describes the legal issues and confusion created by the operation of the special procedures, specifically the Screening Panels dealing with young offenders in Australia. 146p.

1685 Seymour, John *Juvenile Justice: Before And After The Onset Of Delinquency*. Canberra: Australian Government Publishing Service, 1979. In the proceedings of the Sixth United Nations Congress on the Prevention of Crime and Treatment of Offenders, the Australian juvenile justice Children's Aid Panels, Children's Courts, sanctions, and children in need of care and protection are discussed. 34p.

1686 Shrimpton, Sandra; Oates, Kim & Hayes, Susan The Child Witness And Legal Reforms In Australia, pp 132-144 in Bottoms, Bette L. & Goodman, Gail S. (eds.) *International Perspectives On Child Abuse And Children's Testimony: Psychological Research And Law.* Thousand Oaks, California: Sage, 1996. This chapter describes child abuse in Australia, the research influencing legislative reforms, and four areas of legal reforms regarding children as witnesses.

1687 Simpson, Brian & Simpson, Cheryl The Use Of Curfews To Control Juvenile Offending In Australia: Managing Crime Or Wasting Time? *Current Issues In Criminal Justice* 5:184-199, 1993. The authors examine the use of curfews, their effectiveness and possible harm in controlling youth crime in Australia, and focus on the infringement of liberty of movement and lack of clear authority in municipal law to impose curfews.

1688 Simpson, Cheryl & Hil, Richard (eds.) *Ways Of Resistance: Social Control And Young People In Australia.* Sydney, Australia: Hale & Iremonger, 1995. This anthology addresses the reactions of youths to the exercise of social control by criminal justice agencies, welfare organizations, and educational authorities, and includes a summary of recent changes in juvenile justice legislation in Australia. 208p.

1689 Smith, Greg Kids And Coppers, *Australian And New Zealand Journal Of Criminology* 8:221-230, 1975. Based on participant observation of delinquents, the author found that the racially mixed group of adolescents feel the police they deal with as violent and as drinking on the job, and view them with suspicion, disrespect, distrust, dislike, contempt and fear.

1690 Snashall, Ron (ed.) *National Conference On Child Abuse: Proceedings 3-7 February 1987.* Phillip, Australia: Australian Institute of Criminology, 1987. An Australian national conference on child abuse in 1986 that reviews treatment services and problems, and resources needed by legal, welfare, medical, and community agencies. 291p.

1691 South Australia Community Welfare Department *Juvenile Aid Panels In South Australia.* Adelaide, Australia, 1975. Describes and evaluates the Juvenile Aid Panel system adopted in South Australia and concludes that such panels have the potential of offering a better way of processing juvenile offenders. 42 p.

1692 Sutton, Adam Crime Prevention: Promise Or Threat? *Australian And New Zealand Journal Of Criminology* 27:5-20, 1994. The author reviews the threat and promises of the new developments in crime prevention, and warns against the danger of ignoring the structural issues in social control, privatizing of safety, and security.

1693 Swanton, Bruce; Wyles, Paul; Lincoln, Robyn; Wilson, Paul & Hill, Lavinia *Missing Persons*. Canberra, Australia: Australian Institute Of Criminology, 1988. Chapter eight of this volume has statistics on and a discussion of juveniles runaways and how to reduce the number of youths leaving home. 284p.

1694 Tomsen, Stephen Ruling Men? Some Comments On Masculinity And Juvenile Justice, *Australian And New Zealand Journal Of Criminology* 29:191-194, 1996. The author focuses on the varied definitions of masculinity within which juvenile justice system and young males operate.

1695 Trimboli, Lily *An Evaluation Of The NSW Youth Justice Conference Scheme* Sydney, Australia: New South Wales Bureau of Crime Statistics and Research, 2000. This is an evaluation of an alternative that included victim's perspective to court processing established in New South Wales. 95p.

1696 United Nations Social Defence Research Institute South Australia: Notes On The Juvenile Justice System, pp 199-220 in United Nations Social Defencse Research Institute (ed.) *Juvenile Justice: An International Survey*. Rome, Italy, 1976. Chapter provides a brief description of the South Australian juvenile justice system with extensive statistics on its operations.

1697 University Of Sydney Faculty Of Law *Proceedings Of The Institute Of Criminology: No. 75 Changes In Direction Of Juvenile Justice*. Sydney, Australia, 1988. This report discusses the various changes in the directions of diverse areas within the Australian juvenile justice. 86p.

1698 Vardon, Sue The South Australian Juvenile Justice System, pp 100-108 in Biles, David (ed.) *Current Australian Trends In Corrections*. Annandale, Australia: Federation, 1988. This document summarizes some data and provides a graph of children in secure care in South Australia from 1973 to 1987, the various major reforms of the 1970s, and their 19th century origins within the inter-twining of social welfare concerns with juvenile justice.

1699 Walters, Reece & Muncie, John Alternatives To Youth Imprisonment: Evaluating The Victorian Youth Attendance Order. Punishment In The Community--Seven Years On, *Australian And New Zealand Journal Of Criminology* 29:166-190, 1996. An evaluation of the Youth Attendance Order shows that although it did not add to the number of young offenders entering detention centers, the results suggests a "net widening" at the lower end of the sentencing scale.

1700 Walters, Reece Alternatives To Youth Imprisonment: Evaluating The Victorian Youth Attendance Order, *Australian And New Zealand Journal Of Criminology* 29:166-181, 1996. This is a critique of the Youth Attendance Order in Victoria, Australia's as an alternative sanction and its unintended consequence of "net-widening".

1701 Ward, Lisa & Jones, Gerard Juveniles And HIV/AIDS Policy Development And Practice In Victoria, pp 257-267 in Norberry, Jennifer; Gaughwin, Matt & Gerull, Sally-Anne (eds.) *HIV/AIDS And Prisons*. Canberra, Australia: Australian Institute of Criminology, 1991. The authors stress the need to respond to issues related to HIV in juvenile training centers in Victoria, Australia.

1702 White, Rob The Business Of Youth Crime Prevention, pp 164-184 in O'Malley, P. & Sutton, A. (eds.) *Crime Prevention In Australia:Issues In Policy And Research*. Leichhardt, Australia: Federation, 1997. This is a discussion of the importance of the relationship among youth crime control and containment, and the socioeconomic trends that marginalize and alienate the Australian youth.

1703 White, Rob Racism, Policing And Ethnic Youth Gangs, *Current Issues In Criminal Justice* 7:302-313, 1996. This article discusses some myths and realities of ethnic youth gangs and policing in Australia.

1704 White, Rob & Alder, Christine (eds.) *The Police And Young People In Australia*. Melbourne, Australia: Cambridge University Press, 1994. This volume provides ten articles on the relationship between policing and the specific economic and social position of young people in Australia. 252p.

1705 White, Rob Young People And Policing Of Community Space, *Australian And New Zealand Journal Of Criminology* 26:208-218, 1993. In this article the author discusses the various issues related to the policy of crime-prevention by policing young people in urban public spaces.

1706 White, Rob; Underwood, Rod & Omelczuk, Susanne Victims Of Violence: The View From The Youth Services, *Australian And New Zealand Journal Of Criminology* 24:25-39, 1991. A survey of youth workers in Western Australia found that users of these services experienced a significant level of violence such as incest, assault and harassment.

1707 White, Robert Curtailing Youth: A Critique Of Coercive Crime Prevention, pp 117-137 in Mazerolle, Lorraine Green & Roch, Jan (eds.) *Crime Prevention Studies, Vol. 9*. Monsey, New York: Criminal Justice

Press, 1998. Critique of Australian attempts to control the activities and public visibility of youths through reconstruction of public space, extension of police powers in the regulation of street life, curfews, and emphasis on getting parents to police their offspring

1708 Wimshurst, Kerry Control And Resistance: Reformatory School Girls In Late nineteenth Century South Australia, *Journal Of Social History* 18:273-288, 1984. The author describes the history of gender-based difference in admissionsto reformatory schools durng 1871-1892.

1709 Word, Elizabeth Rape Of Girl-Children By Male Family Members, *Australian And New Zealand Journal Of Criminology* 15:90-99, 1982. Using the term "girl-child" rape to highlight what is generally referred to as father-daughter incest, this article criticizes the cultural image and research on the phenomenon.

1710 Wundersitz Joy & Hetzel, Sue Family Conferencing For young Offenders: The South Australian Experience, pp 111-139 in Hudson, Joe; Morris, Allison; Maxwell, Gabrielle & Galaway, Burt (eds.) *Family Group Conferences: Perspectives On Policy & Practice.* Annandale, Australia: Criminal Justice Press, 1996. This chapter provides a flow-chart of the restructured Australian juvenile justice system, a description of the processes of referral and the factors that affect referral decision, selecting a venue, conducting the conference, and the outcomes of family conferencing.

1711 Wundersitz, Joy; Doherty, Justine; Gardner, Julie & Mannik, Maire *The South Australian Juvenile Justice System: A Review Of Its Operation.* Adelaide, Australia: South Australia Attorney General's Department, 1996. This study provides an assessment of the various changes during 1994 in South Australia juvenile justice system. 224p. Appendix.

1712 Wundersitz, Joy The Net-Widening Effect Of The Aid Panels And Screening Panels In The South Australian Juvenile Justice System, *Australian And New Zealand Journal Of Criminology* 25:115-134, 1992. The author of this study examined whether South Australia's informal processing mechanisms of Screening Panels and Aid Panels widened the net of social control or facilitated the diversion of youths who would otherwise have come before the Children's Court.

1713 Wundersitz, Joy; Naffine, Ngaire & Gale, Fay The Production Of Guilt In The Juvenile Justice System: The Pressures To `Plead', *Howard Journal* 30:192-206, 1991. If South Australian system of juvenile justice with its high rate of guilty pleas is a function of pressure brought to bear on the young defendants, this case study questions the wisdom of a system that assumes that the defendant will admit guilt.

1714 Yeager, Matthew G. Immigrants And Criminality, *Criminal Justice Abstracts* 29:143-171, 1997. A small section on immigrant juvenile delinquents is included in this review of research findings from Australia, and elsewhere.

Austria

1715 Fenz, Claudia The Juvenile Court System In Austria, pp 137-141 in United Nations Expert Group Meeting (eds.) *Children And Juveniles In Detention: Application Of Human Rights Standards*. Vienna, Austria: The United Nations Centre for Human Rights, 1994. This chapter provides a brief description of the history, laws, organization, and orientation of juvenile justice in Austria.

1716 Goodman, Randy Summaries Of DCI Country Surveys, Austria, pp 151-153 in Tomasevski, Katarina (ed.) *Children In Adult Prisons: An International Perspective*. New York, New York: St. Martin's Press, 1986. This is a report on the findings of the 1982-1984 Defense for Children International survey of children in Austrian adult prisons.

1717 Grafl, Christian Decisive Factors In Decisions Involving Juveniles In Criminal Proceedings (Entscheidungsgrundlagen Für Strafrechtliche Reaktionen Bei Jungendlichen), *Monatsschrift Für Kriminologie Und Strafrechtsreform* 78:69-83, 1995. When factors that determine decisions on sanctioning in the juvenile court of Vienna are examined, it was concluded that such sanctions were primarily determined by the characteristics of the delinquent in keeping with the intention of the Austrian Youth Court Act of 1988. German.

1718 Hackler, James C. The Flow Of Information In Court: The Juvenile Court In Vienna As An Illustration, *Canadian Journal Of Criminology And Correction* 17:57-68, 1975. The author argues that in Austria there seems to be a general assumption that a juvenile brought before the court is guilty, and once it has established that a juvenile has committed a crime, the Austrian court may punish the youth by putting him/her in jail for two weeks or a month.

1719 Pelikan, Christa Conflict Resolution Between Victims And Offenders In Austria And In The Federal Republic Of Germany, pp 151-172 in Heidensohn, Frances & Farrell, Martin (eds.) *Crime In Europe*. London: Routledge, 1991. The resolution of issues of conflict in the processing of juvenile offenders victims in Austria and Germany is described.

1720 Steinert, Heinz Rumours Of Prevention, pp 129-152 in Hebberecht, Patrick & Sack, Fritz (eds.) *The Prevention Of Delinquency In Europe: New Strategies (La Prévention De La Délinquance En Europe: Nouvelles Stratégies)*. Paris, France: L'Harmattan, 1997. This chapter describes prevention policy in Austria and suggests that while official, little actual prevention activity takes place. French with English summary.

1721 Winter, Renate The Project To Regulate Conflicts In Austria (Le Projet De La Régulation Des Conflites En Autriche), pp 139-142 in Dünkel, Frieder & Zermatten, Jean (eds.) *Recent Trends In Penal Law For Minors: Mediation, Community Service And Intermediate Treatment (Nouvelles Tendances Dans Le Droit Pénal Des Mineurs: Médiation, Travail Au Profit De La Communauté Et Traitement Intermédiaire)*. Freiburg, Germany: Max Planck Institute for Foreign and International Criminal Justice, 1990. Conciliation programs started since 1989 under the Austrian penal codes are described in this chapter.

Bangladesh

1722 Bhuiyan, Md. Golam Kibria Juvenile Delinquency And Justice System In Bangladesh, *Asian Journal Of Crime Prevention And Criminal Justice* 8:92-98, 1990. This author provides a brief overview of juvenile courts, and laws in Bangladesh with some data on corrections.

Belgium

1723 Aertsen, Ivo & Peters, Tony Mediation And Restorative Justice In Belgium, *European Journal On Criminal Policy And Research* 6:507-525, 1998. This article reports on new sentencing policies, especially mediation programs, relating to juveniles in Belgium.

1724 Buonatesta, A. Mediation And Community Service Within The Belgian Law On Juvenile Protection, pp 219-228 in Walgrave, Lode (eds.) *Restorative Justice For Juveniles: Potentialities, Risks And Problems For Research*. Leuven, Belgium: Leuven University Press, 1998. This chapter discusses how mediation and community service as an effective restorative justice system can be integrated and implemented more widely by the juvenile court.

1725 Christiaens, Jennecke A History Of Belgium's Child Protection Act Of 1912: The Redefinition Of The Juvenile Offender And His Punishment, *European Journal Of Crime, Criminal Law And Criminal Justice* 7:5-21, 1999. The author provides an historic review of the nature and evolution of Belgian laws regarding minors.

1726 Claes, Mia The Juvenile Mediation Project In Leuven (Belgium), pp 367-386 in Walgrave, Lode (eds.) *Restorative Justice For Juveniles: Potentialities, Risks And Problems For Research.* Leuven, Belgium: Leuven University Press, 1998. The author describes mediation and raises judicial and methodological questions regarding mediation programs in Leuven, Belgium.

1727 Dechesne, Marie-Ange *Juvenile Delinquency In Belgium From 1971 To 1975 (La Délinquance Juvénile En Belgique De 1971 À 1975).* Brussels, Belgium: Centre D'Étude De La Délinquance Juvenile, 1978. This is a report on the number of juveniles appearing in Belgian courts and their dispositions during 1971-1975 period following legislative reforms. 148p. French.

1728 Dupont-Bouchat, Marie Sylvie Origins And Transformation From Juvenile Penitentiaries To Charitable Schools In Belgium (1840-1914) (De La Prison À L'École De Bienfaisance: Origines Et Transformations Des Institutions Pénitentiaires Pour Enfants En Belgique (1840-1914)), *Criminologie* 28:85-108, 1995. This examination of the history of three charitable Belgian juvenile institutions in the nineteenth century reflects evolution from an early, offender reform approach to a protection-of-the-child-in-danger philosophy in the latter part of the century. French.

1729 Eliaerts, Christian; Dumortier, Els & Vanderhaeghen, Rachel Critical Assessment Of Community Service And Mediation For Juvenile Offenders In Brussels, pp 351-366 in Walgrave, Lode (ed.) *Restorative Justice For Juveniles: Potentialities, Risks And Problems For* Research. Leuven, Belgium: Leuven University Press, 1998. This chapter argues that a lack of clear legal rules in Belgium have led to an ambiguous application of community service as an alternative sanction for juveniles.

1730 Hirsch, Jacques L. The Future Of Youth Protection In Belgium (L'Avenir De La Protection De La Jeunesse En Belgique) pp 43-82 in Sace, Jean & Van Der Vorst, Pierre (eds.) *Justice And Young Delinquents: Institutional And Criminological Aspects (Justice Et Jeunes Délinquants: Aspects Institutionnels Et Criminologiques).* Brussels, Belgiumn: Bruylant, 1989. The discussion is on the effects of centralizing trends in Belgian courts dealing with juveniles.

1731 Junger-Tas, Josine Hidden Delinquency And Judicial Selection In Belgium, pp 70-94 in Friday, Paul C. & Stewart, V. Lorne (eds.) *Youth Crime And Juvenile Justice: International Perspectives.* New York, New York: Praeger, 1977. This chapter reports findings from a study investigating involvement in delinquency and the likelihood of judicial processing for such behavior, and the factors that influence it.

1732 Kellens, Georges Justice And Troubled Children: An Examination Of The Belgian Experience, *Eurocriminology* 3:103-133, 1990. The author reviews and explores the history and French traditions of delinquency and youth protection in Belgium from the eighteenth century to the present.

1733 Mauwissen, Eric & Delaet-van Gasse, Joëlle Some Issues On The Fates Of Young Delinquents In Belgium During The 19th Century (Quelques Aspects Du Sort Réservé Aux Jeunes Délinquants En Belgique Au XIXè Siècle), pp 625-654 in Hess, Albert G. & Clement, Priscilla F. (eds.) *History Of Juvenile Delinquency: A Collection Of Essays On Crime Committed By Young Offenders, In History And In Selected Countries Volume II.* Aalen, Germany: Scientia Verlag, 1993. The author discusses the legal and judicial systems, and extent and nature of delinquency in Belgium during the 19th century. French with English summary.

1734 Scieur, Yves Benefits Of Community Service Provision: Arguments For Juvenile Magistrates (La Préstation Communautaire: Une Logique Pour Le Magistrat De La Jeunesse), pp 143-156 in Dünkel, Frieder & Zermatten, Jean (eds.) *Recent Trends In Penal Law For Minors: Mediation, Community Service And Intermmediate Treatment (Nouvelles Tendances Dans Le Droit Pénal Des Mineurs: Médiation, Travail Au Profit De La Communauté Et Traitement Intermédiaire).* Freiburg, Germany: Max Planck Institute for Foreign and International Criminal Justice, 1990. This chapter describes the alternatives to jail and the approval of community service as an appropriate penalty for minors in Belgium. French.

1735 Walgrave, Lode; Berx, Eric; Poels, Veerle & Vettenburg, Nicole Belgium, pp 55-95 in Mehlbye, Jill & Walgrave, Lode (eds.) *Confronting Youth In Europe: Juvenile Crime And Juvenile Justice.* Copenhagen, Denmark: Forlaget, 1998. This chapter has a detailed description of the origins, organization, and step-by-step procedures and operation of the contemporary Belgian juvenile justice.

1736 Walgrave, L. & Beudens, H. The Restorative Proportionality Of Community Service For Juveniles, *European Journal Of Crime, Criminal Law And Criminal Justice* 4:361-380, 1996. This study presents an analysis of 614 cases of community service sentences in juvenile courts in Belgium.

1737 Walgrave, Lode Beyond Rehabilitaiton: In Search Of A Constructive Alternative In The Judicial Response To Juvenile Crime, *European Journal On Criminal Policy And Research* 2:57-75, 1994. The contradictions in rehabilitation laws for juvenile offender, the effectiveness of programs, and models of judicial intervention in

Belgium are the subject of this article.

1738 Vettenburg, Nicole Preventing Juvenile Delinquency By Offering An Attractive Curriculum (La Préventation De La Délinquance Juvenile Par L'Offre Scolaire Attractive), pp 181-194 in Junger-Tas, Josine; Boendermaker, Leonieke & Van Der Laan, Peter H. (eds.) *The Future Of The Juvenile Justice System (L'Avenir Du Système Pénal Des Mineurs)*, Leuven, Belgium: Acco, 1991. In a survey of children in Flemish Belgium, this study of social control and vulnerability theory, sought to investigate how changes in school curricula could help prevent delinquency. French.

Brazil

1739 Cavalieri, Alyrio & Rios, Jóse Arthur Brazil, pp 1-22 in Stewart, V. Lorne (ed.) *Justice And Troubled Children Around The World, Vol. 1.* New York, New York: New York University Press, 1980. This chapter describes Brazilian efforts to prevent juvenile delinquency, and treat child abuse and neglect through nationwide coordination of health, educational, welfare, and legal services.

1740 Costa, Edes Some Aspects Of Brazilian Criminal Justice System And Crime Prevention, pp 94-110 in Sugihara, Hiroyasu (ed.) *Resource Material Series No. 38*. Tokyo, Japan: UNAFEI, 1990. This is an examination of the criminal justice system and crime prevention including delinquency prevention, juvenile justice, and protection of the young in Brazil.

1741 Figueira-McDonough, Josefina Processing Juvenile Delinquency In Two Cities: A Cross-National Comparison. *Journal Of Research In Crime And Delinquency* 16:114-142, 1979. This study involving two juvenile court systems, one in Rio de Janeiro, Brazil, and the other in the United States concludes that the latter processed ten times more juveniles than the former, and has displaced the traditional mandates of juvenile justice.

1742 Human Rights Watch/Americas *Final Justice: Police And Death Squad Homicides Of Adolescents In Brazil.* New York, New York, 1994. This document provides a report based on observation research and official statistics, on death squad killings of youth in Brazil. 140p.

1743 Leal, César Barros Brazil, pp 20-33 in Shoemaker, Donald J. (ed.) *International Handbook On Juvenile Justice*. Westport, Connecticut: Greenwood, 1996. This chapter offers an extensive discussion of the juvenile justice system of Brazil.

1744 Lucchini, Riccardo The Brazilian Debate On Justice For Minors (Le Débat Brésilien Sur La Justice Des Mineurs), *Déviance Et Societé* 15:175-186, 1991. This is a summary of the Brazilian debate on the pros and cons of two conceptions of justice for minors-- the Code of Minors which had been in effect since 1979 and an alternative statute compliant with the new Brazilian Constitution and with United Nations standards on the protection and rights of children. French with English summary.

1745 Rios, Jóse Arthur Street Children: The Situation In Latin America, pp 131-137 in Kubota, Yo (ed.) *International Review Of Criminal Policy: Special Double Volume On Juvenile Justice In International Perspective.* New York, New York: United Nations Center for Social Development and Humanitarian Affairs, 1990. Article discusses the situation of Brazilian homeless children, and societal and official reaction toward them.

Bulgaria

1746 Goodman, Randy Summaries Of DCI Country Surveys, Bulgaria, pp 153-154 in Tomasevski, Katarina (ed) *Children In Adult Prisons: An International Perspective.* New York: St. Martin's Press, 1986. Findings on children in adult prisons in Bulgaria from 1982-1984 by Defense for Children International Survey are listed in this chapter.

1747 Human Rights Watch Children's Rights Project *Children Of Bulgaria: Police Violence And Arbitrary Confinement.* New York, New York, 1996. A fact-finding mission to Bulgaria found that street children are often subjected to physical abuse and other mistreatment by police, and by skinhead gangs who attack the youths because of their Roma ethnic identity. 145p. Appendix.

Burma

1748 Aung, U Tin An Outline Of Existing Juvenile Justice System In The Socialist Republic Of The Union Of Burma, pp 115-121 in United Nations Asia And Far East Institute (eds.) *Report For 1983 And Resource Material Series No. 25*, Tokyo, Japan: UNAFEI, 1984. Juvenile crime trends, probation, boys' training schools, the Children's Act of 1955 and age of criminal responsibility, juvenile courts are all briefly described.

Canada

1749 Abramovitch, Rona; Peterson-Badali, Michele & Rohan, Meg Young People's Understanding And Assertion Of Their Rights To Silence And

Legal Counsel, *Canadian Journal Of Criminology* 37:1-18, 1995. In this study of factors that affect juveniles' and young adults' the knowledge of rights to silence and legal counsel as investigated.

1750 Abramovitch, Rona; Higgins-Biss Karen L. & Biss, Stephen R. Young Persons' Comprehension Of Waivers In Criminal Proceedings, *Canadian Journal Of Criminology* 35:309-322, 1993. This study explores the ability of school youths to understand their rights and the implications of forfeiting them when presented with accounts of criminal proceedings against arrested juveniles.

1751 Adkins, Amanda Nielsen The Strength of Community: The Native Counselling Services of Alberta Story, pp 103-118 in Hazlehurst, Kayleen M. (ed.) *Popular Justice and Community Regeneration: Pathways of Indigenous Reform* Westport, Connecticut: Praeger, 1995. This chapter describes the Native Counseling Services of an Alberta program, its philosophy and services, including those involving young offenders such as the criminal court work program, open custody group homes, and youth programs.

1752 Alberta Correctional Services Division *Report Of The Efficiency Review Team*. Edmonton, Canada: Alberta Department of Justice, 1995. This inquiry includes cost/efficiency issues,such as supplies, laundry, contract staff etc. in both juvenile and adult offender centers in Calgary and Edmonton. 305p.

1753 Amorso, Donald M. & Ware, Edward E. Youth's Perception Of Police As A Function Of Attitudes Towards Parents, Teachers And Self, *Canadian Journal Of Criminology* 25:191-200, 1983. This study found that while attitudes toward parents and self contributed less toward their attitudes towards the police, youths' attitudes toward teachers were primary in predicting attitudes toward police.

1754 Auger, Donald J.; Doob, Anthony N. & Auger, Raymond P. Crime And Control In Three Nishnawbe-Aski Nation Communities: An Exploratory Investigation, *Canadian Journal Of Criminology* 34:317-338, 1992. The authors explore the communities' perceptions of crime problem and solutions, and offer some data on police and court activities including charges against adolescents under Young Offender Act.

1755 Badgley, Robin & Rae-Grant, Quentin Report Of The Committee On Sexual Offenses Against Children And Youths In Canada, *Canadian Criminology Forum* 7:145-156, 1985. These are symposium proceedings on sexual offenses against Canadian children and youths including prostitution, and is otherwise referred to as the Badgley Report.

1756 Baker, Falcon *Saving Our Kids from Delinquency, Drugs, And Despair: Solutions Through Prevention*. New York, New York: Harper Collins, 1991. In this book the author covers topics such as delinquency and social structural factors, the juvenile court and reforming juvenile justice, rehabilitation, failure of preventive measures, and the portrayal of public schools as the villain. 348p.

1757 Bala, Nicholas What's Wrong With YOA Bashing, What's Wrong With YOA? Recognizing The Limits Of The Law, *Canadian Journal Of Criminology* 36:247-270, 1994. This is a critique of both the advocates and the opponents of Young Offenders Act, given the limitations of the law.

1758 Bala, Nicholas; Hornick, Joseph P.; McCall, M. L. (Marnie) & Corke, Margaret E. *State Responses To Youth Crime: A Consideration Of Principles*. Ottawa, Canada: Department of Justice Canada, 1994. This report describes the principles, philosophy and historic transformation of the youth justice system and state intervention in the lives of children and teens in Canada, including the constitution and Young Offenders Act, and new responses to youth crime, victims' rights, crime prevention, get tough policies, and community responsibility. 135p.

1759 Barkwell, Lawrence J. Differential Treatment Of Juveniles On Probation: An Evaluation Study, *Canadian Journal Of Criminology* 18:363-378, 1976. In their test of the relationship among reduced severity of illegal conduct, delayed re-involvement and enhanced self-image of juvenile probationers, the authors conclude there is a greater positive effect on juveniles when they are matched with appropriate probation officers.

1760 Baron, Stephen W. & Hartnagel, Timothy F. Lock 'Em Up': Attitudes Toward Punishing Juvenile Offenders, *Canadian Journal Of Criminology* 38:191-212, 1996. This study of punitiveness toward young offenders found a high degree of support for measures such as curfew for those below 16, waiver to adult court after the first offense, and feelings that the youth court was too lenient.

1761 Bayles, J. A. & Maurice, A. The Juvenile Services Project: An Experiment In Delinquency Control, *Canadian Journal Of Criminology* 21:155-165, 1979. This article provides a description of the juvenile intervention strategy of an Ottawa experimental project, its purpose, objectives, and target groups.

1762 Beaulieu, Lucien A. & Cesaroni, Carla The Changing Role Of The Youth Court Judge, *European Journal On Criminal Policy And Research*

7:363-393, 1999. Mainly focusing on Canada as an example, the emerging and evolving role and status of youth-court judge, the role's uniqueness and future are discussed in this article.

1763 Beaulieu, Lucien A. Youth Offences - Adult Consequences, *Canadian Journal Of Criminology* 36:329-341, 1994. The author discusses the applications of the Young Offenders Act in transfers of minors to adult court.

1764 Beaulieu, Lucien Community Service In Canada (Le Travail Au Profit De La Communauté Au Canada), pp 185-192 Dünkel, Frieder & Zermatten, Jean (eds.) *Recent Trends In Penal Law For Minors: Mediation, Community Service And Intermediate Treatment (Nouvelles Tendances Dans Le Droit Pénal Des Mineurs: Médiation, Travail Au Profit De La Communauté Et Traitement Intermédiaire).* Freiburg, Germany: Max Planck Institute for Foreign and International Criminal Justice, 1990. This chapter surveys community service programs for delinquent youths in Canada.

1765 Beaulieu, Lucien A. (ed.) *Young Offender Dispositions: Perspectives On Principles And Practice.* Toronto, Canada: Wall & Thompson, 1989. The chapters in this anthology address various aspects of the Canadian Young Offenders Act of 1984. 225p.

1766 Beaumont, Hélène & LeBlanc, Marc The Decisions Of An Urban Juvenile Court (Les Décisions De Juges D'un Tribunal De La Jeuness En Milieu Urbain), *Canadian Journal Of Criminology* 29:153-170, 1987. In this case study of male delinquents in Montreal, the authors found that the severity of the offense determined the harshness of the sentence.

1767 Beckett, Elizabeth *Vicarious Liability Of Parents For Actions Of Their Children Who Are Found To Be Delinquent.* Ottawa, Canada: Ministry of the Solicitor General of Canada, 1985. This policy paper discusses parental liability for delinquent children under Section 22 of the 1908 Canadian Juvenile Delinquents Act. 79p.

1768 Besta, Randall W. & Wintemute, Paul J. Young Offenders In Adult Court: Are We Moving In The Right Direction? *Criminal Law Quarterly* 30:476-491, 1988. The authors examine the issues involved in transferring juvenile offenders to adult court under Canada's Young Offenders Act of 1984 and related case law.

1769 Biron, Louise L. & Trépanier, Jean Justice For Minors (La Justice Des Mineurs), pp 183-220 in Szabo, Denis & LeBlanc, Marc (eds.) *Treatise On Empirical Criminology 2nd. Ed. (Traité De Criminologie Empirique 2nd Ed.).* Montreal, Canada: University of Montreal Presses, 1994. Deals with juvenile judicial practices in Quebec such as sanctions for minors and pre-trial decisions to prosecute, the protection of minors' rights and right to legal representation, and the goal of the juvenile court.

1770 Borgo, Joe Treating The Violent Juvenile Offender, pp 298-304 in MacLatchie, James M. (eds.) *Insights Into Violence In Contemporary Canadian Society.* Ottawa, Canada: John Howard Society, 1987. The author describes Shawbridge Treatment Centre near Montreal for emotionally disturbed youths and delinquent children.

1771 Boyd, Neil The Circularity Of Punishment And Treatment: Some Notes On The Legal Response To Juvenile Delinquency, *Canadian Journal Of Family Law* 3:419-438, 1980. In this article the author argues that juvenile delinquency is a social construct reflecting the relationship between state and its citizens.

1772 Byles, John A. Evaluation Of An Attendance Centre Program For Male Juvenile Probationers, *Canadian Journal Of Criminology* 23:343-355, 1981. This evaluation of the Hamilton, Ontario Attendance Centre concludes that the center was unsuccessful in reducing the delinquent behavior of its graduates to a significantly lower rate than that of a comparison group.

1773 Byles, John A. The Arrell Home: Detention For Juveniles, *Canadian Journal Of Criminology And Corrections* 17:69-77, 1975. Describes the Ontario Home For Children, and where the wards come from, the type of admissions, ages and length of stay, recidivism and where they go from there.

1774 Caldwell, E. Dianne & Erickson, Patricia G. Drugs As A Factor In Delinquency Proceedings, *Crime et/and Justice Ottawa* 5:118-125, 1977. The authors report that alcohol and other drugs do not present grave problems in the Ontario juvenile court system, but question the low incidence of such charges given the extent of illicit substance use by juveniles.

1775 Canada Centre For Justice Statistics *Juvenile Delinquents.* Ottawa, Canada. Statistics Canada, 1982. Age limits, the number of juvenile cases processed by the courts, the sentences, and gender of the prosecuted juveniles are presented in this document. 77p.

1776 Canada Federal Provincial Territorial Task Force On Youth Justice *A Review Of The Young Offenders Act And The Youth Justice System In Canada.* Ottawa, Canada, 1996. This report reviews the Young Offenders Act of 1994 in light of various published research, case law, and statistics, as well as relevant practices in other countries and the

United Nations standards. 651p.

1777 Canada Solicitor General *The Young Offenders Act,1982: Highlights*. Ottawa, Canada: Minister of Supply and Services Canada, 1982. This document describes the Canadian Young Offenders Act of 1982. 25p.

1778 Canada Solicitor General *Highlights of Federal Initiatives In Criminal Justice: 1966-1980*. Ottawa, Canada: Minister of Supply and Services, 1981. In Section C, this compendium of major developments in Canadian criminal justice includes juvenile delinquency and justice, and the proposed Young Offenders Act. 78p.

1779 Canada Solicitor General *The Young Offenders Act: Highlights*. Ottawa, Canada: 1981. This is a summary of the changes to the juvenile law in Canada under the proposed Young Offenders Act. 19p.

1780 Canada Solicitor General *Legislative Proposals To Replace The Juvenile Delinquents Act*. Ottawa, Canada: Canada Solicitor General, 1979. This document presents the philosophical, practical and legal arguments that form the basis of the new Young Offenders Act. 16p.

1781 Canada Solicitor General *Community Kit For The Development Of A Juvenile Diversion Project*. Ottawa, Canada: 1979. This "community kit" includes an inventory of diversion projects in Canada, short bibliography as well as issues in and planning for, developing and monitoring juvenile diversion projects. 56 p.

1782 Canada Solicitor General *Highlights Of The Proposed New Legislation For Young Offenders*. Ottawa, Canada: Supply and Services Canada, 1977. This document describes the proposed Young Offenders Act in Canada. 38 p.

1783 Canada Solicitor General Committee On Proposals For New Legislation To Replace The Juvenile Delinquents Act *Young Persons In Conflict With The Law*. Ottawa, Canada, 1975. The various recommendations regarding the new young offenders legislation are set forth in this document. 104p.

1784 Canada Solicitor General Information Systems And Statistics Division *Statistics Handbook 1977*. Ottawa, Canada, 1978. This is a statistical compilation of Canadian juvenile and adult crimes with details on drug offenses and convictions, and penitentiary statistics. 143p.

1785 Canada Statistics *Murder Statistics 1975*. Ottawa, Canada: Minister of Supply and Services, 1976. Theses statistics reveal that the number of homicide cases in Canada that involve juveniles is small. 38p.

1786 Canadian Association Of Elizabeth Fry Societies *Response To Fraser Report On Prostitution*. Ottawa, Canada, 1986. This is a critique of the Fraser Report on pornography and prostitution in Canada and includes some information on juveniles. 50p.

1787 Caplan, Aron Recent Research On Sanctions For Juveniles, pp 52-61 in Canada Solicitor General (ed.) *Criminal Justice Research - A Selective Review*. Ottawa, Canada: Minister of Supply and Services, 1981. This paper is on research evidence on the relative effectiveness of sanctions such as diversion, probation, restitution and custody as far as reducing rates of delinquency are concerned.

1788 Caputo, T.; Weiler, R. & Kelly, K. *Phase II Of The Runaways And Street Youth Project: The Ottawa Case Study*. Ottawa, Canada: Policing Division, Solicitor General Canada, 1994. This study examines the responses of Ottawa-based programs for at-risk juveniles, such as run-aways and street youths. 112p.

1789 Caputo, Tullio; Ryan, Colleen & Proulx, Diane *Children And Youth At Risk: A Working Bibliography*. Ottawa, Canada: Ministry of the Solicitor General, 1991. This review of the criminal justice literature and juvenile justice system in Canada provides a discussion of the issue of "youth at-risk," the types of "risks" young people face as victims of harm as well as from their involvement in risky or dangerous activities. 80p.

1790 Carrier, Suzanne; Fortin, Daniel & Paquet, Danielle Measuring The Effects Of Community Service Among Juvenile Delinquents (Mésure De Résultats Des Travaux Communitaires Chez Les Jeunes Contravenants), *Criminologie* 31:111-132, 1998. This evaluation using psychometric measures and variables in community service program for 12-17 year olds in Quebec as their impact on reducing rates of offense behavior. French with English summary.

1791 Carrington, Peter J. Changes In Police Charging Of Young Offenders In Ontario And Saskatchewan After 1984, *Canadian Journal Of Criminology* 40:153-164, 1998. This is a study of the reduced diversion of young offenders and an increase in the proportion of juveniles who were charged during the first 5 years of Young offenders Act.

1792 Carrington, Peter J. *Factors Affecting Police Diversion Of Young Offenders: A Statistical Analysis*. Ottawa: Solicitor General of Canada, 1998. The author found that in five Canadian provinces the likelihood of being charged rather than being given pre-charge diversion depended on older age, Aboriginal status, alcohol/drug consumption, type of incident, presence of a weapon, the value of stolen property, and the seriousness of the violation. 64p.

1793 Carrington, Peter J. & Moyer, Sharon Factors Affecting Custodial Dispositions Under The Young Offenders Act, *Canadian Journal Of Criminology* 37:127-162, 1995. In this research examining the Canadian Young Offenders Act, the authors conclude that any increase in custodial dispositions under the Young Offenders Act stems from its offense orientation.

1794 Carrington, Peter J. & Moyer, Sharon Inter-Provincial Variations In The Use Of Custody For Young Offenders: A Funnel Analysis, *Canadian Journal Of Criminology* 36:271-290, 1994. The authors examine the controversial "custody" element of the Young Offenders Act to demonstrate how the rates vary by provinces due to the discretionary decisions at each stage of the judicial process.

1795 Carrington, Peter J. & Moyer, Sharon Legal Representation In Canadian Juvenile Courts: Its Nature, Extent, And Determinants, *Canadian Journal Of Criminology* 34:51-74, 1992. This study found that legal criteria were more strongly and consistently influential than extra-legal criteria in determining the presence or type of defense counsel in juvenile court cases.

1796 Carrington, Peter J. & Moyer, Sharon The Effect Of Defense Counsel On Plea And Outcome In Juvenile Court, *Canadian Journal Of Criminology* 32:621-637, 1990. This study of the effects of differential legal representation on juvenile court processing found that the majority of juveniles had some kind of legal representation at some point in the court process, and that those with legal representation generally had lower rates of conviction.

1797 Carrington, Peter J.; Moyer, Sharon & Kopelman, Faigie Factors Affecting Pre-Dispositional Detention And Release In Canadian Juvenile Courts, *Journal Of Criminal Justice* 16:463-476, 1988. Observational and data collected by the National Study on the Functioning of the Juvenile Court in five large Canadian cities from 1981 to 1982 were employed to analyze the factors that affect detention at arrest and judicial interim release.

1798 Catton, Katherine Children In The Courts: A Selected Empirical Review, *Canadian Journal Of Family Law* 1:329-362, 1978. This review focuses on the need to document and understand what actually happens as children are processed through Canada's courts.

1799 Catton, Katherine Models Of Procedure And The Juvenile Courts, *Criminal Law Quarterly* 18:181-201, 1976. The three models for the analysis of the criminal process "crime control", “due process," and "family" are applied to the administration of justice in Canadian juvenile courts.

1800 Catton, Katherine & Erickson Patricia *The Juvenile's Perception Of The Role Of Defense Counsel In Juvenile Court: A Pilot Study*. Toronto, Canada University of Toronto Centre of Criminology, 1975. A sample of juveniles processed through two family courts in Toronto were interviewed to elicit their opinions of the legal defense counsel assigned to them. 25p.

1801 Center For Justice Statistics *The Prevention Of Crime And The Treatment OF Offenders: A Sourcebook Of Canadian Experiences*. Ottawa, Canada: Canada Statistics, 1990. Canadian experiences in crime and criminal justice, including juvenile delinquency prevention and corrections, are discussed within the framework of United Nations norms and guidelines. 73p.

1802 Chase, John; Hirsch, Pam; Arnold, Bruce & Hudson, Joe *A Review Of "S.H.O.P.": The Serious Habitual Offender Program Of The Calgary Police Service*. Ottawa, Canada: Solicitor General of Canada, 1993. This is an evaluation report of the Calgary police department's serious habitual offender program. 32p.

1803 Chisolm, Barabara A. Canada, pp 1-20 in Stewart, V. Lorne (ed.) *The Changing Faces Of Juvenile Justice*. New York, New York: New York University Press, 1978. This article on juvenile justice in Canada addresses issues of when childhood ends and self- determination begins, the rights of children and youths, native children and children in trouble with the law.

1804 Church Council On Justice And Corrections *Watching Youth In Court: An Invitation To Community Involvement Under The Young Offenders Act*. Ottawa, Canada: Church Council on Justice and Corrections, 1987. This is a manual to help those monitoring the processing of young offenders in Canada under the Young Offenders Act. 32p.

1805 Clark, Barry M. & O’Reilly- Fleming, Thomas Implementing The Young Offenders Act In Ontario: Issues Of Principles, Programmes And Power, *Howard Journal* 32:114-135, 1993. The authors argue that the original principles and programs were sidelined in the legislation, and recommend agencies coordinate their approaches to juvenile corrections.

1806 Coates, Robert B. Victim-Offender Reconciliation Programs In North America: An Assessment, pp 125-134 in Galaway, Burt & Hudson, Joe (eds.) *Criminal Justice, Restitution, And Reconciliation*. Monsey, New York: Criminal Justice Press, 1990. This review of victim-offender reconciliation programs, from their origins to contemporary practice, indicates that a majority of such resolutions involve juveniles.

1807 Commission On Systemic Racism In The Ontario Criminal Justice System *Report Of The Commission On Systematic Racism In The Ontario Criminal Justice System: A Community Summary*. Ontario, Canada: Commission on Systemic Racism in the Ontario Criminal Justice System, 1995. This research has a flow-chart of the Canadian criminal justice system, and deals with racism in general, and towards male youths and blacks in Ontario criminal courts. 115p.

1808 Connell, Anne & Farrington, David P. The Reliability And Validity Of Resident, Staff And Peer Reports Of Bullying In Young Offender Institutions, *Psychology Crime And Law* 3:287-300, 1997. This study comparing residents' self- report along with peer and staff reports of bullying and victimization among young males in an open facility and a secure facility in eastern Ontario, found that residents' report higher bullying and victimization rates than either peer or staff.

1809 Corrado, Raymond R.; Odgers, Candice & Cohen, Irwin M. The Incarceration Of Female Young Offenders: Protection For Whom? *Canadian Journal Of Criminology* 42:189-207, 2000. This report on serious young female offenders concludes that, although there were instances of violence, a majority were in custody for minor offenses.

1810 Corrado, Raymond R. & Markwart, Alan Canada, pp 34-56 in Shoemaker, Donald J. (ed.) *International Handbook On Juvenile Justice*. Westport, Connecticut: Greenwood, 1996. This chapter offers an extensive discussion of the juvenile justice system of Canada.

1811 Corrado, Raymond R. & Markwart, Alan The Need To Reform The YOA In Response To Violent Young Offenders: Confusion, Reality Or Myth? *Canadian Journal Of Criminology* 36:343-378, 1994. This review of the Young Offenders Act criticizes several of its provisions from a public and law-enforcement, and suggests modifications to remedy its shortcomings.

1812 Corrado, Raymond R.; Bala, Nicholas & Linden, Rick (eds.) *Juvenile Justice In Canada: A Theoretical And Analytical Assessment*. Ontario, Canada: Butterworths, 1992. Most of the eight articles in this anthology address the Young Offenders Act focusing on its evolution, sanctions, the rights of children's rights under it, and the theoretical and analytical aspects of juvenile justice in Canada. 391p.

1813 Corrado, Raymond R.; LeBlanc, Marc & Trépanier, Jean (eds.) *Current Issues In Juvenile Justice.* Toronto, Canada: Butterworths, 1983. Most of the 19 articles in this anthology are on Canada and are organized under four sections: Delinquency Some Aspects, Some Comparative Perspectives on Shifting Orientations, Intake and Diversion; and Dispositions Decisions and Programs for Young Offenders. 386p.

1814 Corrado, Raymond R. Using Experiments In Evaluating Delinquency Prevention, pp 17-28 in Roesch, Ronald & Corrado, Raymond R. (eds.) *Evaluation And Criminal Justice Policy.* Beverly Hills, California: Sage, 1981. In this article the author argues against the use of experiments in juvenile delinquency prevention programs.

1815 Creechan, James H. & Silverman, Robert A. *Canadian Delinquency.* Scarborough, Canada: Prentice Hall, 1995. This anthology has 36 chapters addressing: youth, adolescence and the invention of delinquency; the emergence of Canadian juvenile justice; the extent and nature of juvenile delinquency; and various theoretical approaches, delinquency research in Canada, and the police, courts, programs and policies. 530p.

1816 Csapo, Marg & Clarke, Bryan Probation Officers For Juveniles In Canada, *Canadian Journal Of Criminology And Corrections* 18:290-301, 1976. This report is based on a survey of vital statistics on Canadian probation officers and their opinions on their training, work conditions, procedures, and civil rights of juveniles facing the court.

1817 Csapo, Marg & Agg, Bernie Educational Rehabilitation Of Delinquents In A Community Setting, *Canadian Journal Of Criminology And Corrections* 18:42-48, 1976. When a highly structured school situation was created within the community where "hard core" delinquent youths received consistent, positive, feedback for appropriate academic and social responses using a token economy system, the frequency of inappropriate social behaviors were reduced while socially acceptable behaviors increased, and pupils reported growth in all three academic categories.

1818 Cuddington, Lynn Young Offenders: A Correctional Policy Perspective, *Forum On Corrections Research* 7:43-45, 1995. This article describes the impact of the Young Offender Act on the correctional system, including discussion on transfers to adult courts, increased length of sentences for murder, and increased access to the minor's records.

1819 Cusson, Maurice Criminological Theories And Penal Politics For Minors (Théories Criminologiques Et Politiques Pénales Des Mineurs), pp 81-92 in Junger-Tas, Josine; Boendermaker, Leonieke & Van Der Laan, Peter H. (eds.) *The Future Of The Juvenile Justice System (L'Avenir Du Système Pénal Des Mineurs)*. Leuven, Belgium: Acco, 1991. This chapter summarizes various criminological theories, and discusses their relationship to correctional policies for juveniles. French.

1820 Cusson, Maurice & Laberge-Altmejd, Danielle The Exercise Of Power In Institutions (L'Exercise Du Pouvoir En Institution), *Crime Et/And Justice* 4:238-254, 1977. The authors address the theoretical issues in the exercize of power in juvenile and adult institutions, by whom and for what ends, and discuss obedience, the use of authority, and the legitimacy of the use of power in correctional institutions. French with English summary.

1821 Cusson, Maurice Observation Of The Behavior Of Juveniles In Institutions (L'Observation Du Comportement Des Jeunes En Institution), *Criminologie* 8:119-144, 1975. This article describes a "classification" instrument (OCJI) for treatment developed in Quebec to analyze students' behavior in juvenile correctional institutions.

1822 Dandurand, Yvon Training School Wards Running Away From After-Care Placement, *Canadian Journal Of Criminology And Corrections* 17:292-306, 1975. Data on Quebec runaways from after-care in Metropolitan Toronto, Ontario Training Schools for wards suggest that more than 56 per cent of the runaways were not successfully reintegrated.

1823 Day, David M. Risk For Court Contact And Predictors Of An Early Age For A First Court Contact Among A Sample Of High Risk Youths: A Survival Analysis Approach, *Canadian Journal Of Criminology* 40:421-446, 1998. This long-term follow-up study investigated the court contact and criminal behavior of high-risk Canadian youths admitted into a children's mental health center between the ages of 6 and 12.

1824 Decision Dynamics Corporation *Family And Juvenile Courts: Edmonton Report*. Edmonton, Canada, 1977. This is a description of the family and juvenile court system in Edmonton, Canada and a discussion of the problems within the court environment. 301p.

1825 Dell, Colleen Anne Young Offender Legislation In Canada, *Forum on Corrections Research* 11:47-50, 1999. The author summarizes the proposed Canadian legislation referred to as Youth Criminal Justice Act with descriptions of its predecessor, the Young Offenders Act.

1826 Dezwirek, Louise Sas; Wolfe, David A. & Gowdey, Kevin Children And Courts In Canada, pp 77-95 in Bottoms, Bette L. & Goodman, Gail S. (eds.) *International Perspectives On Child Abuse And Children's Testimony: Psychological Research And Law*. Thousand Oaks, California: Sage, 1996. This chapter describes and assesses changes in Canadian law regarding testimony of children in sex abuse cases.

1827 Doherty, Glen & De Souza, Paul Youth Crime, pp 231-250 in Kennedy, Leslie & Sacco, Vincent F. (eds.) *Crime Counts: A Criminal Event Analysis*. Toronto, Canada: Nelson, 1996. This chapter covers the Young Offenders Act, its precursors, profiles of young male and female offenders, youth violence, youth court case loads, sentences, custodial dispositions, probation, and hard-core delinquents with tables, graphs, and charts of Canadian data.

1828 Doob, Anthony N. Youth Justice Research In Canada: An Assessment, *Canadian Journal Of Criminology* 41:217-224, 1999. The author reviews the Canadian Centre for Justice Statistics data, gaps in court data, and describes the youth justice system, research on juveniles and justice.

1829 Doob, Anthony N. & Sprott, Jane B. Interprovincial Variation In The Use Of The Youth Courts, *Canadian Journal Of Criminology* 38:401-412, 1996. Data collected from five provinces demonstrate that there were great inter-provincial differences in the use of custodial sentences.

1830 Doob, Anthony N.; Marinos, Voula & Varma, Kimberly *Youth Crime And The Youth Justice System In Canada: A Research Perspective*. Ottawa, Canada: Department of Justice Canada, Research, Statistics and Evaluation, 1995. This is a summary of the literature on youth crime and the operation of the justice system for Canadian youth. 144p.

1831 Doob, Anthony N. & Meen, Jennifer M. An Exploration Of Changes In Dispositions For Young Offenders In Toronto, *Canadian Journal Of Criminology* 35:19-30, 1993. The authors investigated the effects of Canada's Young Offenders Act and Juvenile Delinquents Act on the case processing of delinquent minors under age 16 and found that, depending on the time periods, the characteristics of the cases that arrive at the court differed.

1832 Doob, Anthony N. & Beaulieu, Lucien A. Variation In The Exercise Of Judicial Discretion With Young Offenders, *Canadian Journal Of Criminology* 34:35-50, 1992. The authors found a good deal of variability in juvenile court dispositions, although the judges appeared to have been thoughtful and principled in arriving at recommendations.

1833 Doob, Anthony N. Trends In The Use Of Custodial Dispositions For Young Offenders, *Canadian Journal Of Criminology* 34:75-84, 1992. When the use of custodial dispositions for juveniles in six Canadian provinces is examined, the proportion of such sanctions increased dramatically for the first five years following the Young Offenders Act.

1834 Doob, Anthony N. & MacFarlane, P. Dianne *The Community Service Order For Youthful Offenders: Perceptions And Effects*. Toronto, Canada: Centre for Criminology, University of Toronto, 1984. This evaluation of the Community Service Order program in Durham Region, Ontario shows that both those with service orders and their parents were quite favorable towards the experience and express feelings of accomplishment or satisfaction at having finished their sentences. 85p.

1835 Doob, Anthony N. & Chan, Janet B. Factors Affecting Police Decisions To Take Juveniles To Court, *Canadian Journal Of Criminology* 24:25-37, 1982. When data on Ontario police decisions to prosecute juveniles were examined to determine the factors that affect them, it appeared that the police make use of certain legal criteria, along with some situational and historical contexts in assessing each juvenile.

1836 Douglas, Jackie *Juvenile Crime Prevention Programs In British Columbia*. Vancouver, Canada: Research and Evaluation, Policy and Planning Branch, Ministry of Attorney General, 1982. This is an inventory of various programs to prevent delinquency in British Columbia. 120p.

1837 Dowden, Craig & Andrews, D. A. What Works In Young Offender Treatment: A Meta Analysis, *Forum On Corrections Research* 11:21-24, 1999. This article based on meta-analysis of various treatments for juvenile delinquents and addresses issues of risk, need and responsiveness.

1838 Dowrich Management Services *Police And Youth "Looking To The Future": Executive Summary Of The Final Report Of Pilot Project Police/Youth Mentoring Program*. Ottawa, Canada: Solicitor General Canada, 1994. This evaluation of the Ontario police/youth mentoring pilot demonstration project discusses the relationships between mentors and protégés including family, community and peer support. 16p. Appendix.

1839 Doyle, Robert & Freedman, Linda A Legacy Of Colonialism And Racism: Aboriginal Injustice In Australia, pp 91-125 in McCormick, Kevin R. E. (ed.) *Carceral Contexts: Readings In Control*. Toronto, Canada: Canadian Scholars' Press, 1994. The implications of the Young Offenders Act for incarceration and the consequences for community programs for juvenile offenders in Ontario are discussed.

1840 Elchardus, Jean Marc The Problems Of Therapeutic Interventions For Specific Categories Of Delinquents (Problèmes Des Interventions Thérapeutiques Auprès De Catégories Spécifiques De Délinquants) *Revue Internationale De Criminologie Et De Police Technique* 47:391-418, 1994. The author reviews the different therapeutic treatment options and the practical, bureaucratic and administrative issues for delinquents who engage in sex, and drug and violence-related problem behavior. French.

1841 Erickson, Patricia Legalities And Traditional Role Expectations For Defense Counsel In Juvenile Court, *Canadian Journal Of Criminology And Corrections* 17:78-93, 1975. This report is based on the feedback from judges and social workers with experience with defense lawyers on the legal and traditional role definitions for private and duty counsel have for juveniles.

1842 Farrington, David P. Implications Of Longitudinal Studies For Social Prevention, *Canadian Journal Of Criminology* 31:453-463, 1989. The author discusses the need for social prevention approach in dealing with juvenile delinquency.

1843 Fleming, Thomas; O'Reilly, Patricia & Clark, Barry *Youth Injustice: Canadian Perspectives 2nd Ed.* Toronto, Canada: Canadian Scholars' Press, 2001. This comprehensive anthology concerns the state of juvenile justice in Canada.

1844 Fletcher, Randall *On Corrections Research* 11:30-33, 1999. This essay describes early intervention programs to deal with sexual delinquency of adolescents.

1845 Fox, Richard G. The Treatment Of Juveniles In Canadian Criminal Law, pp 149-185 in Doob, Anthony & Greenspan, Edward L. (eds.) *Perspectives In Criminal Law.* Aurora, Canada: Canada Law Book, 1985. Provides an overview of Canadian criminal law, concept of *parens patriae*, due process, the Juvenile Delinquency Act, and the Young Offenders Act.

1846 Gandy, John M. Parents' Perceptions Of The Effect Of Volunteer Probation Officers On Juvenile Probationers, *Canadian Journal Of Criminology* 17:5-19, 1975. This is an empirical study of male and female parents' positive perceptions of volunteer probation officers.

1847 Gatti, Uberto Ethical Issues Raised When Early Intervention Is Used To Prevent Crime, *European Journal On Criminal Policy And Research*

6:113-132, 1998. The author raises questions about the early medical and psychiatric programs for delinquency prevention, and the effect of such labeling and the undesired effects of intervention, risks of predicting delinquency, issues of consent, welfare and justice.

1848 Gordon, Robert M. & Nelson, Jacquelyn *The Report Of The 1993 Census Of Provincial Correctional Centres In British Columbia*. Ottawa, Canada: Department of Justice, Research and Statistics Directorate, 1994. This report presents an ethno-cultural profile of a census of all persons incarcerated in British Columbian adult prisons and youth detention centers, and any problems that emerge due to ethnicity. 72p. Appendix.

1849 Greco, J. D. Bail And The Juvenile, *Criminal Law Quarterly* 20:180-184, 1978. This is a short description of the law of bail in Canada as it pertains to juveniles, and the juvenile court's exclusive jurisdiction in this matter.

1850 Griffiths, Curt Taylor Police School Programs: The Realities Of The Remedy, *Canadian Journal Of Criminology* 24:329-340, 1982. This is a description and critique of the school-based police initiative designed to reduce delinquency through positively affecting the perceptions juveniles have of the police.

1851 Hackler, James C. *Crime And Canadian Public Policy*. Scarborough, Canada: Prentice Hall, 1994. Chapter 11 includes a discussion of the relationship between family, friends, school and delinquency while chapter 20 includes youth courts and increasing crime. 397p.

1852 Hackler, Jim *Nail Pounders And Other Builders Of Social Control Houses*. Edmonton, Canada: University of Alberta, 1992. This is a critique of Canadian attempts to imitate American crime control and includes a discussion of the issues of juveniles and the Young Offender Act. 20p.

1853 Hackler, James & Don, Kim Screening Juveniles And The Central City Phenomenon: Using Official Statistics To Understand The Dynamics Of Police Systems, *Canadian Police College Journal* 13:1-17, 1989. British Columbia's police data show that while cities surrounded by suburbs were attractive areas for theft and other criminal activity, police forces in suburban areas had lower crime rates than downtown areas where the police were in a better position to develop strategies to screen juveniles.

1854 Hackler, Jim The Impact Of The Young Offenders Act, *Canadian Journal Of Criminology* 29:205-209, 1987. The author critiques the

Young Offenders Act focusing on the impact the law has on how juveniles are teated by Canadian courts.

1855 Hackler, James C. Juvenile Justice In Canada: Comparisons With Other Systems, pp 503-525 in Kerner, Hans-Jürgen; Galaway, Burt & Janssen, Helmut (eds.) *European And North American Juvenile Justice Systems: Aspects And Tendencies (Jugendgerischtsbarkeit In Europa Und Nordamerika: Aspekte Und Tendenzen)*. Munich, West Germany: Schriftenreihe den Deutschen Vereinigung für Jugendgerichte und Jugendgerichtshilfen, 1986. This chapter summarizes research on Canadian juvenile justice, the Young Offenders Act of 1984, the various issues of legal rights and defense for juveniles, provincial differences in juvenile judicial practices etc.

1856 Hackler, James C. Canada, pp 39-70 in Klein, Malcolm W. (ed.) *Western Systems of Juvenile Justice.* Beverly Hills, California: Sage, 1984. This chapter has an overview of the Canadian juvenile justice system, a chart of its structure, and description of the flow of cases through the court from intake to dispositions, and a discussion of public reaction to juvenile theft, issues such as age limits and use of discretion.

1857 Hackler, Jim & Paranjape, Wasanthi Analyzing Juvenile Justice Statistics In Metropolitan Areas, *Canadian Journal Of Criminology* 25:447-462, 1983. This analysis of Ontario and other metropolitan official data points out the disparities and local variations in juvenile justice statistics across Canada.

1858 Hackler, Jim Juvenile Court Statistics In Three Prairie Provinces (1977), *Canadian Journal Of Criminology* 22:476-482, 1980. Based on his analysis of 1979 juvenile court statistics for Alberta, Manitoba, and Saskatchewan provinces, the author concludes that patterns of juvenile delinquency in the three prairie provinces were similar, but the procedures involving juveniles and administration of justice varied.

1859 Hackler, James C. *The Prevention Of Youthful Crime: The Great Stumble Forward.* Toronto: Methuen Publications, 1978. This volume is a critique of policy and the operation of delinquency prevention programs in Canada revealing the inherent difficulties in traditional evaluation design and recommends alternatives. 252p.

1860 Hagan, John & Collins, Alixe A. The Escalation Of Evil: A Study In The Behavior Of Juvenile Law, *Osgoode Hall Law Journal* 16:649-661, 1978. Studying the evidence from Toronto juvenile courts, the authors' argue that decision making in the juvenile court in Canada is based on a set of common "cues" of the moral and legal status of the adolescent that promote a punitive judicial response to their behavior.

1861 Hatch, Alison & Griffiths, Curt T. Youth Crime In Canada: Observations For Cross-Cultural Analysis, *International Journal of Comparative and Applied Criminal Justice*, 16: 165-183, 1992. In comparing the lower juvenile delinquency rates of Canada versus the United Sates, the authors discuss the issues of ethnic gangs and Aboriginal overrepresentation.

1862 Havemann, Paul *Team Work: Saskatoon's Unified Family Court: Final Report Of The Saskatoon Unified Family Court Evaluation 1978 – 1981.* Saskatchewan, Canada: Prairie Justice Research Consortium, School of Human Justice, University of Regina, 1982. This evaluation suggests that a unified family court in Saskatoon will eliminate the problems of fragmented jurisdictions and the adversarial mode of resolution of conflicts involving juveniles. 250 p.

1863 Hiew, Chok C. Prevention Of Shoplifting: A Community Action Approach, *Canadian Journal Of Criminology* 23:57-68, 1981. A community-based prevention program in the Maritime Provinces attempted to increase the collaboration of community members, professionals, students, and the researchers in curbing shoplifting incidents.

1864 Hodgson, Maggie & Heckbert, Doug *Healing, Spirit And Recovery: Factors Associated With Successful Integration.* Ottawa, Canada: Solicitor General of Canada, 1995. This book is based on unstructured interviews of Aboriginal ex-offenders' recollections of their early years of growing up, getting into trouble, getting out of it, and staying out of trouble. 94p.

1865 Hoge, Robert D. An Expanded Role For Psychological Assessments In Juvenile Justice Systems, *Criminal Justice And Behavior* 26:251-266, 1999. In this essay, the author provides arguments in favor of systematic use of standardized psychological assessments in the juvenile justice and corrections systems.

1866 Hoge, Robert D. & Andrews, D. A. *Assessing The Youthful Offender.* New York, New York: Plenum: Forensic Psychiatry and Psychology Library, 1996. This is a manual on psychological assessment of juveniles in the judicial-correctional system. 139p.

1867 Hornick, Joseph P.; Caputo. Tullio & Hastings, Ross *A Police Reference Manual On Crime Prevention And Diversion With Youth.* Ottawa, Canada: Solicitor General Canada, 1996. This "how-to" manual is for Canadian front-line police officers and senior police managers on how to take a proactive approaches to juvenile crime prevention and various responses to use in dealing with youth crime. 131p. Appendix.

1868 Hornick, Joseph P. & Bolitho, Floyd A *Review Of The Implementation Of The Child Sexual Abuse Legislation In Selected Sites*. Ottawa, Canada: Research Section, Canada Department of Justice, 1992. The findings of studies conducted from 1988 to 1990 in Alberta, Saskatchewan and Ontario to assess the extent to which various components of Bill C-15 (An Act to Amend the Criminal Code and the Canada Evidence Act) have been implemented are summarized and analyzed. 150p

1869 Hudson, Joe; Hornick, Joseph P. & Burrows, Barbara A. (eds.) *Justice And The Young Offender In Canada*. Toronto,Canada: Wall and Thompson, 1988. This edited volume has 12 articles covering a comprehensive spectrum of the conception, implementation, relevant issues and current status of the Canadian Young Offenders Act. 190p.

1870 Hylton, John H. Get Tough Or Get Smart? Options For Canada's Youth Justice System In The Twenty-First Century, *Canadian Journal Of Criminology* 36:229-246, 1994. The author discusses the Canadian juvenile justice system and the various issues related to the Young Offenders Act since its enactment a decade earlier.

1871 Jaccoud, Mylène Restoring Justice In Native Communities In Canada, pp 285-300 in Walgrave, Lode (ed.) *Restorative Justice For Juveniles: Potentialities, Risks And Problems*. Leuven: Leuven University Press, 1998. This chapter discusses contemporary restorative justice programs in native communities of Canada with special focus on the Community Holistic Circle Healing of Hollow Water.

1872 Jack, Lindsay A. & Ogloff, James R. P. Factors Affecting The Referral Of Young Offenders For Medical And Psychological Assessment Under The Young Offenders Act, *Canadian Journal Of Criminology* 39:247-273, 1997. This report based on Vancouver Youth Court records of adjudicated youths found that those youths referred for assessment were younger, white, had multiple offenses and substantial behavioral and psychological problems, and were perceived to be at high-risk compared with their non-referred counterparts.

1873 Joyal, Renée Returning Adolescents To Regular Jurisdiction: Recent Development In Quebec (Le Renvoi De L'Adolescent À La Juridiction Normalement Compétente: Évolution Récente Au Québec), pp 211-221 in Junger-Tas, Josine; Boendermaker, Leonieke & Van Der Laan, Peter H. (eds.) *The Future Of The Juvenile Justice System (L'Avenir Du Système Pénal Des Mineur)*. Leuven, Belgium: Acco, 1991. This chapter discusses recent Quebec laws concerning the treatment of juveniles in regular (adult) courts instead of through re-education. French.

1874 Jung, Sandy & Rawana, Edward P. Risk And Need Assessment Of Juvenile Offenders, *Criminal Justice And Behavior* 26:69-89, 1999. From an evaluation in a medium-sized Canadian city, this research concluded that the Ministry Risk/Need Assessment Form is adequate in delineating recidivist juveniles from non-recidivists.

1875 Kaill, Robert C. (eds.) *Record Of Proceedings: Implementing The Young Offenders Act In Atlantic Canada*. Halifax, Canada: Atlantic Institute of Criminology, 1982. Conference discussions on the effects, status offenses, policing and correction in the context of the Young Offenders Act are presented in this volume. 152p. Appendix.

1876 Kennedy, Leslie & Sacco, Vincent F. (eds.) *Crime Counts: A Criminal Event Analysis*. Toronto, Canada: Nelson, 1996. This anthology incorporates juvenile delinquency throughout in discussions of homicide, robbery, assault, etc. 321p.

1877 Kirvan, Mary-Anne The Canadian legislative Response To Adolescents Who Kill, pp 178-203 in Cavadino, Paul (ed.) *Children Who Kill*. Winchester, United Kingdom: Waterside, 1996. Canadian legislation including the Young offenders Act regarding classification, trial and punishment of minors involved in murders is the focus of this paper.

1878 Kirvan, Mary-Anne Canada's Youth Justice System Under Review, *Forum On Corrections Research* 7:41-42, 1995. The author provides a brief summary of the Young Offender Act of 1984, its principles, and provisions for penalties, and transfer to adult court.

1879 Kowalski, Melanie & Caputo, Tullio Recidivism In Youth Court: An Examination Of The Impact Of Age, Gender, And Prior Record, *Canadian Journal Of Criminology* 41:57-84, 1999. The authors conclude that although age, gender, and the seriousness of offense play a role, judges tend to dispense more severe custodial dispositions more often to repeat offenders under Canadian Young Offenders Act.

1880 Kueneman, Rod; Linden, Rick & Kosmick, Rick Juvenile Justice In Rural Northern Manitoba, *Canadian Journal Of Criminology* 34:435-460, 1992. Based on diverse sources, the authors examined differences in case processing-time. as well as social and legal variables, of rural and Manitoba juvenile courts.

1881 Laflamme, Suzanne Cusson; Langelier-Biron, Louise & Trépanier, Jean *Formulation Of The Decision Regarding Young Offenders (La Prise De Décision À L'Égard Des Jeunes Contrevenants)*. Montreal, Canada:

Centre International de Criminologie Comparée, Université de Montréal, 1992. This research of dispositions for young offenders in three areas of Quebec concludes that similar offenses were tried for a longer time in areas with higher crime rates thereby making the case less timely and more complex. 261p. French.

1882 Lajeunesse, Therese *Innovative Approaches To Juvenile Justice: Executive Summaries For Four Juvenile Diversion Project Reports*. Ottawa, Canada: Communication Division, Solicitor General, 1982. This report summarizes four juvenile diversion projects in Canada. 35 p.

1883 Langelier-Biron, Louise Aggression And Delinquency In Adolescence: Similar Or Different Behavior? (Agression Et Délinquance Chez L'Adolescence: Conduites Analogues Ou Différentiale?), *Criminologie* 16:67-76, 1983. This questionnaire study of girls in public schools on attachment to parents, delinquent friends, and punishment emphasized the importance of role integration plays in preventing delinquency. French.

1884 Langley, Michael; Thomas, Brenda J. & Parkinson, Ronald Youths' Expectations And Perceptions Of Their Initial Juvenile Court Appearances, *Canadian Journal Of Criminology* 20:43-53, 1978. When pre- and post-hearing expectations and perceptions of males and females who appeared for the first time in the Family Court of Ottawa were examined, it was clear that most had no clear understanding of the court processes.

1885 Langley, Michael An Alternative Approach To Delinquency Analysis And Management, *Canadian Journal Of Criminology And Corrections* 18:3:204-224, 1976. The author blames ageism and the medical model as the culprits in the stigmatization of delinquent minors as quasi criminals even in the post-1960s and -1970s new developments.

1886 LaPrairie, Carol The 'New' Justice: Some Implications for Aboriginal Communities, *Canadian Journal Of Criminology* 40:61-79, 1998. This is a critical article on the issues in increased use of restorative justice in general, and its positive and negative implications for the Aboriginal communities of Canada.

1887 LaPrairie, Carol Reconstructing Theory: Explaining Aboriginal Over-representations In The Criminal Justice System In Canada, *The Australian And New Zealand Journal Of Criminology* 30:39-54, 1997. The author tries to explain the vulnerability of Aboriginal Canadians due to the processes and mechanisms of social control while having limited access to resources.

1888 LaPrairie, Carol Community Justice Or Just Communities? Aboriginal Communities In Search Of Justice, *Canadian Journal Of Criminology* 37:521-545, 1995. Albeit on the complex issues facing contemporary Aboriginal justice, this article includes juveniles as well.

1889 LaPrairie, Carol Pitcher Native Juveniles In Court: Some Preliminary Observations, pp 337-350 in Fleming, Thomas & Visano, L. A. (eds.) *Deviant Designations: Crime, Law And Deviance In Canada*. Toronto, Canada: Butterworth, 1983. This study of Native and non-Native juvenile delinquents in one northern hinterland in Canada reveals that, although their offenses were no different from the rest of the juvenile population, the clients of juvenile courts were disproportionately Native juveniles, particularly females.

1890 Lavoie, Yves Is Society Ready To Support A New Sanction? (La Société Est-Elle Prête À Considérer La Médiation Comme Une Sanction?), pp 83-94 in Dünkel, Frieder & Zermatten, Jean (eds.) *Recent Trends In Penal Law For Minors: Mediation, Community Service And Intermediate Treatment (Nouvelles Tendances Dans Le Droit Pénal Des Mineurs: Médiation, Travail Au Profit De La Communauté Et Traitement Intermédiaire)*. Freiburg, Germany: Max Planck Institute for Foreign and International Criminal Justice, 1990. This chapter discusses juvenile restitution as a form of sanction in Canadian society. French.

1891 LeBlanc, Marc Consequences Of Research On Maladjusted Adolescents, *Forum On Corrections Research* 11:43-46:1999. This article reviews various research findings on juvenile residential rehabilitation, the diverse commission reports, and media's interpretations.

1892 LeBlanc, Marc Juvenile Justice In Quebec: The Anatomy Of Legislative And Administrative Changes And Their Impact On Dispositions (La Justice Des Mineurs Au Québec: Anatomie Des Changements Législatifs Et Administratifs Et Leurs Impacts En Term D'Efficacité), pp 237-245 in Junger-Tas, Josine; Boendermaker, Leonieke & Van Der Laan, Peter H. (eds.) *The Future Of The Juvenile Justice System (L'Avenir Du Système Pénal Des Mineurs)*. Leuven, Belgium: Acco, 1991. Evaluates the effectiveness of the new diversion programs for juvenile offenders in Quebec. French.

1893 LeBlanc, Marc & Beaumont, Hélène The Effectiveness Of Diversion In Montreal In 1981 (L'Efficacité De La Déjudiciarisation À Montréal En 1981), *Canadian Journal Of Criminology* 33:61-82, 1991. Using court files of boys aged 14 to 18, this evaluation of the effectiveness of alternative diversions found that the diverted and non-diverted youths relapsed at much the same rate and, those who were asked to do reparations had the lowest recidivism rate. French with English summary.

1894 LeBlanc, Marc & Beaumont, Hélène The Effectiveness Of Juvenile Court Sentences In Montreal In 1981 (*L'Efficacité Des Mesures Ordonnées Au Tribunal De La Jeunesse De Montréal En 1981*), *Canadian Journal Of Criminology* 32:607-620, 1990. This study of recidivism following sanctions imposed by the Montreal Youth Court found that those with more severe sentences tend to repeat their offense behavior after 18, and their sentences appear to be the result of certain personal characteristics, and prior criminal and judicial records. French with English summary.

1895 LeBlanc, Marc Armed Robbery By Minors (Le Vol À Main Armée Chez Les Mineurs), *Criminologie* 18:7-34, 1985. The author concludes that the sentence is more reflective of the characteristics and prior record of youth rather than the seriousness of the crime. French with English summary.

1896 LeBlanc, Marc The Police, The Law On Juvenile Delinquents And The Juvenile Justice System (Les Policiers, La Loi Sur Les Jeunes Contrevenants Et Le Systéme De Justice Pour Les Mineurs), *Criminologie* 17:91-115, 1984. Police representatives and diverse personnel in Montreal neighborhoods who deal with minors were surveyed on their perceptions of delinquency, juvenile judicial processes, and evaluation of the services for adolescents in their community. French.

1897 Lee, Naomi Youth Crime Trends In British Columbia, *Forum On Corrections Research* 11:3-6, 1999. The author uses various data ources to address the issue of youth crime trends in one northwest Canadian province.

1898 Lee, Naomi & Leonard, Tim *Serious Violent Offenses And Offenders In Youth Court*. Ottawa, Canada: Canada Department of Justice, 1995. This report has statistical profiles of youths sentenced for various violent offenses under the Young Offenders Act. 63p.

1899 Leeson, Golden & Snyder, Arn Specialized Police Response To The Juvenile: The Ottawa Police Force Youth Liaison Section, pp 197-216 in McGrath, William T. & Mitchell, Michael P. (eds.) *The Police Function In Canada*. Toronto, Canada: Methuen, 1981. The philosophy of the Youth Liaison Section, its structure and position within the police force, selection and training of personnel are described.

1900 Leon, Jeffrey S. The Development Of Canadian Juvenile Justice: A Background For Reform, *Osgoode Hall Law Journal* 15:71-106, 1977. The author provides a history of the origin, philosophy and development of Canadian juvenile delinquency laws and juvenile justice system.

1901 Leschied, Alan W. & Cunningham, Alison A Community-Based Alternative For High-Risk Young Offenders, *Forum On Corrections Research* 11:25-29, 1999. The authors describe community-based alternative sanctions for high-risk juvenile offenders.

1902 Leschied, Alan W. & Cunningham, Alison Alternatives To Custody For High-Risk Young Offenders: The Multisystemic Therapy Approach, *European Journal On Criminal Policy And Research* 6:545-560, 1998. This is a summary of the randomized trials of community-based therapeutic program in Ontario for youth at-risk of custodial sentences due to the severity or persistence of their criminal behavior.

1903 Leschied, Alan W. The Young Offenders Act In Review: A More Than Modest Proposal For Change, *Forum On Corrections Research* 7:1:37-40, 1995. The author discusses the principles such as justice and due process, crime control via deterrence and rehabilitation, and the implications of Young Offenders Act.

1904 Leschied, Alan W. & Gendreau, Paul Doing Justice In Canada, *Canadian Journal Of Criminology* 36:291-303, 1994. This is an analysis of the use of custody and access to treatment under the Young Offenders Act.

1905 Leschied, Alan W.; Jaffe, Peter G. & Willis, Wayne (eds.) *The Young Offenders Act: A Revolution In Canadian Juvenile Justice*. Toronto: University of Toronto Press, 1991. The articles in this anthology deal with the evolution and effects as well as the future of the Canadian Young Offenders Act. 300p.

1906 Leschied, Alan Canadian Juvenile Justice Reform: Is Fair And Equal Always Effective? Pp 83-90 in Hackler, Jim (ed.) *Official Responses To Problem Juveniles: Some International Reflections*. Euskadi, Spain: The Oñati International Institute for the Sociology of Law, 1991. This chapter explores the paradox of the recent Canadian law given the literature favoring rehabilitation of offenders over punishment.

1907 Leschied, Alan W.; Austin, Gary W. & Riley, Eric Description And Assessment Of A Crisis Consultation Program In A Youth Detention Centre, *Canadian Journal Of Criminology* 31:145-154, 1989. Using clinical records, The authors describe the residents of a twenty-bed

Ontario secure detention center for young people.

1908 Leschied, Alan W. & Wilson, Susan Kaye Criminal Liability Of Children Under Twelve: A Problem For Child Welfare, Juvenile Justice Or Both? *Canadian Journal Of Criminology* 30:17-29, 1988. This study of youths in Ontario addresses their delinquency and family difficulties in the context of the Young Offenders Act that raised the age of criminal culpability from 7 to 12.

1909 Leschied, Alan W. & Jaffe, Peter G. Impact Of The Young Offender's Act On Court Dispositions: A Comparative Analysis, *Canadian Journal Of Criminology* 29:421-430, 1987. Based on two studies of court dispositions following the Young Offenders Act, it was concluded that there was an increased use of the custodial disposition reflecting the prevalence of the popular concept of deterrence through punishment. 32p.

1910 Leschied, Alan W. & Gendreau, Paul The Declining Role Of Rehabilitation In Canadian Juvenile Justice: Implications Of Underlying Theory In The Young Offenders Act, *Canadian Journal Of Criminology* 28:315-322, 1986. The authors, in the context of the consent to treatment provision of the Act, advance the argument that the new Young Offender Act is based on an American justice model of deterrence and punishment rather than rehabilitation.

1911 Leschied, Alan W. & Hyatt, Christopher W. Perspective: Section 22(1), Consent to Treatment Under The Young Offenders Act, *Canadian Journal Of Criminology* 28:69-78, 1986. The authors criticize the "consent to treatment" provision of the Young Offenders Act given the capacity to provide consent, the opportunity to consent and the effectiveness of treatment are all limited.

1912 Leschied, Alan W. ; Jaffe, Peter G. & Stone, Gerald L. Differential Response Of Juvenile Offenders To Two Detention Environments As A Function Of Conceptual Level, *Canadian Journal Of Criminology* 27:467-476, 1985. The authors found that male and female juveniles in pre-trial detention react differently to their different facilities, with the younger detainees coping better than the older ones who have problems with the more structured detention home.

1913 Leschied, Alan Treating The Violent Juvenile Offender, pp 288-290 in MacLatchie, James M. (ed.) *Insights Into Violence In Contemporary Canadian Society*. Ottawa, Canada: John Howard Society, 1987. Describes the 1984 Young Offenders Act of Canada, and the increasing rates of committals to training schools compared to the old law.

1914 Long, Carmen A.; Langevin, Chantal M. & Weeks, John R. A Cognitive Behavioral Approach To substance Abuse Treatment, *Corrections Today* 60:102-105, 1998. This is a description of Canadian substance-abuse treatment based on cognitive-behavioral theory.

1915 Longclaws, Lyle; Galaway, Burt & Barkwell, Lawrence Piloting Family Group Conference For Young Aboriginal Offenders In Winnipeg, Canada, pp 195-205 in Hudson, Joe; Morris, Allison; Maxwell, Gabrielle & Galaway, Burt (eds.) *Family Group Conferences: Perspectives On Policy & Practice.* Monsey, New York: Criminal Justice Press and Federation Press, 1996. This is a report on a pilot project for Aboriginal young offenders in Winnipeg.

1916 Lysack, Mishka Narrative Therapy With Incarcerated Teenagers And Their Families, *Forum On Corrections Research* 7:28-303-42, 1995. The author argues in favor of narrative as a therapeutic tool in dealing with young offenders and their families.

1917 MacDonald, John A. Juvenile Training Schools And Juvenile Justice Policy In British Columbia, *Canadian Journal Of Criminology* 20:418-436, 1978. The authors detail the legislative history of the training schools, various commission reports and, changes and their final abolition with descriptions of t types of offenders, intake volume, social class background, etc.

1918 MacLatchie, James M. (ed.) *Insights Into Violence In Contemporary Canadian Society.* Ottawa, Canada: John Howard Society of Canada, 1987. This volume has a section on treating the violent juvenile offender. 360p.

1919 Manfredi, Christopher P. The Young Offenders Act And Juvenile Justice In The United States: Perspectives On Recent Reform Proposals, *Canadian Journal Of Law And Society* 6:45-63, 1991. This essay reviews and evaluates within the perspective of recent American developments in juvenile justice policy, Canadian Young Offenders Act that reduces the disparity and unfairness characteristic of juvenile justice although at the risk of greater criminalization.

1920 Marinos, Voula What's Intermediate About `Intermediate' Sanctions? The Case Of Young Offender Dispositions In Canada, *Canadian Journal Of Criminology* 40:355-375, 1998. This study of dispositions handed down in Canadian youth courts found that the use of short custody sentences increased since passage of the Young Offenders Act and there did not appear to be much that was intermediate about "intermediate" sanctions.

1921 Marshall, Larry; Miller, Nancy; Miller-Hewitt, Sandra; Sudermann, Marlies & Watson, Lynn *Evaluation Of Groups For Children Who Have Witnessed Violence*. London, Canada: Centre for Research on Violence Against Women and Children, 1995. This study evaluates the effectiveness of therapy groups for children who witness violence in their homes. 40p.

1922 Martin, Fay E. & White, Georgina West Indian Adolescent Offenders, *Canadian Journal Of Criminology* 30:367-379, 1988. The experience of the Toronto Family Court Clinic in addressing the needs of West Indian adolescent offenders indicates that they and their families seem to have fewer mental health symptoms than their Canadian counterparts, but whether this difference was real an artifact of reporting was not clear.

1923 Mathews, Frederick *The Badge & The Book: Building Effective Police/School Partnerships To Combat Youth Violence*. Ottawa, Canada: Solicitor General of Canada, 1995. This survey found that the respondents attributed the problem of school violence to factors such as violence in society, the failure of adults to take students' complaints seriously, lack of accountability of perpetrators, the sports mentality, and the absence of boundaries and limits. 58p. Appendix.

1924 McCowan, Joan Impact Of The Young Offenders Act On Dispositions In The Juvenile Justice System Of Canada, *International Journal Of Comparative And Applied Criminal Justice* 14:289-305, 1990. Data on juvenile court dispositions show that, when controlled for age, gender, prior record and offense type, considerable variation is found in, and the severity of dispositions increases under the new law.

1925 McGowan, Patrick An Evaluation Of City Center Youth Resources Forty-Eight Hour Protective Custody Facility, *Canadian Journal Of Criminology And Corrections* 18:225-237, 1976. This article describes the workings of a Vancouver center for crime prevention that actively dealt with the problems by intervention and diversion for those under 17 years of age.

1926 McGuire, Maureen C.19, An Act To Amend The Young Offenders Act And The Criminal Code--Getting Tougher? *Canadian Journal Of Criminology* 39:185-214, 1997. This is a description of the major changes envisioned by the Canadian Parliament in its C.19, An Act to Amend the Young Offenders Act and the Criminal Code.

1927 McLellan, Myles F. The Viking Homes Saga: Group Home Placements For Juveniles, *Canadian Journal of Family Law*1:126-148, 1978. This is a critique of the Ontario Supreme Court ruling on placement of juvenile delinquents in private corporate group homes.

1928 Messier, Camille Adolescent Problem Behavior And Its Treatment In A Reception Center Following A Protective Order (Les Troubles De Comportement À L'Adolescence Et Leur Traitement En Centre D'Accueil De Réadaptation À La Suite D'Une Ordonnance De Protection), *Criminologie* 23:7-39, 1990. This article describes a 1987-88 Quebec study of the treatment of 167 12-17 year olds with serious behavior problems. French with English summary.

1929 Minore, J. B. Not Just "Potato Chips" Thieves, pp 279-297 in Silverman, Robert A. & Nielsen, Marianne O. (eds.) *Aboriginal Peoples And Canadian Criminal Justice.* Toronto, Canada: Butterworths, 1992. The author covers a wide spectrum of topics including native youths in trouble, native youths and Northern courts, law and its cultural dimensions, native peoples' opinion of youthful offenders as a community problem, etc.

1930 Moyer, Sharon *A Profile Of The Juvenile Justice System In Canada.* Toronto, Canada: Moyer & Associates, 1996. This is a report on Youth Justice, with statistical data on juveniles who come into contact with the youth justice system in Canada. 190p.

1931 Moyer, Sharon; Kopelman, Faigie & Carrington, Peter J. *The Relationships Between The Age Of The Accused Young Person And Other Personal And Case Characteristics.* Ottawa, Canada: Ministry of the Solicitor General of Canada, 1985. This is a report on a large-scale research on the relationship among background, offense characteristics and age of accused minors and their use of court resources and alternative sentences. 112p.

1932 Normandeau, André & Ouellette, Christiane Quebec Programs Of Delinquency Prevention (Les Programmes Québécois De Prévention De La Délinquance), *Crime Et/And Justice* 7-8:119-123, 1979-1980. An examination of 34 delinquency prevention programs in Quebec, Canada found that they focused on crisis intervention, big brother programs, job training, housing, information and referral, "drop-in" services, and street work.

1933 Nuttal, Christopher P. Crime Prevention In Canada, *Canadian Journal Of Criminology* 31:477-486, 1989. This is a review of Canadian delinquency and crime prevention measures.

1934 Ontario London Family Court Clinic *Reducing The System-Induced Trauma For Child Sexual Abuse Victims Through Court Preparation,*

Assessment And Follow-Up. Ontario, Canada, 1991. Two intervention models designed to prepare child victims and witnesses of sexual abuse to testify in court are evaluated. 18p.

1935 O'Reilly-Fleming, Thomas & Clark, Barry Community Programming For Young Offenders In Ontario: From Neglect To Rhetoric, pp 21-42 in McCormick, Kevin R. E. (ed.) *Carceral Contexts: Readings in Control* Toronto, Canada: Canadian Scholars' Press, 1994. The Young Offenders Act's implications of incarceration and consequences for community program for a group of juvenile offenders in Ontario are discussed.

1936 O'Reilly-Fleming, Thomas & Clark, Barry (eds.) *Youth Injustice: Canadian Perspectives*. Toronto: Canadian Scholars' Press, 1993. This anthology has 21 articles on the various philosophical, legislative, programmatic and practical aspects of Canada's Young Offenders Act of 1984, young offenders' knowledge of laws and legal system, their rights, dispositions, rehabilitation, and minority offenders. 437p.

1937 O'Reilly-Fleming, Thomas (ed.) *The New Criminologies In Canada: The State, Crime, And Control*. Toronto, Canada: Oxford University, 1985. In discussing issues of social control and punishment, politics and crime legislation, Canadian intellectual and philosophical traditions, and economic factors such as youth unemployment, the author includes juvenile delinquency throughout the book. 343p.

1938 Osborne, Judith A. Juvenile Justice Policy In Canada: The Transfer Of The Initiative, *Canadian Journal Of Family Law*, 2:7-32, 1979. This article describes both the substantive and procedural changes in juvenile justice policy in Canada that is transforming the system.

1939 Paiement, Robert *An Exploratory Study Of Youth Justice Committees*. Ottawa, Canada: Canada Department of Justice, Research, Statistics and Evaluation Directorate, 1996. This volume describes Canadian Youth Justice Committees, including Aboriginal ones , and provides an in-depth examination of five of them. 70p.

1940 Parizeau, Alice *Parenting And Delinquent Youth*. Lexington, Massachusetts: D. C. Heath, 1980. The author surveyed parents of inmates and critiques the juvenile justice system in Quebec, Canada for its failure to focus on parental responsibility for their minor children while holding children responsible to the court for their behavior. 179p.

1941 Parizeau, Alice & Szabo, Denis *The Treatment Of Criminality In Canada (Le Traitement De La Criminalité Au Canada)*. Montreal, Canada: University of Montreal Press, 1977. Chapter 5, on detention and probation, includes the treatment norms for minors. 427p.

1942 Pate, Kim Victim-Young Offender Reconciliation As Alternative Measures Programs In Canada, pp 135-144 in Galaway, Burt & Hudson, Joe (eds.) *Criminal Justice, Restitution, And Reconciliation.* Monsey, New York: Criminal Justice Press, 1990. This article is on the eligibility criteria, referral processes, variations on a reconciliation model, follow-up and evaluation, programming trends and administration of victim-offender reconciliation program under the Canadian Young Offenders Act of 1984.

1943 Pennell, Joan & Buford, Gale Attending To Context: Family Group Decision-Making In Canada, pp 206-220 in Hudson, Joe; Morris, Allison; Maxwell, Gabrielle & Galaway, Burt (eds.) *Family Group Conferences: Perspectives On Policy & Practice.* Monsey, New York: Criminal Justice Press and Federation Press, 1996. This chapter is based on preliminary findings from the Family Group Decision-Making Project implemented in Newfoundland and Labrador.

1944 Peterson-Badali, Michele & Koegl, Christopher J. Young People's Knowledge Of The Young Offenders Act And The Youth Justice System, *Canadian Journal Of Criminology* 40:127-152, 1998. This study of students from six Canadian cities investigates youths' knowledge of the Young Offenders Act.

1945 Peterson-Badali, Michele; Abramovitch, Rona & Duda, Juliane Young Children's Legal Knowledge And Reasoning Ability, *Canadian Journal Of Criminology* 39:145-170, 1997. Children being treated and at-risk when examined on knowledge of and reasoning about legal issues of the juvenile justice system, reveal their lack of knowledge of attorney-client relationship and the workings of the legal system although they had some legal basics.

1946 Peterson-Badali, Michele *Students' Knowledge And Perceptions Of The Young Offenders Act: Final Report.* Ottawa, Canada: Research and Statistics Section, Canada Department of Justice, 1996. The author evaluates Canadian students' knowledge of a number of laws including the Young Offenders Act, age boundaries, dispositions, procedures, youth court records, transfer to adult court, and the role of legal personnel. 77p.

1947 Peterson-Badali, Michele & Abramovitch, Rona Children's Knowledge Of The Legal System: Are They Competent To Instruct Legal Counsel? *Canadian Journal Of Criminology* 34:139-160, 1992. This study of children and young adults used vignettes of delinquent youth to study their understanding of law. Most respondents were ignorant or had misconceptions of the legal system.

1948 Petrunik, Michael *Models Of Dangerousness: A Cross Jurisdictional Review Of Dangerousness Legislation And Practice*. Ottawa, Canada: Canada Solicitor General, 1994. Part five on "Dangerousness Legislation And Practice In Canada" has a critique of the report of the 1980 Badgley Committee On Sexual Abuses Against Children and Youth and the legislation enacted after it. 140p.

1949 Petrunik, Michael Crime And Delinquency Prevention: An Overview Of Current Approaches, *Impact* 1:21-31, 1982. This article summarizes the nature and effectiveness of various Canadian delinquency prevention programs.

1950 Rains, Prue & Teram, Eli *Normal Bad Boys: Public Policies, Institutions, And The Politics Of Client Recruitment*. Quebec City, Canada: McGill-Queen's University Press, 1992. This study traces the developments, up to the present, of the history, the impact, and subversion of public policies that affect the disposition of English-speaking delinquent, neglected, and emotionally disturbed youth in Montreal. 187p.

1951 Rains, Prue & Teram, Eli The Transformation Of Strategies For Controlling Admissions: Professionalization And Youth Processing Organizations, *Crime & Delinquency* 37:281-299, 1991. Summarizes the findings of a larger study tracing the history of public policies and their effect on disposition of delinquent, neglected, and emotionally disturbed anglophone youths in Montreal, Canada.

1952 Rains, Prue Juvenile Justice And The Boy's Farm: 1909-1968. (La Justice Des Mineurs Et The Boys' Farm 1909-1968, *Criminologie* 18:103-127, 1985. A case study using the historic documents that reveal the tension and conflict between the Quebec's Shawbridge boys training school and the Montreal Social Welfare Court. French with English summary.

1953 Rainville-Laforte, Fernande Bill C-37 To Amend The Young Offender Act: Implications For The Correctional Services Of Canada, *Forum On Corrections Research* 7:46-48, 1995. In comparing the youth and adult correctional systems of Canada, the author highlights the youth courts' protective, instructive, and reeducating principles.

1954 Raychaba, Brian Canadian Youth In Care: Leaving Care To Be On Our Own, *Children And Youth Services Review* 11:61-73, 1989. The author provides a description of Canada's National Youth in Care Network for youths with troubled family history.

1955 Reid, Susan The Juvenile Justice 'Revolution' In Canada: The Creation And Development Of New Legislation For Young Offenders, *Canadian Criminology Forum* 8:1-14, 1986. This articles evaluates the new Young Offenders Act, that was designed to replace and improve juvenile justice system under the 1908 Juvenile Delinquents Act.

1956 Reitsma-Street, Marge Justice For Canadian Girls: A 1990's Update, *Canadian Journal Of Criminology* 41:335-363, 1999. The author focuses on discrimination and gender-based variations in judicial practice, the disparity between public fear and incidence, and girls' pro-social tendencies in considering delinquency research, and Canadian Youth court data.

1957 Reitsma-Street, Marge Canadian Youth Court Charges And Dispositions For Females Before And After Implementation Of The Young Offenders Act, *Canadian Journal Of Criminology* 35:437-458, 1993. This study of Youth court responses to female offenders before and after the passage of Canada's Young Offenders Act found reductions in status offenses but there was an increase in charges of non-compliance with the administration, such as failure to appear in court, leaving a residence without permission, and breach of probation.

1958 Reitsma-Street, Marge Implementation Of The Young Offenders Act, *Canadian Social Work Review* 7:137-158, 1990. The author argues that the goal of Canada's 1984 Young Offenders' Act to balance the rights, needs, and responsibilities of juveniles and society has been unfulfilled.

1959 Reker, Gary T.; Coté, James E. & Peacock, Edward J. Juvenile Diversion: Conceptual Issues And Program Effectiveness, *Canadian Journal Of Criminology* 22:36-50, 1980. The rationale, evaluation, supportive empirical research, and a summary table of the 1970s diversion outcome studies are presented by the authors.

1960 Ribordy, François-Xavier; Laflamme, Simon & Cazabon, Benôit *Legal Education And Information: Exploratory Study*. Ottawa, Ontario: Department of Justice Canada, 1986. This research evaluates legal literacy among Canadian young people, women, native peoples, the elderly and others. 182p.

1961 Roberts, Julian *Public Knowledge Of Crime And Justice*. Ottawa, Canada: Department of Justice Research, Statistics and Evaluation, 1994. This is a review of research on public knowledge of laws, the court system vis-à-vis crime, including juvenile crime in Canada, and the gap between perceptions and evidence. 77p.

1962 Royal Canadian Mounted Police *Crime Prevention And Community Relations Programs.* Ottawa, Canada: Minister of Supply and Services, 1987. Section 8 of this catalogue of crime prevention and police-community relations includes sundry youth programs such as Big Brother Superstar Event, Boys Club Alta Vista, Halloween Spookerama, etc. 199p.

1963 Ryan, Colleen & Mathews, Frederick *A National Directory Of Exemplary School-Based Police Programs To Combat Youth Violence.* Ottawa, Canada: Solicitor General Canada, 1996. This directory provides a listing of school-based police model programs for violence prevention and early intervention in Canada. 177p.

1964 Sacco, Vincent F. Shoplifting Prevention: The Role Of Community-Based Intervention Strategies, *Canadian Journal Of Criminology* 27:15-29, 1985. Direct deterrence of juvenile shoplifters is the focus of this essay on strategies using community resources such as mass media to prevent carime.

1965 Safer City Task Force *Final Report.* Vancouver, Canada: Safer City Task Force, 1993. This report on urban design and safer cities addresses issues of homeless and street youths besides traffic safety, prostitution, drugs, violence, and property crimes. 386p.

1966 Sas, Louise; Jaffe, Peter & Reddon, John R. Unravelling The Needs Of Dangerous Young Offenders: A Clinical-Rational And Empirical Approach To Classification, *Canadian Journal Of Criminology* 27:83-96, 1985. This psychological study of dangerous and non-dangerous offenders, concludes that those who were victims and placed outside the family and had documented school, peer problems and poor school performance tended to have more serious charges against them.

1967 Schissel, Bernard A Sociolegal Analysis Of Canadian Youth Justice: The Impact Of Offender's Race On Judicial Decisions, *Journal Of Criminal Justice* 21:533-552, 1993. The influence of extralegal variables on judicial outcomes, including detention, plea, adjudication and sentencing, reveals those variables, most notably race, have a substantial systematic influence on judicial decisions, especially when seriousness of offense and criminal record are controlled.

1968 Schissel, Bernard *Social Dimensions Of Canadian Youth Justice.* Toronto, Canada: Oxford University Press, 1993. This critical analysis of several issues related to youth crime in Canada includes the history of Canadian youth justice from the Industrial Revolution to the Young Offenders Act, the conflict perspective on youth crime, and the discriminatory justice experienced by young offenders. 151p. Appendix.

1969 Schmolka, Vicki *Is Bill C-15 Working? An Overview Of The Research On The Effects Of The 1988 Child Sexual Abuse Amendments.* Ottawa, Canada: Department of Justice Canada, 1992. Studies on child sexual abuse in Canada are summarized to indicate how the criminal justice system deals with such behavior since the enactment of legislation addressing issues of protection, prosecution, improving the experience of child victims and witnesses, and sentencing. 113p.

1970 Shearing, Clifford D.; Lynch, Jennifer F.; Matthews, Catherine J. & The University of Toronto Centre of Criminology *Policing In Canada: A Bibliography.* Ottawa, Canada: Solicitor General of Canada, 1979. Chapter four of this annotated reference list includes police and youth under "Police Role." 362p. French & English.

1971 Silverman, Robert A. & Creechan, James H. *Delinquency Treatment And Intervention.* Ottawa, Canada: Research, Statistics and Evaluation Directorate, Department of Justice Canada, 1995. This technical report provides an overview of the social context of juvenile delinquency, and describes how both non-legal and legal mechanisms interact to prevent and reduce delinquent behavior, and rehabilitate offenders. 92p.

1972 Smith, Ronald B.; Hornick, Joseph P. & Copple, Peter *Community Resource Committee: A Community-Based Strategy For Dealing With Youth Crime And Violence In Calgary.* Ottawa, Canada: Solicitor General Canada, 1995. This is a report and summary of the 1990 Community Resource Committee of the Calgary Police Service on youth crime and violence in Calgary. 60p.

1973 Smart, Reginald G. & Goodstadt, Michael S. Effects Of Reducing The Legal Alcohol-Purchasing Age On Drinking And Drinking Problems: A Review Of Empirical Studies, *Journal Of Studies On Alcohol* 38:1313-1323, 1977. This review of self-report and sales research on the effects of reducing the legal age for purchasing alcoholic beverages and drinking concludes that there is increased youthful drinking after lowering the legal age for purchasing alcoholic beverage reduced.

1974 Smith-Gadacz, Trudie Speak No Evil, Hear No Evil? Juveniles And The Language Of Law, pp 351-374 in Fleming, Thomas & Visano, L. A. (eds.) D*eviant Designations: Crime, Law And Deviance In Canada.* Toronto, Canada: Butterworths, 1983. From focused interviews with probation officers, defense counsel and the judges in Winnipeg juvenile court, the author describes process of initial contact, first court hearing, and court follow-up in juvenile delinquency cases.

1975 Sprott, Jane B. Understanding Public Opposition To A Separate Youth Justice System, *Crime & Delinquency* 44:399-411, 1998. The public belief that juvenile court sentences are too lenient and that young offenders should be processed in the adult justice system is examined in this survey whose findings suggests that the more punitive attitudes were, in part, due to the perceived ineffectiveness of the alternatives.

1976 Sprott, Jane B. Understanding Public Views Of Youth Crime And The Youth Justice System, *Canadian Journal Of Criminology* 38:271-290, 1996. The disparity between media portrayals of juvenile delinquency and juvenile court statistics is examined in this research.

1977 Task Force On The Criminal Justice System And Its Impact On The Indian And Metis *Justice On Trial, Vol.* 3. Edmonton, Canada: Solicitor General of Canada, 1991. The section on youth court activity in Alberta provides data on offense categories of youths and adults charged by the police, and statistics on young offenders admitted to youth facilities in the province of Alberta. 298p.

1978 Tator, Joan & Wilde, Katherine Child Abuse And The Courts: An Analysis Of Selected Factors In The Judicial Processing Of `Child Abuse' Cases, *Canadian Journal Of Family Law* 3:165-205, 1980. Legal factors involved in the judicial processing of child abuse cases brought before the Family Division of the Provincial Court in metropolitan Toronto, Canada when analyzed indicate that there was no a typical outcome in such cases.

1979 Taylor, Gib Project Pride - An Anti-Vandalism Program, *Canadian Journal Of Criminology* 25:91-94, 1983. The author describes Lakehead, Canada Board of Education's implementation of a program to reduce vandalism in schools.

1980 Teevan, James J. Deterrent Effects Of Punishment For Breaking And Entering And Theft, *The Canadian Journal Of Criminology And Corrections* 19:121-149, 1977. This questionnaire study of London, Ontario secondary school students' perceptions of punishment and their own deviance, showed that perceived level of certainty of punishment is only weakly related to certain types of deviance.

1981 Theoret, Bruno The Correctional Detention Of Youths In Winnipeg During 1930-1959 (Le Détention Correctionnelle Au Tribunal Des Jeunes De Winnipeg Entre 1930 Et 1959), *Criminologie* 28:3-147, 1995. From the files of boys and girls after the establishment of juvenile courts, the author provides descriptions of the judicial processes and sentencing in Winnipeg during the above period.

1982 Theoret, Bruno Psychiatry, Juvenile Justice, And Delinquent Identity: A Case Study At The Juvenile Court Of Winnipeg, 1930-1959, *Journal Of Human Justice* 6:64-77, 1994. This is an historic study of the identity construction of youths processed by the Winnipeg Juvenile Court between 1930 and 1959.

1983 Tremblay, Pierre; Tremblay, Manon & Léonard, Lucie Arrest, Racial Discrimination And Intergroup Relations (Arrestation, discrimination Raciale Et Relations Intergroupes), *Canadian Journal Of Criminology* 41:457-478, 1999. This research found that outcomes of arrest did not vary because of the ethnic background of either the accused or the victim, but disposition were more severe in black neighborhoods. French with English summary.

1984 Tremblay, R. E. Treatment Of Hard-Core Delinquents In Residential Establishments: The Ardale Case, *British Journal Of Criminology* 24:384-393, 1984. This is a survey of the staff and resident delinquent boys' perceptions of the social and educational climate of Ardale and other residential treatment centers for juveniles.

1985 Trépanier, Jean Juvenile Delinquency And Youth Protection: The Historical Foundations Of The Canadian Juvenile Delinquents Act Of 1908, *European Journal Of Crime, Criminal Law And Criminal Justice* 1:41-62, 1999. This article offers an historical review of the Canadian legislative processes preceding the 1908 Juvenile delinquent Act.

1986 Trépanier, Jean Juvenile Justice In Canada: The Issues In Question At The End Of A Century (La Justice Des Mineurs Au Canada: Remises En Question À La Fin D'Une Siècle), *Criminologie* 32:7-35, 1999. Discusses the Juvenile Delinquents Act and the Young Offenders Act and argues the planned replacements of the latter will, besides transferring a lot of young offenders to the adult system, make the juvenile system more similar to the adult system. French with English summary.

1987 Trépanier, Jean The Canadian Law On Juvenile Offenders: Principles And Objectives Guiding The Choice Of Measures Ordered By The Court. (La Loi Canadienne Sur Les Jeunes Contrevenants: Principes Et Objectifs Guidant Le Choix Des Mesures Ordonnées Par Les Tribunaux), *Revue Internationale De Criminologie Et De Police Technique* 43:273-308, 1990. The author compares and contrasts Canada's 1908 Juvenile Delinquents Act that focused on the minor and the responsibility of family and society while under its replacement, the Young Offenders Act of 1982-84, the judge's priority in diversion and its increased social control is to protect society. French with English summary.

1988 Trépanier, Jean The Removal Of Juvenile Offenders From Juvenile Court Jurisdiction In Canada And Legislative Projects Of The Federal Government (La Déjudiciarisation Des Mineurs Délinquents Au Canada Et Les Projets Législatifs Du Gouvernement Fédéral), *Canadian Journal Of Criminology*, 23:279-289, 1981. The author argues that the Young Offenders Bill and its provisions for formalized diversion mean increased social control of delinquents.

1989 Turner, David The Probation Officer And Community Delinquency Prevention, *Canadian Journal Of Criminology* 26:75-95, 1984. Based on a study in Victoria, this article describes the geography of delinquency and the Blanshard Community Project to prevent delinquent behavor.

1990 Vasey, Paul *Kids In The Jail: Why Do Our Young Offenders Do The Things They Do*. Windsor, Canada: Black Moss Press, 1995. This is a journalistic profile of juvenile offenders in a maximum-security jail for young offenders in Canada. 271p.

1991 Vingilis, Evelyn A Study Of A Sample Of Young People Charged With Underage Drinking, *Canadian Journal Of Criminology* 22:457-463, 1980. This article profiles the underage Canadian drinker.

1992 Vitaro, F.; Tremblay, R. E. & Charlebois, P. Nothing Works....Really? Preventing Intervention For At Risk Boys' Delinquency (Nothing Works.... Vraiment? Intervention Préventive Auprès De Garçons À Risque De Délinquance), pp 171-199 in Killias, Martin (ed.) *Recidivism And Rehabilitation (Rückfall Und Bewährung/Récidive Et Réhabilitation)*. Zurich, Switzerland: Verlag Rüegger, 1992. The authors report on their preventive intervention-oriented study of stealing, breaking and entering, alcohol use, television-watching as well as the psychological measures of Child Fantasy Inventory among control and experimental groups of boys from schools in diverse areas of Montreal. French.

1993 Warner, Jessica; Fischer, Benedikt & Albanes, Ricardo Marijuana, Juveniles, And The Police: What High-School Students Believe About Detection And Enforcement, *Canadian Journal Of Criminology* 40:401-420, 1998. This study investigates Canadian high school students' calculations of the odds of being arrested for possession or use of marijuana.

1994 Waterhouse, John & Waterhouse, Lorraine Implementing Unified Family Courts: -- The British Columbian Experience, *Canadian Journal Of Family Law* 4:153-171, 1983. This essay describes the recommendations for a unified family court system, based on a project of the British Columbia Royal Commission on Family and Children's Law.

1995 Wells, Mary *Canada's Law On Child Sexual Abuse: A Handbook.* Ottawa, Canada: Minister of Justice Canada, 1990. This handbook provides information about reforms in child sexual abuse legislation in Canada. 117p.

1996 Wilson, Larry C. *Juvenile Courts In Canada.* Toronto, Canada: Carswell, 1982. This book covers the history of the transition of juvenile justice in Canada from the individualized justice and *parens patriae* approach of the old Juvenile Delinquents Act (1908) to the Young Offenders Act with the procedural safeguards found in the adult criminal justice system. 272p.

1997 Wilson, Larry C. Diversion: The Impact On Juvenile Justice, *Canadian Journal Of Criminology And Corrections* 18:161-167, 1976. This article critiques the Law Reform Commission's call for diversion and its implications, and discusses the lack of such alternatives in the formal structure or policy in Canada.

1998 Wine, Shelley A Motherhood Issue: *The Impact Of Criminal Justice Involvement On Women And Their Children.* Ottawa, Canada: Ministry of Solicitor General, 1992. This user report has a small section that discusses intergenerational crime involving the children of women in custody.

1999 Winogron, William Correctional Psychology Of Young Offenders In The Community: Philosophical Musings, *Forum On Corrections Research* 7:31-33, 1995. The author argues in favor of emotive therapy based on equality of worth, responsible hedonism, and ongoing psychological assessment, and the implications of such treatment.

2000 Winterdyk, John A. Juvenile Justice And Young Offenders: An Overview Of Canada, pp 139-175 in Winterdyk, John A. (ed.) *Juvenile Justice Systems: International Perspectives.* Toronto, Canada: Canadian Scholars' Press, 1997. The author covers the history of the development of the Young Offenders Act and the dimensions of Canadian the delinquency problem with several tables of data, the processess of youth justice with a model, and addresses various current Canadian issues.

2001 Winterdyk, John A. (ed.) *Issues And Perspectives On Young Offenders In Canada.* Toronto, Canada: Harcourt Brace Canada, 1996. The twelve articles in this collection are organized under topics such as an overview of young offenders in Canada, the Young Offenders Act, and special topics including articles on the amendments to the Young Offenders Act, sexual abuse and prostitution, substance abuse and delinquency, runaway and homeless youth, and youth in the criminal justice sustem. 322p.

2002 Winterdyk, John & Roesch, Ronald A Wilderness Experiential Program As An Alternative For Probationers: An Evaluation, *Canadian Journal Of Criminology* 24:39-49, 1982. This evaluation study of the wilderness adventure experience as a therapeutic measure for adjudicated male juveniles found the results were mixed.

2003 Wormith, Stephen; Wright, Jeffrey; Sauve, Isabelle & Fleury, Paul Ontario's Strict Discipline Facility Is Not Just Another Boot Camp, *Forum On Corrections Research* 11:34-38, 1999. The authors provide a description and analysis of a privately run program call Project Turnaround for 16-19 year olds.

2004 Wormith, J. S. The Youth Management Assessment: Assessment Of Young Offenders At Risk Of Serious Reoffending, *Forum On Corrections Research* 7:23-27, 1995. This article addresses the development and implementation of an instrument to assess and identify youths at-risk.

2005 Young, Allison Harvey Child Sexual Abuse And The Law Of Evidence: Some Current Canadian Issues, *Canadian Journal Of Family Law* 11:11-40, 1992. This legal review contends that the traditional treatment of children and their evidence in Canadian sexual abuse cases is unsatisfactory.

2006 Youth Correctional Services *A Review Of Security And Staffing In Young Offender Community Residences*. Ottawa, Canada: Ministry of Correctional Services, 1990. This is a report based on the data from community residences for delinquent youths on security issues, such as locked doors, restricted access, staff knowledge of clientele, maintenance of presence and trust, and the like. 21p.

Cayman Islands

2007 Hylton, Joyce & Davie, Pamela The Caymen Islands, British West Indies, pp 1-40 in Stewart, V. Lorne (ed.) *Justice And Troubled Children Around The World, Vol.4*. New York, New York: New York University Press, 1982. This chapter describes how the community in the Cayman Islands has improved the situation of children in trouble, even though the Islands are experiencing disruption.

Chile

2008 Goodman, Randy Summaries Of DCI Country Surveys, Chile, pp 156-158 in Tomasevski, Katarina (ed.) *Children In Adult Prisons: An International Perspective*. New York, New York: St. Martin's Press, 1986. Findings for Chilie from the 1982-1984 Defense for Children International Survey of children in adult prisons are presented.

China

2009 Curran, Daniel J. & Cook, Sandra Growing Fears, Rising Crime: Juveniles And China's Justice System, *Crime & Delinquency* 39:296-315, 1993. This survey of 15,000 citizens, examines the growing fear of crime among youths in China and, relative to their elders, their distrust of the justice system.

2010 Han, Wu Youth Crime And The Prevention Of Delinquency In China, pp 145-149 Kubota, Yo (ed.) *International Review Of Criminal Policy: Special Double Volume On Juvenile Justice In International Perspective*. New York, New York: United Nations Centre for Social Development and Humanitarian Affairs, 1990. This article reviews the Chinese constitution and laws on juvenile offenders, and describes programs designed to deal with offenders under age 18.

2011 Hewitt, John D.; Hickey, Eric W. & Regoli, Robert M. Dealing With Juvenile Delinquency: The Re-Education Of The Delinquent In The People's Republic Of China, pp 67-82 in Hackler, Jim (ed.) *Official Responses To Problem Juveniles: Some International Reflections*. Euskadi, Spain: The Oñati International Institute for the Sociology of Law, 1991. The underlying assumptions about and practices followed in re-education programs for juvenile offenders in Chinaare examined in this chapter.

2012 Human Rights Watch/Asia *Death By Default: A Policy Of Fatal Neglect In China's State Orphanages*. New York, New York: Human Rights Watch, 1996. This report documents the pattern of cruelty, abuse, and malign neglect which has dominated child welfare work since the early 1950s, now constituting one of China's gravest human rights problems. 394p. Appendix.

2013 Jian, Xu The Principles And Development Of Juvenile Justice Administration In The People's Republic Of China, *Police Studies* 10:181-184, 1987. This article describes twenty principles used in Chinese juvenile justice policy.

2014 Jiuming, Wei The People's Republic Of China, pp 125-144 in Stewart, V. Lorne (ed.) *Justice And Troubled Children Around The World Vol IV*. New York, New York: New York University Press, 1982. Chapter discusses a variety of approaches such as blockparents, voluntary service of retired persons, work-study, and other programs in dealing with youth.

2015 Mok, Bong Ho Community Care For Delinquent Youth: The Chinese Approach Of Rehabilitating The Young Offenders, *Journal Of Offender Counseling Services And Rehabilitation* 15:5-20, 1990. The community-care approach to the treatment of delinquent youth in China is described.

2016 Ren, Xin People's Republic Of China, pp 57-79 in Shoemaker, Donald J. (ed.) *International Handbook On Juvenile Justice*. Westport, Connecticut: Greenwood, 1996. Chapter offers an in-depth discussion of the juvenile justice system of China.

2017 Wong, Dennis S. W. Delinquency Control And Juvenile Justice In China, *Australian And New Zealand Journal Of Criminology* 32:27-41, 1999. This review suggests that economic improvement is associated with a real increase in delinquency in China, and describes the relationship between informal grassroots networks of social control and the formal correctional institutions, and the lack of improvement in juvenile justice in recent years.

2018 Zhang, Lening & Messner, Steven F. The Severity Of Official Punishment For Delinquency And Change In Interpersonal Relations In Chinese Society, *Journal Of Research In Crime And Delinquency* 31:416-433, 1994. This study focuses on the impact of the severity of official punishment for delinquency leading to estrangement from parents, relatives, friends and neighbors in Chinese society.

2019 Zhang, Lening Peers' Rejection As A Possible Consequence Of Official Reaction To Delinquency In Chinese Society, *Criminal Justice And Behavior* 21:387-402, 1994. This study examines the attitudes peers have toward those officiall labeled delinquent in China.

2020 Zhong, Gu Bai Shanghai Regulations Concerning Protection Of Juveniles, *Criminal Justice Review* 14:177-191, 1989. This article provides a translation of the Shanghai Regulations Concerning Protection of Juveniles. These were the first such regulations adopted in China in 1987.

Colombia

2021 Goodman, Randy Summaries Of DCI Country Surveys, Columbia, pp 158-160 in Tomasevski, Katarina (ed) *Children In Adult Prisons: An*

International Perspective. New York, New York: St. Martin's Press, 1986. Findings for Columbia from the 1982-1984 Defense for Children International Survey of children in adult prisons are presented.

2022 Kirk, Robin *Generation Under Fire: Children And Violence In Colombia.* New York, New York: Human Rights Watch/Americas, 1994. This report is on street children targeted by agents of the Colombian government for murder, torture, and vigilante violence. 66p. Appendix.

2023 Serra, Merienne *Violence And Tenderness: The Street Children Of Bogota (Violence Et Tendresse: Les Enfants De La Rue Á Bogota).* Paris, France: L'Harmattan, 1995. This book reports an ethnographic study of street children in Bogota, and the illegal behaviors they engage in. 101p. French.

2024 Wilson, Suzanne & Greider-Durango, Julia Social Cleansing In Columbia: The War On Street Children, pp 135-149 in Kelly, Robert J. & Maghan, Jess (eds.) *Hate Crime: The Global Politics Of Polarization.* Carbondale, Illinois: Southern Illinois University Press, 1998. In addition to discussing the victimization of juveniles suspected of crimes in Columbia, this chapter offers some information of youthful criminality as well.

Costa Rica

2025 Goodman, Randy Summaries Of DCI Country Surveys, Costa Rica, pp 160-162 in Tomasevski, Katarina (ed) *Children In Adult Prisons: An International Perspective.* New York, New York: St. Martin's Press, 1986. Findings on Costa Rica from the 1982-1984 Defense for Children International Survey of children in adult prisons are presented in this section.

2026 Montero, Jorge A. & Navarro, Sonia Costa Rica, pp 41-60 in Stewart, V. Lorne (ed.) *Justice And Troubled Children Around The World, Vol. 4.* New York, New York: New York University Press, 1982. This chapter describes Costa Rica's behavioral approach in dealing with children's problems.

Denmark

2027 Goodman, Randy Summaries of DCI Country Surveys, Denmark, pp 163-166 in Tomasevski, Katarina (ed.) *Children In Adult Prisons: An International Perspective.* New York, New York: St. Martin's Press, 1986. This report summarizes Danish laws and presents data regarding juvenile offenders, the detention of minors, and the condition of state prisons where temporary detention may be provided.

2028 Jensen, Kirsten & Mednick, Sarnoff A. & Vand Dusen, Katherine Denmark, pp 171-190 in Klein, Malcolm W. (ed.) *Western Systems Of Juvenile Justice* Beverly Hills, California: Sage, 1984. This chapter has a concise flow-chart of the Danish juvenile justice system, descriptions of the role of the police, prosecutor, social welfare authorities, and the juvenile court.

2029 Kramp, Peter; Israelson, Lise; Mortensen, Karen Vibeke & Aarkrog, Tove Serious Juvenile Offenders: Demographic Variables, Diagnostic Problems, And Therapeutic Possibilities, *International Journal Of Law And Psychiatry* 10:63-73, 1987. Based on a retrospective study of a small sample of youths, this paper discusses the age of onset of behavioral problems.

2030 Leonhardt, Fred *Prostitution: Alternatives To Prohibition.* Salem, Oregon: Oregon Legislative Research 1981. This research monograph has a small section on Danish runaways engaged in prostitution. 16p.

2031 Mehlbye, Jill & Sommer, Brigit Denmark, pp 97-137 in Mehlbye, Jill & Walgrave, Lode (eds.) *Confronting Youth In Europe.* Copenhagen, Denmark: Forlaget, 1998. This chapter has a summary of the history of the judicial system, the criminal code and other statutes regarding juveniles, the various sanctions and services for young offenders as well as some graphs and data on youth crime.

2032 Munch-Petersen, Erik Denmark, pp 23-35 in Lorne, V. Stewart (ed.) *Justice And Troubled Children Around The World Vol I.* New York, New York: New York University Press, 1980. This chapter has a summary of various Danish legislative measures and their background.

2033 Nielson, Beth Grothe Young Offender Ideologies And The Danish Discourse, pp 56-65 in Booth, Tim (ed.) *Juvenile Justice In The New Europe.* Sheffield, United Kingdom: Joint Unit for Social Services Research, Sheffield University, 1991. This chapter examines the origins and development of a more punitive movement toward juvenile offenders in Denmark, given the different value systems prevailing in the criminal justice and social service systems.

2034 Serrill, Michael S. In Denmark, Juvenile Crime Is Seen As A Social Problem, *Corrections Magazine* 3:44-46, 1977. This article describes the Danish philosophy that considers juvenile delinquency by a child below 15 a social, rather than a criminal, problem.

2035 Van Kalmthout, Anton M. & Tak, Peter J. P. Denmark, pp 17-67 in Van Kalmthout, Anton M. & Tak, Peter J. P. (eds.) *Sanction-Systems In The Member-States Of The Council Of Europe Part I.* New York, New York: Kluwer, 1988. This chapter describes Danish sanction systems in general, and residential homes for young people, with some data on youths age 15 and older for whom community service reports were ordered.

2036 Vestergaard, Jorn Juvenile Contracting In Denmark: Paternalism Revisited, pp 73-97 in Snare, Annika (ed.) *Youth, Crime And Justice.* Oslo, Norway: Norwegian University Press, 1991. This chapter reviews a pilot program where the offender contracts to participate in certain alternate community service sanctions for juveniles involved in property offenses, vandalism or joyriding.

2037 Wita, Marcel Community Policing: The Example Of The Danish SSP (Community Policing Das Daenische SSP Modell), *Die Kriminalpraevention* 4:7-12, 2000. The multi-agency Danish approach to crime prevention that was credited with reducing delinquency among juveniles is describe in this volume.

Egypt

2038 Ali, Badr-El-Din History Of Juvenile Delinquency In Modern Egypt, pp 757-789 in Hess, Albert G. & clement, Priscilla F. (eds.). *History Of Juvenile Delinquency: A Collection Of Essays On Crime Committed By Young Offenders, In History And In Selected Countries Volume II.* Aalen, Germany: Scientia Verlag, 1993. This chapter discusses the law and official reactions to juvenile offenders, and the establishment of juvenile police, trial, probation and juvenile institutions in pre-modern and contemporary Egypt.

2039 Ewies, Saied Egypt, pp 37-48 in Stewart, V. Lorne (ed.) *Justice And Troubled Children Around The World, Vol. I.* New York, New York: New York University Press, 1980. The author presents an overview of the rights of children in Egypt's history, a chronology of concerns on juvenile justice and views of juvenile justice comparing Egypt's modern society with its traditions.

2040 Hafez, Nagwa A. Egypt, pp 80-89 in Shoemaker, Donald J. (ed.) *International Handbook On Juvenile Justice.* Westport, Connecticut: Greenwood, 1996. This Chapter offers a detailed discussion of the juvenile justice system of Egypt.

Fiji

2041 Hackler, Jim Using Reintegrative Shaming Effectively: Why Fiji Has A Juvenile Justice System Superior To The US, Canada, And Australia, pp 109-128 in Hackler, Jim (ed.) *Official Responses To Problem Juveniles: Some International Reflections*. Euskadi, Spain: The Oñati International Institute for the Sociology of Law, 1991. In an analysis of Fiji's use of informal reintegrative shaming in dealing with young offenders, the author concludes that the larger the number of lawyers per capita, the thicker the juvenile code, and the greater the emphasis on due process, the worse the juvenile justice system.

2042 Tavai, Etuate Vugakoto The Quest For A Better System And Administration Of Juvenile Justice: The Case Of Fiji, pp 122-131 in United Nations Asia And Far East Institute (eds.) *Report for 1983 and Resource Material Series No. 25*. Tokyo, Japan: UNAFEI, 1984. Fiji's court and juvenile justice systems, probation, prosecution, adjudication and treatment after adjudication, and juvenile crime trends are some topics covered by this chapter.

Finland

2043 Grönfors, Martti; Hirvonen, Ari & Vesikansa, Sari Youth And Justice: On Law, Criminality And Moral Education, pp 121-139 in Snare, Annika (ed.) *Youth, Crime And Justice, Vol. 12*. Oslo, Norway: Norwegian University Press, 1991. This chapter reports the findings from interviews regarding law and moral education with Finnish youths.

2044 Joutsen, Matti *Dealing With Child Offenders In Finland: The Scandinavian Child Welfare System In Operation*. Helsinki, Finland: Research Institute of Legal Policy, Helsinki, 1980. This discussion on child offenders in Finland describes the background and operation of the Scandinavian child welfare system, and examines the issue of handling such offenders in the context of the wider criminal policy. 121p.

2045 Karkkainen, Hilkka Treatment Of Delinquent Youth In Finland, *Child Welfare* 68:183-188, 1989. This is a description of a two-year experimental mediation program of the Finnish Academy that sought to develop an alternative way of dealing with juvenile crime and conflict, and to increase community understanding and tolerance.

2046 Nylund, Marianne Young Offenders And The Mediation Program In Finland, pp 257-268 in Hackler, Jim (ed.) *Official Responses To Problem Juveniles: Some International Reflections*. Euskadi, Spain: The Oñati

International Institute for the Sociology of Law, 1991. This article summarizes one of the first mediation programs and the main points of the Young Offender Act in Finland.

2047 Pösö, Tarja Youth And Justice: On Law, Criminality And Moral Education, pp 98-120 in Snare, Annika (ed.) *Youth, Crime And Justice, Vol. 12*. Oslo, Norway and Oxford, United Kingdom: Norwegian University Press, 1991. Chapter traces the history of Finland's child welfare system, emphasizing its disparate treatment of boys and girls.

France

2048 Algan, André The Green Files: Descriptive Study Of The Delinquent Behavior Of Juveniles, The Paris Children's Court 1977 (Les Dossiers Verts: Études Descriptives Des Conduites Déliquantes Des Jeunes, Tribunal Pour Enfants Paris--1977), Vaucresson, France: Centre De Formation Et De Recherche De L'Éducation Surveillée, 1981. Using the files of delinquents of a Parisian court, the author describes the misbehaviors that brought the French boys and girls to the attention of authorities. 215p. French.

2049 Annales De Vaucresson *From Delinquncy To Detention (De La Délinquance À La Détention)*, Vaucresson, France: Centre D'Information Et De Recherche De L'Éducation Surveillée, 1981. This volume of ten articles addresses mostly issues in French juvenile justice. 291p. French with English summary.

2050 Aubusson De Cavarlay, Bruno France 1998: The Transformation Of Justice For Troubled Minors (France 1998: La Justice Des Mineurs Busculés), *Criminologie* 32:83-99, 1999. The author feels that, due to the police and court resorting to alternative sanctions, there is a blurring and mixing of minor delinquents and minors in "danger" in France. French with English summary.

2051 Bailleau, F. & Garioud, G. The Central Object Of Insecurity In Local Politics: The Case Of A Suburban Community Of Paris (*L'Insécurité Objet Central Des Politiques Locales: Créer La Ville, Le Cas D'Une Commune De La Banlieue Parisienne), Déviance Et Société* 15:329-337, 1999. This article describes Orly's social and physical rehabilitation of the entire community in a crime-prevention effort.

2052 Bailleau, Francis A Crisis Of Youth Or Of Judicial Response? pp 95-103 in Ruggiero, Vincenzo, South, Nigel & Taylor, Ian (eds.) *New European Criminology*. London, United Kingdom: Routledge, 1998. This chapter addresses the issue of the role of various socializing agents, including the state, vis-à-vis the young in urban problem enclaves.

2053 Bailleau, Francis & Garioud, Georges Social Strategies Aimed At Avoiding The Production Of Criminalisable Behavior, pp 11-30 in Asquith, Stewart (ed.) *New Social Strategies And The Criminal Justice System*, Strasbourg, France: Council of Europe Press, 1994. This chapter summarizes the French philosophy, logic, and policy of alternatives to judicial intervention by use of various local measures.

2054 Blatier, Catherine Juvenile Justice In France: The Evolution Of Sentencing For Children And Minor Delinquents, *British Journal Of Criminology* 39:240-252, 1999. The evolution of the unique trust in judicial authority to substitute and compensate faulty parenting exhibited in French law is discussed along with an analysis of juvenile judicial proceedings in a few French regions.

2055 Bonnemaison, Gilbert Confronting Delinquency: Prevention, Repression, And Solidarity--Report To The Prime Minister By The Mayors' Commission On Security (*Face À La Délinquance: Prévention, Répression, Solidarité--Rapport De La Première Ministre De Commission Des Maires De La Securité)*. Paris, France: La Documentation Française, 1983. This is the report and recommendations of the French mayors' commission on escalating youthful crime and delinquency that is the basis of current French preventiom, treatment, and penal policies. N/P. French.

2056 Cario, Robert Strengthening Special Education For The Judicial Protection Of Youth (Le Renforcement De La Spécificité Éducative De La Protection Judiciaire De La Jeunesse), *Revue Internationale De Criminologie Et De Police Technique* 50:276-299, 1997. This article critiques juvenile delinquency prevention by means of repression instead of focusing on the social and psychological foundations for such behavior. French with English summary.

2057 Charlemagne, Jacqueline Juvenile Justice And Rromani Youth In France: The Case Of The Paris Area (La Justice Des Mineurs Et Les Jeunes Rroms En France: Le Cas De La Région Parisienne), pp 99-162 in Patrignani, Angela & Villé, Renaud (eds.) *Romani Youths: The Pathways Of Juvenile Justice*. Rome, Italy: United Nations Interregional Crime and Justice Research Institute, 1997. Summarizes the French laws regarding juveniles such as age of criminal responsibility, protection of the identity of the minor, closed hearings, and the goal of education with numerous case descriptions. French with English summary.

2058 Collomp, Jean-Paul *Children's Rights* (*Les Droits Des Mineurs)*. Vaucresson, France: Centre De Formation Et De Recherche De L'Éducation Surveillée, 1980. This volume describes French statutes and sections of statutes that are applicable to minors, minority children, parental rights and obligations, delinquents, children's education, working children, and victims. 138p. French.

2059 Duprez, Dominique The French Model For Preventing Delinquency: The Second Attempt (Le Modèle Français De Prévention De La Délinquance: La Recherche D'Un Second Souffle) pp 61-82 in Hebberecht, Patrick & Sack, Fritz (eds.) *The Prevention Of Delinquency In Europe: New Strategies (La Prévention De La Délinquance En Europe: Nouvelles Stratégies)*. Paris, France: L'Harmattan, 1997. This chapter describes the originsof, and provides a critique of, delinquency prevention programs in France. French with English summary.

2060 Faget, Jacques & Wyvekens, Anne Urban Policy And Proximity Justice In France, *European Journal On Criminal Policy And Research* 4:64-73, 1996. The integrated services of the French Ministry Of Social Integration, Ministry Of Youth And Sports, National Educational Ministry all geared to prevent the exclusion of the young, immigrants, the uneducated, the unemployed and other segments of French society are described in this article.

2061 Fuchs, Rachel Juvenile Delinquency In Nineteenth-Century France, pp 265-285 in Hess, Albert G. & Clement, Priscilla F. (eds.) *History Of Juvenile Delinquency: A Collection Of Essays On Crime Committed By Young Offenders, In History And In Selected Countries Volume I.* Aalen, Germany: Scientia Verlag, 1990. This chapter offers an historic review of the attitudes, laws, and public policy toward youthful criminals in France from 1815 to 1914.

2062 Gazeau, Jean-François & Peyre, Vincent France, pp 217-249 in Mehlbye, Jill & Walgrave, Lode (eds.) *Confronting Youth In Europe: Juvenile Crime And Juvenile Justice.* Copenhagen, Denmark: Forlaget, 1998. This chapter gives a detailed description of the origins, organization, step-by-step procedures for, and operation of the contemporary French juvenile justice system in conjunction with the department of *aide sociale á l'enfance* (social assistance to children).

2063 Gazeau, Jean-François The Future Of Former Incarcerated Minors (Le Devenir D'Anciens Mineurs Détenus), pp 21-27 in Junger-Tas, Josine; Boendermaker, Leonieke; Van Der Laan, Peter H. (eds.) *The Future Of Juvenile Justice System (L'Avenir Du Système Pénal Des Mineurs).* Leuven, Belgium: Acco, 1991. This chapter points out the increasing blurring and mixing of the youthful "minor offenders" and children "in danger" categories in France. French.

2064 Godefroy, Thierry & Laffargue, Bernard The Cost Of Crime In France: Security Expenditures During 1988-1991 (Les Côuts Du Crime En France: Les Dépenses De Sécurité--Donnés Pour 1988 À 1991). Includes data on the public cost for private and public arrangements to rear French delinquent minors. 117p. French.

2065 Goodman, Randy France, pp 170-171 in Tomasevski, Katarina (ed.) *Children In Adult Prisons: An International Perspective*. New York, New York: St. Martin's Press, 1986. This dicussion focuses on the infer-quent use of im-prisonment of juveniles in France.

2066 Graham, John Crime Prevention Policies In Europe, *European Journal Of Crime, Criminal Law And Criminal Justice* 1:126-142, 1993. The section on France describes the French philosophy and preventive measures in dealing with juvenile delinquency.

2067 Hackler, Jim Confusing The Drama With The Reality In The French Juvenile Court, pp 205-222 in Hackler, Jim (ed.) *Official Responses To Problem Juveniles: Some International Reflections*. Euskadi, Spain: The Oñati International Institute for the Sociology of Law, 1991. It is argued that the French have produced a much more effective and sensible system of juvenile justice than those that have evolved in North America.

2068 Hackler, James C. Practicing In France What Americans Have Preached: The Response Of French Judges To Juveniles, *Crime & Delinquency* 34:467-485, 1988. The author describes the French paternalistic philosophy and social welfare-orientation of providing helpful services, and limiting use of custodial punishment for juveniles.

2069 Hackler, James Implications Of Variability In Juvenile Justice, pp 213-233 in Klein, Malcolm W. (ed.) *Western Systems Of Juvenile Justice* Beverly Hills, California: Sage, 1984. This chapter provides a good description the juvenile justice system in France.

2070 Humphris, Nicolas Educational Aspects Of French Cabinet Justice, pp 223-2234 in Hackler, Jim (ed.) *Official Responses To Problem Juveniles: Some International Reflections*. Euskadi, Spain: The Oñati International Institute for the Sociology of Law, 1991. This chapter describes how French juvenile courts have transformed the desire for normative autonomy into an opportunity to intervene.

2071 King, Michael Crime Prevention In France, *Canadian Journal Of Criminology* 31:527-538, 1989. The author discusses French crime prevention in general by means of school safety, operation metro, and the operation of various "*mission locale*" projects.

2072 King, Michael *How To Make Social Crime Prevention Work: The French Experience.* London, United Kingdom: National Association for Care and Resettlement of Offenders, 1988. This document has a good summary of the Bonnemaison Commission report and describes the philosophy, operation and results of the crime prevention programs undertaken by French government in the early 1980's. 43p.

2073 Krikorian, Gregoire Prevention As A Strategy For Combating Urban Crime: Theoretical Considerations And Their Application To A Local Situation In France, *International Criminal Police Review* 396:71-80, 1986. Based on an experiment in Bassens, Marseilles, this French study describes "active prevention," and deterrence by persuasion through job creation, emphasis on community leadership by elders, parental civic duty, and the youths moral values of offenders within the context of police support and approval.

2074 LaCombe, P. & Moulin, C. Delinquent Minors Amidst Repression, Media, Enforcement, Education And Responsibility (Les Mineurs Délinquants, Entre Répression, Médialisation, Sanction, Education Et Reponsabilisation*), Déviance Et Société* 24:167-186, 2000. Provides some life histories of delinquent youths and emphasizes education combined with the youths' acknowledgement of their responsibility in ending delinquent careers. French with English summary.

2075 Lazerges, Christine & Balduyck, Jean-Pierre Response To Juvenile Delinquency: Report To The French Prime Minister, *European Journal On Criminal Policy And Research* 6:581-591, 1998. Tha authors recommend that there be an integrated approach of family, social services organizations, the police, and the courts, to combat juvenile delinquency.

2076 Lernout, Yves The French Trial System, pp 162-173 in Cavadino, Paul (ed.) *Children Who Kill: An Examination Of The Treatment Of Juveniles Who Kill In Different European Countries*. Winchester, United Kingdom: Waterside, 1996. This chapter describes how children accused of very serious violent offenses are processed by the French criminal justice system.

2077 Lioy, Michele Open Residences: An Alternative To Closed Correctional Institutions For Hard-Core Juvenile Delinquents, *Canadian Journal Of Criminology* 20:409-417, 1978. This article describes a French loosely structured, community-based, program emphasizing social reintegration through jobs for hard-core male and female delinquents.

2078 Lorvellec, Soizie Penal Procedures And Minors: Some Recent French Laws (Procédure Pénale Et Mineurs: À Propos De Quelques Lois Françaises Récentes), *Revue Internationale De Criminologie Et De*

Police Technique 69:147-159, 1996. This article provides details on the 1993 French Penal Code that is designed to balance crime protection and juvenile rights.

2079 Mérigeau, Martine Legal Frameworks And Interventions, pp 75-139 in McCarney, Willie (ed.) *Juvenile Delinquents And Young People In Danger In An Open Environment.* Winchester, United Kingdom: Waterside, 1996. This chapter has descriptions of the rights of the child and age of criminal culpability, the legal framework for intervention, prevention and imposition of various measures in dealing with delinquent youths in France. 223p.

2080 Ministère De La Justice *Rights And Obligations Of The Parents: Married and Unmarried Parents (Droits Et Devoirs Des Parents: Parents Mariés, Parents Non Mariés).* Paris, France: Service de L'Information et de la Communication, 2000. This document presents a very clear list of the rights and obligations of each parent within the framework of French law. 15p. French.

2081 Ministère De La Justice *The Directory Of Judicial Statistics (Annuaire Statistique De La Justice. Éditions 2000).* Paris, France: La Documentation Française. Pages 209 to 239 have tables of data on recorded juvenile crimes and dispositions from 1994 to 1998. French.

2082 Ministère De L'Intérieur *Aspects Of Reported Criminality And Delinquency In France In 1996 (Aspects De La Criminalité Et De La Délinquance Constatées En France En 1996).* Paris, France: The Ministry of The Interior, 1997. Official data from both the police and gendarmerie services for various cities, towns and rural communes on reported and cleared incidents, and the age, gender, and nationality characteristics of the accused are tabulated in this document. 382p. French.

2083 Ottenhof, Reynald & Renucci, Jean-François (translated by Sammann, Elizabeth) France, pp 110-124 in Shoemaker, Donald J. (ed.) *International Handbook On Juvenile Justice.* Westport, Connecticut: Greenwood, 1996. Chapter offers a discussion of the juvenile justice system of France.

2084 Ottenhof, Reynald Young Offenders And Young Victims: Unity Or Duality? (Jeunes Auteurs Et Jeunes Victims: Unité Ou Dualité?), *Revue International De Criminologie Et De Police Technique* 42:455-463, 1989. This article presents the logic of and need for childrens' rights.

2085 Patrignani, Angela & Villé, Renaud (eds.) *Rromani Youth: The Pathways Of Juvenile Justice.* Rome, Italy: UNICRI, 1997. This volume describes the involvement of Romani youth groups in property crimes in France, Hungary, and Italy with a good summary of the French juvenile laws and the processing protocol. 180p.

2086 Poignant, Serge *Social Analyses* (*Logiques Sociale*). Paris, France: L'Harmattan, 1991. This study of three gangs concludes that the youthful behavior represents an enduring existential need of the young men and women of the street for food, camaraderie, comfort, affirmation and survival while they exhibited in their seeming anti-establishment attitudes and behavior a remarkable degree of rules, authority, and structure. 159p. French.

2087 Portelli, Serge Family Crime And The Law (Crimes Et Délits De Famille: L'État Du Droit) *Les Cahiers De La Sécurité Intérieur* 28:75-100, 1997. Describes the loss of paternal power under the new family law and recommends that criminal law be resorted to in cases of family violence. French.

2088 Poullain, Bernard & Cirba, Laurence France: Notes On The Juvenile Justice System, pp 141-173 in United Nations Social Defence Research Institute (ed.) *Juvenile Justice: An Internatinal Survey*. Rome, Italy, 1976. This chapter offers an extensive description of the French juvenile justice system and treatment approach to young offenders.

2089 Pradel, Jean Which Delinquents Are To Be Treated With Non-Penal Sanctions, Particularly In French Law (Quels Délinquants Pour Le Traitement En Milieu Libre Notamment En Droits Français?) pp 117-129 in Fondation Internationale Pénale Et Pénitentiaire (ed.) *Elaboration Of The Minimum Rules For Non-Penal Sanctions* (*L'Élaboration Des Règles Minima Pour Le Traitement En Milieu Libre*). Paris, France: Cujas, 1990. The author presents legal, pragmatic, and economic arguments in favor of sentencing youthful minor offenders to a nonpenal environment rather than placing them in custody. 12p. French.

2090 Pradel, Jean Community Service: The French Experience, pp 27-44 in Fondation Internationale Pénale Et Pénitentiaire (ed.) *Community Service As An Alternative To The Prison Sentence*. Bonn, West Germany: International Penal and Penitentiary Foundation, 1987. This chapter presents a report on the use of community service as a sentence for adults and juveniles in France, and this sanction's frequent use for the young.

2091 Renouard, J. M. The Relations Between The Police And Youth: The Research In Question (Les Relations Entre La Police Et Les Jeunes: La Recherche En Question), *Déviance Et Société* 17:419-438, 1993. The author offfers a review of literature for the United States and England

and focuses on youth and police in France. French.

2092 Rollet, Catherine The Early Prevention Of Juvenile Crime, *Journal Of Criminal Policy And Research* 5:83-100, 1996. Offers a summary of the ideas of Philippe Aries and Foucault, and traces the history of the creation and separation of children and delinquents and the state intervention in family sphere.

2093 Rozēs, Simone France, pp 67-80 in Stewart, V. Lorne (ed.) *Justice And Troubled Children Around The World, Vol. 2.* New York, New York: New York University Press, 1981. This chapter describes how France's well-integrated approach to children's problems reflects the willingness of representatives of the various disciplines involved to work together.

2094 Selosse, Jacques (ed.) *Working With The Families Of Marginal Youths (Le Travail Avec Les Familles De Jeunes Marginaux).* Vaucresson, France: Centre De Formation Et De Recherche De L'Éducation Surveillée Annales De Vaucresson, 1979. The four sections of this volume include the importance of the family in general and those of immigrants, child welfare, prejudice and discrimination against young people, correctional education and training, etc. French. 601p.

2095 Strasburg, Paul A. How France Treats Children In Trouble, *Judicature* 61:23-31, 1977. This article discussing some similarities and differences in the philosophies and operations of French and American juvenile justice, three issues are emphasized: judicial discretion, punishment versus treatment, and continuity of responsibility.

2096 Tomlinson, Edward A. *The French Penal Code Of 1994 Amended As Of January 1, 1999.* Littleton, Colorado: Rothman, 1999. The American Series Of Foreign Penal Codes, 1999 has an excellent introduction to the origins of the new French penal code adopted in 1992 providing a translation of the five "books" of the penal code that cover offenses against person, property, the nation and public peace, public health, and the general provisions applicable to all of the above. 278p.

2097 Tournier, Pierre The Detention Of Minors: Followup Observations Of An Incoming Cohort (La Détention Des Mineurs: Observation Suivie D'Une Cohorte D'Entrants). Paris, France: Centre De Recherches Sociologiques Sur Le Droit Et Les Institutions Pénales, 1991. A longitudinal study of the dossiers of male and female incarcerated young French offenders focuses the on length of imprisonment and post-release behavior in 1983. 108p. French.

2098 US National Criminal Justice Reference Service The Police Officer And The Juvenile Problem, pp 99-124 in *International Summaries: A*

Collection Of Selected Translations In Law Enforcement And Criminal Justice, Volume 1. Washington, D.C.: United States: US Government Printing Office, 1978. Chapter discusses the role of the public security police in preventing juvenile delinquency in France, and a description of the organization and activities of the special juvenile delinquency prevention unit of the Paris police department.

2099 Van Kalmthout, Anton M. & Tak, Peter J. P. France, pp 69-148 in Van Kalmthout, Anton M. & Tak, Peter J. P. (eds.) *Sanctions-Systems In The Member States Of The Council Of Europe Part I: Deprivations Of Liberty, Community Service, And Other Substitutes*. Norwell, Massachuettes: Kluwer, 1988. This chapter provides a summary of France's general amnesty under Justice Minister Robert Badinter in the early 1980s, and detailed descriptions of the alternate sanctions such as community service with a small section on juveniles. 361p.

2100 Verrest, Pieter The French Public Prosecution Service, *European Journal Of Crime, Criminal Law And Criminal Justice* 8:210-244, 2000. Provides a description of the multi-faceted coordination and delivery of diverse social services by the Public Ministry (*Ministère Public*) in general, and its relations to others besides the prosecutors, and Childcare Protection Board (La Protection Judiciaire De La Jeuness/PJJ) entrusted with preventing and tackling juvenile crimes.

2101 Wells, Michael French And American Judicial Opinions, *The Yale Journal Of International Law* 19:81-133, 1994. Although mostly about the *cour de cassation*, this is an excellent source on the French judiciary's training, ideology, and role in juvenile justice.

2102 Wyvekens, Anne Mediation And Proximity: Community Justice Centers in Lyons, *European Journal On Criminal Policy And Research* 5:27-42, 1997. This article describes the community justice centers as a significant response to the growing problem of delinquency in Lyons, France.

2103 Wyvekens, A. The Treatment Of Urban Delinquents In Courts (Le Traitemente La Délinquance Urbane En Maison De Justice), *Justices* December:91-101, 1995. This articles offers a discription of and commentary on how juveniles in urban areas are treated by French juvenile courts.

2104 Yvorel, Jean-Jacques *The Child, Paternal Authority And The Judge At The End Of The 19th Century (L'Enfant, La Puissance Paternelle Et Le Juge Du XIXe Siècle)*. Paris, France: Ministère De L'Interieur. Violence En Famille #28, 1997. This volume traces the 19th century incident which originated the French laws that transformed the relationship between the absolute patriarch and the judiciary. 14p. French.

Germany

2105 Albrecht, Hans-Jörg Juvenile Justice And Juvenile Law In The Federal Republic Of Germany, pp 233-269 in Winterdyk, John A. (ed.) *Juvenile Justice Systems: International Perspectives*. Toronto, Canada: Canadian Scholars' Press, 1997. This chapter provides an extensive discussion of the juvenile justice system and youth crime in Germany.

2106 Bettmer, Franz; Messmer, Heinz & Otto, Hans-Uwe Informal Justice And Conflict Solution -- A Research Report On New Intervention Strategies Of Administrative Social Work In The Field Of Juvenile Delinquency, pp 129-144 in Albrecht, Peter Alexis & Backes, Otto (eds.) *Crime Prevention And Intervention: Legal And Ethical Problems*. Berlin, Germany: Walter de Gruyter, 1989. Positive results from a juvenile diversion project in Bielefeld are reported in this study.

2107 Bierbauer, Günter The Schiedmann's Legal Status And The Scope Of His Activities, pp 103-111 in Lloyd-Bostock, Sally (ed.) *Law And Psychology: Papers Presented At SSRC Law And Psychology Conferences 1979-1980*. Oxford, United Kingdom. This volume concerns dispute resolution involving mediators in Germany's juvenile justice system.

2108 Boes, Maria R. The Treatment Of Juvenile Delinquents In Early Modern Germany: A Case Study, *Continuity And Change* 11:43-60, 1996. This essay describes the history of special sentencing policy for juvenile delinquents used in Frankfurt am Main from 1562 to 1692.

2109 Buchholz, Erich The German Democratic Republic, pp 61-90 in Stewart, V. Lorne (ed.) *Justice And Troubled Children Around The World, Vol. 4*. New York, New York: New York University Press, 1982. This chapter discusses the law and procedures of juvenile justice in Germany.

2110 Bunk, G. P. & Stentzel, M. Vocational Training For Juvenile And Young Adult Offenders (Modelle Der Berufserziehung Straffälliger Jugendlicher Und Heranwachsender), *Zeitschrift Für Strafvollzug Und Straffälligenhilfe* 44:73-81, 1995. This article reports results of a survey that examined vocational training of delinquent juveniles and young adults during 1987-1989 in Germany. German.

2111 Dorner, Christine The Third Reich's Policy on Youthful Offenders Using The Example Of Indeterminate Sentences (Jugendkriminalpolitik Im Dritten Reich Am Beispiel Der Unbestimmten Verurteilung), *Monatsschrift Für Kriminologie Und Strafrechtsform* 4:236-246, 1991. The history of indeterminate sentencing is discussed from two points of view: as a part of the history of juvenile criminal law, and as an expression of the conflict between the police and the judiciary in the National Socialist State. German.

2112 Du Bois, Reinmar The German System, pp 131-146 in Cavadino, Paul (ed.) *Children Who Kill: An Examination Of The Treatment Of Juveniles Who Kill In Different European Countries*. Winchester, Unied Kingdom: Waterside, 1996. This chapter provides an overview of the method used to deal with violent juvenile offenders in Germany.

2113 Dünkel, Frieder & Mérigeau, Martine The Results Of Mediation Involving Delinquents And Victims In The Federal Republic Of Germany, (Les Expériences De Médiation Délinquant-Victime En République Fédérale D'Allemagne), pp 95-124 in Dünkel, Frieder & Zermatten, Jean (eds.) *Recent Trends In Penal Law For Minors: Mediation, Community Service And Intermediate Treatment (Nouvelles Tendances Dans Le Droit Pénal Des Mineurs: Médiation, Travail Au Profit De La Communauté Et Traitement Intermédiaire)*. Freiburg, Germany: Max Planck Institute for Foreign and International Criminal Justice, 1990. The use of victim-offender mediation for juvenile offenders in Germany since 1985 is reviewed. French.

2114 Dünkel, Frieder The Development Of Drug-Related Crime And Drug Control In Germany, *International Journal Of Comparative And Applied Criminal Justice* 16:1-14, 1992. This review, surveying trends in drug offenses and sentencing practices in West Germany from 1965 to 1989, shows special emphasis on "dedramatization," or "normalization," in juvenile courts that tended to favor a therapeutic, over a punitive, approach in dealing with 14- to 21-year-old offenders.

2115 Feuerhelm, Wolfgang *The Provision And Organization Of Community Service In Criminal Law (Stellung Und Ausgestaltung Der Gemeinnützigen Arbeit Im Strafrecht)*. Wiesbaden, Germany: Eigenverlag Kriminologische Zentralstelle, 1997. This volume and review includes a discussion of the provisions for community service in Germany's juvenile and adult criminal law. 584p. German.

2116 Geissler, Isolde Deviant Inmate Behavior And Recidivism: An Empirical Study On Juvenile Prison, pp 273-296 Kaiser, Günther & Geissler, Isolde (eds.) *Crime And Criminal Justice: Criminological Research In The 2nd Decade At The Max Planck Institute In Freiburg*. Freiburg, Germany: Max Planck Institute, 1988. Examination of the disciplinary infractions and recidivism among inmates of two juvenile correctional institutions found that rule breaking was common.

2117 Goodman, Randy Summaries Of DCI Country Surveys, Federal Republic of Germany, pp 167-170, in Tomasevski, Katarina (ed.) *Children In Adult Prisons: An International Perspective*. New York: St. Martin's Press, 1986. This report lists findings from the 1982-1984 German survey of Defense for Children International on children in adult prisons.

2118 Grosch, Olaf *Relaxing Enforcement In Juvenile Corrections: Foundation And Practice (Lockerungen Im Jugendstrafvollzup: Grundlagen Und Praxis)*. Freiburg Im Breisgau, Germany: Max Planck Institute for Foreign and International Criminal Law, 1995. This volume examines the impact of relaxing supervision of incarcerated juveniles in the form of work release, supervised and unsupervised leaves of absence. 512p. German.

2119 Grosch, Olaf Disciplinary Measures In Juvenile Prisons: Inmates' Perception Of Severity, pp 297-318 in Kaiser, Günther & Geissler, Isolde (eds.) *Crime And Criminal Justice: Criminological Research In The 2nd Decade At The Max Planck Institute In Freiburg*. Freiburg, Germany: Max Planck Institute, 1988. This study examined the severity of consequences for institutional rule breaking as perceived by inmates of juvenile correctional facilities.

2120 Haller, Volkmar & Machura, Stefan Procedural Justice At German Courts As Seen By Defendants And Juvenile Prisoners, *Social Justice Research* 8:197-215, 1995. In this research, the authors explore the conceptions of defendants and juvenile prisoners of procedural justice in criminal courts in Germany.

2121 Hartmann, Arthur & Kilchling, Michael The Development Of Victim/Offender Mediation In The German Juvenile Justice System, pp 261-282 in Walgrave, Lode (ed.) *Restorative Justice For Juveniles: Potentialities, Risks And Problems For Research*. Leuven, Belgium: Leuven University Press, 1998. This chapter describes the development, practice and evaluation of victim/offender mediation in the German juvenile justice system.

2122 Heinz, Wolfgang Diversion In German Juvenile Justice, *Studies On Crime And Crime Prevention: Its Practice, Impact And Penal Policy Implications* 1:146-166, 1992. This article presents a discussion of various diversion strategies and practices in Germany, along with data on programs, and a description of the United Nations rules on offenders.

2123 Heinz, Wolfgang Effectivity Of Sanctions, pp 297-322 in Junger-Tas, Josine; Boendermaker, Leonieke & Van Der Laan, Peter H. (eds.) *The Future Of The Juvenile Justice System(L'Avenir Du Système Pénal Des*

Mineurs). Leuven, Belgium: Acco, 1991. This essay describes results of a study to evaluate the effectiveness of various sanctions to deter delinquency in Germany.

2124 Hering, Eike *Mechanisms For Judicial Escalation In Juvenile Court Proceedings (Mechanismen Justizieller Eskalation Im Jugendstrafverfahren). Hamburger Studien Zur Kriminologie, Vol. 17.* Hamburg, Germany: Centaurus-Verlagsgesellschft, 1993. This volume reports an investigation of how the juvenile justice system reacts to multiple offending by juveniles and young adults. 338p. Appendix. German.

2125 Herz, Ruth G. German Experience In Victim-Delinquent Mediation: Köln's "Die Waage" Model (Médiation Entre Auteur Et Victime: Le Modèle "Die Waage" À Cologne), pp 125-138 in Dünkel, Frieder & Zermatten, Jean (eds.) *Recent Trends In Penal Law For Minors: Mediation, Community Service And Intermmediate Treatment (Nouvelles Tendances Dans Le Droit Pénal Des Mineurs: Médiation, Travail Au Profit De La Communauté Et Traitement Intermédiaire)*. Freiburg, Germany: Max Planck Institute for Foreign and International Criminal Justice, 1990. A mediation program called Die Waage for juvenile offenders in Cologne, Germany is described by the author. French.

2126 Hinrichs, Günter Psychotherapy With Incarcerated Violent Juvenile Inmates (Psychotherapie Mit Gewalttätern Im Jugendstrafvollzug) *Monatsschrift Für Kriminologie Und Strafrechtsreform* 74:17-26, 1991. A project involving psychotherapeutic work with young, violent inmates in Germany is described in this article. German.

2127 Janssen, Helmut F. & Plewig, Hans-Joachim The Juvenile Justice System Of The Federal Republic Of Germany, pp 23-40 in Kerner, Hans-Jürgen; Galaway, Burt & Janssen, Helmut (eds.) *European And North-American Juvenile Justice Systems: Aspects And Tendencies (Jugendgerichtsbarkeit In Europa Und Nordamerika: Aspekte Und Tendenzen)*. München, West Germany: Schriftenreihe den Deutschen Vereinigung für Jugendgerichte und Jugendgerichtshilfen, 1986. This chapter describes the juvenile justice system of Germany.

2128 Kerner, Hans-Jürgen & Weitekamp, Elmar The Federal Republic Of Germany, pp147-170 in Klein, Malcolm W. (ed.) *Western Systems Of Juvenile Justice*. Beverly Hills, California: Sage, 1984. The authors of this chapter provide a description of the organization and operation of the juvenile justice system in Germany.

2129 Kersten, Joachim The Institutional Control Of Girls And Boys: An Attempt At A Gender-Specific Approach, pp 129-144 in Cain, Maureen (ed.) *Growing Up Good: Policing The Behavior Of Girls in Europe.* Newbury Park, California: Sage, 1989. This chapter looks at the gender-related differential handling of girs in German corrections institutions dealing with young people of both sexes.

2130 Kersten, Joachim Incarcerated Juvenile Offenders In The German Federal Republic, pp 283-302 in Kerner, Hans-Jürgen; Galaway, Burt & Janssen, Helmut (eds.) *European And North-American Juvenile Justice Systems: Aspects And Tendencies (Jugendgerichtsbarkeit In Europa Und Nordamerika: Aspekte Und Tendenzen).* Munich, West Germany: Schriftenreihe den Deutschen Vereinigung für Jugendgerichte und Jugendgerichtshilfen, 1986. This chapter describes the condition and situation of juveniles housed in prisons in Germany.

2131 Klingemann, Harald K.-H. Goal Conflicts In Correctional Institutions For Juvenile Delinquents, *British Journal Of Criminology* 22:140-164, 1982. When research on conflicts in four correctional institutions for juvenile delinquents and one public educational center for pre-delinquents in West Germany was carried out, the findings fail to reveal any functional goal conflicts.

2132 Knölker, U.; Schüler-Springorum, H. & Nissen, G. Federal Republic Of Germany, pp 81-94 in Stewart, V. Lorne (ed.) *Justice And Troubled Children Around The World, Vol. 2.* New York, New York: New York University Press, 1981. The clinical treatment of children with behavior problems in Germany is described in this volume.

2133 Kury, Helmut Treatment Of Young Remand Prisoners: Problems And Results Of A Research Project, pp 356-375 in Wegener, Hermann; Lösel, Friedrich & Haisch, Jochen (eds.) *Criminal Behavior And The Justice System: Psychological Perspectives.* New York, New York: Springer-Verlag, 1989. This chapter describes Freiburg's small, pretrial, detention unit for juvenile offenders and its treatment program based on behavior therapy.

2134 Löschnig-Gspandi, Marianne & Kilchling, Michael Victim/Offender Mediation And Victim Compensation In Austria And Germany--Stocktaking And Perspectives For Future Research, *European Journal Of Crime Criminal Law And Criminal Justice* 5:58-78, 1997. The authors examine the general legal background of victim offender mediation, and introduce restorative elements of German criminal law in the juvenile and adult justice systems.

2135 Ludwig, Wolfgang *Diversion: Punishment In New Clothes? (Diversion: Strafe Im Neuen Gewand).* Berlin, Germany: Walter de Gruyter, 1989. This critical analysis of the diversion of young offenders includes discussion of diversion as a social movement and the involvement of judges and prosecutors, and compares diversion in the United States and Germany. 131p. German.

2136 Ludwig-Meyerhofer, Wolfgang & Rzepka, Dorothea Diversion And Offender Orientation In Juvenile Criminal Law (Diversion Und Täterorientierung Im Jugendstrafrecht), *Monatsschrift Für Kriminologie Und Strafrechtsreform* 81:17-37, 1998. Using data from court files of trials, this study found that sociobiographic peculiarities of defendants in terms of family, school, and workplace had an influence on the sentencing decisions, although variables related to the offenses did have a stronger impact. German.

2137 Max Planck Institute For Foreign And International Penal Law *Criminological Research Unit Research In Criminal Justice: Stock-Taking Of Criminological Research At The Max Planck Institute For Foreign And International Penal Law After A Decade*. Freiburg, West Germany, 1982. This volume provides summaries of 27 studies of juvenile delinquency, detention, probation, recidivism, and rehabilitation conducted during the first decade of criminological research at the Max Planck Institute. 508p.

2138 Mérigeau, Martine Evolution Of Penal Rights Of Juveniles And Young Adults In The Federal Republic Of Germany (Evolution De Droit Pénal Des Mineurs Et Des Jeunes Adultes En République Fédéral d'Allemagne), *Revue Internationale De Criminologie Et De Police Technique* 43:309-322, 1990. The author focuses on Germany's 1989 juvenile law replacing the 1953 Youth Act, that is geared to rehabilitation and new means of conflict resolution through informal community measures. French with English summary.

2139 Mérigeau, Martine New Alternatives To Penal Sanction For Minors In The Federal Republic Of Germany: Practice And Evaluation (Nouvelles Alternatives À La Peine D'Emprisonnement Des Mineurs En République Fédérale D'Allemagne-Pratique Et Évaluation), pp 211-230 in Dünkel, Frieder & Zermatten, Jean (eds.) *Recent Trends In Penal Law For Minors: Mediation, Community Service And Intermediate Treatment (Nouvelles Tendances Dans Le Droit Pénal Des Mineurs: Médiation, Travail Au Profit De La Communauté Et Traitement Intermédiaire)*. Freiburg, Germany: Max Planck Institute for Foreign and International Criminal Justice, 1990. Alternatives to incarceration involving personal supervision by a social worker, group training, community service, and victim offender mediation in Lubeck, Braunschweiz, Munich and Uelzen are described.

2140 Micheel, Heinz-Günter *Diversion As An Extension Of Social Control: An Empirical Study Using Discrete Models (Diversion Als Ausweitung Sozialer Kontrolle? Eine Empirishe Studie Mit Einer Einführung In Diskrete Ergebnis-Modelle).* Berlin, Germany: Verlag Köster, 1994. A discrete-outcome model is used to determine the probable outcome of formal proceedings against juvenile offenders treated in a diversion project in Bielefeld, Germany. 179p. German.

2141 Neubacher, Frank Xenophobic Arson Attacks Following The Reunification (Die Fremdenfeindlichen Brandanschlaege Nach Der Vereinigung), *Monatsschrift Für Kriminologie Und Strafrechtsreform* 82:1-15, 1999. This study focused on the phenomenon of arson attacks against resident-foreigners in Germany by juveniles and young adults. German.

2142 Pelikan, Christa Conflict Resolution Between Victims And Offenders In Austria And In The Federal Republic Of Germany, pp 151-172 in Heidensohn, Frances & Farrell, Martin (eds.) *Crime In Europe.* London, United Kingdom: Routledge, 1991. Conflict resolution involving juvenile offenders in Austria and Germany is described in this chapter.

2143 Rotthaus, Karl-Peter Imprisonment Of Juveniles In The Federal Republic Of Germany, pp 55-61 in Kerner, Hans-Jürgen; Galaway, Burt & Janssen, Helmut (eds.) *European And North-American Juvenile Justice Systems: Aspects And Tendencies (Jugendgerichtsbarkeit In Europa Und Nordamerika: Aspekte Und Tendenzen).* Munich, West Germany: Schriftenreihe den Deutschen Vereinigung für Jugendgerichte und Jugendgerichtshilfen, 1986. The author describes the sentencing and custodial practices in cases involving minors in Germany. German.

2144 Sack, Fritz The German Situation: Unique And Delayed (La Situation Allemande: Un Cas Unique Et En Retard), pp 153-206 in Hebberecht, Patrick & Sack, Fritz (eds.) *The Prevention Of Delinquency In Europe: New Stratégies (La Prévention De La Délinquance En Europe: Nouvelles Stratégies).* Paris, France: L'Harmatten, 1997. This chapter discusses the German delinquency prevention measures of recent years. French.

2145 Steinhilper, Monica Social Work Within The Police Department - Experiences From A German Perspective, pp 343-356 in Kerner, Hans-Jürgen; Galaway, Burt & Janssen, Helmut (eds.) *European And North-American Juvenile Justice Systems: Aspects And Tendencies (Jugendgerichtsbarkeit In Europa Und Nordamerika: Aspekte Und Tendenzen).* Munich, West Germany: Schriftenreihe den Deutschen Vereinigung für Jugendgerichte und Jugendgerichtshilfen, 1986. In this chapter, the author describes a police and social worker initiated prevention program initiated in Hanover, Germany.

2146 Teske, Raymond H. C. Jr. & Albrecht, Hans-Jörg Prosecution And Sentencing Patterns In The Federal Republic Of Germany, *International Criminal Justice Review* 2:76-104, 1992. The statistics on and procedures governing the prosecution and sentencing of juveniles and adults are described in this article.

2147 Weidner, Jens & Wolters, Jörg M. Aggression And Delinquency: Special Prevention Training For Violent Repeat Offenders (Aggression Und Delinquenz: Ein Spezialpräventives Training Für Gewalttätige Wiederholungstäter), *Monatsschrift Für Kriminologie Und Strafrechtsform* 4:210-223, 1991. This study evaluates the Anti-Aggressiveness-Training program for youth in prison in Hameln, Germany. German.

2148 Weitekamp, Elmar G. M.; Kerner, Hans-Jürgen & Herberger, Scania Marita Germany, pp 251-304 in Mehlbye, Jill & Walgrave, Lode (eds.) Confronting Youth In Europe: Juvenile Crime And Juvenile Justice. Copenhagen, Denmark: AKF Forlaget, 1998. This chapter provides some historical background, data on the extent and nature of delinquency, and an extensive discussion of the current juvenile justice/correctional system in Germany.

2149 Wolfe, Nancy Travis Germany, pp 125-145 in Shoemaker, Donald J. (ed.) *International Handbook On Juvenile Justice*. Westport, Connecticut: Greenwood, 1996. This chapter offers a discussion of the juvenile justice system in Germany.

2150 Wolfe, Nancy Travis Socialist Juvenile Justice: The German Democratic Republic, pp 349-376 in Hackler, Jim (ed.) *Official Responses To Problem Juveniles: Some International Reflections*. Euskadi, Spain: The Oñati International Institute for the Sociology of Law, 1991. This chapter describes the apparent partial success of efforts to deal with juvenile delinquency in East Germany prior to reunification.

Ghana

2151 Arthur, John A. Rehabilitation Of Juvenile Offenders In Ghana, *Journal Of Offender Rehabilitation* 24:23-37, 1996. This article deals with the social context of delinquency and rehabilitation in Ghana.

Greece

2152 Chaidou, Anthozoe Griechenland/Greece, pp 251-269 in Frieder, Dünkel & Vagg, Jon (eds.) *Waiting For Trial: International Perspectives On The Use Of Pretrial Detention.* Freiburg, Germany: Max Planck Institute For Foreign And International Criminal Law, 1994. A small section devoted to juveniles discusses the high rate of juveniles in pre-trial detention, and the lack of separate facilities for them. German with English summary.

2153 European Urban Delinquency And Crime-Conference 1995 *Delegate Conference Papers And Appendices.* London, United Kingdom: Wandsworth, 1995. This report includes a paper on varioious initiatives for young offenders in Greece. 2 Vols.

2154 Kotsopoulos, S. & Loutsi, Z. Trends Of Juvenile Delinquency In Greece, *International Journal Of Offender Therapy And Comparative Criminology* 21:270-278, 1977. This study of Greek trends on who is referred to the juvenile authorities and subsequently labeled as delinquent focuses on the apparent reasons, offenses, or complaints, that lead to the referral, who takes the initiative for the referral, and how the court responds to the referral.

2155 Petousi, Vassiliki & Stavrou, Kalliopi Greece, pp 146-159 in Shoemaker, Donald J. (ed.) *International Handbook On Juvenile Justice.* Westport, Connecticut: Greenwood, 1996. The authors provides a discussion of the juvenile justice system of Greece.

2156 Pitsela, Angelika Greece, pp 149-170 in Van Kalmthout, Anton M. & Tak, Peter J. P. (eds.) *Sanctions-Systems In The Member States Of The Council Of Europe Part I.* Boston, Massachusettes: Kluwer, 1988. This essay offers a general description of the Greek sanction practices include-ing some of the rules regarding juveniles offenders.

2157 Spinellis, Dionysios & Spinellis, Calliope D. *Greece: Criminal Justice Systems In Europe And North America.* Monsey, New York: Criminal Justice Press, 1999. This volume includes the demographics of, statistics and research on crime and criminal justice, organization and procedures for investigating, processing, sentencing, and sanctions, as well as a description of the Greek statutes and provisions regarding juvenile offenders. 65p.

2158 Vouyoucas, Constantin New Perspective In Greece On The Factors In Juvenile Delinquency And Its Treatment (Perspectives Nouvelles en Grèce Sur Les Facteurs De La Délinquance Juvénile Et Le Traitement Des Jeunes Auteurs D'Infractions), *Cahiers De Defense Social* 2:53-

62:1983. The author argues that to successfully treat juvenile offenders in Greece, preliminary research into the factors underlying youth crime is needed and suggests areas of inquiry. French with English summary.

Guatemala

2159 Human Rights Watch Children's Rights Project *Guatemala's Forgotten Children: Police Violence And Abuses In Detention.* New York, New York, 1997. This report is on the abuse of Guatemalan street children by the national police and private security guards under the jurisdiction of the Interior Ministry. 132p. Appendix.

Guyana

2160 Dodd, David J. & Parris, Michael An Urban Plantation: Socio-Cultural Aspects Of Crime And Delinquency In Georgetown, Guyana, *International Journal Of Criminology And Penology* 5:31-61, 1977. This article presents data on official crime rates by age, and argues the the colonial "plantation" relationship of haves and have-nots is responsible for the bulk of offense behavior.

Hong Kong

2161 Gaylord, Mark S. Hong Kong, pp 160-174 in Shoemaker, Donald J. (ed.) *International Handbook On Juvenile Justice.* Westport, Connecticut: Greenwood, 1996. In this discussion, the author provides insights into the operation of Hong Kong's system of juvenile justice.

2162 Gray, Patricia The Emergence Of The Disciplinary Welfare Sanction In Hong Kong, *Howard Journal* 36:187-208, 1997. This history of the Hong Kong juvenile justice system argues that the court is an institutional network of power relations that formulat policies and programs that regulate the behavior delinquent youth.

2163 Ho, Ting-Pong Children's Evidence: Mandating Change In The Legal System Of Hong Kong, pp 182-200 in Bottoms, Bette L. & Goodman, Gail S. (eds.) *International Perspectives On Child Abuse And Children's Testimony: Psychological Research And Law.* Thousand Oaks, California: Sage, 1996. This chapter reviews legal practices regarding child witnesses in cases of child abuse in Hong Kong, describes official statistics of allegations and prosecutions, and discusses procedures for handling allegations.

2164 Japan Ministry Of Justice Research And Training Institute Hong Kong, pp 45-50 in United Nations Asia And Far East Institute (ed.) *Asia Crime Report No. 1*. Tokyo, Japan: UNAFEI, 1993. This chapter provides some information on facilities for young offenders in Hong Kong.

2165 Kwan, Tsung Pui The Correction Of Young Offenders In Hong Kong, pp 43-50 in Hideo, Utsuro (ed.) *Materials Produced During The 78th International Seminar On Contemporary Achievements And Future Perspectives In Policies For Corrections*. Tokyo: UNAFEI, 1988. The institutions that deal with juvenile offenders in Hong Kong are described in this document which also includes data on the characteristics of young offenders and their processing.

2166 Traver, Harold Juvenile Delinquency in Hong Kong, pp 113-137 in Winterdyk, John A. (ed.) *Juvenile Justice Systems: International Perspectives*. Toronto, Canada: Canadian Scholars' Press, 1997. This chapter provides an extensive description of the history and contemporary structure of the juvenile justice system along with information on delinquency in Hong Kong.

2167 Ying, Kwok-Ching Rick Juvenile Justice In Hong Kong, pp 269-287 in United Nations Asia and Far East Institute (ed.) *UNICEF Resource Material Series No. 46*. Tokyo, Japan: UNAFEI, 1995. The author provides information on age limits and a variety of aspects of drug treatment for juveniles in Hong Kong.

Hungary

2168 Herczog, Mária & Irk, Ferenc Comparative Juvenile Justice: An Overview Of Hungary, pp 303-330 in Winterdyk, John A. (eds.) *Juvenile Justice Systems: International Perspectives*. Toronto, Canada: Canadian Scholars' Press. In this chapter the author provides a history of abd describes the contemporary structure of juvenile justice in Hungary along with some information on offenders.

2169 Kóczé, Angela & Versitz, Piroska Juvenile Justice And Rromani Youths In Hungary: The Case Of Pest County, pp 21-66 in Patrignani, Angela & Villé, Renaud (eds.) *Rromani Youths: The Pathways Of Juvenile Justice*. Rome, Italy: United Nations Interregional Crime And Justice Research Institute, 1997. This is a description of the social conditions of Rromani youth in post-communist Hungary, and their interaction with the various governmental agencies including the juvenile justice system.

India

2170 Bedi, M. S. Problems Of Juvenile Correctional Institutions, pp 33-38 in Panakal, J. J. & Gokhale, S. D. (eds.) *Crime And Corrections In India.* Bombay, India: Tata Institute of Social Sciences, 1989. This chapter offers a brief description of juvenile corrections in India.

2171 Bedi, M. S. Problems Of Juvenile Correctional Institutions In India, *Social Defence* 20:30-38, 1985. The author attributes the problems of juvenile corrections in India to inadequate and unfavorable conditions of the institutions, lack of coordination among related social services, and an authoritarian administration.

2172 Chatterjee, Gautam *Child Criminals And The Raj.* New Delhi, India: Akshaya Publications, 1995. This historic study focuses on the British colonial and current approaches to juvenile offenders. 226p.

2173 Goel, J. S. Juvenile Justice, pp 47-50 in Chakrabarti, N. K. (ed.) *Administration Of Criminal Justice: The Correctional Services.* New Delhi, India: Deep & Deep Publications, 1997. This discussion of the juvenile justice system in India includes the Juvenile Justice Act of 1986.

2174 Gokhale, S. D. & Sohoni, N. K. The Juvenile Justice System In India: Summary Of Findings Of The Three Sub-Studies In Bombay, Delhi And Madras, pp 15-54 in United Nations Social Defence Research Institute (ed.) *Juvenile Justice An International Survey.* Rome, Italy, 1976. The authors describe the juvenile justice system, organization, and case processing of delinquent youths, as well as descriptions of offender and clinical populations in India.

2175 Goodman, Randy Summaries Of DCI Country Surveys-India, pp 171-174 in Tomasevski, Katarina (ed) *Children In Adult Prisons: An International Perspective.* New York, New York: St. Martin's Press, 1986. Findings of the Defense for Children International the 1982-1984 survey of children in adult Indian prisons are represented in this section.

2176 Hartjen, Clayton A. & Kethineni, Sesha India, pp 175-190 in Shoemaker, Donald J. (ed.) *International Handbook On Juvenile Justice.* Westport, Connecticut: Greenwood, 1996. The authors provide a discussion of the juvenile justice system of India.

2177 Hartjen, Clayton A. & Priyadarsini, S. *Delinquency In India: A Comparative Analysis.* New Brunswick, New Jersey: Rutgers University Press, 1984. In addition to presenting data on offense behavior, this volume describes the laws, system of juvenile justice and corrections in India, and public and official reactions to offense behavior. 252p.

2178 Hartjen, Clayton A. Legal Change And Juvenile Justice In India, *International Criminal Justice Review* 5:1-16, 1995. This article describes the Juvenile Justice Act of 1986, which served to nationalize and standardize juvenile justice throughout India.

2179 Kaldate, S. V. *Society, Delinquent And Juvenile Court*. Delhi, India: Ajanta Books, 1982. Besides discussing the causes of delinquency, this book compares juvenile courts in five districts in India. 179p.

2180 Krishnamurty, V. & Bhaskara, Rao S. V. Handling Delinquent At Home, *Social Defence* 21:36-38, 1986. The authors suggest that rates of delinquency in India could be reduced if parents took greater responsibility for their adolescents by directing them toward more positive behaviors.

2181 Kulkarni, Akka India, pp 49-56 in Stewart, V. Lorne (ed.) *Justice And Troubled Children Around The World, Vol. I*. New York, New York: New York University Press, 1980. This chapter profiles juvenile justice in Bombay, India and provides an overview of the practices of the child-welfare system in that country.

2182 Ministry Of Law And Justice *The Juvenile Justice Act, 1986*. The Gazette of India Extraordinary Part II – Section 1. New Delhi, India, 1986. This document details the delinquency law passed in Inida in 1986, and includes details on the age of responsibility, offenses, judicial processing, and correctional institutions. 39p.

2183 Mookerjee, Asutosh *Juvenile Justice: An In-Depth Study On Matters Related To Children*. Calcutta, India: S. C. Sarkar, 1989. In this book, a description of laws regarding children and juvenile justice in India is presented, along with a discussion of the Juvenile Justice Act of 1986. 367p.

2184 Priyadarsini, S. & Hartjen, Clayton A. Delinquency And Corrections In India, pp 109-123 in Jensen, Gary F. (ed.) *Sociology Of Delinquency: Current Issues*. Beverly Hills, California: Sage, 1981. Besides a brief description of offense rates, this chapter provides a discussion of the juvenile justice system in India and its processing of young offenders.

2185 Segal, Uma A. Children As Witnesses: India Is Not Ready, pp 266-282 in Bottoms, Bette L. & Goodman, Gail S. (eds.) *International Perspectives On Child Abuse and Children's Testimony: Psychological Research And Law*. Thousand Oaks, California: Sage, 1996. This chapter reviews the sociocultural context of Indian society, the traditional Indian family and perceptions of children in India and child victims, and discusses the Indian Constitution, children's rights and the use of children as witness, the juvenile justice system, and presents data on the incidence of child abuse.

2186 Sethna, Jehangir M. J. *Society And The Criminal.* Bombay, India: N. M. Tripathi Private Limited, 1980. In the last section of this volume, juvenile delinquency, its causes and treatment, juvenile legislation and the courts, children aid societies and residential treatment centers are addressed. 417p.

2187 Sinha, Sanat Kumar Children In Detention In Bihar, India, pp 181-183 in United Nations Expert Group Meeting (eds.) *Children In Trouble.* United Nations Centre for Human Rights: Vienna, Austria, 1994. This chapter offers a brief discussion of the situation of detained children in the Indian state of Bihar.

2188 Vadackumchery, James *The Police And Delinquency In India.* New Delhi, India: APH Publishing, 1996. This book is a critique of the failure of India in addressing the problems of delinquent children and children in trouble. 181p.

Indonesia

2189 Gosita, Arif The Prevention Of Child Exploitation And Abuse: A Community Responsibility, pp 31-40 in Strang, Heather & Vernon, Julia (eds.) *International Trends In Crime: East Meets West.* Canberra, Australia: Australian Institute of Criminology, 1992. This chapter discusses the problem of child exploitation and laws designed to regulate it in Indonesia.

2190 Japan Ministry Of Justice Research And Training Institute Indonesia, pp 51-55 in United Nations Asia And Far East Institute (ed.) *Asia Crime Report No. 1.* Tokyo, Japan: UNAFEI, 1993. This chapter provides some information on the numbers of youth and young people in institutions in Indonesia.

2191 Sisworahardjo, Suwantji Services For Juvenile Delinquents In Indonesia, pp 71-78 in Strang, Heather & Vernon, Julia (eds.) *International Trends In Crime: East Meets West.* Canberra, Australia: Australian Institute of Criminology, 1992. This chapter discusses, with illustrations on how they are implemented in government institutions, the various services for juvenile delinquents that are available in Indonesia.

2192 United Nations Social Defence Research Institute Indonesia: Notes On The Juvenile Justice System, pp 175-181 in United Nations Social Defence Research Institute (ed.) *Juvenile Justice: An International*

Survey. Rome, Italy, 1976. *This c*hapter offers a brief overview of the Indonesian system of justice for juveniles.

Ireland

2193 Breathnach, Seamus Juvenile Delinquency In The Irish Republic: Sketching A Historical Perspective, pp 693-734 in Hess, Albert G. & Clement, Priscilla F. (eds.) *History Of Juvenile Delinquency: A Collection Of Essays On Crime Committed By Young Offenders, In History And In Selected Countries, Vol. 2*. Aalen, Germany: Scientia Verlag, 1993. This is a description of juvenile crime and how it has been dealt with in Ireland since the 1700s to the present.

2194 Farelly, John *Crime Custody & Community: Juvenile Justice & Crime With Particular Relevance To Sean McDermott Street.* Dublin, Ireland: Voluntary & Statutory Bodies, 1989. In this report, the author describes the juvenile justice system of Ireland, the Juvenile Liaison Scheme, children's court, probation, welfare service, as well as residential and custodial institutions for juvenile offenders. 150p.

2195 Hanly, Conor Child Offenders: The Changing Response Of Irish Law, *Dublin University Law Journal* 19:113-138, 1997. This article provides a description of the age of culpability, the present law on juveniles, as well as information on informal justice and children's courts.

2196 Harvey, Brian & Menton, Mary Ireland's Young Homeless, *Children And Youth Services Review* 11:31-44, 1989. This article describes the impact of Ireland's history of neglect and indifference to homeless youth.

2197 O'Sullivan, Denis Negotiation In The Maintenance Of Social Control: A Study In An Irish Correctional School, *International Journal Of Criminology And Penology* 6:31-42, 1978. The process of negotiation between pupils and staff in maintaining social control in a school for offenders is investigated in this paper.

2198 O'Sullivan, Eoin Ireland pp 307-352 in Mehlbye, Jill & Walgrave, Lode (eds.) *Confronting Youth In Europe: Juvenile Crime And Juvenile Justice*. Copenhagen, Denmark: AKF Forlaget, 1998. This chapter provides an historical background of, some data on offenders, and an extensive discussion of the contemporary organization and operation of juvenile justice and corrections agencies in Ireland.

2199 Tutt, Norman Home And Away: A New Social Policy For Children In Ireland, *European Journal On Criminal Policy And Research* 2:115-122, 1997. This article describes the history of Ireland's legislation regarding children, and discussed issues regarding juvenile justice in Ireland.

Israel

2200 Ajzenstadt, Mimi & Steinberg, Oneda The Elasticity Of The Law: Treating Girls In Distress In Israel Through The Shadow Of The Law, *British Journal Of Criminology* 35:236-247, 1995. This article addresses the issue of using the "shadow of the law" by Israel's Unit For Girls In Distress.

2201 Cohen, Yona Stages In The Development Of The Juvenile Probation Services In Israel, *Juvenile And Family Court Journal* 31:85-92, 1980. The development of juvenile probation services in Israel is described in this article.

2202 Cohen, Yona Observations On The Juvenile Court In Israel, *Juvenile Justice* 27:39-41, 1976. This article is a description of the juvenile court in Israel, and its role as a criminal court.

2203 Fischer, Michael & Geiger, Brenda A Model For Change Following The Kibbutz Resocialization Program, *Journal Of Offender Rehabilitation* 21:221-237, 1994. This assessment suggests that the Kibbutz experiment serves as a model of change in treatment of juvenile offenders.

2204 Fischer, Michael; Teichman, Meir & Geiger, Brenda The Rehabilitation Of Young Israeli Offenders: A Kibbutz Experiment, *International Journal Of Offender Therapy And Comparative Criminology* 29:277-279, 1985. This essay describes the theory behind a kibbutz rehabilitation project for juveniles.

2205 Fishman, Gideon; Kraus, Vered & Lever, Henry Factors Affecting Juvenile Court Decisions in Israel: A Multivariate Approach, *Sociological Inquiry* 52:291-305, 1982. Using data on youths brought to courts, the authors analyzed the relationship between age, record, offense and case outcome.

2206 Hassin, Yael Presence Of Parents During Interrogation Of Their Children, *Juvenile And Family Court Journal* 32:33-42, 1981. This paper argues that some of the negative effects of interrogating the child could be lessened by allowing parents to be present during the process.

2207 Karp, Judith Alternatives In The Treatment Of Juvenile Offenders In Israel, pp 142-149 in United Nations Expert Group Meeting (eds.) *Children And Juveniles In Detention: Application Of Human rights Standards*. The United Nations Centre for Human Rights: Vienna, Austria, 1994. This chapter describes underlying principles of law on juveniles, the Youth Law of 1971, and diversion practices in Israel.

2208 Kashti, Yitzak The Education Of Problem Adolescents In Israel, pp 55-64 in Bullock, Roger (ed.) *Problem Adolescents: An International View.* London, United Kingdom: Whiting & Burch, 1992. This chapter describes how problem juveniles are dealt with by the educational system of Israel, and the growth of specialized facilities to divert such cases from regular schools.

2209 Maroon, Istifan *Evaluating A Therapeutic Intervention Programme For Alienated Youth And Their Families In A Voluntary Institutional Framework.* Hildesheim, Germany: Olms, 1995. This study describes the psychosocial characteristics of Arab juvenile offenders in Israel, and provides recommendations for their treatment. 163p.

2210 Mesch, Gustavo S. & Fishman, Gideon Entering The System: Ethnic Differences In Closing Juvenile Criminal Files In Israel, *Journal Of Research In Crime And Delinquency* 36:175-193, 1999. This study investigated the differences between Arabs and Jews regarding court decisions to close juvenile criminal files or to prosecute the suspect.

2211 Rahav, Giora Ethnic Origins And The Disposition Of Delinquents In Israel, *International Journal Of Comparative And Applied Criminal Justice* 4:63-74, 1980. This analysis of official delinquency data demonstrates the discriminatory treatment of ethnic groups by Israeli juvenile courts.

2212 Reifen, David Israel, pp 57-86 in Stewart, V. Lorne (ed.). *Justice And Troubled Children Around The World, Vol. 1.* New York, New York: New York University Press, 1980. This chapter describes the various social services that Israel provides delinquent and other children.

2213 Romi, Shlomo & Teichman, Meir Participant And Symbolic Modeling And The Self-Efficacy Of Israeli "Street Corner" Youth Counselors, *Journal Of Offender Rehabilitation* 24:155-169, 1996. In this article a training program for youth advancement counselors is described.

2214 Sebba, Leslie Israel, pp 97-120 in Klein, Malcolm W. (ed.). *Western Systems Of Juvenile Justice.* Beverly Hills, California: Sage, 1984. The author describes the juvenile justice system of Israel, and provides a chart of its structure.

2215 Sebba, Leslie Legalism Versus Welfarism In Israel's Juvenile Justice System, *Israel Law Review* 16:461-498, 1981. This paper presents an analysis of the structure of juvenile justice legislation and institutions in Israel.

2216 Shichor, David Clients' Views Of Juvenile Justice Personnel: Perceptions Of Continuing And Noncontinuing Delinquents In Israel, *Criminal Justice Review* 5:85-100, 1980. This study analyzed how the "clients" of the juvenile justice system in Israel viewed the personnel of the various agencies of the system.

2217 Slonim-Nevo, Vered Evaluating The Effectiveness Of Juvenile Probation Officers: An Israeli Study, *Journal Of Offender Rehabilitation* 28:77-90, 1999. In this study of female and male adolescents who were being treated by probation officers, numerous differences between control and experimental groups were found regarding the effectiveness of treatment.

2218 Sternberg, Kathleen J.; Lamb, Michael E. & Hershkowitz, Irit Child Sexual Abuse Investigations In Israel: Evaluating Innovative Practices, pp 62-76 in in Bottoms, Bette L. & Goodman, Gail S. (eds.) *International Perspectives On Child Abuse And Children's Testimony: Psychological Research And Law*. Thousand Oaks, California: Sage, 1996. This chapter offers a review of the Israeli system for investigating child sex crimes and summarizes research dealing with the problem.

2219 Weiss, Karin & Wozner, Yochanan Institutional Treatment For Juvenile Delinquents: 2000 Offenders After Three Years, *Journal Of Offender Rehabilitation* 21:165-182, 1994. This article presents an analysis of the results of treatment of some 2000 juveniles in Israeli institutions over a three year period.

2220 Wozner, Yochanan & Bilha, Arad-Davidson Community Hostels: An Alternative To Rehabilitating Young Offenders, *Journal Of Offender Rehabilitation* 20:37-60, 1994. The authors found that up to three years after being discharged, a large percentage of youths were successful on a variety of dimensions.

Italy

2221 Azzacconi, Matilde The Italian Juvenile Penal Process And Children Who Kill, pp 115-125 in Cavadino, Paul (ed.) *Children Who Kill*. Winchester,United Kingdom: Waterside, 1996. This chapter describes how child-murderers are treated by the Italian juvenile justice and corrections systems.

2222 Baldry, Anna Costanza Victim Offender Mediation In The Italian Juvenile Justice System: The Role Of The Social Worker, *British Journal Of Social Work* 28:729-744, 1998. This study on victim-offender mediation in the Italian juvenile justice system is based on a national survey of social workers involved with the program.

2223 Cavalli, Alessandro Reclamation From Maladjustment In A Social System In A State Of Transition, pp 87-89 in United Nations Crime Prevention And Criminal Justice Program International Scientific And Professional Advisory Council (ed.) *Juveniles And Delinquency: In The Italian And European Context*. Milan, Italy, 1995. The author argues that since one becomes and is not born delinquent, the process of reclamation should begin early.

2224 Cipollini, Roberta Gypsy Girls In An Italian Juvenile Court, pp 114-129 in Cain, Maureen (ed.) *Growing Up Good: Policing The Behavior Of Girls In Europe*. Newbury Park, California: Sage, 1989. This chapter describes research demonstrating that gypsy girls are treated differently from others in the Italian juvenile and criminal justice systems.

2225 Costarelli, Sandro Juvenile Justice And Romani Youths In Italy: The Case of Florence, pp 67-97 in Patrignani, Angela & Villé, Renaud (eds.) *Rromani Youths: The Pathways Of Juvenile Justice*. Rome, Italy: United Nations Interregional Crime and Justice Research Institute, 1997. This chapter provides an extensive discussion of the Italian problem of how Romani youths are treated in the juvenile justice system.

2226 Dente, Maria Grazia Intervention By The Municipal Administration, pp 59-62 in United Nations Crime Prevention And Criminal Justice Program International Scientific And Professional Advisory Council (ed.) *Juveniles And Delinquency: In The Italian And European Context*. Milan, Italy, 1995. This chapter briefly describes various delinquency intervention programs that are run by the city of Milan.

2227 Di Gennaro, Giuseppe & Bonomo, Luisa Bianchi Italy, pp 1-30 in Stewart, V. Lorne (ed.) *Justice And Troubled Children Around The World, Vol. 3*. New York, New York: New York University Press, 1981. This chapter offers a discussion of the interrelationships among the family, official agencies, and young offenders in Italy.

2228 Ferracuti, Franco *Criminogical And Psychiatric-Forensic Aspects Of Minors* (*Aspetti Criminologici E Psichiatrico-Forensi Dell'età Minore*). Milan, Italy: Dott. A. Giuffrè Editore, 1987. Seventeen essays on juvenile delinquency and juvenile justice are presented in this anthology on Italy. 206p. Italian.

2229 Ferrari-Bravo, Gabriella & Arcidiacono, Caterina Compounded Misunderstanding: Relations Between Staff And Girls In An Italian Juvenile Prison, pp 145-157 in Cain, Maureen (ed.) *Growing Up Good: Policing The Behavior Of Girls In Europe*. Newbury Park, California: Sage, 1989. This chapter describes an attempt to "integrate" female delinquents into a formally all male penal institution in Italy.

2230 Gatti, Uberto & Ceretti, Adolfo Italian Experiences Of Victim-Offender Mediation In The Juvenile Justice System, pp 201-218 in Walgrave, Lode (ed.) *Restorative Justice For Juveniles: Potentialities, Risks And Problems*. Leuven, Belgium: Leuven University Press, 1998. This chapter provides a brief history of juvenile justice in Italy, and the development of mediation as an alternative approach.

2231 Gatti, Uberto & Verde, Alfredo Italy, pp 355-387 in Mehlbye, Jill & Walgrave, Lode (eds.) *Confronting Youth In Europe: Juvenile Crime And Juvenile Justice*. Copenhagen, AKF Forlaget, 1998. The authors describe the structure and operation of juvenile justice and corrections in present day Italy.

2232 Gatti, Uberto & Verde, Alfredo Comparative Juvenile Justice: An Overview Of Italy, pp 177-204 in Winterdyk, John A. (ed.) *Juvenile Justice Systems: International Perspectives*. Toronto: Canadian Scholars' Press, 1997. This chapter describes the history and the contemporary structure of juvenile justice in Italy.

2233 Gatti, Uberto & Verde, Alfredo The Dividing Line Between Punishment And Help: New Questions, Old Answers-Observations On The Juvenile Procedural Penal Code In Italy, pp 251-260 in Junger-Tas, Josine; Boendermaker, Leonieke & Van Der Laan, Peter H. (eds.) *The Future Of The Juvenile Justice System (L'Avenir Du Système Pénal Des Mineurs)*. Leuven, Belgium: Acco, 1991. This essay provides a brief discussion of the 1988 Italian law on the processing of young offenders.

2234 Lemert, Edwin M. Juvenile Justice Italian Style, *Law And Society Review* 20:509-544, 1986. The author argues that the Italian juvenile court has been a spurious development that reflected contradictions between the culture of legal certainty and familism combined with a pattern of discretionary justice based on the positivism of Enrico Ferri.

2235 Leone, U. Operational Research Perspectives: Youth, Criminality And Juvenile Justice (Perspectives En Matière De Recherche Opérationnelle: Jeunesse, Criminalité Et Justice Juvenile), *Revue Internationale De Crimonologie Et De Police Technique* 39:107-116, 1986. This report presents the summary of a seminar on Youth, Crime and Juvenile Justice held in Milan, Italy. French with English summary.

2236 Malerba, Alberto & Ferrari, Maria Giuliana Intervention By The Provincial Administration, pp 65-66 in United Nations Crime Prevention And Criminal Justice Program International Scientific And Professional

Advisory Council (ed.) *Juveniles And Delinquency: In The Italian And European Context.* Milan, Italy, 1995. This chapter briefly describes delinquency intervention programs in Milan, Italy.

2237 McGee, Henry W. & Adamo, John Juvenile Court Jurisdiction In Italy And Europe, *American Journal Of Comparative Law* 29:139-145, 1981. This article presents a comparison of the jurisdiction of the juvenile courts in Italy, and the system under consideration outlined in the proposed Juvenile Justice Code for Europe.

2238 Pesci, Furio Juvenile Justice, pp 91-92 in United Nations Crime Prevention And Criminal Justice Program International Scientific And Professional Advisory Council (ed.) *Juveniles And Delinquency: In The Italian And European Context.* Milan, Italy, 1995. The author articulates some of the legal problems of dealing with delinquency in a changing Italy.

2239 Pierro, Lina Intervention By The Regional Administration, pp 63-64 in United Nations Crime Prevention And Criminal Justice Program International Scientific And Professional Advisory Council (ed.) *Juveniles And Delinquency: In The Italian And European Context.* Milan, Italy, 1995. This chapter briefly describes delinquency intervention programs run by the region of Lombardy, Italy.

2240 Rigoldi, Don Gino Reclamation Of The Offending Minor: Some Practical Proposals, pp 97-100 in United Nations Crime Prevention And Criminal Justice Program International Scientific and Professional Advisory Council (ed.) *Juveniles And Delinquency In The Italian And European Context.* Milan, Italy, 1995. This chapter briefly describes some of the practical difficulties of "reclamation" projects for delinquents in the city of Milan.

2241 Roma, Giuseppe The Prevention Of Juvenile Maladjustment, pp 93-95 in United Nations Crime Prevention And Criminal Justice Program International Scientific And Professional Advisory Council (ed.) *Juveniles And Delinquency: In The Italian And European Context.* Milan, Italy, 1995. This chapter briefly describes some Italian prevention approaches to dealing with delinquency.

2242 Scardaccione, G. Drug Addiction And Juvenile Justice, *Journal Of Drug Issues* 24:687-696, 1994. The author discusses the various Italian legislative and therapeutic programs designed to deal with juvenile drug offenders.

2243 Sorcioni, Maurizio Social Policies For The Young, pp 101-103 in United Nations Crime Prevention And Criminal Justice Program

International Scientific And Professional Advisory Council (ed.) *Juveniles And Delinquency: In The Italian And European Context.* Milan, Italy, 1995. This chapter briefly summarizes the Italian approach to, and problems in dealing with, delinquency.

Ivory Coast

2244 Koudou, O. Social Intolerance, Continuation Of Delinquent Behavior In Adolescence And Prevention Strategies (Intolérance Sociale, Continuation Du Comportement Délinquant Chez L'Adolescent Et Stratégie Préventive), *Déviance Et Societé* 20:141-151, 1996. The author reports a study of clinical cases of inmates in Dabou Reeducation Centre and argues that various "community" factors contribute to continued delinquency. French with English summary.

2245 Ouizan-Bi, Hughes The Area Research Project On The Street Children Of Abidjan (Les Enfants De La Rue À Abidjan De La Recherche-Action À L'Action De Terrain), pp 281-284 in Hérault, Georges & Adesanmi, Pius (eds.) *Youth, Street Culture And Urban Violence In Africa: Proceedings Of The International Symposium In Abidjan 5-7 May, 1997 (Jeunes, Culture De La Rue Et Violence Urbaine En Afrique: Actes Du Symposium International D'Abidjan 5-7 Mai 1997).* Ibadan, Nigeria: French Institute for Research in Africa 1997. This chapter describes the activities of street children in Abidjan and the various services available to them. French.

2246 Sissoko, Alain Abidjan: A Well Managed Situation? (Abidjan: Une Situation Relativement Bien Maîtrisée?), pp 247-279 in Hérault, Georges & Adesanmi, Pius (eds.) *Youth, Street Culture And Urban Violence In Africa: Proceedings Of The International Symposium In Abidjan 5-7 May, 1997 (Jeunes, Culture De La Rue Et Violence Urbaine En Afrique: Actes Du Symposium International D'Abidjan 5-7 Mai 1997).* Ibadan, Nigeria: IFRA French Institute for Research in Africa 1997. French; English. This study of street children in Abidjan found that little data existed, however observations and interviews provide a demographic picture of the nature of street life and its distribution in Abidjan. French with English Summary.

Jamaica

2247 Cumper, Gloria Jamaica, pp 31-74 in Stewart, V. Lorne (ed.) *Justice And Troubled Children Around The World Vo.l III.* New York, New York: New York University Press, 1981. This chapter provides an extensive discussion of delinquency laws, and the historical development of delinquency programs and system of justice in Jamaica.

2248 Goodman, Randy Summaries Of DCI Country Surveys, Jamaica, pp 174-176 in Tomasevski, Katarina (ed) *Children In Adult Prisons: An International Perspective.* New York, New York: St. Martin's Press, 1986. The author presents the findings on Jamaica from the 1982-1984 Defense for Children International Survey of children in adult prisons.

Japan

2249 Castberg, A. Didrick *Japanese Criminal Justice.* Westport, Connecticut: Praeger, 1990. Some statistics on juvenile penal-code offenders, a flow chart of the judiciary, and official data from family courts are included in this overview of crime, laws, law enforcement, legal education, prosecution, judiciary, defense and corrections in general. 168p.

2250 Chang, Dae H. Crime And Delinquency Control Strategy In Japan: A Comparative Note, *International Journal Of Comparative And Applied Criminal Justice* 12:139-149, 1988. Both crime and delinquency within the Japanese legislative, legal, judicial and enforcement structures, social structural elements such as world-view of the Japanese, are also included.

2251 Clifford, William Corrections In Asia, pp117-133 in United Nations Asia And Far East Institute For The Prevention Of Crime And The Treatment Of Offenders (ed.) *Resource Material Series No 17.* Tokyo, Japan:UNAFEI, 1980. The author discusses the ascendancy of Western correctional and penal philosophy in Japan in general, and discusses delinquency as an issue of poverty.

2252 Goodman, Randy Summaries Of DCI Country Surveys, Japan, pp 176-177 in Tomasevski, Katarina (ed.) *Children In Adult Prisons: An International Perspective.* New York: St. Martin's Press, 1986. Findings for Japan from the 1982-1984 Defense for Children International Survey of children in adult prisons are summarized here.

2253 Harada, Yutaka & Suzuki, Shingo An Analysis Of The Recidivism Of Juveniles Referred To Family Court By Summary Referral, *Reports Of The National Research Institute Of Police Science* 35:58-72, 1994. This study examines police records for recidivism rates among juvenile penal-code offenders subjected to summary referrals to Japanese family court. Japanese with English summary.

2254 Hoshino, Kanehiro; Suzuki, Shingo; Inokuchi, Yumiko; Watanabe, Kazumi & Suzuki, Mamoru A Study On The Impact Of Five Day School Week Upon The Life style Of Students And Delinquents: Attitudes Of Juveniles Towards Community Programs For Preventing

Delinquency One And A Half Years After The Introduction, *Reports Of The National Research Institute Of Police Science* 36:1-17, 1995. This is an evaluation of the relations between community-based delinquency prevention programs and a short school-week. Japanese with English summary.

2255 Inokuchi, Yumiko Changes In The Attitudes Of Guardians Receiving Police Counseling Services For Delinquency Prevention, *Reports Of The National Research Institute Of Police Science* 35:29-49, 1994. This research focuses on the views of 90 police experts regarding the usefulness of counseling for the guardians of juvenile delinquents. Japanese with English summary.

2256 Japan Ministry of Justice *Correctional Institutions In Japan 1995.* Tokyo, Japan: Correction Bureau, 1995. This handbook describes correctional administration in Japan, and also includes a description of juvenile training schools and classification homes. 100p.

2257 Japan Ministry of Justice *Graphic Introduction To Japanese Corrections.* Tokyo, Japan: Correction Bureau, 1995. Using tables and graphs, this report describes the Japanese corrections system including juvenile corrections. 24p.

2258 Japan Ministry of Justice *Summary Of White Paper On Crime 1988.* Tokyo, Japan: Research and Training Institute, 1988. Section III on juvenile crime covers the various statistics on trends, prosecution, classification homes, training schools and juvenile prisons, parole and recidivists and their treatment. 167p.

2259 Japan Ministry of Justice *Summary Of White Paper On Crime 1982.* Tokyo, Japan: Research and Training Institute, 1982. Part III of this report deals with official juvenile delinquency such as type of offenses, prior record, dispositions, and treatments facilities. 79p.

2260 Japan Ministry of Justice *Bulletin Of The Criminological Research Department.* Tokyo, Japan: Research and Training Institute, 1982. In this volume there are several short reports on sentencing, training school youths, and treatment of offenders. 21p.

2261 Japan Ministry of Justice *Bulletin Of The Criminological Research Department.* Tokyo, Japan: Research and Training Institute, 1980. This research bulletin has several short discussions by authors who report that delinquent students, although above average in intelligence, had low self-esteem, dysfunctional families, delinquent friends, and histories of truancy. 40p.

2262 Japan Ministry of Justice *Summary Of The White Paper On Crime: 1979*. Tokyo, Japan: Research and Training Institute, 1980. Several articles in this report deal with a typology of delinquent behavior among the residents in a training school, characteristics and outcomes of the juveniles admitted to classification homes, and the differential treatment of juvenile delinquents. 66p.

2263 Japan Ministry of Justice *Summary Of White Paper On Crime 1979*. Tokyo, Japan: Research and Training Institute, 1979. Part III of this report on juvenile delinquency summarizes the laws, describes the juvenile justice system, and provides data on family courts, dispositions etc. 66p.

2264 Japan Ministry of Justice *Bulletin Of The Criminological Research Department*. Tokyo, Japan: Research and Training Institute, 1978. There are several short reports on juvenile delinquents, their personality traits, and the use of psychodrama therapy in treating juvenile delinquents. 31p.

2265 Japan Ministry of Justice *Bulletin Of The Criminological Research Department*. Tokyo, Japan: Research and Training Institute, 1977. This report has several brief contributions of multiple authors covering topics such as decision-making in the classification of juvenile delinquents, delinquency and personality traits, and the differential treatment of juvenile delinquents. 36p.

2266 Japan Ministry Of Justice Research And Training Institute *Asia Crime Report No. 1*. Tokyo, Japan: UNAFEI, 1993. Crime rates for adults and juveniles are summarized in table form and some information on facilities for youth and young people in Japan is provided. 88p.

2267 Japan National Police Agency *White Paper On Police 1997*. Tokyo, Japan: Japan Police Association, 1997. Albeit on criminal justice activities in general, this paper also includes official juvenile delinquency data.

2268 Japan National Police Agency *White Paper On Police 1990*. Tokyo, Japan: Police Association, 1991. Police activities directed toward the prevention of juvenile delinquency are included in this publication. 138p.

2269 Johnson, Elmer H. *Japanese Corrections: Managing Convicted Offenders In An Orderly Society*. Carbondale, Illinois: Southern Illinois University Press, 1996. This book offers a detailed description of how Japanese corrections programs deal with juvenile offenders as well as with adult criminals. 336p.

2270 Kawamoto, Mitutaka Reforms In Treatment Measures For Juvenile Offenders--An Experience In Japan, pp 130-135 in Sugihara, Hiroyasu (ed.) *Resource Material Series No. 38*. Tokyo, Japan: UNAFEI 1990. This brief essay examines Japan's juvenile justice system and related reforms between 1955 and 1979. 5p.

2271 Kobayashi, Kazuhiro Institutional Treatment Of Offenders In Special Categories In Japan, pp.266-277 in Sugihara, Hiroyasu (ed.) *Resource Material Series No. 44*. Tokyo, Japan: UNAFEI, 1991. This publication has some data on institutionalized youths below age 20 who are penal-code violators.

2272 Miyawaza, Setsuo *Policing In Japan: A Study On Making Crime*. Albany, New York: State University of New York, 1992. Based on a study of the Japanese police, this book describes the varied aspects of Japanese police work including juvenile case processing in Japan. 267p.

2273 Moriyama, Tadashi The Response To Delinquency By Formal Agencies In Japan: Could It Change The Reality, pp 269-278 in Hackler, Jim (ed.) *Official Responses To Problem Juveniles: Some International Reflections*. Euskadi, Spain: The Oñati International Institute for the Sociology of Law, 1991. This chapter describes the underlying philosophy behind juvenile justice in Japan, and some of the possible consequences in changes that appear to be taking place in the system.

2274 Nomura, Yukio Japan, pp 76-86 in United Nations Asia And Far East Institute (ed.) *Delineation of Crucial Issues of Criminal Justice in Asia*. Tokyo, Japan: UNAFEI, 1985. The section on Japan includes a short disccussion on the treatment for juveniles.

2275 Parker, L. Craig Jr. *Parole And The Community Based Treatment Of Offenders In Japan And The United States*. New Haven, Connecticut: University of New Haven, 1986. Some details on Japanese juvenile probationers are included in this book on probation. 156p.

2276 Parker, L. Craig Jr. *The Japanese Police System Today: An American Perspective*. Tokyo, Japan: Kodansha, 1984. Chapter seven on "Crisis With Youth" provides an overview of young offenders, and various counseling centers,while chapter eight deals with drug abuse, family counseling and crime prevention including runaways. 220p.

2277 Rosch, Joel Institutionalizing Mediation: The Evolution Of The Civil Liberties Bureau In Japan, *Law & Society Review* 21:243-266, 1987. Although this article does not directly deal with juveniles, the unique Japanese office of the Civil Liberties Bureaus indicate the overall Japanese inclination for conflict resolution via mediation based on remorse, apology and restitution this characteristic of juvenle justice in Japan.

2278 Shikita, M. & Tsuchiya, S. The Juvenile Justice System In Japan, pp 55-81 in United Nations Social Defence Research Institute (ed.) *Juvenile Justice: An International Survey*. Rome, Italy, 1976. Japan's juvenile and child welfare laws and a description of the organization and functioning of it's juvenile justice system, the police, prosecutor, and family court, and treatment modalities are described in this chapter.

2279 Shikita, Minoru & Tsuchiya, Shinichi *Crime And Criminal Policy In Japan From 1926 To 1988: Analysis And Evaluation Of The Showa Era*. Tokyo, Japan: Japan Criminal Policy Society, 1990. Chapter IV deals with juvenile delinquency - trends, treatment, prosecution, training schools, juvenile prisons and rehabilitation with some tables of data in the appendix. 394p.

2280 Shikita, Minoru Report Of Mr. Minoru Shikita, Tokyo (Rapport De M. Minoru Shikita, Tokyo) pp.69-104 in Fondation Internationale Pénale Et Pénitentiaire - Institut De Sciences Criminelles De Poitiers (ed.) *Elaboration Of The Minimum Rules For Non-Penal Treatment* (*L'Élaboration Des Règles Minima Pour Le Traitment En Milieu Libré*) Paris, France: Cujas, 1987. Describes the various alternatives to imprisonment that are used in Japan, and includes juvenile sanctions as well. French.

2281 Suzuki, Yoshio Criminal Law Reform In Japan, pp 84-96 in United Nations Asia And Far East Institute (ed.) *Resource Material Series No. 13*. Tokyo, Japan: UNAFEI, 1977. This general discussion of law reforms in Japan, includes juvenile laws as well.

2282 Suzuki, Yoshio Japan, pp 75-102 in Stewart, V. Lorne (ed.) *Justice And Troubled Children Around The World, Vol. 3*. New York, New York: New York University Press, 1981. This chapter provides an extensive overview of the extent of delinquency and the operations of juvenile justice agencies in Japan.

2283 Takakuwa, Kazumi Successes And Failures In Police Counseling Services For Pre-Delinquents, *Reports Of The National Research Institute Of Police Science* 34:71-86, 1993. Reports on the results of a survey of male and female pre-delinquents, and their parents' evaluation of delinquency prevention program. Japanese with English summary.

2284 Tanioka, Ichiro & Goto, Hiroko Japan, pp 191-206 in Shoemaker, Donald J. (ed.) *International Handbook On Juvenile Justice*. Westport, Connecticut: Greenwood, 1996. This chapter offers an extensive discussion of the law and the juvenile justice system of Japan.

2285 Tsujimoto, Yoshio The Genesis And Historical Development Of Juvenile Care In Japan, pp 791-807 in Hess, Albert G. & Clement, Priscilla F. (eds.) *History Of Juvenile Delinquency: A Collection Of Essays On Crime Committed By Young Offenders, Vol. 2*. Aalen, Germany: Scientia Verlag, 1993. This chapter covers the developments in the penal code and juvenile laws and care from 1800s to post-World War II.

2286 United Nations Asia And Far East Institute *Resource Material Series No. 14*. Tokyo, Japan: UNAFEI, 1978. The section titled "Some Thoughts on Decriminalization and Depenalization" and the section "Japanese Rehabilitation Services and Community Involvement" include discussions of juvenile offenders. 155p.

2287 Westermann, Ted D. & Burfeind, James W. *Crime And Justice In Two Societies: Japan And The United States*. Pacific Grove, California: Brooks/Cole, 1991. Juvenile delinquency and justice are interspersed throughout this book on the Japanese cultural values and aversion to legislate morality, informal social control, criminal law, law enforcement and policing, courts including family courts that deal with juveniles. 211p.

2288 Yokoyama, Minoru Delinquency Control Programs In The Community In Japan, *International Journal Of Comparative And Applied Criminal Justice* 5:169-178, 1981. This article examines the various means by which the Japanese work to prevent juvenile delinquency.

2289 Yokoyama, Minoru Guarantee Of Human Rights In Juvenile Justice System In Japan, *Kokugakuin Journal Of Law And Politics* 30:1-30, 1992. This article explores the protection of the rights of juvenile offenders to social services in Japan's juvenile justice system as prescribed by the Constitution of 1946..

2290 Yokoyama, Minoru Juvenile Justice: An Overview Of Japan, pp 1-28 in Winterdyk, John A. (ed) *Juvenile Justice Systems: International Perspectives*. Toronto, Canada: Canadian Scholar's Press, 1997. This chapter provides an overall description of the history of and present structure of the juvenile justice system of Japan.

2291 Yokoyama, Minoru Net-Widening Of The Juvenile Justice System In Japan, *Criminal Justice Review* 14:43-53, 1989. The author describes the various components of the juvenile judicial system and provides some data on juveniles investigated and their dispositions over 20 years.

2292 Yokoyama, Minoru The Juvenile Justice System In Japan, pp 102-113 in. Brusten, M.; Graham, J.; Herriger, N. & Malinowski, P. (eds.) *Youth Crime Social Control And Prevention: Theoretical Perspectives And Policy Implications:Studies From Nine Different Countries*. Pfaiffenweiler, Germany: Centaurus-Verlagsgesellschaft, 1986. This chapter describes the law and system of juvenile justice including extensive data of post WWII official delinquency rates in Japan.

Jordan

2293 Obeidat, Zougan Bullying And Violence In The Jordanian School, pp 20-33 in Ohsako, Toshio (ed.) *Violence At School: Global Issues And Interventions*. United Nations Educational, Scientific and Cultural Organization: Paris, France, 1997. This chapter describes some aspects of violence in Jordanian schools and outlines the policies and procedures designed to deal with it.

Kenya

2294 Human Rights Watch Children's Rights Project *Juvenile Injustice: Police Abuse And Detention Of Street Children In Kenya*. New York, New York 1997. This report describing police abuse and detention of homeless Kenyan children is based on a 1996 fact-finding mission of interviews with more than 60 street youths in Nairobi, Kisumu, and Mombasa, and with members of non-governmental organizations and human rights activists. 155p. Appendix.

2295 Mali-Musiime, Florence M. Review Of An African Country's Experience With Juveniles In Conflict With The Law, pp 155-158 in Kubota, Yo (ed.) *International Review Of Criminal Policy: Special Double Volume On Juvenile Justice In International Perspective*. New York, New York: United Nations. Centre for Social Development and Humanitarian Affairs, 1990. This article describes the Kenyan government's attempts at overhauling the juvenile law.

Malaysia

2296 Ahmad, Rahimah Haji & Salleh, Norani Mohd. Bullying And Violence In The Malaysian School, pp 57-71 in Ohsako, Toshio (ed.) *Violence At School: Global Issues And Interventions*. United Nations Educational, Scientific And Cultural Organization: Paris, France, 1997. This chapter describes some aspects of school violence in Malaysia and outlines the policies and procedures designed to deal with it.

2297 Kuan, Choong Sik The Effective Treatment of Juvenile Delinquents In Malaysia, pp 198-209 in United Nations Asia And Far East Institute (ed.) *UNICEF Resource Material Series No. 46*. Tokyo, Japan: UNAFEI, 1995. This is a description of the structure and operation of the juvenile justice system in Malaysia.

Mexico

2298 Alvarez, Ana Josefina (trans. by Vinay, Ivonne) Mexico, pp 207-219 in Shoemaker, Donald J. (ed.) *International Handbook On Juvenile Justice*. Westport, Connecticut: Greenwood, 1996. The author discusses the juvenile justice system of Mexico.

2299 United Nations Social Defence Research Institute Mexico: Notes On The Juvenile Justice System, pp 189-198 in. *Juvenile Justice An International Survey*. Rome, Italy: United Nations Social Defence Research Institute, 1976. This chapter provides a brief description of the system and organization of juvenile justice in Mexico, and contains some data on cases processed.

Morocco

2300 Goodman, Randy Summaries Of DCI Country Surveys, Morocco, pp 177-180 in Tomasevski, Katarina (ed) *Children In Adult Prisons: An International Perspective*. New York,New York: St. Martin's Press, 1986. This section reports on the findings of the 1982-1984 Defense for Children International Survey of Moroccan children in adult prisons.

Netherlands

2301 Andriessen, Margo A Foreigner's View Of American Diversion, *Crime And Delinquency* 26:70-82, 1980. The author lists recommendations for the Dutch sponsored voluntary diversion program in Groningen after discussing the pros and cons of five police-sponsored American diversion projects.

2302 Andriessen, Margo F. The Handling Of Juvenile Cases By The Dutch Police, *Police Journal* 51:261-265, 1978. This article describes a five months participant observation study of police processing of juveniles in the Hague and Amsterdam in the Netherlands.

2303 Baerveldt, Chris; Bunkers, Hans & De-Winter, Micha Assessing A Moral Panic Relating To Crime And Drugs Policy In The Netherlands: Towards A Testable Theory, *Crime, Law And Social Change* 29:31-47, 1998. This study compared the five criteria model of moral panic to the

Dutch policy on youth crime, and found that although most of the criteria have been met, there were indications that public concern had been disproportionate to trends in crime and victimization, and that the panic erupted fairly suddenly.

2304 Blees, L. W. & Brouwers, M. Alternative Sanctions: A Review Of The Imposition And Execution (Takkstraffen Voor Minderjarigen: Toepaspsing En Uitvoering Opnieuw Belicht). Arnhem, The Netherlands: Gouda Quint, 1996. This publication reports the socio-economic characteristics, offense behaviors, alternative sanctions, and the outcomes of cases involving the 200 Dutch juvenile offenders surveyed. 79p. Dutch with English summary.

2305 Boendermaker, L. & Verwers, C. *Daily Practice In Judicial Treatmen Centers (Een Veld In Beeld: Een Beschrijving Van Het Werk In De Justitiele Behandelinrichtingen).* Amsterdam, The Netherlands: Gouda Quint, 1996. Provides descriptions based on the interviews with the staff and juvenile offenders in ten different Dutch juvenile treatment centers. 171p. Appendix. Dutch.

2306 Brown, John The Netherlands: Tripartite Consultation: Burgomaster, Chief Public Prosecutor, Chief Of Police - With Special Reference To The City Of Amsterdam, pp. 34-83 in Brown, Audrey (ed.) *Insecure Societies Delinquency In Troubled Times.* London, United Kingdom: Macmillan, 1990. This chapter provides a description of the multi-faceted Dutch approach to dealing with delinquency.

2307 Bruinsma, Frits Immediate Assessment Of Adolescent Sex Offenders Seen At The Police Station, *International Journal Of Offender Therapy And Comparative Criminology* 39:307-316, 1995. An evaluation study of Dutch 7-18 year olds in the Juvenile Sex Offenders Project of Utrecht is described in this article.

2308 Carlie, Mike An Overview Of Institutions For Juvenile Offenders In The Netherlands And Their Place Within The Dutch System Of Justice, *International Journal Of Comparative And Applied Criminal Justice* 21:31-140, 1997. This article provides a concise review of the Dutch juvenile laws, a chart of the Dutch courts, an overview of the juvenile courts, police and the different types of juvenile correctional institutions in the Netherlands, and an analysis of 1984-1992 trend toward expansion of juvenile institutions in the Netherlands.

2309 De Waard, J. & Lohman, P. M. de Savornin *Crime Prevention At The Neighborhood Level (Preventie En Buurtbeheer*). Gravenhage, The Netherlands: Netherlands Ministry of Justice, 1991. The five chapters address various issues related to crime-prevention and emphasize self-report delinquency surveys as an important criterion for an integrated, tailored, approach to crime prevention in the high-crime neighborhoods of Holland. 68p. Dutch with English summary.

2310 Dettmeyer-Vermeulen, Corinne Community Service In The Low Countries (*Le Travail Au Profit De La Communauté Aux Pays-Bas*), pp 179-184 in Dünkel, Frieder & Zermatten, Jean (eds.) *Recent Trends In Penal Law For Minors: Mediation, Community Service And Intermediate Treatment (Nouvelles Tendances Dans Le Droit Pénal Des Mineurs: Médiation, Travail Au Profit De La Communauté Et Traitement Intermédiaire)*. Freiburg, Germany. Max Planck Institute for Foreign and International Criminal Justice, 1990. This article concludes that community services, as an alternative sanction for juveniles, vary from court-to-court within the Netherlands. French.

2311 Dettmeyer, Corinne The Trial System In Holland, pp 151-153 in Cavadino, Paul (ed.) *Children Who Kill: An Examination Of The Treatment Of Juveniles Who Kill In Different European Countries*. Winchester, United Kingdom: Waterside, 1996. The author describes the court procedures that involve juveniles accused of committing serious crimes in the Netherlands.

2312 Doreleijers, Theo A. H.; Moser, Françoise; Thijs, Petra; Van England, Herman & Beyaert, Frank H. L. Forensic Assessment Of Juvenile Delinquents: Prevalence Of Psychopathology And Decision-Making At Court In The Netherlands, *Journal Of Adolesence* 23:263-275, 2000. This study sought to investigate the extent to which the juvenile criminal justice system provides needed professional help.

2313 Drost, Jelle The Treatment Of Seriously Delinquent People In The Netherlands, pp 154-161, in Cavadino, Paul (ed.) *Children Who Kill: An Examination Of The Treatment of Juveniles Who Kill In Different European Countries*. Winchester, United Kingdom: Waterside, 1996. This chapter describes diverse treatment programs of the detention and treatment centers for delinquent youths in the Netherlands.

2314 Essers, A. A. M.; Van Der Laan, P. & Van Der Veer, P. N. *Cashba: An Intensive Day Training Programme For Juvenile And Young Adult Offenders (Cashba: Een Intensief Dagprogramma.*N *Voor Jeugdige En Jongvolwassen Delinquenten)*. Hague, The Netherlands: Gouda Quint, 1995. The authors describe and examine an alternative, 13-week, intensive day-training program for juvenile and young adult offenders in Rotterdam. 58p. Appendix. Dutch with English summary.

2315 Goodman, Randy Summaries Of DCI Country Surveys, Netherlands, pp 180-183 in Tomasevski, Katarina (ed) *Children In Adult Prisons: An*

International Perspective. New York, New York: St. Martin's Press, 1986. Findings regarding children in adult prisons in the Netherlands from the 1982-1984 Defense for Children International Survey are presented here.

2316 Hauber, Albert R. A Dutch Perspective On Some Of The Effects Of Alternative Sanctions, *Crime Law And Social Change* 15:91-108, 1991. This article describes the author's interviews with youths arrested for vandalism on developing a diversion program in the Netherlands.

2317 Hauber, Albert R. Influencing Juvenile Offenders By Way Of Alternative Sanctions In Community Settings, pp 382-396 in Wegener, Hermann; Lösel, Friedrich & Haisch, Jochen (eds.) *Criminal Behavior And The Justice System: Psychological Perspectives*. New York, New York: Springer-Verlag, 1989. The author describes and discusses alternative sanctions for juvenile offenders and the public's reaction to various forms of juvenile criminality, such as vandalism, in the Netherlands.

2318 Junger-Tas, Josine Recent Trends In Sentencing Policies In The Netherlands, *European Journal On Criminal Policy And Research* 6:475-579, 1998. This article provides a description of new, alternative legal sanctions for both adults and juveniles in the Netherlands.

2319 Junger-Tas, Josine Netherlands, pp 389-422 in Mehlbye, Jill & Walgrave, Lode (ed.) *Confronting Youth In Europe: Juvenile Crime And Juvenile Justice*. Copenhagen, Denmark: AKF Forlaget, 1998. This chapter describes the blurring of the line between juvenile justice and child protection (punitive vs. welfare models), and presents some official and self-reported delinquency statistics, and sentencing and alternative sanctions.

2320 Junger-Tas, Josine Juvenile Delinquency And Juvenile Justice In The Netherlands, pp 55-75 in Winterdyk, John A. (ed.) *Juvenile Justice Systems: International Perspectives*. Toronto, Canada: Canadian Scholars' Press, 1997. This chapter reviews the Dutch juvenile justice system, provides some statistics on trends, and describes the role of different officials in the juvenile justice system.

2321 Junger-Tas, Josine Intermediate Treatment In the Low Countries (*Le Traitment Intermédiaire Aux Pays-Bas*), pp 193-209 in Dünkel, Frieder & Zermatten, Jean (eds.) *Recent Trends In Penal Law For Minors: Mediation, Community Service And Intermediate Treatment (Nouvelles Tendances Dans Le Droit Pénal Des Mineurs: Médiation, Travail Au Profit De La Communauté Et Traitement Intermédiaire)*. Freiburg, Germany, 1990. Max Planck Institute for Foreign and International

Criminal Justice. In this chapter the author describes (with an illustrating table) intermediate treatment in the Netherlands, specifically in Amsterdam, that focus on individualized help centered around employment and personal goals. French.

2322 Junger-Tas, Josine Effects Of Intervention By The Police And The Prosecutor, pp 177-201 in Junger-Tas, Josine & Block, Richard L. (eds.) *Juvenile Delinquency In The Netherlands, 1988.* Amstelveen, The Netherlands: Kugler, 1988. This study found that changes in social integration produces changes in delinquent behavior but judicial contact had no impact on such behavior.

2323 Junger-Tas, Josine New Trends In Dutch Juvenile Justice, pp 443-467 in Kerner, Hans-Jürgen; Galaway, Burt & Janssen, Helmut (eds.) *European And North-American Juvenile Justice Systems: Aspects And Tendencies (Jugendgerichtsbarkeit In Europa Und Nordamerika: Aspekte Und Tendnzen).* Munich, West Germany: Schriftenreihe den Deutschen Vereinigung für Jugendgerichte und Jugendgerichtshilfen, 1986. This chapter reviews the Rotterdam youth diversion project and raises some important issues relevant to diversion.

2324 Junger-Tas, Josine Some Consequences Of Changes In The Processing Of Juveniles Through The Child Protection System In The Netherlands, pp 144-161 in Brusten, M.; Graham, J.; Herriger, N. & Malinowski, P. (eds.) *Youth Crime, Social Control And Prevention: Theoretical Perspectives And Policy Implications--Studies From Nine Different Countries.* Pfaffenweiler, Germany: Centauras-Verlagsgesellschaft, 1986. Using available statistics, the author argues that while there is decreasing care for children in need of protection, young are increasingly being divereted through extra-judicial channels in the Netherlands.

2325 Junger-Tas, Josine *Young Immigrants In The Netherlands And Their Contacts With The Police.* Hague, The Netherlands: The Netherlands: The Netherlands Ministry of Justice, 1985. Using available data from the Office of Social and Cultural Plan, the author examined the disproportionate attention that ethnic minority youths in the Netherlands receive from the social welfare services and juvenile courts. 21p.

2326 Junger-Tas, Josine & Junger, Marianne *Juvenile Delinquency: Backgrounds Of Delinquent Behavior.* The Hague, The Netherlands: Netherlands Ministry of Justice, 1984. This study in collaboration with the prosecutor and the police focuses on the policy of minimal intervention to see if it was effective in preventing juveniles from coming into further contact with the Dutch juvenile justice system. 78p.

2327 Junger-Tas, Josine *Child Protection And Juvenile Justice In Holland.* Hague, The Netherlands: Netherlands Justice Ministry, 1983. This monograph describes the way the Dutch juvenile justice and protection system operates, its interactions and overlappings with other systems, and the changes over the past twenty years. 32p.

2328 Junger-Tas, Josine *Police Diversion In The Netherlands.* Hague,The Netherlands: The Netherlands. Ministry of Justice - Research and Documentation Center, 1983. The contributions of juvenile police in reducing the number of children entering the Dutch child care system, and the extra-judicial processes and efforts made to handle the problems of juveniles are discussed. 25p.

2329 Junger-Tas, Josine Holland, pp 121-146 in Klein, Malcolm W. (ed.) *Western Systems Of Juvenile Justice.* Beverly Hills, California: Sage, 1983. This chapter describes the operation of the Dutch juvenile justice system, changes in childcare and juvenile justice and intervention, nature of diversion and the problems and options for the future of juvenile justice.

2330 Junger-Tas, Josine & Tigges, Leo C. M. *Probation, After-Care, Child-Care And Protection: Today And In The Future.* Hague, The Netherlands: Netherlands Justice Ministry, 1982. This article emphasizes the similarities between two kinds of social work involving minors in Holland,and recommends how the services can be improved in the future. 40p. Appendix.

2331 Junger-Tas, Josine *Diversion In The Dutch Child Care System.* Hague, The Netherlands: Netherlands Ministry of Justice, 1980. Discusses the two-fold (criminal and problem behavior) functions and implications of the Dutch system of childcare and child protection. 29p.

2332 Junger-Tas, Josine Netherlands, pp 87-124 in Stewart, V. Lorne (ed.) *Justice And Troubled Children Around The World, Vol. I.* New York, New York: New York University Press, 1980. This chapter discusses a variety of special youth programs designed to prevent delinquency in the Netherlands.

2333 Komen, Mieke Elias's Theory Of Civilizing Processes: An Exploratory Note On The Judicial System, Families, And Juvenile Delinquency In The Netherlands, *Sociological Studies Of Children* 7:231-246, 1995. Data from the files of youths under juvenile courts near Rotterdam were reviewed for any changes in the criteria of intervention between 1960's and 1980's.

2334 Kruissink, M. & Verwers, C. Diversion Of Shoplifters In The Halt Procedure: Evaluation Of A Rotterdam Experiment. (Afhandeling Van Winkeldiefstal Via De Halt-Procedure: Evaluatie Van Een Rotterdams Experiment). The Hague, The Netherlands: Netherlands Ministry of Justice Research & Documentation Center, 1991. This is based on a study of the alternative sanction program among Rotterdam's juvenile shoplifters. 92p.

2335 Kruissink, M. The Halt Program: Diversion Of Juvenile Vandals *Dutch Penal Law And Policy: Notes On Criminological Research*. The Hague, The Netherlands: Ministry of Justice Research & Documentation Center, 1990. The author reports an evaluation based on a sample of juveniles in the "HALT" diversion and restitution program for juvenile vandals in Rotterdam. 7p.

2336 Lamers-Winkelman, Francien & Buffing, Frank Children's Testimony In The Netherlands: A study Of Statement Validity Analysis, pp 45-61 in Bottoms, Bette L. & Goodman, Gail S. (eds.) *International Perspectives On Child Abuse And Children's Testimony: Psychological Research And Law*. Thousand Oaks, California: Sage, 1996. This chapter discusses the agencies in the Netherlands that deal with child abuse/neglect, presents some data on child abuse and neglect, and provides an assessment of children's allegations of sexual abuse.

2337 Tak, Peter J. P. Community Service As An Alternative To Prison In The Low Countries (*Le Travail D'Intérêt Général En Tant Qu'Alternative Aux Peines De Prison Aux Pays-Bas)*, pp 137-148 in Fondation Internationale Pénale Et Pénitentiaire (ed.) *Community Services As An Alternative To The Prison Sentence* (*Le Service Au Profit De La Communauté En Tant Que Mesure De Substitution À La Peine D'Emprisonnement)*. Bonn, West Germany, 1988. This has a small section on the alternative sanctions for adolescents and youths in the Netherlands, and emphasizes how the sanctions must be only punitively pedagogic in nature. French.

2338 Terpstra, Jan *Delinquency Prevention For Juveniles With Police Contacts (Preventie Voor Jongeren Met Politiecontactens)*. Hague, The Netherlands: Netherlands Ministry of Justice, 1997. This review of The Youth Prevention Project in Land Van Cujik, Holland which found that quick, intensive, individual assistance that involved the family had more positive effects on the youths who come into contact with the police and court and while group treatment had negative impact. 51p. Dutch.

2339 Van Der Hoeven, Erik The Juvenile Investigation Unit – An Observation Study, pp 137-176 in Junger-Tas, Josine & Block, Richard L. (eds.) *Juvenile Delinquency In The Netherlands, 1988*. Amstelveen, The

Netherlands: Kugler, 1988. This chapter offers an extensive analysis of police/juvenile interaction based on a study of Dutch investigations unit and it's dealings with juvenile suspects.

2340 Van Der Laan, Peter H. Repressive Tendencies In Netherlands' New Penal Laws (Repressive Tendenzen Im Neuen Niederländischen Strafrecht), pp 65-77 in Friedrich Ebert Stiftung (ed.) *Child And Juvenile Delinquency In Germany (Kinder- Und Jugendkriminalität In Deutschland)* Friedrich Ebert Stiftung: Berlin, Germany, 1996. Chapter describes how the Dutch trends reflect American repressiveness and the problems related to prevention. German.

2341 Van Der Laan, Peter H. Alternative Sanctions For Juveniles In The Netherlands, *Dutch Penal Law And Policy* 8:1-8, 1993. The author describes and reviews the history, objectives, types, processes and organization of alternative sanctions for juveniles in the Netherlands in this article.

2342 Van Der Laan, P. H. & Smit, M. Boys And Girls In A Closed Residential Institution: The First Experience With Coeducation In Poortje (Jongens En Meisjes In Een Gesloten Jeugdinrichting-De Eerste Ervaringen Met Coëducatie In Het Poortje). The Hague, The Netherlands: Minsitry of Justice, 1993. This is an evaluation study of a Dutch experimental coeducational institution for youths 12-18 years of age.

2343 Van Der Laan, Peter Innovations In The Dutch Juvenile Justice System: Alternative Sanctions, pp 203-239 in Junger-Tas, Josine & Block, Richard L. (eds.) *Juvenile Delinquency In The Netherlands, 1988.* Amstelveen, The Netherlands: Kugler, 1988. This paper presents an analysis of the approach to "alternative sanction" developed in the Netherlands in the mid 1980s.

2344 Van Der Vaart, Johanna M. *Some Aspects Of The Administration Of Criminal Justice In The Netherlands - Memorandum To Participants In The Conference On Comparative Criminal Sanctions*. New York, New York: Aspen Institute for Humanistic Studies, 1976. Describes the Dutch criminal justice system including the private juvenile justice agencies that tend to be fully funded by the government. 13p.

2345 Van Hees, Alma Diversion In The Netherlands: Bureau Halt, pp 323-332 in Junger-Tas, Josine; Boendermaker, Leonieke & Van Der Laan, Peter H. (eds.) *The Future Of The Juvenile Justice System (L'Avenir Du Système Pénal Des Mineurs).* Leuven, Belgium: Acco, 1991. This chapter discusses the diversion of juveniles in Holland, specifically focusing on the Bureau Halt program initiated in 1981.

2346 Van Nijnatten, C. H. C. J. Discourses In Dutch Child Welfare Inquiries, *British Journal Of Criminology* 28:494-512, 1988. Based on content analysis of dossiers from Child Welfare Councils, this study concludes that less attention is now paid to the "immoral" behavior of individual members but the family is the subject of increasing therapeutic intervention, albeit with some freedom to negotiate with the social workers.

2347 Van Teeffelon, Paul The Dutch System, pp 147-150 in Cavadino, Paul (ed.) *Children Who Kill: An Examination Of The Treatment of Juveniles Who Kill In Different European Countries*. Winchester, United Kingdom: Waterside, 1996. The author briefly describes the new 1995 Dutch Criminal Minors Code and the Civil Minors Code, and their implications.

2348 Weijers, Ido The Debate On Juvenile Justice In The Netherlands, 1891-1901, *European Journal Of Crime, Criminal Law And Criminal Justice* 7:63-78, 1999. The author provides a historic perspective on the evolution of juvenile justice in the Netherlands in this essay.

2349 Zandbergen, Anke Shaming In A Dutch Diversion Project, *European Journal On Criminal Policy And Research* 4:93-112, 1996. Describes the Dutch "Halt" youth diversion project, and a related preliminary research using a self-report questionnaire survey of young people.

New Zealand

2350 Allen, Rob The Nature Of Responsibility & Restorative Juvenile Justice, pp 115-121 in Walgrave, Lode (ed.) *Restorative Justice For Juveniles: Potentialities, Risks And Problems For Research*. Leuven, Belgium: Leuven University Press, 1998. This chapter explores the ways in which restorative justice can incorporate the emerging competencies of young people.

2351 Braithwaite, John & Mugford, Stephen Conditions Of Successful Reintegration Ceremonies: Dealing With Juvenile Offenders, *British Journal Of Criminology* 34:139-171, 1994. In this article, the authors identify two conditions that they feel are conducive to successful reintegrative shaming.

2352 Coumarelos, Christine & Weatherburn, Don Targeting Intervention Strategies To Reduce Juvenile Recidivism, *Australian And New Zealand Journal Of Criminology* 28:55-72, 1995. This critical review examines the hypothesis that formal processing of juvenile offenders is inherently criminogenic, and argues that the thesis lacks empirical support.

2353 Doolan, Michael P. Youth Justice Reform In New Zealand, *Community Alternatives* 2:77-90, 1990. This article examines New Zealand's 1989 Children, Young Persons And Their Families Act.

2354 Fergusson, D. M.; Horwood, L. J. & Lynskey, M. T. Ethnicity And Bias In Police Contact Statistics, *Australian And New Zealand Journal Of Criminology* 26:193-206, 1993. This study investigated the relationships among ethnicity, self and parental reports of delinquency, and police contacts among 739 Christ Church children.

2355 Fraser, Sarah & Norton, Jenni Family Group Conferencing In New Zealand Child Protection Work, pp 37-48 in Hudson, Joe; Morris, Allison & Maxwell, Gabrielle (eds.) *Family Group Conferences: Perspectives On Policy & Practice*. Monsey, New York/Annandale, Australia: Criminal Justice Press and Federation Press, 1996. This chapter describes casework practices essential to successful family group conferences.

2356 Hampton, Ross E. Sex And Sentencing In A Children's Court, *Australian And New Zealand Journal Of Criminology* 17:24-32, 1979. This study examines differences in sentencing and prior arrest in Wellington's Children's Court cases.

2357 Hassall, Ian B.; Maxwell, Gabrielle M. & Robertson, Jeremy P. *An Appraisal Of The First Year Of The Children, Young Persons And Their Families Act 1989*. Wellington, New Zealand: New Zealand Office of the Commissioner for Children, 1991. In this document, there are three papers that describe some of the changes in judicial processing of young people following the Children, Young Persons and Their Families Act of 1989. 31p.

2358 Kraus, J. The Deterrent Effect Of Fines And Probation On Male Juvenile Offenders, *Australian And New Zealand Journal Of Criminology* 7:231-240, 1975. This five-year follow-up of the criminal careers of male juvenile offenders given fines and offenders given probation found that the former group had significantly higher rates of offenses after probation.

2359 Maxwell, Gabrielle & Morris, Allison Research On Family Group Conferences With Young Offenders In New Zealand, pp 88-110 in Hudson, Joe; Morris, Allison; Maxwell, Gabrielle & Galaway, Burt (eds.) *Family Group Conferences: Perspectives On Policy & Practice*. Annandale, Australia: Criminal Justice Press, 1996. This article addresses various issues in New Zealand's family group conferences approach as a way of dealing with juvenile offenders.

2360 Maxwell, Gabrielle & Robertson, Jeremy *Child Offenders: A Report To The Minister Of Justice, Police And Social Welfare*. Wellington, New Zealand: New Zealand Office of Commissioner for Children, 1995. This report describes how children are processed in the New Zealand system of juvenile justice. 68p.

2361 Maxwell, Gabrielle M. & Morris, Allison *Family, Victims And Culture: Youth Justice In New Zealand*. Wellington, New Zealand: Social Policy Agency and Victoria University of Wellington, 1993. This study investigated the juvenile justice processes in New Zealand under the new Children, Young Persons and Their Families Act of 1990. 228p. Appendix.

2362 McElrea, F. W. M. The New Zealand Model Of Family Group Conferences, *European Journal On Criminal Policy And Research* 6:527-543, 1998. Article discusses the model of family group conferences in the New Zealand youth justice system.

2363 McElrea, Frederick W. M. The New Zealand Youth Court: A Model for Use with Adults, pp 69-83 in Galaway, Burt & Hudson, Joe (eds.) *Restorative Justice; International Perspective*. Monsey, New York: Criminal Justice Press, 1996. This chapter provides a description and review of the restorative model behind Family Group Conferences using the Maori concept of involving the community, the victim, and the offender.

2364 Moore, David B. Shame, Forgiveness, And Juvenile Justice, *Criminal Justice Ethics* 12:3-25, 1993. The Family Group Conference approach, and its broader implications, are the focus of this article.

2365 Morris, Allison & Maxwell, Gabrielle M. Juvenile Justice In New Zealand: A New Paradigm, *Australian And New Zealand Journal Of Criminology* 26:72-90, 1993. In this article, the authors discuss the system of juvenile justice adopted in New Zealand following the 1989 passage of the Children, Young Persons and Their Families Act.

2366 Morris, Allison & Maxwell, Gabrielle Family Empowerment In Juvenile Justice In New Zealand: A Marriage Of Indigenous And Western Processes, pp 91-108 in Hackler, Jim (ed.) *Official Responses To Problem Juveniles: Some International Reflections*. Euskadi, Spain: The Oñati International Institute for the Sociology of Law, 1991. This chapter presents a description and assessment of the New Zealand juvenile justice system.

2367 Morris, Allison & Maxwell, Gabrielle Re-Forming Juvenile Justice: The New Zealand Experiment, *Prison Journal* 77:125-134, 1997. This article describes New Zealand's system of youth justice focusing on it's attempts to involve youths, their families and victims in assessing how best to deal with the offender.

2368 Morris, Allison & Young, Warren *Juvenile Justice In New Zealand: Policy And Practice* Wellington, New Zealand: Victoria Institute Of Criminology, 1987. This study examines the extent of the operation of welfare versus social control models in the jusdicial processing of young people in New Zealand. 138p

2369 Olsen, Teresa; Maxwell, Gabrielle & Morris, Allison Maori And Youth Justice in New Zealand, pp 45-65 in Hazlehurst, Kayleen M. (ed.) *Popular Justice And Community Regeneration: Pathways Of Indigenous Reform.* Westport, Connecticut: Praeger, 1995. This chapter discusses issues related to the over-representations of Maori youth in New Zealand's crime statistics as well as the 1989 Children, Young Persons and Their Families Act.

2370 Pipe, Margaret-Ellen & Henaghan, Mark Accommodating Children's Testimony: Legal Reforms In New Zealand, pp 145-167 in Bette L. & Goodman, Gail S. (eds.) *International Perspectives On Child Abuse And Children's Testimony: Psychological Research And Law.* Thousand Oaks, California: Sage, 1996. The authors provide an overview of recent legislative provisions and judicial decisions regarding the testimony of children, the opinions of professionals regarding these laws, and argues that the changes have not solved all the problems relating to the testimony of children in criminal cases.

2371 Robertson, Jeremy Research On Family Group Conferences In Child Welfare In New Zealand, pp 49-64 in Hudson, Joe; Morris, Allison & Maxwell, Gabrielle (eds.) *Family Group Conferences: Perspectives On Policy & Practice.* Monsey, New York: Criminal Justice Press and Federation Press, 1996. This chapter describes various studies on family group conferences in New Zealand, summarizes the issues, identifies gaps in knowledge, and offers suggestions for further research.

2372 Sandford, Donald A.; Priest, Phillip A.; Keenan, Michael J.; Brown, Robert A. & Harris, Gregory C. The Hillary House Project: An Experimental Community For Adolescent Offenders, *Australian And New Zealand Journal Of Criminology* 10:165-172, 1977. The use of token economies based on behavioral principles in a Borstal institution in New Zealand are described in this article.

2373 Seymour, J. A. Children's Boards In New Zealand: Some Unanswered Questions, *Australian And New Zealand Journal Of Criminology* 10:233-243, 1977. This article discusses the functions of and issues regarding the Children's Boards in New Zealand for children in trouble.

2374 Stewart, Trish Family Group Conferences With Young Offenders In New Zealand, pp 65-87 in Hudson, Joe; Morris, Allison, Maxwell, Gabrielle & Galaway, Burt (eds.) *Family Group Conferences: Perspectives On Policy & Practice*. Annandale, Australia: Criminal Justice Press, 1996. Describes the roles of youth advocates, social workers, youth justice coordinator, the police, and the victim in the family group conference and processes with some sample case studies.

2375 Tauri, Juan Family Group Conferencing: A Case Study Of The Indigenisation Of New Zealand's Justice System, *Current Issues In Criminal Justice* 10:168-182, 1998. In discussing the issues of cultural variability in sentencing of young offenders in New Zealand, the author addresses variou questions raised regarding the application of the 1989 law.

Nicaragua

2376 West, W. Gordon Juvenile Justice In Nicaragua: Do Traditional Concepts Make Sense? pp 311-338 in Hackler, Jim (ed.) *Official Responses To Problem Juveniles: Some International Reflections*. Euskadi, Spain: The Oñati International Institute for the Sociology of Law, 1991. This chapter describes juvenile delinquency and justice in Nicaragua, both before and after the 1979 Sandinista revolution.

Nigeria

2377 Akande, Jadesola A. The Disposition Of Juvenile Cases In An African Country, pp 159-161 in Kubota, Yo (ed.) *International Review Of Criminal Policy: Special Double Volume On Juvenile Justice In International Perspective*. New York, New York: United Nations Centre for Social Development and Humanitarian Affairs, 1990. The author provides a brief overview of juvenile justice administration in Nigeria.

2378 Asuni, Tolani Tradition And Innovation In Child Care In Nigeria, pp 151-156 in Stewart, V. Lorne (ed.) *The Changing Faces Of Juvenile Justice*. New York, New York: New York University Press, 1978. The importance of the family, the tribe, and the community in dispensing juvenile justice in Nigeria is addressed in this chapter.

2379 Asuni, Tolani & Jack, David D. Nigeria, pp 91-124in Stewart, V. Lorne (ed.) *Justice And Troubled Children Around The World Vol IV*. New York, New York: New York University Press, 1982. The provision of social services to children in Nigeria is discussed in this chapter.

2380 Bulumo, Sigismund O. A. Akin Nigeria, pp 220-239 in Shoemaker, Donald J. (ed.) *International Handbook On Juvenile Justice*. Westport, Connecticut: Greenwood, 1996. The author offers a description and discussion of the juvenile justice system of Nigeria.

2381 Ebbe, Obi N. Ignatius Juvenile Justice System In Southern Nigeria, *International Journal Of Comparative And Applied Criminal Justice* 12:191-204, 1988. This ethnographic study analyses the juvenile justice system in southern Nigeria.

2382 Ehonwa, Osaze Lanre *Prisoners In The Shadows: A Report On Women And Children In Five Nigerian Prisons*. Lagos, Nigeria: Civil Liberties Organization, 1993. The conditions under which women and children are incarcerated is the subject of this report. 264p.

2383 Goodman, Randy Summaries Of DCI Country Surveys-Nigeria pp 183-185 in Tomasevski, Katarina (ed) *Children In Adult Prisons: An International Perspective*. New York, New York: St. Martin's Press, 1986. Findings of the Defense for Children International 1982-1984 survey of children in Nigeria's adult prisons is the subject of this summary.

2384 Igbinovia, Patrick Edoborg Old Wine In New Bottles: Juvenile Justice And Care Of Juvenile Offenders In Nigeria, *International Child Welfare Review* 6465:14-24, 1985. This essay discusses measures to control and treat juvenile offenders in Nigeria focusing on juvenile court procedures, probation, approved schools, reformatories, and imprisonment.

2385 Odekunle, F. Patterns Of Delinquency And Formalized Control Policy In Nigeria, pp 114-124 in Brusten, M.; Graham, J.; Herriger, N. & Malinowski, P. (eds.) *Youth Crime, Social Control and Prevention: Theoretical Perspectives and Policy Implications: Studies From Nine Different Countries*. Pfaffenweiler, Germany: Centaurus-Verlags-gesellschaft, 1986. This chapter describes the delinquency problem and the formalized Nigerian social control responses toward it.

Norway

2386 Boutellier, Hans; Marshall, Tony F. & Dünkel, Frieder The Norwegian Mediation Boards, *European Journal On Criminal Policy And Research* 4:86-94, 1996. This article presents a brief history of the Norwegian mediation boards, types of cases mediated by them with tables of ages of offenders.

2387 Canada Correctional Service *The Criminal Justice System: Norway.* Ottawa, Canada: Background Report No. 2 Of The Strategic Planning Committee, 1980. This report discusses how, since the abolition of detention facilities for juveniles, Norway is facing the paradox of increasing number of young offenders being incarcerated in traditional prisons while the child welfare authorities are unwilling to provide detention institutions for them. 11p. English and French.

2388 Clifford, Graham Norway: A Resolutely Welfare-Oriented Approach pp 141-146 in Cavadino, Paul (ed.) *Children Who Kill.* Winchester, United Kingdom: Waterside, 1996. The Norwegian juvenile court system and sentencing practices that are geared toward the welfare model are described in this chapter.

2389 Dahl, Tove Stang *Child Welfare And Social Defense.* Oslo, Norway: Norwegian University Press, 1985. In this book, the author describes the historic origins of child welfare and the treatment of problem children, and their impact on the legal and juvenile justice system. 185p.

2390 Dahl, Tove Stang The Scandinavian System Of Juvenile Justice: A Comparative Approach, pp 327-347 in Rosenheim, Margaret K. (ed.) *Pursuing Justice For The Child.* Chicago, Illinois: University of Chicago Press, 1976. This Chapter describes the laws, philosophy, and operation of the "Scandinavian" juvenile justice system focusing mainly on Norway.

2391 Dullum, Jane The Norwegian Mediation Boards, *European Journal On Criminal Policy And Research* 4:86-94, 1996. The author provides a description of the 42 Mediation Boards in Norway, along with some discussion of cases involving juveniles.

2392 Ericsson, Kjersti Social Control And Emancipation - Ambiguities In Child Welfare, *Journal Of Scandinavian Studies In Criminology And Crime Prevention* 1:156-26, 2000. This article discusses the implications for the entire family under the paternalistic orientations of Norwegian legislation regarding "crime control" and "child welfare".

2393 Ericsson, Kjersti Gender, Delinquency And Child Welfare, *Theoretical Criminology* 2:445-459, 1998. The author discusses the implicit conflict between the gender assumptions of child welfare ideology and the dissonant realities of professional and personal goals experienced by the, mostly female, welfare workers.

2394 Falck, Sturla Community Mediation Centers On The Right Track Or Side-Tracked, pp 56-72 in Snare, Annika (ed.) *Youth, Crime And Justice.* Oslo, Norway: Norwegian University Press, 1991. Describes the Norwegian alternative sanction for young offenders, and community mediation centers that have evolved into a child welfare measure.

2395 Kogen, Ketil & Wichström, Lars Social Class And Delinquency (Kriminalitet Og Klasse), *Nordisk Tidsskrift For Kriminalvidenskab* 82:32-59, 1995. A national, random representative sample of about 12,000 Norwegian 13-20 year olds were surveyed on their problem delinquent behavior and social class.

2396 Pedersen, Willy Crime And Punishment In Norwegian Mid-Adolescents: A Normal Population Study, *Journal Of Scandinavian Studies In Criminology And Crime Prevention* 1:87-104, 2000. From a national representative sample of adolescents self-reported crimes compared to official police records, the author concludes that 3.7% of the boys and 1.9% of the girls had received some penal sanction during the preceding year, and they also had higher crime participation than the rest of the sample.

2397 Schjoldager, Harald *The Norwegian Penal Code.* Hackensack, New Jersey: Fred Rothman, 1961. Provides the details on age of culpability, conditions for determining punishment, and sentencing. 167p.

2398 Storvoll, Elizabet E. & Hovland, Arild The Ullersmo Project: "Scared Straight" (Ullersmoprosjektet: `Scared Straight'), *Nordisk Tidsskrift For Kriminalvidenskar* 85:122-135, 1998. An evaluation study of the Ullersmo Project, and its approach to the prevention of juvenile delinquency, found that the project was a failure due to various factors including preparation and follow-up. Norwegian.

2399 Van Wormer, Katherine The Hidden Juvenile Justice System In Norway: A Journey Back In Time, *Federal Probation* 54:57-61, 1990. Based on interviews with social workers, lawyers, the police and the parents and observations of official proceedings, the author describes Norway's juvenile justice system.

Pakistan

2400 Goodman, Randy Summaries Of DCI Country Surveys, Pakistan, pp 185-187 in Tomasevski, Katarina (ed) *Children In Adult Prisons: An International Perspective.* New York, New York: St. Martin's Press, 1986. Findings for Pakistan from the 1982-1984 Defense for Children International Survey of children in adult prisons are presented here.

2401 Kachwaha, Malik Lala-I-Yesrab *Juvenile Delinquency And Drug Abuse Problem In Pakistan.* Tokyo, Japan: Report for 1981 and Resource Material Series No. 21, 1982. Although the penal code does not include "juvenile delinquency," the author describes delinquency laws and practices in Pakistan and provides some data on the various offenses for which juveniles are convicted.

Papua New Guinea

2402 Onopia, Jimmy Puieki Crime Prevention And Juvenile Delinquency: The Causes Of Crime Increases In Papua New Guinea, pp 295-300 in United Nations Asia And Far East Institute (ed.) *Resource Material Series No. 46.* Tokyo, Japan: UNAFEI, 1995. Chapter offers a brief overview of the justice and corrections systems for juveniles and some speculation on increases in youth crime.

2403 Sundeen, Richard A. Juvenile Arrests in Papua New Guinea, pp 124-142 in Jensen, Gary F. (ed.) *Sociology Of Delinquency: Current Issues.* Beverly Hills, California: Sage, 1981. This chapter provides a brief overview of the New Guinea juvenile justice system and data on arrests of juveniles, their offenses and demographic characteristics.

Philippines

2404 Aglipay, Edgar B. Problems Faced In The Administration Of The Juvenile Justice System In The Philippines In The Context Of Urbanisation, pp 92-103 in United Nations Asia And Far East Institute (ed.) *Report for 1993 And Resource Material Series No. 45.* Tokyo, Japan: UNAFEI, 1994. Issues related to administering juvenile justice within the urbanizing context of the Philippines are addressed in this chapter.

2405 Aldaba, Lim Estefania Care Of The Juvenile Offenders In The Philippines, *International Journal Of Offender Therapy And Comparative Criminology* 22:239-243, 1978. The 1974 Philippine juvenile code and its impact on social services, law enforcement, and judicial systems and institutions are described in this chapter.

2406 Caalim, Divina P. Treatment And Rehabilitation Of Youthful Offenders In The Philippines, pp 134-141 in Hideo, Utsuro (ed.) *Materials Produced During The 78th International Seminar On Contemporary Achievements And Future Perspectives In Policies For Corrections.* Tokyo, Japan: UNAFEI, 1988. Correctional laws, services for delinquent children and youth, along with a flow chart of corrections for juveniles in the Philippines are presented by the author.

2407 De Jesus-Amor, Ester The Philippines, pp 103-116 in Stewart, V. Lorne (ed.) *Justice And Troubled Children Around The World, Vol. 3.* New York, New York: New York University Press, 1981. This chapter offers in brief, a description of the juvenile justice system in the Philippines.

2408 Shoemaker, Donald J. & Austin, Timothy W. The Republic Of The Philippines, pp 240- 252 in Shoemaker, Donald J. (ed.) *International Handbook On Juvenile Justice.* Westport, Connecticut: Greenwood, 1996. In this chapter, the authors present an extensive discussion of the juvenile justice system of the Philippines.

2409 Shoemaker, Donald J. Juvenile Corrections In The Philippines, *Journal Of Offender Rehabilitation* 24:39-52, 1996. Based on his observations, the author discusses the laws, procedures and correctional facilities in a metropolitan area of the Philippines.

2410 Yangco, Celia C. Community Based Corrections For Youthful Offenders In The Philippines, pp 151-155 in United Nations Asia And Far East Institute For The Prevention Of Crime And The Traetment Of Offenders (ed.) *Resource Material Series No 17.* Tokyo, Japan: UNAFEI, 1980. This brief chapter provides an overview of laws, the bureau of youth welfare, and a flow chart of the juvenile justice system in the Philippines.

Poland

2411 Krukowski, Adam The Criminological And Legal Problems Of Juvenile Delinquency In Poland, *Eurocriminology* 1:113-129, 1987. The author provides statistics on official delinquency in Poland, and a description of delinquency laws and the system of justice for juveniles.

2412 Marek, Andrzej Juvenile Justice In Poland: Its History And Current Development, *Review Of Socialist Law* 14:305-318, 1988. The history of juvenile protection in Poland, Polish juvenile law of the 1930s and the 1982 Act dealing with juveniles are reviewed in this artcile.

2413 Moczydlowski, Pawel *The Hidden Life Of Polish Prisons.* Bloomington, Indiana: Indiana University Press, 1992. Using diverse techniques, including observations in a juvenile institution, the author reveals the secret and unique social organization of three Polish correctional institutions. 176p. Appendix.

2414 Resmierski, Leonard Roger *A View Of Juvenile Delinquency In Poland: Some Considerations And Implications.* Ann Arbor, Michigan:

University Microfilms International, 1982. This study on Poland's juvenile correctional institutions, detention centers, concludes that encounters with the juvenile justice system helps deflect youths form careers in crime. 145p.

2415 Wójcik, Dobrochna Poland, pp 253-271 in Shoemaker, Donald J. (ed.) *International Handbook On Juvenile Justice*. Westport, Connecticut: Greenwood, 1996. In this chapter the author offers a descrption and discussion of the juvenile justice system of Poland.

2416 Zobkiw, Ivan Militaristic Aspects Of A Prison Service: Poland/UK Comparison, pp 65-81 in Wilson, Thelma (ed.) *Penal Services For Offenders: Comparative Studies Of England And Poland 1984/85*. Brookfield, Vermont: Gower, 1987. Describes the paramilitary milieu of six institutions for juvenile delinquents in northwest Poland.

Portugal

2417 Fonseca, Duarte Internment In Reeducational Establishments: The Meaning And Sense Of Law And Practice In Portugal (L'Internement Dans Les Établissements De Rééducation: Les Signifiants Et Les Signifiés Dans La Loi Et La Pratique Portugaise), pp. 429-442 in Junger-Tas, Josine; Boendermaker, Leonieke & Van Der Laan, Peter H. (eds.) *The Future Of The Juvenile Justice System (L'Avenir Du Système Pénal Des Mineurs)*. Leuven, Belgium: Acco, 1991. This chapter discusses the medical and psychological placements of juveniles, and rehabilitation programs in Portugal during 1979-1980. French.

2418 Gersaõ, Eliana Portugal Between The Traps Of "Protection" And "Justice" For Minors (Le Portugal Entre Les Pièges De La "Protection" Et De La "Justice" Des Mineurs), pp 261-274 in Junger-Tas, Josine; Boendermaker, Leonieke & Van Der Laan, Peter H. (eds.) *The Future Of The Juvenile Justice System (L'Avenir Du Système Pénal Des Mineurs)*. Leuven, Belgium: Acco, 1991. This chapter discusses the long history of juvenile courts in Portugal, and the conflict between their role in protecting the interest of children versus dispensing justice. French.

2419 Rodrigues, Anabela Miranda The Rights Of Minors In Portugal: An Urgent Reform (Le Droit Des Mineurs Au Portugal: Une Réforme Urgente), *Criminologie* 32:101-116, 1999. Although various commissions had been appointed with the goal of changing the prevalent welfare model with regards to both offenders and youths in danger, the author declares that the welfare model remains prevalent in Portugal. French with English summary.

2420 Van Kalmthout, Anton M. & Tak, Peter J. P. Portugal, pp 171-238 in Van Kalmthout, Anton M. & Tak, Peter J. P. (eds.) *Sanction-Systems In The Member-States Of The Council Of Europe Part I.* New York, New York: Kluwer, 1988. This chapter describes the Portuguese sanctions systems in general with some information on juveniles, and the age limits of juvenile criminal law.

Romania

2421 Goodman, Randy Summaries Of DCI Country Surveys, Romania, pp 187-189 in Tomasevski, Katarina (ed) *Children In Adult Prisons: An International Perspective.* New York, New York: St. Martin's Press, 1986. The author presents the findings for Romania from the 1982-1984 Defense for Children International Survey of children in adult prisons.

Russian Federation

2422 Bassiouni, Cherif M. *The Criminal Justice System Of The USSR.* Springfield, Illinois: Charles C. Thomas, 1979. Soviet criminal law, the judiciary, the procurator, the police, the penal system as well as the Constitution, Criminal Procedural codes and other criminal legislation are all described in this book. 268p.

2423 Baturov, Genius P. & Reshetnikov, Felix M. Juvenile Delinquency Cases In Courts And Juvenile Commissions In The Soviet Union, *Juvenile Justice* 28:11-14, 1977. The authors discuss how cases of juvenile delinquents were examined in the Soviet Union by courts, or by juvenile commissions, since Soviet legislation had no privisions for a separate system of juvenile or family courts.

2424 Borodin, Stanislav V. Soviet Union, pp 125-142 in Stewart, V. Lorne (ed.) *Justice And Troubled Children Around The World, Vol. I.* New York, New York: New York University Press, 1980. This chapter describes the "special" measures that are applied to juvenile offenders in the Soviet Union.

2425 Finckenauer, James O. Russia, pp 272-285 in Shoemaker, Donald J. (ed.) *International Handbook On Juvenile Justice.* Westport, Connecticut: Greenwood, 1996. This Chapter provides a description and discussion of the juvenile justice system of Russia.

2426 Juviler, Peter H. *Revolutionary Law And Order: Politics And Social Change In The USSR.* New York, New York: The Free Press, 1976. A historic review of the emergence of post-revolutionary Soviet laws, including those involving children up to the 1970s, is presented in this volume.

2427 Kirafly, Albert The Child In Soviet Law: The Juvenile Delinquent, *Review Of Socialist Law* 2:67-77, 1976. This is a critique of Soviet law and ideology that denies the connection between social structural and behavioral variables and juvenile delinquency, such as bad company and parental inadequacy.

2428 Minkovsky, G. M. USSR: Effectiveness Of Treatment Measures And Problems Of The Typology Of Juvenile Delinquents, pp 221-241 in United Nations Social Defence Research Institute (ed.) *Juvenile Justice: An International Survey*. Rome, Italy: The United Nations, 1976. The author criticizes the standard-issue Soviet typologies of juvenile delinquency, and recommends sentencing and corrections policies that are more flexible and less ideological.

2429 Ochs, Brian A. Procedural Rights Of Juvenile Offenders Before Soviet Courts And Commissions For Juvenile Affairs, *Review Of Socialist Law* 1:61-83, 1983. The author provides a history of the general structure of soviet juvenile justice and procedural laws.

2430 Shestakov, Dmitry A. & Shestakova, Natalia D. Comparative Juvenile Justice: An Overview Of Russia, pp 205-232 in Winterdyk, John A . (ed.) *Juvenile Justice Systems: International Perspectives*. Toronto: Canadian Scholars' Press, 1997. This chapter offers a comprehensive description of juvenile law and justice in contemporary Russia.

2431 Solomon, Peter H. Jr. The Case Of The Vanishing Acquittal: Informal Norms And The Practices Of Soviet Criminal Justice, *Soviet Studies* 39:531-555, 1987. This article reveals the informal processes that operate in the Soviet criminal justice system, including the processing of young offenders.

2432 Solomon, Peter H. *Soviet Criminologists And Criminal Policy: Specialists In Policy-Making*. New York, New York: Columbia University, 1978. Based on official data and interviews, the author reviews the role of criminologists in general, and in the prevention of juvenile delinquency in particular in the chapter titled "Delinquency Prevention." 253p.

2433 Strogovich, M. S. On The Rights Of The Individual In Soviet Criminal Procedure, *The Soviet Review* 18:3-17, 1977. The philosophical and legal principles underlying the rights of the accused, including minors, are discussed by the author.

2434 USSR All Union Institute Of Problems Of Strengthening Of Legality (ed.) *Scientific Information On Problems Of Crime Combating (Research Findings Of 1989)*. Moscow, USSR. The main topics addressed in this document are the procurator's role under the conditions of "perestroika" and the democratization of social life, crime prevention in the city, work collectives, and juvenile delinquency research. 52p.

2435 USSR All Union Research Institute Of The Causes And Prevention Of Crime *Juvenile Crime In The Soviet Union*. Moscow, USSR: The Novosti Press, 1976. This document discusses the rate of juvenile crime vis-à-vis adult crime and various measures to prevent juvenile illegality. 5p.

2436 Van Den Berg, Ger P. *The Soviet System Of Justice*. Dordrecht, The Netherlands: 1985. This volume offers a review of the Soviet criminal justice system, and a critique of the official crime and criminal justice data from the USSR. 374p.

2437 Wenk, Ernst *In Search Of Delinquency Prevention Models In Schools: A Cross-National Study*. Davis, California: National Council on Crime and Delinquency, 1977. This publication describes Soviet strategies in eradicating delinquency at two levels: by the basic measures of improving educational and work conditions and structuring of leisure time, and by preventive measures against dropping out, improving work habits, and remedial teaching. 48p.

2438 Zeldes, Ilya *The Problem Of Crime In The USSR*. Springfield, Illinois: Charles C. Thomas, 1981. The author describes the Soviet concept of crime using various Soviet and other research data on the state of crime in the USSR, with pp 108-112 devoted to juvenile justice processing from the militia/police to special schools for delinquents. 140p.

2439 Zeldes, Ilya Methods Of Crime Prevention In The USSR, *International Journal Of Comparative And Applied Criminal Justice* 2:29-34, 1978. The procedural and non-procedural means of economic, technical, and rehabilitative strategies in crime prevention, including that of juveniles is described in this article.

Saudi Arabia

2440 Al-Athl, Abdullah Mohamed Saudi Arabia, pp 117-140 in Stewart, V. Lorne (ed.) *Justice And Troubled Children Around The World, Vol. 3*. New York, New York: New York University Press, 1981. This chapter describes and discusses various welfare facilities and programs to deal with, mainly male, juvenile offenders.

Singapore

2441 Hah, Ng Bie Existing Juvenile Justice System In Singapore, pp 132-141 in United Nations Asia and Far East Institute (eds.) *Report For 1983 And Resource Material Series No. 25*. Tokyo, Japan: UNAFEI, 1984. Some data on juvenile offenders and pre-delinquents, treatment orientation such as the protection of the child and young persons, power and procedures of the juvenile court, probation reports and community probation are the focus of this report.

2442 Martin, Roderick E. The Sentencing Of Young Adult Offenders In Singapore, pp 111-120 in United Nations Asia And Far East Institute (ed.) *Report For 1975 And Resource Material No. 11*. Tokyo, Japan: UNAFEI, 1976. Offenders, aged 16-21, and the range of sentences they could receive are described in this document.

2443 Somalingam, Radakrishnan Kannusammy An Integrated Approach To Effective Juvenile Justice Administration, pp 136-144 in United Nations Asia And Far East Institute (ed.) *Resource Material Series No. 21*. Tokyo, Japan: UNAFEI, 1982. This document discusses the laws, police, juvenile court, dispositions, and drug abuse in Singapore.

Slovakia

2444 Brunovska, Annamaria Juvenile Justice in Slovakia, pp 174-175 in Cavadino, Paul (ed.) *Children Who Kill*. Winchester, United Kingdom: Waterside, 1996. A brief description of the system of juvenile justice in Slovakia and the treatment of violent young offenders is presented in this chapter.

Slovenia

2445 Dekleva, Bojan Renewal Of Residential Treatment In Solvenia, pp 401-410 in Junger-Tas, Josine; Boendermaker, Leonieke & Van Der Laan, Peter H. (eds.) *The Future Of The Juvenile Justice System (L'Avenir Du Système Pénal Des Mineurs)*. Leuven, Belgium: Acco, 1991. In describing the present institutional treatment of delinquent children, the author speculates about the future of the juvenile criminal justice system in Slovenia.

South Africa

2446 Conradie, Herman The Republic Of South Africa, pp 286-300 in Shoemaker, Donald J. (ed.) *International Handbook On Juvenile Justice.* Westport, Connecticut: Greenwood, 1996. This chapter offers a description and discussion of the South African juvenile justice system.

2447 Goodman, Randy Summaries Of DCI Country Surveys, South Africa pp 190-196 in Tomasevski, Katarina (ed) *Children In Adult Prisons: An International Perspective.* New York, New York: St. Martin's Press, 1986. Findings for South Africa from the 1982-1984 Defense for Children International Survey of children in adult prisons are presented.

2448 Harcourt-Baldwin, J. D. Sentencing The Juvenile Offender, pp 260-279 in Olmesdahl, M. C. J. & Steytler, N. C. (eds.) *Criminal Justice In South Africa.* Cape Town, South Africa: Juta, 1983. This article focuses on the South African legal rules applicable in sentencing juvenile offenders, and offers data on actual sentences.

2449 Hutchinson, D. Juvenile Justice, pp 236-259 in Olmesdahl, M. C. J. & Steytler, N. C. (eds.) *Criminal Justice In South Africa.* Cape Town, South Africa: Juta, 1983. In this study the author focuses on offenders aged 7-17 and describes the approach taken by the South African judiciary in dealing with them.

2450 Lawyers Committee For Human Rights *The War Against Children: South Africa's Youngest Victims.* New York, New York: Lawyers Committee for Human rights, 1986. Based on a fact-finding mission in 1985 involving children under age 18, this report examines human rights violations in South Africa.

2451 Louw, Dap & Olivier, Pierre Listening To children In South Africa, pp 168-181 in Bottoms, Bette L. & Goodman, Gail S. (eds.) *International Perspectives On Child Abuse And Children's Testimony: Psychological Research And Law.* Thousand Oaks, California: Sage, 1996. The authors describe two research projects that had significant effects on protecting the rights of child witnesses, and the legislative and procedural changes that resulted from the report of the South African Law Commission.

2452 Midgley, J. *Children On Trial: A Study Of Juvenile Justice.* Cape Town, South Africa: National Institute for Crime Prevention and the Rehabilitation of Offenders, 1975. From research the juvenile justice system in South Africa, it is concluded that the juvenile court's approach and orientation are outdated and inapplicable tgiven the needs of children and young people. 181p.

2453 Puritz, Patricia Children In Detention In South Africa, *Children's Legal Rights Journal* 8:8-10, 1987. Reviewing the laws and practices under the South African "State of Emergency," the author is critical of the unusually large number of minors that were detained.

2454 Skelton, Ann Standards Concerning Children In Conflict With The Law: Developing Juvenile Justice in Post-Apartheid South Africa, pp 101-108 in United Nations Centre for Human Rights, United Nations Crime Prevention And Criminal Justice Branch (eds.) *Children And Juveniles In Detention: Application Of Human Rights Standards*. Vienna, Austria: United Nations Children's Fund, 1995. This chapter provides a brief, but comprehensive discussion of standards for dealing with youthful offenders in post-apartheid South Africa.

2455 South Africa Juvenile Justice Drafting Consultancy *Juvenile Justice For South Africa: Proposals For Policy And Legislative Change*. Cape Town, South Africa, 1995. This report was designed to help create a new juvenile justice system in South Africa, offering specific proposals on a wide range of issues. 56p.

South Korea

2456 Korean Institute Of Criminology *Crime & Criminal Justice In Korea: KIC Research Abstracts 1994*. Seoul, 1995. This compilation presents 32 abstracts in English and German that summarize juvenile delinquency research projects conducted at the Institute, focusing on running away from home and deviance, suspension of prosecution with supervision, classification, and predicting recidivism. 166p. English and German.

2457 Seung Ja Doe, Sondra Comparative Review Of Children's Rights And Women's Rights In Korea, *Development* 44:111-116, 2001. Outlining the development of children's and women's rights in modern Korea, the author feels the evolving welfare state is responding to international concerns for human rights.

2458 Shin, Kyoung-Woo The Effective Treatment Of Drug Offenders And Juvenile Delinquents In Korea, pp 288-294 in. United Nations Asia And Far East Institute (ed.) *Resource Material Series No. 46*. Tokyo, Japan: UNICEF, 1995. Chapter provides information on age limits, and a variety of aspects of drug treatment for juveniles in Korea.

2459 Cho, Byung In & Chang, Richard J. The Youth Crime Problems In The Republic Of Korea, *International Journal Of Comparative And Applied Criminal Justice* 16:301-316, 1992. The shift from rural-agrarian traditions to modernization and urbanization in Korea, and the consequent conflict of values, and the impact these forces are having on juvenile delinquency is the focus of this paper.

Spain

2460 Angeles, Cea D'Ancona M. *Juvenile Justice In Spain (La Justicia De Menores En Espana)*. Madrid: Siglo XXI, 1992. This study identifies the major problems with the old system of juvenile justice in Spain. 169p.

2461 Alabart, Anna; Aragay, Josep M. & Sabaté, Juli Of Victimization And Local Politics in Delinquency Prevention (Encuestas De Victimización Y Políticas Locales De Provención De La Delincuencia), pp 61-68 in Ajuntament De Barcelona Forum Des Collectivites Territoriales Europeennes Pur La Securite Urbaine (ed.) *Urban Crime: Statistical Approaches And Analysis: Papers And Conclusions (Instrumentos Y Metodologiá Para El Conocimiento Del Fenómeno Delincuencial: Ponencias Y Conclusiones)*. Barcelona: Institut d'Estudis Metropolitans de Barcelona, 1990. The authors affirm the usefulness of crime surveys as instrumental in developing local crime prevention strategies in Barcelona. Spanish with English/French summary.

2462 Beristain, Antonio Treatment Of Young Delinquents In Spain And The Basque Country From 1936 To 1978, *International Journal Of The Sociology Of Law* 8:277-296, 1980. Using an historical analysis, the author describes the nature, extent, and treatment of juvenile offenders in Spain.

2463 Garrido, Vicente R & R With Spanish Offenders And Children "At Risk," pp 358-382 in Ross, Robert R. & Ross, Roslynn D. (eds.) *Thinking Straight: The Reasoning And Rehabilitation Program For Delinquency Prevention and Offender Rehabilitation*. Ottawa, Canada: Air Training and Publications, 1995. The rationale for testing the applicability and efficacy of the cognitive model among juvenile and adult offenders in Spain is discussed in this chapter.

2464 Garrido, Vicente & Santiago, Redondo The Institutionalization Of Young Offenders, *Criminal Behavior And Mental Health* 3:336-348, 1994. The authors examine the efficacy and usefulness of institutionalization in rehabilitating Spanish youth who are found to be delinquent.

2465 Goodman, Randy Summaries Of DCI Country Surveys-Spain, pp 196-197 in Tomasevski, Katarina (ed) *Children In Adult Prisons: An International Perspective*. New York, New York: St. Martin's Press, 1986. Findings on Spain's children in adult prisons from the 1982-1984

Defense for Children International Survey are presented in this section.

2466 López de Oruezábal, Julio Spain, pp 113-136 in Stewart, V. Lorne (ed.) *Justice And Troubled Children Around The World, Vol. 2*. New York, New York: New York University Press, 1981. In this chapter, the author describes the way Spain's family-orientation is reflected in the juvenile tutelary courts.

2467 Maquieira, Virginia Boys, Girls And The Discourse Of Identity: Growing Up In Madrid, pp 38-54 in Cain, Maureen (ed.) *Growing Up Good: Policing The Behavior Of Girls In Europe*. Newbury Park, California: Sage. This is a description of the results from an investigation on changes in the values and morality emerging in Spanish society focusing on a sample of urban youth in Madrid.

2468 Redondo, Santiago; Roca, Manual; Perez, Elena; Sanchez, Anarbella & Deumal, Eva Environmental Outline Of A Youth Prison In Catalogna: Five Years Evaluation, pp 411-428 in Junger-Tas, Josine; Leonieke, Boendermaker & Van Der Laan, Peter H. (eds.) *The Future Of The Juvenile Justice System (L'Avenir Du Système Pénal Des Mineurs)*. Leuven, Belgium: Acco, 1991. This study sought to determine if social behavioral training had a positive impact on recidivism rates among youths incarcerated in the Youth Penitentiary Center in Barcelona.

2469 Van Kalmthout, Anton M. & Tak, Peter J. P. Spain, pp 239-265 in Van Kalmthout, Anton M. & Tak, Peter J. P. (eds.) *Sanction-Systems In The Member-States Of The Council Of Europe Part I*. New York, New York: Kluwer, 1988. The authors describe the Spanish sanctions systems in general.

Sweden

2470 Bondeson, Ulla V. *Prisoners In Prison Societies*. New Brunswick, New Jersey: Transaction, 1989. This volume reports research on the impact of socialization into institutions among incarcerated Swedish juveniles and adults. 371p.

2471 Gummesson, Margit & Alexandersson, Lars (eds.) *Crime Prevention Work In Schools (Brottsförebyggand Arbete I Skolan)*. Stockholm, Sweden: Vad Säger Forskningen, 1989. This anthology describes current research in the field of juvenile crime carried out on behalf of the Swedish Council Of Crime Prevention and the National Board Of Education. 116p. Swedish.

2472 Hessle, Sven Welfare in Sweden: The Family And Problematic Adolescents, pp 65-72 in Bullock, Roger (ed.) *Problem Adolescents: An*

International View. London, United Kingdom: Whiting & Burch, 1992. The opportunities and problems with Swedish welfare approach to dealing with problem youth is discussed by the author.

2473 Janson, Carl-Gunnar & Torstensson, Marie Sweden, pp 191-212 in Klein, Malcolm W. (ed.) *Western Systems Of Juvenile Justice*. Beverly Hills, California: Sage, 1984. A description of the organization and discussion of the operation of juvenile justice in Sweden are provided by the authors.

2474 Lansing, Paul The Swedish Law Of Juveniles, *Juvenile And Family Court Journal* 31:49-51, 1980. This article describes the Swedish law governing children under 15 years of age who commit crimes, and the authority of the Child Welfare Boards over them.

2475 Lindby, Kerstin In This Children's Age, What Is Being Done For The "Outsiders" Problems And Trends In The Field Of Juvenile Delinquency In Sweden, *International Child Welfare Review* 35:33-46, 1977. This article discusses the changes resulting from thrends in immigration that have taken place in Swedish juvenile justice since the late 1970s.

2476 Lindström, Peter & Svanberg, Karin Victim/Offender Mediation In Sweden: A Research Note, pp 245-260 in Walgrave, Lode (ed.) *Restorative Justice For Juveniles: Potentialities, Risks And Problems For Research*. Leuven: Leuven University Press, 1998. This chapter describes results from an ongoing evaluation of a mediation project in a medium-sized Swedish city.

2477 Nelson, Alvar Sweden, pp 175-228 in Stewart, V. Lorne (ed.) *Justice And Troubled Children Around The World, Vol. 3*. New York, New York: New York University Press, 1981. The laws, nature, organization, and operation of the Swedish system of juvenile justice is the focus of the author's description.

2478 Nyquist, Ola The Swedish Approach To Juvenile Corrections, pp 135-150 in Stewart, V. Lorne (ed.) *The Changing Face Of Juvenile Justice*. New York, New York: New York University Press, 1978. This chapter describes the legal status of youths of various ages, and presents an overview of processing and disposition of different categories of juveniles offenders in Sweden.

2479 Sarnecki, Jerzy Reaction To Crimes Committed By Young People, pp 42-55 in Snare, Annika (ed.) *Youth, Crime And Justice, Vol. 12*. Oslo, Norway: Norwegian University Press, 1991. The author provides a brief description of the laws and juvenile justice system in Sweden.

2480 Serrill, Michael S. Swedish Juvenile Institutions: Open, Tolerant, And Under Attack, *Corrections Magazine New York* 3:35-36, 1977. In this article the author discusses the organization of institutions for delinquents run by the Swedish National Board of Health and Welfare, and also comments on some of the issues regarding their operation.

2481 Somander, Lis & Johansson, Helena *Young Offenders In Prison In 1989 (Fängelsedömda Ungdomar 1989)*. Norrkoping, Sweden: Swedish Prison and Probation Administration Research Group, 1992. This study investigates diverse grounds for the decision to imprison young offenders under age 18.

2482 Sundeen, Richard A. Swedish Juvenile Justice And Welfare, *Journal Of Criminal Justice* 4:109-121, 1976. The author of this article describes the ideology and welfare value system that guide the Swedish juvenile justiice system.

Switzerland

2483 Aebi, Marcelo; Killias, Martin & Ribeaud, Denis Medical Prescription For Drugs And Delinquency: The Evolution Of Swiss Drug Policy (Prescripton Médicale De Stupéfiants Et Délinquence: Résultats Des Essais Suisses), *Criminologie* 32:127-148, 1999. The authors evaluate the effectiveness of the Swiss drug prescription program using police records, interviews and self-reported delinquency survey. French with English summary.

2484 Alimam, Ahmed Evaluation Of An Educational Institution For Youth In Swiss Romande (Évaluation D'Une Institution Éducative Pour Jeunes En Suisse Romande), *Revue Internationale De Criminologi Et De Police Technique* 46:23-48, 1993. In an evaluation of an educational institution for youths in French-speaking Switzerland, this study found a significant reduction in recidivism and an increase in social adjustment. French.

2485 Boehlen, Marie Recidivism And The Retention Of Juvenile Sentences (Rückfall Und Bewärhrung Im Jugendstrafvollzug), pp 201-206 in Killias, Martin (ed.) *Recidivism And Rehabilitation (Rückfall Und Bewährung/Récidive Et Réhabilitation)*. Zurich, Switzerland: Verlag Rüegger, 1992. The author addresses the legal, the social, the work and total enforcement of the sentences for youthful Swiss offenders. German.

2486 Etienne, Sandrine A Critical Report On The Federal 1985-1992 Statistics On Swiss Juvenile Delinquency And The Penal Rights Of Minors, *Revue Internationale De Criminologie Et De Police Technique* 68:63-86, 1995. In analyzing some statistics for all of Switzerland and various Cantons, in addition to age the author favors tailoring, a judicial structure for minors based on diverse criteria.

2487 Goodman, Randy Summaries Of DCI Country Surveys, Switzerland, pp 197-199 in Tomasevski, Katarina (ed) *Children In Adult Prisons: An International Perspective.* New York, New York: St. Martin's Press, 1986. This paper presents findings for Switzerland from the 1982-1984 Defense for Children International Survey on Swiss children in adult prisons.

2488 Haesler, Walter T. Juvenile Delinquency In Switzerland, *Euro-criminology* 11:133-150, 1997. This article presents an historical review of juvenile penal law in Switzerland, along with tables of data on penalities for juveniles from 1985 through 1991.

2489 Huber, Patrizia Pesenti Maintaining Youthful Peace In Canton Tessin 1987-92 (Die Jugendrechtspflege Im Kanton Tessin 1987-92) pp 207-210 in Killias, Martin (ed.) *Recidivism And Rehabilitation (Rückfall Und Bewährung/Récidive Et Réhabilitation*). Zurich, Switzerland: Verlag Rüegger, 1992. Continuation of juvenile court interventions to maintain its effectiveness is the theme of this article on Swiss juvenile justice. German.

2490 Killias, Martin & Rabasa, Juan Does Heroin Prescription Reduce Crime? Results From The Evaluation Of The Swiss Heroin Prescription Project, *Studies On Crime And Prevention* 7:127-133, 1998. This research investigated the before- and after-delinquency rates among youths admitted to a medical heroin treatment program.

2491 Killias, Martin & Rabasa, Juan Effects Of The Medical Prescription Of Heroin On The Delinquency Of Drug Addicts (Auswirkungen Der Heroin-Verschreibung Auf Die Delinquenz Drogenabhaengiger), *Monatsschrift Fuer Kriminologie Und Strafrechtsroform* 81:1-16, 1998. This article presents the results of an evaluation study of medical drug-prescription treatment programs in several Swiss cities. German.

2492 Killias, Martin & Uchtenhagen, Ambros Does Heroin Prescription Reduce Delinquency Among Drug-Addicts? On The Evaluation Of The Swiss Heroin Prescription Projects And Its Methodogy, *Studies On Crime And Crime Prevention* 5:245-256, 1996. Using a variety of data sources, the authors evaluated the Swiss medical-prescription program for heroin addicts.

2493 Queloz, Nicolas Judicial Responses To Youthful Offenders: The Case Of Switzerland, pp 295-310 in Hackler, Jim (ed.) *Official Responses To Problem Juveniles: Some International Reflections*. Euskadi, Spain: The Oñati International Institute for the Sociology of Law, 1991. This paper outlines the legal framework of the juvenile (criminal) justice system in Switzerland.

2494 Schuh, Jörg (ed.) *Youth And Delinquency (Jugend Und Delinquenz)*. Grusch, Switzerland: Verlag Rüegger, 1988. This anthology includes papers presented at a criminological symposium in Switzerland on juvenile code revision and covers a variety of related topics. 455p. German and French.

2495 Tanner, Hannes Inside Order Offside: Re-Examining Judicial Decisions Regarding Difficult Young Clients (Inside Order Offside: Ergebnisse Der Nachuntersuchung Von Klienten Des Massnahmenvollzugs Für Besonders Erziehungsschwierige Jugendliche (Art. 93ter StGB) Anlässlich Einer Längsschnittuntersuchung), pp. 149-170 in Killias, Martin (ed.) *Recidivism And Rehabilitation (Rückfall Und Bewährung/Récidive Et Réhabilitation*). Zurich, Switzerland: Verlag Rüegger, 1992. German & French. The author examines evidence on hardcore, youthful offenders in Switzerland. German.

2496 Veillard-Cybulska, H. Switzerland, pp 143-165 in Stewart, V. Lorne (ed.) *Justice And Troubled Children Around The World, Vol. I.* New York, New York: New York University Press, 1980. Using an international perspective, this chapter provides a description of the various social and judicial services Switzerland provides its children.

2497 Zermatten, Jean Reforming The Community Service Sentence In Switzerland (La Prestation En Travail En Suisse), pp 157-178 in Dünkel, Frieder & Zermatten, Jean (eds.) *Recent Trends In Penal Law For Minors: Mediation, Community Service And Intermediate Treatment (Nouvelles Tendances Dans Le Droit Pénal Des Mineurs: Médiation, Travail Au Profit De La Communauté Et Traitement Intermédiaire)*. Freiburg, Germany: Max Planck Institute for Foreign and International Criminal Justice, 1990. This chapter describes community service as an alternative sentence for juvenile offenders in Switzerland.

Taiwan

2498 Chao, Winston Juvenile Justice In Taiwan: Further Reflections, *Police Studies* 13:139-144, 1990. The impact of rapid social change following the end of martial law in Taiwan, and its impact on juvenile justice reform, are discussed in this article.

2499 Deng, Furjen; Lee, Lou-Tou & Vaughn, Michael S. Drug Crime In Taiwan: A Time-Series Analysis From 1965 To 1994, *Deviant Behavior* 17:347-368, 1996. This article offers data on offenders below age 18.

2500 Jan, Lee-Jan Preventing Juvenile Delinquency In Taiwan, *International Journal Of Comparative And Applied Criminal Justice* 10:205-213, 1986. This article provides statistics on juveniles and describes various prevention programs under the auspices of different government branches and organizations in Taiwan.

2501 Jan, Lee-Jan Corrections In Taiwan (Republic Of China), *International Journal Of Comparative And Applied Criminal Justice* 12:95-100, 1988. The autor describes Taiwan's correctional system with three types of facilities for children under age 18.

2502 Shee, Amy H. L. *Legal Protection Of Children Against Sexual Exploitation In Taiwan: A Socio-Legal Perspective.* Aldershot, United Kingdom: Ashgate, 1998. This critical review explores legal protections for child prostitution in Taiwan. 275p.

2503 Wu, Bohsiu The Impact Of An Antiamphetamine Law On Juvenile Delinquency In Taiwan, *International Journal Of Offender Therapy And Comparative Criminology* 40:234-242, 1996. The consequences of changes in Taiwan's criminal code on delinquency drug arrest rates are examined in this article.

Thailand

2504 Champaratna, Prija The Effective Treatment Of Drug Abusers In Thailand, pp 210-219 in. United Nations Asia And Far East Institute (ed.) *Resource Material Series No. 46.* Tokyo, Japan: UNICEF, 1995. This chapter provides a description of the approach taken to deal with juvenile and other drug abusers in Thailand.

2505 Goodman, Randy Summaries Of DCI Country Surveys, Thailand; pp 199-200 in Tomasevski, Katarina (ed) *Children In Adult Prisons: An International Perspective.* New York, New York: St. Martin's Press, 1986. Findings on children in adult prisons in Thailand from the 1982-1984 Defense for Children International Survey are the subject of this presentation.

2506 Piyasirananda, Praneeet Diagnosis And Classification For The Effective Treatment Of Juvenile Delinquents In Thailand, pp 95-115 in United Nations Asia And Far East Institute (ed.) *Annual Report For 1996 And Resource Material Series No. 51.* Tokyo, Japan, 1996. This chapter describes the initial activities of the new juvenile court in Thailand.

2507 Watanavanich, Prathan The Juvenile And Family Court System In Thailand: Development And Experience, pp 80-91 in United Nations Asia And Far East Institute (ed.) *Report for 1993 And Resource Material*

Series No. 45. Tokyo, Japan, 1994. This chapter describes the organization and operation of the family court system in Thailand and provides some data on cases processed.

2508 Winitnaiyapak, Trakul An Outline Of The Existing Juvenile Justice System In Thailand, pp 155-169 in United Nations Asia And Far East Institute (ed.) *Report For 1986 And Resource Material Series No. 29*. Tokyo, Japan, 1986. The juvenile justice system of Thailand is described in this article.

Turkey

2509 Human Rights Watch *'Nothing Unusual': The Torture Of Children In Turkey*. New York & Washington, D.C., 1991. This report examines the torture and detention of children for "crimes of thought" in Turkey. 77p. Appendix.

2510 Šelih, Alenka Juvenile Justice In Turkey, pp 111-134 in Stewart, V. Lorne (ed.) *The Changing Faces Of Juvenile Justice*. New York, New York: New York University Press, 1978. The author stresses the importance of adequate social and educational services for children and how the latter plays a major role in delinquency prevention.

United Kingdom

2511 Adams, Robert; Allard, Simon; Baldwin, John & Thomas, Jim *A Measure Of Diversion: Case Studies In Intermediate Treatment*. Leicester, United Kingdom: National Youth Bureau, 1981. The authors discuss six studies of intermediate treatment programs for juveniles in the general context of community based projects, and the politics, and the social policy of the 1970s in the United Kingdom. 347p.

2512 Allen, Rob *Children And Crime: Taking Responsibility*. London, United Kingdom: Institute for Public Policy Research, 1998. The author advocates a new criminal justice policy for juveniles in the United Kingdom modeled after the New Zealand Family Group Conference approach for young offenders. 104p.

2513 Allen, Rob Out Of Jail: The Reduction In The Use Of Penal Custody For Male Juveniles 1981-88, *Howard Journal* 30:30-52, 1991. The author discusses the role of declining juvenile populations, and changes in law and policy on the dramatically reduced custodial sentences for juvenile delinquents in the United Kingdom since 1981.

2514 Allen, Rob Parental Responsibility For Juvenile Offenders, pp 105-117 in Booth, Tim (ed.) *Juvenile Justice In The New Europe*. Sheffield, United Kingdom: Joint Unit for Social Services Research, Sheffield University, 1991. This chapter examines policy initiatives designed to reinforce the responsibility of parents for the illegal acts of their children.

2515 Alun, Michael (ed.) *Tough On Crime, Tough On The Causes—A Collection Of Essays*. London, United Kingdom: Fabian Society, 1997. Included in this discussion are changes in juvenile justice, the perspect ives of victims, policing, and crime in England. 47p.

2516 Anderson, Richard *Representation In The Juvenile Court*. London, United Kingdom: Routledge & Kegan Paul, 1978. The assignment of representation in two juvenile courts, and its practical effects, are the subjects of this exposition of juvenile court processes in Great Britain, demonstrating that courts had widely different interpretations of the law on representation. 82p.

2517 Ashford, Mark The Trail Process In England And Wales, pp 67-72 in Cavadino, Paul (ed.) *Children Who Kill*. Winchester, United Kingdom: Waterside, 1996. Age of criminal culpability and other laws as they apply to juveniles under trial is the subject of this chapter.

2518 Asquith, Stewart Scotland, pp 425-458 in Mehlbye, Jill & Walgrave, Lode (eds.) *Confronting Youth In Europe: Juvenile Crime And Juvenile Justice*. Copenhagen, Denmark: AKF Forlaget, 1998. This chapter provides an in-depth description of the Scottish juvenile justice system.

2519 Asquith, Stewart (ed.) *Children And Young People In Conflict With The Law*. London, United Kingdom: Jessica Kingsley, 1996. This anthology addresses the conceptual and empirical developments in juvenile justice in the United Kingdom. 200p.

2520 Asquith, Stewart (ed.) *The Kilbrandon Report: Children And Young Persons Scotland*. Edinburgh, Scotland: Her Majesty's Stationery Office, 1995. This reissue of a policy analysis on how society should deal with children in trouble includes a new introduction that reflects the changes since its original publication in Scotland 30 years earlier. 131p.

2521 Asquith, Stewart *Children And Justice: Decision-Making In Children's Hearings And Juvenile Courts*. Edinburgh, Scotland: Edinburgh University Press, 1983. This study attempts to analyze the translation of social policy into actual practice focusing on the extent to which decisions made about delinquent children reflect and are based on competing judicial and welfare ideologies. 258p.

2522 Association Of Chief Officers Of Probation *A Crisis In Custody: Findings From A Survey Of Juveniles In Prison Awaiting Trial*. London, United Kingdom: National Association for the Care and Resettlement of Offenders, 1995. This report faults the pretrial bail and remand of youths, and the system's failure to find alternatives to imprisonment for them. 35p.

2523 Association Of Chief Officers Of Probation *Awaiting Trial Final Report: A Survey Of Juveniles*. London, United Kingdom: National Association for the Care and Resettlement of Offenders, 1993. This study includes the number of youths and minority youths in prison, the number awaiting trial, their offenses, regional variations in the court's power and local authority, and legal representations prior to the 1991 Criminal Justice Act's abolition of remand for juveniles. 40p.

2524 Bailey, Roger The System In Northern Ireland, pp 88-93 in Cavadino, Paul (ed.) *Children Who Kill*. Winchester, United Kingdom: Waterside, 1996. Northern Ireland's discovery, reporting, bail, remand, arrest and court processes as well as treatment of 16-17 year olds, and alternative procedural rules on press reporting of juveniles are the topics included in this chapter.

2525 Bailey, S. M. Serious Young Offenders, pp 15-20 in Heritage, Ian & Martin, Carol (eds.) *Serious Young Offenders, Security, Treatment & Future Prospects*. London, United Kingdom: Institute for The Study & Treatment of Delinquency, 1995. The author lists factors that prevent consistency and effectiveness of treatment, treatment institutions, and community intervention programs in the United Kingdom.

2526 Bailey, Susan Health In Young Persons' Establishments: Treating The Damaged And Preventing Harm, *Criminal Behaviour And Mental Health* 3:349-367, 1994. This is a critique of the tendency of authorities to resort to simplistic solutions for the problems of young offenders in residential schools, hospitals, and prisons.

2527 Baker, Heidi & Caraher, Martin *Do It Yourself: The Process Of Developing A Drugs Information Resource For Children*. London, United Kingdom: Central Drugs Prevention Unit-Home Office, 1995. This document, on drug use prevention aimed at 9-10 year olds in England,describes a media-based information resource about drugs designed and piloted on two specific media prototypes. 64p.

2528 Ball, Caroline & Connolly, Jo Educationally Disaffected Young Offenders - Youth Court And Agency Response To Truancy And School Exclusions, *British Journal Of Criminology* 40:594-616, 2000. This study of youth court defendants from inner London, Midlands, Yorkshire and the North East of England focused on family background, school attendance, and further offense behavior during the six-months following sentencing.

2529 Balsdon, Sam *Improving The Management Of Juvenile Informants*. London, United Kingdom: Police Research Group-Home Office, 1996. This is a study of the extent to which the police use juvenile informants and if they could be used more, and offers guidelines for such use. 33p. Appendix.

2530 Bandelli, Sue Abolition Of The Presumption Of Doli Incapax And The Criminalisation Of Children, *The Howard Journal Of Criminal Justice* 37:114-123, 1998. The various issues related to the abolition of the presumption of incapacity to delineate right from wrong *(doli incapax)* for 10-13 year olds are discussed by the author.

2531 Barker, Mary & Bridgeman, Cressida *Preventing Vandalism: What Works?* London, United Kingdom: Home Office-Police Research Group, 1994. The author discusses a five-step vandalism prevention program that seems to be effective in the United Kingdom. 50p.

2532 Barker, Mary; Pease, Ken & Webb, Barry *Community Service And Crime Prevention*. London, United Kingdom: Home Office-Police Research Group. This document reports an evaluation of a project aimed at primary prevention of criminality among "at-risk" youth in deprived neighborhoods. 36p.

2533 Barrows, John; Ekblom, Paul & Heal, Kevin *Crime Prevention And The Police*. London, United Kingdom: Her Majesty's Stationery Office, 1979. The two studies reported in this volume found that there was little convincing evidence that truancy patrols reduced crime during those times when children should have been in school, and that the number of offenses attributable to truants appeared small. 37 p.

2534 Bell, Adrian & Gibson, Phillip Tackling The Dilemmas For Policy And Practice In Justice Systems Divided By Age, pp 97-104 in Booth, Tim (ed.) *Juvenile Justice In The New Europe*. Sheffield, United Kingdom: Joint Unit for Social Services Research, Sheffield University, 1991. This chapter focuses on the problems encountered in systems bifurcated by age, and the three stages of diversion available in the juvenile justice system.

2535 Bell, Charles & Haines, Kevin Managing The Transition: Implications Of The Introduction Of A Youth Court In England And Wales, pp 118-132 in Booth, Tim (ed.) *Juvenile Justice In The New Europe*. Sheffield, Unied Kingdom: Joint Unit for Social Services Research, Sheffield

University, 1991. This chapter defines the age boundaries for dealing with young offenders in England and Wales, and describes plans for introducing youth courts within current juvenile justice practices.

2536 Bell, Charles; Hill, Graham & Crisp, Ann (eds.) *Managing Remands In The New Youth Justice System: A Handbook For Practice*. London, United Kingdom: National Association for the Care and Resettlement of Offenders-Youth Crime Section, 1992. This is an anthology on a systems approach to juvenile justice, its success, and the failure of the remand management process involving young offenders. 52p.

2537 Bennett, Trevor Police Strategies And Tactics For Controlling Crime And Disorder In England And Wales, *Studies On Crime And Crime Prevention* 3:146-167, 1994. This essay argues that the police increasingly rely on situational measures, such as hot spot locations, offenses that have high rates, offenders and victims, and a wide array of crime prevention strategies, including youth projects.

2538 Berg, Ian; Brown, Imogen & Hullin, Roy *Off School, In Court: An Experimental And Psychiatric Evaluation Of Severe School Attendance Problems*. New York, New York: Springer-Verlag, 1988. Among truants under juvenile court supervision in Leeds, who were placed on supervision or monitored through repeated court appearance in a controlled experiment, it was found that the adjournment procedure requiring repeated appearance had greater, positive impact. 142p.

2539 Berg, Ian; Goodwin, Alison; Hullin, Roy & McGuire, Ralph The Effect Of Two Varieties Of The Adjournment Procedure On Truancy, *British Journal Of Criminology* 23:150-163, 1983. This study, based on a Leeds juvenile court sample of truants, concludes that random assignment of flexible and inflexible monthly adjournments are equally effective in improving future school attendance.

2540 Berg, Ian Features Of Children Taken To Juvenile Court For Failure To Attend School, *Psychological Medicine* 8:447-453, 1978. This examination of social reports for antisocial and other problem behavior of juvenile court cases for truancy in Leeds tried to locate indications of problems regarding the behavior from school, family, and involvement with social work agencies.

2541 Berg, Ian; Consterdine, Margaret; Hullin, Roy; McGuire, Ralph & Tyrer, Stephen The Effect Of Two Randomly Allocated Court Procedures On Truancy, *British Journal Of Criminology* 18:232-244, 1978. Under the juvenile truancy court care proceedings in Leeds, it was found that subsequent school attendance improved under adjournment procedure which required repeated court appearances of the truant.

2542 Blagg, Harry & Smith, David *Crime, Penal Policy And Social Work.* Essex, United Kingdom: Longman, 1989. This report summarizes British developments under Margaret Thatcher with impacted on penal policy and social work in managing juvenile delinquents and other deviants. 152p.

2543 Blagg, Harry Reparation And Justice For Juveniles, *British Journal Of Criminology* 25:267-279, 1985. Based on interviews with victims and juvenile perpetrators in a Northampton facility, the author describes juvenile reparation and diversion from the perspective of both the victims and the juvenile offenders.

2544 Bottomley, Keith & Pease, Ken *Crime And Punishment: Interpreting The Data.* Philadelphia, Pennsylvania: Open University, 1986. this report reviews statistics on crime and punishment in England and Wales in the previous two decades with illustrations of juvenile diversion and net widening in juvenile justice. 185p.

2545 Bottoms, Anthony; Haines, Kevin & O'Mahony, David England And Wales, pp 139-215 in Mehlbye, Jill & Walgrave, Lode (eds.) *Confronting Youth In Europe: Juvenile Crime And Juvenile Justice.* Copenhagen, Denmark: AKF Forlaget, 1998. This chapter provides an historical overview and extensive descriptions of the contemporary system of juvenile justice and corrections in England and Wales.

2546 Bottoms, Anthony E. & Pratt, John Intermediate Treatment For Girls In England And Wales, pp158-176 in Cain, Maureen (ed.) *Growing Up Good: Policing The Behavior Of Girls in Europe.* Newbury Park, California: Sage, 1989. This chapter examines the level and type of provision for 'intermediate treatment' for girls and boys in England and Wales, with special emphasis on girls.

2547 Bright, Jon Preventing Youth Crime In High Crime Areas: Toward A Strategy, pp 24-42 in Asquith, Stewart (ed.) *Children And Young People In Conflict With The Law.* London, United Kingdom: Jessica Kingsley, 1996. Focusing on prevention rather then rehabilitation, this chapter proposes ways to reduce youth crime in high crime areas.

2548 Brookes, Phillip Positive Regimes For Young Offenders, pp. 12-19 in Prison Reform Trust (eds.) *'A Good and Useful Life': Constructive Prison Regimes.* London, United Kingdom: Prison Reform Trust, 1995. The author examines juvenile offenders and the positive impact of institutional regimens on young offenders, discusses problems and recent developments in the treatment of offenders, as well as education, bullying, and local community involvement. 68p.

2549 Brownlee, Ian D. Intensive Probation With Young Adult Offenders: A Short Reconviction Study, *British Journal Of Criminology* 35:599-612, 1995. This article reports on a study of a non-custodial, intensive probation sentence for both female and male youths and 17-21 in Leeds area, their recidivism and reconviction.

2550 Bruce, Nigel & Spencer, John *Face To Face With Families: A Report On The Children's Panels In Scotland.* Loanhead, Scotland: Macdonald Publishers, 1976. This volume describes and analyzes the operation of Children's Panels in Scotland. 183p.

2551 Bull, Ray & Davies, Graham The Effect Of Child Witness Research On Legislation In Great Britain, pp 96-113 in Bottoms, Bette L. & Goodman, Gail S. (eds.) *International Perspectives On Child Abuse And Children's Testimony: Psychological Research And Law.* Thousand Oaks, California: Sage, 1996. This chapter discusses a number of legislative and procedural changes regarding testimony of children in sex abuse cases in England and Wales, and the impact research on these changes has had in modifying the law and procedures.

2552 Bullock, Roger Secure Accommodation For Very Difficult Adolescents: Some Recent Research Findings, *Journal Of Adolescence* 13:205-216, 1990. The effectiveness of treatment for young people in two United Kingdom Youth Treatment Centers operating under the health department on the future behavior of the young delinquents suggests that, although their behavior generally improved, they are subject to a lot of changes and setbacks.

2553 Burney, E. Sentencing *Young People: What Went Wrong With The Criminal Justice Act 1982?* Brookfield, Vermont: Gower, 1986. The author feels that, due to its ambiguities, the 1982 Criminal Justice Act of England and Wales has not reduced custodial sentences of male juvenile delinquents, but it has resulted in variable application by the courts, and recommends age restrictions for custodial and non-custodial sentences for recidivists, and closing institutions to reduce custodial punishment. 103p.

2554 Caul, Brian; Pinkerton, John & Powell, Fred (eds.) *The Juvenile Justice System In Northern Ireland.* Antrim, Northern Ireland: University of Ulster at Jordantown, 1983. This anthology examines implications of the Report of the Children and Young Persons Review Group (the "Black Report"), published in 1979 in Northern Ireland. 115p.

2555 Cavenagh, W. E. England And Wales, pp 35-66 in Stewart, V. Lorne (ed.) *Justice And Troubled Children Around The World, Vol. 2*. New York, New York: New York University Press, 1981. This chapter offers detailed descriptions of the organization and procedures followed by the juvenile justice systems of England and Wales.

2556 Children's Society *A False Sense Of Security: The Case Against Locking Up More Children*. London, United Kingdom: Children's Society, 1993. This is an outline of an advisory committee opinion that additional lock-up facilities for young offenders are not necessary or needed in the United Kingdom. 71p. Appendix.

2557 Children's Society Advisory Committee On Penal Custody And Its Alternatives For Juveniles *Penal Custody For Juveniles--The Line Of Least Resistance*. London, United Kingdom: Children's Society, 1989. According to this report, although the data from the Home Office indicate decreasing custodial sentences, custody is used inconsistently and much too frequently. 29p.

2558 Clarke, John Whose Justice? The Politics Of Juvenile Control, *International Journal Of The Sociology Of Law* 13:407-421, 1985. The author argues that the 1969 Children and Young Persons Act of England and Wales based on a justice-model, defined accountability in specific, legal, terms to the exclusion of debate and political accountability of the juvenile justice system.

2559 Cleaver, Hedy *Vulnerable Children In Schools: A Study Of Catch 'Em Young*. Dartmouth, United Kingdom: Aldershot, 1991. This report describes a 1986 project to curb vandalism by identifying "at-risk" five-year olds whose future delinquency the teachers predict. 145p.

2560 Collison, Mike Drug Offenders And Criminal Justice: Careers, Compulsion, Commitment And Penalty, *Crime Law And Social Change* 21:49-71, 1994. The author contends that the drug policy of the United Kingdom criminal justice system is based on the model of problem or dependent use, and is inadequate and increasingly irrelevant to diverting young people from drug use.

2561 Cook, Dee *Poverty, Crime And Punishment*. London, United Kingdom: Poverty Publications, 1997. This review of the popular images of the connection between poverty and crime in the United Kingdom in the 1990s also delves into the interactions among poverty, society and crime, and the social control forces. 166p.

2562 Cooper, Barrymore *The Management And Prevention Of Juvenile Crime Problems*. London, United Kingdom: Home Office, 1989. This study of young offender-oriented crime prevention concludes that the basis for crime prevention strategies should be based on the local multi-agency group's profile of the local juvenile. 63p. Appendix.

2563 Coote, Anna (ed.) *Families, Children And Crime*. London, United Kingdom: Institute for Public Policy Research, 1994. There are 16 articles organized under four sections addressing issues such as "families, gender and crime", "evidence, ideas and policy", "working with offenders" and "working with families and children" that express the various authors' views on delinquency and how to deal with it. 147p.

2564 Cornish, D. B. & Clarke, R. V. G. *Residential Treatment And Its Effect On Delinquency*. London, United Kingdom: Home Office, 1975. The findings show that the type of residential program does not have any effect on reducing subsequent delinquent behavior of youths who were the subject of this study. 73p.

2565 Coyle, Andrew *The Prisons We Deserve*. London, United Kingdom: Harper Collins, 1994. This discussion of prisons in the Unied Kingdom includes detention of juveniles and women, violence in prisons, mentally disturbed offenders, and the importance of family and community ties. 218p.

2566 Crowley, Anne *A Criminal Waste: A Study Of Child Offenders Eligible For Secure Training Centres*. London, United Kingdom: Children's Society, 1998. Presenting alternate government sponsored secure training centers for persistent juvenile offenders in the United Kingdom, the author depicts children who lack caring families, adequate supervision and appropriate education, that are aggravated by family breakdowns, institutional care, school expulsions, and abuse. 67p.

2567 Curran, Damian; Kilpatrick, Rosemary & Young, Valerie Longitudinal Aspects Of Reconviction: Secure And Open Intervention With Juvenile Offenders In Northern Ireland, *Howard Journal* 34:97-123, 1995. This study examines baseline and comparative serious offense behavior in a sample of male juveniles sentenced to secure and open forms of residenial custody in Northern Ireland training schools.

2568 Dartington Social Research Unit *Matching Needs And Services: The Audit And Planning Of Provision For Children Looked After By Local Authorities*. Dartington, United Kingdom, 1995. This study argues in favor of "needs assessments," including the need for residential care, in planning for vulnerable children in Great Britain. 67p.

2569 Dartington Social Research Unit *Taking Forward Specialist Services For Young Offenders: The Hampshire Young Offender Community*

Support Scheme. Devon, United Kingdom, 1994. This report presents an evaluation of the impact of a community support project for persistent juvenile offenders, including those in foster care, and partnership between probation and child-care agencies, as well as pre-sentence diversion and specialist services. The report describes also the characteristics of the youth, their criminal careers, and referrals. 45p.

2570 Davies, Graham; Wilson, Clare & Mitchell, Rebecca *Videotaping Children's Evidence: An Evaluation*. London, United Kingdom: Home Office, 1995. This study examines the impact of, and suggests improvements in, the law on child witnesses who had mixed views about the experience of providing videotape testimony. 64p.

2571 Davies, Graham Children On Trial? Psychology, Video Technology And The Law, *Howard Journal* 30:177-191, 1991. This review essay examines the legal issues on the admissibility of children's evidence in British courts.

2572 Davies, Joan *Girls Appearing Before A Juvenile Court*. London, United Kingdom: Her Majesty's Stationery Office, 1976. In this study of delinquent girls appearing before the juvenile court in Greenwich, it was found that a majority had close associates who had been to the juvenile court, certain girls exhibited disturbed mental state, incidence of truancy, and parental employment was not steady. 66p.

2573 Davis, Gwynn & Dawson, Nona *Using Diversion To Communicate Drug Prevention Messages To Young People: An Examination Of Six Projects*. London, United Kingdom: Drug Prevention Initiative-Home Office, 1996. Discusses the importance of planning, stability, access and credibility of various school activities to divert students away from drugs. 32p.

2574 Davis, Gwynn; Boucherat, Jacky & Watson, David Pre-Court Decision-Making In Juvenile Justice, *British Journal Of Criminology* 29:219-235, 1989. The authors' observations of juvenile liaison bureaus in Northampton suggest that decisions to prosecute are made irrespective of the wishes of the victims or parents of the juvenile offenders, and are more administrative rather than judicial.

2575 Davis, Inger P. Individual And Group Treatment Of Problem Adolescents: A Selective Review, pp. 47-54 in Bullock, Roger (ed.) *Problem Adolescents: An International View*. London, United Kingdom: Whiting & Burch, 1992. The author describes a meta analysis of findings from various mental health treatments of disturbed juveniles.

2576 Ditchfield, John & Catan, Liza Juveniles Sentenced For Serious Offences: A Comparison Of Regimes In Young Offender Institutions And Local Authority Community Homes. London, United Kingdom: Home Office, 1992. When comparing two different types of facilities for juveniles convicted of serious offenses, their philosophies, effectiveness, and costs, the author concludes that, although both shared the same broad rehabilitative aims, their regimes were quite different. 95p. Appendix.

2577 Dolan, M.; Holloway, J. & Bailey, S. Health Status Of Juvenile Offenders. A Survey Of Young Offenders Appearing Before The Juvenile Courts, *Journal Of Adolescence* 22: 137-144, 1999. This report on the health needs of juvenile offenders who appeared before a Manchester court found that 19% had significant medical problems, 42% had a history of substance abuse, and 7% had psychiatric problems while 26% engaged in various dangerous behaviors.

2578 Donnison, David Creating A Safer Society, *Social Policy and Administration* 31:3-21, 1997. The author argues that any strategy for social safety, besides support to victims and families that are vulnerable and ex-offenders, must involve also those who seem to be the source of the problem, such as the young offenders.

2579 Donovan, Keith *Hidden From View: An Analysis Of The Problems Of Young Male Prostitutes In Order To Formulate An Effective Interagency Approach*. London, United Kingdom: Police Requirements Support Unit-Home Office, 1991. Based on interview with adolescent male prostitutes in London and cities in Europe, this report sought to suggest policy initiatives on how to deal with the problem. 109p. Appendix.

2580 Dowds, Lizanne & Redfern, Judith *Drug Education Amongst Teenagers: A 1992 British Crime Survey Analysis*. London, United Kingdom: Home Office Research and Planning Unit, 1994. This is a discussion of issues in providing drug education in the schools, such as the views of students and sources of information about drugs, and attitudes towards drug-taking, its prevalence and seriousness, drug related lessons involved and learned at school and their usefulness. 46p.

2581 Drakeford, Mark & Butler, Ian Tough Enough? Youth Justice Under New Labour, *Probation Journal* 48:2:119-124, 2001. The authors discuss their concerns iregarding the reforms in the British juvenile justice system.

2582 Dunlop, Anne B. *Junior Attendance Centres*. London, United Kingdom: Her-Majesty's Stationery Office, 1980. This study of youths sentenced to spend some of their leisure time at junior attendance centers where staff members attempt to guide them toward worthwhile recreational activities, found that most completed their orders satisfactorily without undue absence and without committing any further offenses during the sentence period. 47p.

2583 Elliott, Doreen *Gender, Delinquency and Society*. Aldershot, United Kingdom: Gower, 1988. Official records of boys and girls subject to police cautioning and juvenile court proceedings, do not demonstrate any gender-bias in the treatment juvenile offenders receive from the police and the courts. 151p.

2584 Ely, Peter; Swift, Alan & Sutherland, Alistair *Control Without Custody*. Edinburgh, Scotland: Scottish Academic Press, 1987. This is an evaluation of the viability of the Medway Close Support Unit, an intermediate treatment for juvenile delinquents, as an alternative to custodial sentences for young persons under supervision. 255p.

2585 Epps, Kevin J. Treating Adolescent Sex Offenders In Secure Conditions: The Experience At Glenthorne Centre, *Journal Of Adolescence* 17:105-122, 1994. This Manchester area study of treatment for the sexually-deviant adolescents concludes that four factors--severity of behavior, resistance to treatment, transferring behavioral change into community setting, and staff motivation--affect success.

2586 Evans, Roger Cautioning: Counting The Cost Of Retrenchment, *Criminal Law Review* (August):566-575, 1994. The author argues that a proposal to limit the use of cautioning by police in diverting juveniles from court processing in the United Kingdom will have important ramifications for the youth, as well as the juvenile justice system.

2587 Evans, Roger *The Conduct Of Police Interviews With Juveniles*. London, United Kingdom: Her Majesty's Stationery Office, 1993. This research on police interviews with young offenders in Great Britain looked at the process, and compared the content, denials, and confessions of respondents with police records. 54p.

2588 Farrington, David P. & Bennett, Trevor Police Cautioning Of Juveniles In London, *British Journal Of Criminology* 21:123-135, 1981. The findings of this study suggest that upon the introduction of police cautioning which failed to prevent recidivism, there was an increase in the number of officially processed juveniles due to diversion and net widening, even controlling for the effect of the juveniles' attitude.

2589 Farrington, David P. England And Wales, pp 71-95 in Klein, Malcolm W. (ed.) *Western Systems of Justice*. Beverly Hills, California: Sage, 1984. Using a flow chart of the British juvenile justice system, the author describes the intake and adjudication process, recent changes in the juvenile justice system and welfare policy, and the problem of net-widening.

2590 Farrington, David P. Delinquent Behaviour Modification In The Natural Environment, *British Journal Of Criminology* 19:353-372, 1979. The author discusses the application of behavior modification in the school, the family, and the community.

2591 Field, Sue Young Offender Community Support Scheme--Hampshire, England, *Community Alternatives* 4:77-96, 1992. This is a description of a probation program providing an alternative to custody for young violent offenders who lacked other appropriate adult support in the community in southern England.

2592 Finer, Catherine Jones The New Social Policy In Britain, *Social Policy And Administration* 31:154-170, 1997. The author discusses the new, conservative, crime control and penal policy in Britain, and its implications for various issues, such as crime prevention, and the education, healthcare, and employment of British youth.

2593 Fisher, C. J. & Mawby, R. I. Juvenile Delinquency And Police Discretion In An Inner-City Area, *British Journal Of Criminology* 22:63-75, 1982. This study of police cautioning of juveniles in West Yorkshire, England, their offenses and characteristics reveal that offenders who commit offenses costing below UK 25 and shoplifters were often cautioned, and age, student status, being Asian or female, and previous record were highly correlated to cautioning.

2594 Flin, Rhona; Kearney, Brian & Murray, Kathleen Children's Evidence: Scottish Research And Law, pp 114-131 in Bottoms, Bette L. & Goodman, Gail S. (eds.) *International Perspectives On Child Abuse And Children's Testimony: Psychological Research And Law*. Thousand Oaks, California: Sage, 1996. This chapter reviews some Scottish proposals for reform and procedural changes regarding the testimony of children in child sex-abuse cases.

2595 France, Alan & Wiles, Paul Dangerous Futures. Social Exclusion And Youth Work In Late Modernity, *Social Policy And Administration* 31:59-78, 1997. The author discusses the intertwining of modernity, citizenship, labor market, youth education, space, employment and crime.

2596 Freeman, John C. The Quest For A Better System And Administration Of Juvenile Justice, pp 9-80 in United Nations Asia And Far East Institute (eds.) *Report for 1983 and Resource Material Series No. 25.* Tokyo, Japan: UNAFEI, 1984. The author discusses a variety of topics regarding British juvenile offenders, including recidivists, juvenile jusice and alternatives to custody for adolescents in the United Kingdom.

2597 Freeman, M. D. A. The Rights Of Children When They Do `Wrong', *British Journal Of Criminology* 21:210-229, 1981. Advocating children's rights, the author argues that children have the same rights as adults and should be punished for only those behaviors defined as criminal when adults also engage in them, and should be treated like adult offenders.

2598 Gamlen, Sergeant Andrew *Juvenile Recidivists Offending On Bail - A Management Strategy*. London, United Kingdom: Police Research Group- Home Office, 1994. This report examines bail process, juvenile crime trends, and the issue of persistent young offenders committing offenses while on bail in England. 108p. Appendix.

2599 Gandy, John M. Juvenile Justice In England And Scotland, pp 17-21 in Friday, Paul C. & Stewart, V. Lorne (eds.) *Youth Crime And Juvenile Justice: International Perspectives*. New York, New York: Praeger, 1977. This chapter offers a brief, but comprehensive, overview of the recent changes to the laws, and in the scope of juvenile justice, in England and Scotland.

2600 Gelsthorpe, Loraine & Fenwick, Mark Comparative Juvenile Justice: England And Wales, pp 77-112 in Winterdyk, John A. (ed.) *Juvenile Justice Systems: International Perspectives*. Toronto, Canada: Canadian Scholars' Press, 1997. Along with information on offenders, this chapter provides an extensive discussion of the history and current structure of juvenile justice in England and Wales.

2601 Gelsthorpe, Loraine & Morris, Allison Juvenile Justice 1945-1992, pp 949-993 in Maguire, Mike; Morgan, Rod & Reiner, Robert (eds.) *The Oxford Handbook of Criminology*. Oxford, United Kingdom: Clarendon, 1994. Changes in the legislative and public policy regarding welfare, custody and diversion for juvenile offenders from 1945 to the 1990s is the subject of this article.

2602 Gelsthorpe, Loraine *Sexism And The Female Offender: An Organizational Analysis*. Hampshire, United Kingdom: Gower, 1989. From a feminist perspective, this study of sexism in the treatment of juveniles by the criminal justice system and allied agencies, concludes that the personnel of these agencies were indeed sexist. 194p. Appendix.

2603 Gelsthorpe, Loraine & Tutt, Norman The Attendance Centre Order, *Criminal Law Review* (March):146-153, 1986 .An examination of attendance center orders over six months in six rural and urban juvenile justice systems in England indicated great diversity in its use.

2604 Gelsthorpe, Loraine & Morris, Allison Attendance Centers: Policy and Practice, *Howard Journal* 22:101-118, 1983. The authors trace the history of attendance centers for boys, discuss their current status and functions in Great Britain, and focus on the confusing and contradictory expectations faced by the personnel who work in them.

2605 Gentry, Malcolm R. & Ostapiuk, Eugene B. Violence In Institutions For Young Offenders And Disturbed Adolescents, pp 250-266 in Howells, Kevin & Hollin, Clive R. (eds.) *Clinical Approaches To Violence*. Chichester, United Kingdom: Wiley, 1989. A treatment program at the long-term care center in Glenthorne for institutionalized disturbed and disruptive 10-18 year olds who may have committed serious violent offenses is described by the authors.

2606 Gibbons, T. C. N. Borstal Boys After 25 Years, *British Journal Of Criminology* 24:49-62, 1984. In this followup study of ex-Borstal boys, it was found that only a minority of them had no repeat offenses, and that getting married seems to give stability to these young men.

2607 Gibson, Bryan; Cavadino, Paul & Rutherford, Andrew *The Youth Court: One Year Onwards*. Winchester, United Kingdom: Waterside, 1994. This review of the evolution of the youth court since 1991 argues that young offenders will increasingly be formally processed and have less chance of bail, face decreasing chances of diversion, and escalated penalties, experience incarceration and longer detention for youth 12-to-14 years of age, and suggests that youth justice agencies reduce these risks by a constructive ethos of monitoring. 258p.

2608 Gibson, Bryan; Cavadino, Paul & Rutherford, Andrew; Ashworth, Andrew & Harding, John *Criminal Justice In Transition*. Winchester, United Kingdom: Waterside, 1994. The history, and effects, of the 1991, 1993 and 1994 criminal justice legislation in Great Britain, youth courts, principles of sentencing, fines and compensation, parole practices, early release, and various statutes of relevance to minors are all discussed in this volume. 301p.

2609 Gibson, Bryan *Introduction To The Magistrate's Court And Glossary Of Words, Phrases And Abbreviations*. Winchester, United Kingdom: Waterside, 1990. This article provides a description of the organizational structure and process of the United Kingdom's magistrate courts that deal with juvenile and other cases. 132p.

2610 Gill, Owen Urban Stereotypes And Delinquent Incidents, *British Journal Of Criminology* 16:321-336, 1976. This descriptive study narrates confrontations involving boys and the police in the Luke Street neighborhood in the West End of London.

2611 Giller, Henri From Centre Stage To Spear Carrier: The Repositioning Of The English Juvenile Court, *European Journal On Criminal Policy And Research* 7:395-403, 1999. This article traces the history and status of the English juvenile court over the century.

2612 Godfrey, David Lost In The Myths Of Crime: The Use Of Penal Custody For Male Juveniles, 1969 To 1993, *Howard Journal* 35:287-298, 1996. In comparing the use of custody for 14-16 year old males from passage of the 1969 Children and Young Persons Act to the 1993 the Home Secretary orders for secure placement, the author concludes that the tougher approach since 1979 has reduced the use of detention centers and decreasing rates of incarceration.

2613 Godsland, J. H. & Fielding, N. G. Young Persons Convicted Of Grave Crimes: The 1933 Children And Young Persons Act (3:53) And Its Effect Upon Children's Rights, *British Journal Of Criminology* 24:282-297, 1985. The authors discuss research revealing the tension between care and control, and the staff experience during the processes of trial and post sentence dealings with juvenile offenders.

2614 Goldson, Barry (ed.) *The New Youth Justice*. Dorset, United Kingdom: Russell House, 2000. The various articles in this collection review the legal, political, and theoretical issues regarding, and relevant policies and practices in current juvenile justice in England and Wales. 196p.

2615 Goodman, Randy Summaries Of DCI Country Surveys, Scotland; pp 187-189 in Tomasevski, Katarina (ed.) *Children In Adult Prisons: An International Perspective*. New York: St. Martin's Press, 1986. This section presents the findings for Scotland from the 1982-1984 Defense for Children International Survey of children in adult prisons.

2616 Graham, John The Organization And Functioning Of Juvenile Justice In England And Wales, pp 73-91 in Asquith, Stewart (ed.) *Children And Young People In Conflict With The Law*. London, United Kingdom: Jessica Kingsley, 1996. This chapter describes the juvenile justice system in England and Wales, and includes pre-trial arrangements and the details on the wide range of sentencing options available to the youth court.

2617 Great Britain Advisory Group On Video Evidence *Report Of The Advisory Group On Video Evidence*. London, United Kingdom: Home Office, 1989. This report is on the pros and cons of using victim videotape testimony of abused, including sexually abused, children and other victims in criminal trials. 75p. Appendix.

2618 Great Britain Home Office *Tackling Youth Crime: A Consultation Paper.* London, United Kingdom: Home Office-Juvenile Offenders Unit, 1997. This is a government proposal on the prevention, deterrence, and punishments for youthful criminality in the United Kingdom. 21p.

2619 Great Britain Home Office *Youth Custody And Supervision: A New Sentence.* London, United Kingdom: Her Majesty's Stationery Office, 1979. This reportrecommends that the sentences of imprisonment, Borstal training, and detention in detention centers for young offenders be replaced by a single custodial sentence of "youth custody" and that the length of sentence be determined by the courts in the same manner as imprisonment sentence for adults, and be subject to the statutory maximum relating to the particular offense committed. 67p.

2620 Great Britain Inspectorate Of Probation *An Overview Report On The Practice And Supervision Of Juvenile Offenders In Two Non Metropolitan Counties In England--1984-85.* London, United Kingdom: Home Office and Social Services Inspectorate, 1987. In examining the practices of supervising juvenile offenders in two non-metropolitan counties in England, this report found lack of supervising experience among those in the probation service or the social service departments. 51p.

2621 Great Britain Secretary Of State For The Home Department *Juvenile Offenders.* London, United Kingdom: Her Majesty's Stationery Office, 1993. This document presents this British government response to the Home Affairs Committee list of issues concerning juvenile crime, including crime prevention, dealing with offenders in the community, and issues of delinquent minors in custody. 17p.

2622 Great Britain Standing Conference On Crime Prevention Working Group *Safer Communities: The Local Delivery Of Crime Prevention Through The Partnership Approach.* London, United Kingdom: Home Office, 1991. The multi-agency approach to juvenile and other crime prevention, as well as profiles of some local initiatives, are in this report. 48p.

2623 Greater Manchester Juvenile Justice Group *123 Days: Review Of The Use Of Custody For Juveniles In Courts In Greater Manchester 1 November 1989 To 30 April 1990.* Manchester, United Kingdom: National Association for the Care and Resettlement of Offenders, 1990. Thios report is based on comparative custody data for Manchester and other urban areas, including the demographics of the sentenced youths, their offenses, and sentences. 34p.

2624 Grimshaw, Roger & Pratt, John Responses To Truancy Among The Juvenile Panel Of A Magistrates' Court, *British Journal Of Criminology* 25:321-343, 1985. This research found that magistrates lack personal experience and training in truancy cases, feel that poverty and other individual factors caused truancy, followed the social workers' recommendation while expecting social worker supervision of the juveniles.

2625 Hagell, Ann & Newburn, Tim Going Public With Young Offenders And The Media, pp. 152-156 in Barker, Martin & Petley, Julian (eds.) *Ill Effects: The Media/Violence Debate.* London, United Kingdom: Routledge, 1997. This chapter is a report of the seventeen-member Gulbenkian Foundation Commission's recommendations in dealing with children and violence and includes the role of media in reporting youth crime. 171p.

2626 Haines, Kevin *Understanding Modern Juvenile Justice.* Avebury, United Kingdom: Aldershot, 1996. On the bases of empirical research, the author discusses developments and practices in the 1980s and 1990s in the British juvenile justice system. 227p.

2627 Hakkert, Alfred No More Excuses: A New Approach To Tackling Youth Crime In England And Wales: A Summary, *European Journal On Criminal Policy And Research*, 6:279-291, 1998. The author advocates early intervention, reinforcing of parents and children, faster and more efficient procedures, and multi-agency cooperation in dealing with juvenile delinquency in England and Wales.

2628 Harding, John The Changing Nature Of Criminal Justice In England And Wales, With Particular Regard To The Introduction Of Community-Based Punishment, The Young Offender And The Treatment of Drug Offenders, pp 220-236 in United Nations Asia And Far East Institute (ed.) *Resource Material Series No. 46.* Tokyo, Japan: UNAFEI, 1995. In a general discussion of changes in British criminal justice, this chapter includes a discussion of juveniles, community-based treatment, pre-sentence reports, community-service orders, and the treatment for drug offending within the context of the 1991 Criminal Justice Act.

2629 Harding, John Changing The Sentencing Culture, pp. 32-35 in Bullock, Roger (ed.) *Problem Adolescents: An International View.* London, United Kingdom: Whiting & Burch, 1992. This conference paper focuses on the ethos, philosophy, and ideology of the juvenile justice systems predispositions toward sentencing.

2630 Harding, John The Development Of Community Service: Its Application And Relevance To Criminal Justice System, pp. 164-185 in Tutt,

Norman (ed.) *Alternative Strategies For Coping With Crime.* Oxford, United Kingdom: Basil Blackwell and Martin Robertson, 1978. Although general in orientation, the author addresses the various issues of relevance to community service as an alternate sentence for juveniles in the United Kingdom.

2631 Harris, Phil & Jackson, Barclay *Evaluation Of The "Joy-Ride Initiative" In Manchester Schools To Counter Violent Car Crime.* Manchester, United Kingdom: Manchester Metropolitan University, 1997. The author evaluates the effectiveness of a program to reduce violent crime involving stolen vehicles and joy-riding by secondary school students in Manchester. 79p.

2632 Harris, Robert & Timms, Noel *Secure Accommodation In Child Care: Between Hospital And Prison Or Thereabouts?* London, United Kingdom: Routledge, 1993. Secure facilities for juveniles under care in the United Kingdom, and issues of conflict among the goals of care, treatment, or custody are the focus of this policy study for management and professionals in 50 agencies. 196p.

2633 Harris, Robert & Timms, Noel The Lost Key: Secure Accommodation And Juvenile Crime: An English And Welsh Perspective, *Australian And New Zealand Journal Of Criminology* 26:219-231, 1993. The findings of a large-scale empirical study of children in secure British facilities in the late 1980s are discussed, and the authors argue that focus should be on what the children have to do to be released.

2634 Harris, Robert J. Towards Just Welfare, *British Journal Of Criminology* 25:31-45, 1985. This article explores the flaws and factors that made the Children And Young Persons Act of 1969 a failure in Great Britain.

2635 Hayman, Stephanie; Martin, Carol & Nurse, Angus (eds.) *The Forgotten Children: Young People In Prison.* London, United Kingdom: Institute for the Study and Treatment of Delinquency, 1998. The articles in this collection address issues on the imprisonment of children, such as custodial sentences, rescue and support of children facing prison, education and reformation in prisons, etc. 61p.

2636 Hayman, Stephanie (ed.) *What Works With Young Prisoners?* London, United Kingdom: Institute for the Study and Treatment of Delinquency, 1996. This paper addresses rehabilitation of juvenile offenders and a wide spectrum of issues, such as cognitive skills training and working with difficult young prisoners. 51p.

2637 Hazel, Nancy Adolescent Fostering As A Community Resource, *Community Alternatives International Journal Of Family Care* 1:1-9, 1989. This article describes a small experimental alternative program to place delinquent and disturbed adolescents in the United Kingdom.

2638 Helsinki Watch *Children In Northern Ireland: Abused By Security Forces And Paramilitaries*. New York, New York: Human Rights Watch, 1992. This report details the abuse of, and violence against children in Northern Ireland. 100p.

2639 Henderson, Paul *Drugs Prevention And Community Development: Principles Of Good Practice*. London, United Kingdom: Central Drugs Prevention Unit-Home Office, 1995. This is a report on the experiences of a of community development initiative in identifying and prevention of drug use among young people. 34p.

2640 Her Majesty's Inspectorate Of Prisons For England And Wales *Young Prisoners: A Thematic Review By HM Chief Inspector Of Prisons For England And Wales*. London, United Kingdom: Home Office, 1997. This report provides a description of the prison conditions and treatment of 15-21 year olds during the 1990s in United Kingdom. 104p.

2641 Heritage, Ian & Martin, Carol (eds.) *Serious Young Offenders: Security, Treatment & Future Prospects*. London, United Kingdom: Institute for the Study & Treatment of Delinquency, 1995. This volume has three papers presented at a 1994 conference on serious young offenders and their treatment. 32p.

2642 Holt, John *No Holiday Camps: Custody, Juvenile Justice And The Politics Of Law And Order*. Leicester, United Kingdom: Association for Juvenile Justice, 1985. This handbook on radical criminology within the intermediate treatment field offers possible future reforms in juvenile justice within the political and ideological realities faced by practitioners. 54p.

2643 Home Office *No More Excuses--A New Approach To Tackling Youth Crime In England And Wales*. London, United Kingdom: Her Majesty's Stationery Office, 1997. This is a policy paper on the British government proposal to reform the youth justice system. 40p.

2644 Hopkins, Nick; Hewstone, Miles & Hantzi, Alexandra Police-Schools Liaison And Young People's Image Of The Police: An Intervention Evaluation, *British Journal Of Psychology* 83:203-220, 1992. This British study comparing the views of young people and attitudes about the police and offending in schools that did or did not have a full-time Schools Liaison Officer Program concludes that the program did have a limited positive effects on the views of young people.

2645 Howard League Commission Of Inquiry Into Violence In Penal Institutions For Teenagers Under 18 *Banged Up, Beaten Up, Cutting Up.* London, United Kingdom: The Howard League, 1995. According to this report, as a result of the failure to adequately identify the vulnerable and implement anti-bullying strategy against youth in custody in United Kingdom., many are subject to abuse and manipulation while incidents go unreported. 115p.

2646 Howard League For Penal Reform *Sentenced To Fail--Out Of Sight, Out Of Mind: Compounding The Problems Of Children In Prison.* London, United Kingdom: The Howard League, 1998. The nature and quality of rehabilitative care of juvenile offenders in the United Kingdom during 1997 is described, and it is concluded that communication and service agencies' cooperation with the prison staff was often non-existent. 72p.

2647 Howard League For Penal Reform *Lost Inside-The Imprisonment of Teenage Girls.* London, United Kingdom: The Howard League, 1997. This report is on the numbers, ethnicity, offenses, prison conditions and experiences of girls below 18 held in the prisons during 1997 in The United Kingdom. 44p.

2648 Howard League For Penal Reform *The Howard League Troubleshooter Project: Lessons For Policy And Practice On 15 Year Olds In Prison.* London, United Kingdom: The Howard league, 1997: The Howard League. This study of an advocacy project to obtain the release of 15 year olds in custody in England identifies and analyzes the problems and offers solutions, and examples of good and bad practices in juvenile justice. 45p.

2649 Howard League For Penal Reform *Troubleshooter: A Project To Rescue 15 Year Olds From Prison.* London, United Kingdom: The Howard League, 1995. This report describes the first year of a project that intervenes on behalf of 15-year old prisoners in Great Britain, and identifies persisting issues and provides recommendations. 75p.

2650 Howard League For Penal Reform *Young And In Trouble: Young Teenagers And Crime.* London, United Kingdom: The Howard League, 1993. Socio-legal issues of declining numbers of juvenile offenders and the use of custody for young offenders in the United Kingdom over the decade are examined in this report that also highlights alternative and positive practices, such as diversion, bail, remand, and youth courts, and community sanctions for young offenders. Also addressed are suicides and self-harm, sentencing, serious offenders, and prevention. 42p.

2651 Howard League For Penal Reform *`Unruly' Children In A Human Context: Types, Costs And Effects Of Security*. London, United Kingdom: Barry Rose, 1977. The authors, in analyzing the arguments in favor of security, conclude that some powerful considerations, such as cost, effectiveness, essential standards of humaneness, and civil rights in dealing with youthful delinquents, make it less desirable. 36 p.

2652 Hudson, Annie Troublesome Girls: Toward Alternative Definitions And Policies, pp. 197-219 in Cain, Maureen (ed.) *Growing Up Good: Policing The Behavior Of Girls In Europe*. Newbury Park, California: Sage, 1989. This chapter focuses on English girls who are seen as manifesting some kind of social or emotional trouble, and their conflicts and skewed relationships with their families and various welfare professionals.

2653 Husain, Sohail *Cutting Crime In Rural Areas: A Practical Guide For Parish Councils*. Swindon, United Kingdom: Crime Concern, 1995. This guide to improve rural safety in Great Britain focuses on getting the local councils involved, describes crime prevention partnership efforts in curtailing opportunities to commit crime, dicusses social causes of crime, and provides examples to support local police, diversion of youth from crime, making crime difficult etc. 36p.

2654 Hyland, Jim *Yesterday's Answers: Development And Decline Of Schools For Young Offenders*. London, United Kingdom: Whiting and Birch, 1993. This is the 150-year history of United Kingdom's response to young offenders through residential schools to care, control, and educate delinquent and needy children. 206p.

2655 Inner London Probation And After-Care Service *ILPAS '76: A Report On Aspects Of The Work Of The Inner London Probation After-Care Service-To Commemorate The Centenary Of Probation In London*. London, England: Inner London Probation and After-Care Service, 1976. The chapters in this report describe the various inner-London community service units serving young people's needs, and report an increase in their caseload in the aftermath of the 1969 Children and Young Persons Act. 128p.

2656 Jackson, Shirley E. Family Group Conferences In Youth Justice: The Issues For Implementation In England And Wales, *Howard Journal* 37:34-51, 1998. The author, who favors family group conferences in the United Kingdom, covers its origins, principles and the issues in its implementation in the youth justice system in England and Wales.

2657 Jackson, Valerie *Racism And Child Protection: The Black Experience Of Child Sexual Abuse.* London, United Kingdom: Cassell, 1996. This study examines the effects of racism on the protection and support of sexually abused black children in England. 86p.

2658 Jaffe, Peter & Thompson, Judy Family Consultant Service With The London Police Force--A Description, *Canadian Police College Journal* 3:115-125, 1979. This preliminary evaluation of the Family Consultant Service suggests that it provides effective crisis intervention to families in need, capitalizing on the mobility and immediacy of police contact as well as the professional service available from community mental health agencies.

2659 Jagger, E. A. S. M. The Policing Of Glue Sniffing, *British Journal Of Criminology* 36:237-254, 1996. The implications of the Scottish police practice of holding parents responsible for glue sniffing by their children was the focus of the author's interviews of families, police and other professionals.

2660 Jefferson, Tony Race, Crime And Policing: Empirical, Theoretical And Methodological Issues, *International Journal Of The Sociology Of Law* 16:521-539, 1988. The author reviews socioeconomic factors such as race on crime and policing, and includes what is known about minority juvenile crime in United Kingdom.

2661 Johnston, Valerie & Shapland, Joanna The United Kingdom And The New Prevention, pp.33-59 in Hebberecht, Patrick & Sack, Fritz (eds.) *The Prevention Of Delinquency In Europe: New Stratégies (La Prévention De La Délinquance En Europe: Nouvelles Stratégies).* Paris, France: L'Harmatten, 1997. Reports on the main crime-prevention efforts by the government, local communities, the police, citizens' groups and the private sector in United Kingdom.

2662 Jones, Beti & Murray, G. J. The Scottish Rejection Of The Juvenile Court, pp 86-110 in Stewart, V. Lorne (ed.) *The Changing Face Of Juvenile Justice.* New York, New York: New York University Press, 1978. This chapter describes the introduction of the children's panel system in Scotland replacing the former juvenile court approach.

2663 Kearney, B. *Children's Hearings And The Sheriff Court.* London, United Kingdom: Butterworths, 1987. This book provides an examination of the Scottish legal principles and procedures behding the children's hearing and sheriff court system, for all those involved in the Scottish juvenile justice system, and for lawyers outside Scotland dealing with cases involving children's hearings. 577 p.

2664 Kelley, Barbara *Children Inside: Rhetoric And Practice In A Locked Institution For Children*. London, United Kingdom: Routledge, 1992. Based on her case study of troubled youths under 16 in a locked secure Scottish facility for childcare, the author assesses the rhetoric versus the reality of such confinement in discussing the dilemmas of cost by containing the child versus prevention of the conditions that contribute to deviance. 248p.

2665 Kelly, Liz; Wingfield, Rachel & Burton, Sheila *Splintered Lives: Sexual Exploitation Of Children In The Context Of Children's Rights And Child Protection*. Ilford, United Kingdom: Barnardo's, 1995. This report on the sexual exploitation of children and young people in England and Europe includes current international law and policy, theoretical perspectives, the impacts of sexual exploitation on children, and routes into and out of the sex industry. 92p.

2666 King, Michael & Piper, Christine *How The Law Thinks About Children*. Brookfield, Vermont: Grower, 1990. The chapters in this anthology address issues such as the limits of welfare, law as a self-referential system, the construction of child welfare science, and chapter 6 on the child as offender is of particular interest to those in the juvenile justice field. 172p.

2667 King, P. & Noel, J. The Origins Of The `Problem Of Juvenile Delinquency' In The Late Eighteenth And Early Nineteenth Centuries In London (Les Origines Du 'Problème De La Délinquance Juvenile': La Multiplication Des Poursuites Contre Des Mineurs À Londres À La Fin Du XVIII Siècle Et Au Début Du XIX Siècle), *Déviance Et Société* 18:3-30, 1994. This historical examination of the emergence of juvenile delinquency as a social problem in nineteenth century England, found young offenders increasingly brought to court reflecting an increased concern not only about young offenders, but the large problem of the working class insubordination. French.

2668 King, Peter The Rise Of Juvenile Delinquency In England 1780-1840: Changing Patterns Of Perception And Prosecution, *Past And Present* 160:116-166, 1998. This paper examines the history of the emergence of juvenile delinquency in England between 1780 and 1840.

2669 Kirk, Bruce M. *Negative Images: A Simple Matter of Black and White?* Aldershot, United Kingdom: Avebury, 1996. Differential sentencing of Afro-Caribbean juveniles in the United Kingdom is the focus of this study that found them to be subject to disproportionately more serious sentences vis-à-vis Asian and white adolescents. 174p.

2670 Landau, Simha & Nathan, Gad Selecting Delinquents For Cautioning

In The London Metropolitan Area, *British Journal Of Criminology* 23:128-149, 1983. Official records of police decisions on cautioning of 1146 juvenile delinquents, when examined reveal that legal variables such as prior record, and some non-legal variables have a major role in such decision making.

2671 Landau, Simha F. Juveniles And The Police, *British Journal Of Criminology* 21:27-46, 1981. This study of the contribution of legal and other variables in early decisions by Londen Police to charge immediately or to refer juvenile delinquents to the juvenile bureau, found that, while legal factors play a major role in police decisions, some extra-legal variables also have a significant effect on such decisions.

2672 Lawrie, Christine; Smith, Graham & Eastwood, John *Young Offenders And The Probation Service: Report Of A Thematic Inspection*. London, United Kingdom: Her Majesty's Inspectorate of Probation, 1994. This report is on British inter-agency arrangements to provide services to youth courts, supervise young offenders, implement the Criminal Justice Act of 1991, and discusses other national standards, and related issues. 69p.

2673 Laycock, Gloria & Tarling, Roger Police Force Cautioning: Policy And Practice, *Howard Journal* 24:81-92, 1985. This study on cautioning of juveniles and adults in the United Kingdom found discrepancies in police data, and the findings suggest that the cautioning is affected by policy and practice.

2674 Lee, M. Police Cautioning Of Minors: In Whose Best Interests? (Admonestation Policière Et Justice Des Mineurs: Au Mieux Des Intérêts De Qui?), *Déviance Et Société* 18:43-54, 1994. This 3-year study of police cautioning and juvenile justice in England and Wales traces the development of police cautioning, policing priorities, changes in the concept of "welfare," and "business" approach in criminal justice. French.

2675 Lee, Maggy *Youth, Crime And Police Work*. London, United Kingdom: Macmillan, 1998. This study describes police work, specifically informal processing such as cautioning, as a major means of dealing with young offenders in United Kingdom. 171p. Appendix.

2676 Lerman, Paul Policing Juveniles In London: Shifts In Guiding Discretion 1893-1968, *British Journal Of Criminology* 24:168-184, 1984. The author describes changes in the public policy regarding the treatment of delinquent youth, from tough handling to leniency, as well as the origins of separate juvenile courts, and practices such as "cautioning" over the decades that span the late 19th to the mid 20th centuries.

2677 Liddle, Mark *Wasted Lives*. London, United Kingdom: National Association for the Care and Resettlement of Offenders, 1998. The backgrounds and characteristics of young male offenders in prison in the United Kingdom during 1997 are described and estimated total costs for all respondent offenses are also included in this report. 76p.

2678 Littlewood, Paul Secure Units, pp 155-168 in Asquith, Stewart (ed.) *Children And Young People In Conflict With The Law*. London, United Kingdom: Jessica Kingsley, 1996. This chapter describes the practice of and children under confinement in secure facilities in England and Wales.

2679 Lloyd, Charles *To Scare Straight Or Educate? The British Experience Of Day Visits To Prison For Young People*. London, United Kingdom: Home Office Research and Statistics Department, 1995. This report is based on interviews with inmates, referrers, and youth, both offenders and others, on the effectiveness of a "scared straight" program in Great Britain.

2680 Lloyd, Siobhan & Burman, Michele Specialist Police Units And The Joint Investigation Of Child Abuse, *Child Abuse Review* 5:4-15, 1996. This study explores the ways in which Scottish special police units have responded to the issue of child abuse investigations jointly with social workers.

2681 Lloyd-Bostock, Sally *Law And Psychology: Papers Presented At SSRC Law And Psychology Conferences 1979-1980*. Oxford, United Kingdom: SSRC Centre for Socio-Legal Studies, 1981. This collection addresses issues related to the juvenile court role of educational psychologists in the British juvenile justice system. 165p.

2682 Longford, Lord *Young Offenders*. London, United Kingdom: Chapmans, 1993. This book examines the causes, prevention and the treatment of youthful criminality in Great Britain. 239p.

2683 Lupton, Carol & Stevens, Martin *Family Outcomes: Following Through On Family Group Conferences*. Portsmouth, United Kingdom: Social Services Research and Information Unit, University of Portsmouth, 1997. This evaluation of family group conferences in Hampshire concludes that they are well coordinated and consistent on issues of the welfare of the child. 70p.

2684 Lyon, Juliet; Dennison, Catherine & Wilson, Anita *'Tell Them So They Listen': Messages From Young People In Custody*. London, United

Kingdom: Home Office, 2000. Young offenders in prisons who were the focus of this inquiry advocate interventions from very young age, want help improving communication between parents and adolescents, drug and alcohol prevention education, involvement of those marginalized in education, and the use of positive peer pressure. 94p.

2685 Mackay, Robert E. Restorative Justice And The Scottish Children's Justice System, pp 185-200 in Walgrave, Lode (ed.) *Restorative Justice For Juveniles: Potentialities, Risks And Problems For Research*. Leuven, Belgium: Leuven University Press. This chapter examines the question of the theoretical fit between the restorative justice model and the philosophy and practice of the Scottish Childrens Hearing approach.

2686 MacLean, Brian D. Left Realism, Local Crime Surveys And Policing Of Racial Minorities. A Further Analysis Of Data From The First Sweep Of The Islington Survey, *Crime Law and Social* Change 19:51-86, 1993. This survey of military-style policing in the black community of the United Kingdom concludes that the response of the black youth and community to such focused policing is quite complex.

2687 Macmillan, John Social Information And Decision-Making In Juvenile Liaison Panels, pp 144-167 in Booth, Tim (ed.) *Juvenile Justice In The New Europe*. Sheffield, United Kingdom: Joint Unit for Social Services Research, Sheffield University, 1991. This chapter describes research on the operation of juvenile liaison panels in Cleveland, United Kingdom.

2688 Magarey, Susan M. The Invention Of Juvenile Delinquency In Early Nineteenth-Century England, pp 325-346 in Hess, Albert G. & Clement, Priscilla F. (eds.) *History Of Juvenile Delinquency: A Collection Of Essays On Crime Committed By Young Offenders, In History And In Selected Countries Volume I*. Aalen, Germany: Scientia Verlag, 1990. This chapter describes how youth crime became a problem in 19th century England, and emergence of the concept of juvenile delinquent with special treatment of offenders by the judiciary during this time.

2689 Mahood, Linda *Policing Gender, Class And Family: Britain, 1850-1940*. London, United Kingdom: UCL Press, 1995. This historical study examines the child saving movement in Scotland, from passage of the Youthful Offenders Act in 1854 to passage of the Children and Young Persons Act in 1932. 215p. Appendix.

2690 Manchester, A. H. & Giles, Ann (eds.) *Juvenile Offenders And Juvenile Justice Into The 1990s*. London, United Kingdom: British Juvenile and Family Court Society, 1989. This is a report on children's rights, objectives of juvenile justice, juvenile crime in England, Scotland, Wales, and Birmingham, cautioning practices, and alternatives to custody, the training of magistrates, and international law. 117p.

2691 Manson, Doreen *Success And Failure In IT: An Exploration In Personal Construct Theory*. Norwich, United Kingdom: University of East Anglia Social Work Monographs, 1992. This is a study of an intermediate treatment program for juvenile delinquents in the United Kingdom. 49p.

2692 Marlow, Alan & Pitts, John 'Remember The Alamo': Action Research And Crime Prevention In A High-Crime Neighborhood, *International Criminal Justice Review* 9:69-87, 1999. Multi-agency crime prevention measures targeting violent, interracial youth crime, and the Walford Youth Violence Reduction Project are the focus of this research in a high-crime borough of London.

2693 Marsh, Peter & Crow, Gillian Family Group Conferences In Child Welfare Services In England And Wales, pp 152-166 in Hudson, Joe; Morris, Allison & Maxwell, Gabrielle (eds.) *Family Group Conferences: Perspectives On Policy & Practice*. Monsey, New York: Criminal Justice Press, 1996. This chapter describes the background, and provides an assessment of, the current stage of development of the family group conference program following a 1989 law in Britain.

2694 Martin, F. M. & Murray, Kathleen Scotland, pp 95-112 in Stewart, V. Lorne (ed.) *Justice And Troubled Children Around The World, Vol. 2*. New York, New York: New York University Press, 1981. The rationale underlying the Scottish system of juvenile justice is discussed by the authors.

2695 Martin, F. M.; Fox, Sanford J. & Murray, Kathleen *Children Out Of Court*. Edinburgh, Scotland: Scottish Academic Press, 1981. This study examined the factors associated with decision making in the Scottish children's hearing system, particularly by the panels and intake officials who decide if children referred to them are "in need of compulsory measures of care." 331p.

2696 Martin, J. P. & Webster, Douglas *Probation Motor Projects In England And Wales*. London, United Kingdom: Home Office, 1994. This is a review of various probation programs for motor vehicle-related young offenders in England and Wales, describing their principal features, as well as the issues raised by both census and case studies. 131p.

2697 Matthews, Roger & Trickey, Julie *The Eyres Monsell Crime Reduction Project*. Leicester, United Kingdom: Center for the Study of Public Order-University of Leicester, 1994. This Evaluation of burglary-reduction program in two public housing projects in United Kingdom covers youth programs, community centers, the fear of crime and other related issues. 59p.

2698 Maung, Natalie Aye *Young People, Victimisation And The Police: British Crime Survey Findings On Experiences And Attitudes Of 12 To 15 Year Olds*. London, United Kingdom: Her Majesty's Stationery Office, 1995. The focus of this analysis of the 1992 British Crime Survey of 12-15 year olds found that the majority of incidents against young people, although illegal, will not be pursued within the criminal justice system. 140p. Appendix.

2699 May, David Juvenile Shoplifters And The Organization Of Store Security: A Case Study In The Social Construction Of Delinquency, *International Journal Of Criminology And Penology* 6:137-160, 1978. This paper examines the process by which children first come to be accused of shoplifting.

2700 May, David The Children's Hearing System: Part I. The Limits of Legislative Action, *Journal Of Social Welfare Laws* (November):14-23, 1978. The author traces various contemporary concepts of Scottish juvenile justice, such as decriminalization and diversionary measures, and discusses how the approach to deal with young people evolved from social control to social welfare during the 19th century in most Western nations.

2701 May, David Rhetoric And Reality: The Consequence Of Unacknowledged Ambiguity In The Children's Panel System, *British Journal Of Criminology* 17:209-227, 1977. The author argues that much of the present frustration and discontent with the Children's Panel system of juvenile justice in Scotland emanates from its persistent refusal to ack-knowledge the disjunction between rhetoric and practice.

2702 Mayers, Michael O. *The Hard-Core Delinquent: An Experiment In Control And Care In A Community Home With Education*. London, United Kingdom: Westmead, 1980. Data on hard-core delinquents and ordinary juvenile delinquents were analyzed to determine whether hard-core delinquents could be treated successfully. 198p.

2703 McAulay, Margot & Cunningham, Gerry Day Assessment And Short-Term Treatment For Juveniles In Trouble, *Community Homes Gazette* 74:196-203, 1980. This article discusses the impact of day-assessment on the juvenile justice system of Northern Ireland.

2704 McGhee, Janice; Waterhouse, Lorraine & Whyte, Bill Children's Hearings And Children In Trouble, pp 56-72 in Asquith, Stewart (ed.)

Children And Young People In Conflict With The Law. London, United kingdom: Jessica Kingsley, 1996. This chapter discusses the children's hearing system in Scotland as an enlightened and progressive way to deal with the welfare of children in trouble.

2705 McGurk, Harry & Hurry, Jane *Project Charlie: An Evaluation Of A Life Skills Drug Education Programme For Primary Schools*. London, United Kingdom: Home Office, 1995. This evaluation of Project Charlie, a drug prevention program in primary schools in the United Kingdom, covers theoretical, empirical, and practical aspects of knowledge of and attitudes towards drugs, peer pressure and social dilemmas, and self-esteem. 64p.

2706 McIsaac, M. W. & McClintock, F. H. The Juvenile Justice System In Scotland, pp 83-128 in United Nations Social Defence Research Institute (ed.) *Juvenile Justice An International Survey*. Rome, Italy, 1976. This chapter provides an extensive description of the system of juvenile justice as well as an overview of research on juvenile delinquency and justice in Scotland.

2707 McIvor, Gill Jobs For The Boys? Gender Differences In Referral To Community Service, *Howard Journal* 37:280-290, 1998. Community service commonly imposed upon young males in three Scottish Sheriff courts during 1992 was found to be common for both males and females.

2708 McKail, C. R.; Wilkinson, P. S. & Miles, A. J. E. Day Care And Education At St. John's Community Home School, Birmingham, *Community Home Gazette* 74:204-210, 1980. This piece provides a description of co-educational schooling, that has both secure and non secure units, for juvenile delinquents in United Kingdom.

2709 McLean, S. A. M.; Docherty, C. J. & Grant, J. P. *The Prosecution Of Children In Scotland*. Edinburgh, Scotland: Scottish Office, 1984. This report presents findings from research on the prosecution of children in Scotland. 99p.

2710 McMurran, Mary & Hollin, Clive R. *Young Offenders And Alcohol-Related Crime: A Practitioner's Guidebook*. Chichester, United Kingdom: John Wiley & Sons, 1993. This volume summarizes the various cognitive-behavioral treatment programs for alcohol abusing juvenile offenders, with chapters devoted to understanding the behavior, youthful offender and drinking, alcohol education, and lifestyle modification. 195p.

2711 McQuoid, Joan & Bloomer, Stephen A Portrait Of Juvenile Crime: Craigavon Juvenile Court Statistics 1985-1989, pp 86-96 in Booth, Tim (ed.) *Juvenile Justice In The New Europe*. Sheffield, United Kingdom: Joint Unit for Social Services Research, Sheffield University, 1991. This chapter describes the changes that occurred from 1985 to 1990 in the juvenile justice system of Craigavon, Northern Ireland.

2712 Meehan, Albert J. Internal Police Records And The Control Of Juveniles: Politics And Policing In A Suburban Town, *British Journal Of Criminology* 33:504-524, 1993. The external and internal pressure on the Hargrove police to manage their crime rate, i.e., avoid arrest and formal processing of juveniles, by informal record-keeping practices, and the implications of such for official crime data are the focus of this research.

2713 Merker, A. A. Token Economics In The Residential Care Of Delinquent Children, *Community Home Schools Gazette* 73:158-166, 1979. This evaluation of the British community-based achievement presents the behavioral treatment approach of token economies within an institutional setting.

2714 Mhlanga, Bonny *The Colour Of English Justice: A Multivariate Analysis*. Aldershot, United Kingdom: Avebury, 1997. This study on racial bias in the administration of juvenile justice in United Kingdom found that over all, in relation to their numbers in the local population, black youths were overrepresented in the local justice system. 194p.

2715 Millham, Spencer *Juvenile Justice And Child Care In England*. Ann Arbor, Michigan: University of Michigan Center for the Study of Youth Policy, 1991. Recent changes, such as the closing of large juvenile reform schools in England, and the introduction of community-based corrections are the subjects of this paper. 16p.

2716 Millham, Spencer; Bullock, Roger; Hosie, Kenneth & Little, Michael *The Experiences And Careers Of Young People Leaving The Youth Treatment Centres*. Bristol, United Kingdom: Dartington Social Research Unit, University of Bristol, 1989. This follow-up research on the post-treatment behavior of juveniles leaving youth treatment centers found that 70 percent re-offend within four years. 125p.

2717 Millham, Spencer; Bullock, Roger & Hosie, Kenneth Another Try: An Account Of A New Careers Project For Borstal Trainees, pp. 137-163 in Tutt, Norman (ed.) *Alternative Strategies For Coping With Crime*. Oxford, United Kingdom: Basil Blackwell and Martin Robertson, 1978. The authors evaluate a project whose aim was to provide training and opportunities to Borstal school residents for non-criminal careers.

2718 Millham, Spencer; Bullock, Roger & Hosie, Kenneth *Locking Up Children: Secure Provisions Within The Child-Care System*. Westmead,

United Kingdom: Saxon House, 1978. This report on the history of the development, nature, and effects of secure care within the British child-care system concludes that most of the resident children in secure facilities were the casualties of the British child-care system. 196p.

2719 Monck, Elizabeth; Bentovim, Arnon; Godall, Gillian; Hyde, Caroline; Lwin, Rebekah; Sharland, Elaine & Elton, Anne *Child Sexual Abuse: A Descriptive & Treatment Study*. London, United Kingdom: Her Majesty's Stationery Office, 1996. This volume examines, and evaluates, issues of relevance to family network and group treatment programs. 176p.

2720 Morris, Allison & Giller, Henri *Understanding Juvenile Justice*. London, England: Croom Helm, 1987. This book focuses on English and Welsh trends in juvenile justice with brief reference to the United States and Scotland as well.

2721 Morris, Allison & Giller, Henri Young Offender: I. Law, Order and the Child Care System, *Howard Journal* 20:81-89, 1981. The authors describe the increasingly tough law and order-oriented interventions and their long-term implications appearing in the facilities for children in the United Kingdom.

2722 Morris, Allison & McIsaac, Mary *Juvenile Justice?: The Practice Of Social Welfare*. London, United Kingdom: Heinemann, 1978. The ideology and practice of social welfare in the Scottish juvenile justice system are examined in this volume. 186p.

2723 Morris, Allison & Giller, Henri The Juvenile Court -- The Client's Perspective, *Criminal Law Review* (April):198-205, 1977. After interviewing children and parents, the authors conclude that the clients perceive the role of the court to "administer justice" in the traditional sense of proof of an offense and the sentence commensurate with the offense.

2724 Mott, Joy Police Decisions For Dealing With Juvenile Offenders, *British Journal Of Criminology* 23:249-262, 1983. An examination of the effects of cautioning of juveniles in English police departments indicates that first offenders of all ages and both sexes were cautioned often, except when the offense was serious, if the youth denied the illegal behavior, or at the insistence of the victim to prosecute.

2725 Moxon, David; Jones, Peter & Tarling, Roger *Juvenile Sentencing: Is There A Tariff?* London, United Kingdom: Home Office, 1985. This book offers a report examining sentencing variations, and the equity and clarity of fines imposed on male juvenile offenders who appeared in nine courts in Great Britain during 1978. 19p.

2726 National Association For The Care And Resettlement Of Offenders *Diverting People From Crime*. London, United Kingdom: National Association for the Care and Resettlement of Offenders, 1998. This manual on policies and strategies for diverting both youths and adults from criminal court describes the Northamptonshire Diversion Unit's referral process, partnerships with local agencies, the monitoring framework, and the evaluation process, as well as the statutory framework for reprimands and the final warning process, and the range of interventions. 79p.

2727 National Association For The Care And Resettlement Of Offenders *Outside In: A Report On The NACRO Advice And Settlement Project In Feltham*. London, United Kingdom: National Association for the Care and Resettlement of Offenders, 1996. This is a report on a juvenile prison, the demographics of the incarcerated juveniles, and a program to reassure youths for whom this was the first imprisonment. 21p.

2728 National Association For The Care And Resettlement Of Offenders Juvenile Remand Review Group *Safe And Secure: Ending Remands To Prison For 15 And 16 Year Old Boys*. London, United Kingdom, 1996. The authors found that, in spite of the expectation that the number of 15-16-year-old boys remanded in prison would steadily fall under the tighter criteria of the United Kingdom's Criminal Justice Act 1991, the numbers actually increased. 28p.

2729 National Association For The Care And Resettlement Of Offenders *Reducing Delays In Criminal Proceedings Involving Young Defendants And Young Offenders*. London, United Kingdom: National Association for the Care and Resettlement of Offenders, 1995. This paper is on issues related to court delays in juvenile cases in the United Kingdom. 15p.

2730 National Association For The Care And Resettlement Of Offenders *Partnership With Parents In Dealing With Young Offenders*. London United Kingdom: National Association for the Care and Resettlement of Offenders, 1994. The desirability of encouraging greater involvement of and responsibility for parents of children engaging in illegality, the extent of juvenile delinquents in the criminal justice system, cautioning, family support and community programs are addressed by this report. 16p.

2731 National Association For The Care And Resettlement Of Offenders *Rethinking Remands For Young Alleged Offenders*. London, United Kingdom: National Association for the Care and Resettlement of Offenders, 1994. This report is on the ways to reduce the number of 15-

16 year old youths in custody, while protecting the public from criminal behavior when the youths are on bail, addressing remand arrangements for juveniles offenders and young adults. 23p.

2732 National Association For The Care And Resettlement Of Offenders *Community Provision For Young People In The Youth Justice System: A Survey Of Local Authorities*. London, United Kingdom: National Association for the Care and Resettlement of Offenders, 1993. This report identifies community services for young offenders in Great Britain, and covers issues related to pre-trial, bail and remand, sentencing, and reviews multi-agency local diversion, support for housing, treatment and activities beyond cautioning. 20p.

2733 National Association For The Care And Resettlement Of Offenders *Juvenile Crime: Some Current Issues*. London, United Kingdom: National Association for the Care and Resettlement of Offenders, 1993. This report on current issues and trends in juvenile delinquency in Great Britain, includes topics such as cautioning, bail, community-based and custodial sentences, court sentencing powers, strategies for prevention and dealing with persistent, youthful offenders. 14p.

2734 National Association For The Care And Resettlement Of Offenders *Reducing The Use Of Custody For Young Offenders*. London, United Kingdom: National Association for the Care and Resettlement of Offenders, 1992. This review of the reduction in the use of custody for juvenile offenders in Great Britain recommends extending the use of community sentencing for youthful offenders. 6p.

2735 National Association For The Care And Resettlement Of Offenders *Awaiting Trial. Interim Report: A Survey Of Juveniles*. Manchester, United Kingdom: National Association for the Care and Resettlement of Offenders, 1992. This report based on a survey of youthful pre-trial criminal detainees in England and Wales concludes that the number of remands have decreased and two-thirds of those remanded were 16 years of age while 15% were black. The report also presents details of their offenses, risk of recidivism while on bail, as well as those in detention in non-juvenile court cases. 24p. Appendix.

2736 National Association For The Care And Resettlement Of Offenders *Criminal Justice Act 1991: Statutory Criteria For Custodial Sentences*. London, United Kingdom, 1992. this report describes the impact of Great Britain's Criminal Justice Act of 1991 on the custody for young offenders under age 21, and summarizes key judgments and interpretations of the Court of Appeals. 39p.

2737 National Association For The Care And Resettlement Of Offenders *NACRO's Final Report On The DHSS Intermediate Treatment Initiative To Divert Juvenile Offenders: 1983-1989*. London, United Kingdom: National Association for the Care and Resettlement of Offenders, 1991. This is a description and evaluation of a successful intermediate treatment, providing juvenile delinquents alternative to custodial sentences in intensive community-based projects collaboratively administered by voluntary and local agencies. 67p.

2738 National Association For The Care And Resettlement Of Offenders *Unheard In Prison: A Study Of Unconvicted Juveniles Held In Prison Establishments*. London, United Kingdom: National Association for the Care and Resettlement of Offenders, 1990. This study of juveniles in remand found that adult courts had remanded a large number of these youths without the safeguards of the juvenile court procedures. 11p.

2739 National Association For The Care And Resettlement Of Offenders *Reducing Custody For Juveniles: The DHSS Intermediate Treatment Initiative*. London, United Kingdom: National Association for the Care and Resettlement of Offenders, 1990. This document on the Intermediate Treatment Initiative in Great Britain reports on the use of community-based sentences involving probation, both governmental and voluntary agencies thereby reducing the use of custodial care for juvenile offenders. 39p.

2740 National Association For The Care And Resettlement Of Offenders *School Reports In The Juvenile Court*. London, United Kingdom: National Association for the Care and Resettlement of Offenders, 1984. This report documents the practices and problemsof the juvenile courts in England in using school reports. 54p.

2741 National Association For The Care And Resettlement Of Offenders *Community Alternatives For Young Offenders: Final Report*. London, United Kingdom: National Association for the Care and Resettlement of Offenders, 1982. This report describes the work and method of the Community Alternatives for Young Offenders (CAYO) project, and its local consultancy programs in various communities. 20 p.

2742 Newman, Cathy *Young Runaways: Findings From Britain's First Safe House*. London, United Kingdom: Children's Society, 1989. This is a two-year study of youths offered safety under a project for runaways during the 1980s in the United Kingdom. 157p.

2743 Normand, Andrew The Scottish System, pp73-87 in Cavadino, Paul (ed.) *Children Who Kill*. This chapter describes the Scottish system of justice and how it responds to youths engaged in serious, violent crime.

2744 O'Mahony, David & Haines, Kevin *An Evaluation Of The Introduction And Operation Of the Youth Court*. London, United Kingdom: Home Office Research and Statistics Directorate, 1996. This study of about 2,000 youths sentenced in six local-area courts before and after the introduction of the youth court and concludes that there is a lack of evidence demonstrating that as a result of the Criminal Justice Acts of 1993 and 1994 there will be more severe future sentencing of youthful offenders. 70p.

2745 O'Shea, James *Juvenile Crime: An Information Sharing System*. London, United Kingdom: Home Office-Police Research Group, 1994. This volume ia a guideline and list of goals for developing shared, information-system projects that involve juvenile offenders in Great Britain. 45p. Appendix.

2746 Ostapiuk, Eugene Working With Offenders in Secure Accommodation: New Challenges for the Youth Treatment Services, pp 21-29 in Heritage, Ian & Martin, Carol (eds.) *Serious Young Offenders, Security, Treatment & Future Prospects*. London, United Kingdom: Institute for The Study & Treatment of Delinquency, 1995. The importance of control, care and change in youth treatment centers is the focus of this discussion.

2747 Owens, Elwyn & MacKenzie, Keith Changed Local Authorities And Opportunities For Large British Voluntary Organizations In 1990s, pp 82-87 in Bullock, Roger (ed.) *Problem Adolescents: An International View*. London, United Kingdom: Whiting & Burch, 1992. This conference paper discusses the role of juvenile justice system participants, such as the various local public agencies and voluntary organizations, in dealing with juvenile delinquency and delinquents.

2748 Pain, Kenneth W. *Minors: The Law And Practice: The Juvenile Courts -- The Offences -- The Role Of The Local Authorities*. London, United Kingdom: Fourmat, 1987. The major elements of English laws on minors, offenses committed by and against minors, the juvenile court practices and procedures, and the role of the local authorities in proceedings on the care of a young person in trouble are discussed by the author. 293p.

2749 Parker, Howard; Gallagher, Bernard & Hughes, Beverley The Policing Of Child Sexual Abuse In England And Wales, *Policing And Society* 6:1-13, 1996. This study evaluates the performance of specialist Child Abuse Units (CABs) established in the 1980s by British police forces to foster child protection through multi-agency teams.

2750 Parker, Howard & Giller, Henri More And Less The Same: British Delinquency Research Since The Sixties, *British Journal Of Criminology* 21:230-245, 1981. This review of research on juvenile delinquency, its etiology, correction and control in Great Britain declares that although some criminologists have been radicalized, criminology has not and bemoans the lagging critical research and input in the era of repressive attitudes and juvenile justice.

2751 Parker, Howard; Casburn, Maggie & Turnbull, David *Receiving Juvenile Justice: Adolescents And State Care And Control.* Oxford, United Kingdom: Basil Blackwell, 1981. Observations of police intervention and case disposition in some city and county juvenile justice systems in Great Britain reveal the concepts of juvenile justice and control of 12-17 year olds held by local officials. 259p.

2752 Parker, Howard; Casburn, Maggie & Turnbull, David The Production Of Punitive Juvenile Justice, *British Journal Of Criminology* 20:236-260, 1980. The authors argue that a consequence of 1969 Children and Young persons' Act has been increased custody in the countryside of England and Wales.

2753 Parker, Lois *Music Against Drugs: An Evaluation Of A Drugs Prevention Diversionary Activity.* London, United Kingdom: Home Office, 1995. This is a description and evaluation of a drug prevention project called the Music Against Drugs in Birmingham, England for youth at-risk of taking drugs by providing musical instruments and tuition to encourage and reinforce positive activities. 33p.

2754 Parliamentary All Party Penal Affairs Group *The Prevention Of Crime Among Young People.* London, United Kingdom: Barry Rose, 1985. This report on crime prevention in Great Britain discusses (1) situational factors such as products and security systems designed to deter and detect crime, and to reduce opportunities for crime, and (2) societal factors of parental care, environment, education, employment opportunities, and recreational facilities that predispose youth toward or away from criminality. 112p.

2755 Parliamentary All Party Penal Affairs Group *Young Offenders: A Strategy For The Future.* London, United Kingdom: Barry Rose, 1981. Criminal justice system alternatives, such as diversion, community-based alternatives, and custodial programs, in dealing with youthful offenders, are discussed in this legislative report including discussion of juvenile crime, sentencing trends, cautioning, etc. 100p.

2756 Penal Affairs Consortium *The Doctrine Of 'Doli Incapax.'* London, United Kingdom: Penal Affairs Consortium, 1995. This summary covers the principles underlying criminal responsibility of children between the ages of 10 and 13, the current law, and the Consortium's opinion. 7p. Appendix.

2757 Pengelly, Hilary *Juvenile Justice Under The Tories: The Example Of Oxford*. Norwich, United Kingdom: University of East Anglia, 1985. This report found that in the Oxford City Juvenile Court there were increasing detentions and custodial sentences for juveniles, and that over half of the detentions were due to directives of the Criminal Justice Act of 1982 that might not have happened previously. 38p.

2758 Petrie, Cairine *The Nowhere Boys: A Comparative Study of Open and Closed Residential Placement*. Hampshire, England: Saxon House, 1980. This study sought to determine the characteristics of boys placed in residential treatment, and the effectiveness of their treatment. 163p.

2759 Pfeffer, Karen; Cole, Bankole & Dada, Kayode British And Nigerian Adolescents' Lay Theories Of Youth Crime, *Psychology, Crime And Law* 3:21-35, 1996. This study of Nigerian and British youths' explanations of what causes youthful crime found that while the British respondents attributed it to personal variables, such as boredom, the Nigerians believe situational factors such as poverty were the cause.

2760 Plotnikoff, Joyce & Woolfson, Richard *Options For Improved Support For Victims And Other Witnesses Attending Magistrates' Courts*. London, United Kingdom: Home Office, 1997. This report on improved victim and witnesses support in magistrates' and youth courts in England addresses issues of physical environment, pre- and post-trial information, effective management of the criminal justice process, and sensitivity in their personal treatment. 94p.

2761 Powell, Fred Restructuring Juvenile Justice And The Young Offender: A Comparative Study Of Northern Ireland And England And Wales, *Social Work Today* 15:16-19, 1984. This is a comparison of the juvenile justice systems of England, Wales and Northern Ireland, and a critique of the "justice model" approach to juvenile justice expounded by the Black Report, also known as The Northern Ireland Report of the Children and Young Persons Review Group of 1979.

2762 Power, Michael J. Juvenile Justice In Great Britain: Cautions, Hearings, And Courts, pp 299-326 in Rosenheim, Margaret K. (ed.) *Pursuing Justice For The Child*. Chicago, Illinois: University of Chicago Press, 1976. This chapter discusses a variety of topics related to juvenile justice in the United Kingdom.

2763 Pratt, John Crime, Time, Youth And Punishment, *Contemporary Crises* 14:219-242, 1990. The author reviews the relationship of politics, economy and ideology, and the social control of youth in the 1980s.

2764 Pratt, John Corporatism: The Third Model Of Juvenile Justice, *British Journal Of Criminology* 29:236-254, 1989. Corporatism of advanced welfare societies with centralized policy and governmental intervention to avoid disruption and reduce conflict among diverse interest groups, the author feels, has come to dominate the juvenile justice system in England and Wales.

2765 Pratt, John Diversion from the Juvenile Court, *British Journal Of Criminology* 26:212-233, 1986. Increasing regulation of young people within the context of probation orders and professionalization of social work during 1925-1960 in Britain is the theme of this article that analyzed the use of diversion as a disposition and sanction for juveniles.

2766 Pratt, John & Grimshaw, Roger A Juvenile Justice Pre-Court Tribunal At Work, *Howard Journal* 24:213-228, 1985. Examining pre-court tribunals' decisions to prosecute a family for a child's truancy, the authors found that most families accept the tribunal's strictures and strategy geared to replacing deviant identities, and guarantees the judge of regular school attendance of the youngsters.

2767 Pratt, J. D. Folk-Lore And Fact In Truancy Research, *British Journal Of Criminology* 23:336-353, 1983. this article is a critique of the social policy to deal with "truancy crisis" and its negativism in the context of the educational and judicial bureaucratic processes of juvenile court adjournments, care orders, ethics and research evidence.

2768 Pratt, J. D. Intermediate Treatment And The Normalization Crisis, *Howard Journal* 22:19-37, 1983. The historic developments since the 19th century in community-based intermediate treatment in British corrections is the focus of this article.

2769 President Of The Council And Leader Of The House Of Commons *Tackling Drugs Together: A Strategy For England 1995-1998*. London, United Kingdom: Her Majesty's Stationery Office, 1995. This report advocates vigorous enforcement, localized strategy and treatment for youths' drug use. 69p.

2770 President Of The Council And Leader Of The House Of Commons *Tackling Drugs Together: A Consultation Document On A Strategy For England 1995-1998*. London, United Kingdom: Her Majesty's Stationery Office, 1994. This report covers existing drug strategy in United

Kingdom and elsewhere, community safety, helping young people resist drugs, coordination of local and national agencies, etc. 114p.

2771 Priestley, Philip; Fears, Denise & Fuller, Roger *Justice For Juveniles. The 1969 Children And Young Persons Act: A Case For Reform?* London, United Kingdom: Routledge & Kegan Paul, 1977. This report on the impact of the 1969 Children and Young Persons Act on the British juvenile justice system is based on data on juvenile offense cases processed during the first three months of 1972 in Bristol and Wiltshire. 120p.

2772 Prins, Herschel Psychiatric Services And The Magistrates' And The Juvenile Courts, *British Journal Of Criminology* 15:315-332, 1975. The author discovered in his observations, that the magistrates and the probation officers differed on who among the juvenile court clients deserved the attentions of a psychiatric inquiry.

2773 Prison Reform Trust (eds.) *Drink, Delinquency And Prison*. London, United Kingdom: Prison reform Trust, 1989. This report is based on a survey of both juvenile and young adult alcohol-abusing inmates in a prison program for alcohol abusers, and explores the various options for the diversion of such offenders. 24p.

2774 Rawstorne, Shirley England And Wales, pp. 33-45 in Hoffman, Allan M. & Summers, Randal W. (eds.) *Teen Violence A Global View*. Westport, Connecticut: Greenwood, 2001. This chapter discusses the problem of teen violence and strategies for dealing with it in the United Kingdom.

2775 Reed, Gordon Young Offenders, Hopes and Fears, A Comparison Between Poland And England, pp 8-22 Wilson, Thelma (ed.) *Penal Services For Offenders: Comparative Studies Of England And Poland 1984/85*. Brookfield, Vermont: Gower, 1987. The author reports on increased custody and punitiveness in England and Wales.

2776 Richardson, Françoise Electronic Tagging Of Offenders: Trails In England, *Howard Journal* 38:158-172, 1999. This article provides a description of the electronic monitoring of English offenders including the monitoring of juveniles.

2777 Riley, David & Mayhew, P. *Crime Prevention Publicity: An Assessment*. London, United Kingdom: Her Majesty's Stationery Office, 1980. This report is an evaluation of the effectiveness of various advertising campaigns to combat crimes, such as vandalism and car theft, in the United Kingdom.

2778 Robertson, Alex & McClintock, Derick The Community Based Alternative: Intermediate Treatment For Young Offenders, pp 131-154 in Asquith, Stewart (ed.) Children And Young People In Conflict With The Law. London, United Kingdom: Jessica Kingsley, 1996. This chapter discusses intermediate treatment programs as facilitating the diversion of youths from more severe penal measures, although such programs may be no more or even less effective as deterrent measures compared to alternatives.

2779 Robins, David *Sport As Prevention: The Role Of Sport In Crime Prevention Programmes Aimed At Young People.* Oxford, United Kingdom: University of Oxford, 1990. This document provides a description and critique of various delinquency programs involving sports and recreation as a social crime-prevention strategy in the United Kingdom. 108p.

2780 Roughton, Andy; Glynn, Chris & Robinson, Chris Cautioning Works, *Policing* 11:120-130, 1995. There was no evidence of racial discrimination on the part of West Midlands police in this analysis focusing on "cautioning" juveniles in United Kingdom.

2781 Ruggiero, Vincenzo Punishing Children: The Manufacture Of Criminal Careers In Hellion Town, *Theoretical Criminology* 1:341-361, 1997. This participant observation study of "Hellion Town," United Kingdom over six months describes the treatment of young offenders in an inner-city youth justice service, and suggests that acceleration of criminal careers among these youths may be due to inaction, absenteeism and the non-productive investment of energies created by tensions among agencies and agents in charge.

2782 Rumgay, Judith & Brewster, Mary Restructuring Probation In England And Wales: Lessons Learned From An American Experience, *Prison Journal* 76:331-347, 1996. This critical essay of the proposed restructuring of probation service in England and Wales speculates on the possible consequences when imposing constraints that conflict with the professional ideology of probation officers.

2783 Rumgay, Judith Taking Rehabilitation Out Of After-Care? The Post-Release Supervision Of Young Adult Offenders, *British Journal Of Criminology* 30:36-50, 1990. This study on the effects the law had on youth custody after the abolition of Borstal training schools for juvenile delinquents in the United Kingdom following passage of the Criminal Justice Act 1982. It was found that the officers and evidence point to ambivalence about punishment versus rehabilitation in the penal treatment of these young offenders.

2784 Runnicles, Dorothy *Co-Operation And Conflict: A Study Of Police And Social Service Work With Juveniles In Trouble*. London, United Kingdom: School of Social Sciences, Hatfield Polytechnic, 1984. Exploring the interface of the police and social services in one outer London neighborhood, this study found that most of the clients were juveniles in trouble, and, as each agency had different tasks, liaison was minimal. 97p. Appendix.

2785 Rutherford, Andrew *Growing Out Of Crime: The New Era. 2nd. Ed.* Winchester, United Kingdom: Waterside, 1992. The author is against institutional solutions to the problems of juvenile delinquency in the United Kingdom, and favors minimal intervention and alternatives to custody. 163p.

2786 Rutherford, Andrew Adolescents And The Penal System: Hopeful Straws In The Wind, *Criminal Behavior And Mental Health* 2:15-23, 1992. This article analyzes recent changes in the United Kingdom in placing youths in prisons, and offers some commentary on various European countries as well.

2787 Rutherford, Andrew Criminal Justice Act '82 And The Use Of Custody, *Probation Journal* 30:93-95, 1983. This article argues that the 1982 Criminal Justice Act will considerably increase the number of juveniles in custody and enmesh young offenders in crime, besides eroding custodial standards.

2788 San Lazaro, Camille; Steele, Alison M. & Donaldson, Liam J. Outcome Of Criminal Investigation Into Allegations Of Sexual Abuse, *Archives Of Disease In Childhood* 75:149-152, 1996. This two-year study of criminal investigations into allegations of sexual abuse made by children in a special pediatric unit, found that pragmatic selection of cases for prosecution ended in favorable case outcomes supporting the decision to prosecute.

2789 Savil, Eve & Rumney, David *A History Of The I.S.T.D.: A Study Of Crime And Delinquency From 1931 To 1992*. London, United Kingdom: Institute for the Study and Treatment of Delinquency, 1993. The authors trace the origins and development of interdisciplinary approaches to meet the needs of youths within the community in dealing with delinquents by the Institute. 144p.

2790 Schaffer, Evelyn B. *Community Policing*. London, England: Croom Helm, 1980. This publication considers issues involving the police and juvenile offenders in Great Britain, including police adaptations to the new legislation, social work practices, and community policing. 145p.

2791 Shiner, Michael & Newburn, Tim *Young People, Drugs And Peer Education: An Evaluation Of The Youth Awareness Programme (YAP).* London, United Kingdom: Drug Prevention Initiative-Home Office, 1996. This evaluation of a drug-abuse prevention program in London is based on interviews with school children, volunteers, staff as well as program documents and observations. 81p.

2792 Silberman, Sharon Community Service As An Alternative Sentence For Juveniles, *New England Journal On Criminal And Civil Confinement* 12:123-150, 1986. The author examines the pros and cons of community service as an alternative to detention in criminal cases involving juvenile offenders.

2793 Smith, Roger *Children And The Courts*. London, United Kingdom: Sweet and Maxwell. 1979. This book is a guide to lay advisers' understanding of the legal technicalities, powers and obligations regarding children appearing in British courts. 219p.

2794 Soothill, Keith Rapists Under 14 In The News, *Howard Journal* 36:367-377, 1997. This is a study of newspaper reports of prosecution of 12 boys 10-14 years of age (with only one conviction) following the 1993 aboliton of the common law presumption that a boy under age 14 is incapable of sexual intercourse.

2795 Spencer, J. R. & Flin, Rhona *The Evidence Of Children: The Law And The Psychology*. London, United Kingdom: Blackstone Press, 1991. The authors summarize social psychological research on children's court testimony, and describe the various rules of children's evidence in the United Kingdom. 362p.

2796 Stack, John A. Children, Urbanization, And The Chances Of Imprisonment In Mid-Victorian England, pp 113-139 in Knafla, Louis A. (ed.) *Criminal Justice History: An International Annual, Volume 13.* Westport: Connecticut: Greenwood, 1993. This is a historic study of the relationship between socioeconomic background and the commitment of children to prison during the latter half of the 19th century in England and Wales.

2797 Stafford, Elizabeth & Hill, John The Tariff, Social Inquiry Reports And The Sentencing Of Juveniles, *British Journal Of Criminology* 27:411-420, 1987. Based on a survey of juveniles, this research concludes that type of offense, previous convictions and dispositions, and social inquiry report were good predictors of court outcomes.

2798 Stanley, Stephen & Baginsky, Mary *Alternatives To Prison: An Examination Of Non-Custodial Sentencing Of Offenders*. London, United

Kingdom: Peter Owen, 1984. The authors review the literature and research on non-custodial sentences, such as care orders, supervision and community service orders, intermediate treatment, probation, suspended and deferred sentences, and parole for juveniles in the United Kingdom and other countries. 183p.

2799 Stephens, Mike *Crime And Social Policy: The Police And Criminal Justice System*. East Sussex, United Kingdom: Gildredge, 2000. Besides crime, fear of crime and community corrections in general, this book includes a section on youth courts in the United Kingdom, the scale of 'youth problem' and public concern about it. 148p.

2800 Stein, Mike; Rees, Gwyther & Frost, Nick *Running The Risk: Young People On The Streets Of Britain Today*. London, United Kingdom: The Children's Society, 1994. This evaluation of different street work projects of the British Children's Society for runaways describes the characteristics of the runaways and the diverse projects, compares different models of the projects, their outcomes and the effects of service delivery. 133p.

2801 Stevens, Malcolm The Management Of Serious Young Offenders, pp 4-13 in Heritage, Ian & Martin, Carol (eds.) *Serious Young Offenders, Security, Treatment & Future Prospects*. London, United Kingdom: Institute for The Study & Treatment of Delinquency, 1995. This article provides a description of the changes in custodial sentencing, remands, cautioning, and community-based penalties.

2802 Stewart, Gill & Stewart, John *Social Circumstances Of Younger Offenders Under Supervision*. London, United Kingdom: Association of Chief Officers of Probation, 1993. This research on offenders from seven probation areas in Great Britain includes an examination of the relationships among social and economic circumstances, offense behavior, and the probation of youthful offenders. 94p.

2803 Stewart, Gillian & Tutt, Norman *Children In Custody*. Gower, United Kingdom: Aldershot, 1987. This book is concerned with youth in custody in England, Wales, Scotland and Northern Ireland and the Republic of Ireland, and focuses on the varied definitions of childhood and children's rights, the legislative agenda and penal system of each country, their philosophy and principles in dealing with young offenders. 237p.

2804 Stewart, Gill & Smith, David Help For Children In Custody; Some Implications Of Probation Withdrawal, *British Journal Of Criminology* 27:302-315, 1987. This survey of British juveniles in custody in 1984 is critial of the low level of probation staffing in juvenile institutions given the difficulties and disruptions the children had experienced.

2805 Stockdale, Eric *Criminal Justice Under Stress*. London, United Kingdom: Blackstone, 1992. In the chapter entitled "Juveniles," the author considers the changes brought by the 1989 Children's Act and the 1991 Criminal Justice Act to be positive and progressive, but discusses the problems and issues related to the juvenile court, diversion, remand, sentencing and custody. 299p.

2806 Stott, Denis *Delinquency: The Problem And Its Prevention*. New York, New York: Spectrum, 1982. The focus of the various chapters under the four parts of this book is on effective casework and community techniques in juvenile delinquency work in general. 345p

2807 Sumner, Maggie; Jarvis, Graham & Parker, Howard Sentencing Trends: A Review Of Criminal Statistics For England And Wales, *British Journal Of Criminology* 26:87-93, 1986. This analysis of offense behavior, cautioning and sentences in post-1982 Criminal Justice Act in England and Wales found that during 1984 juveniles and females, than adults and males, were cautioned most frequently.

2808 Taylor, D. Juvenile Detected Crime: Decline And Fall, *Criminal Law Review* (November):731-734, 1986. The author's argument is that the decreasing detected crime rate is the consequence of the 1978 English Judges' Rules and Administrative Directions restricting the interviewing of juveniles without the presence of parents or guardians.

2809 Taylor, Ian Crime Waves In Post-War Britain, *Contemporary Crises* 5:43-62, 1981. Reviewing the history of crime and the labeling of offenders in Britain over 100 years, the author claims that crime control is still geared to controlling the unemployed, youths, blacks and others.

2810 Thoepe, D. H.; Smith, D.; Green, C. J. & Paley, J. H. *Out Of Care: The Community Support Of Juvenile Offenders*. London, United Kingdom: George Allen & Unwin, 1980. This publication addresses the Children and Young Persons Act of 1969, and its implications. 183p.

2811 Tillham, Spencer *Juvenile Justice And Child Care In England*. Ann Arbor, Michigan: University of Michigan, Center for the Study of Youth Policy, 1991. A seminar presentation, this piece describes recent, dramatic changes in the youth correction system in England. 16p.

2812 Tuck, Mary *Drinking And Disorder: A Study Of Non-Metropolitan Violence*. London, United Kingdom: Her Majesty's Stationery Office, 1989. This study on public drunkenness in three districts in the United Kingdom includes the impact of factors such as population composition and preventive measures to reduce under-age alcohol consumption. 111p.

2813 Tutt, Norman; Fitzgerald, Edward; Levy, Allan; Rutter, Michael; Thomas, Mike & Akester, Kate *Children And Homicide: Appropriate Procedures For Juvenile In Murder And Manslaughter Cases*. London, United Kingdom: Justice, 1996. This paper on the appropriate treatments for children who commit or are accused of murder in England emphasizes, both the legal and child development needs while protecting society. 36p.

2814 Tutt, Norman A Decade Of Policy, *British Journal Of Criminology* 21:246-256, 1981. The author contends that the policies proposed in" Young Offenders", a white paper of the Home Office, will bring more juveniles into the juvenile justice system instead of providing an alternative to custody.

2815 Tutt, Norman (ed.) *Alternative Strategies For Coping With Crime*. Oxford, United Kingdom: Basil Blackwell and Martin Robertson, 1978. This anthology, mostly covering the United Kingdom, has eleven essays on the prevention of juvenile delinquency, diversion of juvenile offenders from the criminal justice system, intermediate treatment, the use of family placements in the treatment of delinquency, new careers for Borstal trainees, and the development of community service. 230p.

2816 Tutt, N. S. Recommittals Of Juvenile Offenders, *British Journal Of Criminology* 16:385-388, 1976. The author declares that a study of the dropout rate from treatment in approved schools when compared with previous national and research data in Great Britain, demonstrates an increased dropout rate, but says sthat the reasons for the change are not very clear.

2817 Tutt, Norman *Care Or Custody: Community Homes And The Treatment Of Delinquency*. New York, New York: Agathon Press, 1975. This comprehensive analysis of a residential treatment center for juvenile offenders in England highlights the omnipresent dilemmas and conflicting aims of punishment versus treatment in such residential treatment programs. 226p.

2818 Tweedie, Ian Police Cautioning of Juveniles - Two Styles Compared, *Criminal law Review* (March):168-174, 1982. Data on informal advise guidance and admonitory cautioning of juveniles in Avon and Somerset shows, that an informal approach had greater impact on the parents while the formal admonition was remembered and more favorably viewed by the youths.

2819 UK Commission For Racial Equality *Cautions Vs. Precautions: Ethnic Monitoring Of Juveniles By Seven Police Forces*. London, United Kingdom: United Kingdom Commission for Racial Equality, 1992. Data on juveniles from seven police forces in the United Kingdom indicate that monitoring pre-court decisions will reduce the disparity in diversion among Afro-Caribbean, Asian and White youths. 26p.

2820 UK Home Office Juvenile Offenders Unit *Preventing Children Offending: A Consultation Document*. London, United Kingdom: The Stationery Office Ltd., 1997. This document presents a proposal to reduce juvenile crime by creating Child Crime Teams. 27p.

2821 UK Home Office *Crime, Justice And Protecting The Public: The Government's Proposals For Legislation*. London, United Kingdom: Her Majesty's Stationery Office, 1990. This is a government policy proposal recommending greater powers for the courts in making parents take greater responsibility for their children's crimes, and flexibility in dealing with 16-17-year-old offenders, and transform the juvenile courts to youth courts to deal with youths under age 18. 48p.

2822 Utting, David *Reducing Criminality Among Young People: A Sample Of Relevant Programmes In The United Kingdom*. London, United Kingdom: Research and Statistics Directorate-Home Office, 1996. this paper describes various programs focusing on families, school, sports and leisure. 112p.

2823 Vass, Anthony A. *Sentenced To Labour: Close Encounters With A Prison Substitute*. St. Ives, England: Venus Academia, 1984. This is a discussion of statutes on "community service order," and includes the 1982 juvenile law on non-custodial sentence as well. 191p.

2824 Vass, Anthony A. Community Service For Juveniles? A Critical Comment, *Probation Journal* 28:44-49, 1981. In a critique of the British government's proposal to extend the community service order for juveniles, the author argues that it is not a true alternative to other milder non-custodial sentences, and moreover involves cases where custodial sentences would been unlikely anyhow.

2825 Vennard, Julie; Sugg, Darren & Hedderman, Carol *Changing Offenders' Attitudes And Behaviour: What Works?* London, United Kingdom: Research d Statistics Directorate-Home Office, 1997. The value and effectiveness of cognitive-behavioral intervention on probationers, both minors and adults, is the focus of this national survey. 69p.

2826 Walker, Monica A. The Court Disposal Of Young Males, By Race, In London In 1993, *British Journal Of Criminology* 28:441-460, 1988. A study of 14-16 year old males prosecution data shows that, due to insufficient evidence, relatively more black males had their cases dismissed prior to trial compared to whites, suggesting racial disparity in the police treatment of young blacks.

2827 Walker, Nigel *Aggravation, Mitigation And Mercy In English Criminal Justice.* London, United Kingdom: Blackstone, 1999. This survey of English sentencing laws and the role of mitigating circumstances includes chapters on desert, utility, youth and old age, precautionary detention, non-custodial precautions and so on. 207p.

2828 Wardhaugh, Julia Criminalising Truancy: Legal And Welfare Responses To School Non-Attendance, pp 133-143 in Booth, Tim (ed.) *Juvenile Justice In The New Europe.* Sheffield, United Kingdom: Joint Unit for Social Services Research, Sheffield University, 1991. This chapter describes the changing legal context of school non-attendance as a result of the Children Act of 1989.

2829 Webb, David More On Gender And Justice: Girl Offenders On Supervision, *Sociology* 18:367-381, 1984. Case files and social inquiry reports of girls and boys under supervision orders in six areas of England and Wales indicate the existence of gender bias in the administration of juvenile justice.

2830 Weinberger, B. The Policing Of Minors: Manchester At The End Of The 19th And Beginning Of The 20th Centuries (La Police Des Mineurs: Manchester À La Fin Du XIX Et Au Début Du XX Siècles), *Déviance Et Société* 18:31-42, 1994. Describes the Victorian, Edwardian programs and continued post-war Manchester and British programs to discipline and reform juveniles. French.

2831 Weinberger, Barbara Policing Juveniles: Delinquency In Late Nineteenth And Early Twentieth Century Manchester, pp 43-55 in King, Peter & Noel, Joan (eds.) *The Origins Of The `Problem Of Juvenile Delinquency': The Growth of Juvenile Prosecutions in London In The Late Eighteenth And Early Nineteenth Centuries.* Westport, Connecticut: Greenwood, 1994. Problem juveniles and street adolescents who, during the late 18th to early 19th centuries, became the focus of attention of evangelicals, educationalists, philanthropists and progressive liberals Britain are the subjects of this article.

2832 Welsh, Sheila The Manufacture Of Excitement In Police-Juvenile Encounters, *British Journal Of Criminology* 21:257-267, 1981. Interviews with a mixed group of adolescents from the East End of London, and with police officers, to gauge police-youth interaction lead to the conclusion that adolescents deliberately created excitement and seemed to enjoy abusing the police in such encounters more than harassing their Asian neighbors.

2833 Wheeler, Gerald R. Creative Punishment: A Quick Justice System For Juvenile Offenders, *Probation And Parole* 9:7-17, 1977. In a critique of the abuse in indeterminate juvenile sentences, the author advocates community involvement in juvenile sentencing, as benefiting both youths as well as some needy segments of the community.

2834 Whyte, Bill *Re-Examining Juvenile Justice In Scotland.* Edinburgh, Scotland: Department of Social Work, University of Edinburgh, 1996. This review explains how the children's hearing system in Scotland responds to juveniles in principle and practice. 40p.

2835 Wilkinson, Christine & Evans, Roger Police Cautioning Of Juveniles: The Impact Of Home Office Circular 14/1985, *Criminal Law Review* (March):165-176, 1990. This assessment of the effects of new directives on police cautioning of British juveniles concludes that to some extent it has been a success.

2836 Wilkinson, John & Morgan, David *The Impact of Ilderton Motor Project On Motor Vehicle Crime And Offending.* London, United Kingdom: Inner London Probation Service, 1995. This study is on the positive impact on young probationers being trained to repair cars, both in reducing offense behavior involving cars as well as punishment for re-offending. 23p.

2837 Williamson, Howard *Youth And Policy: Contexts And Consequences.* Aldershot, United Kingdom: Ashgate, 1997. This anthology on political, policy and research initiatives affecting youth in Great Britain focuses on the views and experiences of youths that are unskilled and unqualified who eke out an existence living on the margins of "post modern" society. 251p.

2838 Wilson, J. C. & Davies, G. M. An Evaluation Of The Use Of Videotaped Evidence For Juvenile Witnesses In Criminal Courts In England And Wales, *European Journal On Criminal Policy And Research* 7:81-96, 1999. This article presents an evaluation of the use of videotaped testimony of children in criminal cases.

2839 Wooton, Barbara *Crime And Penal Policy: Reflections On Fifty Years' Inexperience.* London, United Kingdom: George Allen and Unwin, 1978. This book presents a critique of Great Britain's tendency to punish youthful offenders of compulsory school age rather than preventing their incarceration. 261p.

United States

2840 Abadinsky, Howard The Status Offense Dilemma: Coercion And Treatment, *Crime & Delinquency* 22:456-460, 1976. Advocating alternatives based on the Scandinavian model, the author argues that juvenile court's jurisdiction over status offenses leads to increased coercive power, stigmatization and ineffectual treatment.

2841 Acoca, Leslie Outside/Inside: The Violation Of American Girls At Home, On The Street, And In The Juvenile Justice System, *Crime & Delinquency* 44:561-589, 1998. This paper describes the physical and emotional abuse that delinquent girls encounter at home, on the street, and within the American juvenile justice system.

2842 Adams, Laura S. & Curran, Laura Wayward Girls And Virtuous Women: Social Workers And Female Juvenile Delinquency In The Progressive Era, *Affilia* 15:49-64, 2000. This article presenta a discussion of the role and practices of the burgeoning social reformers of the Progressive Era and professional social workers in criminalizing adolescent female sexuality.

2843 Altschuler, David M.; Lawrence, Janet S. & National Juvenile Justice Assessment Centers *A Review Of Selected Research And Program Evaluations On Police Diversion Programs*. Chicago, Illinois: University of Chicago, School of Social Service Administration, 1979. This is a description of seven diversion programs, their organization and conception of their mission to divert delinquent youths. 86p.

2844 American Bar Association Presidential Working Group On The Unmet Legal Needs Of Children And Families *America's Children At Risk: National Agenda For Legal Action*. Chicago, Illinois: American Bar Association, 1993. This report lays out the agenda for legal actions to address the unmet needs of at-risk children and families in America. 105p.

2845 American Correctional Association *Juvenile Justice Programs And Trends*. Lanham, Maryland, 1996. The 13 essays in this volume illustrate promising programs in juvenile corrections. 100p.

2846 American Medical Association *American Medical Association Standards For Health Services In Juvenile Correctional Facilities*. Chicago, Illinois: American Medical Association, 1979. Seventy-three standards, arranged by topic, covering all aspects of health care for juvenilels in correctional facilities are presented in the volume. 44p.

2847 Amnesty International *Betraying The Young: Human Rights Violations Against Children In The US Justice System*. New York, New York, 1998. This report focuses on the imprisonment of youthful offenders with adults, and use of the death penaly for minors. 66p. Appendix.

2848 Amnesty International *On The Wrong Side Of History: Children And The Death Penalty In The USA*. New York, New York, 1998. This critical discussion of the American policy of death penalty for minors, is cast within the international context. 35p.

2849 Anderson, Dennis B. & Anderson, Sara Long Educational Needs of Juvenile Offenders, *Journal Of Offender Rehabilitation* 23:153-166, 1996. This article discusses the special needs, of and problems in providing education to juvenile offenders.

2850 Andriessen, Margo A Foreigner's View Of American Diversion, *Crime & Delinquency* 26:70-82, 1980. Five California diversion projects the author feels were class-prejudiced and preoccupied with therapy, when evaluated reveal little actual diversion took place regardless of the program.

2851 Applegate, Brandon K.; Turner, Michael G.; Sanborn, Joseph B. Jr.; Latessa, Edward J. & Moon, Melissa M. Individualization, Criminalization, Or Problem Resolution: A Factorial Survey Of Juvenile Court Judges' Decisions To Incarcerate Youthful Felony Offenders, *Justice Quarterly* 17:309-331, 2000. This study uses a survey of juvenile court judges to determine the factors that shape disposition decisions for juvenile felony offenders.

2852 Arizona Joint Juvenile Justice Committee *Mental Health Commitments Of Children In Custody*. Phoenix, Arizona, 1979. This report is on Arizona statutes governing mental health commitment of minors, differential procedures in juvenile commitments, and the major problems and findings regarding commitments of children in custody to state and private psychiatric hospitals. 26p. Appendix.

2853 Arnold, Bruce L. & Kay, Fiona M. Early Transition Stages And Heterogeneity In Criminal Cases Among Young Offenders, *Canadian Review Of Sociology & Anthropology* 36:157-177, 1999. This study focuses on the patterns of police contact among diverse youth groups from their early involvement in criminality.

2854 Arthur D. Little, Inc. *Programs For The Serious And Violent Juvenile Offender*. Washington, D.C.: US Juvenile Justice and Delinquency Prevention Office, 1981. This booklet offers a range of options that people involved in planning and enacting policy can choose from, depending on the needs of the community in dealing with serious and violent juvenile offenders. 51p.

2855 Ashford, Jose B. & LeCroy, Craig Winston Juvenile Parole Policy In The United States: Determinate Versus Indeterminate Models, *Justice Quarterly* 10:179-195, 1993. Eight different approaches to juvenile parole policy are discussed in this article.

2856 Association For Experiential Education A Directory Of Adventure Alternatives In Corrections, Mental Health, Special Education And Physical Rehabilitation, *Journal Of Experiential Education* 2:9-26, 1979. Various adventure programs for American juveniles as alternatives to standard corrections treatment, mental health, special education, and physical rehabilitation are listed alphabetically by title with addresses, telephone numbers, contact persons and annotated explanations of the programs.

2857 Austin, James & Krisberg, Barry *The Impact Of Juvenile Court Intervention*. Washington, D.C.: US Office of Juvenile Justice And Delinquency Prevention, 1987. This study of the impact of various interventions on serious juvenile offenders in the Second District Juvenile Court of Utah found no significant differences among serious juvenile offenders in Utah. 156p. Appendix.

2858 Austin, James F.; Lawrence, Wayne & Krisberg, Barry *Open Space, Community Detention, Pittsburgh-Antioch Diversion And AB3121: Diverting The Status Offender*. San Francisco, California: National Council on Crime and Delinquency, 1978. Within the context of California mandatory deinstitutionalization of all status offenders, this report describes the Contra Costa Probation Department voluntary support project to provide services to juvenile status offenders and their parents.

2859 Austin, James; Krisberg, Barry; DeComo, Robert; Rudenstine, Sonya & Del Rosario, Dominic *Juveniles Taken Into Custody: Fiscal Year 1993. Statistics Report*. San Francisco, California: National Council on Crime and Delinquency, 1995. This study presents a statistical portrait of U.S. juveniles taken into custody during fiscal year 1993. 126p.

2860 Baines, Margaret & Alder, Christine Are Girls More Difficult To Work With? Youth Workers' Perspectives In Juvenile Justice And Related Areas, *Crime & Delinquency* 42:467-508, 1996. This article explores and explains the gendered assumptions, and their impact on juvenile justice decision making and practice which views girls as more difficult to work with.

2861 Bakal, Yitzhak Reflections: A Quarter Century Of Reform In Massachusetts.Youth Corrections, *Crime & Delinquency* 44:110-116, 1998. The author assesses the strategies in and consequences of the closing of juvenile institutions in Massachusetts.

2862 Bakal, Yitzhak &; Krisberg, Barry *Placement Needs Assessment For Youth Committed To Oregon Training Schools.* San Francisco, California: National Council on Crime and Delinquency, 1987. This is an assessment of the study team of Oregon state juvenile corrections agencies that investigated the placement of juvenile offenders in the training schools. 38p.

2863 Baker, Falcon *Saving Our Kids From Delinquency, Drugs And Despair: Solutions Through Prevention.* New York, New York: Harper-Collins, 1991. In this 22 chapter criticism of the American juvenile justice system which the author contends has failed both youth and society at large, he recommends making accountable both the juvenile and society for creating conditions conducive to the delinquency of youth. 348p.

2864 Bartollas, Clemens United States, pp 301-316 in Shoemaker, Donald J. (ed.) *International Handbook On Juvenile Justice.* Westport, Connecticut: Greenwood, 1996. This chapter offers a discussion of the juvenile justice system in the United States.

2865 Bartollas, Clemens Little Girls Growing Up: The Perils Of Institutionalization, pp 469-482 in Culliver, Concetta C. (ed.) *Female Criminality: The State of the Art.* New York, New York: Garland, 1993. Based on self-administered questionnaires on female delinquents' coping behavior in institutions, this study concludes that in the United States female adolescents are treated more harshly than males.

2866 Bartollas, Clemens Juvenile Corrections: The State Of The Art, pp 159-167 in Barak-Glantz, Israel L. & Huff, C. Ronald (eds.) *The Mad, The Bad, And The Different: Essays In Honor Of Simon Dinitz.* Lexington, Massachusetts: Lexington Books, 1981. This chapter presents a history of the juvenile court, the rights of juveniles, unfairness in the system and the failure of the rehabilitation model.

2867 Bartollas, Clemens; Miller, Stuart J. & Dinitz, Simon The Exploitation Matrix In A Juvenile Institution, *International Journal Of Criminology And Penology* 4:257-270, 1976. This study reports findings regarding victimization of juveniles in correctional facilities by other juveniles.

2868 Barton, William & Butts, Jeffrey A. Viable Options: Intensive Supervision Programs For Juvenile Delinquents, *Crime & Delinquency* 36:238-254, 1990. This study describes the development and evaluation of three in-home program alternatives to commitment for adjudicated delinquents in the Wayne County Detroit Juvenile Court in Michigan.

2869 Bazemore, Gordon & Walgrave, Lode *Restorative Juvenile Justice: Repairing the Harm of Youth Crime*. Monsey, New York: Criminal Justice Press, 1999. This book is on victim-offender mediation as an alternative measure for dealing with juvenile delinquency. 375p.

2870 Bazemore, Gordon The Participation Of Victims In The Judicial Decisions Of Minors (*La Participation Des Victimes Dans Le Processus Décisionnel De La Justice Des Mineurs*), *Criminologie* 32:133-159, 1999. This article is based on the national survey of American juvenile court judges' attitudes toward victim participation in the various stages of decision making in juvenile delinquency cases. French with English summary.

2871 Bazemore, Gordon & Feder, Lynette Judges In The Punitive Juvenile Court: Organizational, Career And Ideological Influences On Sanctioning Orientation, *Justice Quarterly* 14:87-114, 1997. This is an examination of judicial support for punitive sentencing policies in the jvenile court.

2872 Bazemore, Gordon Three Paradigms For Juvenile Justice, pp 37-67 in Galaway, Burt & Hudson, Joe (eds.) *Restorative Justice: International Perspective*. Monsey, New York: Criminal Justice Press, 1996. The author reviews the individual treatment and retributive justice models, and advocates a third, restorative, model.

2873 Bazemore, Gordon & Umbreit, Mark Rethinking The Sanctioning Function In Juvenile Court: Retributive Or Restorative Responses To Youth Crime, *Crime & Delinquency* 41:296-316, 1995. The limitations of sanctioning choices of both the individual treatment and the retributive justice paradigm for juvenile offenders in the United States are discussed by the authors who argue in favor of individual treatment, and preserving the juvenile justice system.

2874 Bazemore, Gordon & Dicker, Todd J. Juvenile Justice Reform And The Difference It Makes: An Exploratory Study Of The Impact Of Policy On Detention Worker Attitudes, *Crime & Delinquency* 40:37-53, 1994. The authors compare the impact of criminal justice reforms on staff attitudes in two similar juvenile detention facilities.

2875 Bazemore, S. Gordon Beyond Punishment, Surveillance, And Traditional Treatment: Themes For A New Mission In US Juvenile Justice, pp 129-158 in Hackler, Jim (ed.) *Official Responses To Problem Juveniles: Some International Reflections*. Euskadi, Spain: The Oñati International Institute for the Sociology of Law, 1991. This chapter describes the "new" mission of juvenile justice in contrast to past ideas, and describes how the new approach might be implemented.

2876 Beaser, Herbert Wilton *The Legal Status Of Runaway Children*. Washington, D.C.: Educational Systems Corporation, 1975. This article explores juvenile laws and reforms concerning runaways in the various states and territories of the United States.

2877 Becker, Robert J. A Criticism Of The Juvenile Offender's Right To Treatment (The Recognition Of A Local Problem), *Loyola Law Review* 26:379-388, 1980. Rather than raising constitutional issues, the author argues in favor of using local statutory provisions as solutions in the treatment for juvenile offenders.

2878 Bell, Duran Jr. & Lang, Kevin The Intake Dispositions Of Juvenile Offenders, *Journal Of Research In Crime And Delinquency* 22:309-328, 1985. This study analyzed the dispositions at intake by ethnicity of a ssmple of 533 juvenile suspects in Los Angeles, California during 1982.

2879 Bellermann, Hans Variations In Juvenile Investigations, *International Journal Of Offender Therapy And Comparative Criminology* 30:59-68, 1986. This survey of juvenile probation officers found that although there was no correlation between their socioeconomic characteristics and the personal histories they prepare, officers whose personal histories were short tended to express more dissatisfaction with the juvenile justice system.

2880 Bensinger, Gad J. The Juvenile Court Of Cook County: Past, Present, And Future, pp 159-174 in Hackler, Jim (ed.) *Official Responses To Problem Juveniles: Some International Reflections*. Euskadi, Spain: The Oñati International Institute for the Sociology of Law, 1991. The author describes the history and operation of the juvenile court in the United. States, with speculations on its future.

2881 Berger, Randall R. Illinois Juvenile Justice: An Emerging Dual System, *Crime & Delinquency* 40:54-69, 1994. This research demonstrates the Illinois juvenile court judges'power to force offender compliance with routine court directives by their use of contempt charge.

2882 Berkman, David J. & Smith, Charles P. *Juvenile Justice System Processing And The Disposition Of Juveniles With Special Problems*.

Sacramento, California: American Justice Institute, 1979. This assessment of the current knowledge and practices of the juvenile justice system handling of, and the way it meets the needs of, juveniles with special problems, indicates a lack of consensus on the definition of what constitutes health problems and on numerous other issues. 141p.

2883 Berleman, William C. *Juvenile Delinquency Prevention Experiments: A Review And Analysis*. Washington, D.C.: National Center for the Assessment of Alternatives to Juvenile Justice Processing, US Juvenile Justice and Delinquency Prevention Office, 1980. This is a review of ten delinquency prevention studies that found that except one, all of the experimental projects were deemed ineffective in that their treatment produced no better results than non-treatment. 161p.

2884 Bernard, Thomas J. Juvenile Crime And The Transformation Of Juvenile Justice: Is There A Juvenile Crime Wave? *Justice Quarterly* 16:337-356, 1999. The author examines the get-tough juvenile policy reforms that assume that claims rergarding increasing rates of juvenile crime can be substantiated by official and victimization data.

2885 Bilchik, Shay A Juvenile Justice System For The 21st Century, *Crime & Delinquency* 44:89-101, 1998. The author examines the need for juvenile justice system to effectively reduce juvenile crime and victimization in the United States.

2886 Billingsley, Joanna V. Juvenile Justice: Procedural Safeguards For Delinquents At The Adjudicatory State - Not For Adults Only, *Washburn Law Journal* 21:288-314, 1982. The main thrust of the author's argument is that the original ideas and philosophies of juvenile courts are no longer applicable to the post-Gault, contemporary social context of due-process safeguards for minors accused of crimes.

2887 Binder, Arnold Juvenile Diversion and the Constitution, *Journal Of Criminal Justice*, 10:1-24, 1982. The author argues that diversion processes are an infringement of the due process rights of delinquent minors.

2888 Binder, Arnold The Juvenile Justice System: Where Pretense And Reality Clash, *American Behavioral Scientist* 22:621-652, 1979. This article discusses the historical idea behind the creation of the juvenile court, and its failure to both help those in need and protect the community from violent offenders while at the same time, change the treatment of juveniles to the pre-19th-century notion of a child's criminal responsibility and noninterference in status offenses.

2889 Birkbeck, Christopher; LaFree, Gary; Gabaldón, Lewis; Bassin, Andrea; Wilson, Nora; Fernández, Martha & Pacheco, Melissa Controlling New Mexico Juveniles' Possession And Use Of Firearms, *Justice Research And Policy* 1:25-49, 1999. This study describes the possession and use of firearms and how the system responds to offenses of juveniles involving firearms.

2890 Bishop, Donna M. & Frazier, Charles E. The Transfer Of Juveniles To Criminal Court: Does It Make A Difference? *Crime & Delinquency* 42:171-191, 1996. Comparing a sample of juvenile offenders transferred to criminal court with a matched sample of delinquents who were retained in the juvenile system, this research focused on recidivism rates--of reoffending, seriousness of reoffending, and lapsed time to reoffending.

2891 Black, T. Edwin; Smith, Charles P. & American Justice Institute & National Institute for Juvenile Justice and Delinquency Prevention *A Preliminary National Assessment Of The Numbers And Characteristics of Juveniles Processed In The Juvenile Justice System*. Washington, D.C.: US Government Printing Office, 1980. This volume provides detailed statistics on the numbers and characteristics of youths processed as offenders during 1977. 195p.

2892 Blackmore, John; Brown, Marci & Krisberg, Barry *Juvenile Justice Reform: The Bellwether States*. Ann Arbor, Michigan: University of Michigan, 1988. Profiles of 5 reform efforts in Pennsylvania, Oklahoma, Louisiana, Colorado and Oregon suggest an emerging political and organizational perspective on juvenile justice reform reflecting a move away from the traditional, large-scale training schools in very different locales to diverse organizational and programmatic methods. 23p.

2893 Block, Kathleen J. & Hale, Donna C. Turf Wars In Progressive Era Juvenile Justice: The Relationship Of Private And Public Child Care Agencies, *Crime & Delinquency* 37:225-241, 1991. This paper on the history of two 19th-century child-saving agencies focuses on the organizational contexts, their inter-organizational relations, and their impact on juvenile courts.

2894 Blomberg, Thomas G. Diversion's Disparate Results And Unresolved Questions: An Integrative Evaluation Perspective, *Journal Of Research On Crime And Delinquency* 20:24-38, 1983. This article discusses diversion of juvenile offenders to various community-based alternatives, their disparate results and related issues.

2895 Boerman, Thomas Ecological Assessment: Establishing Ecological Validity In Gang Intervention Strategies – A Call For Ecologically

Sensitive Assessment of Gang Affected Youths, *Journal Of Gang Research* 8:35-48, 2001. The author discusses 40 years of failed American policy and strategies in dealing with gangs.

2896 Boggs, Keith & National Office For Social Responsibility *Diversion Of Youth From The Juvenile Justice System: Project Orientation Training Manual.* Washington, D.C.: US Juvenile Justice and Delinquency Prevention Office, 1981. This manual on designing juvenile diversion staff orientation training programs, also has a sample agenda for a two-day orientation conference. 37p.

2897 Boisvert, Maurice J. & Wells, Robert Toward A Rational Policy On Status Offenders, *Social Work* 25:230-234, 1980. The author analyzes data from a Massachusetts juvenile court and recommends decriminalizing status offenses to remove the stigma, that helps to create the severe problems faced by these youths.

2898 Bond-Maupin, Lisa; Lujan, Carol Chicago & Bortner, M. A. Jailing Of American Indian Adolescents: The Legacy Of Cultural Domination And Imposed Law, *Crime Law And Social Change* 23:1-16, 1995. Pre-trial detention of native American, female, adolescents is the subject of this research based on case histories.

2899 Bond-Maupin, Lisa J. & Maupin, James R. Juvenile Justice Decision Making In A rural Hispanic Community, *Journal Of Criminal Justice* 26:373-384, 1998. Two rural counties in New Mexico were monitored to observe juvenile justice processing in rural areas of the country.

2900 Bowe, Jess J. & Suarr, Richard The Nature Of Programs Used In Response To Delinquent Behavior Among Juveniles, *International Journal Of Comparative And Applied Criminal Justice* 10:147-159, 1986. The American juvenile justice system in its various aspects across the country is discussed by the authors.

2901 Braden, Carole L. *Compulsory School Attendance Laws And The Juvenile Justice System.* Huntsville, Texas: Sam Houston State University Institute of Contemporary Corrections and the Behavioral Sciences, 1978. The author reviews the history and the present status of compulsory school attendance and truancy laws. 30p.

2902 Breed, Allen F. & Krisberg, Barry Juvenile Corrections: Is There A Future? *Corrections Today* 48:14-20, 1986. This article reports on a survey of the history and current context of American juvenile justice, and contens that juvenile corrections evolved without a set of explicit goals or rational and planned responses to such goals.

2903 Brenner, Robert H. (ed.) *Children And Youth In America: A Documentary History. Volume III: 1933-1973.* Cambridge, Massachusetts: Harvard University Press, 1974. This two-part volume discusses the problems of youths in the United States, child labor and youth employment, aid to dependent children and child welfare services, child protection and family planning, juvenile delinquency, health care for children and youths, and education. 2038p.

2904 Bronick, Matthew J. Relieving Subpopulation Pressure, *Federal Prisons Journal* 1:7-21, 1989. This essay provides data on the inmates and various types of facilities, and providers of facilities for both adult and juvenile offenders who have contract with the Federal Bureau of Prisons in the United States.

2905 Brown, Justin H.; Arrigona, Nancy & Chapmond, Thomas *The Prevention And Early Intervention Services Division: An Implementation And Status Review.* Austin, Texas: Texas Criminal Justice Policy Council, 2000. This report describes the administration and management of seventeen statewide early intervention service programs for at-risk youths in Texas.

2906 Brown, Stephen E. The Class-Delinquency Hypothesis And Juvenile Justice System Bias, *Sociological Inquiry* 55:212-223, 1985. The author concludes that social class bias persists in the juvenile justice system.

2907 Brown, Susan M. & Robbins, Michael J. Serving The Special Education Needs Of Students In Correctional Facilities, *Exceptional Children* 45:574-579, 1979. The authors argue that the presence of handicapped juveniles in juvenile correctional institutions warrants special education and support services.

2908 Brownfield, David; Sorenson, Ann Marie & Thompson, Kevin M. Gang Membership, Race, And Social Class: A Test Of The Group Hazard And Master Status Hypotheses, *Deviant Behavior* 22:73-89, 2001. This study found that while being a gang member does not pose a group hazard to being arrested, a youth's master status based on race and social class is associated with arrest risk.

2909 Buckner, John C. & Chesney-Lind, Meda Dramatic Cures For Juvenile Crime: An Evaluation Of A Prisoner-Run Delinquency Prevention Program, *Criminal Justice And Behavior* 10:227-247, 1983. This study found no differences in recidivism between program participants and controls in an inmate-run delinquency prevention program.

2910 Butts, Jeffrey A. Is Juvenile Justice Just Too Slow? *Judicature* 83:16-24, 1999. This critique of trial lprocedures in juvenile courts details the pros and cons of the right of juveniles to a speedy trial.

2911 Butts, Jeffrey A. Necessarily Relative: Is Juvenile Justice Speedy Enough? *Crime & Delinquency* 43:3-23, 1998. Examining case processing in 400 jurisdictions, this study focused on the length of time to reach disposition, and the factors in processing time varaiations.

2912 Caldwell, Laura & Altschuler, David M. Adolescents Leaving Gangs: An Analysis Of Risk And Protective Factors, Resiliency And Desistance In A Developmental Context, *Journal Of Gang Research* 8:21-34, 2001. In an attempt to understand what impels gang members to depart the gang, the author reviews literature on protective factors and successful intervention strategies.

2913 Campbell, Mary Ann & Schmidt, Fred Comparison Of Mental Health And Legal Factors In The Disposition Outcome Of Young Offenders, *Criminal Justice And Behavior* 27:688-715, 2000. This study of court-ordered mental health reports and legal factors in determining dispositions of young offenders found that poor quality home conditions and severity of substance abuse significantly correlated with custody over probation, and that the legal factors predicted probation length, while mental health factors had a small effect via behavior problems.

2914 Carlson, Nancy D. Jailing Juveniles: Impact On Constitutional Rights, *New England Journal On Criminal & Civil Confinement* 13:45-67, 1987. The author argues that jailing of young offenders is cruel and unusual punishment.

2915 Carter, Robert M. The United States, pp 17-38 in Klein Malcolm W. (ed.) *Western Systems of Juvenile Justice*. Beverly Hill, California: Sage, 1984. This chapter describes the systems of criminal justice found in the various American states.

2916 Carter, Robert M. & Klein, Malcolm W. (eds.) *Back On The Street: The Diversion Of Juvenile Offenders*. Englewood Cliffs, New Jersey: Prentice-Hall, 1976. Readings in this anthology focus on diversion programs as alternative ways of dealing with youthful offenders in order to minimize their penetration into the criminal justice system. 368p.

2917 Carter, Timothy & Clelland, Donald A Neo-Marxian Critique, Formulation And Test Of Juvenile Dispositions As A Function Of Social Class, *Social Problems* 27:96-108, 1979. When multivariate analysis of the juvenile court records of juveniles was used to establish the validity of a Marxist model of class structure in capitalist societies, the findings supported the hypotheses that juvenile court dispositions are class-biased.

2918 Carter, Timothy J. Juvenile Court Dispositions: A Comparison Of Status And Nonstatus Offenders, *Criminology* 17:341-359, 1979. Based on data from court records of juveniles in a metropolitan area of the southeastern United States, this study on the criteria used by juvenile courts in disposition decisions found that poor youths with troubles are at a distinct disadvantage.

2919 Center For Legislative Improvement *Legislative Policymaking in Juvenile Justice: Four Case Studies*. Englewood, Colorado: Center For legislative Improvement, 1976. The subject of this report is the legislative movement in Alabama, Florida, Michigan and New Mexico to pass various youth related statutes covering the juvenile code, in-need of supervision laws and state bureaucracies dealing with children.

2920 Charle, Suzanne The Proliferation Of Project New Pride, *Corrections Magazine* 7:28-34, 1981. Two evaluations of New Pride, a community based delinquency-prevention program show recidivism rates for offenders during their 6-12 months in the program to be between 50 and 55 percent, although they were not compared with a control group.

2921 Chesney-Lind, Meda What About The Girls? Delinquency Programing As If Gender Mattered, *Corrections Today* 63:38-40,44-45, 2001. In a special issue of the journal, the author describes how girls are invisible within juvenile justice programming.

2922 Chesney-Lind, Meda Girls, Gangs And Violence: Anatomy Of A Backlash, *Humanity And Society* 17:321-344, 1993. This essay describes the racist orientations in perceptions of females, gang membership and violence.

2923 Chesney-Lind, Meda Girls In Jails, *Crime & Delinquency* 34:150-168, 1988. In this review, the author argues that female juveniles are more likely to be younger than their male counterparts, incarcerated for status offenses, jailed for misdemeanors, and are often held almost as long as boys and lists the special problems girls in jail face.

2924 Chesney-Lind, Meda Judicial Paternalism And The Female Status Offender: Training Women To Know Their Place, *Crime And Delinquency* 23:121-130, 1977. The author critiques the paternalistic practices of juvenile courts pertaining to female offenders.

2925 Christensen, Dan M. Dollars Versus Delinquency: A Juvenile Justice Policy Evaluation, *Crime Prevention Review* 4:34-38, 1977. This critique of the large amounts of money being spent to halt increasing rates of juvenile crime advocates a proper balance be drawn between dollars and social control, as well as between the forces of social regulation and the individual's autonomy in society.

2926 Chung, Kristina H. Kids Behind Bars: The Legality Of Incarcerating Juveniles In Adult Jails, *Indiana Law Journal* 66:999-1030, 1991. This is a legal analysis of the constitutional, legal and civil wrongs of incarceration of juveniles in adult facilities.

2927 Cicourel, Aaron V. *The Social Organization of Juvenile Justice, Reprinted.* New Brunswick, New Jersey: Transaction, 1995. This reprint of the 1967 classic has eight chapters addressing issues such as theory and method, offense rates, organizational settings, routine practices of law-enforcement agencies, law-enforcement practices, court hearings, and disposition negotiations. 345p.

2928 Clarke, Stevens H. & Koch, Gary G. Juvenile Court: Therapy Or Crime Control, And Do Lawyers Make A Difference?, *Law & Society Review* 14:263-308, 1980. North Carolina juvenile court data are used to examine some major variables associated with juvenile dispositions.

2929 Clement, Priscilla Ferguson The Incorrigible Child: Juvenile Delinquency In The United States From The 17th Through The 19th Centuries, pp 453-490 in Hess, Albert G. & Clement, Priscilla F. (eds.) *History Of Juvenile Delinquency: A Collection Of Essays On Crime Committed By Young Offenders, In History And In Selected Countries, Vol. 2.* Aalen, Germany: Scientia Verlag, 1993. This chapter describes the changes in ideas of childhood and sanctions for offending juveniles during the 17th-19th centuries in America.

2930 Coalition For Juvenile Justice *No Easy Answers: Juvenile Justice In A Climate Of Fear.* Washington, D.C., 1994. This report includes current laws, transfers of juveniles, and alternatives to transfers. 69p.

2931 Colins, Gerald L. *Utilizing Adventure Education To Rehabilitate Juvenile Delinquents.* Denver, Colorado: Outward Bound, 1979. The author describes Outward Bound and similar programs, and feels they provide a viable alternative to traditional training schools. 43p. Appendix.

2932 Commission On Accreditation For Corrections *Manual Of Standards For Juvenile Detention Facilities And Services.* Rockville, Maryland, 1979. This document includes a list of 414 standards in administrative, operational, and programmatic aspects of juvenile detention. 94p.

2933 Commission On Accreditation For Corrections *Manual Of Standards For Juvenile Training Schools And Services.* Rockville, Maryland, 1979. This volume is on standards for juvenile correctional institutions, training schools, camps, ranches, and other facilities holding delinquents. 109p.

2934 Community Research Associates, Inc. *A Comparative Analysis of Juvenile Codes*. Champaign, Illinois: Community Research Associates, Inc., 1987. Laws regarding minors in the 50 States, District of Columbia and the Virgin Islands are the focus of this publication. 117p.

2935 Community Research Center *It's Your Move: The Un-Jailing Of Juveniles In America*. Washington, D.C.: US Juvenile Justice and Delinquency Prevention Office, 1981. The author of this booklet favors alternatives to incarceration, is against the overuse of jail detention for juveniles, and lists ways to eliminating this by monitoring of jails by concerned citizens and promote public education on this issue. 42p.

2936 Community Research Forum *Forum On Deinstitutionalization: Selected Readings On Children In Adult Jails And Lockups*. Washington, D.C.: US Juvenile Justice and Delinquency Prevention Office, 1980. This is a compendium of recent literature and research on children in adult jails, lockups and related topics. 89p.

2937 Conley, Darlene J. Adding Color To A Black And White Picture: Using Qualitative Data To Explain Racial Disproportionality In The Juvenile Justice System, *The Journal Of Research In Crime And Delinquency* 31:135-148, 1994. Using both quantitative and qualitative participant observation data on encounters between police and youths, the author highlights the disproportionate over-representation of minors of color in the American juvenile justice system.

2938 Conrad, J. P. Can Juvenile Justice Survive? *Crime & Delinquency* 25:544-554, 1981. The author argues that once young people are caught and brought to justice, what we do with them within the juvenile justice system is riddled with incompetence, confusion, contradictions and brutality.

2939 Cook, John W. (ed.) Third Annual Juvenile Law Thematic Journal, *Pepperdine Law Review* 6:597-883, 1979. This special issue of the journal has nine articles and two comment articles on diverse aspects of juvenile justice and juvenile law in the United States.

2940 Corvo, Kenneth N. Community-Based Youth Violence Prevention; A Framework For Planners And Funders, *Youth & Society* 28:291-316, 1997. The author provides a summary of various research and literature on youthful violence, and a list to identify and categorize family and microenvironmental factors impacting violence among young people.

2941 Cotton, Martin; Fein, Deborah & Cotton, Shirley Effectiveness Of A Community Based Treatment Program In Modifying Aggressiveness Of Delinquent Behavior, *Corrective And Social Psychiatry And Journal Of Behavior Technology Methods And Therapy* 22:35-38, 1976. This article based on a study of the effect of a community treatment program on the aggressive behavior of a group of juvenile offenders concludes that after treatment, the youths' aggression dropped somewhat.

2942 Council Of State Governments *The Handbook On Interstate Crime Control*. Lexington, Kentucky, 1978. This handbook for officials engaged in interstate crime control includes the interstate compact on juveniles. 160p.

2943 Cox, Stephen M. An Assessment Of An Alternative Education Program For At-Risk Delinquent Youth, *Journal Of Research In Crime And Delinquency* 36:323-336, 1999. Using an experimental design with a one-year follow-up, this study assessed the effectiveness of an alternative education program to change the self-reported delinquency of students, their school related attitudes, and their academic performance.

2944 Cox, Stephen M. & Davidson, William S. A Meta-Analytic Assessment Of Delinquency-Related Outcomes Of Alternative Education Programs, *Crime & Delinquency* 41:219-232, 1995. The authors present a meta-analytic assessment of prior empirical research on alternative education programs for juvenile delinquents.

2945 Craig, Marla C. & Stafford, Mark C. Delinquency And Juvenile Justice In The United States, pp 271-302 in Winterdyk, John A. (ed.) *Juvenile Justice Systems - International Perspective*. Toronto, Canada: Canadian Scholars' Press, 1997. This chapter provides a brief history of, and list of reforms that have occurred in, juvenile justice in the United States, alsong with dicussion of public beliefs about delinquency and juvenile justice, causes and trends in delinquency using some official data and graphs, and unofficial self-report and victimization data.

2946 Cromwell, Paul Quaker Origins Of Juvenile Justice Reform, *Juvenile & Family Court Journal* 38:9-15, 1987. The author traces the history of juvenile justice to the Quaker involvement in penitentiary reform.

2947 Curran, David J. Destructuring, Privatization, And The Promise Of Juvenile Diversion: Compromising Community-Based Corrections, *Crime & Delinquency* 34:363-378, 1988. This article focuses on the American juvenile correctional system and recent developments in it.

2948 Curtis, Russell L. Jr.; Reese II, William A. & Cone-Michael, Patrick Cynicism Among Juvenile Probation Officers: A Study Of Subverted

Ideals, *Journal Of Criminal Justice* 18:501-517, 1990. The perceptions and attitudes of juvenile probation officers are examined in this study.

2949 Dahman, Linda; Snyder, Howard N. & Sullivan, Dennis *Juvenile Court Statistics: 1976-1978*. Pittsburgh, Pennsylvania: National Center for Juvenile Justice, 1980. This report provides data on delinquency and dependency/neglect cases of juvenile court processing during 1976-1978 in the United States. 102p.

2950 Dale, Michael J. & Sanniti, Carl Litigation As An Instrument For Change In Juvenile Detention: A Case Study, *Crime & Delinquency* 39:49-67, 1993. The authors discuss the 1987 class action civil rights lawsuit, G.C. v. Coler et al. challenging the conditions in the Broward County Regional Juvenile Detention Center, Ft. Lauderdale, Florida, its success and general application.

2951 Dannefer, Dale Who Signs The Complaint? Relational Distance And The Juvenile Justice Process, *Law & Society Review* 18:249-271, 1984. Files of juvenile court cases were examined to unravel the relationship between the offender and the complainant in juvenile court cases.

2952 Davis, Bruce L. *Criminological Bibliographies: Uniform Citations To Bibliographies*. Westport, Connecticut: Greenwood, 1978. This volume is a comprehensive compilation of bibliographies, indexes, current serial reference services, and review articles dealing with American criminology and criminal justice administration including juvenile delinquency. 182p.

2953 Dawson, Lynn Admission Criteria For Juvenile Secure Treatment Facilities: Documentation Of The Incidence Of Violent Juvenile Crime; Juvenile Sentencing Structure In The States Of Washington And New York. Austin, Texas: Texas Youth Council, 1980. This is a summary of the incidence of violent crime and the criteria for placing juvenile offenders in various secure facilities in the United States. 5p.

2954 De Li, Spencer Legal Sanctions And Youths' Status Achievement: A Longitudinal Study, *Justice Quarterly* 16:377-401, 1999. In this research on the impact of legal sanctions for delinquency and status achievement, the results suggest that legal sanctions decrease the likelihood of achievement by increasing youths' involvement in delinquent behavior.

2955 DeComo, Robert. E. Estimating The Prevalence Of Juvenile Custody By Race And Gender, *Crime & Delinquency* 44:489-506, 1998. This is an analysis of the prevalence of state custody of juveniles by age, sex and racial subgroups in 36 American states.

2956 Dedel, Kelly National Profile Of The Organization Of State Juvenile Corrections Systems, *Crime & Delinquency* 44:507-525, 1998. In this survey of juvenile corrections in the United States, the author lists juvenile correctional agencies in various states for the year 1995, and describes court structures and juvenile delinquent policies.

2957 Dembo, Richard.; Cervenka, Kathleen A. & Hunter, Brian Engaging High Risk Families In Community Based Intervention Services, *Aggression And Violent Behavior* 4:41-58, 1999. The authors discuss the challenge of service providers in getting high-risk families to participate in community-based intervention in cases involving mental health and substance abuse.

2958 Dembo, Richard (ed.) Substance Use And Juvenile Justice, *Substance Use And Misuse* 33:1435-1567, 1998. Juvenile substance offenses and the juvenile court system are the focus of the five articles in this special issue.

2959 DeMuro, Paul & Krisberg, Barry *Adjudicated Youth In Delaware Who Need Secure Care*. San Francisco, California: National Council on Crime and Delinquency, 1987. These authors examine Delaware's juvenile secure care requirements, and recommend the creation of a comprehensive classification and placement system. 29p.

2960 Deschenes, Elizabeth Piper & Greenwood, Peter W. Alternative Placements For Juvenile Offenders: Results From The Evaluation Of The Nokomis Challenge Program, *Journal Of Research In Crime And Delinquency* 35:267-294, 1998. The authors describe the Nokomis Challenge Program that combined three months of residence and outdoor programs with nine months of intensive community-based aftercare.

2961 DiGiorgio-Miller, Janet Clinical Techniques In The Treatment Of Juvenile Sex Offenders, *Journal Of Offender Rehabilitation* 21:117-126, 1994. The author discusses the various theoretical and practical issues in treating adolescent sex offenders.

2962 Downs, William R. & Robertson, Joan F. Referral For Treatment Among Adolescent Alcohol And Drug Abusers, *Journal Of Research In Crime And Delinquency* 27:190-209, 1990. This research on certain adolescent-status characteristics, and increased likelihood of referral to alcohol and other drug-abuse programs, indicated that when prior involvement in the social delivery system is used in labeling the adolescent, the likelihood of referral increased.

2963 Dunford, Franklyn W.; Osgood, D. Wayne & Weichselbaum, Hart F. *National Evaluation Of Diversion Projects, Executive Summary.*

Washington, D.C.: U. S. National Institute for Juvenile Justice and Delinquency Prevention, 1982. This summary of a national evaluation of the Diversion Initiative of the United States Office of Juvenile Justice and Delinquency Prevention found considerable evidence, that the projects of the initiative succeeded in many of the criteria of true diversion. 17p.

2964 Dussich, John P. J. Juvenile Delinquency: Definitions, Character, and Theory, pp 70-79 in Wegener, Hermann; Lösel, Friedrich & Haisch, Jochen (eds.) *Criminal Behavior And The Justice System: Psychological Perspectives*. New York, New York: Springer-Verlag, 1989. Statutes regarding juveniles including age of criminal responsibility in various states, youth crime rates, the major theoretical approaches and interpretations of criminal behavior are the focus of this chapter.

2965 Elrod, H. Preston & Minor, Kevin I. Second Wave Evaluation Of A Multi-Faceted Intervention For Juvenile Court Probationers, *International Journal Of Offender Therapy And Comparative Criminology* 36:247-262, 1992. The results of a two-year follow-up evaluation of a probation treatment program are presented by the authors.

2966 Empey, LaMar T. (ed.) *The Future Of Childhood And Juvenile Justice*. Charlottesville, Virginia: University Press of Virginia, 1979. This anthology covers the historic developments and changes in the legal status of children, various issues of children's rights, the children's rights movement, and the evolving jurisprudence regarding adolescence and the question of children's liberation. 422p.

2967 Epstein, Sam & Epstein, Beryl *Kids In Court: The ACLU Defends Their Rights*. New York, New York: Four Winds Press, 1982. Chapter 2 of this book of case histories covers due process rights for minors. 233p.

2968 Ervin, Laurie & Schneider, Anne Explaining The Effects Of Restitution On Offenders: Results From A National Experiment In Juvenile Courts, pp 183-206 in Galaway, Burt & Hudson, Joe (eds.) *Criminal Justice, Restitution, And Reconciliation*. Monsey, New York: Criminal Justice Press, 1990.The authors conclude that restitution reduces juvenile recidivism in that it positively rewarding the young delinquents for the actions they take.

2969 Erwin, Tiffany M. United States v. R. L. C.: The Supreme Court Applies A Band-Aid Where Major Surgery Is Needed, *Criminal Law Bulletin* 29:317-355, 1993. This article reviews the treatment of juvenile offenders under the American Federal criminal law and sentencing guidelines.

2970 Esbensen, Finn-Aage & Osgood, D. Wayne Gang Resistance Education And Training (GREAT): Results From The National Evaluation, *Journal Of Research In Crime And Delinquency* 36:194-225, 1999. This article is on the National Evaluation of the Gang Resistance Education and Training (GREAT) program, a school-based gang prevention program in which uniformed law enforcement officers taught a nine-week curriculum to middle-school students.

2971 Ezell, Mark & Cohen, Lawrence E. Age, Crime, And Crime Control Politics: A Longitudinal Analysis Of Youthful, Serious, Chronic Offenders With Implications For "Three Strikes" Legislation, *Studies On Crime And Crime Prevention* 6:169-199, 1997. This 10-year follow up research of serious and chronic male offenders in California seeks to assess the impact of three-strikes legislation on the behavior of youthful offenders.

2972 Ezell, Mark Juvenile Arbitration: Net Widening And Other Unintended Consequences, *Journal Of Research In Crime And Delinquency* 26:358-377, 1989. The author examines the variables that affect delinquent dispositions in juvenile court and argues that juvenile arbitration is a form of sanction-oriented dispute resolution that results in larger numbers of youth staying in the system longer, and being subject to system requirements and control.

2973 Fader, Jamie J.; Harris, Philip W.; Jones, Peter R. & Poulin, Mary E. Factors Involved In Decisions On Commitment To Delinquency Programs For First-Time Juvenile Offenders, *Justice Quarterly* 18:323-341, 2001. This paper focusing on commitment decisions for first-time offenders, compares the effect of factors traditionally included in such decision-making as well as variables on child and family functioning.

2974 Fagan, Jeffrey & Forst, Martin Risks, Fixers And Zeal: Implementing Experimental Treatments For Violent Juvenile Offenders, *Prison Journal* 76:22-59, 1996. The authors review research on the implementation of the violent-juvenile offender research and development program in the United States.

2975 Fay, Juliette E. *Residential Programs For Court-Involved Youth In Massachusetts.* Boston, Massachusetts: Criminal Justice Committee, 1979. This report on the monitoring requirement of the Juvenile Justice and Delinquency Prevention Act (JJDP) shows that Massachusetts is in compliance with the de-institutionalization and separation mandates of the act. 61p.

2976 Feld, Barry C. Criminalizing The American Juvenile Court, pp 197-280 in Tonry, Michael (ed.) *Crime And Justice: A Review Of Research.*

Chicago, Illinois: University of Chicago Press, 1993. This chapter traces the evolution of the American juvenile courts' shift, from focus on the child's best interests to punishment.

2977 Feld, Barry C. The Transformation Of The Juvenile Court -- Part II: Race And The 'Crack Down' On Youth Crime, *Minnesota Law Review* 84:327-395, 1999. The author reviews the evolution of the juvenile court, from inception to current times, within the socio-political context of the United States.

2978 Feld, Barry A Funny Thing Happened On The Way To The Century, *Punishment And Society* 1:187-214, 1999. A host of deficiencies of the American juvenile courts are addressed in this essay.

2979 Feld, Barry *Bad Kids: Race And The Transformation Of The Juvenile Court*. New York, New York: Oxford University Press, 1999. This is a critical review of American juvenile courts, their notions of childhood, youthful misconduct, and social control.

2980 Feld, Barry C. Juvenile (In)Justice And The Criminal Court Alternative, *Crime & Delinquency* 39:403-424, 1993. The discussion here is on the transformation of the juvenile court from an informal, welfare agency into a scaled down, second-class criminal court.

2981 Feld, Barry C. The Punitive Juvenile Court And The Quality Of Procedural Justice: Disjunctions Between Rhetoric And Reality, *Crime & Delinquency* 36:443-466, 1990. The quality of procedural justice, resulting from relevant recent changes in juvenile courts sentencing policies, is the focus of this discussion.

2982 Ferdinand, Theodore N. History Overtakes The Juvenile Justice System, *Crime & Delinquency* 37:204-224, 1991. The author's solution to the criminalizing of juveniles by the justice system is to establish a state-level department to treat delinquents in the community or small custodial facilities limited to 15-20 beds each.

2983 Ferrell, Jeff Youth, Crime And Cultural Space, *Social Justice* 24:21-38, 1997. The author describes the interlocking mechanisms of youthful deviance and cultural space in dealing with delinquent youths.

2984 Finckenauer, James O. Juvenile Criminals: Punishment Or Reform? pp 253-268 in Hartjen, Clayton A. and Rhine, Edward E. (eds.) *Correctional Theory And Practice*. Chicago: Nelson-Hall, Inc., 1992. This chapter attempts to dispel various myths about juvenile delinquency and juvenile justice.

2985 Finckenauer, James O. & Kochis, Donna S. Causal Theory And The Treatment Of Juvenile Offenders: A Case Study, pp 49-63 in Rieber, Robert W. (ed.) *Advances In Forensic Psychology And Psychiatry, Vol. I.*. Norwood, New Jersey: Ablex Publishing, 1984. In relation to various causal theories, the authors report their findings on offense recidivism rates among violent youths released from a treatment program.

2986 Finckenauer, James O. *Scared Straight! And The Panacea Phenomenon.* Prentice-Hall, Englewood Cliffs, New Jersey, 1982. In this case history of the Juvenile Awareness Program in New Jersey and other programs modeled after it, the author argues that the Scared Straight concept is one of the many "punctured panaceas" seized by criminal justice practitioners in their search for strategies to prevent juvenile crime. 257p.

2987 Fisher, Stanley Z. 'Families With Service Needs:' The Newest Euphemism? *Journal Of Family Law* 18:1-77, 1979; 1980.The author raises the issue of increased court power to intervene in family life under the 'Families with Service Needs' category under the proposals of the US National Advisory Committee on Criminal Justice Standards and Goals.

2988 Fishman, Gideon; Schwartz, Ira M. & Hsieh, Chang-Ming Commitment Of Juveniles To Training Schools, *Children And Youth Services Review* 19:633-650, 1997. Data on state-level juvenile detentions during 1979-1990 were analyzed to examine the commitment trends over the two decades.

2989 Flaherty, Michael G. *An Assessment Of The National Incidence Of Juvenile Suicide In Adult Jails, Lockups, And Juvenile Detention Centers.* Washington, D.C.: US Government Printing Office, 1980. In this study of suicide among juveniles in adult jails, adult lockups, and juvenile detention centers it was found that the rates of suicide among juveniles in the former two are significantly higher than those among juveniles in juvenile detention centers as well as in the general population of the United States. 24p.

2990 Flannery, Daniel J. & Huff, C. Ronald (eds.) *Youth Violence: Prevention, Intervention, And Social Policy.* Washington, D. C.: American Psychiatric Press, 1999. This 21-chapter anthology provides summaries of strategies for the prevention of, and intervention in, youthful violence. 322p.

2991 Flaten, Caren L. Victim-Offender Mediation: Application With Serious Offenses Committed by Juveniles, pp 387-401 in Galaway, Burt & Hudson, Joe (eds.) *Restorative Justice: International Perspective.* Monsey, New York: Criminal Justice Press, 1996. This chapter describes an Anchorage, Alaska mediation program involving serious juvenile offenders that incorporated concepts of reconciliation, accountability, and closure

2992 Forst, Martin; Fagan, Jeffrey & Scott,Vivona T. Youth In Prisons And Training Schools: Perceptions And Consequences Of The Treatment-Custody Dichotomy, *Juvenile & Family Court Journal* 40:1-14, 1989. A survey of juveniles in adult and juvenile institutions was used to assess evaluations of the programs.

2993 Foster, Thomas W. Make-Believe Families: A Response Of Women And Girls To The Deprivation Of Imprisonment, *International Journal Of Criminology And Penology* 3:71-78, 1975. The findings of studies on six institutions for adults and juveniles are summarized in this article.

2994 Frank, Ivan C. *Building Self-Esteem In At-Risk Youth: Peer Group Programs And Individual Success Stories.* Westport, Connecticut: Praeger, 1996. This publication presents a review of programs designed to improve self-esteem among at-risk American youths. 114p.

2995 Frazier, Charles E. & Lee, Soon Rae Reducing Juvenile Detention Rates Or Expanding The Official Control Nets: An Evaluation Of A Legislative Reform Effort, *Crime & Delinquency* 38:204-218, 1992. The authors examine the change in Florida's juvenile detention law designed to reduce overcrowding in its secure detention facilities.

2996 Frazier, Charles E. & Bishop, Donna M. Jailing Juveniles In Florida: The Dynamics Of Compliance With A Sluggish Federal Reform Initiative, *Crime & Delinquency* 36:427-442, 1990. This is a description of the various obstacles to achieving full compliance with the mandates of the Juvenile Justice and Delinquency Prevention Act of 1974.

2997 Friday, Paul C.; Malzahn-Bass, Katherine & Harrington, Donna K. Referral And Selection Criteria In Deferred Prosecution, *British Journal Of Criminology* 21:166-175, 1981. This article is about Citizens Probation Authority decisions on 17-21 year old referees in Kalamazoo, Michigan.

2998 Fritsch, Eric J.; Caeti, Troy J. & Taylor, Robert W. Gang Suppression Through Saturation Patrol, Aggressive Curfew, And Truancy Enforcement: A Quasi-Experimental Test Of The Dallas Anti-Gang Initiative, *Crime & Delinquency* 45:122-139, 1999. Research on a 1996 Dallas Police Department anti-gang initiative found that aggressive curfew and truancy enforcement reduced gang violence, while simple the use of saturation patrol did not have such an impact.

2999 Fritsch, Eric J.; Caeti, Troy J. & Hemmens, Craig Spare The Needle But Not The Punishment: The Incarceration of Waived Youth In Texas Prisons, *Crime & Delinquency* 42:593-609, 1996. The length of sentence and time served by juveniles sentenced to prison in Texas is examined.

3000 Fritsch, Eric & Hemmens, Craig Juvenile Court Waiver In The United States 1979-1995: A Comparison And Analysis Of State Waiver Statutes, *Juvenile And Family Court Journal* 46:17-35, 1995. The authors examine the impact of judicial and legislative acts in the waiver of juveniles to adult courts.

3001 Gabinet-Morgenstern, Sarah The Representation Of Juveniles Before The Court: A Look Into The Past And The Future, *Case Western Reserve Law Review* 31:580-607, 1981. The Supreme Court's Gault opinion on juveniles' right to independent legal representation in quasi-criminal proceedings and its implications are discussed.

3002 Gable, Richard J. & McFall, Patricia What To Do About Serious Delinquency: Do Good? Do Bad? Do Nothing, *Today's Delinquent* 2:7-44, 1983. The authors summarize the various cohort studies, the philosophy of paying for one's crime, transfers of youths to adult courts, and describe various prevention models.

3003 Gable, Richard J. Juvenile Delinquency Research: Truths, Myths And Hope, Today's Delinquent 1:39-55, 1982. This article provides an overview of research on violent offenders, their processing by the juvenile justice system, and its impact.

3004 Gardner, Martin R. Punishment And Juvenile Justice: A Conceptual Framework For Assessing Constitutional Rights Of Youthful Offenders, *Vanderbilt Law Review* 35:791-847, 1982. The author analyzes the issue of therapy versus punishment in the dissenting Gault opinion of the Supreme Court.

3005 Garlock, Peter D. "Wayward" Children And The Law, 1820-1900: The Genesis Of The Status Offense Jurisdiction Of The Juvenile Court, *Georgia Law Review* 13:341-447, 1979. The author traces the history, social context and origins of status offense laws in the United States.

3006 Garofalo, James & McDermott, M. Joan *Anti-Drug Initiatives In Small Cities And Towns: A National Assessment*. Carbondale, Illinois: Center for the Study of Crime, Delinquency and Corrections, Southern Illinois University, 1995. The authors argue in favor of anti-drug policies that focus on schools and youths in schools. 168p.

3007 Garrett, Carol J. Effects Of Residential Treatment On Adjudicated Delinquents: A Meta-Analysis, *Journal Of Research In Crime And Delinquency* 22:287-308, 1985. This study, reviewing abstracts and complete reports that concentrated on evaluations of juvenile treatment, concludes that treatment in institutional or community settings can be effective.

3008 Gavazzi, Stephen M.; Wasserman, Deborah; Partridge, Charles & Sheridan, Sarah The Growing Up FAST Diversion Program: An Example Of Juvenile Justice Program Development For Outcome Evaluation, *Aggression And Violent Behavior* 5:159-175, 2000. The authors describe the theoretical bases of the juvenile diversion program 'FAST,' and the preliminary group of 18 families who participated in the program.

3009 Geiger, Brenda Plato And Rawls On Correctional Rehabilitation Of Juvenile Offenders, *Journal Of Offender Rehabilitation* 23:49-59, 1996. The issues of consent, liberty, and rights of juveniles in any rehabilitation program are addressed using the philosophical perspectives of Plato and Rawls.

3010 Gibbons, Don C. Juvenile Delinquency: Can Social Science Find A Cure? *Crime & Delinquency* 32:186-204, 1986. The implications of American social scientific accomplishments in the study of delinquency is addressed by the author.

3011 Gibbons, Don C. Changing The Lawbreaker: The Treatment Of Delinquents And Criminals. Montclair, New Jersey: Allanheld, Osmun, 1981. The author in his extensive discussion on the problem of changing (juvenile and adult) offenders into law-abiding citizens, argues that doing so requires an understanding of three basic problems: what causes people to violate criminal laws, how to keep them from breaking laws, and how to change the conditions that encourage criminality. 318p.

3012 Gibbons, Don C. & Blake, Gerald F. Evaluating The Impact Of Juvenile Diversion Programs, *Crime & Delinquency* 22:411-420, 1976. Nine studies of the outcomes of specific juvenile diversion programs are reviewed by the authors, who investigated the impact of diversion programs on the juvenile justice system in Los Angeles County.

3013 Gold, Martin & Osgood, D.Wayne *Personality And Peer Influence In Juvenile Corrections*. Westport, Connecticut: Greenwood, 1992. This volume reports on the findings of a field experiment to examine the experiences of delinquent youths assigned to four medium security institutions in Michigan. 230p.

3014 Gold, Martin; Mattlin, Jay & Osgood, D. Wayne Background Characteristics And Responses To Treatment Of Two Types Of Institutionalized Delinquent Boys, *Criminal Justice And Behavior* 16:5-33, 1989. This study explores if distinguishing institutionalized delinquent boys on the basis of their anxiety and depression constitutes a useful typology.

3015 Gottesman, Roberta *The Child And The Law*. St. Paul, Minnesota: West Publishing, 1981. This is a general review of the legal principles, issues and trends in laws concerning minors in general. 223p.

3016 Gottesman, Roberta & Mountz, Lynne *Restitution Legal Analysis*. Reno, Nevada: National Council of juvenile and Family Court Judges, 1979. The legal and practical issues in using 'restitution' as alternative dispositions for juvenile offenders in criminal cases are explored by the authors.

3017 Greater Egypt Regional Planning And Development Commission *Evaluation Report: Menard Correctional Center Juvenile Tours Impact Study*. Carbondale, Illinois, 1979. An evaluation of the effect of a "scared straight" program on post-tour offense behavior among experimental/control groups of juveniles concluded that these tours had little positive impact, and may actually have had negative effects. 123p.

3018 Greene, Michael B. Chronic Exposure To Violence And Poverty: Interventions That Work For Youth, *Crime & Delinquency* 39:106-124, 1993. The author presents statistics on youth in poverty, the frequency and nature of violence to which these youth are exposed to, and the critical elements and philosophical underpinnings of programs that work for those exposed to the powerful stresses of poverty and violence.

3019 Greene, Michael P. *Volunteerism In The Criminal And Juvenile Justice System: The OAR Model And Its Implications For Future Planning*. New York, New York: Criminal Justice Coordinating Council, 1979. This document presents an evaluation of the New York City Offender Aid and Restoration program that used trained volunteers working with young offenders in detention centers and correctional institutions on a one-to-one basis, its clients, recommendations for pre-service volunteer training, feedback sessions, volunteer supervision, and aftercare. 99p. Appendix.

3020 Greenwood, Peter W. & Turner, Susan Private Presentence Reports For Serious Juvenile Offenders: Implementation Issues And Impacts, *Justice Quarterly* 10:229-243, 1993. This study on a private pre-sentence report initiative in California concluded that the project was not a success.

3021 Greenwood, Peter W. Substance Abuse Problems Among High-Risk Youth And Potential Interventions, *Crime & Delinquency* 38:444-458, 1992. The author argues that preventive interventions for adolescents from impoverished urban communities must address an array of problems and service needs, besides getting such youth involved.

3022 Greenwood, Peter W.; Petersilia, Joan & Zimring, Franklin E. *Age, Crime, And Sanctions: The Transition From Juvenile To Adult Court.* Santa Monica, California: Rand, 1980. This study sought to determine the relationship between age and seriousness of crimes, and their impact on criminal sanctions. 89p.

3023 Griffiths, Curt Taylor Community-Based Corrections For Yong Offenders: Proposal For A 'Localized Corrections,' *International Journal Of Comparative And Applied Criminal Justice* 12:219-228, 1988. This critique of community-based corrections offers "localized" corrections as an alternative.

3024 Grisso, Thomas *Forensic Evaluation Of Juveniles.* Sarasota, Florida: Professional Resource Press, 1998. This is a general clinical manual on mental health evaluations of juvenile delinquents. 286p.

3025 Grissom, Grant W. & Dubnov, William L. *Without Locks And Bars: Reforming Our Reform Schools.* New York, New York: Praeger, 1989. The focus of this publication is the Glen Mills, Pennsylvania correctional institution for juveniles which during 1975-1980s engaged in a humane and successful experiment. 240p. Appendix.

3026 Grichting, Wolfgang L. Do Laws Make A Difference? *Journal Of Social Service Research* 2:245-265, 1979. The author argues that juvenile codes summarize rather than guide actual policy, and found no empirical evidence of differential effect of the legal climate of juvenile statutory laws on adjudication and dispositions involving 15-17 year olds.

3027 Grichting, Wolfgang On The State And Fate Of Status Offenders, *Australian & New Zealand Journal Of Criminology* 10:133-151, 1977. What happens to status offenders brought before court authorities is determined by socio-demographic variables more than any other factors, says the author of this study.

3028 Guarino-Ghezzi, Susan & Carr, Bryan Juvenile Offenders Vs The Police: A Community Dilemma, *Caribbean Journal Of Criminology And Social Psychology* 1:24-43, 1996. This study of anti-police attitudes of chronic, urban juvenile offenders discusses the implications for reforming the police role vis-à-vis juveniles.

3029 Guarino-Ghezzi, Susan Reintegrative Police Surveillance Of Juvenile Offenders: Forging An Urban Model, *Crime & Delinquency* 40:131-153, 1994. The focus of this piece is the patterns of police behavior, and a model for police procedures in incidents, involving juvenile offenders that the author calls reintegrative surveillance based on Braithewaite's theory of reintegrative shaming.

3030 Hagan, Michael & King, Robert P. Recidivism Rates Of Youth Completing An Intensive Treatment Program In A Juvenile Correctional Facility, *International Journal Of Offender Therapy And Comparative Criminology* 36:349-358, 1992. This study was a two-year follow-up of recidivism among 55 young graduates of a treatment program.

3031 Halliday, C. A. & Graham, S. "If I Get Locked Up, I Get Locked Up": Secondary Control And Adjustment Among Juvenile Offenders, *Personality And Social Psychology Bulletin* 26:548-559, 2001. This study of the relationship between types of control and the psychological, and community, adjustment of adolescent offenders suggests that secondary control beliefs may be maladaptive, particularly when perceived primary control is high among adolescent offenders.

3032 Hamm, Mark S. Legislator Ideology And Capital Punishment: The Special Case For Indiana Juveniles, *Justice Quarterly* 6:219-232, 1989. This survey of 74 Indiana legislators found that political party affiliation and interest in prisons have impact on their support for the death penalty for juvenile murderers,with about half approving it.

3033 Hanley, Kenneth T. Fourth Amendment Protection For The Juvenile Offender: State, Parent And The Best Interests Of The Child, *Fordham Law Review* 49:1140-1160, 1981. The author discusses the Fourth Amendment issues of privacy and unreasonable intrusions by the government in criminal cases involving minors, restricting parents' rights and protecting the interests of the state.

3034 Harbage, Paula A. Juvenile Transfer In Illinois, *Journal Of Criminal Law And Criminology* 67:287-309, 1976. This critique of the Illinois juvenile transfer statute argues that it has not gone far enough in assuring an adequate level of procedural protection to juveniles while according virtually unchecked discretion to the juvenile court judge.

3035 Harrington, Maxine M. & O'Leary, Ann R. The Insanity Defense In Juvenile Delinquency Proceedings, *Bulletin Of The American Academy Of Psychiatry And The Law* 8:272-279, 1980. This is a legal and clinical defense for protecting the children who are not responsible for their criminal acts due to mental illness.

3036 Harris, Philip W. & Jones, Peter R. Differentiating Delinquent Youths For Program Planning And Evaluation, *Criminal Justice And Behavior* 26:403-434, 1999. This study supports the developing of treatment typologies in the rehabilitation of adjudicated delinquents.

3037 Harrison, Paige; Maupin, James R. & Mays, G. Larry Teen Court: An Examination Of Processes And Outcomes, *Crime &* Delinquency 47:243-264, 2001. This examination of Doña Ana County, New Mexico teen court processing found a 25% recidivism rate that varied by gender, age, the presence of a prior referral, whether the youngster completed the teen court program or not, the person with whom the juvenile resided, and by the severity of the jury sentence.

3038 Hatchett, Glenda Why We Can't Wait: The Juvenile Court In The New Millennium, *Crime & Delinquency* 44:83-88, 1998. The author criticizes the preoccupation with punitiveness, and the inadequate commitment to systematic intervention and prevention, in the American juvenile justice system.

3039 Hawkins, J. David & Fraser, Mark W. Theory And Practice In Delinquency Prevention, *Social Work Research And Abstracts* 17:3-13, 1981. In trying to identify and assess the effects of the theoretical perspectives of administrators of programs for the prevention of juvenile delinquency on the policies of their programs, this study found the evidence to be mixed.

3040 Hemmens, Craig & Bennett, Katherine Juvenile Curfews And The Courts: Judicial Response To A Not-So-New Crime Control Strategy, *Crime & Delinquency* 45:99-121, 1999. Given the lack of Supreme Court guidance on the issue, this article examines the lower court decisions, the constitutionality, and implications, of juvenile curfew laws as measures to curb juvenile crime.

3041 Henggler, Scott W.; Cunningham, Phillippe B.; Pickrel, Susan G.; Schoenwald, Sonja K. & Brondino, Michael J. Multisystemic Therapy: An Effective Violence Prevention Approach For Serious Juvenile Offenders, *Journal Of Adolescence* 19:47-61, 1996. The authors discuss the theoretical framework and findings of two studies on juvenile delinquents in the United States.

3042 Higgins, Thomas The Crime Costs Of California Early Minor Offenders: Implications For Prevention, *Journal Of Research In Crime And Delinquency* 14:195-205, 1977. The author explores costs of delinquency prevention programs, their implications for prevention efforts, and the ineffectiveness of prevention efforts, and recommends that only small, carefully evaluated, programs be supported.

3043 Hill, Christopher M. Can The Death Penalty Be Imposed On Juveniles: The Unanswered Question In Eddington V. Oklahoma, *Criminal Law Bulletin* 20:5-33, 1984. The author discusses death penalty for juveniles, with particular reference to the Supreme Court decision regarding it by an Oklahoma case.

3044 Hindelang, Michael J. With A Little Help From Their Friends: Group Participation In Reported Delinquent Behavior, *British Journal Of Criminology* 16:109-125, 1976. In this report on a survey of sheriffs' deputies on what their actions will be in case of juvenile misdemeanor, it was found most decide not to arrest juveniles for minor infractions, and those youths who do get picked up by the police tend to participate in illegal group behavior.

3045 Hirschi, Travis & Gottfredson, Michael Rethinking The Juvenile Justice System, *Crime & Delinquency* 39:262-271, 1993. This essay assesses the desirability of a separate juvenile justice system, and argues that special treatment of juveniles is based on an erroneous image of the developmental sequences that misrepresents differences between juvenile and adult crime.

3046 Hodgkinson, Peter; Bedau, Hugo Adam; Radelet, Michael; Durnall, Gaynor & Massey, Kim *Capital Punishment In The United States Of America: A Review Of The Issues*. London, United Kingdom: Parliamentary Human Rights Group, 1996. This review of capital punishment in the United States addresses the issue of death penalty for juvenile offenders. 84p.

3047 Hoge, Robert D.; Andrews, D. A. & Leschied, Alan W. Investigation Of Variables Associated With Probation And Custody Dispositions In A Sample Of Juveniles, *Journal Of Clinical Child Psychology* 24:279-286, 1995. The dispositions for boys and girls in an American urban juvenile court system hinged on the seriousness of their current offense and their history of incarceration.

3048 Horn, Margo *Before It's Too Late: The Child Guidance Movement In The United States, 1922-1945*. Philadelphia, Pennsylvania: Temple University Press, 1989. This book discusses the child saving movements from the turn of the century up to World War II. 224p.

3049 Horowitz, Ruth & Pottieger, Anne E. Gender Bias In Juvenile Justice Handling Of Seriously Crime-Involved Youths, *Journal Of Research In Crime And Delinquency* 28:75-100, 1991. This research reveals a number of differences in the outcomes of juvenile justice cases for males and females, and dicusesses reasons for these differences for specific offenses.

3050 Houghtalin, M. & Mays, G. L. Criminal Dispositions Of New Mexico Juveniles Transferred To Adult Court, *Crime & Delinquency* 37:393-407, 1991. This is an investigation of the characteristics of juveniles subject to the waiver process, and the criminal court dispositions of juveniles tried as adults in New Mexico.

3051 Houlgate, Laurence D. *The Child & the State: A Normative Theory Of Juvenile Rights*. Baltimore, Maryland: Johns Hopkins University Press, 1980. The application of the two moral principles--utility and just distribution--in various issues involving court cases of minors and their right to liberty in juvenile adjudication process are discussed.

3052 Howard, Kim Ammann; Flora, June & Griffin, Marie Violence-Prevention Programs In Schools: State Of The Science And Implications For Future Research, *Applied & Preventive Psychology* 8:197-215, 1999. This article reviews studies on the prevention of, and intervention in, school violence.

3053 Howell, J. C. Youth Gang Homicides: A Literature Review, *Crime & Delinquency,* 45:208-241, 1999. This is a review of the data and results of empirical studies on homicides involving youth gangs.

3054 Howell, James C. & Krisberg, Barry (eds.) Juveniles In Custody, *Crime And Delinquency* 44:483-601, 1998. This special issue of the journal focuses on the movement of juveniles through the correctional systems of various states in the United States.

3055 Howell, James C. NCCD's Survey Of Juvenile Detention And Correc-tional Facilities, *Crime & Delinquency* 44:102-109, 1998. The findings of a survey of juvenile detention and correctional facilities in the United States are reported in this article.

3056 Howell, James C.; Krisberg, Barry; Hawkins, J. David & Wilson, John J. (eds.) *A Sourcebook: Serious, Violent, & Chronic Juvenile Offenders*. Thousand Oaks, California: Sage, 1995. This sourcebook includes articles advocating a more balanced, humane and effective response to serious, violent and chronic delinquency. 296p.

3057 Hubbard, Robert D. & Horton, David M. *Rural Crime And Criminal Justice: A Selected Bibliography*. Washington, D. C: US National Criminal Justice Reference Service, 1981. Included in the 140 citations in this collection are references on rural juvenile justice and delinquency prevention. 57p.

3058 Hudson, Barbara *Justice Through Punishment: A Critique of the 'Justice' Model of Corrections*. New York, New York: St. Martin's Press, 1987. The author explains the justice model in detail, and goes on to elaborate its negative impact on juveniles, blacks, women and minorities in general 184p.

3059 Hudson, Joe & Galaway, Burt (eds.) *Victims, Offenders, And Alternative Sanctions*. Lexington, Massachusetts: Lexington Books, 1980. Two chapters in this anthology deal with the juvenile restitution initiative of the United States Office of Juvenile Justice and Delinquency Prevention identifying issues in implementation. 204p.

3060 Human Rights Watch *No Minor Matter: Children In Maryland's Jails*. New York, New York, 1999. This report concludes that there are disproportionately large numbers of African American youths in Maryland's jails. 169p.

3061 Human Rights Watch *High Country Lockup: Children In Confinement In Colorado*. New York, New York, 1997. Conditions of juveniles in Colorado detention and correctional facilities are the focus of this critical report.

3062 Hurst, Hunter Issues For Resolution In The Eighties: Family Courts And Retribution, *Today's Delinquent* 1:57-68, 1982. This article discusses various alternatives such as due process, retribution, and sentencing in justice system for juveniles.

3063 Hutzler, John L. Canon To The Left, Canon To The Right: Can The Juvenile Court Survive? *Today's Delinquent* 1:25-38, 1982. The dilemma of the juvenile court caught between 'procedural reform' and 'law & order' legislation is the focus of this discussion.

3064 Hutzler, John L. *Statutory Exclusion Of Crimes From Juvenile Court Jurisdiction: 1980 Statutes Analysis*. Pittsburgh, Pennsylvania: National Center for Juvenile Justice, 1980. This compilation provides an analysis and tabulation of juvenile crimes excluded from the jurisdiction of juvenile courts under the statutes of various states. 6p.

3065 Isaacson, Michael D. *A Citizen's Guide To The Juvenile Justice System*. Bay Shore, New York: Suffolk County Conference on Juvenile and Criminal Justice, Inc., 1979. This practitioner and citizen manual on the operations of the juvenile justice system in Suffolk County, New York includes some historical material on the development of juvenile justice in the United States. 42p.

3066 Ito, Jeanne A.; Hendryx, Janice & Stapleton, Vaughan Inside Metropolitan Juvenile Courts: How Their Structure Affects The Outcome Of Cases, *State Court Journal* 6:16-20 & 34-36, 1982. American juvenile courts were surveyed to see if dispositions are affected by the type of court.

3067 Jackson, Patrick C. Some Effects Of Parole Supervision On Recidivism, *British Journal Of Criminology* 23:17-34, 1983. In this study of youths in California, the author found no difference in arrests or time of offense and convictions, but in the nature and severity of the various offenses committed by those discharged and those retained for parole supervision.

3068 Jacobs, Mark D. Juvenile Justice In The No-Fault Society, pp 235-256 in Hackler, Jim (ed.) *Official Responses To Problem Juveniles: Some International Reflections*. Euskadi, Spain: The Oñati International Institute for the Sociology of Law, 1991. The author argues that the practice and ideology of juvenile justice in the United States are conditioned by issues of social control, and an overly individualistic conception of social life, the inability to distinguish between private and public spheres of action, and laxity in the rule of law.

3069 Jacobs, Mark D. *Screwing The System And Making It Work*. Chicago, Illinois: University of Chicago Press, 1990. Based on participant observations and interviews, the author comes to the conclusion that probation officers were a positive force in that they created informal and personal solutions in juvenile court cases in a Midwestern suburb. 284p.

3070 James, Kathleen L. & James, David Coed Residential Milieu, *Child Care Quarterly*, 9:32-40, 1980. A survey of inmates three months after the commencement of a coed treatment program in a minimum-security juvenile correctional facility began, showed that coed living was manageable, productive, delinquent boys and girls behaved better when they lived in the same cottage, and that sexual promiscuity and homosexual behavior decreased with behavioral treatment.

3071 Jellinek, Michael S.; Little, Michelle; Benedict, Kenneth; Murphy, Michael J.; Pagano, Maria; Poitrast, Francis & Quinn, Dorothy Placement Outcomes Of 206 Severely Maltreated Children In The Boston Juvenile Court System: A 7.5-Year Follow-Up Study, *Child Abuse And Neglect* 19:1051-1064, 1995. Among 206 severely maltreated children permanently under Boston Juvenile Court on Care and Protection Petitions , the rate of court referral for incidences of re-abuse or delinquency was significantly lower.

3072 Jensen, Eric L. & Metsger, Linda K. A Test Of The Deterrent Effect Of Legislative Waiver On Violent Juvenile Crime, *Crime & Delinquency* 40:96-104, 1994. This is an evaluation of the deterrent effect of the 1981 Idaho legislative waiver statute on juvenile crime.

3073 Jenson, Jeffrey M.; Potter, Cathryn C. & Howard, Matthew O. American Juvenile Justice: Recent Trends And Issues In Youth Offending, *Social Policy And Administration* 35:48-68, 2001. The trends in juvenile offending in the United States since the 1970s, its policy implications, and a variety of issues confronting the American juvenile justice system are identified by the author of this article.

3074 Jerry, Franklin & Gibbons, Don C. New Directions For Juvenile Courts. Probation Officers' Views, *Crime And Delinquency* 19:508-517, 1973. The Pacific Northwest metropolitan juvenile court counselors' attitudes regarding Supreme Court assertions of due process rights of minors were gauged by the authors.

3075 Jones, Clergue T. & Kravitz, Marjorie *Variations On Juvenile Probation: A Selected Bibliography.* Washington, D.C.: US National Criminal Justice Reference Service, 1980. This bibliography contains over 125 documents on trends in program administration and approaches to case handling in the American juvenile probation system, and adult programs that apply to juveniles. 50p.

3076 Jones, Michael A. & Krisberg, Barry *Images And Reality: Juvenile Crime, Youth Violence And Public Policy.* San Francisco, California: National Council on Crime and Delinquency, 1994. This report summarizes juvenile crime trends, and their implications for American public policy and the juvenile justice system response. 46p.

3077 Jones-Brown, Delores D. & Henriques, Zelma Weston Promise And Pitfalls Of Mentoring As A Juvenile Justice Strategy, *Social Justice* 24:212-233, 1997. This study compares various mentoring and bootcamp, waiver, and diverse punitive programs used in juvenile corrections.

3078 Jonson-Reid, Melissa & Barth, Richard P. From Maltreatment Report To Juvenile Incarceration: The Role Of Child Welfare Services, *Child Abuse And Neglect* 24:505-520, 2000. This study investigated whether children who received child welfare services were more or less likely to become incarcerated as serious, violent, youthful offenders, compared to children who were investigated as victims of abuse and neglect but received no further child welfare intervention.

3079 Josi, Don A. & Sechrest, Dale K. A Pragmatic Approach To Parole Aftercare: Evaluation Of A Community Reintegration Program For High-Risk Youthful Offenders, *Justice Quarterly* 16:51-80, 1999. This evaluation of the success of a parole reentry program, "Lifeskills '95," for individuals released from secure facilities concludes that the program was successful in reducing recidivism rates during the program participation period.

3080 Kara, Suman Delinquency Prevention Through Family And Neighborhood Empowerment, *Studies In Crime And Crime Prevention* 7:107-125, 1998. Alternative sanctions for juveniles is the subject of this article.

3081 Katz, Susan Roberta Presumed Guilty: How Schools Criminalize Latino Youth, *Social Justice* 24:77-95, 1997. The labeling, racism, and prejudice that was experienced by San Francisco youths of different Latin-American origins is the subject of this article on institutional racism.

3082 Kennedy, David M.; Braga, Anthony A. & Piehl, Anne The (Un)Known Universe: Mapping Gangs And Gang Violence In Boston, pp 219-262 in Weisburd, David and McEwen, Tom (eds.) *Crime Mapping And Crime Prevention*. Monsey, New York: Criminal justice Press, 1997. The question of using local police and others who are routinely in contact with juvenile gangs in mapping gangs and gang activity is addressed by the author.

3083 Kennedy, David M.; Piehl, Anne M. & Braga, Anthony A. *Youth Gun Violence In Boston: Gun Markets, Serious Youth Offenders, And A Use Reduction Strategy*. Boston, Massachusetts: John F. Kennedy School of Government, Harvard University, 1996. This document reports the results of an effort to deal with the problem of youth violence in Boston. 111p.

3084 Kennedy, Dennis Jay; Pate, Anthony Michael & Hamilton, Edwin *Police Handling Of Juveniles: Developing Model Programs Of Response*. Washington, D.C.: Police Foundation, 1990. This review covers various issues such as serious juvenile offenders, police versus juveniles, and models for handling juvenile offenders. 193p.

3085 Kiersh, Edward Minnesota Cracks Down On Chronic Juvenile Offenders, *Corrections Magazine* 7:1-28, 1981. The author discusses the impact of Minnesota legislative "crack down" by treating chronic juvenile offenders as adults and sending more of them to adult prisons.

3086 Kihm, Robert C. Prohibiting Secure Juvenile Detention: Assessing The Effectiveness Of National Standards Detention Criteria, *Juvenile And*

Family Court Journal 31:3-17, 1980. Two jurisdictions, based on their adherence to proposed detention criteria, when compared for any significant differences in the number of arrests or failures to appear for court hearings, indicate that such criteria reduce detention rates without negative consequences.

3087 King, Jane L. *A Comparative Analysis Of Juvenile Codes*. Washington D.C.: US Government Printing Office, 1980. This is a review of the structure of the juvenile courts, laws concerning juveniles such as waiver to adult court, maximum age for juvenile court jurisdiction, custody process, and inspection of juvenile facilities in various American states. 90p.

3088 Kipke, Michele D.; Palmer, Raymond F.; LaFrance, Steven & O'Connor, Susan Homeless Youths ' Descriptions Of Their Parents' Child-Rearing Practices, *Youth & Society* 28:415-431, 1997. This is a self-report study of 12-23 year old street youths in California on rules at home and parenting styles that are intrusive, supportive, or parental supervision is unavailable.

3089 Klein, Malcolm American Juvenile Justice: Method And Madness, *European Journal Of Criminal Policy And Research* 2:24-41, 1994. The contradictions, inconsistencies, and chaotic behavior of American juvenile justice is described in this article.

3090 Klein, Malcolm W. Attempting Gang Control By Suppression: The Misuse Of Defense Principles, *Studies In Crime & Crime Prevention* 2:88-111, 1993. The author discusses the American approach to controlling gangs, its bases, and implications.

3091 Klein, Malcolm W. A Judicious Slap On The Wrist: Thoughts On Early Sanctions For Juvenile Offenders, pp 376-393 in Martin, Susan E.; Sechrest, Lee B. & National Research Council Panel On Research On Rehabilitative Techniques (eds.) *New Directions In The Rehabilitation Of Criminal Offenders*. Washington D.C.: National Academy Press, 1981. This chapter discusses the merits of using early sanctions to deter future delinquency.

3092 Klein, Malcolm W. Deinstitutionalization And Diversion Of Juvenile Offenders: A Litany Of Impediments, pp 145-201 in Morris, Norval & Tonry, Michael (eds.) *Crime And Justice: An Annual Review Of Research, Vol. 1*. Chicago, Illinois: University of Chicago Press, 1979. In discussing the degree of "program integrity" or compatibility of social programs with their underlying ideas in current diversion and deinstitutionalization programs, the author also feels that the programs have not been effectively implemented.

3093 Klein, Malcolm W. (ed.) *The Juvenile Justice System*. Beverly Hills, California: Sage, 1976. The articles in this volume discuss the present and future status of delinquency prevention, the historical context of adolescence, alternative indices of delinquency, interaction between community structure, delinquency, and social policy in the inner city, police diversion programs, juvenile corrections, police views of the juvenile justice system, and the possibility of the return of the juvenile court as a criminal court. 287p.

3094 Kobrin, Solomon & Klein, Malcolm W. *National Evaluation Of The Deinstitutionalization Of Status Offender Programs: Executive Summary. Review Draft*. Los Angeles, California: University of Southern California. Social Science Research Institute, 1980. An evaluation of eight national programs de-institutionalizing status offenders concludes that the programs provided services for 16,000 youths during the two-years of Federal support, the extent of implementation varied and many of those served were the ones neither the funding nor the legislation intended. 52p.

3095 Kowalski, Gregory S. & Rickicki, John P. Determinants Of Juvenile Postadjudication Dispositions, *Journal Of Research In Crime And Delinquency* 19:66-83, 1982. When decisions on placement in either a group home or an institutional setting was examined, it was found that race influenced the treatment of the adolescent in the juvenile justice system early in the process.

3096 Kratcoski, Peter & Kratcoski, Lucille The Impact Of Social Change On Juvenile Justice Policy In The United States, pp 189-204 in Hackler, Jim (ed.) *Official Responses To Problem Juveniles: Some International Reflections*. Euskadi, Spain: The Oñati International Institute for the Sociology of Law, 1991. This chapter is a discussion of the various changes in American juvenile courts and their short and long-term consequences.

3097 Krisberg, Barry *The Impact Of The Justice System On Serious, Violent, And Chronic Juvenile Offenders*. San Francisco, California: National Council on Crime and Delinquency, 1997. This is a policy statement on the responses of the American juvenile justice system to serious, violent and chronic juvenile offenders. 32p.

3098 Krisberg, Barry; DeComo, Robert & Rudenstine, Sonya & Del Rosario, Dominic *Juveniles Taken Into Custody Research Program: FY 1994 Annual Report*. San Francisco, California: National Council on Crime and Delinquency, 1995. In this report, the authors present information on

American youths in custody during 1993. 74p. Appendix.

3099 Krisberg, Barry; Neuenfeldt, Deborah & Wiebush, Richard & Rodriguez, Orlando *Juvenile Intensive Supervision: Planning Guide*. Washington, D.C.: US Office of Juvenile Justice and Delinquency Prevention, 1994. This manual details post-adjudication non-residential intensive supervision programs in the United States. 80p.

3100 Krisberg, Barry; Rodriguez, Orlando & Bakke, Audrey *Juvenile Intensive Supervision: An Assessment*. Washington, D.C.: US Office of Juvenile Justice and Delinquency Prevention, 1994. This review describes juvenile intensive supervision programs in the United States. 89p.

3101 Krisberg, Barry; Onek, David; Jones, Michael & Schwartz, Ira *Juveniles In State Custody: Prospects For Community-Based Care Of Troubled Adolescents*. San Francisco, California: National Council on Crime and Delinquency, 1993. This policy oriented analysis examined the number of juveniles in various custodial training schools in 14 American states. 7p.

3102 Krisberg, Barry & DeComo, Robert *Juveniles Taken Into Custody: Fiscal Year 1991 Report*. Washington, D.C.: Office of Juvenile Justice and Delinquency Prevention, 1993. This report contains national data on juveniles under confinement. 88p.

3103 Krisberg, Barry (ed.) Reinventing Juvenile Justice: Research Directions, *Crime & Delinquency* 39: 3-124, 1993. This special issue of the journal includes six articles on juvenile justice in the United States dealing with public opinion, racial disparity, detention, intensive supervision, risk classification and intervention programs.

3104 Krisberg, Barry; Baird, Christopher & Quigley, Peter *A Classification And Placement System For Indiana Juvenile Corrections*. San Francisco, California: National Council on Crime and Delinquency, 1993. The authors review the development of a structured decision making system for Indiana Juvenile Corrections. 31p. Appendix.

3105 Krisberg, Barry; DeComo, Robert & Herrera, Norma C. *National Juvenile Custody Trends 1978-1989*. San Francisco, California: National Council on Crime and Delinquency, 1992. This essay explores how the the gap emerged between theory and reality in the practice of juvenile justice in the United States. 42p.

3106 Krisberg, Barry *Juvenile Justice: Improving The Quality Of Care*. San Francisco, California: National Council on Crime and Delinquency, 1992. The author provides a critical review of the theory and practice of juvenile justice in the United States. 59p.

3107 Krisberg, Barry; Freed, Peter & Jones, Michael *Louisiana Juvenile Justice At The Crossroads*. San Francisco, California: National Council on Crime and Delinquency, 1991. The authors use a criminal justice population simulation model, and risk assessment technology, to analyze the need for expansion of the juvenile corrections system in the State of Louisiana. 7p.

3108 Krisberg, Barry; Austin, James & Steele, Patricia A. *Unlocking Juvenile Corrections: Evaluating The Massachusetts Department Of Youth Services*. San Francisco, California: National Council on Crime and Delinquency, 1989. This document provides detailed information on the deinstitutionalization movement in Massachusetts, and provides suggestions on how to respond to serious, violent and chronic juvenile offenders. 170p. Appendix.

3109 Krisberg, Barry; Rodriguez, Orlando; Bakke, Audrey; Neuenfeldt, Deborah & Steele, Patricia *Demonstration Of Post-Adjudication Non-Residential Intensive Supervision Programs: Assessment Report*. San Francisco, California: National Council on Crime and Delinquency, 1989. The authors identify and assess various nonresidential post-adjudication programs for the intensive supervision of American juvenile offenders. 235p.

3110 Krisberg, Barry; Bakke, Audrey & Neuenfeldt, Deborah *Demonstration Of Post-Adjudication Non-Residential Intensive Supervision Programs: Selected Program Summaries*. San Francisco, California: National Council on Crime and Delinquency, 1989. This document provides descriptions of eleven intensive juvenile supervision programs in the United States. 235p.

3111 Krisberg, Barry *The Juvenile Court: Reclaiming The Vision*. San Francisco, California: National Council on Crime and Delinquency, 1988. This is a critique of the increasingly disparate nature of the theory and practice found in the American system of juvenile justice. 18p. Appendix.

3112 Krisberg, Barry; Schwartz, Ira & Fishman, Gideon; Ersikovits, Zai; Guttman, Edna & Joe, Karen The Incarceration Of Minority Youth, *Crime & Delinquency* 33:173-205, 1987. This review exploring the disproportionate incarceration of American minority youths in juvenile correctional facilities, found that blacks are somewhat more likely than white youngsters to be involved in serious crime, but not to the generally assumed extent.

3113 Krisberg, Barry *The Incarceration Of Minority Youth*. Minneapolis, Minnesota: The Hubert Humphrey Institute of Public Affairs, University of Minnessota, 1986. This analysis of national data on minority youth imprisonment, developed by the US Bureau of the Census, found evidence contrary to the hypothesis that demographic trends are the principal forces generating a growth in minority incarceration. 37p.

3114 Krisberg, Barry; Schwartz, Ira M.; Litsky, Paul & Austin, James The Watershed Of Juvenile Justice Reform, *Crime & Delinquency* 32:5-38, 1986. This article focuses on various policy issues concerning reforms in juvenile justice in the United states.

3115 Krisberg, Barry & Litsky, Paul Youth In Confinement: Justice By Geography, *Journal Of Research In Crime And Delinquency* 21:153-181, 1984. Current data on interstate variations in the use of public juvenile correctional facilities and conditions of confinement, when analyzed, demonstrate glaring differences in juvenile correctional practices among diverse jurisdictions in the United States.

3116 Krisberg, Barry Themes Of Violence And Gang Youth, *International Annals Of Criminology* 18:9-18, 1979-1980. This article is based on interviews and observations of 22 young gang leaders in Philadelphia, and their discussions in and out of program sessions that seemed to center on the gang leaders' experiences of such conflicts and assessment of violence as a valuable social force reminiscent of Third World concern with "violence as a public issue".

3117 Krisberg, Barry & Austin, James *The Children Of Ishmael: Critical Perspectives On Juvenile Justice*. Palo Alto, California: Mayfield, 1978. This anthology on the role of racism, economic exploitation, poverty, sexism, and political repression, juvenile delinquency and juvenile justice contends that delinquency is widespread and is not primarily a lower-class phenomenon, and the prevalent juvenile court system is a bureaucratic nightmare lacking due process and legal safeguards.

3118 Krisberg, Barry; McCall, Carolyn & Munson, Judy *Pioneering In Delinquency Prevention: The California Experience*. San Francisco, California: National Council on Crime and Delinquency, 1978. This research attempts to evaluate accomplishments and failures emanating from organizational and political issues in the California's Youth Development and Delinquency Prevention Project (YDDPP). 94p.

3119 Lab, Steven P.; Shields, Glenn & Schondel, Connie Research Note: An Evaluation Of Juvenile Sexual Offender Treatment, *Crime & Delinquency* 39:543-553, 1993. Lack of improvement in youths under treatment, and lack of knowledge on identifying at-risk youths, causes of behavior and appropriate treatment for juvenile sexual offenders are listed as the shortfalls by this critique of a court-based program for the treatment of juvenile sex offenders.

3120 LaBelle, Barbara *Expungement Of Juvenile Records*. Columbia, South Carolina: Department of Youth Services, 1981. The author discusses the need for statutes regarding the expunging of juveniles' criminal records in states such as South Carolina.

3121 Lattimore, Pamela K.; Visher, Christy A. & Linster, Richard L. Predicting Rearrest For Violence Among Serious Youthful Offenders, *Journal Of Research In Crime And Delinquency* 32:54-83, 1995. The conclusion of the authors is that when prior criminal history, institutional behavior, and personal background characteristics are all considered together, the re-arrest probability for violent juvenile offenders can be predicted.

3122 Laurence, Susan E.; Schneider, Peter R. & Finkelstein, Matthew C. *Serious And Chronic Juvenile Offenders: A Study To Determine Future Directions*. Bethesda, Maryland: Pacific Institute for Research and Evaluation, 1991. This is an examination of Maryland's need for the construction of a new rehabilitation-oriented institution for chronic and serious juvenile offenders. 133p.

3123 Lawrence, Richard A. The Role Of Legal Counsel In Juveniles' Understanding Of Their Rights, *Juvenile And Family Court Journal* 34:49-58, 1983. The focus of this study is on juvenile offenders' understanding of their legal rights.

3124 Loeber, Rolf. & Farrington, David P. Never Too Early, Never Too Late: Risk Factors And Successful Intervention For Serious And Violent Juvenile Offenders, *Studies On Crime And Crime Prevention* 7:7-30, 1998. There is a summary and discussion of the various predictors of youth violence, and the role of community and interventions in preventing it.

3125 Lee, Deborah A. The Constitutionality Of Juvenile Preventive Detention: Schall V. Martin-Who Is Preventive Detention Protecting? *New England Law Review* 20:341-374, 1984-1985. The author discusses a New York State case, the Supreme Court ruling supporting the State's action, and its implications for juvenile offenders.

3126 Leiber, Michael J.; Nalla, Mahesh K. & Farnworth, Margaret Explaining Juveniles' Attitudes Toward The Police, *Justice Quarterly* 15:151-174, 1998. The authors proposes that, rather than a single-causeal model of personal interactions with the police, any explanation should include the attitudes of youths toward authority and agents of social control.

3127 Lemert, Edwin M. Diversion In Juvenile Justice: What Hath Been Wrought, *The Journal Of Research In Crime And Delinquency* 18:34-46, 1981. The author argues that diversion began as an effort to reduce discretion in juvenile justice, but has now become a warrant to increased discretion and extend control to other areas of juvenile conduct.

3128 Lerman, P. Counting Youth In Trouble In Institutions: Bringing The United States Up, *Crime & Delinquency* 37:465-480, 1991. This is a discussion of the importance of timely reporting, unduplicated counts of inter-system trends, fuller coverage of facilities, and improved demographic enumerations.

3129 Lewis, Dorothy Otnow Racial Factors Influencing Diagnosis, Disposition And Treatment Of Deviant Adolescents, pp 295-311 in Lewis, Dorothy Otnow (ed.) *Vulnerabilities To Delinquency*. New York, New York: SP Medical and Scientific Books, 1981. This article reports on racial bias in the perspectives of staff toward the behavior and psychopathology of adolescents in psychiatric hospitals, and under incarceration.

3130 Lieb, Roxanne & Matson, Scott *Sexual Predator Commitment Laws In The United States: 1998 Update*. Olympia, Washington: Washington State Institute for Public Policy, 1998. The authors compare the sexual predator laws in diverse American states, and include statutes on juvenile sexual predators as well. 38p.

3131 Lieb, Roxanne; Fish, Lee & Crosby, Todd *A Summary Of State Trends In Juvenile Justice*. Olympia, Washington: Washington State Institute for Public Policy, 1994. Data from diverse sources were analyzed to track trends among the various states' juvenile justice legislation and programs transferring juveniles to adult courts. 59p.

3132 Lindner, Charles Probation And The Law, *Probation And Parole* 9:(Fall):39-45, 1977. Various New York State and United States legislations whereby increasing number of minors can be brought under juvenile justice are the focus of this article.

3133 Linn, Janice *Minors In Need: A Study Of Status Offenders At The Juvenile Court Of Cook County*. Chicago, Illinois: Chicago Law Enforcement Study Group, 1979. Data on MINS (Minors In Need Of Supervision) cases in Cook County Illinois lead the author to conclude that there is little difference in the dispositions received on the bases of gender or ethnicity. 167p.

3134 Lipsey, Mark W. Is Delinquency Prevention A Cost-Effective Strategy? A California Perspective, *Journal Of Research In Crime And Delinquency* 21:279-302, 1984. This study of crime prevention programs in Los Angeles County, California found that the cost-benefit ratio of delinquency prevention was high, even under realistic assumptions about the effectiveness of the prevention treatment.

3135 Lipsey, Mark W.; Cordray, David S. & Berger, Dale C. Evaluation Of A Juvenile Diversion Program Using Multiple Lines Of Evidence, *Evaluation Review* 5:283-306, 1983. This is an evaluation of a Los Angeles County juvenile community-based alternative diversion program for arrested juveniles, who otherwise would have been referred to the juvenile justice system.

3136 Little, Judith W. & Skarrow, Margaret K. *Delinquency Prevention: Selective Organizational Change In The School. Rev. Ed.* Washington, D.C.: US Office of Juvenile Justice and Delinquency Prevention, 1981. The role of American schools in delinquency prevention by implementing select organizational changes to develop self-contained school delinquency-prevention programs is the focus of this discussion. 71p.

3137 Loughran, Edward J. The Massachusetts Experience: A Historical Review Of Reform In The Department Of Youth Services, *Social Justice* 24:170-186, 1997. The history of the Department of Youth Services of Massachusetts, the Department's activities, and data on institutions, budgets, legislation and other matters presented here.

3138 Loy, Pamela & Norland, Stephen Gender Convergence And Delinquency, *Sociological Quarterly* 22:275-283, 1981. Self-report data support the predictions of this study that tests the hypothesis that delinquency of androgynous and undifferentiated youths is similar in frequency when compared to traditional males and females.

3139 Lukin, Penny R. Recidivism And Changes Made By Delinquents During Residential Treatment, *Journal Of Research In Crime And Delinquency* 18:101-112, 1981. This study investigated the changes in the behavior during residential treatment, and recidivism among juvenile offenders.

3140 Lynch, James P.; Spergel, Irving A. & Korbelik, John *Understanding The Role Of Community In Delinquency Prevention*. Washington, D. C.: Bureau of Social Science Research, 1981. This paper explores reasons why some communities are better able to buffer their children others, and provides data on three Chicago communities in the labeling process. 18p.

3141 Macallair, Dan Disposition Case Advocacy In San Francisco's Juvenile Justice System: A New Approach To Deinstitutioalization, *Crime & Delinquency* 40:84-95, 1994. The impact of defense-based advocacy on juvenile case dispositions and commitment rate to state correctional facilities was examined in this research from San Francisco.

3142 Macallair, Dan Reaffirming Rehabilitation In Juvenile Justice, *Youth & Society* 25:104-125, 1993. The declining popularity and use of rehabilitation in the juvenile corrections systems of several states is the subject of this essay.

3143 MacDonald, J. M. & Chesney-Lind, M. Gender Bias And Juvenile Justice Revisited: A Multiyear Analysis, *Crime & Delinquency* 47:173-195, 2001. A multiyear empirical examination of gender bias in the handling of juvenile court cases in Hawaii indicates significant differences in the outcomes for male and female juvenile offenders, particularly for youth of color.

3144 MacKenzie, Doris Layton; Wilson, David B.; Armstrong, Gaylene Styve & Gover, Angela R. The Impact Of Boot Camps And Traditional Institutions On Juvenile Residents: Perceptions, Adjustment, And Change, *Journal Of Research In Crime And Delinquency* 38:279-313, 2001. When experiences of juveniles during the first month of confinement in boot camps were compared with those of youths in traditional facilities, were no differences between their anxiety and depression levels were found.

3145 Magill, Sherry Adolescents: Public Enemy #1, *Crime & Delinquency* 44:121-126, 1998. From a humanistic perspective, the focus of this work is on what ails United States public policies toward juveniles.

3146 Mahoney, Anne Rankin Jury Trial For Juveniles: Right Or Ritual? *Justice Quarterly* 2:553-565, 1985. Based on an examination of jury trials for juveniles, the author found no significant impact on either adjudication or disposition when a juvenile case is sent for trial rather than resolved by a judge alone.

3147 Males, Mike & Macallair, Dan *The Color Of Justice: An Analysis Of Juvenile Court Transfers In California*. Washington, D.C.: Justice Policy Institute, 1999. The disproportionate transfer rates of minority youths to California adult courts, and its consequences in terms of sentencing and imprisonment are the focus of this inquiry. 10p.

3148 Manfredi, Christopher P. *The Supreme CourtAnd Juvenile Justice*. Lawrence, Kansas: University Press of Kansas, 1998. This discussion addresses the various landmark decisions and activities of the Supreme

Court during the 1960s to bring juvenile justice under the constitution. 256p.

3149 Martin, Susan E.; Sechrest, Lee B.; Redner, Robin & National Research Council Panel On Research On Rehabilitative Techniques (eds.) *New Directions In The Rehabilitation Of Criminal Offenders*. Washington, D.C.: National Academy Press, 1981. This is a review and an assessment of the reliability of research on rehabilition techniques and includes juvenile justice research as well. 498p.

3150 Martinez, Alma I. *An Overview Of Texas Juvenile Justice Population Trends And Dynamics: An Update*. Austin, Texas: Texas Criminal Justice Policy Council, 2000. This is a report based on the official data on the trends in juvenile crimes and arrests. 14p.

3151 Marx, Gary T. Ironies Of Social Control: Authorities As Contributions To Deviance Through Escalation, Non-Enforcement And Covert Facilitation, *Social Problems* 28:221-246, 1981. This discussion addresses how efforts to control delinquency may actually lead to its continuation and persistence.

3152 Massachusetts Governor's Juvenile Justice Advisory Committee *The Violent Juvenile Offender In Massachusetts: A Policy Analysis*. Boston, Massachusetts: Committee on Criminal Justice, 1981. This examination of juvenile justice policy on treatment, placement and control of serious violent juvenile offenders in Massachusetts found lack of uniformity in decisions of the courts and the Department of Youth Services. 137p. Appendix.

3153 Mauer, Marc & Young, Malcolm C. *Truths, Half-Truths, And Lies: Myths And Realities About Crime And Punishment*. Washington, D.C.: The Sentencing Project, 1996. This critique of 10 common beliefs about crime and punishment includes the treatment of serious juvenile offenders as adults. 13p.

3154 Maupin, James R. Risk Classification Systems And The Provision Of Juvenile Aftercare, *Crime & Delinquency* 39:90-105, 1993. This analysis of juvenile aftercare decision-making by parole officers in allocating their time among clients, attempted to track a random sample of 280 Arizona juvenile parolees for 90 days.

3155 Maxson, Cheryle L. & Klein, Malcolm W. *Responding To Troubled Youth*. New York, New York: Oxford University Press, 1997. This research report offers a critical analysis of the Federally funded Deinstutionalization of Status Offenders Project. 207p.

3156 Mays, G. Larry & Houghtalin, Marilyn Trying Juveniles As Adults: A Note on New Mexico's Recent Experience, *Justice System Journal* 15:814-823, 1992. The authors found that although juvenile justice personnel rarely used transfers to adult courts, they consistently applied the rules of the waiver process.

3157 McCarthy, Francis B. Pre-Adjudicatory Rights In Juvenile Court: An Historical And Constitutional Analysis, *University of Pittsburgh Law Review* 42:457-514, 1981. The author implies that the goal of Supreme Court rulings in cases involving juvenile criminal defendants, such as Gault and Miranda, was to establish certain procedural rights of minors in criminal cases.

3158 McCarthy, Francis B. The Role Of The Concept Of Responsibility In Juvenile Delinquency Proceedings, *University Of Michigan Journal Of Law Reform* 10:181-219, 1977. This article offers an historic review of penal sentences for children in criminal courts.

3159 McCorkle, Richard C. Correctional Boot Camps And Change In Attitude: Is All This Shouting Necessary? A Research Note, *Justice Quarterly* 12:365-375, 1995. This is an assessment of boot camps for juveniles that concludes the findings do not support the expansion of such programs.

3160 McDowall, David; Loftin, Colin & Wiersema, Brian The Impact Of Youth Curfew Laws On Juvenile Crime Rates, *Crime & Delinquency* 46:76-91, 2000. This study shows that, although overall juvenile crime did not decrease following the new curfew laws, there were statistically significant reductions in arrests for burglary, larceny, and simple assault.

3161 McEniry, Mary C. *Restitution: A Dynamic And Challenging Alternative For Wisconsin's Juvenile Justice System*. Madison, Wisconsin: Wisconsin Bureau of Children, Youth and Families, 1979. This document provides information on designing restitution project for juvenile offenders as well as current restitution projects in the United States. 59p. Appendix.

3162 McGarrell, Edmund F. Trends In Racial Disproportionality In Juvenile Court Processing: 1985-1989, *Crime & Delinquency* 39:29-48, 1993. An analysis of juvenile court processing data from a sample of counties detected the trend of increasingly non-white overrepresentation in the population of juvenile correctional facilities.

3163 McGarrell, Edmund F. Differential Effects Of Juvenile Justice Reform On Incarceration Rates Of The States, *Crime & Delinquency* 37:262-280,

1991. This analysis demonstrates the wide variation in the states' use of incarceration for juveniles in various public facilities during the mid-1970s to 1987.

3164 McGillis, Daniel; Spangenberg, Robert & Abt Associates, Inc. *The Camp Hill Project: An Assessment*. Cambridge, Massachusetts, 1976. This assessment of an alternative to incarceration, the Camp Hill roject, found that the goal of relocating the 392 juveniles was achieved, but the project encountered severe fiscal problems, in part due to poor fiscal management. 244 p.

3165 McNulty, Jill K. First Amendment Versus Sixth Amendment: A Constitutional Battle In The Juvenile Court, *New Mexico Law* Review 10:311-340, 1980. In considering the issues related to the Sixth Amendment provision for public trial of minors in criminal cases, the author contrasts publicity and media access in juvenile and adult trials under the First Amendment.

3166 Mears, Daniel P. Getting Tough With Juvenile Offenders: Explaining Support For Sanctioning Youths As Adults, *Criminal Justice And Behavior* 28:206-226, 2001. The findings of this study suggest that marital status, and philosophy of punishment, are consistently associated with the public's support for adult sanctioning of minors who sell illegal drugs, commit property or violent crimes.

3167 Mears, Daniel P. & Field, Samuel H. Theorizing Sanctioning In A Criminalized Juvenile Court, *Criminology* 38:983-1021, 2000. The authors addresses the effects of legal, extra-legal, and processing factors, as well as sentencing option in a highly proceduralized and criminalized juvenile court in Texas.

3168 Mears, Daniel P. & Kelly, William R. Assessments And Intake Processes In Juvenile Justice Processing: Emerging Policy Considerations, *Crime & Delinquency* 45:508-529, 1999. Using interview and survey data of county-level intake processes in Texas, this study discusses the policy implications of assessment and its role at in-take, and the timing and structure of intake and its goals.

3169 Mears, Daniel P. Evaluation Issues Confronting Juvenile Justice Sentencing Reforms: A Case Study Of Texas, *Crime & Delinquency* 44:443-463, 1998. This paper reviews the Texas justice system, and highlights the changes that are being made to the juvenile justice system in that state.

3170 Meehan, Albert J. Internal Police Records And The Control Of Juveniles, *Youth & Society* 33:504-524, 1993. This study found that as a consequence of community and administrative pressure, while dealing with troublesome youths, the police shifted to surveillance and internal record keeping as a social control mechanism.

3171 Meisel, Joshua S. Relationships And Juvenile Offenders: The Effects Of Intensive Aftercare Supervision, *The Prison Journal* 81:206-245, 2001. In examining the impact of participation on relationships between youth and their service providers in an Intensive Aftercare Demonstration Project, the findings demonstrate a strong association between participation in the experiment and youth's expressions of positive relationships with their case managers.

3172 Melton, Gary B. Legal Policy And Child Development Research: A Selective Review, *Child And Youth Services* 3:13-20, 1980-1981. The various issues of social science evidence, and role of professional opinion, in acknowledging the legal rights of children are the focus of this discussion.

3173 Merlo, Alida V. Juvenile Justice At The Crossroads: Presidential Address To The Academy Of Criminal Justice Sciences, *Justice Quarterly* 17:639-661, 2000. The author feels that in spite of falling youth offenses, due to ideology, the media, and politics legislatures continue to advocate a harsh, punitive stance toward youthful offenders.

3174 Miethe, Terance D. & McCorkle, Richard C. Gang Membership And Criminal Processing: A Test Of The "Master Status" Concept, *Justice Quarterly* 14:407-427, 1997. When the authors of this study examined if gang membership influenced both charging and sentencing decisions in an urban court, it was found that it does.

3175 Miller, Walter B. Youth Gangs In The Urban Crisis Era, pp 91-128 in Short, James F. (ed.) *Delinquency, Crime, And Society*. Chicago, Illinois: University of Chicago Press, 1976. 1960s and contemporary Boston and Philadelphia gangs, and their coverage by the media, is the subject of this article.

3176 Minnesota Corrections Department *The Serious Juvenile Offender: Proceedings Of A Symposium*. St. Paul, Minnesota: Minnesota Corrections Department, 1977. The focus here is on definition, incidence, treatment and control of, and legal issues regarding, serious offenders.

3177 Minor, Kevin I.; Wells, James B.; Soderstrom, Irina R.; Bingham, R. & Williamson, D. Sentence Completion And Recidivism Among Juveniles Referred To Teen Courts, *Crime & Delinquency* 45:467-480, 1999. This study of juveniles referred to teen courts for disposition by their peers as an alternative to judicial sentencing found that among those sentenced to community service sentence completion was significantly less likely, while recidivism was significantly higher among those with prior records and those sentenced for curfew violations.

3178 Minor, Kevin I. & Hartmann, David J. Predictors Of Juvenile Court Actions And Recidivism, *Crime & Delinquency* 43:328-344, 1998. Over two-years, the authors examined the variables in court decision-making and recidivism among a group of first-time juvenile court referrals.

3179 Mirell, Douglas E. & Fainer, David C. Delinquency Hearings And The First Amendment: Reassessing Juvenile Court Confidentiality Upon The Demise Of Conditional Access, *Juvenile And Family Court Journal* 31:17-42, 1980. The issues related to closed proceedings in juvenile criminal cases form the core of this discussion.

3180 Mitchell, Ojmarrh; MacKenzie, Doris Layton; Gover, Angela R. & Styve, Gaylene, J. The Environment And Working Conditions In Juvenile Boot Camps And Traditional Facilities, *Justice Research And Policy* 1:1-22, 1999. This national study of staff perceptions reveals their positive attitudes toward their environment, programs, and prognosis of their adolescent charges.

3181 Mones, Paul Too Many Rights And Not Enough? A Study Of The Juvenile Related Decisions Of The West Virginia Supreme Court Of Appeals, *Journal Of Juvenile Law*, 8:32-57, 1984. The repercussions of two important court decision -- least restrictive alternative rehabilitative treatment and prohibiting commingling of status and criminal offenders in secure facilities -- are discussed in this article.

3182 Moon, Melissa M.; Wright, John Paul; Cullen, Francis T. & Pealer, Jennifer A. Putting Kids To Death: Specifying Public Support For Juvenile Capital Punishment, *Justice Quarterly* 17:663-684, 2000. This research on the extent of public support for the death penalty for juveniles reveals that a majority of respondents favored it, and often for young offenders, although there is less support for executing juveniles than for adults.

3183 Moon, Melissa M.; Sundt, Jody L.; Cullen, Francis T. & Wright, John P. Is Child Saving Dead? Public Support For Juvenile Rehabilitation, *Crime & Delinquency* 46:38-60, 2000. In a statewide survey, Tennessee residents supported rehabilitation as an integral goal of the juvenile correctional system, endorsed a range of community-based treatment interventions, and favored early intervention programs over imprisonment for juvenile offenders.

3184 Morash, Merry & Rucker, Lila A Critical Look At The Idea Of Boot Camp As A Correctional Reform, *Crime & Delinquency* 36:204-222, 1990. Their analysis lead the authors to question the efficacy of correctional boot camp as a way of dealing with juvenile offenders.

3185 Moton, Joann B. (ed.) *Complex Challenges, Collaborative Solutions: Programming For Adult And Juvenile Female Offender.* Lanham, Maryland: American Correctional Association, 1985. This anthology has several chapters on the treatment of female juvenile offenders. 240p.

3186 Nathan, Winifred Whose Rights Are They Anyway? The Supreme Court And The Rights Of Juveniles, *Children And Youth Services Review* 6:329-344, 1984. Supreme court decisions over 60 years centering around the interests of the parent, the state and the child, and the child's individual rights are the focus of this exposition.

3187 National Association Of Counties *Youth Employment And Counties: A Focus On Youth Needs And System Realities.* Washington, D.C., 1979. This report focuses on the role of the county in delivering various social services affecting youths, including the juvenile Justice system, welfare and social services, alcohol abuse control, the CETA program, and education. 13p.

3188 National Coalition For Jail Reform *National Symposium On Children In Jail.* Washington, D.C.: Office of Juvenile Justice and Delinquency Prevention, 1980. Research findings on a wide range of issues concerning juveniles in adult jails, and alternatives to jail confinement are discussed by this publication. 106p.

3189 National Commission On Youth The Transition Of Youth To Adulthood: A Bridge Too Long. A Report To Educators, Sociologists, Legislators, And Youth Policymaking Bodies. Boulder, Colorado: Westview, 1980. In this volume, there are twenty-seven recommendations for juvenile justice reform, policy prescriptions for revitalizing services for juveniles and young adults, and suggestions on ways to build new links among the family, the school, private organizations, the government, and voluntary agencies. 228p.

3190 National Council Of Jewish Women *Directory Of Section Services For Justice For Children, Child Abuse And Neglect.* New York, New York, 1978. This directory of geographic districts in the United States with various juvenile justice projects, includes the title and description of the projects, number of members, mailing addresses, and contact persons as well is an index of the projects. 38p. Appendix.

3191 National Council Of Juvenile Court Judges *Juvenile Justice Information Systems: A National Assessment.* Reno, Nevada, 1976. The experiences of juvenile courts in the United States with computers shows that, although not many courts or agencies are automated, there are a variety of computer applications in management reporting, name-indexing and record-checking, and caseload-monitoring forming the core of their functions. 144p.

3192 National Council On Crime & Delinquency Volunteers In Probation *A Report On The National Survey And Questionnaire Conducted By VIP-NCCD On The Volunteer Juvenile And Criminal Justice Movement In The United States October, 1979.* Royal Oak, Michigan, 1979. This document reports the findings of a nationwide survey of programs that use volunteers, and the number of volunteers in them. 6p.

3193 National Office For Social Responsibility *Youth Services Information System (YSIS).* Washington, D.C.: US Office of Juvenile Justice and Delinquency Prevention, 1979. Implementation of the YSIS (Youth Services Information System) through large-scale computers and minicomputers, and procedures detailing the manual operation of the system are the topics of this report. 118p.

3194 National Youth Workers Alliance *Runaway Youth Program Directory.* Washington, D.C.: US Office of Juvenile Justice and Delinquency Prevention Office, 1979. This is a directory of 212 runaway programs, operating independent of the juvenile justice system, serving the self-referred runaway and "throwaway" youth. 109p.

3195 Newcomb, Theodore M. Characteristics Of Youths In A Sample Of Correctional Programs: Differences Associated With Programs And Time Spent In Them, *Journal Of Research In Crime And Delinquency* 15:3-24, 1978. This analysis of the relaltionship among size of the program, individuals' length of stay, and pre- and post-commitment offense levels, from the responses of a representative sample of American youths in correctional programs, shows that outcomes are the result of the interaction between what youths bring to the programs and what they are offered in the programs.

3196 Newton, Anne M. Prevention Of Crime And Delinquency, *Criminal Justice Abstracts* 10:245-266, 1978. Concentrating on scientifically evaluated crime and delinquency prevention programs, the author concludes that, with few a exceptions, most did not reduce crime or have the anticipated effect on crime, but many had potentially serious social side effects, were cost ineffective and susceptible to displacement.

3197 Newton, Charles H.; Shelden, Randall G. & Jenkins, Sam The Homogenization Process Within The Juvenile Justice System, *International Journal Of Criminology And Penology* 3:213-227, 1975. This study explores how authorities of processing in the system, sort diverse youth into various categories.

3198 Nugent, William R.; Umbreit, Mark S.; Wiinamaki, Lizabeth & Paddock, Jeff Participation In Victim-Offender Mediation And Reoffense: Successful Replications*?* *Research On Social Work Practice* 11:5-23, 2001. This research, on the extent and effects of participation in four programs of victim-offender mediation, found that participanting juveniles have significantly lower re-offending rates.

3199 Nuttall, John; MacDonald, Donald & Brandon, Ann Meeting The Educational Needs Of Youth Violent Offenders In The Adult Correctional System of New York State, *Journal Of Correctional Education* 46:25-30, 1995. This article offers an overview of a young, violent offender initiative in New York State.

3200 O'Brien, Kevin E. Returned to the Streets: Legal Issues Raised by Juvenile Diversion Programs, *New England Journal On Prison Law* 3:381-436, 1977. The author discusses the issues related to the dilemma of constitutionality in sentencing juvenile delinquents to diversion programs for rehabilitation.

3201 Oden, Mary E. & Schlossman, Steven Guardians Of Virtue: The Juvenile Court And Female Delinquency In Early 20th-Century Los Angeles, *Crime & Delinquency* 37:186-203, 1991. The authors analyze the origins and implementation of policies and the formal institutional apparatus for disciplining female delinquents in the early 20th Century.

3202 Ohio Association Of Juvenile Court Judges *Let's Get Kids Out Of Adult Jails*. Canton, Ohio: Ohio Association of Juvenile Court Judges, 1979. This paper argues that in spite of the Juvenile Justice and Delinquency Prevention Act, only minimal effort had been taken to removing young delinquents from American adult institutions. 41p.

3203 Ohlin, Lloyd E. The Future Of Juvenile Justice Policy And Research, *Crime & Delinquency* 44:143-152, 1998. The author reviews the American juvenile justice policies of the preceding 20 years, and the principal challenges in developing, and enhancing, these policies.

3204 Mitchell, Ojmarrh; MacKenzie, Doris Layton; Styve, Gaylene J. & Gover, Angela R. The Impact Of Individual, Organizational, And Environmental Attributes On Voluntary Turnover Among Juvenile Correctional Staff Members, *Justice Quarterly* 17:332-357, 2000.

Assessing the turnover intentions of juvenile correctional staff members, the authors found that both individual characteristics and organizational attributes were significant predictors of such intentions.

3205 Orchowsky, Stan Serious Juvenile Offenders: Predicting The Probability Of Transfer To Criminal Court, *Crime & Delinquency* 40:3-18, 1994. This paper based on a Virginia study, identifies the legal and extralegal factors that play a significant role in the decision to transfer a serious juvenile offender to adult criminal court.

3206 Osgood, D. Wayne & Weichselbaum, Hart F. Juvenile Diversion: When Practice Matches Theory, *Journal Of Research In Crime And Delinquency* 21:33-56, 1984. This study demonstrates that both the juveniles and service providers perceive diversion programs as a true alternative to the services that otherwise would be provided by justice agencies.

3207 Osgood, D. Wayne Offense History And Juvenile Diversion, *Evaluation Review* 7:793-806, 1983. This article discusses the success of diversion programs for juveniles who otherwise would have received formal dispositions.

3208 Ottis, Jo Ann An Analysis Of The Juvenile Courts' Discretionary Power In Waiver Of Jurisdiction Hearings, *South Texas Law Journal* 21:80-97, 1981. The power of Texas juvenile courts to waive juvenile cases to adult criminal courts is analyzed in this article.

3209 Pabon, Edward Changes In Juvenile Justice: Evolution Or Reform, *Social Work* 23:492-497, 1978. The author argues that diversion and deinstitutionalization programs have not reduced the impact of coercive supervision and labeling, since only the locus of control has been transferred from residential to nonresidential programs, and from legal bureaucracies to organizations outside the legal arena.

3210 Palace, William A. Procedural Due Process For Confined Juveniles, *New England Journal On Prison Law* 2:173-203, 1976. This article advocates granting detained juveniles, the right to due process as guaraneed by the American Constitution.

3211 Pallone, Nathaniel J. (ed.) Young Victims, Young Offenders: Current Issues In Policy And Treatment, *Journal Of Offender Rehabilitation* 21:1-237, 1994. This special issue is devoted to policy and treatment issues concerning child abuse and juvenile delinquency.

3212 Parent, Dale G. Conditions Of Confinement, *Juvenile Justice* 1:2-23, 1993. This article offers a summary of public and private juvenile institutions in 1991 found in the United States.

3213 Pennell, Susan & Curtis, Christine Controlling Juvenile Delinquency: An Evaluation Of An Interagency Strategy, *Crime & Delinquency* 36:257-275, 1990. Findings from a two-year evaluation of the impact of the San Diego County Interagency Agreement upon delinquent behavior are discussed in this report.

3214 Perkins-Dock, Robin E. Family Interventions With Incarcerated Youth: A Review Of The Literature, *International Journal Of Offender Therapy And Comparative Criminology* 45:606-625, 2001. This article provides a review and critique of family intervention models designed for juvenile offenders, discusses familial influences on antisocial and delinquent behavior, and treatment dilemmas in working with incarcerated juvenile offenders.

3215 Petersen, Rebecca D. Definitions Of A Gang And Its Impacts On Public Policy, *Journal Of Criminal Justice* 28:139-149, 2000. This analysis is based on the author's interviews with 34 incarcerated juvenile gang members in the Southwest.

3216 Phillips, Mary T.; Gewirtz, Marian & Sealy, Dale *Release On Recognizance Recommendation System For Juvenile Offenders Arraigned In New York City Adult Courts. Part I: Validation Study*. New York, New York: New York City criminal Justice Agency, 1999. This research report concludes that, among youths under 16 brought to adult courts and released on recognizance, only a small proportion fail to appear for their court date. 99p.

3217 Pierce, James R. Relinquishment Of Jurisdiction For Purposes Of Criminal Prosecution Of Juveniles, *Northern Kentucky Law Review* 8:377-393, 1981. Waiver and the various laws regarding it are the topics the author discusses in this article.

3218 Piquero, Alex Applying An Evaluability Assessment Tool To Community-Based Programs In Pittsburgh, *Prison Journal* 78:74-89, 1998. This article focuses on various issues and problems in evaluating a community-based delinquency prevention program.

3219 Pisciotta, Alexander W. Parens Patriae, Treatment And Reform: The Case Of The Western House Of Refuge 1849-1907, *New England Journal On Criminal And Civil Confinement* 10:65-86, 1984. The origin, development, and operations of this institution are the focus of this historic analysis.

3220 Plotkin, Alan L. & Ellas, Geri The Curfew Bill As It Relates To The Juvenile And His Family, *Adolescence* 7:523-528, 1977. The authors discuss the pros and cons of juvenile curfew laws in several American states.

3221 Poulin, John E.; Levitt, John L.; Young, Thomas M.; Pappenfort, Donnell M. & US National Institute For Juvenile Justice And Delinquency Prevention *Juveniles In Detention Centers And Jails: An Analysis Of State Variations During The Mid 1970s*. Washington, D.C.: US Government Printing Office, 1980. This document offers a detailed description and national assessment of juveniles in detention facilities across the nation. 75p.

3222 Powkes, James J. A Review Of Federal Involvement In The Prevention And Control Of Juvenile Delinquency, *Juvenile And Family Court Journal* 30:37-47, 1979. The author argues that more than any of the administrative and legislative efforts that followed, the most significant Federal involvement in the prevention and control of juvenile delinquency occurred during late 1960s and early 1970s when the Supreme Court accorded youngsters' the process rights of adults thereby improving the status of youth.

3223 Price, Virginia Ann Characteristics And Needs Of Boston Street Youth: One Agency's Response, *Children And Youth Services Review* 11:75-90, 1989. The author stresses the diversity in the needs and characteristics of runaway minors, homeless juveniles and those youths who engage in prostitution.

3224 Project READ *To Make A Difference*. Silver Spring, Maryland: READ, Inc. 1978. Students from 74 schools were pre-tested and post-tested in reading, mental ability, and self-concept in this study of a 14 month program to prevent juvenile delinquency that concludes that all students can be motivated to read better. 46p.

3225 Rafky, David M. & Sealey, Ronald W. The Adolescent And The Law: A Survey, *Crime & Delinquency* 21:131-138, 1975. This article reports results from a survey of high school youths measuring their knowledge of, and attitudes toward, the law.

3226 Raley, Gordon Removing Children From Adult Jails: The Dance Of Legislation, *Children's Legal Rights Journal* 3:4-9, 1982. This article discusses legislation directed at the removal of juveniles from adult jails.

3227 Reamer, Frederic G. & Shireman, Charles H. Alternatives To The Juvenile Justice System: Their Development And The Current `State Of The Art', *Juvenile And Family Court Journal* 32:17-32, 1981. This review of juvenile alternative programs suggests that there is no significant difference between the effects of justice system or alternative treatment on post-treatment offending behavior.

3228 Rector, John M. Children In Custody: Our Continuing National Scandal. *Prison Law Monitor* 2:12-15, 1979. Prepared for the Children in Custody Initiative of the United States Office of Juvenile Justice and Delinquency Preventio, this is a critique of American juvenile justice system' current reliance on detention and incarceration of status offenders.

3229 Redding, Richard E. Juvenile Offenders In Criminal Court And Adult Prison: Legal, Psychological, And Behavioral Outcomes, *Juvenile And Family Court Journal* 50:1-20, 1999. This analysis focuses on the impact of American states' laws on the transfer of juveniles to adult criminal courts, and programs and conditions in juvenile verus adult correctional facilities.

3230 Reddington, Frances P. & Sapp, Allen D. Juveniles In Adult Prisons: Problems And Prospects, *Journal Of Crime And Social Justice* 20:139-153, 1997. From data collected from self-administered questionnaires, the authors investigate the incarceration of juveniles in adult American prisons.

3231 Reese II, William A.; Curtis, Russell L. Jr. & Richard, Albert Jr. Juvenile Justice As People-Modulating: A Case Study Of Progressive Delinquent Dispositions, *Journal Of Research In Crime And Delinquency* 26:329-357, 1989. Examining qualitative literature, this study argues that in multifunctional, people-modulating, contexts increases in deviance result in a progression of remedial reactions.

3232 Reinharz, Peter *Killer Kids, Bad Laws: Tales Of The Juvenile Court System*. Brooklyn, New York: Barricade Press, 1996. This book provides a prosecutor's critique of the juvenile justice system, along with narratives of case studies. 335p.

3233 Reno, Janet Taking America Back For Our Children, *Crime & Delinquency* 44:75-82, 1998. This is the text of a speech given by the then United States Attorney General, Janet Reno, during the National Forum on Youth Violence on May 31, 1995.

3234 Reynolds, K. Michael; Seydlitz, Ruth & Jenkins, Pamela Do Juvenile Curfew Laws Work? A Time-Series Analysis Of The New Orleans Law, *Justice Quarterly* 17:205-230, 2000. This article is an examination of the impact on victimizations, juvenile victimizations, and juvenile arrests of curfew law in New Orleans, Louisiana.

3235 Ruefle, William & Reynolds, Kenneth Mike Curfews And Delinquency In Major American Cities, *Crime & Delinquency* 41:347-363, 1995. The use of curfew as a delinquency control mechanism in American cities is examined.

3236 Ritz, Wilfred J. Federal Youth Corrections Act: The Continuing Charade, *University Of Richmond Law Review* 13:743-782, 1979. The author discusses the failures in the implementation of the Youth Corrections Act, and advocates its abolition but retention of its provision on expunging juvenile records.

3237 Roberts, Albert R. Wilderness Programs For Juvenile Offenders: A Challenging Alternative, *Juvenile & Family Court Journal* 39:1-12, 1988. The origins of various wilderness programs for young offenders are discussed by the author who describes several of them.

3238 Robertson, A. A.; Grimes, P. W. & Rogers, K. E. A Short-Run Cost-Benefit Analysis Of Community-Based Interventions For Juvenile Offenders, *Crime & Delinquency* 47:265-285, 2001. This article presents a cost-benefit evaluation of two community-based intervention techniques.

3239 Robinson, Marcelle; Hanneman, Kathleen & Gould, David The Hillcrest School Of Oregon: Guided Group Interaction In A Juvenile Institution, pp.143-162 in Griffiths, Curt T. & Nance, Margit (eds.) *The Female Offender: Selected Papers From An International Symposium.* Vancouver, British Columbia: Simon Fraser University Criminology Research Center, 1980. This is a description of the institution, its philosophy, programs, and administration.

3240 Rojek, Dean G. & Erickson, Maynard L. Reforming The Juvenile Justice System: The Diversion Of Status Offender, *Law & Society Review* 16:241-264, 1981-82. This article presents an analysis of a follow up of a two-year, status-offender, diversion program.

3241 Romero, Leo M. *An Administrative Model Of Juvenile Justice: The NATO Status Of Forces Agreement Application To American Juvenile Offenders In Germany.* Reno, Nevada: National Council of Juvenile Court Judges, 1975. This document discusses the legal and administrative status of juvenile-dependents of members of the American armed forces, or members of a civilian component attached to the armed forces, who commit criminal offenses in a foreign country subject to the NATO Status of Forces Agreement. 54p. Appendix.

3242 Romig, Dennis A. *Justice For Our Children: Part I, Program Interventions As Treatment.* Lexington, Massachusetts: Lexington Books, 1978. After examining over 825 books and articles on the treatment of juvenile offenders, the author argues that an ideal intervention program includes communication skills, daily living and survival skills, educational advancement and study skills to obtain a diploma or certificate that supports career goals, and career skills. 205p.

3243 Root, Lawrence S. (ed.) *Site Visit Reports: Thirteen Jurisdictions With Programs Used As Alternatives To Detention For Juveniles.* Chicago, Illinois: University of Chicago School of Social Service Administration, 1976. This volume presents descriptions of 13 alternative programs to secure detention for juveniles awaiting hearing.

3244 Rose, Steven R. Analysis Of A Juvenile Court Diversion Program, *Journal Of Offender Rehabilitation* 24:153-161, 1997. Focusing on 50 juveniles in a diversion program, the author investigated a large number of variables relating to them and their processing by the system.

3245 Rosenbaum, Dennis P. & Hanson, Gordon S. Assessing The Effects School-Based Drug Education: A Six-Year Multilevel Analysis Of Project D.A.R.E., *Journal Of Research In Crime And Delinquency* 35:381-412, 1998. The results of an experiment to estimate the short- and long-term effects of the Drug Abuse Resistance Education program on students attitudes, beliefs, social skills, and drug use behaviors, indicate that it neither had long-term effects on a wide range of drug use measures, nor a lasting impact on mediating variables.

3246 Rosenbaum, Jill Leslie & Chesney-Lind, Meda Appearance And Delinquency: A Research Note, *Crime & Delinquency* 40:250-262, 1994. This author reviews related literature, and documents the interest of criminal justice professionals in the physical appearance of girls in the juvenile justice system.

3247 Rosenberg, Irene M. The Constitutional Rights Of Children Charged With Crime: Proposals For A Return To The Not So Distant Past, *UCLA Law Review*, 27:656-721, 1980. The author raises the various constitutional issues related to the Gault decision.

3248 Rosenthal, Richard S. & Smith, Jacqueline J. *Juvenile Justice Publications Of The U.S. Department Of Justice: A Comprehensive Bibliography.* Washington, D.C.: US Government Printing Office, 1982. This is a bibliography of the various publications of the United States Department of Justice on juvenile justice.

3249 Rossum, Ralph A.; Koller, Benedict J. & Manfredi, Christopher P. *Juvenile Justice Reform: A Model For The States*. Claremont, California: Rose Institute of State and Local Government, 1987. The purpose of this publication that presents in table format the various state statutes of relevance to misbehaving youths, is to reform juvenile justice by creating a uniform code. 201p.

3250 Rotherford, Robert B. & Bower, Kenneth Bruce The Role Of Special Education In Juvenile Corrections, *New England Journal Of Prison Law* 2:155-163, 1976. The authors discuss how diverse education programs in juvenile institutions may reduce recidivism, and various ways of enhancing such efforts throughout the country.

3251 Rubel, Robert J. (ed.) *Theoretical Perspectives On School Crime And Poverty*. Washington, D.C.: Department of Health, Education and Welfare, 1979. This is an annotated summary of diverse edited and unedited manuscripts with notations on their relevance for federal and local policy. 107p.

3252 Rubel, Robert J. Analysis And Critique Of HEW's Safe School Study Report, *Crime & Delinquency* 24:257-265, 1978. This article presents a critique of the report to Congress of the Department of Health, Education and Welfare safe school project.

3253 Rubin, H. Ted (ed.) *Juveniles In Justice: A Book Of Readings*. Santa Monica, California: Goodyear, 1980. The articles in this anthology include history, legislative trends, court practices and stages in the processing of juveniles, corrections and in general, and recent trends in the United States juvenile justice system, particularly the juvenile court. 340p.

3254 Rubin, H. Ted The Emerging Prosecutor Dominance Of The Juvenile Court Intake Process, *Crime & Delinquency* 26:299-318, 1980. The author argues that the historic replacement of juvenile court informality and *parens patriae* practice in the United States since the 1967 Gault decision has been at the expense of the probation officers' informal, discretionary practices at the intake stage, and has increased prosecution representation in intake decisions and of the community interest at adjudicatory hearings.

3255 Rubin, H. Ted *Juvenile Justice: Policy, Practice, And Law*. Santa Monica, California: Goodyear Publishing, 1979. This book addresses a host of topics on the complex American handling of serious and repetitive juvenile and status offenders, the case flow process from police apprehension through court disposition, boundaries of judicial authority and case decisions expressing right of institutionalized youths for treatment, prosecution and defense lawyers, and juvenile court judges and an assessment of juvenile court structure and organization, and issues affecting dependent, neglected, and abused children. 299p.

3256 Rubin, H. Ted Retain The Juvenile Court? Legislative Developments, Reform Directions, And The Call For Abolition, *Crime & Delinquency* 25:281-298, 1979. This article discusses trends in legislative reforms that result from public pressure to redefine the juvenile court and juvenile justice.

3257 Rutherford, Andrew Emerging Themes Of Federal Youth Crime Policy, *Justice System Journal* 4:88-99, 1978. Three themes emerge in this discussion of juvenile justice policy in the United States: (1) reducing the massive overreach of the juvenile justice process, (2) narrowing the gap between juvenile and criminal court procedures, and (3) changing sentencing philosophies from rehabilitation to just desserts and incapacitation.

3258 Ryan, Joseph P.; Davis, Randy K. & Yang, Huilan Reintegration Services And The Likelihood Of Adult Imprisonment: A Longitudinal Study Of Adjudicated Delinquents, *Research On Social Work Practice* 11:321-337, 2001. This study, to identify the factors associated with adult imprisonment after long-term residential care of adjudicated delinquent males, found that full reintegration process enables youths to achieve better future outcomes.

3259 Ryerson, Ellen *The Best-Laid Plans: America's Juvenile Court Experiment*. New York, New York: Hill and Wang, 1978. This volume traces the history and development of the juvenile court system in the United States with special emphasis on changing social patterns of the nineteenth and twentieth century, and suggests that the change to the crime control model by the late 1960s reflects a profound loss of faith in the idea of juvenile court. 180p.

3260 Saleebey, George *Hidden Closets: A Study Of Detention Practices In California*. Sacramento, California. Youth Authority Department, 1975. This study describes, identifies, and develops criteria for temporary detention of children in existing alternatives to temporary detention, and detention bed needs.

3261 Salerno, Anthony W. The Child Saver Movement: Altruism Or Conspiracy? *Juvenile And Family Court Journal* 42:37-49, 1991. The 19th century Wilmington, Delaware child-saving movement is the focus of this article.

3262 Salken, Barbara Down The Up Staircase: Due Process And Removal From Criminal Court, *New York Law School Review* 26:643-675, 1981. The pros and cons of denying and removing a case involving a juvenile criminal defendant from criminal to family court are presented in detail.

3263 Sampson, Robert J. & Laub, John H. Structural Variations In Juvenile Court Processing: Inequality, The Underclass, And Social Control, *Law & Society Review* 27:285-311, 1993. This study focuses on racial inequality and economic disparity in the processing and disposition of juvenile cases.

3264 Sanborn, Joseph B. Jr. Remnants Of Parens Patriae In The Adjudicatory Hearing: Is A Fair Trial Possible In Juvenile Court? *Crime & Delinquency* 40:599-615, 1994. Urban, rural and suburban courts, fairness of adjudicatory hearings in juvenile courts, and its implications for the structure of juvenile justice is examined by the authors.

3265 Sanborn, Joseph B. Jr. Factors Perceived To Affect Delinquent Dispositions In Juvenile Court: Putting The Sentencing Decision Into Context, *Crime & Delinquency* 42:99:113, 1996. This study sampled practitioners regarding factors that may influence juvenile court decision making.

3266 Scalia, John *Juvenile Delinquents In The Federal Criminal Justice System.* Washington, D.C: US Bureau of Justice Statistics, 1997. This report presents an analysis of what happened to juveniles referred to the American Federal criminal justice system during 1994-1995.

3267 Schaffer, Laurie; Shick, Shelley & Stein, Nancy Changing Policy In San Francisco: Girls In The Juvenile Justice System, *Social Justice* 24:187-211, 1997. The author provides an insider's view of young female detainees, their view of themselves and experiences in correctional placement.

3268 Schiraldi, Vincent & Soler, Mark The Will Of The People? The Public's Opinion Of The Violent And Repeat Juvenile Offender Act Of 1997, *Crime & Delinquency* 44:590-601, 1998. This paper reports on a study of public's support of the United States Senate Bill S. 10, `Violent and Repeat Juvenile Offender Act of 1997,' that aims to amend the Juvenile Justice Delinquency and Prevention Act.

3269 Schlossman, Steven & Wallach, Stephanie The Crime Of Precocious Sexuality: Female Juvenile Delinquency In The Progressive Era, *Harvard Educational Review* 48:65-94, 1978. Using court records and secondary data sources, the juvenile justice system's discriminatory practices against female juvenile delinquents during the Progressive Era of the early twentieth century United States is examined.

3270 Schlossman, Steven L. *Love And The American Delinquent: The Theory And Practice Of `Progressive' Juvenile Justice 1825-1920*. Chicago, Illinois: University of Chicago Press, 1977. In an attempt to shed new light on juvenile justice in its formative period, this volume offers selective historical materials on theory and practice in American juvenile justice. 303p.

3271 Schneider, Anne L. A Comparative Analysis Of Juvenile Court Responses To Drug And Alcohol Offenses, *Crime & Delinquency* 34:103-124, 1988. Data from Washington state are examined on how courts deal with juvenile drug or alcohol offenders.

3272 Schneider, Anne Larson & Warner, Jean Shumway The Role Of Restitution In Juvenile Justice Systems, *Yale Law Review* 5:382-401, 1987. This article offers a review of the literature on restitution in the American juvenile justice system.

3273 Schneider, Anne L. & Schneider, Peter R. The Impact Of Restitution On Recidivism Of Juvenile Offenders: An Experiment In Clayton County, Georgia, *Criminal Justice Review* 10:1-10, 1985. This study examined the effects of restitution on the recidivism rate of juvenile offenders.

3274 Schneider, Anne Larson & Schneider, Peter R. A Comparison Of Programmatic And "Ad Hoc" Restitution In Juvenile Courts, *Justice Quarterly* 1:529-547, 1984. This study of the rate of successful completions and the extent of restitution to victims, and the differences between the *ad hoc* and programmatic conditions of the Youth Restitution Program to test if program completion had an impact on rates of recidivism.

3275 Schneider, Anne L. & Schram, Donna D. Responses Of Professionals To The Washington (State) Law, pp. 101-120 in Corrado, Raymond; LeBlanc, Marc & Trépanier, Jean (eds.) *Current Issues In Juvenile Justice*. Toronto, Canada: Butterworths, 1983. The transformation from a rehabilitation-orientation to a justice model in the treatment of juvenile delinquents is the subject of this chapter.

3276 Schneider, Anne L. & Schneider, Peter R. An Overview Of Restitution Program Models In The Juvenile Justice System, *Juvenile And Family Court Journal* 31:3-22, 1980. Based on the research of the National Juvenile Restitution Evaluation Project of the Institute of Policy Analysis, seven general models of restitution programs, including juvenile restitution programs, described by the authors.

3277 Schneider, Peter R.; Griffith, William R. & Schneider, Anne L. Juvenile Restitution As A Sole Sanction Or Condition Of Probation: An Empirical Analysis, *Journal Of Research In Crime And Delinquency* 19:47-65, 1982. This study compared outcomes of cases in which offenders received probation with restitution against those ordered restitution only.

3278 Scholten, Carla A. Waiver Of Juvenile Court Jurisdiction Under Iowa's New Juvenile Justice Act, *Drake Law Review* 29:405-432, 1979;1980. The new Iowa Juvenile Justice code on waiver of juvenile court jurisdiction in the context of the general concerns and criticisms of the juvenile court system, discussion of several cases, and analysis of the provisions of the new statute lead the author to conclude that, despite the need for minor change, it is unquestionably a major improvement over the law it replaced.

3279 Schutt, Russell K. & Dannefer, Dale Detention Decisions In Juvenile Cases: JINS, JDs, And Gender, *Law & Society Review* 22:511-520, 1988. The decisions of New Jersey judges involving juvenile detention are examined forany gender-related differences in this study.

3280 Schwartz, Ira M. (ed.) Will The Juvenile Justice System Survive? *Annals Of The American Academy Of Political And Social Science* 564:8-184, 1999. The nine articles in this special issue deal with diverse issues on the future of present-day juvenile court in the United States.

3281 Schwartz, Ira M. & Hsieh, Chang-Ming *Juveniles Confined In The United States: 1979-1991*. Philadelphia, Pennsylvania: Center for the Study of Youth Policy, University of Pennsylvania, 1994. Based on diverse data sources, this document estimates the number of who are juveniles confined in the United States during the survey period. 59p. Appendix.

3282 Schwartz, Ira M. & Guo, Shenyang The Impact Of Demographic Variables On Public Opinion Regarding Juvenile Justice: Implications For Public Policy. *Crime & Delinquency* 39:5-28, 1993. This examination of data from a national public opinion survey on attitudes toward juvenile crime and justice explores the relationship between demographic variables and opinions toward trying juveniles in adult courts, adult sentences, and sentencing youths to adult prisons.

3283 Schwartz, Ira M. (ed.) *Juvenile Justice And Public Policy*. New York, New York: Lexington, 1992. This anthology, covering a wide spectrum of topics, includes 12 articles on critical issues in juvenile justice in the United states. 271p.

3284 Schwartz, Ira M.; Stekltee, Martha W. & Schneider, Victoria W. Federal Juvenile Justice Policy And The Incarceration Of Girls, *Crime & Delinquency* 36:503-520, 1990. This study of the impact of United States Federal juvenile justice policy on the incarceration of girls in public training schools and detention centers found that girls were more likely than boys to be confined for status offenses.

3285 Schwartz, Ira M. *(In)Justice For Juveniles: Rethinking The Best Interest Of The Child*. Lexington, Massachusetts: Lexington Books, 1989. This books offer a critical appraisal of the United States juvenile justice system. 184p.

3286 Schwartz, Ira M.; Jensen, Donald R.; Mahoney, Michael J. *Volunteers In Juvenile Justice*. Washington, D.C.: US National Institute of Law Enforcement and Criminal Justice, 1977. This manual of guidelines and methods for developing and implementing effective volunteer programs in American juvenile justice highlights, describes, and surveys the best methods for operating such programs. 111p.

3287 Schwartz, Jeffrey S. The Young Offender: Transfer To The Adult Court And Subsequent Sentencing, *Criminal Justice Journal* 6:281-313, 1983. The philosophy of juvenile justice, transfer, due process, and constitutional rights are discussed in this article.

3288 Scutt, Jocelynne Justice In A Juvenile Court: What Price Due Process? *Australian And New Zealand Journal Of Criminology* 10:173-184, 1977. In light of the American developments in due process rights for juveniles, this discussion of case studies of juveniles asks to what extent they may be adopted in Australia.

3289 Sealock Miriam D. & Simpson, Sally S. Unraveling Bias In Arrest Decisions: The Role Of Juvenile Offender Type-Scripts, *Justice Quarterly* 15:427-457, 1998. This research is on police decisions to arrest, and the role of their stereotyped assumptions of suspects' race, gender, socioeconomic status, and offense types play in their decision to arrest.

3290 Sealock, Miriam D.; Gottfredson, Denise C. & Gallagher, Catherine A. Drug Treatment For Juvenile Offenders: Some Good And Bad News, *Journal Of Research In Crime And Delinquency* 34:210-236, 1997. The authors report that when substance-abusing youthful offenders were assigned to a two-month residential treatment program, compared to a control group, their drug use and delinquency decreased significantly.

3291 Secret, Philip E. & Johnson, James B. The Effect Of Race On Juvenile Justice Decision Making In Nebraska: Detention, Adjudication, And Disposition, 1988-1993, *Justice Quarterly* 14:445-478, 1997. This study investigated racial differences in juvenile court decision making, and found that black youths received harsher treatment than whites.

3292 Seis, Mark C. & Elbe, Kenneth L. The Death Penalty For Juveniles: Bridging The Gap Between An Evolving Standard Of Decency And Legislative Policy, *Justice Quarterly* 8:465-487, 1991. The author of this essay reviews the literature opposing the death penalty for juveniles.

3293 Selph, Andrew F.; Winfree, L. Thomas Jr. & Mays, G. Larry Serving Juvenile Time In New Mexico: A Comparison Of Institutionalized And Reintegrated Male Offenders, *Juvenile And Family Court Journal* 47:1-14, 1996. Two groups of incarcerated New Mexico juveniles were compared for the length of their state supervision and reintegration into the community.

3294 Shelden, Randall G. & Osborne, Lynn T. "For Their Own Good": Class Interests And The Child Saving Movement In Memphis, Tennessee, 1900-1917, *Criminology* 27:747-768, 1989. This analysis of the child saving movement in Memphis, Tennessee found that the upper-class citizens were in the forefront of the movement, supporting Anthony M. Platt's thesis that the movement was class-biased in order to extend social control to the children of the poor.

3295 Shichor, David & Bartollas, Clemens Private And Public Juvenile Placements: Is There A Difference? *Crime & Delinquency* 36:286-299, 1990. This paper is based on a research examining the patterns of public and private juvenile placements in one of the larger probation departments in Southern California.

3296 Shichor, David Historical And Current Trends N American Juvenile Justice, *Juvenile And Family Court Journal* 34:61-75, 1983. The evolution of American juvenile justice upto the 1950s, and the more recent emphasis on due process are discussed by the author.

3297 Shireman, Charles H. & Reamer, Frederic G. *Rehabilitating Juvenile Justice*. New York, New York: Columbia University Press, 1986. This book is a review of a variety of issues regarding the goal of rehabilitation in American juvenile justice. 188p.

3298 Short, James F. Gangs, Politics, And The Social Order, pp 129-163 in Short, James F. (ed.) *Delinquency, Crime, And Society*. Chicago, Illinois:

University of Chicago Press, 1976. From his observations of Chicago youth gangs, the author describes politicization and politics of delinquency control.

3299 Siegel, Larry J.; Senna, Joseph J. & Libby, Therese J. Legal Aspects Of The Juvenile Justice Process: An Overview Of Current Practices And Law, *New England Law Review* 12:223-264, 1976. The focus of this discussion is the various procedural safeguards needed in detention, probable cause, waiver and other issues in the preliminary processing stages for juveniles accused of crimes.

3300 Sieverdes, Christopher M.; Shoemaker, Donald J. & Cunningham, Orville R. Disposition Decisions By Juvenile Court Probation Officers And Judges: A Multivariate Analysis, *Criminal Justice Review* 4:121-132, 1979. This study found that legal factors outweigh extra-legal factors in dispositions decisions in juvenile courts.

3301 Silberman, Sharon Community Service As An Alternative Sentence For Juveniles, *New England Journal On Criminal And Civil Confinement* 12:123-150, 1986. This essay addressing community service as an alternative to traditional detention of juveniles argues that the former allows juveniles to work off their sentences by doing unpaid social service, and considers it especially appropriate for offenders in the early stages of delinquency.

3302 Simmons, Susan M. & Thompson, V. Oklahoma Debating The Constitutionality Of Juvenile Executions, *Pepperdine Law Review* 16:737-762, 1989. The author discusses the contradictions of Federal opposition to executions of juveniles, and the state level support for it.

3303 Sinclair, Catherine M. A Radical/Marxist Interpretation Of Juvenile Justice In The United States, *Federal Probation* 46:10-28, 1983. The author examines the assumptions of the Marxist view of the origins of juvenile justice in the United States.

3304 Singer, Simon I. The Automatic Waiver Of Juveniles And Substantive Justice, *Crime & Delinquency* 39:253:261, 1993. The author tests the idea that juvenile offenders from nontraditional families are more often waived into criminal court on the assumption that parental support is greater among traditional families with both parents than among those juveniles with only a single parent.

3305 Singer, Simon I. & McDowall, David Criminalizing Delinquency: The Deterrent Effects Of The New York Juvenile Offender Law, *Law & Society Review* 22:521-535, 1988. The authors conclude that the New

York State law of 1978 has not been effective in reducing juvenile crime.

3306 Smith, Bernard Children In Custody: 20-Year Trends In Juvenile Detention, Correctional, And Shelter, *Crime & Delinquency* 44:526-543, 1998. The focus of this article is on trends in public and private juvenile correctional and shelter facilities in the United States during 1978-1998.

3307 Smith, Charles P. *Juvenile Justice System Achievements, Problems, And Opportunities. Draft.* Sacramento, California: American Justice Institute, 1980. This document examines diverse elements of American juvenile justice. 110p.

3308 Smith, Charles P. & Alexander, Paul S. *A National Assessment Of Serious Juvenile Crime And The Juvenile Justice System: The Need For A Rational Response, Vol. I: Summary.* Washington, D.C.: American Justice Institute and US National Institute for Juvenile Justice and Delinquency Prevention, 1979. This is a summary of the major findings, conclusions, and recommendations of a report on serious juvenile crime, and the juvenile justice system in the United States. 65p.

3309 Smith, Charles P.; Black, Edwin & Camp, Fred R. A National Assessment Of Case Disposition And Classification In The Juvenile Justice System: Inconsistent Labeling, Vol. 3: Results Of A Survey. Washington, D.C.: US National Institute for Juvenile Justice and Delinquency Prevention, 1979. This survey of juvenile justice system personnel to determine the association between case service needs and the classification and labeling of juveniles as delinquent, incorrigible, dependent, or abused, and disposition decisions found no association among these variables. 211p.

3310 Smith, Daniel D. *Delinquency 1978: United States Estimates Of Cases Processed By Courts With Juvenile Jurisdiction.* Pittsburgh, Pennsylvania. National Center for Juvenile Justice, 1981. This annual report on national estimates on youth processed by juvenile courts in the United States during 1978 provides detailed information about the juvenile justice system, and a quantitative description of the nature and the extent of the cases involving delinquency and status offenses processed by the juvenile courts. 157p.

3311 Smith, Daniel D. *Young Female Offenders: Analysis Of Differential Handling Based On Sex.* Pittsburgh, Pennsylvania: National Center for Juvenile Justice, 1980. This study assessed the differential processing of females in United States juvenile courts compared to that of males. 12p.

3312 Smith, Daniel D.; Finnegan, Terrence & Corbett, Jacqueline *Young People And The Juvenile Justice System: 1975 Data Base.* Pittsburgh,

Pennsylvania: National Center for Juvenile Justice, 1978. This report on juvenile court statistics has frequency tables and cross-tabulations of offenses, offenders, case processing, and dispositions. 114p.

3313 Smith, Joseph F. An Analysis Of When Juveniles Must Be Afforded Due Process Rights, *Nebraska Law Review* 51:136-158, 1978. When a juvenile faces the potential loss of liberty for a status offense, the author recommends forsaking the two watermarks of the Gault decision -- that a juvenile must have committed an act that constitutes a crime and which may result in incarceration if committed by adults.

3314 Snyder, Howard N. A National Portrait Of Juvenile Court Caseloads: A Summary Of Delinquency In The United States, *Juvenile And Family Court Journal* 38:39-53, 1987. Using data from cases processed in juvenile courts, the author makes estimates of the number of delinquent and status offenders these courts dealt with during 1983.

3315 Snyder, Howard N. & Hutzler, John L. *The Serious Juvenile Offender: The Scope Of The Problem And The Response Of Juvenile Courts.* Pittsburgh, Pennsylvania: National Center for Juvenile Justice, 1981. Drawing on official data, this report questions the perception that serious juvenile crime dramatically increased in the 1970s, and the consequent response of legislators and courts to treat juveniles as adults. 9p.

3316 Sontheimer, Henry & Goodstein, Lynne An Evaluation Of Juvenile Intensive Aftercare Probation: Aftercare Versus System Response Effects, *Justice Quarterly* 10:197-227, 1993. This article reports on the Intensive After Care project of the Philadelphia Juvenile Probation Department.

3317 Sosin, Michael *Juvenile Court Commitment Rates: The National Picture.* Madison, Wisconsin: Institute for Research on Poverty, University of Wisconsin, 1979. This volume examines the institutional commitment of juveniles in the United States during 1974.

3318 Sosin, Michael Due Process Mandates And The Operation Of Juvenile Courts, *Journal Of Social Services Research* 1:321-343, 1978. The impact of Kent, Gault and Winship decisions regarding the due process rights of juveniles in criminal court are discussed by the author.

3319 Spergel, Irving A. & Grossman, Susan F. The Little Village Project: A Community Approach To The Gang Problem, *Social Work* 42:456-470, 1997. This study evaluating the Little Village Gang Violence Reduction Project found consistently positive, preliminary results.

3320 Spergel, Irving A. *The Youth Gang Problem: A Community Approach.* New York, New York: Oxford University Press, 1995. This review advocates a rethinking of the gang policy and programs in the United States. 346p.

3321 Spergel, Irving; Chance, Ron; Ehrensaft, Kenneth; Regulus, Thomas; Kane, Candice; Luseter, Robert; Alexander, Alba & Oh, Sandra *Gang Suppression And Intervention: Community Models. Research Summary.* Washington, D.C.: U. S. Office of Juvenile Justice and Delinquency Prevention, 1994. Based on a national survey and assessmant of organized agency and community group responses to combat the problem of gangs in the United States, this piece develops a comprehensive gang prevention and intervention model. 26p.

3322 Spergel, Irving; Curry, David; Chance, Ron; Kane, Candice; Ross, Ruth; Alexander, Alba; Simmons, Edwina & Oh, Sandra *Gang Suppression And Intervention: Problem And Response Research Summary.* Washington, D. C.: U. S. Office of Juvenile Justice and Delinquency Prevention, 1994. This report on the results of a national survey and assessment of the problem of youth gangs and responses to them across the United States, discusses the need for effective suppression and intervention programs. 21p.

3323 Spergel, Irving *Gang Suppression And Intervention: An Assessment.* Washington, D.C.: U. S. Office of Juvenile Justice and Delinquency Prevention, 1993. This review examines research on youth gangs and interventions to prevent, or minimize, gang violence in the United States. 195p.

3324 Spergel, Irving A. Youth Gangs: An Essay Review, *Social Service Review* 66:121-140, 1992. This review of gang literature is geared towards facilitating greater involvement of social service agencies with gang problems.

3325 Spergel, Irving; Curry, G. David; Ross, Ruth E. & Chance, Ron *Survey Of Youth Gang Problems And Programs In 45 Cities And 6 Sites.* Chicago, Illinois: University of Chicago School of Social Service Administration, 1990. This survey of 254 respondents in 45 American cities, and 6 institutional sites, attempted to discover promising avenues of approach to the youth gang problem. 281p.

3326 Spergel, Irving A. Youth Gangs: Continuity And Change, pp 171-275 in Tonry, Michael & Morris, Norval (eds.) *Crime And Justice: A Review Of Research, Vol. 12.* Chicago: University of Chicago Press, 1990. This review essay describes youth gangs from the social disorganization and poverty perspectives, and evaluates the effectiveness of several;

organized responses to the problem.

3327 Spergel, Irving A. The Violent Gang Problem In Chicago: A Local Community Approach, *Social Service Review* 60:94-131, 1986. This report describes and evaluates the Crisis Intervention Services Project.

3328 Spergel, Irving A. Violent Gangs In Chicago: In Search Of Social Policy, *Social Service Review* 58:199-226, 1984. This article presents a model regarding the development of two types of gangs, and offers a community intervention approach to deal with violent gangs.

3329 Spergel, Irving A.; Reamer, Frederic G. & Lynch, James P. Deinstitutionalization Of Status Offenders: Individual Outcome And System Effects, *Journal Of Research In Crime And Delinquency* 18:4-33, 1981. The authors summarize the findings from the evaluation of an Illinois state-wide deinstitutionalization program providing status offenders, between the time of arrest and court appearance, alternatives to secure detention.

3330 Spergel, Irving A.; Lynch, James P. & Korbelik, John *Deinstitutionalization In Illinois: The Case For Removal Of Status Offenders From Court Processing*. Chicago, Illinois: University of Chicago School of Social Service Administration, 1980. The authors describe and assess The Illinois Status Offender Service (ISOS) project. 47p. Appendix.

3331 Spergel, Irving A. *Social Innovation: Politics, Program, Evaluation: An Organizational Analysis Of The Illinois Status Offender Service Project*. Chicago, Illinois: University of Chicago, School of Social Service Administration. n/d. This document reports findings from an inter-organizational analysis of the Illinois Status Offender Service Project (ISOS), highlighting the politics of its implementation. 463p.

3332 Sprott, Jane B. Understanding Public Opposition To A Separate Youth Justice System, *Crime & Delinquency* 44:399-411, 1998. This paper reports the results of a study examining public perception regarding the leniency of court sentences against youths who commit crime.

3333 Staples, William G. Law And Social Control In Juvenile Justice Dispositions, *Journal Of Research In Crime And Delinquency* 24:7-22, 1987. The author, using the ideas of Donald Black, attempts to predict variations in legal social control in juvenile justice.

3334 Starr, Isidore *Justice: Due Process of Law*. St. Paul, Minnesota: West Publishing, 1981. Issues of due process in criminal proceedings, includeing proceedings against minors, are addressed. 274p.

3335 Stoll, N. Robert *Youh And The Police*. Seattle, Washington: Self-Counsel Press, 1978. The constitutional rights of all, including juvenile offenders, and the impact of a criminal record are discussed in this publication. 118p.

3336 Stott, Denis *Delinquency: The Problem And Its Prevention*. New York, New York: Spectrum, 1982. This book discusses effective social casework approaches to dealing with young offenders.

3337 Streib, Victor L. The Eighth Amendment Capital Punishment Of Juveniles, *Cleveland State Law Review* 34:363-399, 1985-1986. This is a discussion of the American constitutional provisions, the Supreme Court rulings, and death penalty for young offenders.

3338 Streib, Victor L. Death Penalty For Children: The American Experience With Capital Punishment For Crime Committed While Under Age Eighteen, *Oklahoma Law Review* 36:613-641, 1983. In discussing death penalty for minors, the author reviews the various policies and statutes of several states, and provides data on executions of adult and juvenile offenders both preceding, and following the advent of, the juvenile court system.

3339 Strom, Kevin J.; Smith, Steven K. & Snyder, Howard N. *Juvenile Felony Defendants In Criminal Courts*. Washington, D.C: US Bureau of Justice Statistics, 1998. This study used court records on juvenile felony defendants in both criminal and juvenile courts to study their offenses and proceedings.

3340 Stumphauzer, Jerome S. *Helping Delinquents Change: The Treatment Manual Of Social Learning Approach*. New York, New York: Haworth, 1986. The principles of and practices in clinical behavior therapy and community treatment, institutional programs, evaluation, measurement, family contracting, social skills and staff training are the different topics the author covers in this book. 213p.

3341 Stumphauzer, Jerome S. *Progress In Behavior Therapy With Delinquents*. Springfield, Illinois: Charles C. Thomas, 1979. This volume reports on a number of studies representing innovations in behavioral therapy approache to be used with delinquent youths. 390p.

3342 Sulton, Anne T. (eds.) *African-American Perspectives On: Crime Causation, Criminal Justice Administration And Crime Prevention*. Englewood, Colorado: Sulton Books, 1994. Among the topics included in this anthology of contributions by African-Americans professionals are fear of crime among students, female-headed households, and juvenile misbehavior. 222p.

3343 Sumansky, Thomas Witches And Wizards: The Treatment Of Adolescent Drug Abuse, *Today's Delinquent* 3:53-79, 1984. The history of various treatment services such as Alcoholics Anonymous, therapeutic communities and the processes involved in the treatment processes are the focus of this article.

3344 Sutton, John R. *Stubborn Children: Controlling Delinquency In The United States, 1640-1981*. Berkeley, California: University of California press, 1988. The historic evolution from punitive to therapeutic treatment, and social control of deviant American children over the past two centuries is the theme of this book.

3345 Sutton, John R. The Juvenile Court And Social Welfare: Dynamics Of Progressive Reform, *Law & Society Review* 19:107-145, 1985. The author argues that the juvenile court is actually an extension of child control under the guise of progressivism.

3346 Sutton, L. Paul *CHINS Intervention Project: A Study Of Juvenile Recidivism*. Albuquerque, New Mexico: University of New Mexico, 1978. This evaluation of a program for CHINS juveniles compares recidivism rates and their degree of change over time, and identifies factors correlated with youthful recidivism. 40p.

3347 Taft, Philip B. Jr. Elan: Does Its Bizarre Regimen Transform Troubled Youths, Or Abuse Them?, *Corrections Magazine* 5:18-28, 1979. This article describes 'Elan,' a million dollar, for-profit private enterprise started in 1971 by an ex-junkie and a Boston psychiatrist with more than 100 staff members, 6 buildings, and 250 residents.

3348 Tamilia, Patrick R. The Recriminalization Of The Juvenile Justice System--The Demise Of The Socialized Court, *Juvenile And Family Court Journal* 31:15-22, 1980. The author argues against the move to make the juvenile justice system more like the criminal justice system in the United Sates as being regressive and a possible destroyer of the juvenile court as originally conceived.

3349 Tamilia, Patrick Toward A More Credible Juvenile Justice System In The United States, *Juvenile Justice* 27:3-11, 1976. The author feels that the juvenile courts can and do deter criminal behavior, and diversion of youth from the juvenile justice system is fake treatment of the problem that may insulate the child from the consequences of his behavior.

3350 Taylor, Joyce S. Speech-Language Services For Youthful And Adult Offenders, *Federal Probation* 49:37-41, 1980. The thrust of this article is on the need for and adherence of States to Federal legislation mandating that all American children be given free and appropriate special education in the school setting or in institutions and hospitals is.

3351 Taylor, Ronald B. *The Kid Business: How It Exploits The Children It Should Help*. Boston: Houghton Mifflin, 1981. The history of foster care and the juvenile justice system, the beginnings of public welfare, and laws regarding children are traced by the author, who uses examples of successful programs in the United States and abroad to show that it is possible to do the job right. 303p.

3352 Teilmann, Katherine S. & Landry, Pierre H. Gender Bias In Juvenile Justice, *Journal Of Research In Crime And Delinquency* 18:47-80, 1981. This research examing the assertion that female status offenders are treated more harshly than boys in the juvenile justice system did find bias, but bias against girls for some offenses and against boys for others but, overall such bias varied widely with little consistency.

3353 Teitelbaum, Lee E. & Gough, Aidan R. (eds.) *Beyond Control: Status Offenders in the Juvenile Court*. Cambridge, Massachusetts: Ballinger, 1977. This anthology addresses the historical perspective on government regulation of children and parents, and contemporary issues relating to PINS (Persons In Need Of Supervision) processing. 330p.

3354 Texas Youth Commission Department Of Research And Planning *Juvenile Sentencing In The United States: A Survey*. Austin, Texas, 1991. This is a short review of the authority of American juvenile court judges in deciding treatment, and to confine juveniles. 9p. Appendix.

3355 The Juvenile Court Centennial Symposium *Juvenile And Family Court Journal* 50:1-32, 1999. This special issue of the journal has four articles on the past, present, and future of juvenile justice in the United States.

3356 Thomas, Charles W. & Bilchik, Shay Prosecuting Juveniles In Criminal Courts: A Legal And Empirical Analysis, *Journal Of Criminal Law And Criminology* 76:439-479, 1985. The history of special treatment for offending juveniles and their constitutional rights are discussed.

3357 Thornberry, Terence P.; Tolnay, Stewart E.; Flanagan, Timothy J. & Glynn, Patti *Children In Custody 1987: A Comparison Of Public And Private Juvenile Custody Facilities*. Washington D.C.: Office of Juvenile Justice and Delinquency Prevention, 1991. This is a description of a 1987 census of juvenile detention, correctional, and shelter facilities for minors throughout the United States. 75p. Appendix.

3358 Thornton, Robert Y. & Endo, Katsuya *Preventing Crime in America And Japan: A Comparative Study*. Armonk, New York: M. E. Sharpe, 1992. This book compares successful crime prevention methods in Japan and the U.S., and chapter eight in particular focuses on juvenile courts and services including youthful behavioral problems, and curfew. 227p.

3359 Towberman, Donna B. National Survey Of Juvenile Needs Assessment, *Crime & Delinquency* 38:230-238, 1992. From a nationwide survey of needs of juveniles, the author concludes that the most common problems that these youth face include substance abuse, emotional/psychological dysfunction, violent behavior, sexual abuse and deviancy, and family and peer association problems.

3360 Towberman, Donna B. A National Survey Of Juvenile Risk Assessment, *Juvenile And Family Court Journal* 43:61-67, 1992. This is a report of a national suvey of "at-risk" juveniles.

3361 Traver, Michael D. & Rule, Warren R. Self-Mutilating Adolescents In secure Confinement: A Nationwide Survey Of Institutional Response Systems, *Journal Of Offender Rehabilitation* 23:11-22, 1996. Based on questionnaire data of officials, this study is on self-injury among male and female youths in confinement.

3362 Trone, Jennifer; Armstrong, Molly & Sullivan, Mercer *Beyond Blame And Panic: Institutional Strategies For Preventing And Controlling Adolescent Violence*. New York, New York: Vera Institute of Justice, 1998. This report summarizes the findings of a 1997 workshop on adolescent violence. 19p.

3363 Turner, Kenneth A. Treatment Of Juvenile Delinquents, *Juvenile And Family Court Journal* 32:3-7, 1981. The author feels that in spite of failing many, community-based impatient and outpatient mental health services to juveniles who come to the attention of juvenile courts benefits such troubled youths.

3364 Tyler, Jerry E. & Segady, Thomas W. Parental Liability Laws: Rationale, Theory, And Effectiveness, *The Social Science Journal* 37:79-96, 2000. Referring to the distinction between parental liability and responsibility, and the efficacy of applying social control theory in isolation, the author considers such laws as being more repressive for some parents, subjecting parents to their children's judgment, and "quick-fixes" to satisfy a growing concern over delinquency instead of society sharing the blame.

3365 Tyler, Jerry; Darville, Ray & Stalnaker, Kathi Juvenile Boot Camps: A Descriptive Analysis Of Program Diversity And Effectiveness, *The Social Science Journal* 38:445-460, 2001. The authors' survey of literature shows that juvenile boot camps are considerably less effective than the public believes, recidivism rates disappointing, and are more costly than most other traditional options..

3366 University Of Chicago School Of Social Service Administration *Wilderness/Adventure Programs For Juvenile Offenders*. National Center for the Assessment of Alternatives to Juvenile Justice Processing, 1980. This volume describes and evaluates wilderness programs adapted from the Outward Bound programs in the United States. 41p.

3367 University Of New Mexico Youth Resource And Analysis Center *Evaluation of The Juvenile Community Corrections Programs*. Albuquerque, New Mexico: Institute for Soocial research, 1996. This report is an evaluation of community corrections, and reviews relevant research and data on alternative sanctions. 130p. Appendix.

3368 US Bureau Of Alcohol Tobacco And Firearms *The Youth Crime Gun Interdiction Initiative Performance Report*. Washington, D.C., 1999. This is an evaluation of the performance of the Youth Crime Gun Interdiction Initiative of the US Bureau of Alcohol, Tobacco and Firearms that resulted in the investigations of illegal gun trafficking of almost 400 defendants. 27p.

3369 US Comptroller General *Reevaluation Needed Of Educational Assistance For Institutionalized Neglected Or Delinquent Children*. Washington, D.C., 1977. This is a discussion of the Elementary and Secondary Education Act along and an evaluation survey of education of administrators of nationwide programs receiving Title I funds under the act. 67p.

3370 US Conference Of Mayors *A Status Report On Youth Curfews In America's Cities A 347-City Survey*. Washington, D.C., 1997. This document presents results of a survey on curfew laws in American cities. 11p.

3371 US General Accounting Office *At-Risk And Delinquent Youth: Multiple Federal Programs Raise Efficiency Questions*. Washington, D.C., 1996. This report to the United States Congress raises questions about the overall efficiency of Federal efforts and programs to provide various services for at-risk and delinquent youths. 98p.

3372 US General Accounting Office *Juvenile Justice: Juveniles Processed In Criminal Court And Case Dispositions*. Washington, D.C., 1995. This study focused on the transfer of juvenile offenders to criminal courts and the outcomes in such cases. 93p.

3373 US General Accounting Office *Juvenile Justice: Minimal Gender Bias Occurred In Processing Noncriminal Juveniles*. Washington, D.C., 1995. This report focuses on gender bias in the juvenile justice system processsing of status offenders during 1986-1991. 90p.

3374 US House Education And Labor Committee Human Resources Subcommittee *Oversight On Scared Straight: Hearing Held In Washington, D.C., On June 4, 1979*. Washington, D.C.: US Government Printing Office, 1979. This report of the congressional testimony of criminal justice personnel and administrators of the Juvenile Awareness Project and similar programs, representatives of concerned interest groups, and the producers of the film "Scared Straight" is on the pros and cons of the "Scared Straight" program. 380p.

3375 US House Judiciary Committee Courts Civil Liberties And The Administration Of Justice Subcommittee *Bureau Of Prisons Youth And Juvenile Policies*. Washington. D.C.: US Government Printing Office, 1979. The implementation of the congressional Youth Corrections Act and the Juvenile Justice and Delinquency Prevention Act by the Bureau of Prisons, a listing of Federal juvenile facilities, and their descriptions are the subject of this report. 85p.

3376 US House Of Representatives Committee On Natural Resources *Urban Recreation And Crime Prevention*. Washington, D.C.: US Government Printing Office, 1994. This document reports on hearings regarding recreational facilities as a way to reduce youth crime. 217p. Appendix.

3377 US House Select Committee On Children Youth And Families *No Place To Call Home: Discarded Children In America*. Washington, D.C.: US Government Printing Office, 1990. This document provides an analysis of the child welfare, mental health, and juvenile justice systems of the United States. 227p.

3378 US Justice Statistics Bureau *Justice Agencies in the United States: Summary Report 1980*. Washington, D.C.: US Government Printing Office, 1980. This is a master list of the various American local and Federal, civil and criminal justice agencies including those that deal with juveniles. 71p.

3379 US Juvenile Justice And Delinquency Prevention Office *First Analysis And Evaluation: Federal Juvenile Delinquency Programs Volume 1 & 2*. Washington, D.C., 1976. The two volumes offer descriptions of the creation and activities of the Office of Juvenile Justice and Delinquency

Prevention, an analysis of the Federal role in delinquency prevention, and summary information on 117 Federal programs with a bearing on juvenile delinquency control or justice. 226p.

3380 US National Advisory Committee For Juvenile Justice And Delinquency Prevention *Report On Public Hearings*. San Diego, California, 1979. This volume includes testimony on the reauthorization of the Juvenile Justice and Delinquency Prevention Act, the organizational location of the Office of Juvenile Justice and Delinquency Prevention among Federal agencies, and appropriation levels. 35p.

3381 US National Institute Of Corrections Information Center *The Youthful Offender: Legislation And Other Documentation Submitted By The States In Response To A National Survey*. Boulder, Colorado: US National Institute of Corrections Information Center, 1994. This compilation lists various state's statutes, juvenile justice system, and programs for juvenile offenders. 208p. Appendix.

3382 US Office Of Justice Programs *Crime And Justice Atlas*. Washington, D.C.: Justice Research and Statistics Association, 1998. This volume on significant trends in crime, justice, and expenditures over the past two decades, includes the proportion of arrests accounted for by juveniles. 140p.

3383 US Office Of Juvenile Justice And Delinquency Prevention *Juvenile Justice Before And After The Onset Of Delinquency*. Washington, D.C., 1980. This volume provides an assessment of juvenile justice practices in the United States during the late 1970s. 96p.

3384 US Senate Committee On The Judiciary Subcommittee On Juvenile Justice *Exploitation Of Children. Hearing, November 5, 1981*. Washington, D.C.: US Government Printing Office, 1982. This report is on the hearings regarding role of the Federal government in ameliorating the problem of all forms of child exploitation in the United States. 165p.

3385 US Senate Committee On The Judiciary Subcommittee On Juvenile Justice *The Gang Problem In America: Formulating An Effective Federal Response*. Washington, D.C.: US Government Printing Office, 1995. This documents reports committee hearings regarding the role of Federal government in reducing gang delinquency. 88p.

3386 US Youth Development Bureau *Executive Summary: National Evaluation Of The Runaway Youth Program*. Washington, D.C.: US Department of Health and Human Services, 1980. This is an evaluation of data gathered, subsequent to the Runaway Youth Act, from 20

Federally funded projects for runaway children.

3387 Van Dusen, Katherine T. Net Widening And Relabeling: Some Consequences Of Deinstitutionalization, *American Behavioral Scientist* 24:801-810, 1981. The author discusses how "net-widening and relabeling" of status offenders produced results contrary to the ideals of deinstitutionalization.

3388 Vermont Legislative Council *Options For Preventing Delinquency In Vermont*. Montpelier, Vermont, 1980. Based on interviews with persons involved with young offenders in Vermont, suggestions for delinquency prevention programs are offered by this report. 46p.

3389 Vestermark, Seymour D. & Blauvelt, Peter D. *Controlling Crime In The School: A Complete Security Handbook For Administrators*. West Nyack, New York: Parker Publishing, 1978. This handbook is designed for school principals and other administrators on choosing a basic security program, controlling vandalism, bomb threats, confronting the drug problem, controlling rumors and managing crises. 354p.

3390 Vogt, Elizabeth R. California Detention Hearings: Due Process for Juveniles, *UCLA Law Review* 26:1462-1499, 1979. The author advocates due process rights for juveniles in pre-adjudication detention hearings and procedures, but without losing juvenile court flexibility, or the negative formality of the adult criminal system.

3391 Wagner, Robert The System Listens But Does Not Hear, *Criminology* 15:431-441, 1978. The author identifies some of the reasons for institutions' inability to meet the challenge of delinquency and the elements perpetuating the present system, and discusses requirements for building a new child-care system.

3392 Wailes, Segrest N. & Rao, V. V. Prakasa A Longitudinal Study Of Male Delinquents In Juvenile Institutions, *Crime And Justice* 4:125-143, 1981. This article reports findings from a long-term study of institutionalized juveniles in Mississippi.

3393 Walker, Jerry P.; Cardarelli, Albert P. & Billingsley, Dennis *The Theory And Practice Of Delinquency Prevention In The United States: Review, Synthesis And Assessment*. Columbus, Ohio: Ohio State University Center for Vocational Education, 1976. This critical and expository analysis of literature and research on delinquency prevention, concludes that none of the preventive efforts is able to develop an effective program to deal with the complexity of delinquency. 208p.

3394 Wall, John S. *Juvenile Delinquency Prevention: A Compendium Of 36 Program Models*. Washington, D.C.: US National Institute for Juvenile Justice and Delinquency Prevention, 1980. Presenting this matrix of 36 American delinquency prevention programs and their key characteristics, the author feels the effectiveness of most in delinquency prevention had been demonstrated by various evaluations. 157p.

3395 Watkins, John C. Jr. *Selected Cases On Juvenile Justice In The Twentieth Century*. Lewiston, New York: Edwin Mellen Press, 1999. Using case studies the trends in juvenile law from 1905-1998 are examined by the author. 477p.

3396 Watkins, John C. Jr. *The Juvenile Justice Century: A Sociological Commentary On American Juvenile Courts*. Durham, North Carolina: Carolina Academic Press, 1998. The author examines the various historical forces in the development of juvenile justice in the United States. 299p.

3397 Weinstein, Noah & Mendoza, John F. *Supreme Court Decisions And Juvenile Justice, 2nd Edition*. Reno, Nevada: National Council of Juvenile and Family Court Judges, 1979. The authors summarize the various Supreme Court decisions affecting the practice of juvenile justice. 55p.

3398 Wellford, Charles F. & Aultman, M. G. Police Contact And Delinquency: A Relevant Evaluation, *Australian And New Zealand Journal Of Criminology* 14:110-118, 1981. This Tallahassee, Florida study examined the relationship between contact with the police and subsequent delinquency, and found that police contact does have considerable effect on subsequent delinquent behavior.

3399 Welsh, Wayne N.; Jenkins, Patricia H. & Harris, Philip W. Reducing Minority Overrepresentation In Juvenile Justice: Results Of Community-Based Delinquency Prevention In Harrisburg, *Journal Of Research In Crime And Delinquency* 36:87-110, 1999. This article describes the results of a three-year evaluation study of the community crime prevention programs that was carried out in Harrisburg, Pennsylvania.

3400 Wheeler, Gerald R. & Wheeler, Carol L. Unraveling Determinate Sentencing For Juvenile Offenders In The United States, *Crime And Justice* 7-8:106-112, 1979-1980. The authors offer new guidelines to counteract the abuse of indeterminate sentence after examining case-by-case decisions of the past that have not been in the best interest of the child or society.

3401 Wheeler, Gerald R. *Counter-Deterrence: A Report On Juvenile Sentencing And Effects Of Prisonization*. Chicago, Illinois: Nelson-Hall, 1978. The author discusses juvenile sentencing, parole procedures, official attitudes toward determinate sentences, the revolving door, decriminalization, and alternative models to coercive treatment. 182p.

3402 Wiebush, Richard G. Juvenile Intensive Supervision: The Impact On Felony Offenders Diverted From Institutional Placement, *Crime & Delinquency* 39:68-89, 1993. This examination of the 18-month recidivism of juvenile felony offenders in an intensive supervision program compared the outcomes of intensive program participants with those incarcerated and released to parole, and a group of youths under regular probation.

3403 Wilderman, Elizabeth Juvenile Diversion: From Politics To Policy, *New England Journal Of Human Services* 3:19-23, 1984. The relations between research and policies within the historical context of diversion in Colorado is the focus of this discussion.

3404 Wilson, Sandra Jo & Lipsey, Mark W. Wilderness Challenge Programs For Delinquent Youth: A Meta-Analysis Of Outcome Evaluations, *Evaluation And Program Planning* 23:1-12, 2000. This meta-analysis of evaluations of wilderness challenge programs concludes that those involving relatively intense activities or with therapeutic enhancements resulted in the greatest reductions in delinquent behavior.

3405 Winfree, L.Thomas Jr.; Esbensen, Finn-Aage & Osgood, D. Wayne Evaluating A School-Based Gang-Prevention Program, *Evaluation Review* 20:181-203, 1996. The authors develop a theory-driven model to assess "GREAT", the Gang Resistance Education and Training Program.

3406 Winner, Lawrence & Lanza-Kaduce, Lonn The Transfer Of Juveniles To Criminal Court: Reexamining Recidivism Over The Long Term, *Crime & Delinquency* 44:548-563, 1998. This study addresses how transfer decisions of Florida criminal courts affect long-term recidivism among juveniles.

3407 Wolfgang, Marvin E; Elliott, Delbert S.; Huizinga, David; Morse, Barbara & Krisberg, Barry *Violent Juvenile Crime: What Do We Know About It And What Can We Do About It?* Minneapolis, Minnesota: Center for the Study of Youth Policy, Hubert H. Humphrey Institute of Public Affairs, University of Minnesota, 1986. This anthology contains three essays that discuss violent crimes committed by youths. 55p.

3408 Woodson, Robert L. (ed.) *Youth Crime And Urban Policy: A View From The Inner City*. Washington, D.C.: American Enterprise Institute for Public Policy Research, 1981. Reporting on the proceedings of a conference on community-based groups active in controlling juvenile crime in urban areas, the author advocates citizens' participation in any policy to solve urban, social problems, such as youth crime. 154p.

3409 Woolredge, John & Hartman, Jennifer Effectiveness Of Culturally Specific Community Treatment For African American Juvenile Felons, *Crime & Delinquency* 40:589-598, 1994. This is an assessment of the effectiveness of prevention of recidivism among Afro-American juvenile felons by the Community Corrections Partnership Program of Cincinnati, Ohio.

3410 Wordes, Madeline & Jones, Sharon Trends In Juvenile Detention And Steps Towards Reform, *Crime & Delinquency* 44:544-560, 1998. This study takes a detailed look at the problems associated with juvenile detention in the United States.

3411 Wordes, Madeline; Bynum, Timothy S. & Corley, Charles J. Locking Up Youth: The Impact Of Race On Detention Decisions, *Journal Of Research In Crime And Delinquency* 31:149-165, 1994. This analysis of the relationship between race and secure detention of juveniles reveals that black and Latino youth were more likely than whites to be detained at each decision point in the juvenile justice system.

3412 Wright, R. Dean; Buzzell, Timothy; Wright, Susan E. & Gay, Fred Promoting Cognitive Development Among Young Offenders Through Pre-Trial Intervention, *Journal Of Offender Rehabilitation* 21:203-219, 1994. This article reports an evaluation study of juveniles transferred to adult court with the intent to improve their attitudes toward police and courts and interpersonal skills.

3413 Zang, Sheldon X. The Efficiency Of Working Under One Roof: An Evaluation Of Lost Angeles County Juvenile Justice Centers, *Crime & Delinquency* 42:257-268, 1996. This evaluation concludes that a unified structure was more efficient than the system of separate agencies handling different stages in judicial processing.

3414 Zimring, Franklin E. *The Changing Legal World Of Adolescence*. New York, New York: Free Press, 1982. Post-1960 developments in the patch-work of laws regarding minors and, particularly the legal status of adolescents on specific issues like juvenile delinquency along with sex-education, compulsory national service are addressed by the author.

Yugoslavia (Former)

3415 Goodman, Randy Summaries Of DCI Country Surveys, Yugoslavia, pp 204-206 in Tomasevski, Katarina (ed) *Children In Adult Prisons: An International Perspective.* New York, New York: St. Martin's Press, 1986. These are the findings for Yugoslavia from 1982-1984 Defense for Children International Survey of children in adult prisons.

3416 Institute Of Criminology At The Faculty Of Law Edvard Kardelj University *Overview Of Research Work 1954-1984 (Pregled Raziskovalnega Dela 1954-1984).* Ljubljana, Yugoslavia, 1984. This volume includes summaries of criminological papers developed at the institute from 1957 through 1984 including papers on juvenile delinquency, and the juvenile justice systems. 61p. Slovene.

3417 Obrad, Peric About The New Social Defense And The Judicial Condition Of Delinquent Minors In Yugoslavian Law (Les Idées De La Défense Sociale Nouvelle Et La Condition Juridique Du Mineur Délinquant En Droit Yougoslave), *Cahiers De Défense Sociale* 109-117, 1990-1991. According to the author, post-1951 changes in criminal law had major impact on juvenile justice with their ephasis on the criteria of criminal responsibility, educational measures, and special penalties for minors. French.

3418 Selih, Alenka Yugoslavia, pp 159-188 in Stewart, V. Lorne (ed.) *Justice And Troubled Children Around The World, Vol. 2.* New York, New York: New York University Press, 1981. This chapter describes the operation and policies of juvenile justice in Yugoslavia.

Zaire

3419 Goodman, Randy Summaries Of DCI Country Surveys, Zaire, pp 206-207 in Tomasevski, Katarina (ed.) *Children In Adult Prisons: An International Perspective.* New York: St. Martin's Press, 1986. Findings on children in adult prisons of Zaire from the 1982-1984 Defense for Children International Survey are described here.

3420 Kabena-Basue, Kabundi The Zaire Juvenile Law And Alternative Measures To Institutinal Confinement: Where Are We? (Le Droit Zaïrois Des Mineurs Et Les Mesures Alternatives À L'Internement Institutionnel: Où En Est-On?), *Revue Internationale De Criminologie Et De Police Technique* 40:448-459, 1987. The concurrence between Zaire's laws and practices regarding minors accused of criminal offenses is the subject of this discussion. French.

Multi-National

3421 Albrecht, Peter Alexis & Backes, Otto (eds.) *Crime Prevention And Intervention: Legal And Ethical Problems: Prevention And Intervention In Childhood And Adolescence, 3 Vols.* Berlin, Germany: Walter de Gruyter, 1989. This anthology includes sixteen papers on various legal and ethical problems of individual liberty and rights, equality, and justice in prevention and intervention, with special reference to adolescence with some field research in Norway and Germany. 286p.

3422 Alder, Christine & Wunderstiz, Joy (eds.) *Family Conferencing And Juvenile Justice: The Way Forward Or Misplaced Optimism?* Canberra, Australia: Australian Institute of Criminology, 1994. This anthology assesses the use and dimensions of family group conferencing in Australia and New Zealand. 220p.

3423 Allen, Rob Responding To Youth Crime In Norway: Suggestions For England And Wales, *Howard Journal* 32:99-113, 1993. This is a review of recent developments in child welfare services provided youths in the Norwegian judicial system compared to England and Wales.

3424 Alper, Benedict S. Abolition The Most Fitting Tribute For John Howard's Biennial, *Howard Journal* 17: 71-77, 1978. Although this volume is on abolition of imprisonment in general, this article includes youth in custody in Canada, the United States, and United Kingdom.

3425 American Correctional Association *Probation and Parole Directory: Adult and Juvenile Probation and Parole Services, United States and Canada*. College Park, Maryland: American Correctional Association, 1981. This North American directory includes brief descriptions of probation and parole for all American states and Canadian territories, and includes details on personnel. 469p.

3426 Andrews, Kay Ideology And Crime In Relation To Juvenile Justice Systems In England And Poland, pp. 38-53 in Wilson, Thelma (ed.) *Penal Services For Offenders: Comparative Studies Of England And Poland 1984/85*. Brookfield, Vermont: Gower, 1987. The author indicates that both Great Britain and Poland have a high proportion of institutionalized youths.

3427 Armstrong, Troy L.; Maloney, Dennis & Romig, Dennis The Balanced Approach In Juvenile Probation: Principles, Issues And Applications, *American Probation And Parole Association Perspectives*, Winter:8-13, 1990. This article reviews the historic trends and conflicting problems faced by juvenile justice programs in Canada and the United States.

3428 Asquith, Stewart *Children And Justice: Decision-Making In Children's Hearings And Juvenile Courts*. Edinburgh, Scotland: Edinburgh University Press, 1983. American, English and Scottish attitudes toward dealing with misbehaving juveniles are compared in this volume.

3429 Atkinson, Lynn & Gerull, Sally-Anne (eds.) *National Conference On Juvenile Detention*. Canberra, Australia: Australian Institute of Criminology, 1994. The focus of this publication is on alternatives to detention for young offenders in New Zealand and Australia. 220p.

3430 Awad, George & Chamberlain, Clive The Process Of Psychiatric Work With The Juvenile Courts, *Canadian Journal Of Family Law* 1:363-374, 1978. The authors examine some possible reasons for the markedly decreased psychiatric work with juvenile delinquents in Canada and the United States.

3431 Bailleau, Francis Social Crime Prevention: Juvenile Delinquency, pp 43-55 in Asquith, Stewart (ed.) *Children And Young People In Conflict With The Law*. London, United Kingdom: Jessica Kingsley, 1996. This chapter offers a brief description of various innovative prevention programs that are aimed at young people in Europe in general.

3432 Bala, Nicholas; Hornick, Joseph P.; Snyder, Howard N. & Paetsch, Joanne J. (eds.) *Juvenile Justice Systems: An International Comparison Of Problems And Solutions*. Toronto, Canada: Thompson Educational Publishing, 2002. This anthology has ten chapters on juvenile crime and justice in eight countries as well as two on general dimensions of the topic. 270p. Appendix.

3433 Bazemore, Gordon & Walgrave, Lode (eds.) *Restorative Juvenile Justice: Repairing The Harm Of Youth Crime*. Monsey, New York: Criminal Justice Press, 1999. This anthology has 15 chapters discussing various aspects of restorative juvenile justice as practiced in countries throughout the world.

3434 Beaulieu, Lucien A. & Cesaroni, Carla The Changing Role Of The Youth Court Judge, *European Journal On Criminal Policy And Research* 7:363-393, 1999. The authors cover a wide spectrum of topics, such as the history of youth justice legislation in the United States, Canada, and the United Kingdom, and describes various laws and statutes on juveniles in these countries.

3435 Bosley, David J. The Problem Of The Young Offender -- An Ideal Solution? Agricultural Reformatories In England And France: The Nonage 1800-1854, pp 289-324 in Hess, Albert g. & Clement, Priscilla F. (eds.) *History Of Juvenile Delinquency: A Collection Of Essays On*

Crime Committed By Young Offenders, In History And In Selected Countries Vo. I. Aalen, Germany: Scientia Verlag, 1990. This chapter discusses reasons for the rise of juvenile reformatories as mainly agricultural institutions, designed to train urban youths in the rural arts, in England and France during the 1800s.

3436 Bottoms, Bette L. & Goodman, Gail S. (eds.) *International Perspectives On Child Abuse And Children's Testimony: Psychological Research And Law.* Thousand Oaks, California: Sage, 1996. This anthology presents extensive discussion of laws, procedures and problems dealing with child witnesses, and allegations of sexual abuse and related issues in diverse societies.

3437 Boutellier, J. C. J. (ed.) New Sanctioning Options, *European Journal On Criminal Policy And Research* 6:475-579, 1998. This special issue of six articles based on a conference on "Beyond Prisons" held in 1998 in Canada concerns sanctioning options in the Netherlands, Belgium, New Zealand, Canada, Hungary, and the Czech Republic.

3438 Bright, Barry An examination Of The Forces That Influence Criminal Justice Policy And Its Administration In England And Poland, pp 23-37 in Wilson, Thelma (ed.) *Penal Services For Offenders: Comparative Studies Of England And Poland 1984/85.* Brookfield, Vermont: Gower, 1987. This essay is on criminal justice system in general, and the author's portrayal of the Polish family's importance within the Polish juvenile justice system is in striking contrast to that of the West. 103p.

3439 Cain, Maureen (ed.) *Growing Up Good: Policing The Behavior Of Girls in Europe.* Newbury Park, California: Sage, 1989. The Appendix titled 'Girls In The European Criminal Courts: A Comparative View' offers statistics on how boys and girls are treated in the judicial systems of several European countries.

3440 Challinger, Dennis Comparison Of Official Warnings And Court Appearances For Young Offenders, *Australian And New Zealand Journal Of Criminology* 14:165-169, 1981. Describes and compares informal diversion from police warnings through children's court in Great Britain and New South Wales, Australia.

3441 Church Council On Justice And Corrections *Satisfying Justice: Safe Community Options To Repair Harm From Crime And Reduce The Use Or Length Of Imprisonment.* Ottawa, Canada: Church Council on Justice and Corrections, 1996. This volume focuses on judicial formats for alternative sentencing for adults and juveniles in Canada, the United States, Norway, the Netherlands, Zimbabwe and Swaziland. 194p.

3442 Council Of Europe European Committee On Crime Problems *Short-Term Methods Of Treatment For Young Offenders*. Strasbourg, France: Council of Europe, 1967. Detailed accounts of the system of "Jugendarrest" in the Federal Republic of Germany and Detention Centers in Great Britain are presented in this effort to identify the salient features for greater effectiveness of correctional work with youthful offenders. 90p.

3443 Council Of Europe European Division Of Crime Problems *Prevention Of Juvenile Delinquency: The Role Of Institutions Of Socialization In A Changing Society*. Strasbourg, France: Council of Europe, 1982. The focus of this collection from around the world is juvenile delinquency, the role of family, school, and socialization to prevent delinquent behavior.

3444 Crawford, Adam Contrasts In Victim-Offender Mediation And Appeals To Community In France and England, pp 205-209 in Nelken, David (ed.) *Contrasting Criminal Justice: Getting From Here To There.* Burlington, United Kingdom: Ashgate/Dartmouth, 2000. Describes how the philosophy, legal-orientation, and values of the French system facilitate mediation in general compared to the adversarial legal-culture of England.

3445 Danto, Bruce; Olszewski, Ron & Shannon, Anthony W. *Crisis Behind Bars: A Book For Police And Correctional Officers*. Warren, Michigan: The Dale Corporation, 1981. This manual examines suicide among juvenile and adult detainees in both Canada and the United States. 60p.

3446 David, Pedro R. Preventing Delinquency, Juvenile Justice And The Protection Of The Young: Policy Approaches And Directions, pp 71-107 in in Sugihara, Hiroyasu (ed.) *Resource Material Series No. 44*. Tokyo, Japan: UNAFEI, 1991. The author discusses Latin and Caribbean delinquency prevention programs in the context of the United Nations guidelines.

3447 Devine, Francis E. Isolation Of English Juvenile Offenders By Classification: An American Perspective, *International Journal Of Comparative And Applied Criminal Justice* 1:123-134, 1977. The author focuses on the English and American differences in classifying and isolating corrigible youth from the hardened ones.

3448 Dingwall, Robert; Eeklaar, John & Murray, Topsy *The Protection Of Children: State Intervention And Family Life*. Oxford, United Kingdom: Basil Blackwell, 1983. The authors use some case studies as examples in addressing the incidence of child abuse and neglect in Great Britain, and compare and explain English law and statutory procedures with the various mthods used in the United States and other countries. 286 p.

3449 Dobash, Russell P.; Dobash, R. Emerson; Ballintyne, Scott; Schumann, Karl; Kaulitzki, Reiner & Garth, Hans-Werner Ignorance And Suspicion: Young People And Criminal Justice In Scotland And Germany, *British Journal Of Criminology* 30:306-320, 1990. This study compares the contacts young people have with and their perceptions of criminal justice systems in Scotland and West Germany.

3450 Doek, Jaap E. The Future Of The Juvenile Court, pp 197-210 in Junger-Tas, Josine; Boendermaker, Leonieke & Van Der Laan, Peter H. (eds.) *The Future Of The Juvenile Justice System (L'Avenir Du Système Pénal Des Mineurs).* Leuven, Belgium: Acco, 1991. This essay traces the history of landmark legislations and proliferation of juvenile courts in Canada, the United States, the Netherlands, France, Belgium, and up to the Beijing Rules that are universal at present.

3451 Dünkel, Frieder Deprivation Of Freedom For Juvenile Delinquents: Actual Tendencies And International Comparisons (La Privation De Liberté À L'Égard De Jeunes Délinquants; Tendances Actuelles Dans Le Cadre D'Une Comparaison Internationale), pp 385-400 in Junger-Tas, Josine; Boendermaker, Leonieke & Van Der Laan, Peter H. (eds.) *The Future Of The Juvenile Justice System (L'Avenir Du Système Pénale Des Mineurs).* Leuven, Belgium: Acco, 1991. This chapter offers an extensive discussion of laws regarding the rights and judicial protections for minors accused of offenses in various countries. French.

3452 Dünkel, Frieder Legal Differences In Juvenile Criminology In Europe, pp 1-29 in Booth, Tim (ed.) *Juvenile Justice In The New Europe.* Sheffield, United Kingdom: Joint Unit for Social Services Research, Sheffield University, 1991. This chapter provides a comprehensive overview of juvenile justice policies in Western Europe.

3453 Dünkel, Frieder Delinquent-Victim Mediation And Restitution: New Developments In Penal Rights And Judicial Practices An International Comparison (Médiation-Délinquant-Victime Et Réparation Des Dommages: Nouvelle Évolution De Droit Pénal Et De La Pratique Judiciaire Dans Une Comparaison Internationale), pp 1-81 in Dünkel, Frieder & Zermatten, Jean (eds.) *Recent Trends In Penal Law For Minors: Mediation, Community Service And Intermediate Treatment (Nouvelles Tendances Dans Le Droit Pénal Des Mineurs: Médiation, Travail Au Profit De La Communauté Et Traitement Intermédiaire).* Freiburg, Germany. Max Planck Institute for Foreign and International Criminal Justice, 1990. As an introduction to the volume, this chapter provides extensive comparisons of approaches to mediation and restitution that are used in several European countries. French.

3454 Ely, Peter & Stanley, Chris *The French Alternative: Delinquency Prevention And Child Protection In France.* London, United Kingdom: National Association for the Care and Resettlement of Offenders, 1990. The authors contrast the paternalistic and social-welfare orientation of the French juvenile justice system, which concentrates on prevention and integration through education and social work, with the punitive approach taken in the United Kingdom. 62p.

3455 European Conference Of Ministers Of Transport *Delinquency And Vandalism In Public Transport.* Paris, France: European Ministers of Transport, 1989. This report describes forms of vandalism and violence in public transportation system, and provides recommendations for dealing with the problem in Great Britain, France, The Netherlands and West Germany. 165p.

3456 Feld, Barry C. Juvenile Justice Swedish Style: A Rose By Another Name? *Justice Quarterly* 11:625-650, 1994. This essay and review compares the Swedish and American juvenile justice systems.

3457 Figueira-McDonough, Josefina Processing Juvenile Delinquency In Two Cities: A Cross-National Comparison, *Journal Of Research In Crime And Delinquency 16*:114-142, 1979. This is a comparison of two juvenile court systems, one in Rio de Janeiro, Brazil and the other in the United States, both functioning in metropolitan centers with similar ecological profiles.

3458 Finckenauer, James O. & Gavin, Patricia W. *Scared Straight: The Panacea Phenomenon Revisited.* Prospect heights, Illinois: Waveland Press, 1999. A critique of the various "scared straight" programs in Norway and the United Statesis presented in the book. 246p.

3459 Fondation Internationale Pénale Et Pénitentiaire (ed.) *Community Service As An Alternative To The Prison Sentence (Le Service Au Profit De La Communauté En Tant Que Mesure De Substitution À La Peine D'Emprisonnement).* Bonn, West Germany, 1988. This anthology has eleven papers on community service as an alternative to prison, including programs for juvenile offenders in the United States, France, England, Spain, New Zealand, Portugal, West Germany, the Netherlands and other members of the Council of Europe.171p. French.

3460 Galaway, Burt & Hudson, Joe (eds.) *Criminal Justice, Restitution, And Reconciliation.* Monsey, New York: Criminal Justice Press, 1990. This anthology includes 19 papers on the use of restitution, community service and victim-offender reconciliation programs in juvenile and adult justice systems of Canada, Germany, United Kingdom and the United States. 236p.

3461 Garrido, Vicente & Redondo, Santiago The Institutionalization Of Young Offenders, *Criminal Behaviour And Mental Health* 3:336-348, 1994. Elucidating on the structural factors and the reduction in the numbers of imprisoned young offenders in Spain, the authors discuss also the community-based alternatives in Germany, and young people in prisons in Britain.

3462 Gelsthorpe, Loraine; Nellis, Mike; Bruins, Jeannette & Van Vliet, Annelies Diversion In English And Dutch Juvenile Justice, pp 199-226 in Harding, Christopher; Fennell, Phil & Jorg, Nico (eds.) *Criminal Justice In Europe: A Comparative Study*. Oxford, United Kingdom: Clarendon, 1995. This chapter discusses in detail, diversion programs in the two countries, comments on human rights, and the possible integration of approaches.

3463 Gilbert, Neil (ed.) *Combating Child Abuse: International Perspectives And Trends*. New York, New York: Oxford University Press, 1997. Compares and illustrates the differences in the philosophy, definition, structure, and operation of the reporting systems and outcomes of child abuse cases in Denmark, the United States, England, Canada, the Netherlands, Finland, Germany, Belgium and Sweden. 255p.

3464 Griffiths, Curt Taylor & Winfree, L. Thomas Jr. Attitudes Toward The Police: A Comparison Of Canadian And American Adolescents, *International Journal Of Comparative And Applied Criminal Justice* 6:127-141, 1982. This is a study of Canadian and American adolescents' attitudes toward the police, and the determinants of these attitudes.

3465 Hackler, Jim The Manifest And Latent Functions Of Legal Aid, *International Criminal Justice Review* 2:58-75, 1992. The juvenile justice system in Melbourne, Australia is compared with practices common in the United States and Canada where a "fee-for-the service" model seems not as beneficial for the juvenile clients.

3466 Hackler, Jim A Strategy For The Cross-Cultural Study Of Juvenile Justice, pp 49-58 in Hackler, Jim (ed.) *Official Responses To Problem Juveniles: Some International Reflections*. Euskadi, Spain: The Oñati International Institute for the Sociology of Law, 1991. This chapter spells out an approach that researchers might use in studying juvenile justice from a broad cross-cultural perspective.

3467 Hackler, Jim Increasing Flexibility In Juvenile Justice pp 389-403 in Hackler, Jim (ed.) *Official Responses To Problem Juveniles: Some International Reflections*. Euskadi, Spain: The Oñati International Institute for the Sociology of Law, 1991. Drawing on the experiences of countries around the world, this chapter discusses ways to increase flexibility in juvenile justice generally.

3468 Hackler, Jim & Garapon, Antoine *Stealing Conflicts In Juvenile Justice: Contrasting France And Canada*. Edmonton, Canada: Centre for Criminological Research, University of Alberta, 1986. The authors' assert that the Young Offenders Act of Canada continues to reduce juveniles' sphere of control in conflicts by placing them under the control of professionals, while in France, the juveniles remain more active participants in determining their fates and therefore have greater control over those conflicts. 18p.

3469 Hackler, Jim *Closed Custody For Juveniles: Comparisons Between Canada And France*. Edmonton, Canada: Centre for Criminological Research, University of Alberta, 1986. This comparison of Alberta, Canada and France focuses on the Canadian Young Offenders Act of 1985 in contrast with the French system that makes extensive efforts to avoid the use of closed custody. 32p.

3470 Hackler, James C. Implications Of Variability In Juvenile Justice, pp 213-233 in Klein, Malcolm W. (ed.) *Western systems of Juvenile Justice*. Beverly Hills, California: Sage, 1984. This is a comparison of the French and Canadian juvenile justice systems.

3471 Hackler, James C. & Brockman, Joan Attitudes Toward Delinquency By Court Officials: Comparisons Between North America And Europe, *International Journal Of Comparative And Applied Criminal Justice* 3:3-25, 1979. This study compared the attitudes, by rank ordering equivalent roles along various attitudinal dimensions to measure the diversity of opinion of juvenile court officials in Vienna, Austria and Boston, Massachusetts.

3472 Hagan, John & Leon, Jeffrey The Rehabilitation Of Law: A Social-Historical Comparison Of Probation In Canada And The United States, *Canadian Journal Of Sociology* 5:235-251, 1981. The authors compare Canadian and American laws' historical, philosophical and policy orientations to juvenile and adult probation.

3473 Hamilton, V. Lee & Sanders, Joseph *Everyday Justice: Responsibility And The Individual In Japan And The United States*. New Haven, Connecticut: Yale, 1992. This study focuses on differences in the the Japanese and American "legal cultures," their concepts of responsibility, and the sanctions typically used for deviance.

3474 Hammarberg, Thomas Children, Crime And Society: Perspectives Of The UN Convention On The Rights Of The Child, pp 15-25 in Howard League for Penal Reform. *Child Offenders: UK & International Practice*. London, United Kingdom, 1995. This has an excerpt and conclusions from the United Nations Convention on the Rights of Children.

3475 Hancock, Linda & Chesney-Lind, Meda Female Status Offenders And Justice Reforms: An International Perspective, *Australian And New Zealand Journal Of Criminology* 15:109-122, 1982. Describes the current legislative attempts and changes as well as the historic development of the paternalistic laws on girls in the United States, United Kingdom, and Australia that are the basis of sex and status-related prosecutions of young women in these countries.

3476 Hartung-Ayisi, Gisela Latin America, pp 210-223 in Brusten, M.; Graham, J.; Herriger, N. & Malinowski, P. (eds.) *Youth Crime Social Control And Prevention: Theoretical Perspectives And Policy Implications—Studies From Nine Different Countries*. Pfaiffenweiler, Germany: Centaurus-Verlagsgesellschaft, 1986. This chapter describes the various crime and delinquency prevention measures used by Latin-American countries.

3477 Hawkins, Gordon & Zimring, Franklin E. Western European Perspectives On The Treatment Of Young Offenders, pp 55-74 in Greenwood, Peter W. (ed.) *Intervention Strategies For Chronic Juvenile Offenders: Some New Perspectives*. New York, New York: Greenwood, 1986. The authors examine ways that Europe and America deal with youth crime and conclude that the American approach is being imitated around the globe.

3478 Howard League *Child Offenders: & International Practice*. London, United Kingdom: The Howard League for Penal Reform, 1995. This volume includes articles on media and political interest in youth crime, the common Law concept of *doli incapax*, age of criminal proceedings in Europe, children and criminal justice system in Scotland, longitudinal aspects of reconviction, and criminal proceedings in Europe in general. 61p.

3479 Hudson, Joe; Morris, Allison & Maxwell, Gabrielle (eds.) *Family Group Conferences: Perspectives On Policy & Practice*. Monsey, New York/Annandale, Australia: Criminal Justice Press and Federation Press, 1996. This anthology reviews the principles and practices of family group conferences as practed in the juvenile justice and child protection systems of several nations around the world. 240p.

3480 Hudson, Barbara Justice Or Welfare? A Comparison Of Recent Developments In The English And French Juvenile Justice Systems, pp 96-113 in Cain, Maureen (ed.) *Growing Up Good: Policing The Behavior Of Girls in Europe*. Newbury Park, California: Sage, 1989. This chapter describes similarities and differences exhibited by France and England in the punitive versus welfare approaches to juvenile justice.

3481 Hudson, Barbara *Justice Through Punishment: A Critique Of The 'Justice' Model Of Corrections*. New York, New York: St. Martin's Press, 1987. Compares the justice model of corrections as practiced in United Kingdom and the United States, and its impact on juveniles, minorities, and women. 184p.

3482 Immarigeon, Russ Family Group Conferences In Canada And The United States: An Overview, pp 167-179 in Hudson, Joe; Morris, Allison; Maxwell, Gabrielle & Galaway, Burt (eds.) *Family Group Conferences: Perspectives On Policy & Practice*. Monsey, New York: Criminal Justice Press and Federation Press, 1996. The author presents a description of the development and practice of family group conference in Canada and the United States.

3483 Jan, Lee-Jan Attitudes Toward Correctional Rehabilitation Among Incarcerated Youth In Taiwan And The United States, *Journal Of Offender Rehabilitation* 24:171-181, 1996. This survey assessed the relationship between incarcerated youths' perceptions and attitudes toward, and reactions to their rehabilitation programs in Taiwan and the United States.

3484 Jan, Lee-Jan Corrections In Taiwan (Republic Of China), *International Journal Of Comparative And Applied Criminal Justice* 12:95-100, 1988. This essay compares the correctional systems of ,and includes a discussion on, juvenile facilities in Taiwan and the United States.

3485 Johnston, Helen Age Of Criminal Law Proceedings In Europe, pp 10-14 in The Howard League for Penal Reform (eds.) *Child Offenders: UK & International Practice*. London, United Kingdom, 1995. This chapter provides a summary of age limits for juveniles in various European jurisdictions.

3486 Joutsen, Matti Treatment, Punishment, Control: Juvenile Delinquency In Scandinavia, pp 599-623 in Hess, Albert G. & Clement, Priscilla F. (eds.) *History Of Juvenile Delinquency II: A Collection Of essays On Crimes Committed By Young Offenders*. Aalen, Germany: Scientia Verlag, 1993. In this chapter the author surveys juvenile delinquency and how is is reacted to in the Scandinavian countries.

3487 Joutsen, Matti From Theory To Research, To Policy: Nordic Developments In The Prevention And Control Of Juvenile Crime, *Eurocriminology* 2:116-127, 1988. This article summarizes the position of youth in the historical development of criminal law, and provides data on Norway, Denmark, Finland, and Sweden.

3488 Junger-Tas, Josine Will The Juvenile Justice System Survive? *European Journal On Criminal Policy And Research* 2:76-91, 1994. In this article, the author discusses the future of juvenile justice.

3489 Junger-Tas, Josine Strategies For Dealing With Delinquents: A European Perspective, pp 20-31 in Bullock, Roger (ed.) *Problem Adolescents: An International View*. London, United Kingdom: Whiting & Birch, 1992. This chapter presents data on the extent and nature of delinquency in European countries, and the various strategies several of these countries have developed to deal with the problem.

3490 Junger-Tas, Josine *Juvenile Delinquency And The Law*. Hague, The Netherlands: Ministry of Justice of the Netherlands, 1983. The author reviews responses of juvenile justice officials from 57 countries regarding the age-categorizations these countries use to establish the criminal culpability of minors, the sanctions used, and the social control functions of judicial officials. 23p.

3491 Kaiser, Günther Strategies For Diversion In European Juvenile Justice Systems, pp 81-93 in United Nations Asia And Far East Institute (eds.) *Report For 1983 And Resource Material Series No. 25*, Tokyo, Japan: UNAFEI, 1984. The author compares and contrasts the diverse juvenile justice systems of Sweden, Switzerland, the Netherlands, Germany and England.

3492 King, Michael Social Crime Prevention À La Thatcher, *Howard Journal* 28:291-312, 1989. This article contrasts the juvenile crime prevention programs and policies of conservative England and socialist France. 21p.

3493 Kube, Edwin *Systematic Crime Prevention, With Practical References (Systematische Kriminalprevention, Mit Praktischen Hinweisen)*. Wiesbaden, Germany: Kriminalistisches Institut Bundeskriminalamt, 1986. The author addresses various theories and methods of crime and delinquency prevention in Germany, and compares it to various other European crime and vandalism programs. 296p. German.

3494 Kubiak, Jacek R. Internal And External Factors Influencing The Operation Of Criminal Justice Systems Of Socialist European Countries, *Review Of Socialist Law* 13:5-59, 1987. This volume reviews the diverse elements such as law enforcement and the criminal justice systems of Bulgaria, Czechoslovakia, German Democratic Republic, Hungary, Poland, Romania, Soviet Union and Yugoslavia.

3495 Kuhne, Hans-Heiner Parties To The Proceedings In Germany, France And Spain, pp 126-130 in Cavadino, Paul (ed.) *Children Who Kill: An Examination Of The Treatment Of Juveniles Who Kill In Different European Countries*. Winchester, United Kingdom: Waterside, 1996. This chapter, focusing mostly on Germany, offers a brief discussion of the role of judges and others in France and Spain in serious cases involving children.

3496 Lanagan, Patrick A. & Farrington, David P. Two-Track Justice? Some Evidence From An English Longitudinal Survey, *Journal Of Criminal Law And Criminology* 74:519-546, 1983. The authors used research data to compare and evaluate the "one" versus the "two" track system of juvenile justice as practiced in United Kingdom and the United States.

3497 LePool, Fré Law And Practice Concerning The Counterparts of "Persons In Need Of Supervision" In Some European Countries With A Particular Emphasis On The Netherlands" in Teitelbaum, Lee E. & Gough, Aidan R. (eds.) *Beyond Control: Status Offenders In The Juvenile Court*. Cambridge, Massachuettes: Ballinger Publishing, 1977. A description of how Persons In Need of Supervision and parent-child relationships are handled within the statutory framework in the Netherlands, France, Sweden, United Kingdom, and West Germany. 330p.

3498 Lipsey, Mark W. Juvenile Delinquency Treatment: A Meta-Analytic Inquiry Into The Variability Of Effects, pp 83-127 in Cook, Thomas. D.; Cooper, Harris; Cordray, David S.; Hartmann, Heidi; Hedges, Larry V.; Light, Richard J.; Louis, Thomas A. & Mosteller, Frederick (ed.) *Meta Analysis For Explanation: A Casebook*. New York, New York: Russell Sage Foundation, 1992. This chapter presents a meta-analysis of 443 studies conducted since 1950 in English-speaking countries that examines variability in the effects of delinquency treatment found in the research literature.

3499 Liu, John Jih-An *Sino-American Juvenile Justice System*. Arlington, Virginia: Carrollton Press, 1980. In contrasting juvenile law in the United States and Taiwan, which enacted a juvenile court law and established its first juvenile court in 1971, the author highlights the latter's policy of flexible treatment for different types of juvenile offenders. 341p.

3500 Liu, Shu Ling; Menzies, Ken & Hinch, Ronald Juvenile Justice Legislation In Canada And Taiwan, *International Criminal Justice Review* 8:61-73, 1998. This review examines the usefulness of the Canadian example for understanding changes in Taiwanese juvenile justice legislation.

3501 Liverpool, Nicholas Criminal Procedure In Barbados, Dominica And Jamaica (El Procedimiento Penal En Barbados, Dominica, Y Jamaica), *Ilanud* 5:56-61, 1982. Laws concerning minors' criminal behavior are among the subjects in this collection on criminal procedures in Caribbean countries. Spanish.

3502 Lücker-Babel, Marie-Françoise The Treatment Of Juveniles In Conflict With The Law: International Standards And Experiences, pp 43-50 in United Nations Crime Prevention And Criminal Justice Program International Scientific And Professional Advisory Council (eds.) *Juveniles And Delinquency In The Italian And European Context.* The author outlines some international standards for the treatment of children, and offers examples of cases from various countries.

3503 Maddox, Alton H. Jr. *The Juvenile Justice System: Where Minorities Become Majorities.* New York: National Conference of Black Lawyers, Juvenile Defense Project, 1981. The main argumen of the author is that both in South Africa and the United States, institutional racism against black juveniles is still present. 25p.

3504 Marshall, Tony F. & Merry, Susan *Crime And Accountability: Victim/Offender Mediation in Practice.* London, United Kingdom: Her Majesty's Stationery Office, 1990. The authors describe the various offender victim mediation and reparation projects, and the related socio-legal issues, including those involving juveniles in the United Kingdom, Canada and the United States. 271p.

3505 Matthews, Catherine J. & Lewis, Lesley *Racism in the Criminal justice System: A Bibliography.* Toronto, Canada: Centre of Criminology, 1995. This bibliography includes a section on minority youth in the criminal justice systems of Canada, United Kingdom, and the United States. 187p.

3506 McCarney, Willie (ed.) *Juvenile Delinquents And Young People In Danger In An Open Environment.* Winchester, United Kingdom: Waterside, 1996. In comparing the European alternative sanction of treatment in open environments, the author focuses on delinquent and "at-risk" youths.

3507 Mehlbye, Jill & Walgrave, Lode An Overview: Comparative Comments On Juvenile Offending And Its Treatment In Europe, pp 21-53 in Mehlbye, Jill & Walgrave, Lode (eds.) *Confronting Youth In Europe: Juvenile Crime And Juvenile Justice*. Copenhagen: AKF Forlaget, 1998. This chapter summarizes a host of information about the delinquency problems and correctional orientations found in Belgium, Denmark, Scotland, the Netherlands, and France.

3508 Méndez, Emilio García & Carranza, Elías (eds.) *Childhood, Adolescence And Social Control In Latin America (Infancia, Adolescencia Y Control Social En América Latina)*. Buenos Aires, Argentina: Ediciones Depalma, 1990. The history and characteristics of juvenile justice systems in Argentina, Colombia, Costa Rica, Uruguay and Venezuela are described in indiividual chapters of this anthology.
417p. Spanish.

3509 Méndez, Emilio García Juvenile Penal Justice In Latin America: Legal Systems, Procedural Guarantees And The Rights Of Man (La Justice Pénale De L'Enfance Et De L'Adolescence En Amérique Latine; Systèmes Légaux, Garanties De Prococédure Et Droits De L'Homme), *Revue Internationale De Criminology Et De Police Technique* 46:49-64, 1993. The Latin-American history of child saving and protection is contrasted with the American model.

3510 Moore, David B. Shame, Forgiveness, and Juvenile Justice, *Criminal Justice And Ethics* 12:3-25, 1993. The author discusses the assumptions, and practical and other implications of family group conference of New Zealand and similar programs in the United Kingdom and the United States.

3511 Morris, Allison & Giller, Henri *Understanding Juvenile Justice*. London, United Kingdom: Croom Helm, 1987. The development of juvenile justice programs in England and Wales, with references to the United States and Scotland, is the focus of this book. 258 p.

3512 Moyer, Sharon *Diversion From The Juvenile Justice System And Its Impact On Children: A Review Of The Literature*. Ottawa, Canada: Solicitor General Canada, 1980. This review of the literature on the juvenile justice systems of Canada and the United States describes the agencies that deal with youths and the various diversion programs for juvenile delinquents. 201p.

3513 Neubacher, Frank; Walter, Michael; Válková, Helena & Krajewski, Krzysztof Juvenile Delinquency In Central European Cities: A Comparison Of Registration And Processing Structures In The 1990s, *European Journal Of Criminal Policy And Research* 7:533-558, 1999. In comparing recorded delinquency in Budapest, Hamburg and Prague the authors conclude that the official data are reflective of specific procedures and methods of crime control in these cities.

3514 Nielsen, Marianne A Comparison of Canadian Native Youth justice and Navajo Peacemakers *Journal of Contemporary Criminal Justice* 14:6-25, 1998. The author discusses Canadaian tribal administration effects on the way Aboriginal Youth Committees are organized and run, and compares them with the Peacemakers of the Navajo Nation in the United States.

3515 Normandeau, André & Hasenpush, Burkhard Crime And Delinquency Prevention In Some European Countries, *International Journal Of Comparative And Applied Criminal Justice* 5:41-49, 1981. The crime and delinquency prevention programs of the European countries of Belgium, France, West Germany, and Switzerland are described in this article.

3516 Oberwittler, Dietrich The Decline Of Correctional Education, 1890-1920: England And Germany Compared, *European Journal Of Crime, Criminal Law And Criminal Justice* 7:22-40, 1999. This article describes how correctional education was the first major project of a reform movement aimed at removing children from jails, and introducing the idea of special treatment for children in Germany and England.

3517 O'Donnell, Daniel *Alternatives To Imprisonment Of Children*. pp 136-149 in Tomasevski, Katarina (ed.) *Children In Adult Prisons: An International Perspective*. New York, New York: St. Martin's Press, 1986. This survey of 27 countries could not locate any that had completely eliminated the detention of minors with adults, although encouraging efforts were reported for Canada United States, France, Argentina and Costa Rica.

3518 Ohsako, Toshio Tackling School Violence Worldwide: A Comparative Perspective Of Basic Issues And Challenges, pp 7-19 in Ohsako, Toshio (ed.) *Violence At School: Global Issues And Interventions*. Paris, France: United Nations Educational Scientific and Cultural Organization, 1997. As a general introduction to the volume, this chapter offers a summary of information on school violence, and the various measures countries around the world have adopted to deal with it.

3519 Parsloe, Phyllida *Juvenile Justice In Britain And The United States: The Balance Of Needs And Rights*. London: Routledge & Kegan Paul, 1978. This volume provides an analysis of the diverse demands on juvenile authorities in England, Scotland and the United States which, regardless of some differences, seem to be similar in their responses to delinquency. 325p.

3520 Pease, Ken & Tseloni, Andromachi Juvenile-Adult Differences In Criminal Justice: Evidence From The United Nations Crime Survey, *Howard Journal* 35:40-60, 1996. This research compares the female-male juvenile to adult ratios from apprehension to imprisonment during 1975 for various countries from Argentina to Zimbabwe, and has a nice summary table on the age of culpability for various countries.

3521 Pelikan, Christa Conflict Resolution Between Victims And Offenders In Austria And In The Federal Republic Of Germany, pp 151-172 in Heidensohn, Frances & Farrell, Martin (eds.) *Crime In Europe*. London: Routledge, 1991. The juvenile justice systems and various conflict resolution programs in Austria and Germany are described in this chapter.

3522 Penal Reform International *Making Standards Work: An International Handbook on Good Prison Practice*. Hague, The Netherlands: Penal Reform International, 1995. This handbook on the United Nations' rules on treatment of prisoners and prison conditions includes a section on the special case of juveniles. 175p.

3523 Pearson, Geoffrey Crime And Criminology In Israel: A Personal Account Of A British Study Tour, *British Journal Of Criminology* 30:235-243, 1990. The author contrasts the American, Israeli, and Arab approach to delinquency.

3524 Pease, Ken & Tseloni, Andromachi Juvenile-Adult Differences In Criminal Justice: Evidence From The United Nations Crime Survey, *Howard Journal* 35:40-60, 1996. This survey presents data on sentencing that was obtained from the second and the third United Nations Crime Surveys involving about 90 countries.

3525 Pitts, John & Hope, Tim The Local Politics of Inclusion: The State And Community Safety, *Social Policy and Administration* 31:37-58, 1997. The relationship among globalization of poverty, state intervention in the economic status of the poor, youth crime and crime prevention, with focus specifically on the example of Britain and France are the subject of this discussion.

3526 Pratt, John A Comparative Analysis Of Two Different Systems Of Juvenile Justice: Some Implications For England And Wales. *Howard Journal* 25:33-51, 1986. This study concludes that reformatory schools and similar closed facilities for juveniles have been completely abolished in Norway and Denmark, but such corporate planning and management of delinquency is lacking in England and Wales.

3527 Queloz, Nicolas Protection, Intervention And The Rights Of Children And Young People, pp 30-45 in Booth, Tim (ed.) *Juvenile Justice In The New Europe*. Sheffield, United Kingdom: Sheffield University, 1991. The focus of this paper is on the epistemological evolution of human rights and its extension to minors, and the complex relationship between two conflicting ideas -- protection, help, and welfare verus intervention, justice, and punishment.

3528 Queloz, Nicolas Is Justice For Minors Being Lost In The Quest For A Community Approach?: Communal Approach And Delinquent Youth (La Justice Pour Mineurs A La Recherche De La Communauté Perdue?: Approche Communautaire Et Délinquance Des Jeunes), pp 155-166 Junger-Tas, Josine; Boendermaker, Leonieke & Van Der Laan, Peter H. (eds.) *The Future Of The Juvenile Justice System (L'Avenir Du Système Pénal Des Mineurs)*. Leuven, Belgium: Acco, 1991. This chapter describes changes in justice for minors in the United States and Europe. French.

3529 Queloz, Nicolas Perspectives On Juvenile Justice And Its Development In Africa In Light Of Recent United Nations Acts (La Justice Pour Mineurs Dans L'Optique Récente Des Nations Unies Et La Question De Son Développement En Afrique), *Revue Internationale De Criminologie Et De Police Technique* 41:33-48, 1988. This article examines the concepts of juvenile delinquency and justice in African countries within the context of United Nations standards. French with English summary.

3530 Queloz, Nicolas Juvenile Delinquency In Switzerland: Some Elements Of Illustration (La Délinquance Juvenile En Suisse: Quelques Elements D'Illustration), *Revue Internationale De Criminologie Et De Police Technique* 40:147-158, 1987. This essay contrasts the Swiss criminal justice system's approach employing assistance, education, and rehabilitation to juvenile delinquency with that of neighboring European countries and the United States. French with English summary.

3531 Ream, B. D. (ed.) The Child And The Law: Special Bibliography Issue, *Children's Legal Rights Journal* 6:1-70, 1985. This issue of the journal provides a bibliography of all post-1980 publications on laws regarding children in Canada, the United States, and African, Asian, Pacific, Latin-American, the Caribbean, Europesn, Middle Eastern, and Islamic states, and has a brief section devoted to juvenile justice and its administration.

3532 Ross, Charles A. *Ripped Off On A Corner Called Justice: Juvenile Judicial Issues In England & America*. Huntington, New York, New ork, New York: Friends World College, 1977. In this analysis of juvenile justice in England and The United States, it is argued that it is subject to frustration and failure due to stigmatizing and labeling of the young offenders, and the conflict between a desire to both care for and punish them for their misbehavior. 109 p.

3533 Ross, Robert R. & Ross, Roslynn D. (eds.) *Thinking Straight: The Reasoning And Rehabilitation Program For Delinquency Prevention And Offender Rehabilitation*. Ottawa, Canada: AIR Training & Publications, 1995. The 24 essays in this anthology describe reasoning and rehabilitation programs, and various multifaceted and structured psycho-educational psrogram for juvenile and adult offenders in Canada, the United Kingdom, Spain and the United States. 428p.

3534 Ruddell, Rick; Mays, G. Larry & Giever, Dennis M. Transferring Juveniles To Adult Courts: Recent Trends And Issues In Canada And The United States, *Juvenile And Family Court Journal* 49:1-15, *1998*. Using official statistics, this article examines the practice of transferring juvenile offenders to adult courts.

3535 Rutherford, Andrew Criminal Policy And The Eliminative Ideal, *Social Policy And Administration* 31:116-135, 1997. The history of the transportation to the colonies, and the exclusion of troublesome delinquent youth and adults by England, France, Russia, Germany and California of the 1990s is the subject of this exposition.

3536 Sagel-Grande, Irene Looking For One Age, pp 66-74 in Booth, Tim (ed.) *Juvenile Justice In The New Europe*. Sheffield, United Kingdom: Joint Unit for Social Services Research, Sheffield University, 1991. This chapter describes the different age limits for criminal responsibility in the various European penal systems, and the evidence on the relationship between age and juvenile offending.

3537 Salzburg Seminar In American Studies *A Proposed Juvenile Justice Code For Europe*. Salzburg, Austria, 1976. A proposed Juvenile Justice Code to be considered by all countries in Europe is presented in this document. 33p.

3538 Sansong, John M. *Sentencing, Corrections, And Special Treatment Services In Sweden, Denmark, And The Netherlands*. Hartford, Connecticut: Hartford Institute of Criminal Justice, 1976. The overview section of this volume has a concise description of juvenile corrections in Denmark, the Netherlands, and Sweden. 189p.

3539 Sciarra, Daniel T. Assessment And Treatment Of Adolescent Sex Offenders: A Review From A Cross-Cultural Perspective, *Journal Of Offender Rehabilitation* 28:103-118, 1999. The clinical treating youthful sex offenders across cultures is the subject of this review essay.

3540 Schaffer, Evelyn B. *Community Policing*. London, United Kingdom: Croom Helm, 1980. Arguing that successful police work depends on fostering a cooperative relationship with the public, the author considers police and juvenile offenders, police and new legislation, police and social work, and police and the schools, and examines several experiments in community policing in Great Britain, Scotland, the United States, Norway, and Sweden. 145p.

3541 Schelkens, Wim Mediation And Community Service In The Juvenile Justice Legislation In Europe, pp 159-184 in Walgrave, Lode (ed.) *Restorative Justice For Juveniles: Potentialities, Risks And Problems For Research*. Leuven: Leuven University Press, 1998. This chapter discusses how European countries apply, the restorative responses to juvenile crime, with special attention to the judicial context.

3542 Schüeler-Springorum, Horst A Critical Comparison Of The British Detention Centers And The German "Jugendarrest" System, *International Journal Of Criminology And Penology* 3:201-211, 1975. This study compares the actual operation of two juvenile correctional systems designed for the same purpose in two different countries.

3543 Selih, A. Juvenile Criminal Law And Change: Trends In Some East- And Central European Countries, *European Journal Of Crime Criminal Law And Criminal Justice* 4:173-183, 1996. This article reviews juvenile delinquency laws in Central and Eastern Europe, including the Czech Republic, Hungary, Poland, Slovakia and Slovenia.

3544 Sickmund, Melissa *How Juveniles Get To Criminal Court*. Washington, D.C.: Office of Juvenile Justice and Delinquency Prevention, 1994. Juvenile court data for 1992 were used to examine the transfer of juveniles to adult criminal courts.

3545 Somerhausen, Colette Models Of State Intervention And Delinquent Minors (Mineurs Délinquents Et Modèles D'Intervention Étatique), pp 79-97 in *Cahiers De Defense Sociale*. Milan, Italy: La Société International De Défense Sociale, 1988. The social control role of states in protecting children in Belgium, Spain, Portugal and other Western European countries is addressed in this discussion.

3546 Tatham, Elizabeth *Correction Facilities And Other Alternatives For Juvenile Delinquents In France, Italy And England*. Hackensack, New Jersey: N.C.C.D.,1975. This survey of correctional facilities and alternatives in France, Italy, and England attempted to discover which of them can be adapted in the New Jersey juvenile justice system. 51p.

3547 Teitelbaum, Lee E. & Gough, Aidan R. (eds.) *Beyond Control: Status Offenders In The Juvenile Court*. Cambridge, Massachusetts: Ballinger Publishing, 1977. This volume on status offenders includes a chapter describing the way in which juveniles are handled in the criminal courts in West Germany, France, Sweden, the United Kingdom, and the Netherlands. 330p.

3548 Trépanier, Jean Juvenile Courts After 100 Years: Past and Present Orientations, *European Journal On Criminal Policy And Research* 7:303-327, 1999. The author provides a history tracting the development of Canadian and American juvenile courts and related institutions.

3549 Trépanier, Jean & Tulkens, Françoise Delinquency And The Protection Of Youth Sources Of Belgian And Canadian Laws On Youth (Délinquance & Protection De La Jeunesse: Aux Sources Des Lis Belge Et Canadienne Sur l'Enfance). Montreal, Canada: University Presses of Montreal and Ottawa, 1995. This analysis examines the origins of child protection and juvenile delinquency laws in Belgium and Canada. 139p. French.

3550 Tomasevski, Katarina *Children In Adult Prisons: An International Perspective*. New York, New York: St. Martin's Press, 1989. This volume provides a comprehensive look at the imprisonment of children in adult institutions around the world and addresses international standards and the deviations from these standards found in various countries, the rights of children, victimization of children by political repression, protections for children in criminal justice systems, minimum-age legislation, alternatives to imprisonment of children and their victimization in adult prisons, babies in prisons, and summaries of Defense For Children International Survey. 220p.

3551 Tremblay, R. E. Treatment Of Hardcore Delinquents In Residential Establishment: The Ardale Case, *British Journal Of Criminology* 24:384-393, 1984. The subject of this article is the positive effects of four Ardale community homes, and their treatment programs in the United Kingdom and Canada.

3552 Troppenhauer, Hannes & Seipel, Claudia Compensation Inside And Outside The Criminal Justice System: International Dimensions Between Austrian And German Criminal Law Systems, *Global Journal On Crime And Criminal Law* 2:41-92, 1994. This article describes compensation systems, compares the systems and compensation possibilities, under juvenile law in Austria and Germany.

3553 Tutt, Norman Youth Justice - Crisis Or Opportunity? *European Journal On Criminal Policy And Research* 2:9-23, 1994. This article focuses on factors in various studies of youthful illegality as well as on a variety of preventive strategies.

3554 Umbreit, Mark & Zehr, Howard Family Group Conferences: A Challenge To Victim-Offender Mediation? *VOMA Quarterly* 7:4-8, 1995 & 1996. This article contrasts family group conferencing in victim-offender mediation programs in New Zealand and Australia.

3555 United Nations Asia And Far East Institute *Resource Material Series No. 46*. Tokyo, Japan: UNAFEI, 1995. This document provides brief descriptions of juvenile justice and/or corrections programs in various countries, and the summary chapters deal with the effective treatment and protection of juveniles in general. 368p.

3556 United Nations Asia And Far East Institute *Report For 1993 And Resource Material Series No. 45*. Tokyo, Japan: UNAFEI, 1994. This volume contains articles on juvenile delinquency and justice in several countries, and presents a comparative study of juvenile justice administration around the world, as well as provides flowcharts on the juvenile justice systems of thirteen countries. 345p.

3557 United Nations Centre For Social Development And Humanitarian Affairs *International Review Of Criminal Policy: Nos. 39 And 40, 1990 Special Double Volume On Juvenile Justice In International Perspective*. New York, New York, United Nations, 1990. This volume provides 21 chapters that deal with diverse aspects of juvenile justice around the world in general, and in specific countries or parts of the world. 161p.

3558 United Nations Expert Group Meeting (eds.) *Children And Juveniles In Detention: Application Of Human rights Standards*. The United Nations Centre for Human Rights: Vienna, Austria, 1994. This volume is on juvenile delinquency and youth crime, child exploitation, juvenile justice standards and norms, and the implementation of United Nations standards and norms around the world,as well as containing articles on various countries and specific issues. 223p.

3559 Van Der Laan, Peter & Giller, Henri Comparative Juvenile Justice Systems Analysis: An Anglo-Dutch Initiative, pp 377-384 in Junger-Tas, Josine; Boendermaker, Leonieke & Van Der Laan, Peter H. (eds.) *The Future Of The Juvenile Justice System (L'Avenir Du Système Pénal Des Mineurs)*. Leuven, Belgium: Acco, 1991. The authors discuss a comparable monitoring instrument to enable Dutch and British organizations to better consider the merits of a comparative analysis of the performance of their local systems.

3560 Waldfogel, Jane *The Future Of Child Protection: How To Break The Cycle Of Abuse And Neglect*. Cambridge, Massachusetts: Harvard University Press, 1998. This is a review of the current child protective services in the United States, compared with those in Canada, Britain and Australia. 285p.

3561 Walgrave, Lode Restorative Juvenile Justice: A Way To Restore Justice In Western European Systems? pp 169-199 in Asquith, Stewart (ed.) *Children And Young People In Conflict With The Law*. London, United Kingdom: Jessica Kingsley, 1996. This chapter compares juvenile justice approaches in several European countries.

3562 Walgrave, Lode The Making Of Concepts On Juvenile Delinquency And Its Treatment In The Recent History Of Belgium And The Netherlands, pp 655-692 in Hess, Albert G. & Clement, Priscilla F. (eds.) *History Of Juvenile Delinquency: A Collection Of Essays On Crime Committed By Young Offenders, In History And In Selected Countries, Vol. 2*. Aalen, Germany: Scientia Verlag, 1993. This chapter provides an extensive discussion of the social meaning of juvenile delinquency, and how young offenders are reacted to, in Belgium and the Netherlands.

3563 Waller, Irvin Delinquency And Its Prevention: Comparative Study (La Délinquance Et Sa Prévention: Étude Comparative), *Revue Internationale De Criminologie Et De Police Technique* 46:23-48, 1993. Countries around the world are included in this description of the role of various government agencies in dealing with delinquency. French

3564 Walter, Michael & Fischer, Wolfgang Crime-Specific Selection Processes In Punishments For Youthful Offenders In East-West Comparison (Deliktsspezifische Selektionsprozesse Bei Der Strafverfolgung Jugendlicher Im Ost-West Vergleich), *Monatsschrift Für Kriminologie Und Strafrechtsform* 3:146-158, 1991. Based on official crime and court statistics, this article describes methods for dealing with delinquency in the cities of Budapest, Prague and Warsaw in Eastern Europe comparing them with corresponding procedures in the cities of West Berlin, Bremen, and Hamburg in the Federal Republic of Germany. German.

3565 Weijers, Ido The Double Paradox Of Juvenile Justice, *European Journal On Criminal Policy And Research* 7:329-351, 1999. The author examines the traditions and origins of European and American juvenile justice within current European justice issues.

3566 Wenk, Ernst A. Delinquency Prevention Models In Schools, *Juvenile And Family Court Journal* 29:17-27, 1978. This article reports and describes on cross national pilot projects of the United Nations Crime Prevention and Criminal Justice Section in sixteen educational/or vocational programs in the Soviet Union, Canada, the Netherlands, and the United States as possible models of school-based delinquency prevention programs around the world.

3567 Wenk, Ernst *In Search Of Delinquency Prevention Models In Schools: A Cross-National Study*. Davis, California: National Council on Crime and Delinquency, Research Center, 1977. This is a summary of model educational and vocational training programs in Canada, the Netherlands, the Soviet Union, and the United States that serve as alternatives to delinquency and criminality-conducive factors. 48p.

3568 Yeager, Matthew G. Immigrants And Criminality: A Cross National Review, *Criminal Justice Abstracts* 29:143-171, 1997. In this article, the author reviews some of the findings and data on the relationship between immigrants and criminality in Canada, the United States, the United Kingdom, Australia, and Continental Europe, and includes a brief section on the illegal behaviors of immigrant children.

3569 Zapatero, Luis Arroyo (ed.) *Studies In Criminology I (Estudios De Criminologiá I)*. Cuenca, Spain: Tarańcon. This anthology of 16 articles includes an international self-reported delinquency study from Albacete, Spain and Omaha, Nebraska, and Italian legistlation pertaining to personal consumption of drugs, and some data on drug use including that of juveniles, application of clinical sociology in delinquency prevention, psychological aspects of child abuse in Spain, the myths and realities of the problem of drug addiction in Latin America, and in diverse countries of the world. 261p. Spanish.

AUTHOR INDEX

Subject Index

About the Compilers

CLAYTON A. HARTJEN is Professor and Chair of the Department of Sociology and Anthropology and Professor in the School of Criminal Justice, Rutgers University, Newark.

S. PRIYADARSINI is Associate Research Professor in the Department of Sociology and Anthropology, Rutgers University, Newark.